The First of Men

The First of Men

A LIFE OF GEORGE WASHINGTON

JOHN E. FERLING

The University of Tennessee Press
KNOXVILLE

Frontispiece: Clay bust of Washington, by Jean Antoine Houdon (1785).
Courtesy of the Mount Vernon Ladies' Association of the Union.

The paper in this book meets the minimum requirements of the American
National Standard for Permanence of Paper for Printed Library Materials.
⊗ The binding materials have been chosen for strength and durability.

Library of Congress Cataloging in Publication Data

Ferling, John E.
     The first of men: a life of George Washington /
     by John E. Ferling.
     p. cm.
     Bibliography: p.
     Includes index.
     ISBN 0-87049-562-3 (alk. paper) :
     1. Washington, George. 1732–1799. 2. Presidents—United States—
Biography. 3. Generals—United States—Biography. 4. United States.
Army—Biography. I. Title.
E312.F47 1988
973.4′1′0924—dc19
[B]   87-26037   CIP

The American Revolution . . . is fixed forever.
Washington began it with energy,
and finished it with moderation.

—LOUISE FONTANES, 1800

Time, like an ever-rolling stream,
   Soon bears us all away;
We fly forgotten, as a dream
   Dies at the op'ning day.

—ISAAC WATTS

Contents

Illustrations

Preface

John Adams doubted that an accurate history of the great events of his lifetime could ever be written. The story of those events would be "one continued lie from one end to the other," he once predicted in a not uncustomarily bilious moment. "The essence of the whole," he went on, "will be that Dr. Franklin's electrical rod smote the earth and out sprang General Washington. That Franklin electrified him with his rod, and thenceforth those two conducted all the policy, negotiations, legislatures, and war." [1]

George Washington expressed greater confidence in the capabilities of future historians, and he was even sufficiently realistic to imagine "the darts which *I think* [will] be pointed at me" by those who would come to write of him and his age. However, he did expect high standards of his biographers. He hoped they would have a "disposition to justice, candour and impartiality, and . . . [a] diligence in investigating" the source materials. [2]

Washington might have been surprised by what was written in the years following his death. For a century or more his biographers were unable to cut through the legends that had come to surround the man. If Adams's ideas about the folklore likely to surround Washington and Franklin were exaggerated, the human Washington did indeed seem to be elusive, and he was handed from generation to generation as a stylized, fanciful figure, as lifeless as the image of the man that peers out from the myriad paintings suspended on quiet museum walls. In a sense, it was as though Washington was too monumental to contemplate, save in the most heroic terms. But in another sense it was as if Washington could not bear scrutiny, for fear that he would prove to be all too human.

My introduction to Washington, fortunately, came after historians had begun to penetrate the mists of heroic legend. A work by Marcus Cunliffe, which I read while still an undergraduate, first made me aware that Washington was, after all, arrestingly human, even though the author confessed his inability fully to distinguish the man from the myth. Later, in graduate school, I read Bernhard Knollenberg on Washington's early years, as well as some of the voluminous works of Douglas Southall Freeman and James Thomas Flexner, each of whom had played an important role in the mortalization of Washington. [3]

Still, something seemed to be lacking. Too often the engines that drove the private man seemed out of sync with the forces that pushed the public figure.

Illogically, there seemed to be two Washingtons, and the inclinations of the one appeared never to intrude upon the actions of the other. This added another intriguing element to the endless fascination of this man, but it was not until my research led me rather circuitously into a study of early American military history that I first began to try to come to grips with Washington. From that beginning I was led to this study, drawn in the hope that I might fathom what I perceived to be an incompleteness to the figure of the historical Washington.

From the outset it was my intent to write a one-volume biography. My goal was to produce something less grand than a man-and-the-times study, yet to probe Washington's era in sufficient depth that I might draw on the explosion of studies set off by the recent celebration of the American Revolution Bicentennial.

Not every reader will agree with my assessment of Washington, particularly with those sections that are less than flattering in their judgment. In fact, in the course of the years required to complete this study, some of my own assumptions about Washington were changed, and I came to a greater admiration of many facets of the man, particularly of his courage, his realization of his limitations, his ability to make difficult decisions, his diligent striving for self-improvement, his willingness to work, the gentle love and abiding steadfastness which he exhibited toward his family, and, with one or two glaring exceptions over a long lifetime, the sense of loyalty and constancy he manifested toward those who remained faithful to him. Of course, there were "darts"—the harsh appraisal that Washington anticipated—but I am confident that these arrows were unsheathed only after I had adhered to the guidelines for fairness that Washington had asked of biographers.

This study could not have been completed without the assistance of many others. Considerable financial support was provided by the Learning Resources Committee of West Georgia College. Albert S. Hanser and Ted Fitz-Simons generously cooperated by providing teaching schedules that facilitated the completion of the study, while the Arts and Sciences Executive Committee and Dean Richard Dangle of West Georgia College assisted by granting my request for a reduced teaching schedule.

I am indebted to numerous people who provided kind assistance in the course of my research. Long days and nights away from home were made more pleasant by the courteous and friendly aid I received from librarians and historians in many libraries. I am grateful for the guidance and encouragement offered by W.W. Abbot, Dorothy Twohig, Philander Chase, and Beverly Runge of the George Washington Papers at the Alderman Library of the University of Virginia. The cordiality with which I was welcomed at the Mount Vernon Library made the hours I spent in that bucolic setting all the more pleasurable. The same can be said of my work at the National Archives, Library of Congress, Massachusetts Historical Society, Connecticut State Library in Hartford, the New York Historical Society, and the New York Public Library.

Several librarians at the Irvine Sullivan Ingram Library of West Georgia College provided considerable assistance, beginning with Anne Manning who oversaw the purchase of the John C. Fitzpatrick edition of Washington's papers for my use. Charles Beard authorized the acquisition of additional items of importance, and Diane Atwater, Genevieve Cooksey, and Nancy Farmer somehow remained friendly and cheerful despite my repeated entreaties for still more materials through their interlibrary loan office.

Pat Giusto and Linda Wagner helped immensely in the preparation of the manuscript, and over the years each remained a source of encouragement by displaying a ready and unabated interest in the progress of this endeavor. Robert J. Masek kindly read portions of the manuscript and offered valuable insight into Washington's character and personality. The manuscript certainly was strengthened as a result of the cogent written critiques provided by historians Paul David Nelson and Dorothy Twohig.

I am indebted to Lee Campbell Sioles for her masterly attention to detail, and I will always be grateful to Cynthia Maude-Gembler, who believed in this project from its infancy.

I am especially indebted to two quite different confidants and friends, R. Gregg Kaufman and Virginia Channell, each of whom provided sustenance and a loving kindness that shepherded me through many moments of doubt and despondency.

The First of Men

I

Young George Washington

"My willingness to oblige"

In 1732 George II sat on the throne of England, a cardinal of the Roman Catholic Church directed the foreign policy of France, and almost every member of the Pennsylvania Assembly was a Quaker. George Frederick Handel's operas *Esio* and *Sosarme* were produced for the first time, while perhaps the most important scientific publication of the year was Jethro Tull's *New Horse Hoeing Husbandry*. Thirty days, or more, were required to cross the Atlantic in the best sailing craft that could be built, though that was only a little longer than it took to travel from Paris to St. Petersburg by land conveyance. An epidemic of yellow fever ravaged New York City that year, just as smallpox had swept over Boston a few months before, leaving more than two thousand dead in its wake. Johann Sebastian Bach and Alexander Pope still were alive, but many of those who now are remembered as among the most powerful and influential personages of the eighteenth century were not yet born in 1732, people like Robespierre and Marie Antoinette, George III and Lord North, Franz Joseph Haydn and Wolfgang Amadeus Mozart.

That year, at 10:00 A.M. on February 22, a cold winter morning in the Northern Neck of Virginia, George Washington was born. At a time when most inhabitants of Great Britain's American colonies were foreign born, Washington was a fourth-generation colonist.

John Washington, George's great-grandfather, was the first of the family to settle in America. Like many of his descendants, he combined native acumen with a tenacious zest for material gain, traits that served him well in the combative wilderness of seventeenth-century Virginia. The son of an Anglican clergyman, well educated and looking upon the world from a comfortable, gentlemanly social stratum, he had seemed to have a bright future in England. Then the Puritan

1656?

Revolution erupted, and his father was stripped of his parish. Cast adrift, John tried his hand at several pursuits over the next half dozen years. By 1756 he was a merchant seamen, and, on a cruise to the New World for tobacco, he landed in Virginia.

Evidently he liked what he saw. Largely still a frontier wilderness, tidewater Virginia offered a vista of opportunity to the dreamer and the adventurous. Land was plentiful. Tobacco still fetched a good price. There were few restraints to bridle a man bent on gaining wealth. With luck, and with an adequate supply of labor, an iron-willed planter could prosper as he could never hope to in England.

Within a few months of landing in the colony, John Washington took his first important step. He married into a class above his own, an act that was to become almost habitual among his descendants. Through his marriage to Anne Pope, John acquired seven hundred acres and a loan of £80 from his affluent father-in-law. In less than a decade he had parlayed his holdings into more than five thousand acres and several lucrative public offices, one of which was a lieutenant colonelcy in the Virginia militia. In no time he had replicated in America the social status the family once had enjoyed in England. By the time he died he had been married four times and had fathered several children, some of whom he had sent to England to receive a formal education.

One of these children was Lawrence Washington. The first son of John and Anne, he received the largest share of his father's estate, a generous grant of thousands of acres and a flour mill. But the law, not farming or business endeavors, interested him. He represented English business interests in Virginia, served as a justice of the peace, and, at age twenty-five, was elected to the House of Burgesses. He died young, before his fortieth birthday, a fate that would haunt many others in this clan.

Lawrence left behind three children, one of whom, Augustine, was to be the father of George Washington. As the second child, Augustine—or Gus as everyone called him—was due a more modest inheritance than his older brother; even so, he received eleven thousand acres. Following his father's untimely death, Augustine's mother remarried and the family moved to England, where the boy attended the Appleby School in Westmoreland until he was nine years old. But after his mother's death, Augustine and his brother and sister were returned to Virginia. They grew up in the plantation house of their cousin, John Washington of Chotank, a prosperous farmer who lived on the south shore of the Potomac.

Gus bore more traits of his grandfather than of his father. He married Jane Butler, the sixteen-year-old daughter of a prosperous planter, and set about to produce a family and a fortune. Three children, two sons and a daughter, were born in rapid succession. Meanwhile, Gus traded and speculated in land, mostly acquiring tracts along the Little Hunting Creek and Pope's Creek, both tributaries of the Potomac in the Northern Neck. In 1726 or 1727 he built a rude country farm house on the Pope Creek site, a dwelling that he rather ostentatiously named "Wakefield."

Tobacco was only one means to affluence for Gus. Like his ancestors, and like many other planters, he accumulated sinecures from the friendly colonial government, offices that required little work, paid a modest salary, and kept both the benefactor and the beneficiary happy. Gus's major source of income, however, resulted from the discovery of iron ore on land he owned near Fredericksburg. Seizing this heaven-sent opportunity, he entered into a partnership with the Principio Iron Works, a company owned by English Quakers, to mine the mineral and to erect a furnace on his lands.

By 1730 Gus seemed to be on top of the world. He lived comfortably, affluently, in fact, by the standards of this primeval, backwater enclave. Certainly he was wealthier than his father, and he enjoyed a coveted position in the society of the Northern Neck. But that spring he returned to Wakefield from a business trip in England to find that his world had changed drastically. His wife was dead, he discovered when he reached Pope's Creek, probably the victim of some fever that had scourged the region during his absence. Unable now to manage the family business and his commercial affairs simultaneously, he dispatched his two sons to the Appleby School. Meanwhile, he set out looking for a new wife. He found her a few miles upstream along the Potomac. Only a few months after he learned of his first wife's death, he remarried.

Mary Ball, his second wife, was the daughter of an English immigrant who had arrived in Virginia in the 1670s and who soon accumulated a small fortune as a planter. Joseph Ball waited until he was nearly sixty to marry, and Mary, George Washington's mother, was born less than a year afterward. Orphaned at age twelve, she was raised thereafter by a family friend, a prosperous farmer who lived at Sandy Point on the Potomac. She was twenty-three and still living there when she met and married Gus Washington. In the early eighteenth century it was unusual for a lady in Virginia still to be single at such an advanced age; for a lady who already had inherited a modest estate to still be single past her twentieth birthday was almost unheard of.

Augustine moved his new wife to his Pope Creek home, where her first obligation centered about raising Gus's nine-year-old daughter, Jane. Soon, however, Mary realized she would bear a child of her own, for by June, three months after the marriage, she knew she was pregnant. The next February she gave birth to a large, healthy boy.[1]

Neighbors dropped by in the weeks following the child's birth to aid the Washington family, to cook and tend to little Jane, to assist with the chores until Mary was back on her feet. These were a frontier people, a group that the governor only a few weeks earlier had labeled as the most disorderly and ungovernable of his subjects.[2]

In this society wealth determined one's status, and the Washingtons, owners of several thousand acres and about twenty slaves, enjoyed a loftier perch than their neighbors. But their wealth was too meager to permit them to live pretentiously. The family dwelling was small, only about twenty-four feet square. Like most others in the area their house probably was constructed of wood frame with a shingled roof, and in all likelihood it was a two-room abode, partitioned down the middle by a whitewashed mud wall. A few outbuildings—a barn and a stable, and probably a hen house, as well as a corncrib, a detached kitchen, and a few squalid cabins for the slaves—were scattered in a clearing to the rear. Because of Gus's overseas business interests, the house was more elegantly furnished than most in this primitive area. The family owned a few nice pieces crafted in England, and some of their clothing likewise had been purchased abroad.[3]

George lived on Pope's Creek for only three years, long enough for him to witness the arrival of a brother and another sister—Samuel and Betty—and to watch helplessly as his half-sister Jane died before her twelfth birthday. Then his father was ready to move. The Northern Neck was becoming a boom area and Gus, always a speculator, hoped to locate in a more advantageous spot.

Up till now, colonists had trickled into this region at a snail's pace since it had been opened three-quarters of a century before. Everywhere else Virginia's frontiers were being besieged by restless citizens. But not the Northern Neck, this region between the Rappahannock and the Potomac. For one thing, the earliest title to the domain had been bestowed upon friends by a king in exile (Charles II in 1649), and such circumstances inevitably resulted in a wearying, protracted battle over the legitimacy of the grant. Moreover, colonial authorities feared that the silk-stocking friends of the Crown who claimed to have received the region someday would use their influence to have the Northern Neck detached from Virginia and made into a proprietary colony; Virginia's rulers had only to look across the Potomac to Maryland for proof that the Crown would tolerate such a colony. So Virginia did nothing to facilitate immigration across the Rappahannock, and it was not until about the time of George Washington's birth that immigrants began to flow in considerable numbers into this region. By then the land ownership question at last had been resolved. About 6 million acres belonged to Thomas Lord Fairfax, who still lived in England. Otherwise, the Virginia Burgesses had finally completed a long overdue series of liberalizing land reforms that lowered both sale prices and property taxes in this corner of the province.[4]

In 1735 Gus transferred the family upriver forty miles or so, to yet another piece of his property, this on the Little Hunting Creek. Here, at Epsewasson, as it was called, he moved the family into a larger, more comfortable domicile, though it too was merely a one-and-a-half-story farmhouse. The house stood atop a bluff above the Potomac. Invisible much of the year, the mile-wide river, a languid highway that flowed from the unexplored West toward the Chesapeake and the markets and the civilization of the East, could only be seen when the dense wilderness foliage tumbled down in the late fall.

George lived here just three years before his father again yielded to the urge to move. Learning of the availability of an estate known as Ferry Farm on the west bank of the Rappahannock, Gus successfully negotiated the purchase of the property and the lease of three hundred adjoining acres. He thought it too good an opportunity to let pass. He retained Epsewasson, of course, and he left it in charge of Lawrence, George's half brother, who had just returned from school in England. The rest of the family moved south. Ferry Farm seemed to occupy a felicitous site, close to Gus's iron works, and just across the river from Fredericksburg, a rustic village to be sure, but a place where Gus could arrange for the formal education of his sons. His family had continued to grow. In addition to George and Sam, there now were John Augustine and Charles, both born at Epsewasson.

The family of seven, plus a domestic servant or two, moved to Ferry Farm late in 1738. They found the new house larger and more accommodating than their previous residence. This too was a frame structure, but with six rooms. Like Epsewasson, it sat atop a knoll that sloped gently down toward the river, the artery that would convey each year's tobacco crop to market. The house bulged with family treasures, the reward of Gus's frenetic business endeavors. Thirteen beds and twenty chairs mingled with a couch, two chests of drawers, a dining-room table, dressing table, card table, and a desk; mirrors graced various rooms, and expensive hardware adorned some of the six fireplaces. The family also owned more than a modest amount of china and silverware. Scattered to the rear of the house, in meager apertures carved out of the forest, stood the barn, dairy, kitchen, toolshed, and three or four rude cabins erected by the twenty slaves.[5]

In many ways George Washington's boyhood years were quite commonplace. He hunted in the enveloping woods around his home, and he fished and swam and sailed in the narrow river nearby. He and his brothers—especially John Augustine, to whom he was closest—played the perdurable games of young people, and he frolicked with the children of the slaves until he was nine or ten. Then the striplings were separated so that one could be taught the habits of the master and the others could learn those of the bondsman.

But Washington's youth was not identical to that of all boys in Virginia. His proximity to Fredericksburg afforded the opportunity for frequent visits to a bustling little town, and his wealth and status provided entrée to the elegant mansions of other planters in the county; moreover, his father's money bought some formal education for him, albeit less than that provided his half brothers. What scant training he did receive probably was intended to prepare him both for the more intensive curriculum of the Appleby School and for the routine duties faced by a Virginia planter. He learned to read and write, studied penmanship, read poetry, and was schooled in the social amenities; in addition, half or more of his training was in mathematics, including geometry and trigonometry, which his teachers emphasized as a precursor to exercises in surveying. To his later chagrin he never was introduced to the mysteries of Latin or other classical languages. Some of his training was at the hands of private tutors (one of whom was a convict indentured servant), although later he was enrolled in a small school in Fredericksburg operated by an Anglican clergyman.[6]

His reading habits as a young man were not much different from those he exhibited as an adult. For him reading always was a utilitarian exercise, a means to self-improvement and advancement. By nature an impatient sort when inactive, Washington never enjoyed reading as a leisure pastime. As a boy he read a little poetry, a bit of history, a few political essays; he was moved most by the ancient story of Cato, which he encountered through Joseph Addison's blank verse tragedy, a drama that depicted the resolve of Cato to resist the tyranny of Caesar, or to die. But George did not pursue any subject in a systematic manner. The one book that he seems to have studied most conscientiously was the *Rules of Civility and Decent Behavior in Company and Conversation*. Compiled by sixteenth-century Jesuits for the instruction of young French noblemen, the *Rules* listed over one hundred maxims for the proper conduct of a gentleman. Some admonitions dealt with hygiene and appearance: keep fingernails and teeth clean, maintain an erect posture. Some tips showed the way to an engaging manner: neither lie nor flatter, do not laugh or talk too loudly, stand when meeting a stranger, accept all advice graciously, control your temper, speak slowly and distinctly, listen attentively when in conversation, and in public eat in moderation. The most hopeless rubes were advised not to pick their teeth with their knives, not to spit seeds into their plates, not to scratch their private parts while in public, and not to stare at the blemishes of others.[7]

If young George was influenced by this book, he was even more profoundly affected by Lawrence, his elegant half brother. In fact, he probably was lured to read the *Rules* when he compared his own rustic manners to Lawrence's urbane demeanor. Polished and cultivated in England, Lawrence had been privy to a world that George had never seen and could not imagine. Lawrence, with his graceful, cosmopolitan habits, became the boy's first role model, more influential even than the youngster's parents.

Gus was too busy to devote much time to George. He provided his son with books and a tutor, and he planned to send him to England for his formal schooling. But as a father of seven, and one who chose to spend his time shuttling between his farm and his mines and his furnace, he did not overindulge this boy. The result was that young George does not appear to have been especially close to his father. In all the millions of words that he ultimately penned, George Washington never mentioned his father. He neither praised him nor damned him. It was as if he had never known his father, as if Gus, in his unremitting preoccupation with wealth, had so ignored his offspring that he ceased to matter to his son; or, perhaps, that his son, rather than live with an unpleasant reality, unconsciously repressed every memory of the father.

His mother was a different matter entirely. Mary Ball Washington was a tough, opinionated, selfish, overly protective, and possessive woman. One person who met Mary described her as "majestic and venerable"; another spoke of her "awe-inspiring air and manner" and went on to describe her as quiet, aloof, almost imperious, and very strong. A nephew of young George, a lad who frequently came to Ferry Farm, confessed that he was "ten times" more afraid of her than of his own mother. She exercised such dominion over her children that only George would really break away from her, and he succeeded only after a painful and drawn-out test of wills.[8]

Lacking a strong parental model, it was thus the example set by Lawrence that George found enticing. When they first met, George barely got to know his half brother. Living a substantial distance away, Lawrence seldom made the ride over Virginia's pitiful roads to Ferry Farm. Besides, his time was consumed by the management of Epsewasson and by whatever minimal social opportunities were available at that cloistered estate. Probably lonely and bored, certainly ambitious, Lawrence was caught up in the excitement that gripped the colony in 1740 when news arrived that Britain sought to raise a three-thousand man colonial army—four hundred of whom would be procured in Virginia—for an invasion of Cartagena, part of Spain's South American empire. Lawrence was the first in his province selected to command a company in the "American Regiment," as Virginia designated its contingent. Lawrence was an unlikely looking soldier. His face was soft, almost effeminate; round-shouldered, slightly paunchy, looking neither muscular nor particularly hardy, he exhibited more the countenance of the aesthete than that of a robust adventurer. In Douglas Southall Freeman's memorable phrase, he looked like the kind of person "to whom, in a crowd, a stranger would go to make an inquiry."[9]

Lawrence sailed in October, leaving behind parents and friends who waited anxiously for nearly two years for his return, a wait that would have been even more agonizing had they known of the pernicious ill-fortune that haunted the expedition. Only about one in three of the colonial recruits survived the campaign. Disease set in quickly, ultimately killing men by the score each day; the Spanish defenders extirpated the others. Lawrence was one of the lucky ones. He made it back in June, 1742, to tell all that "war is horrid in fact but much more so in imagination" than in reality.[10]

He returned to find that Augustine, George's other half brother, had just arrived from England. Now twenty years old, Augustine—Austin, he liked to be called—had quit school, perhaps at the behest of his father so he could manage either Ferry Farm or the iron works.[11] Though closer in age to Austin than to Lawrence, George never was close to this brother. The two were of strikingly different temperaments. Not very ambitious or self-reliant, more sedentary than George, and perhaps more certain of himself, Austin was content to live the life of a planter, leaving soldiering and politics, as well as the adventure and uncertainty of high-stakes financial speculation, to others.

It was to Lawrence, a man whom he perceived as a cosmopolitan adventurer, that little George was drawn, although, at first, the elder soldier-planter scarcely had time for his ten-year-old brother. After a visit with his relatives, Lawrence settled at Epsewasson. His first act was to give the place a new name, Mount Vernon, so designated in honor of Admiral Edward Vernon, commander of the Cartagena expedition. Thereafter, he seemed to have time only for the management of an estate that had been entrusted in his absence to an indifferent overseer.

Lawrence was superintending the planting of his first crop when jolting news arrived. Gus Washington was gravely ill, stricken with "gout of the stomach." Lawrence hurried south, but there was nothing he could do. Within hours of his arrival his father, just forty-nine years old, was dead.

When the will was probated three weeks later, Lawrence, the eldest son, received the lion's share of the estate, including Mount Vernon. Augustine, George later remembered, got the "best part," the lush, fertile land along Pope's Creek in Westmoreland County. Among the children from Gus's second marriage, George, the eldest, received the largest portion. At age twenty-one he was to acquire Ferry Farm, some land along the Aquia Creek that Gus had purchased nearly twenty years before, twenty-one hundred acres in what was called Deep Run tract, ten slaves, and three lots in Fredericksburg.[12]

Now independent and totally self-supporting, Lawrence married Anne Fairfax just two months after Gus's death. When he had returned to Epsewasson in 1742, Lawrence found that Colonel William Fairfax—of the same clan that owned so much of the Northern Neck—had constructed Belvoir, a lovely manor house, on the Hunting Creek property next door. The colonel, a cousin of Lord Fairfax, had only recently arrived in Virginia, coming down from Massachusetts to act as his uncle's agent in the sale of his lands and the collection of his quit rents. Lawrence soon knew his neighbors, and he and Anne, the colonel's daughter, sped through a whirlwind courtship. The wedding was in June 1743.

Having married well, Lawrence had doors opened for him that otherwise surely would have remained closed. Nancy, as his bride preferred to be called, bore a dowry of four thousand acres to the marriage, but more importantly she brought along the prestige and the immense power of the Fairfax family. Soon Lawrence not only added to his landed empire but acquired two important offices: he was elected to the House of Burgesses, and he was appointed adjutant general of the Virginia militia. Meanwhile, he commenced the rebuilding of Mount Vernon, transforming it from a cottage to a small manor house; not yet a mansion, it nevertheless suited the status and habits of a rising young planter and his fashionable new bride.[13]

Only eleven when his father died, George still was many years away from assuming the responsibilities of a small planter. He lived most of each year with his mother, who saw that he continued his education, although now with Gus gone and the estate fragmented all thoughts of schooling at Appleby were discarded. He spent a little time each year with his cousins at Chotank on Pope's Creek, and even longer periods calling on Austin in Westmoreland County. Increasingly, too, young George longed to visit Lawrence, for life at Mount Vernon and nearby Belvoir was exotically different from any world he ever had known. An air of power and influence, of sophistication, opulence, and gentility, of the mysteries

Lawrence Washington, by an unknown artist (ca. 1738). Courtesy of the Mount Vernon Ladies' Association of the Union.

of knowledge and of faraway places, pervaded the two estates. Lawrence, already a hero to George, now must have seemed a grandee. Brave and intelligent to begin with, Lawrence, in fact, was on the verge of becoming a great planter, a man who seemed to be respected by everyone and who sat with those in the highest seat of government in the province. To young George it must have seemed that there were no worlds left for Lawrence to conquer. Indeed, that there were no worlds that his half brother could not conquer.

When George visited Mount Vernon, he often was invited to Belvoir, close enough to be visible through the dark, bare forests in the winter months. Life at that elegant plantation took on a new dimension in 1744 when George William Fairfax, the colonel's son, arrived following fifteen years of schooling in England. George William was seven years older than George, and with little in their backgrounds to make for compatibility, the two initially were not close. Nevertheless, young Washington observed that George William was a meticulous, urbane, sensitive, and empathetic young man, much like Lawrence. Indeed, there were many similarities in the demeanor and mannerisms of these two older men.

George continued to live with his mother in his early teenage years, but his world now was inextricably bound to that of Lawrence and his elegant neighbors. Between the ages of eleven and sixteen, in fact, his view of life changed. He grew to desire something greater than that which seemed to await him—a station as a modestly prosperous planter, albeit an unknown and a powerless one. He now knew that he wished to escape both his mother's iron grip and the acarpous soil of Ferry Farm. He knew, too, that he yearned to be like Lawrence and George William Fairfax: Lawrence, resplendent in his scarlet uniform, revered for his courage, pandered to because of his wealth and status, the object of attention; George William, rich and powerful, a graceful man whose educated habits and tastes distinguished him from the common run of provincial planters. Young Washington had observed the beauty and the style of their milieu, and he longed to live in a world akin to theirs: to wear elegant attire, to express brilliant ideas, to enjoy refined pursuits, and to bask in the deference of others. Lawrence and George William seemed so cultivated in comparison to his own family that young Washington could not but be keenly aware of his limitations in their presence. He felt awkward and clumsy, painfully aware of his lack of refinement in the drawing room and his inarticulateness in the company of the eloquent people who gathered at these Potomac mansions.

But he did not shun the environment that made him uncomfortable, nor, as others might, did he rebel against that which he did not understand. Instead, he labored tirelessly to overcome his deficiencies. His fragile self-esteem under siege, he sought to capture the attention of these older men by making himself over in their image. His tactics were simple: he read, studied, attended, and imitated. He fell into the habit of quiescence, watching, listening, seldom speaking, and all the while discreetly preparing and polishing his behavior and expression into an accommodating style. He quietly took music and fencing lessons back in

Fredericksburg. He developed a passion for fashionable clothing. And he completed his education through a methodical study of *The Young Man's Companion*, another self-help book. It delved into etiquette, arithmetic, and surveying, the latter a tool that he might put to good use since Colonel Fairfax already had begun to make plans for charting the family's domain.[14]

Like Lawrence and George William, Colonel Fairfax also exerted a profound influence upon young George, becoming, in fact, a surrogate father to the youngster. The colonel discovered many similarities in George's background and his own, for he too had received little assistance from his parents. Moreover, the colonel, a forceful and enterprising man, was disappointed with George William, a son he regarded as reticent and uninspiring. Young Washington possessed the qualities that the colonel admired: he was strong and reserved, an excellent horseman, intelligent, and quick tempered. The boy wanted to get ahead; in fact, he seemed to be impelled by a compulsive need to improve himself and his status. Fairfax took the unsure youngster under his wing, instilling in him the lessons that had led to his own success: observation and hard work were the virtues displayed by those who succeeded, he advised, although it did not hurt to find and pander to a powerful potential benefactor.[15] George was not unwilling to follow the advice.

The colonel, of course, became that benefactor, offering assistance and opening doors that in only a decade led George to a plateau he otherwise could never have reached. His patron first offered support when George was just fourteen years old. The colonel procured an offer of a commission in the Royal Navy for the youngster; within a couple days, if he chose to do so, George could become a midshipman aboard a vessel docked in a Virginia harbor. Lawrence thought it the best option facing George. If he refused the commission, Lawrence told him, he probably faced nothing better than Ferry Farm for the remainder of his life, and there he could anticipate only a long struggle with both unexceptional soil and his intractable mother. On the other hand, a naval career offered the lures of travel and adventure, not to mention advancement to a higher social level in England than he ever was likely to attain in Virginia. Lawrence reminded George that this was how the colonel himself had begun his career, for his parents had placed him in the Royal Navy when he was about the same age. Trusting Lawrence's wisdom, George quickly agreed to join, if he could gain his mother's consent.[16]

Mary Washington agreed, then disagreed, then decided to seek the advice of her half brother in England. That put the final decision in limbo for more than nine months. She and her son, both of them tenacious and headstrong, probably clashed vehemently while they awaited Uncle Joseph Ball's counsel. It is likely too that she and Lawrence also discussed the matter acrimoniously. Finally, word arrived from Stratford by Bow: George's uncle denounced the idea. The youth, he wrote, would be better served as an apprentice to a tinker, for a sailor's pay was inconsequential and his liberties were virtually nonexistent. "And as for any considerable preferment in the Navy," he added, "it is not to be expected [as] there are always too many grasping for it here, who have interest and he has none."

That decided the issue. Mary Washington ruled against her son's enlistment, and he, not yet fifteen, complied.[17]

Whatever George's feelings about the final decision, he remained at home for the next year, working on the farm and continuing his self-education, especially his persistent attempts to unravel the mysteries of surveying. His growing knowledge soon stood him in good stead. In 1747 Thomas Lord Fairfax, legal title to his millions of frontier acres at last safely in his possession, arrived at Belvoir. He was in America to oversee the surveying and selling of a chunk of his domain, beginning with a tract that lay across the mountains, along the South Branch of the Potomac.

A surveying party was being assembled. George William was named to the team, and sixteen-year-old George Washington was invited to come along. He could serve as a chainman, and if time permitted he could even survey a bit. Besides, he would be paid a modest salary. To this activity his mother agreed.[18]

When the men left Mount Vernon the jonquils and the golden brillance of the forsythia already had heralded the arrival of spring. They rode west, climbing steadily upward into the mountains, past patches of unmelted snow and across streams whose thin ice coverlets resembled glass table tops, on and on through an unending forest yet in the thrall of the last lingering clutches of winter, then back down the other side of the Blue Ridge and into the long rolling meadows of the valley, which, as if by magic, already luxuriated in a new season's flowers, bathed in the warm sunlight of spring. At first the team had paused each night at the plantations and farms of hospitable backcountry settlers, but once it reached the South Branch the men slept outdoors for seventeen consecutive nights. By the fourth afternoon the party was running surveys. Long, exhausting days of labor followed. Hour after hour the men clambered through the wilderness thickets, groping for footing on the slick, leaf-covered forest floor, as they felled trees so that a line could be sighted. All the while they stayed alert for evidence of the presence of rattlesnakes and other uncompanionable forest creatures. Once the work was interrupted when they ran into a band of thirty Indians returning from a war party, likely the first sizable batch of Native Americans that Washington had encountered. The Virginians entertained their new acquaintances by sharing their liquor, and the Indians, who seemed friendly enough, reciprocated with a dance and a concert. Washington's only brush with danger came one night near the end of the expedition when the straw on which he was sleeping caught fire; luckily, one of the men awakened and doused the flames before any harm was done. Shortly after that incident, George William and Washington, both lonely and tired, and lately—because of a breakdown in their victualing network—rather hungry, decided to return home ahead of the rest of the party. They rode on alone. Although they managed to lose their way once, going twenty miles in the wrong direction, the two weary, homesick young men arrived at Belvoir, home at last a little more than a month after the foray had begun.[19]

George William had an especially good reason to hurry home. On the eve of the expedition he had met Sally Cary. The two were engaged and planned a late autumn wedding. His fiancee was from Ceelys, a mansion along the lower James River near Hampton. She had grown up dividing her time between that pastoral environment and Williamsburg, the lively little hub of Virginia culture during the few weeks each year when the Burgesses was in session. George must have believed immediately that Mr. Fairfax, as he still deferentially called George William, had made a good catch. Slender and long-necked, her enchanting oval face was dominated by wide, dark, alluring eyes and set off by her long, cascading black hair; her manner was lively, and witty, and coquettish.[20]

George returned to Ferry Farm following his first western adventure. The next fifteen months were to be the last he would spend as the dependent of his mother. With some money in his pockets for the first time, he occasionally took the ferry across to Fredericksburg to purchase new items for his growing wardrobe. In September he enrolled under a dance instructor, this to refine his talents for the approaching wedding ball. He slipped off to visit his cousins at Chotank that summer, spent a few pleasant days at the downstream estate of a family friend, and, of course, he occasionally rode over to Mount Vernon and Belvoir. Mostly, though, he helped with the management of Ferry Farm, and he looked after his self-improvement. He read the *Spectator*, perused a biography of Frederick the Great, and read a translated edition of the principal dialogues of Seneca, each a source for the many witty and profound comments that Lawrence and George William made about the dinner table or before the hearth in the drawing room. But Washington was enough of a pragmatist to spend most of his time working on his surveying books, and those efforts paid immediate dividends. In July 1749 he was commissioned a county surveyor in Culpepper County, a post that paid £15 annually.[21] More importantly, the license was his badge of independence from Ferry Farm and his mother.

Within two days of receiving his commission Washington was at work, and for several weeks during each of the next three years he led his own surveying teams into the west. Virtually all of his work was undertaken in the Shenandoah and Cacapon valleys of Frederick County, tracts that fell within the Fairfax proprietary domain. Washington's fee was steep, about £1 per thousand acres above the rate set by the colony's assembly, but it does not seem to have adversely affected the volume of his business. Operating out of an office that he opened in Winchester, he undertook two hundred or more surveys in this period, averaging about £125 in earnings each year, an income roughly equal to that of a skilled artisan. But he also occasionally received land in lieu of cash payments, a kind of deferred salary that offered the potential for spectacular payoffs far beyond those to which any craftsman could aspire.

A rugged existence was imposed on anyone intrepid enough to undertake one of these expeditions. A surveyor wore the same clothing for days on end, "like a Negro," Washington told a friend. The surveying team normally slept outdoors, bedeviled, it must have seemed, by every species of vermin in North

America, and buffeted by the chill mountain rains of spring and the raw, icy blasts of late autumn. The men subsisted on adequate, but monotonous, diets of salt pork and dried beef, although if they were lucky they might have a catch of wild turkey or fish to roast over hot coals, gourmet fare washed down by the brandy and rum they carefully hauled along.[22]

Soon the sound of money jingling in his pockets brought out the gambler in Washington's character, and he too joined in the western speculative fever. He was just eighteen when he purchased his first western tract, over 450 acres in the Shenandoah Valley, a place known as Dutch George's. Soon thereafter he acquired another parcel, over 1000 acres along Bullskin Creek, a tributary of the Shenandoah River that meanders near the present boundary of Virginia and West Virginia.[23]

If he was exhilarated at his new-found freedom, Washington was greeted with ominous news shortly after his initial western expedition. Lawrence had sailed for London. Plagued by a chronic cough symptomatic of tuberculosis, the most dreaded degenerative disease of the age, he had been examined by physicians at Mount Vernon and at Williamsburg, but the medicines they prescribed—worthless compounds of herbs—were unavailing. Now quite ill, he requested a leave of absence from the Burgesses. Anxious and exasperated, he sailed that summer for the British capital, hoping that more skilled physicians there might better treat his affliction. But he was no better when he returned to Virginia in the fall, and by the next summer his condition had only deteriorated further. Desperate for succor, he persuaded George to accompany him to Berkeley Springs, a highly acclaimed spa across the Blue Ridge Mountains. They made two difficult trips to the springs, but the waters were of no help, and, in fact, Lawrence found the damp and chilly climate in the mountains to be more of a danger than a palliative. Only one hope remained. Perhaps a winter in the mild Caribbean might be rejuvenating. Besides, a commercial friend of Lord Fairfax had spoken highly of a physician in Barbados, one with a good record in treating the victims of consumption. Moreover, as if his luck had finally turned for the better, his wife, Nancy, gave birth to a little girl, Sarah, not long after his return from Berkeley Springs. And Sarah survived, the first of their four offspring to live beyond infancy. Maybe little Sarah's survival would prove to be a harbinger of good fortune. At any rate, he now had something else to live for. Lawrence induced George to accompany him on this trip too, and the young men sailed for Bridgetown in September 1751.[24]

The voyage, the only extended cruise George ever took, was typical of those in the age of sailing. The vessel was out for thirty-seven days. It was a reasonably uneventful, if lengthy, trip. The vessel was assaulted by strong gales and incessant rain for half a dozen days, and, added to the occasional dangers and the prolonged monotony of the trip, there was a shortage of biscuit, a condition that occurred when the ship's bread was afflicted by weevils and maggots. But Washington seemed to handle matters like an old salt, occupying much of his spare time conversing with the crew, powerful, coarse men with whom he quickly established a rapport.[25]

The two Virginians disembarked early in November. The next day Lawrence was examined by the physician who had been so highly recommended. His diagnosis sparked a ray of hope. While he too concluded that Lawrence suffered from tuberculosis, he did not regard the disease as incurable, and he merely prescribed rest in the bucolic countryside outside Bridgetown. Lawrence quickly found the climate too harsh to venture out, except in the cool evenings. George, however, spent his first two weeks on the island at the theater, or attending a bewildering succession of dinner parties, or simply sightseeing. Then, suddenly, on his fifteenth day in Bridgetown, he was roused from his sleep with a blinding headache and a burning fever. Not long thereafter pustules appeared over his body, and it was evident that he had the smallpox, perhaps the most dangerous of the febrile viruses then prevalent. In a strange environment, hundreds of miles from his relatives—save for Lawrence, who was too weak to offer any real assistance—George was bedfast for nearly four weeks, some of the time languishing in great agony, always realizing that death might come soon. But by mid-December he felt better, and soon his doctor pronounced him well, both cured and now, of course, immune forever to the disease. Aside from the temporary loss of a few pounds, he had only a slightly pockmarked face, hardly an oddity in the eighteenth century, to show for his travail.[26]

During the last few days of George's illness, while he still was confined to his bedchamber, the brothers reached important decisions. Lawrence already had concluded that the trip was a failure. He decided to sail as soon as possible for Bermuda, forlornly hoping that its climate might prove a restorative. George, undoubtedly more homesick than ever after his brush with death, and anxious to get in one surveying expedition before the spring foliage burst out and obscured the countryside, longed to return home. The brothers, thus, decided to split up. Just ten days after he was allowed once again to venture outside, George booked passage on a ship bound for Virginia.[27]

Washington was hardly at sea before he fell prey to seasickness, a precursor, it turned out, to a thoroughly unpleasant return voyage. For days on end his vessel, the *Industry*, was tormented by rain squalls and thrashing winds. After two weeks at sea, moreover, he discovered that a thief had broken into his chest and made off with £10 of his hard-earned surveyor's wages. Finally, thirty-six days out of Barbados, land was sighted, and three days later George debarked near the mouth of the York River. Having brought ashore some letters for the governor of Virginia, he rented a horse and rode to "ye great . . . polis" of Williamsburg, as he referred to the provincial capital. The governor, Robert Dinwiddie, sixty, wealthy, a graduate of the University of Glasgow, a resident of the Caribbean most of his adult life, greeted the young man cordially, and invited him to stay for dinner. One can only guess at that evening's table talk between the eighteen-year-old and his eminent, stately host. That the governor was impressed by the young man's initiative and flintiness, however, soon would be evident. The following morning George rode to Yorktown to attend a cockfighting tournament, then he rested for a few days at a distant relative's plantation. Early in February, nearly four and a half months following his departure, he returned to Mount Vernon.[28]

George spent several hours with Nancy Washington describing Lawrence's condition. It was a mixed report that brought his anxious sister-in-law some dim hope, but no joy. Thereafter, George did not remain idle for long. He visited with his mother briefly, then, barely a month after his return to Virginia, he sped to the frontier and another surveying job. He clambered over and through the wilderness for nearly two months on this trip, but he pocketed enough money to purchase—for £115—an additional 552 acres for his growing Bullskin Creek realm.[29]

Washington's homecoming from this expedition in May was blighted by various calamities. He had no more than reached Ferry Farm before he fell victim to a debilitating pleurisy. While he was still bedfast, moreover, distressing news arrived from Bermuda. Lawrence had reached the islands early in April, but upon his arrival his illness had taken a turn for the worse. While a new physician promised a cure if he abided by a strict regimen—a vegetarian diet, no alcoholic beverages, and rigorous daily exercise—the melancholy tone of Lawrence's letters left little doubt that he had all but abandoned hope. He spoke of staying on the island for the next several months, then of returning to Barbados or perhaps even of sailing to southern France for the winter. Knowing that another winter in Virginia "will most certainly destroy me," he implored Nancy to come to him, speculating that perhaps George would accompany her. "If I grow worse, I shall hurry home to my grave; if better, I shall be induced to stay longer here to complete a cure," he disconsolately concluded in his last letter. When Lawrence suddenly returned to Mount Vernon in mid-June there was no longer any doubt that he was doomed. He hastily put his affairs in order, and six weeks later his agony ended.[30]

George and Augustine spent the next several months helping Nancy tidy up the loose ends of Lawrence's affairs. The will was a confusing document, one stack of contingencies upon another. George, albeit in "consideration of [his] love and affection," received only three lots in Fredericksburg; but, if he survived Nancy, and if little Sarah died without issue, George was to have Mount Vernon and its plentiful lands. By December the Washingtons knew that Lawrence's wealth was not all it had appeared to be. Without adequate supervision for four years or more, Mount Vernon had produced only meager yields of tobacco; in addition, the expenses attending Lawrence's quest for health had been extraordinary. Faced with indebtedness, his survivors were compelled to sell every item that could be sacrificed, including some of Lawrence's personal effects. George, in fact, acquired several head of livestock during the auction.[31] About the time of the sale, less than six months after Lawrence's funeral, Nancy remarried, selecting George Lee, uncle of Lighthorse Harry Lee, and moved to his Westmoreland estate. For two years Mount Vernon was left to stand idle, a mute reminder of the joys and tragedies it had witnessed during the past decade.

Washington, too, was busy during these months, and not just running surveys. Driven by his acquisitive urge, he now even more assiduously pushed for wealth and status, and for recognition as well. A younger son who had taken a back seat to two older brothers, he hungered to be noticed, to be seen and respected. Even while Lawrence was on his deathbed, Washington had quietly initiated a campaign to secure the dying man's position as adjutant general of Virginia, once even journeying to Williamsburg to speak directly with Dinwiddie. He did not permit the fact that he was barely twenty years old and without military experience to impede him. The position aroused his interest, for not only was it a sinecure worth £100 annually, it carried a modicum of prestige. In the end his efforts succeeded—to a point. The governor and his council decided to divide Virginia into four military districts. Washington was made adjutant of the least desirable territory, the southernmost borough that sprawled from the James to the North Carolina boundary, then west to the frontier. Obviously disappointed, Washington did not even visit the counties of his adjutancy during the first year and a half of his tenure, but he continued to press for the Northern Neck command, doggedly courting those who might be of assistance. In 1753 he got the post he coveted.[32]

To this point Washington had displayed no interest in the major political issues of the day, but it was a political matter that suddenly offered him a chance for renown. By mid-century the ceaseless western movement of English colonists verged on spilling over the mountains and into the Ohio Valley, a prospect that whetted the appetite of speculators in the middle colonies. Those in Virginia were among the first to act. In 1748 Lawrence Washington and several other planters had joined to form the Ohio Company and to apply to London for an official grant. The king obliged, investing the company with 200,000 acres along the Ohio River, and promising an additional 300,000 acres in seven years if the proprietors succeeded in erecting and maintaining a fort and in settling one hundred inhabitants. Its first step a success, the Ohio Company next hired Christopher Gist, a surveyor/explorer/Indian trader, to search the area for a site for a combination trading post and fortress; in addition, he was to mollify the Indians who might be uneasy at the sight of English settlers barging into their homeland. By 1750 the company had blazed a road through eighty miles of wilderness, and within another two or three years, thanks to a heavy personal investment by Virginia's new governor, Robert Dinwiddie, company policy and government policy were indelicately intertwined.

All this frenetic activity might have gone more or less unnoticed, just another in the never-ending ploys of rich men to use their government to grow even richer, except that the stakes had become international in scope. Great Britain and France had been fighting one another for control of North America since 1689. Already they had fought three wars, and the most recent one, which had ended in

1748, had, like all its predecessors, been so inconclusive as to make yet a fourth conflict almost inevitable. The earlier wars had been waged over territory in the East, over islands in the Caribbean, and for the right of dominion over places like Newfoundland and Nova Scotia. But now that the population was about to burst over America's mountain barrier, the Ohio Valley was very much on the minds of Frenchmen and Englishmen. To demonstrate its interest Versailles dispatched fifteen hundred troops south of Lake Erie in 1753, men whose orders were to remove every English trader from the territory; moreover, every few miles they were to plant iron tablets proclaiming France's possession of this vast realm. When Governor Dinwiddie learned of this he realized that Virginia's—and his— Ohio dreams were doomed unless he acted quickly. In June he wrote London of France's actions, and in October he received his orders: send an emissary to the Ohio country, a messenger who would serve notice that the region belonged to Great Britain; if the French did not immediately withdraw, Virginia was to "drive them off by Force of Arms."[33]

When news of London's orders reached George Washington, restive in the isolation and obscurity of Ferry Farm, he made the decision that changed his life. He raced for Williamsburg to volunteer to bear the message to the French. For the third time in less than two years Dinwiddie greeted this enterprising young man.

Dinwiddie was old enough to be Washington's grandfather, but he did not exhibit many avuncular or paternal ways. Short and fat, with a double chin that protruded beneath his puffy, ruddy face, he exuded an air of entrepreneurial lust. He had, in fact, grown wealthy through mercantile endeavors, accumulating a fortune that had enabled him to live and travel extensively on both sides of the Atlantic. Yet, despite his education and his urbanity, an inescapable coarseness was visible through the noble front that he continually sought to maintain. Money and power were the drives that propelled him.[34]

He must have recognized a kindred spirit in the young man who was ushered into his elegant office that sunny autumn afternoon. But the governor also knew that the mission he had in mind would be arduous, possibly dangerous. The messenger that he chose would have to pass through Indian country, would have to dwell, in fact, in the midst of Native Americans whose friendship was being sought by the French. Nor could the French reaction be predicted. Indeed, Dinwiddie advised that already there had been several unpleasant incidents involving French soldiers and luckless English traders. The man who carried the governor's message could not be just any young planter on the make.

Nationalistic lore has so canonized Washington that it is difficult to imagine the young man who was shown into the governor's presence on that Indian Summer afternoon. The "real" Washington seems to have vanished for our age, replaced by an icon that too infrequently bears scant resemblance to a human being. But the youthful Washington that Dinwiddie officiously greeted that October day was very human.

The strapping young man easily met the physical prerequisites for the difficult mission which Dinwiddie had in mind. At age twenty-one George Washington was fully grown, and standing six feet and three inches tall he towered above almost every contemporary. He was broad-shouldered, with long muscular arms. His waist was small and flat, though he was rather wide across the hips. He tended to stand ramrod straight on long, solidly developed legs. He moved about in a fluid, agile manner, and word was that he was an excellent, graceful horseman. There was no hint of softness in the youngster's appearance, particularly not in his face. He would not have been thought handsome, but he hardly was unattractive. Instead, people thought they saw a kind of steely toughness in his features. It was in his blue-grey eyes that this quality seemed most pronounced, for he had learned to stare at—almost through—anyone with whom he spoke. Then, too, he seldom spoke, as if to underscore that he was a man of action, not of words. Clearly, he was not an ignorant brute. He did not bear the looks of a violent person, nor did he convey a sense of viciousness. A little awkward socially, he nevertheless was courteous, and it was apparent that he was familiar with the social code of the planter elite. Tough, yet cordial and with a bit of polish, Washington must also have struck Dinwiddie as being sensible and reliable.[35]

Still, the governor must have tried to learn something of the inner spirit that drove this quiet young man, anxious to learn why any person would be drawn to such a hazardous undertaking. In that endeavor, however, Dinwiddie surely must have been frustrated. George Washington already was a private man, one who carefully guarded his feelings from every intruder.

We cannot know exactly what Dinwiddie deduced about the character of his young caller, but whatever reservations he might have harbored would have been dispelled by the strong recommendation proffered by Washington's powerful benefactor at Belvoir. In reality, Dinwiddie seems to have entertained few doubts about the young man. Sketchy though it is, the evidence hints that the governor's reaction to Washington was based on an amalgam of emotion and instinct. Curiously, Dinwiddie's response was not without precedent; nor would he be the last person to react in this manner to this complicated young man. The governor seemed moved by Washington. A man without a son—Dinwiddie had not married until he was past forty, then he had fathered two daughters— perhaps Washington had stirred some paternal sense within him, some nebulous feeling that transcended the normal relationship of officeholder and supplicant. Washington may have awakened the same subliminal feelings in Dinwiddie's breast as he had in Fairfax's. What is clear is that Washington possessed certain qualities, attributes that quickened the imagination of others, that inspired their confidence, that made some want to follow him, and that caused most men to trust in him, some obscure capacity that has vanished in the impassivity of time and that was never captured in the phlegmatic prose of his contemporaries. What also seems likely is that this young man who had labored so long and hard to improve himself would also have been capable of honing his skills at playing the role of surrogate son. Fairfax had advised as much, and in his aristocratic society—where merit was a virtue, though it was secondary in importance to one's wealth and connections—ingratiating behavior was neither uncommon nor universally displeasing.

At any rate, when Washington left Dinwiddie's office that afternoon he had been selected to bear the governor's message. His orders: he was to depart immediately for Logstown, an Indian village on the Allegheny, where he was to procure an escort from among the Algonquins; he and his guardsmen then were to proceed north until they met the French commander, whereupon he was to present Dinwiddie's letter; he was to wait no longer than one week for the French reply, during which time he was to keep his eyes open, gathering information on the strength, arms, intelligence, and plans of this potential adversary.[36]

Within two weeks the emissary was on his way, plunging deep into the lonely wilderness near the Pennsylvania-Maryland border. He had hired Jacob van Braam, once a lieutenant in the Dutch army, and his former fencing instructor, to be his translator. Christopher Gist came along too; middle-aged but still rugged, he was there to serve as a guide and to handle the diplomatic entreaties that were to be made to the Native Americans. Washington also hired four additional men to tend the horses and the supplies.

The party of seven set off from Gist's residence near Wills Creek in mid-November, plodding up Laurel Hill, moving steadily in a north-by-northwest direction. Eleven days of toil lay between his cabin and Logstown, a trek made no easier by an almost uninterrupted rain that pelted the men. A few day's hiking across intermittent Indian trails and through the defoliated late autumn wilderness brought the party to the Youghiogheny, muddy and swollen from the incessant storms. The men labored toward its junction with the Monongahela, skirting the confluence, marching along the eastern bank until, only a few miles further north, they forded the Allegheny. From there it was only about a dozen miles to the Indian village, and at sunset the next day the sight of smoke from rude lodgings told them they at last had arrived. Until then the only break in the band's wearisome advance had come when Washington, having canoed to the junction of the Monongahela and the Allegheny, spent two days at the point, or the forks, reconnoitering for the best site for the Ohio Company's fort.

The Virginia party stayed at Logstown for five days while the Indians procured the guides who would lead them to the French. Washington rested, and he spent a good portion of his time chatting with the Half King, a sachem of the Senacas. Washington omitted a great deal in his discussions with the chieftan, explaining only that he was on a mission to deliver a letter to the French leader. But the Half King probably guessed the real reason for the young man's journey, even volunteering that his tribesmen already had threatened to drive the French from the region, a warning, he said, which the Gallic commander had only mocked, claiming the Indians were a mere annoyance, like flies and mosquitoes.

Finally the party, augmented now by its Indian guides, set out for French

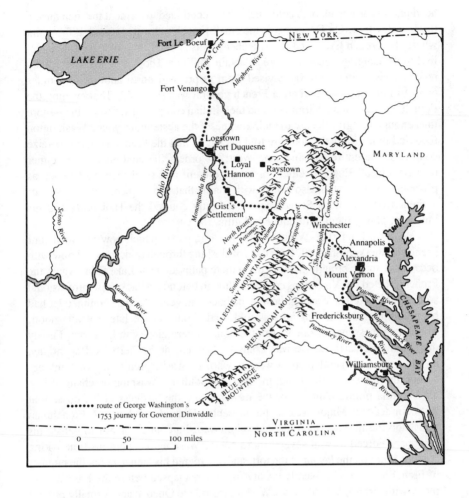

Young Washington's West

headquarters at Venango. A cold, dreary rain continued to torment the men during the five-day trek. On December 4 the small French outpost, located at the point where the French Creek fed the Allegheny, was spotted, a rain-soaked fleur-de-lis limply hanging above its gate. Captain Philippe Thomas Joncaire cordially received his visitors, but he advised them to proceed north another fifty miles or so to Fort Le Boeuf, where a French general was stationed. That evening the French entertained the Virginians and their Indian companions. Over wine—more than enough to "give license to their Tongues," the abstemious young Washington recorded in his journal—Joncaire told his guests that the French planned to seize control of the entire transmontane West; his orders, he continued, were either to drive out all English settlers or to seize them and send them to Quebec as prisoners. Washington also noted with alarm that the Frenchman, the son of a French officer and a Seneca squaw, adroitly courted the Half King and his kinsmen, plying them with liquor and gifts.

After a brief stay, Washington's swelling party, which now included four French soldiers, pushed off. Four days of sloshing through rain, mingled now with occasional snow, brought them to the remote pallisade near Lake Erie. Again the French greeted the Virginians cordially, though behind his back these professional soldiers snickered at Washington as "the buckskin general." The commander had been summoned, Washington was told, and should arrive late that afternoon. The young messenger whiled away the hours fraternizing with his hosts. Finally the commander arrived. He was Louis Le Gardeur de St Pierre de Repentigny, an old, one-eyed gentleman, a warrior who, to Washington's way of thinking, comported himself with "much the Air of a Soldier." Washington changed into his Virginia militia uniform for the meeting, and the business of his mission at last commenced. Major Washington presented Dinwiddie's letter. A Frenchman translated the missive, then the general convened a council of war to debate his response. Forced to wait several more hours, Washington spent his time taking copious notes on the layout of the fort, and he ordered his men to count the number of Frenchmen present. Nearly twenty-four hours elapsed before the French were ready with a reply. Would Major Washington ride to Quebec and formally present the letter to the Governor of Canada? No! Such a trek was beyond the scope of his orders. Another wait ensued as the French officers once again conferred. That evening Washington finally was handed the written response of the general. The French officer promised only to forward Dinwiddie's letter to higher-ups. At least Virginia's ultimatum had been served, and that surely was as much as Dinwiddie had hoped for. The French, meanwhile, could not have been more friendly. Washington was fêted while he was at Le Boeuf, and when he was ready to depart the French, in the spirit of the season—Christmas was just a week away—provided their visitors with two canoes and a plentiful supply of liquor and food.[37]

Washington and his party set out almost immediately after receiving the French response. It was to be a treacherous return trip. For seven days the party canoed through icy streams, at times hampered by such jams that they were obliged to drag their crafts ashore and carry them overland; at other times they were sped along by swollen, frenzied rivers, losing one canoe and its cargo of wine and meat to the furious surf. At Venango, north of present-day Pittsburgh, the Virginians divided into two groups: Gist and Washington donned buckskin garments and set out on foot, while the Dutch translator was placed in command of the other men and of the enervated horses. Trampling through deep snow in near zero temperatures, Washington and his partner walked eighteen miles the first day, lodging that night in the cabin of a hospitable Indian.

Along the way a day or two later they fell in with another Indian who offered to be their guide. He acted friendly enough, though there was something unsettling about him, some inscrutable air that aroused their suspicion. Still, Washington and Gist agreed that he could come along. By now Washington was having a hard time. Too exhausted to carry his pack, he let the Indian shoulder it for him. Then it was his feet. Blisters burst open, making each step sheer torture. Washington begged Gist to stop and make camp, even though it was only mid-afternoon. The Indian objected. There were dangerous Ottowa tribesmen preying in these woods, he cautioned. Besides, his cabin was nearby. Why not spend the night there? The two agreed, but two more miles of hiking still did not lead them to his dwelling. Now angry as well as debilitated, Washington decreed that they were stopping. Camp would be made right there. Suddenly, the Indian whirled about and fired at Gist, obviously the man he most feared and respected, since he aimed what would probably be his only shot at him. Somehow he missed. For an instant Gist and Washington stared blankly, frozen in shock. Then they sprang after their assailant, dragging him down. Gist would have killed him right there, but Washington protested. They disarmed the Indian and sent him north, while, under cover of darkness, they set out to the south, walking for twenty-four consecutive hours until they reached the Allegheny.

Five days later they spotted the welcome sight of Gist's cabin. Washington had barely made it. Rafting down the Allegheny, propelled by swift currents, darting precipitously between ice chunks, he lost his footing and cascaded into the piercing waters. Gist could not help. It was all he could do to keep the raft afloat; besides, his frostbitten fingers were too painfully sore to be of any use. Somehow Washington managed to grab hold of the raft, clinging for dear life until Gist could steer the beleaguered vessel and its passengers to the haven of an island.[38]

When the two reached Gist's residence Washington paused only long enough to procure a horse. Nine days later he was at Belvoir, where he stopped to rest and to have a good meal and a comfortable night's sleep, and, of course, to report on his adventures to Colonel Fairfax. In mid-January, a month and a half after his departure, Washington was back in Williamsburg, delivering the French response—such as it was—and an account of his exploits to Dinwiddie. The governor was impressed. He also believed the young major might be used to further his schemes. In its last session, the Burgesses had refused to appropriate even a cent for defense against the French. However, Washington's eyewitness account of the French efforts to woo the Indians, and his story of Joncaire's bellicose rhetoric, might convert the legislators to the governor's way of thinking. He asked the young man to return the next afternoon with an account of his expedition suitable for publication. The major worked far into the night compiling a narrative of his adventure, a chronicle worked out from the sketchy notes he had made along the way. Right on time, Washington delivered the manuscript the next afternoon. Dinwiddie hurriedly looked it over, rushed it to the printers, and issued a call for a special session of the Burgesses. Within the month a local printer issued Washington's narrative of his trek. Subsequently it was reprinted in several American newspapers, and it was distributed in London as well.[39]

Meanwhile, Dinwiddie moved quickly on various fronts. He dispatched a party of workers to the site Washington had chosen for a fort, he called up two hundred frontier militiamen, whose duty it would be to maintain the new installation, and he asked the Burgesses to finance a supplemental force of four hundred additional men. As adjutant of the Northern Neck District, Washington was directed to raise a hundred of the troops. The time for playing at being a soldier, of merely wearing a handsome uniform at balls and celebrations, was at an end. Now Washington was an officer in the midst of an undeclared war. There is no reason to suspect that he was disappointed with this turn of events. Soldiers still were lauded and lionized throughout eighteenth-century America. Soldiering, moreover, was a fast path to recognition, especially for a tough young man without a formal education, a man who otherwise faced only the prospect of a lifetime as a middling planter.[40]

Washington's first month as an actual soldier was exasperating. Recruiting went slowly. This was a farming society, and one with little tradition of active militia service; besides, the pay was low, and the men were compelled to furnish their own arms and powder. Probably some agreed with those in the Burgesses who muttered that the Ohio country legitimately belonged to France, and some may have suspected that Washington's report was a pack of lies designed to facilitate Dinwiddie's pecuniary interests rather than to further the welfare of Virginia. Unable to secure many enlistees, Dinwiddie shaved his army to only three hundred men, and he offered land bounties to those who would serve. The governor also named Joshua Fry as commander. Fry was a college professor with militia training but no fighting experience; Washington scorned him as old, fat, and slow. Of course, Washington had longed for the appointment. In fact, he had hung around Williamsburg while the Burgesses was in session actively lobbying for the command. Disappointed in that respect, he nevertheless was promoted to lieutenant colonel and made second in command. He was only twenty-two years old, and unlike Fry he had never served in a military unit under the watchful eye of a superior officer. When Dinwiddie received word that hundreds of French troops were proceeding to the Ohio, he ordered Colonel Washington to push ahead without Fry; he was to attempt to beat the French to Virginia's fortress at the forks of the Ohio.[41]

Having spent a month engaged in endless paper shuffling at headquarters in Alexandria, Washington was eager to move out. He debouched for the front with a band of 134 ill-trained, poorly equipped, mostly "loose, Idle" men. He retraced his now-familiar path to Winchester—the way he had taken on numerous surveying excursions—where he was joined by a company of 25 men raised by Adam Stephen, a bachelor physician who had immigrated recently from Scotland. The small army spent a week there while its commander searched for additional supplies. While at Winchester Washington learned that Virginia's new fort on the Ohio had fallen to the French.

He also learned that there were more than a thousand French troops on the Ohio. A more experienced officer might have been inclined to await reinforcements, but Washington pushed on, planning now to march to the junction of the Red Stone Creek and the Monongahela, thirty-seven miles south of the Ohio, and there await Colonel Fry or new orders. His principal aim, evidently, was to impress the Indians with Virginia's vigor and resolve. By mid-May he was deep into the forbidding wilderness, the first transmontane road into the Ohio country cut behind him, when good news arrived. Reinforcements were on the way. He could expect assistance from the Independent Companies of New York. But there was trouble too. His officers had carped about their low pay since the day they began their service. Their complaints were not unjustified; their pay was far below that of British officers who served in America. Despite their cries, however, word now arrived from Williamsburg that the Burgesses had refused to increase their wages. The officers exploded, drafting a strong letter of protest to Dinwiddie, complete with veiled threats to resign. Washington refused to sign the document, but he did transmit it to the governor, accompanied by a letter of his own in which he announced that he would henceforth serve without remuneration rather than accept his "shadow of pay." [42]

At times Virginia's little army found the impenetrable forest more unyielding than any human foe they were likely to encounter. Indian trails and deer paths offered the start of a road, but these byways had to be widened for the army's supply wagons and cannon; hour after hour, sweating in a May heat made almost unbearable in the airlessness of a thick, primeval forest, the men felled trees, sawed limbs, hacked at the ubiquitous, recalcitrant underbrush. Two weeks of this kind of work advanced them only twenty miles, to a place called the Great Meadows, still twenty-five miles short of the Ohio. Washington paused there for three days, sending out scouting parties each morning. One patrol after another returned empty-handed. Then Gist rode in. He had seen French troops nearby. Soon Indians arrived with similar reports. Though probably outnumbered, Washington wanted to fight. First, though, he sought out the Half King. A battle was imminent, he told the sachem. Reinforcements were coming, enough to do the job, Washington added, stretching the truth. Would the Indians join the Virginians? Yes, the Half King responded, divulging his implacable hatred for the French, whom, he now claimed, had murdered, then boiled and eaten his father. Washington, thus, would fight. The fact that war had not been declared seemed not to have bothered him. The French presence, he reasoned, was an act of war, and, anyway, his orders were to "drive the French from the Ohio." [43]

Led by Indian guides, Washington set out at night with forty men, marching single file along a narrow forest path. The men clattered along, often stumbling in the darkness. At sunrise they rendezvoused with the Half King, who had shown up with only fifteen braves. Though probably disappointed at this meager allied force, Washington did not demur. He had the Half King send out some braves to scout for the French. Now the minutes dragged by. The soldiers, forbidden to talk or to smoke, nervously checked and rechecked their equipment. The commander stood off to one side, alone, quiet, anxious. Finally, the scouts returned. A party of French soldiers—only about forty—was camped about a half mile ahead, resting, apparently unsuspectingly, in a little depression beneath a rocky eminence. Washington divided the force into three groups. He took command of a column that would approach from the right; Adam Stephen was placed in charge of the left, and he directed the Indians to creep to the rear of the French. Slowly, quietly, they stole to within a hundred yards of the enemy. Colonel Washington studied the French position, checked the deployment of his men. The seconds seemed like hours. Finally, he was ready. He lept up screaming the command to attack. The Virginians fired. Caught completely off guard, the French scurried for their muskets and dived for cover, but the surprise was too complete. They got off only four or five shots; some did not even fire, but simply attempted to flee, though most only succeeded in rushing into the arms of the Indians posted along the escape route. The fight was over in a few minutes. Ten French soldiers were dead, among them their commander, Sieur de Jumonville, an officer who, the French later would insist with considerable justification, was only acting as an ambassador, much as Washington had six months before. One Virginian was dead, two or three wounded. Though he could not have realized it, Washington and his men had just launched the French and Indian War—the Seven Years' War, as the Europeans would refer to it. His immediate concern was his twenty-two prisoners. He sent them back to Dinwiddie with the suggestion that they be hanged. [44]

Washington hurried back from Laurel Mountain to Great Meadows in a euphoric mood. For the first time, he subsequently wrote, he had "heard the bullets whistle" and he had found "something charming in the sound." He soon learned, too, that Colonel Fry was dead, the victim of a fall from a horse; Dinwiddie had named Colonel James Innes to be his successor, and he had promoted Washington to the rank of colonel. There was no time for exultation, however. A French counterattack now was a certainty. Colonel Washington's first act, therefore, was to write Innes urging that reinforcements be sent immediately. Then he set his men to constructing a fort, a rude, jerry-built stockade that he dubbed "Fort

Necessity." While this work proceeded about him, he wrote a long account of his victory to Dinwiddie. He had something else on his mind too. When he returned from his skirmish with the French he had found a letter from the governor awaiting him. It was Dinwiddie's response to his pleas concerning his officers' pay, and the governor had unsparingly upbraided the young warrior. Indeed, in Washington's adult life no other person ever dared be so directly critical or cavalier toward him on so many occasions as did Dinwiddie. In this instance the governor confessed his disappointment and suggested that perhaps he had misjudged the young commander's character. He noted that no such complaint had arisen from Colonel Fry or his men. "The Hardships complained of," he growled, "are such as usually attend on a Military Life, and are consider'd by Soldiers rather as Opp'ties of Glory than Objects of Discouragem't." Wounded deeply, Washington shot back that his complaints were not frivolous or unfounded, but he also carefully heeded Fairfax's former advice: he did not wish to lose a patron. "I am much concern'd that your Honour should seem to charge me with ingratitude. . . . I retain a true sense of your kindness and want nothing but opportunity to give testimony to my willingness to oblige. . . ."[45]

Meanwhile, trapped by his own obstinacy in this no man's land, Washington awaited the French retaliation. Part of his time was consumed by diplomatic overtures toward the Indians in the area. Using the Indian name "Conotocarious," an appellation meaning "town taker" or "devourer of villages," a title the natives had hung on his great grandfather during the Indian war of 1676, Washington endeavored to persuade the sachems of several tribes to help resist the pending French attack. The initial consequence of his labor, however, was that just enough tribesmen—a fair number of whom, in reality, were French spies—moved into Fort Necessity to assist in seriously depleting the Virginians' provender. While Washington was engaged with the Indians, reinforcements arrived, though far fewer than the five hundred men that the Virginia colonel had expected. Three companies of Virginia volunteers marched in, bringing his troop strength to nearly three hundred men and officers. Shortly thereafter a spit-and-polish company of buckskin-clad colonials and a few regulars under Captain James Mackay, a Scotsman, reached the Great Meadows. Unfortunately, he arrived with precious little food and no cannon. However, he did possess a commission from the Crown, which meant that his captaincy outranked Washington's provincial colonelcy. The young Virginian was not about to take orders from anyone other than another Virginian, and he quickly wrote Dinwiddie that he simply proposed to treat Mackay's force as independent from his command. The following day Washington ordered his men to resume the long-postponed trek to Redstone Creek, cutting a wilderness trail along the way. This put some distance between the rival commanders, for Mackay remained at Great Meadows.[46]

To add to Washington's woes, news arrived during the march that the Delawares and the Shawnees were siding with the French. Alarmed, he immediately summoned local sachems to a parley. For three days at Gist's trading post on

Chestnut Ridge, near present-day Mount Braddock, Pennsylvania, Washington, assisted by the Half King and numerous respected traders, negotiated with forty Indian leaders. "We have engaged in this War, in order to assist and protect you," Washington told them with a straight face. His pleas were not very persuasive. The Indians that had defected—"those treacherous Devils," he called them in private—could not be won back. Even the Half King seemed now to be wavering. The size of the French force, and Washington's pitiful shortage of supplies and men, apparently convinced the recalcitrant native chiefs that the Virginians were doomed.[47]

A week later more jolting news arrived. Reliable sources reported the presence of a Franco-Indian force of perhaps sixteen hundred men at Fort Duquesne on the Ohio; all indicators pointed to an imminent march by this huge force to flush the Virginians from the Ohio country. Oddly, Washington now decided to make his stand here, at Gist's trading post. He recalled his road-clearing troops from the west, and he implored Captain Mackay to hurry to his assistance. By June 29 everyone was in place, but on that day Washington, troubled by second thoughts, called a council of war. Noting that Fort Necessity contained more stores—which afforded a better chance for withstanding a siege operation—and that the few remaining Indian allies preferred to take their chances inside that citadel, the officers voted to return to the Great Meadows. The retreat began at once, a hurried, forced, nightmarish trek on empty stomachs across twelve miles of rugged Allegheny terrain. When his hungry legion at last reached its little fortress, Washington discovered that one-third of his men were too ill for duty.[48]

Throughout the night of July 1, and all the following day, the bone-tired soldiers frantically tried to strengthen the stockade. There was no sign of additional reinforcements. Washington knew that he could not survive a siege, but he refused to retreat. He obstinately clung to his little fort, apparently preferring to die—and to sacrifice the lives of his men—rather than to retreat and live, and face the possible invective and jeers of those on the home front. At daybreak the next day, as his men sought shelter from a cold, unrelenting rain, the first reports reached Washington that the French had been sighted just four miles away; a second report a few hours later estimated French strength at 900. Washington had an effective fighting force of 284, all of them huddled inside the tiny, circular walls of the fort, hoping against hope that its ten-inch-thick white oak walls would save them. At 11:00 A.M. a sentinel first glimpsed the advancing Frenchmen; moments later the blue-coated Europeans opened fire.

It took the French an hour or so to fight to within sixty yards of the fort. From there the sharpshooters took over, killing not only Virginians but their horses and cattle—and even their dogs. Washington was left without hope of retreat, and without a supply of meat. During the remainder of the day the adversaries exchanged potshots. Heavily outnumbered and exposed to a steady, deadly fire from three sides, the Americans got the worst of it. By nightfall about one-third of Washington's army was dead or wounded, and, according to one of Virginia's officers, half the others, convinced that they would be dead in a few hours, had broken into the liquor chest and were proceeding to drink themselves into a state of insensibility, perhaps the best condition to be in when one fell into the ungracious hands of the Indians.[49]

At twilight the French proposed surrender talks. Washington wavered, then he sent van Braam, still his translator, to listen to their terms. It was raining hard again when the Dutchman returned. He and the colonel huddled by a wildly flickering candle, squinting to decipher the rain-soaked document. The terms seemed generous: since France and Great Britain were not officially at war, the Virginians would be permitted to surrender with honor; moreover, they would be shielded from the Indians, and they would be allowed to return to Virginia in exchange for the repatriation of the French prisoners sent there earlier by Washington. It took Washington three hours to make up his mind, then he accepted. Either he was misled by van Braam—whom he later declared was "little acquainted with the English tongue" (still later he changed his story and alleged that the interpreter had willfully deceived him in order to save his skin)—or he was so relieved at the Gallic munificence that he ignored the wording of the preamble to the surrender terms. That short statement pronounced the English guilty of the "assassination" of Jumonville. At any rate, Colonel Washington signed the articles of surrender on July 4, and immediately thereafter departed for Virginia, unwisely leaving his journal behind for the French to find and to publish, a document which, according to his foe, demonstrated that the British were solely responsible for the outbreak of hostilities.[50]

There was ample blame to spread about for the disaster at Great Meadows. Virginia recruited too few troops and did not adequately supply those it did raise. Only meager reinforcements were provided. North Carolina and Maryland promised to augment Washington's army, but neither honored its pledge; nor did all the Virginia troops make an appearance. Although Washington performed about as well as could be expected of a twenty-two-year-old soldier devoid of military experience, he nevertheless blundered repeatedly. At times he was indecisive, for instance planning first to make his stand at Fort Necessity, then at Gist's, then again at his fortress. His pallisaded fort, moreover, was inadequate, divulging his lack of martial training. He thought the installation strong enough to withstand an attack by five hundred men, whereas an old hand like the Half King scoffed at it as "that little thing in the meadow." The Half King additionally characterized Washington as a "good-natured" fool who would have secured more Indian allies had he been more sensitive and dexterous in his dealings with the Native Americans; the sachem's appraisal must have been at least partially accurate, for even though Washington labored diligently to win over the Indians he was but a neophyte in the world of diplomacy.[51] No one could suggest that Washington had not acted bravely. On the other hand, he also had behaved like the ambitious young man that he was, so anxious and impatient for recognition that he sometimes acted injudiciously and recklessly.

Whatever Washington's errors, his reputation amazingly survived unblemished. Incredibly, official outrage for the debacle was focused not on the regiment's commander, but on George Muse, Washington's lieutenant colonel, the number two man in the army. A compatriot of Lawrence Washington in the Cartagena expedition, Muse was a man of some military experience. On the day of the battle at Great Meadows, Muse, together with Mackay's company, had been posted outside the fort; their task was to lure the French into the open spaces of the meadow, whereupon Washington's men could gun them down. But seeing that he was outnumbered by a ten-to-one ratio, Muse fell back into the fortress. His action probably saved most of his men, but it garnered only vilification in Williamsburg. Subsequently, he was the only officer not officially thanked for this service by the assembly, and he resigned in disgrace.[52]

In addition, the "assassination" charge that Washington acknowledged in the surrender document cast the province in a dishonorable light. Yet van Braam, not Washington, was made to take the fall for this error. Responsibility for the mistake cannot now be assigned, but that Washington took three hours to deliberate otherwise exceedingly generous terms hints that the colonel might have been aware of the meaning of the passage. Van Braam was not around to give his side of the story; to guarantee the release of the French prisoners in Williamsburg, he was taken to Quebec as a hostage and he did not return to Virginia for six years, by which time the incident largely was forgotten.[53] Whether Washington played a role in the censure of Muse is not clear, but he did assist in belittling van Braam. It would not be the last time that someone else bore responsibility for what could as easily have been seen as Washington's shortcomings.

The disaster in the Ohio country deterred neither Dinwiddie nor Great Britain. Throughout the remainder of the summer the governor sought funds for a fall campaign against Fort Duquesne, though in the end the assembly demurred and nothing came of the plan. It was just as well, for in October directives from London changed everything. Whitehall made Governor Horatio Sharpe of Maryland a lieutenant colonel and placed him in command of all forces raised for the Ohio theater. Meanwhile, Dinwiddie decided to reshape the Virginia Regiment, to break it into companies with no officer commissioned above the rank of captain.[54]

Washington was disconsolate. This was tantamount to a demotion. Indeed, most of his former officers now would equal him in rank. He would not even consider such a disreputable offer, though he acknowledged that "My inclinations are strongly bent to arms."[55]

Harboring feelings of remorse at the end of his military activities, as well as bitterness toward Dinwiddie for abolishing his command, Washington's attention returned to planting. Mount Vernon stood available to him. Little Sarah, Lawrence's daughter, had died while Washington was in the wilderness, and Nancy lived elsewhere with her second husband. Under the terms of Lawrence's confusing will, George could not formally own Mount Vernon during Nancy's lifetime, but she could not sell it. Just after Christmas in 1754 she rented the unoccupied estate to her former brother-in-law for an annual fee of fifteen thousand pounds of tobacco. Along with that property Washington also rented eighteen slaves owned by Nancy.[56] His military career seemed at an end less than a year after it had begun.

2

The Frontier Warrior

"I have foibles"

Early on August mornings, before the sun climbed high into a pale blue sky, when it had just peeked over the rolling hills to glitter off the dew, Washington was up and riding over his estate—his Mount Vernon. It was the nicest time of the day, still cool, bracing even, a strange time in a way, for the crisp dawn air and the mist that coiled up from the river at the foot of the farm presaged the autumn chill that soon would come, yet the warm sun foretold another morning of parching summer heat. Washington rode about the undulating pastures, examined the overgrown plowlands, leisurely toured the orchards, pondering and planning as countless other farm proprietors were doing.

But for all his yearning during the past decade to become a planter, George Washington's heart was no longer in that endeavor. Not now at least. No one had ever quit the military more regretfully than this young colonial. The Virginia Regiment was no more than just behind him before he was speaking of his "indispensable duty" to serve his province and expanding with longing upon his "future Conduct in the Service of our Country."[1]

There were good reasons why he still preferred the life of the soldier to that of a planter. For one thing, he was hardly in a position to be much of a planter. He had Mount Vernon, but without a sizable labor force that estate would not yield much wealth. In 1754 Washington owned ten slaves and recently had rented another eighteen bondsmen. Those he owned were at Ferry Farm with his mother and three younger brothers; since he evidently preferred that his kinfolk remain on the banks of the Rappahannock, he had little choice but to leave his slaves there too—the labor supply to sustain his relatives. If carefully managed, the slaves he had rented could make him more than comfortable at Mount Vernon, though it was doubtful that they could make a great planter of him. To be a grandee in the Chesapeake was to own three times—or more—as many chattel as Washington had at his disposal. There was another disadvantage to a life at Mount Vernon. Washington still was single, with no prospect of marriage. Mount Vernon would be a terribly isolated, lonely place for a twenty-two-year-old single man. His disinclination to be a farmer just yet also was due to the simple fact that he missed the army life, with its camaraderie, its splendid uniforms, its titles, its attendant risks. His brief service, moreover, had left him with a sense of accomplishment that he had not known previously. He had "opened the way" for Virginia's eventual conquest of the Ohio country, he believed. Still, there was something else attractive about the military. By enduring the "heat and brunt of the Day," as he put it, an officer could win laurels, encomiums of the sort that this chivalric society cherished.[2] Soldiering was a chance to be someone, to be honored and deferred to, to capture attention, something which a middling aristocrat and planter could hardly have in prospect, especially if that planter were neither well educated nor particularly glib.

Nevertheless, fate seemed to have mustered him out of the army. Whether his heart was in it or not, he assumed his planter's role with zeal. He began the renovation of Mount Vernon by moving into Belvoir, overseeing his farming enterprises from Colonel Fairfax's office, which had generously been made available to him. He had next to no furniture for his new house, and, besides, his first project had been to undertake several major repairs on the dwelling, work that was noisy and dusty, and that made Mount Vernon temporarily uninhabitable. He purchased some slaves and a few head of livestock, and he was redeveloping the tobacco fields for his initial crop when international politics once again touched his remote corner of the world.[3]

In faraway London the British government, after an agonizing debate, had resolved to dislodge the French from the disputed West. It had agreed to send two infantry regiments and a train of artillery to America, where it was to join an expeditionary force of seven hundred colonials raised by Governor Sharpe. The force was placed under the command of General Edward Braddock. Washington learned all this just as Braddock was landing in Virginia. The news immediately plunged the young planter into a quandary over what was the best course to pursue. There was no doubt that he wished to serve, but he knew he would never accept a demotion. There were other considerations as well. To leave for the front would be to permit Mount Vernon to continue in its state of disrepair. In addition, his mother appeared at the estate—probably her first visit, since Lawrence had never invited her to his farm—and pleaded with him not to reenter the army. He wrestled with his choices for weeks before deciding that he would elect the military, but only if he could land a post on favorable terms. As he later put it, he would "striv[e] to merit . . . royal favor, and a better establishment as a reward" for his service.[4] In other words, he would return to the military if he could secure a royal commission.

Through intermediaries Washington passed word to Braddock's headquarters of his willingness to serve. The general was interested in him too, for he had heard of this young soldier who twice had journeyed to the Ohio, and in mid-March he had his aide write Washington, inviting him to join his "family." Three weeks of negotiating followed. So bound by his sense of honor was Washington that he spurned a commission as a captain, telling an acquaintance that it was not a rank "I wou'd accept of." But so badly did he wish to soldier that he finally accepted a face-saving position as a volunteer without pay. The deal that was cut permitted Washington to remain at Mount Vernon until Braddock finally was ready to move west, a bargain by which the young farmer could tend to the planting of his first tobacco crop. It was not until mid-May 1755, therefore, that Washington, accompanied by a white servant, rode to Will's Creek to join Braddock, and to resume his military activities.[5]

Washington found the general to be an imposing, though friendly man. A soldier for forty-five years, Braddock had surprisingly little combat experience—only one or two slight, unimportant engagements in the last year of the War of the Austrian Succession. For most of his career his world had been the peacetime army camp, an environment of routine and protracted inactivity. And that was the world he had absorbed. Sixty years old now, large and paunchy, he had a reputation for training men, for excelling at paperwork, and, from decades of experience, for storytelling: he liked nothing better than to sit about and spin tales, spicing them with the salty expletives common in the barracks, though he really only felt comfortable doing this in the presence of younger men, chaps who posed no threat to him. He could be brusque and undiplomatic too, traits that led him to be, if not unpopular, certainly not the most beloved leader who ever wore a British uniform. Many of the officers in this army seem to have made an effort to avoid his company. Washington did not, however. Not surprisingly, Braddock seems also to have taken a liking to this young volunteer. Only Washington's rather braggartly testimony remains as to the degree of intimacy in their friendship, but even if he did overstate the matter, he seems to have been treated kindly by the general. Braddock assigned Washington errands to run and made him responsible for the orderly book. In the evenings, over wine and snacks, the two frequently chatted, and, if Washington is to be believed, they sometimes argued vehemently over strategy, the straightforward young provincial with all of three months' service under his belt advising the veteran commander to abandon his European ways in this wilderness theater.[6]

Washington's duties brought him into contact with numerous British officers. Lieutenant Colonel Thomas Gage, an older man, grew fond of him. He developed a cordial relationship with Horatio Gates, a chubby, aggressive captain of about his own age; and he must have gotten to know Charles Lee, a tall, skinny, talkative young lieutenant. Gage and several other officers shared their martial knowledge with Washington, and some lent him copies of their military manuals, in all likelihood the first such tracts he had ever read.[7]

With light duties and considerably more time on his hands than in his days as a colonel, Washington passed his leisure moments reading and listening to the talk about the campfire. he also had plenty of time to think of home. Lonely and faced with the possibility of danger, he not unnaturally dwelt on the pleasant memories of his bucolic estate. He may have been surprised, too, to discover that he could not get Sally Fairfax, the wife of his friend George William, off his mind.

For all his success in inspiring men of power, Washington had been notably ineffectual in his relationships with young women. His interest in girls first had been aroused when he was sixteen. About the time of his initial surveying venture he had become infatuated with Frances Alexander of Fredericksburg, to whom he sometimes spilled out his feelings in awkward, best-forgotten couplets.[8] Apparently she was heedless of her suitor. He got over her quickly enough, but soon he was taken by the charms of a "Low Land Beauty," probably a lass he met either at Chotank or in the Shenandoah. Next came an unidentified Sally, and still later Betsy Fauntleroy, the daughter of a planter-legislator from Naylor's Hole in Richmond County. She, like all the others, was unimpressed by her taciturn, stilted pursuer, rebuffing his overtures and abjuring him when he wrote pleading for a "revocation" of her "cruel sentence"—which had been to terminate the courtship even before it began.[9]

But none of these ladies had moved Washington as did Sally Fairfax. He had known her now for seven years, but during the six months before he joined Braddock he had lived close to her for the first time as an adult. He was infatuated by her beauty and elegance, by her coy charms and coquettish glances. An inveterate flirt—she could not even resist trying to tease and charm Braddock, whom she met at a military parade in Alexandria—Sally playfully lured on this shy young man. As a married woman, she represented dangerous territory for Washington. But lonely, bewitched by all that Sally represented, and, as always, craving recognition, he now tried to open a correspondence with her. He had been gone from Belvoir barely twenty-four hours when he wrote to her for the first time, and he followed that with two additional missives in the next six weeks. When she failed to answer he wrote her sister and his brother, asking each to persuade her to write. Sally still refused to be drawn into a correspondence, but George William's sister got wind of Washington's epistles and she responded with a stiff message of her own to the young soldier; she rebuked Washington and advised him not to write again, then, more tenderly, she suggested that when he returned home he surely would find waiting for him some "unknown she, that may recompense you for all the Tryals past." Washington was not easily dismissed, however. On an errand to Williamsburg he stopped at Belvoir to see Sally, only to be gently reproached once again by her. She pleaded with him not to write any further letters. He wrote anyway, telling her that if she only would send him a letter it would "make me happier than the Day is long." But once again she discreetly declined to be drawn into a correspondence.[10]

Washington's sudden infatuation with Sally is not out of character. To this point in his life he had given every indication of being a somewhat insecure person in quest of personal identity. His were the actions of a young man who was ashamed of what he saw in himself and who feared that others also would discover his shortcomings. Since he first had encountered the dazzling worlds of Belvoir and Mount Vernon a decade earlier, his behavior had been that of the parvenu desperate to achieve recognition. Troubled by what he regarded as his brutish, unpolished demeanor, uneasy in social situations, frequently feeling rude and out of place, young Washington had sought through introspection and through his continual schemes for self-improvement to become what he believed he had witnessed in Lawrence and George William—a glib, urbane, enlightened, genteel, heroic, and, above all, an attention-getting young man.

Although apparently smitten by this young woman, Washington actually turned toward Sally Fairfax more as a source of self-fulfillment than from real love. Whatever his feelings toward her were to become later, this young man was too self-absorbed to have instituted the kind of warm relationship that he believed he wanted. Instead, at this moment in his life he sought an object through which he might cope with and ameliorate his perceived imperfections. Moreover, dangerous as were his entreaties, they were, from an emotional viewpoint, rather safe inasmuch as any failure in this quest would be less painful than the earlier repudiations he had experienced. Sally was married, and she had made it quite clear that she would not risk her position by even the most harmless liaison with this enamored and seemingly guileless young man. Washington was perfectly well aware of this, of course, so that in a sense he was shielded. If—when—she rejected his advances it could not be perceived as a rejection due to any flaws in his makeup; on the other hand, she served as a defense against his feelings of inadequacy, for whatever attention she displayed toward him could only make him feel more worthy.[11]

Soon Washington was too busy, and too ill, to write to Sally or anyone else. Early in June, Braddock's force at last lumbered forward, moving from Will's Creek into the dark, labyrinthian forests, initially plunging ahead on the road built by the Ohio Company, then clattering along the primitive thoroughfare that Washington's little army had constructed the year before. The pace, however, was agonizingly slow, less than two miles each day. At this rate it would be autumn before Braddock reached his objective, and another ten to twelve weeks of supplying and maintaining an army in the midst of a primeval wilderness was not to his liking. To hasten the trek he sent much of the baggage to the rear and divided the army, sending ahead a force of twelve hundred men and all his artillery. Almost every historian who has studied this fateful campaign has suggested that Braddock acted on Washington's counsel. That the young Virginian offered such advice is beyond dispute, but so in all likelihood, did a council of war that Braddock summoned at about the same time. Inasmuch as several British officers favored such a tactic, Braddock surely would have been more swayed by their ideas than by those of a twenty-three-year-old provincial who had suffered defeat in his only military campaign. At any rate, General Braddock took that unpropitious step on June 18. By then young Washington had fallen sick, complaining of a high fever and a splitting headache. For five days thereafter he struggled on with the column, though by the last day he was delirious at times and forced to travel in a wagon rather than on horseback. Fearing for the young man's life, Braddock finally ordered him to the rear for rest and medical treatment.[12]

Washington remained behind at the British supply camp at George's Creek for a week, quite ill at first, then too weak and depleted to do much of anything but lie in anguishing idleness. His servant cared for him during the initial period of the illness, then he too fell victim to the malady and Washington was compelled to hire a nurse. But the young Virginian wanted to be with the vanguard of the army, and late in June he hitched a ride to the front; he got as far as the Youghiogheny before an army physician examined him and refused to permit him to go any further. He languished there for five more days, fretting that he might be absent when the army reached the forks of the Ohio. All signs pointed to July 10, perhaps a day earlier even, as the date by which Braddock's men at last would gaze upon Fort Duquesne. Washington wanted to be there when the French fortress was taken. Early in July he set out again, departing in another wagon on the slow, agonizing ride to rejoin the army. He caught up with Braddock on July 8. The army was camped just east of the Monongahela, about twelve miles from the Ohio. The mood at headquarters was buoyant. Despite their tortuously slow progress—some days the army had advanced no more than half a mile—the expedition had moved along rather safely, losing less than a dozen men to isolated Indian ambushes. On the day that Washington returned, the army had passed through a long, narrow valley, an excellent site for an attack. But nothing had happened, and now that only one more day's march would bring them to the French bastion few any longer expected to meet stiff resistance en route. Many, in fact, did not even believe the French would defend Fort Duquesne. Washington was one of those who anticipated nothing more than a "trifling" resistance. Rather than divide their army, he conjectured that the French would transfer most of their troops to Canada, their most prized American possession.[13]

Braddock got his army up at 2:00 in the morning on July 9, sending Colonel Gage out with an advance party to secure the elevated points where the army would ford the Monongahela. A work party followed, its task to slope the river banks so the artillery and the wagons could make it across. Three hours later the entire force was on the move. Washington, still weak, came too, riding a horse for the first time in three weeks, though he had to strap pillows atop his saddle to ease his discomfort.[14]

By mid-morning Braddock's army stretched out for almost a mile through the wilderness, a force of some 1300 men and officers, augmented by about 200 wagoners, sutlers, and batmen, as well as by nearly 50 wives and mistresses of the soldiers. Gage's advance party consisted of almost 600 men. Scouts and guides, mostly Indians, were in the lead, followed closely by a van of approximately 20 men; 50 yards further back came the main body of this contingent, a complement that included the elite of Braddock's army, and it in turn was followed by the work party, several artillery pieces, and a few supply wagons. This gangling force extended over 600 yards, all of it guarded on the flanks by small squads totaling nearly 200 men. One hundred yards or so behind the rear of the advance party came the main body of the army. A unit of light horse headed this contingent, followed closely by British sailors on loan to Braddock, and by "pioneers," colonials whose job was road building. After another interval of almost 100 yards came the general and his staff, riding in front of nearly 500 men, almost all of them British regulars. This phalanx also extended over several hundred yards. Finally, a small rear guard completed this cumbrous legion, a long line of soldiery that crunched and rattled and clanged through the splendid woods.[15]

Throughout the morning all went well. The advance party crossed the river without incident, and the main body followed an hour or so later, likewise experiencing no difficulty. Two hours later the lead party was about a mile beyond the Monongahela. It had been a long day already; the men were hot and tired; and many were hungry as well, since no one had eaten during the past nine hours. Still, spirits were high. Word had filtered through the ranks that Braddock had scheduled an end to the day's trek in less than two hours. Everyone knew, too, that Fort Duquesne would be reached the next day.

Suddenly, just after one o'clock, Washington and Braddock heard the crack of musket fire a half mile ahead. But the forest was so thick they couldn't see what was happening: They must have suspected immediately that the advance party had been ambushed, though, in fact, the forward elements of Gage's advance unit had stumbled into the advance units of a French and Indian force of nearly nine hundred men—regulars, militiamen, and braves who had been sent out from Fort Duquesne as a blocking force. Not unlike their adversary, the French and Indians had been surprised, but they recovered more quickly. Unleashing a merciless fire, much of it directed at the gaudily dressed officers, they struck down a dozen, maybe fifteen British leaders before anyone knew what had occurred. Gage and his men had returned the fire, but their losses were too heavy for them to remain in such an exposed spot. Gage ordered his men to fall back, hoping to regroup and to gain reinforcements from the principal force of the British advance party. For a moment it appeared that the clash would end less than ten minutes after it began. Instead, a panic set in among the redcoats, a frenzy that resulted when Gage's men, retreating and firing in good order, collided with the principal force of the British advance party. All at once there was no place to go. Men were bunched together, being shot at by a concealed enemy, sometimes even shooting one another as the distraught men hurriedly ran first one way then another. The Indians, moreover, seemed to take charge from the French once the fighting began, and they raced down the British flanks pouring a devastating fire into the terrified redcoats. In no time men "dropped like Leaves in Autumn," a British survivor later remembered. Then, too, all the horror stories about the savageness of the foe welled up in the minds of these men, especially when the Indians immediately began to scalp some of the dead and wounded. By the time Washington and Braddock reached the site of the attack, probably ten or fifteen minutes after the assault began, a "deadly Panick, . . . nothing but confusion and disobedience of orders," as the Virginian put it, prevailed among the advance party.[16]

Braddock's arrival did nothing to change the course of the battle. He, too, was unable to restore order. He displayed great valor, and, according to the accounts of several witnesses, so did his young aide. Both men rode about, exposed to the deadly fire, vainly trying to restore order. Swinging their swords, cajoling, shouting, each was an inviting target. Four, perhaps five, horses were shot from beneath the general. Two of Washington's mounts also went down with wounds, one of them falling heavily upon him, for an instant trapping him until he could kick and scramble back to his feet. Each man's coat was in tatters, filled with holes made by bullets that somehow missed. But Braddock could not stop the carnage. Not long after his arrival, in fact, the French even seized some of the British cannon, turning them on this trapped, forlorn army, increasing the terror that now gripped every man. An hour elapsed, then another. The British never counterattacked. They remained pinned down, taking heavy casualties. Virginia's troops did attack, however. They fought well, better than the British. They scrapped the tactics of Europe and plunged into the woods to fight like the Indians, seeing the dark forest as a haven, not a danger. But these provincials received no assistance, and ultimately they died in droves. About two of every three men who served that day under the British flag were killed or wounded. Seven Virginia officers perished, while among the enlisted men "near all [were] killed," as Washington reported. At least, he added, they had "behav'd like Men and died like Soldiers."[17]

About four o'clock, nearly three hours after the holocaust commenced, Braddock was shot. A bullet slammed into his back, penetrating his lungs. Now the defeat became truly Molochan, for soon after the general fell British soldiers began to flee. The rout was on. Washington had helped to load the stricken general into the relative safety of a wagon shortly after he was hit, but minutes later the young Virginian also was forced to take flight. With three or four others, he carried Braddock nearly a mile to the east bank of the Monongahela. Along the way one of the officers tried to pay some British soldiers to help carry the wounded commander. There were no takers. Washington and his compatriots labored with their encumbrance and finally reached a safe place, but they succeeded only because the French and the Indians did not pursue the absconding British. Had the enemy given chase it is likely that almost all of Braddock's army would have perished. Later, in fact, some British officers claimed that what remained of the army was so disorganized that it could have been overwhelmed by fewer than one hundred of the adversary. The story eventually circulated that young Washington had directed the British retreat. That was doubtful. Still later Washington himself claimed to have been the only person in the presence of Braddock who was not either wounded or killed in this action. His recollection may have been correct, for sixty-two of the ninety-six officers who fought somewhere or other during this engagement either were killed or wounded. But some officers survived, and if there was any order to this retreat it is likely that a redcoat directed the fleeing Anglo-Americans.

As shadows lengthened over the smoky, debris-littered forest, the shooting died down. The Indians—and enough French soldiers as well—had broken into the captured British rum pots. This fight was over. Behind, on the west side of the river, lay approximately five hundred British dead. Those who had not died fell into the hands of the Indians, and a long ghoulish night of torturing and slaughtering followed. East of the river, with Washington, were the survivors; about four hundred of these men were casualties. Never before had a British army met such an unmistakable disaster on American soil.[18]

About sunset on this horrid day Braddock momentarily drifted out of a coma and woozily surveyed the carnage. He ordered Washington to ride along the path the army had taken that morning. He was to search for runaways, then he was to hurry to the rear for reinforcements that would permit a retreat from these black, ghastly forests. For twelve hours Washington rode, while waves of nausea and anxiety and fatigue swept over him. He galloped past the screaming, pleading wounded, and, alone, he raced on into the sable wilderness. It was a terrifying scene that he never forgot. A quarter century later he still remembered the "groans, lamentation[s], and crys along the Road of the wounded." Late the following morning he reached Dunbar's camp, the British rear encampment, where he painfully related Braddock's orders. Then he collapsed, for twenty-four hours slumbering as best a man could who had just lived through a nightmare.[19]

Still weak and tired, Washington nevertheless returned to headquarters the next day. There he found Braddock dying in great agony. Four days later the commander breathed his last. Near the rotting embers of Fort Necessity, Washington and a few others close to the general oversaw his burial, secreting his body beneath the road he had helped to blaze.[20]

With the death of his commander and the subsequent withdrawal of the remains of the British army from western Pennsylvania, Washington's volunteer service was at an end. He slowly made his way home, a bitter young man. Two years of martial service had netted nothing save the further deterioration of Mount Vernon and his own near demise. As in the previous summer, Washington once again presumed that his military career was at an end. But as black as was his mood when he arrived home, his spirits suddenly were buoyed. Awaiting him was a missive in the clear, familiar hand of Sally Fairfax. She rejoiced at his safe return and proposed that if able and fit he should come to Belvoir the next day; if he was not up to that, she and two other ladies would come to his estate. The next day he purchased some watermelons to add a festive touch to the happy reunion and hurried to the Fairfax mansion.[21]

Nor was it very long before Washington discovered that Sally's effusive welcome was not his only reason to rejoice. His brave conduct beside Braddock had not gone unnoticed. The late general's aide and several other British veterans publicly lauded him as a valorous, resolute soldier. Moreover, by late summer it was apparent that Dinwiddie would be compelled to abandon his independent-companies scheme and to remodel the province's army along the lines that had served the Virginia Regiment during the previous year. Only a centrally directed army could hope to pacify a frontier as vast as that claimed by Virginia; further-more, the colony would have to do the work itself, for the remnants of Braddock's army lay immobilized at Fort Cumberland, soon, in fact, to retreat to Philadel-phia. Once the Virginia Regiment was reconstituted, to whom but Washington could the governor turn when he appointed a commander?

By mid-August Washington knew of "the good Opinion the Governor [and the] Assembly &c" shared of him. He also had learned that "scarce any thing else" was talked about in Williamsburg save for his heroic conduct alongside Braddock. "I think 'tis unanimously agreed, you shall command our Forces," his cousin wrote him from the capital. Would he not come and volunteer his services?

No, he would not. Eager as Washington was to regain his former command, he wanted certain things that he had not enjoyed in 1754. Most importantly, he insisted on the right to advise and concur in the selection of all officers. A leader, he thought, succeeded or failed according to the performance of his subordinates; their selection required great care and should be left neither to chance nor partisanship. In addition, he wanted more aides than had been provided the previous year, and he demanded a military chest. To venture to the capital hat in hand, he said, would only weaken his bargaining power in securing these needs.

Thus, until late in the month he sat at Mount Vernon, watching from a distance while the assembly appropriated funds for a reorganized army of one thousand men. He came to the capital only on August 27, and then only at the urging of numerous friends. When he arrived he learned that his strategy had miscarried. Dinwiddie did indeed offer him his old command, but the governor already had named at least a dozen of the army's sixteen captains. Washington considered the executive's offer, then to the surprise of everyone—and to the vexation of Dinwiddie—he refused the terms. He would command only if the conditions he had outlined were met!

During the next several days these two iron-willed men and their emissaries met, haggling and negotiating. Finally, after nearly five days of what at times must have been acrimonious bargaining, they came to terms. Washington would command, he could name the two principal field officers (a lieutenant colonel and major), and he received funds for a military chest and additional aides.[22] In the end Washington's pragmatic side had won out. He accepted half a loaf rather than risk incurring the wrath of influential men who might see his obstreperous demands as self-indulgent and inimical to the interests of Virginia; to persist, moreover, was to see his military dreams end forever. Hence, in the fall of 1755 Washington became commander of Virginia's army. En route, however, he had stepped on the governor's toes, further transforming what once had been a quite cordial relationship into one that was troubled, verging even on the tempestuous.

The only person who objected to his reentering the service was his mother. The fears that she had expressed earlier that year had come dangerously close to realization. Now she wrote her son beseeching him to decline Dinwiddie's offer. He was unheeding, of course, brushing aside her intrusiveness with the impatient comment that it would "reflect dishonour upon me to refuse" the call of his province. "Honor" was a term that Washington and other Virginia gentrymen used frequently. An ill-defined term, its meaning often lay in the eye of the beholder. When Washington spoke of honorable conduct, he evidently referred to a kind of behavior that in his estimation would embarrass neither himself nor Virginia. In addition, he used the word "honor" to mean disinterested, even sacrificial service. To enter the military, therefore, was "honorable" if one did so selflessly, seeking neither profit nor advancement from the service. He no doubt believed this, although, his rhetoric aside, Washington's conduct points to ends that were far more self-serving—and human. In fact, that summer he confessed to his half brother that he would serve again only if he believed he could "gain by it," adding that for a "trifling Pay" his previous service had caused him to squander his health and to "suffer . . . much in my private fortune." [23]

Washington plunged into his new command with vigor. While recruiting proceeded, he rode off to inspect Fort Cumberland at Will's Creek, then to Fort Dinwiddie, a stockade 125 miles away in the southern part of the province. In three weeks he completed a whirlwind examination, then rode to Winchester where he established his headquarters. Imperturbably, he quickly fixed his control, winning the loyalty of his officers. It was no small feat. Only twenty-three, Washington had won plaudits for his valor, but he had little experience as a commanding officer. Some of his officers were equally young and green, but Adam Stephen was fifteen years his senior and Peter Hog was at least thirty years older than Washington, and both had served in Europe.

Soon Washington was up to his ears in problems. The ranks were swelling, but with exasperating slowness; after two months his force was only at one-third prescribed strength, and the great majority of these men had been recruited earlier in the year for Braddock's campaign. In addition, there were not enough supplies even for that number of soldiers. Ammunition was scarce, and many men were without shoes, much less the ostentatiously romantic raiment that Washington had designed for his army—a blue coat faced and cuffed in scarlet and silver for each man, as well as a red waistband and a silver laced hat. These frustrations paled beside the problem posed by the Indians, however. They seemed to rampage at will through settlements all over the northern Shenandoah. By dividing into small parties, Lieutenant Colonel Stephen reported, the Indians had virtually rendered the army of Virginia powerless. "They go about and commit their outrages at all hours . . . and nothing is to be seen . . . but desolation and murder heightened with . . . unheard of instances of cruelty." Everywhere he went, Stephen continued prosaically, he discovered the "Smouk of the Burning Plantations darken the day, and hide the neighbouring mountains from our Sight." [24]

No one could have worked with greater diligence than did Washington in the first months of his command. He seemed to be everywhere at once, riding hard from the Maryland border to southernmost Virginia, then to Williamsburg, and finally back to the beleagured West. He rattled off orders in all directions: get shoes, blankets, and tents in Philadelphia; procure rum in the West Indies; distribute supplies left behind by Braddock's army; find additional men in Annapolis; cut firewood now so it will be properly aged by winter! Orders were issued to secure more powder, lead, flints, and paper. Purchase horses, wagons, flour, and provender from the settlers, he directed; if the farmers refused to sell, impress these commodities. On occasion he took command of squads engaged in this unpleasant, at times hazardous, undertaking, for civilians who had not yet been reimbursed for the property they had "sold" Braddock a year earlier were understandably reluctant to part with still more of their possessions. On one such foray Washington was confronted by angry yeomen who threatened to "blow out my brains" before they permitted the confiscation of a neighbor's property. The colonel unsheathed his sword and called their bluff; he got the nag he had come for. It was one of two close calls he experienced. Once he narrowly escaped an ambush laid by Shawnees in the southwestern Virginia wilderness. Luck was with him and nothing happened, for the Indians were momentarily indisposed just as Washington rode past; he later learned that only minutes after he passed by a less fortunate soldier had been gunned down on this same murky path.[25]

Washington had no more than undertaken his duties before his letters reassumed the pleading—even peevish—air that had characterized his missives during his previous command. Twice he even threatened to resign if matters did not go his way. Only three weeks after he arrived at Winchester he told the governor that he would quit if the assembly did not redesign the military code so that he might impose draconian punishments upon his recalcitrant and insolent (or so he portrayed them) soldiers. Two months later a command problem elicited a similar threat. Upon his arrival at Fort Cumberland that autumn he discovered about fifty Maryland soldiers under the command of Captain John Dagworthy. The men were a welcome sight, but Colonel Washington was troubled by Dagworthy. Once he had held a royal commission; did he now outrank a colonel whose commission came from a colonial governor? Washington was certain of only one thing: he would not take orders from a captain. He hurried to Williamsburg to huddle with Dinwiddie and the speaker of the House of Burgesses, John Robinson. Both sided with their colonel. The governor quickly wrote Governor William Shirley of Massachusetts, the acting commander in chief of all British forces in America, arguing that Dagworthy outranked Washington only if the king specifically had ordered the Maryland captain to Fort Cumberland; Dinwiddie also requested that Shirley issue George Washington a brevet commission in the British army. What followed was confusing. Weeks, then months, elapsed without word from Shirley. Finally, news arrived that he had directed Governor Sharpe of Maryland to resolve the matter. Washington expected the worst, but Sharpe declared that Dagworthy had no jurisdiction over the troops of Virginia. But neither Washington nor Dinwiddie saw Sharpe's orders, and Dagworthy continued to act as though he still was in command. His act fooled Washington. Thoroughly flustered, Washington made two decisions: he would ride to Boston and urge Shirley not only to curtail Dagworthy's powers but to grant him a royal commission; if either appeal failed, he resolved to resign upon his return to Williamsburg.[26]

Washington's longing for a royal commission is not difficult to understand. If he could procure a commission with at least the rank of major—and he would accept no lower rank—he would outrank any colonial with whom he was likely to come into contact. Besides, the salary would be about twice that he was receiving from Virginia, and, in addition, a royal commission provided for half-pay for life upon retirement.

Leaving his troops and a troubled frontier behind, Colonel Washington, spiffily attired in the uniform he had designed, set out for New England in February 1756. He was accompanied by two servants and his aide, Captain George Mercer, and for a time a British officer tagged along too. The redcoat, in fact, left the earliest description of Washington, a curious depiction, in many respects at odds with every account compiled during these years. He did portray Washington as tall and strong, but he also characterized him as having dark hair with a swarthy complexion, so much so that he looked "like a Forrener." [27]

This was a long and arduous trek for the men, spanning more than a thousand miles across a winter landscape. Once Washington was twenty-five miles or so north of Mount Vernon, moreover, he was on unfamiliar territory. A ride of several days, past the tiny hillocks of eastern Maryland, then over the Delaware flatlands, across myriad creeks and rivers, each mile plunging the little party deeper into the grip of winter, brought them to Philadelphia. There Washington paused briefly to shop for clothing. The city was a new experience for him. He had thought Williamsburg was a metropolis, but now he was in a city more than twenty times the size of the little capital of Virginia. Colonel Washington must have been struck by the vibrancy of this rambunctious urban center, although as a resolute agrarian he must also have recoiled at its sprawl: by the standards of colonial America Philadelphia was a huge, distended city, a place that splayed out for almost twenty blocks from the docks and warehouses along the riverfront to the forests on its western flank.

Washington did not linger long before he again was on his way. He crossed the Delaware into New Jersey, then rode east to Perth Amboy, where he booked passage on a small sailing craft bound for Brooklyn. He paused for a few days in New York, another big, energetic mercantile center, lodging there with Beverley Robinson, the brother of the speaker of Virginia's assembly. He spent some of his time sightseeing and playing cards and backgammon with his host and his merchant friends, but more than anything else his time was occupied by Robinson's sister-in-law, Mary Eliza Philipse. It was not difficult to see why. Attractive and single, Polly, as everyone called her, was quite a wealthy young lady. (She, in fact, owned fifty-one thousand acres of prime New York real estate.) Washington escorted her to a dance, then to the Exhibition Hall to see a mechanical contrivance that depicted aspects of men and women at work and at play since antiquity. Soon, however, he was off for Boston. A cold, wet ride through the Manhattan farmlands and on into Connecticut brought him to New London, where he found space on a vessel bound for Massachusetts. He arrived in Boston four weeks after departing Virginia, a fact noted by a local newspaper, which referred to him as "a gentleman who had deservedly a high reputation for military skill and valor, though success has not always attended his undertakings." [28]

Washington was reasonably confident that he would succeed in this mission. Through Braddock he had met Shirley once before, at a military conference in Alexandria. He had found him to be a "gentleman and [a] great politician," and he believed that Shirley had liked him as well.[29] However that might be, stalking men of influence was something at which Washington was quite skilled.

Two days after his arrival in town Washington was shown into Shirley's presence. As servants bustled in from time to time with tea and additional firewood, the earnest young man and his host chatted for hours about a faraway war. The governor questioned Washington about conditions on the Virginia frontier; Washington made his pitch. The atmosphere was cordial, friendly even, certainly a contrast with the icy mood that recently had prevailed in the governor's office in Williamsburg. Late in the day, when long shadows had begun to jut out over the Boston snow, the meeting ended. Shirley would make a decision within a week, he announced; in the meantime he invited the Virginian to stick around, and he introduced him to some of his friends, with whom, on subsequent evenings, Washington played cards. (The big city sharks clipped him for £5, roughly the cost in those days of an expensive pair of shoes.) After a five-day wait, Shirley summoned Washington back to the governor's palace. His decision: he lacked the power to grant Washington a royal commission, but he did hand him a document declaring that Dagworthy could exercise no authority over the troops of Virginia; indeed, if Captain Dagworthy remained at Fort Cumberland, he was to take orders from Colonel Washington. The governor's decision was both good and bad news for Washington. He had gotten Dagworthy out of his hair, but he had failed to secure the royal commission that he coveted. In addition, as he was leaving Shirley told him that he had just learned from London that Governor Sharpe was to be the commander of all troops raised by Maryland, Pennsylvania, South Carolina, and Virginia.[30] After a long, difficult trip he had discovered that Shirley no longer was in a position to help him.

As soon as the meeting ended Washington departed Boston. Once again he paused briefly in New York, and again he escorted Polly Philipse on a couple of outings. When he was ready to leave he also discovered that he was out of money. In the course of his travels he had spent so much—trips to tailors' and hatters' shops alone ran up a bill of almost £60—that he had to borrow nearly £100 from Beverley Robinson to see himself home. He reached Williamsburg at the end of March, sixty days after his departure from Mount Vernon.[31] On the long ride home he had reconsidered his decision to resign if he failed with Shirley. As in his clash with Dinwiddie six months earlier, he was willing to accept half a loaf. He remained in the army of Virginia.

Washington returned home just in time to find that the spring weather had encouraged the Indians to again take up their tomahawks. He rushed back to the frontier, where he found his army no more effectual than it had been in the last campaign. Nor was their much hope that it could be made efficacious. He believed he needed two thousand men to adequately staff Virginia's frontier garrisons, yet he had less than a quarter of that number. He pleaded with Dinwiddie to call up militia units, and the governor responded by mustering the trainbandsmen from ten western counties. More than a thousand militiamen reached the front, yet that number was only a small percentage of the total summoned by the governor. According to Washington many militiamen started west but soon returned home, fearing to travel alone over roads that were infested with the enemy. Moreover, in Colonel Washington's estimation, many of the men who did reach the war zone were marginal soldiers at best. In fact, he and his officers kept fewer than half the militiamen who arrived, sending the remainder home. All along Washington had hoped that his ranks might be filled with conscriptees, sturdy citizen soldiers yanked from the trainband muster rolls. But that, too, proved illusory. Under Virginia law a conscriptee could escape service by paying a £10 fee. Most men chose that course over carrying a musket, and by midsummer only 254 draftees were under arms. That left the young commander with a force composed primarily of militiamen and volunteers, the first a "poor resource [and] a very unhappy dependance," while the other was hardly better. Still, Washington set to work to make soldiers of the men who arrived, seeking to mold them through the imposition of an iron discipline. Probably influenced by what he had seen in Braddock's army, Washington instituted brutal floggings—up to five hundred lashes—for offenses as disparate as gambling and dereliction of duty. He hanged two habitual deserters. And he promised Dinwiddie that in the future he would act with even more "rigor." In the meantime he dashed off letter after letter to the governor complaining of his worthless soldiers and a multitude of additional difficulties: the troops were inadequately trained; the men had no respect for their officers; the militiamen were called up for too brief a period; the men were poorly paid, although if the government stopped squandering money and put it into pay for the troops all would be well; he lacked the necessary tools to construct fortifications; civilians refused to cooperate.[32] On top of everything else Washington disagreed with the strategy decreed by his government.

Washington, as well as the officials in Williamsburg, knew that only a successful strike against Fort Duquesne would eradicate the Indian problem. Both also knew that such a bold move was out of the question unless Virginia received help from its neighbors, as well as from Great Britain. In the interim Washington and the politicians agreed on the need to fight a defensive war, a design to be facilitated by the construction of a string of forts in the frontier region. However, the two disagreed on how to implement this strategy. Washington favored the erection of several installations, built at intervals of fifteen to eighteen miles, each garrisoned by about one hundred troops. The budget-minded politicians wanted fewer forts, each staffed by only a few soldiers. Colonel Washington also would have liked to dispatch his men periodically from these installations on what today would be called "search and destroy" missions; the legislators—whom he privately referred to as "Chimney-corner politicians"—ordered a purely defensive posture. Finally, Washington urged the withdrawal of Virginia's troops from Fort Cumberland, a citadel in Maryland which only siphoned off soldiers needed in Virginia. The council, however, not only voted to maintain the fort, but to enlarge its garrison.[33] Obviously, the colonel possessed little real power.

Six months after he took command (a period in which he had been with his troops only about 25 percent of the time), Washington still was unable to report any success in pacifying the frontier. Nor were there any particular accomplishments to announce after another six months elapsed. The Indians were "like wolves," he reported, a tough, resourceful foe, unequaled in their cunning or their capacity for deprivation. He also had to tell Dinwiddie that they had surfaced in greater numbers throughout the spring of 1756 than during the autumn following Braddock's defeat. Now Washington spoke of relocating the western inhabitants, placing them in villages where they might be more easily guarded. He also called on the government to resort to conscription, and he urged legislation that would permit the use of indentured servants in his army. Remorsefully, too, he told Dinwiddie that Virginia's frontier now was at the Blue Ridge Mountains. The Shenandoah was lost—at least for the time being. For all this Virginia had paid a high price. Nearly one-third of the troops who served under Washington in 1756 had been killed or wounded fighting in twenty separate engagements. And that did not take into account the province's cataclysmic losses at the Great Meadows or in the disaster that befell Braddock.[34]

Months of stinging reverses seldom are met with equanimity. Sooner or later people begin to ask questions. Colonel Fairfax anticipated a backlash against the young commander, and he had endeavored to prepare Washington. To forestall the almost certain hostility it would create, Fairfax cautioned his young friend about his habit of incessant carping. But to no avail. Washington's orders and his correspondence in this period read as though they were penned by someone who combined the unpleasant qualities of a pompous martinet and a whining, petulant brat. Enough contemporaries apparently saw him in the same light, and Fairfax's prescience was borne out in the fall of 1756. The dam burst when the *Virginia Gazette* published an essay anonymously authored by the "Virginia Centinel." That writer blasted Washington—though he never mentioned the colonel by name—as inexperienced and unsuited to command. He accused Washington of having abused the militiamen, while vacillating between overly harsh and too lenient treatment of his volunteers; the officers, the essayist continued, had indulged in "all manner of debauchery, vice, and idleness," and, while the frontiersmen suffered, a general air of revelry and debasement had enveloped headquarters.

That unidentified penman was not alone in criticizing Colonel Washington. Stories about the army and its commander crept through Virginia that year. Though the frontier was in flames, it was whispered, Washington had lived and entertained regally in a rented house in Winchester. The army was dispirited, some said, and the low morale was due not only to its lack of military success. Part of the problem arose from Washington's frequent absences. In addition to his long trip to Boston, several visits to Belvoir and Mount Vernon had kept him from headquarters, as did jaunts to look after his property on Bullskin Creek. Even when he was in Winchester, it was said, he lived apart from his troops, and he frittered away his time with indulgences, such as his fencing lessons.[35] To make it even worse, there was more than a kernel of truth in each allegation. And, for certain, morale was low in the army of Virginia.

Through Fairfax and Speaker Robinson, as well as from Dinwiddie, Washington learned of the gossip. The episode is significant mostly for what Washington did not do, and, presumably, for the lessons he must have learned from his behavior. His initial reaction was to threaten to resign, a response that had grown stale. He had made the same threat when he encountered Dagworthy, then again both before and after his meetings with Shirley. Of course, he did not resign. He did compose a response to the "Centinel," but instead of publishing it he forwarded it to his brother Austin, asking him to send it to the *Gazette* only if he believed such a move was advisable. Wisely, Austin destroyed the rejoinder.

The most visceral—and, from Washington's perspective, the most menacing—response to the "Centinel" came from his officers. Each of his company commanders publicly pledged to resign if Dinwiddie did not publish an expression of confidence in the army and its leaders. Their ire was raised less by what the anonymous essayist had said than by their mistaken belief that the *Gazette's* editor would never have dared to print the essay without Dinwiddie's acquiescence. Now Washington was vexed, for if his officers quit it was not likely that he could survive as commander. But he handled the momentary crisis admirably. He calmed his captains by promising to ride to Williamsburg where he could press their demands, then over the next few weeks he simply watched as time and second thoughts induced the officers to let their pique evaporate quietly.[36]

In the damp chill of November Washington set out along his well-worn path to Dinwiddie's door. He paused at Belvoir, where he saw Sally and picked up several shirts she had arranged to have made for him. Then he was on his way to the capital. However, when he reached Alexandria he found an ill-tempered letter from Dinwiddie awaiting him, a note in which the governor unequivocally ordered the colonel to return to his army, and, in addition, directed him to move his headquarters from Winchester to Fort Cumblerland. The letter stopped Washington in his tracks. He turned and galloped back to Winchester. Over the next few weeks, while he seethed in a black rage, Washington supervised the transference of his headquarters. Apprised in mid-December that the move was complete, Dinwiddie, in a letter dripping with sarcasm, told Washington: "It gives me great Pleasure [that] Y'r go'g to Ft Cumb'l'd is so agreeable to You, as with't doubt its the proper Place for the Com'd'g Officer." [37]

The holiday period in 1756 was hardly cheerful for Washington. He was ensconced in snow-covered Fort Cumberland, his loneliness broken only by a carefree, energetic puppy he recently had acquired. In this morose state he decided to vent his feelings to the new British commander in chief, John Campbell, Earl of Loudoun, who had arrived in America only in the last few weeks. If he could meet with Loudoun he might gain preferment, while at the same time he might mollify the anger of his still disgruntled officers. First he wrote Loudoun a self-serving letter that was perhaps the least admirable document for which Washington ever was responsible. He recriminated about the faults of others, portraying himself as blameless for the state of affairs on the frontier. He complained about the inactivity of Virginia's neighbors, and he maintained that his province had only half-heartedly attempted to raise troops. Nor did London escape, for he attributed the Indian's loyalty to the French to the ministry's indifference to the transmontane West. He took aim at the quality of his troops, and criticized his government's strategy. Then he begged and groveled, broadly hinting that he hoped for a royal commission. Had Braddock lived, he continued, he would have been commissioned by now. "I had His Promise," he told Loudoun. Shirley had made promises too, but he had returned to London before he could act. Then, clumsily, he told Loudoun: "I have exalted Sentiments of Your Lordship's character. . . . I am so happy . . . to have an opportunity of testifying how much I admire your Lordship's character. . . ." [38]

When Loudoun's aide replied in noncommittal terms, Washington secured permission from Dinwiddie to travel to Philadelphia, where Loudoun had scheduled a conference with several governors. Thus Colonel Washington embarked on his second lengthy trip within a year. Riding through heavy winter weather he reached the Pennsylvania city late in February, arriving, as it turned out, about three weeks before Loudoun. When the British commander did arrive, Washington's request for an appointment went unheeded for several days. Finally, after Washington had whiled away nearly a month in the taverns and posh clubs of this strange city, Loudoun consented to see him.

Short, muscular, fifty-two years old, Loudoun was rich (it had taken nearly an entire ship to transport his personal effects to America), well educated, and an experienced soldier. To him Washington was merely a petty, provincial functionary, and not a terribly successful one at that. Loudoun's manner toward the young colonel was inhospitable. He refused to allow Washington to speak, brusquely rattling off a series of orders, the most important of which comported with Dinwiddie's notions of strategy, though he did order Washington to return to Winchester. Loudoun gruffly asked two or three questions, then he abruptly turned his back on the young man, a signal that the conference was at an end. Before Washington had an opportunity to say another word, he was briskly ushered from the room.[39] Washington had been treated with the same arrogance and contempt that he might himself have directed at an unruly servant at Mount Vernon.

Both his pride and his ambition crushed, Washington returned to the frontier. He did not quit. To resign at this moment surely would end his public career forever. He resolved simply to try to see it through. If he had harbored any illusions that the military situation might improve, they soon were abandoned. He received only a fraction of the troops for which the Burgesses had appropriated funds. Most simply never were recruited, but many of those that were raised were ordered by Loudoun to be sent to South Carolina. Moreover, short-handed to begin with, he now was confronted by a stupendous desertion problem. At times a batch of sorely needed recruits would arrive, and within a few days half or more would be gone, frightened draftees who were loath to die on a frontier that had no meaning for them. Washington ordered a forty-foot-high gallows constructed to intimidate his soldiers, but it does not seem to have been much of a deterrent. Late that spring he wrote of the gloomy prospects for suppressing the foe, and in the fall he still was writing of the "horrid devastation" wrought by the native tribesmen. Strangely, however, there were signs of improvement. Washington's army was augmented by forces from several southern Indian tribes, and colonial diplomatic endeavors led some tribes to lay aside their weapons. By Christmas Virginia's Indians had been pushed onto the defensive.[40]

Much of Washington's time in 1757 had been spent in trading captious letters with Dinwiddie. Now an ill old man (for years he had suffered from a chronic ailment, probably gout or arthritis, and now some new affliction had rendered him partially paralyzed), the governor simply longed to return to England. Certainly, he was tired of Washington's sniping. But there was more too. Their relationship, frequently stormy in the past, had grown particularly sour during this year, perhaps because of Washington's friendly ties with Speaker Robinson, an implacable foe of the governor, and a powerful politician whom the colonel used, without Dinwiddie's consent, to seek additional funding for the army. Dinwiddie also was convinced that Washington had betrayed him, evidently believing the young colonel had complained to Loudoun about his executive leadership. Washington was no less angry, as he had concluded that the governor had refused to aid him in his quest for a royal commission. Washington was partially correct. After meeting with Loudoun in Philadelphia early in 1757, Dinwiddie no longer importuned for Washington; for the two previous years, however, he had spared no energies in his attempts to serve Washington in this matter, and he desisted only when it appeared certain that Washington would never attain what he desired.

The final straw in the clash between these two strong-willed men apparently came when Washington complained one too many times. Dinwiddie listened to his colonel carp about late pay, about the poor quality of the Indian scouts sent out by Williamsburg, about the lack of chaplains, about the manpower shortage, about the want of artillery, about supposedly inadequate instructions from the capital, and even about what Washington—with justification—called a "stupid scandal," allegations circulating in the capital that he had fabricated stories of Indian attacks in order to obtain additional funds from the legislature.[41] The irascible governor no longer was in a mood for this.

His patience exhausted, Dinwiddie turned savagely on Washington, charging him with ingratitude. "You know I had reason to suspect You of Ingratitude, which I'm convinced your own Conscience and reflection must allow," he wrote. "I have foibles, and perhaps many of them," Washington responded. He was not perfect, but he took exception to the charge of ingratitude. He had been blunt, he acknowledged, yet he had only been reporting factually. Never had anyone discharged their duties more earnestly, more patriotically.[42]

The final act came when Washington asked permission to come to Williamsburg to settle some accounts with the governor. With brutal forthrightness Dinwiddie denied Washington's request. Washington had been absent from his army too frequently, said Dinwiddie. "Surely the Commanding officer Should not be Absent when daily Alarm'd with the Enemy's Intent's to invade our frontiers," he went on. Washington was wrong to even file such a request. Besides, "You have no Acco'ts, as I know of, to Settle with me. . . ."[43]

The governor's acrimonious tone was only one element in a wretched, melancholy autumn for Washington. With Dinwiddie's curt words still ringing in his ears, Washington received news of the death of Colonel Fairfax. Soon thereafter Washington fell ill too, his first serious ailment since his days with Braddock. Dysentery had plagued him since not long after he returned from Philadelphia, but he had continued on the job, hopelessly watching the steady erosion of his vitality. By November he was too sick to walk, suffering still from the "bloody flux"—dysentery—then from "Stiches & violent Pleuretick Pains." His army doctor, James Craik, a University of Edinburgh graduate, bled him three times, then recommended that he return home for a rest. Washington did not have to be told twice. He immediately turned over his command and headed east.[44]

Washington did not proceed directly to Mount Vernon, however. He stopped in Alexandria to consult a second physician, who, felicitously, also told Washington to return to his farm and to rest. He did just that, and within thirty days he felt much better, seemingly rejuvenated by the comforts of Mount Vernon. In fact, since early in the year his mind increasingly had drifted back to his estate. In April he had taken the first steps toward remodeling and furnishing the mansion, ordering a marble mantel, wallpaper, two hundred fifty panes of glass, two mahogany tables, and a dozen matching chairs; now, as he recuperated, he ordered a card table, china, and glassware from London. During his years as a soldier he had purchased six slaves (including a woman and her child that he acquired from Dinwiddie), and now he bought five hundred acres adjacent to his estate.[45]

The care and attention that Sally Fairfax extended to her ailing friend did nothing to impede his recovery. As soon as Washington had arrived at Mount Vernon he wrote to let her know that he was ill and at home. She came quickly, and soon she was back with the medicines prescribed by the physician in Alexandria— jellies, hyson tea, and a special wine that was to be mixed with gum arabic. With her husband in England at this time, one can only guess at how often she visited. Certainly Washington begged her to come, and she probably rode over from Belvoir frequently, though discretion would have required that she travel in the company of other ladies. (Discretion was something that her husband had advised her to employ in his absence, prompting one to wonder whether he was aware of Washington's feelings, or whether he simply was all too familiar with Sally's inclinations.)[46]

Early in 1758 Washington felt well enough to attempt a trip to Williamsburg. In January he set out on horseback, but he got only a few miles before the bloody flux recurred. Weak and dispirited, he turned back to Mount Vernon. In the next few days a persistent cough, alarmingly like the tubercular hack that slowly had destroyed Lawrence, set in. That February, while rumors of his death circulated in the capital, Washington languished in bed. It was the lowest point in his life; he saw himself as less than successful as a soldier, and as a failure in his efforts to secure British preferment; he knew that Dinwiddie thought him an ingrate; he was not capable of having the woman he believed that he loved; and, now, he was gripped with the fearful realization that he was dying. He had to know the nature of his illness.

With great difficulty he once again set out for Williamsburg. It was a tortorous ride, and several times he was compelled to pause along the way. But his pains were well rewarded. A careful medical examination in the capital led the doctor to conclude that the cough was harmless, merely the result of a damp winter. Free at last of that nagging worry, Washington seemed to recover instantaneously. But he did not return directly to Mount Vernon. He rode to the Pamunkey River, crossing on Williams' Ferry to the White House, home of Martha Dandridge Custis, for nine months now a widow. Indeed, not just a widow, but the wealthiest widow in all of Virginia.[47]

Washington almost certainly knew Martha before he reined up at her front door. High society in Virginia was not large. There was a chance that they had met at a ball, or perhaps at a race; if not there, their paths in all likelihood would have crossed in the capital, for Martha and her late husband usually attended the round of dances and parties that accompanied the sessions of the Burgesses, and on occasion Washington had also attended these gatherings. If they had met it would only have been the most fleeting of encounters however.

Nine years earlier, at the age of eighteen, Martha had married Daniel Parke Custis, a man twice her age. While she came from a comfortable, middle-class background, he was the son of a wealthy, eccentric planter. In seven years she bore four children, though only two lived beyond infancy. When her husband died, she was left with 100 slaves and 6000 acres valued at about £23,000; her liquid assets were worth approximately £12,000. It was no accident that Washington called on her.[48]

Martha Custis was only a few months older than her suitor. Short—she was barely five feet tall—and plump, her comely face was dominated by great hazel eyes. She was pleasant looking, not pretty, certainly not beautiful. Quiet and reserved, even shy, Martha was not the least bit flirtatious. Nor was she flamboyant in any way. More than anything else, a man could feel comfortable with her, especially a man who was not overly confident of his own talents. She knew her way around high society, she was reasonably polished, and she could be downright flinty when it came to managing a family and an estate, though that is not to suggest that she was either pushy or domineering.

George and Martha met in her parlor and talked of this and that. She probably gave him a tour of the mansion and the grounds, and she must have summoned a servant to fetch her two children, three-year-old John Parke—Jackie, everyone called him—and little Martha Parke, not yet two. George stayed overnight; then he rode to Williamsburg after breakfast the next morning. A week later he was back. When he departed the White House following that visit he was engaged to be married. The two had spent only about twenty hours together, but that was how marriages often were made in eighteenth-century Virginia.[49]

The marriage ceremony, however, would have to wait a few months. First George intended to spruce up Mount Vernon a bit. (He spent £325 on the mansion that summer, more than three times the annual wages of an unskilled laborer in those days.) More than anything else, though, George wanted to see the war on the frontier through that year's campaign. He now believed that the war could be won in 1758, for news had arrived recently of important changes in Britain's direction of hostilities. Loudoun had been recalled. Moreover, the new head of the ministry, William Pitt, had announced plans for three simultaneous campaigns in America, one of which was to be another operation aimed at seizing Fort Duquesne. (The other expeditions were to be directed at Ticonderoga in northern New York and at Louisburg, the great French fortress in Canada.) General John Forbes was to command the army in Pennsylvania, a force that was to include the army of Virginia under Colonel Washington, as well as a large contingent of British regulars. George and Martha must have talked of all this, then decided to schedule the wedding following that year's military activities.[50]

Why Washington decided to marry is something of a mystery. Of course, he had never been one to shun an attractive lady, and Martha was eligible and engaging. The loneliness imposed by command, especially when one was marooned on a remote frontier, probably caused him to think more and more of home and hearth, and of companionship. By early that year, moreover, he must have despaired at ever receiving a royal commission. Then, too, his brush with Loudoun, as well as his long wrangle with Dinwiddie, not to mention the strain and the anguish that came from presiding over a long, costly, ineffectual war, may have led him to the realization that his plantation was his most fulfilling calling. Finally, his bout with serious illness that winter must have reminded him of how short life could be, prompting him to acknowledge the number of life's pleasures he had forgone while sitting at lonely martial outposts. To be alone, and ill too, often quickens one's longing for a mate.[51] Then there was Sally Fairfax.

Unlike the young soldier who had taken up arms four years before, the Washington of 1758—now an adult of twenty-six—was more certain of his talents, more comfortable with his identity. In the years since he had emerged from Ferry Farm to serve as a courier for the governor, his world had expanded far beyond Mount Vernon and Belvoir. He had been lauded by the assemblymen of his province, welcomed into the offices and tents of powerful men, and treated as an equal by important businessmen in northern cities; he had commanded on the frontier, been entertained in Virginia's elegant little capital, and lived for weeks in three major urban entrepots. And he had grappled with life-and-death issues, with grim problems that outdisdanced the confines of estates like Mount Vernon and Belvoir, and which haunted the very halls of power throughout America and western Europe.

Washington, in short, had acquired status as a person. No longer was he compelled to seek his identity through a glamorous older brother or a rich and powerful neighbor. Outwardly Washington was the same person; inwardly, however, he had weathered a kind of late adolescent normative crisis, emerging with an enhanced sense of inner coherence. Now he was able to see both himself and the world more accurately. One change that resulted was in his outlook toward Sally Fairfax. He no longer needed her simply to assist in resolving his sense of inadequacy. Now he wanted her because he was more deeply in love with her than ever before. He had been very close to her recently as she attended him during his desperate sickness, then as she nursed him during his recovery. The experience only solidified his feelings. Yet, it was Martha Custis, not Sally Fairfax, whom he was about to wed. What occurred between George and Sally during those weeks late in 1757 never will be known. What seems likely, however, is that somehow he must have realized finally, unqualifiedly, that it was impossible for the two ever to live together. Somehow that must have been made painfully clear to him, either openly communicated by Sally, or imparted silently in a thousand repressive glances and gestures. However the truth was conveyed, once he confronted reality with regard to Sally, he began to look elsewhere for a wife. By no means did he forget Sally Fairfax. But the tug to marry, to leave the army shortly and at last to become a planter was too strong to resist.

Early in the summer of 1758 Colonel Washington was back in Winchester, writing to a British officer whom he knew, beseeching his assistance in attaining favors from General Forbes. He hoped, he wrote, to be "distinguished from the *common* run of provincial officers." When Washington reassumed his command after his five-month absence, he discovered that more Indian allies had arrived. They performed competently, if savagely, and kept the foe so preoccupied that Washington was able to devote most of his energies to courting Forbes. He did slip off to the Pamunkey on one occasion that spring, but otherwise he remained at Winchester, where he now took his orders from the British regular, Colonel Henry Bouquet, a considerate, Swiss-born officer who had joined the British army only three years earlier, after lengthy service in the Dutch, Sardinian, and his native Swiss armies.[52]

Washington hardly had returned from his sick leave before a nonmilitary matter competed for his attention. A vacancy for a Frederick County seat in the Burgesses was announced. Although he had never lived in that county, and even though he had lost an election bid for that same seat only a year earlier, he decided to run once again for the post. Washington's principal problem was that he could not get away to campaign, but that proved only a slight annoyance. Several of his officers beat the bushes for him, and so did George William Fairfax. Otherwise, his strategy was simple: outspend his adversary. Washington spent more than £40 plying the electorate with rum, beer, and wine, and throwing bashes that one observer called "dull barbeques and yet duller dances." His tactics succeeded. He outpolled three rivals, capturing nearly 40 percent of the votes and the legislative seat.[53]

Meanwhile, week after week Washington waited at Winchester. Early in the spring he had been confident that the year would witness the fall of Fort Duquesne to the British. Forbes had combined over sixteen hundred regular infantrymen with his artillery corps, and the colonists had added their muscle to this force. Virginia created a second regiment, and four other colonies also raised new armies, altogether an American force that exceeded twenty-five hundred men. By the summer, however, Washington's sanguine expectations had vanished as the army sat and sat, relentlessly inert.[54]

Much of Washington's energy during these weeks was spent over a protracted flap concerning the most advisable route to follow to the Ohio. The choices were limited. From his base at Raystown, now Bedford, Pennsylvania, Forbes could cut a road to Will's Creek, then follow the route taken by Braddock. Or, the British could cut a new road almost due west from Raystown. Because Washington was a veteran of two campaigns in this wilderness, his advice was solicited. The episode that resulted was not his finest hour. Washington plumped for the Braddock Road route, but he hardly acted dispassionately or scientifically. To his discredit, he acted like the acquisitive speculator that he was. After all, if the Braddock Road was the only byway carved through the wilderness to the Ohio, a Virginia speculator would have a leg up on his Pennsylvania competitors; besides, the Braddock Road almost touched his Bullskin Creek property. Washington's arguments in favor of that route were not that candid, of course. Instead, he contended that it was folly to build a new road when one already existed; the route from Raystown, he argued, was only slightly shorter, anadvantage that was offset by the difficult mountains that would have to be surmounted. So much time would be consumed in cutting the road, he maintained, that it was doubtful that an attack could be made that year. He managed to overlook the advantage to the alternate route: from Raystown the army would not have to cross the Youghiogheny. In addition, contrary to what Washington said, the Raystown route would be forty miles shorter than the Braddock route, not eighteen miles as the Virginian claimed. Bouquet asked for Washington's opinion, and he listened to his importunate suggestions, then he investigated the matter himself. He recommended the Raystown route. Now Washington acted as though he were desperate. He wrote a friend from his Braddock campaign days, a British major with access to Forbes. If the Braddock Road was not used, he advised hysterically, "all is lost! All is lost by Heavens! Our Enterprise Ruin'd. . . ." Forbes heard the recommendations, chewed them over for a few days, then he, too, opted for the Raystown route. "Poor Virginia," Washington cried to Speaker Robinson when he learned of Forbes's decision. In fact, Colonel Washington continued to make such a racket that Forbes was moved privately to question his integrity and his suitability to lead an army. He also summoned the Virginian to his headquarters, where in no uncertain terms he made it clear that the matter had been resolved.[55]

Not only had Washington's lobbying failed, he must have realized that his reputation had been damaged by his scheming. But if he was morose at this turn of events, his mood surely must have brightened in mid-September when the mail brought a letter from Sally Fairfax, his first contact with her since his engagement to Martha.[56] Sally congratulated him on his pending marriage and gently kidded him about his likely anxiety at the prospect of becoming a husband. Washington replied with as much circumspection as he could muster, but there was no mistaking his feelings. He confessed his love for Sally:

> 'Tis true, I profess myself a votary of love. I acknowledge that a lady is in the case, and further I confess that this lady is known to you. Yes, Madame, as well as she is to one who is too sensible of her charms to deny the Power whose influence he feels and must ever submit to. I feel the force of her amiable beauties in the recollection of a thousand tender passages that I could wish to obliterate, till I am bid to revive them. But experience, alas! sadly reminds me how impossible this is. . . .
>
> You have drawn me, dear Madame, or rather I have drawn myself, into an honest confession of a simple Fact. Misconstrue not my meaning; doubt it not, nor expose it. The world has no business to know the object of my Love, declared in this manner to you, when I want to conceal it. One thing above all things in this

world I wish to know, and only one person of your acquaintance can solve me that, or guess my meaning.[57]

It was not difficult to guess the one thing above all others that Washington wished to know. He awaited her response with a mixture of solicitude and buoyancy. It arrived two weeks later. Though just hearing from her must have delighted George, Sally's discreet refusal to spell out her feelings left him pensive. He wondered whether he had misunderstood her letter. Or had she misconstrued his? "I would feign hope the contrary as I cannot speak plainer without, But I'll say no more, and leave you to guess the rest," he replied. Yet he did add one last note. Sally had mentioned appearing in a production of Addison's *Cato*, and George responded that he would be "doubly happy in being the Juba to such a Marcia, as you must make." Translation: in the play Juba wonders what the man who longs for Marcia's love must do to win her heart, and Marcia responds that Juba would make "Any of womankind but Marcia, happy," for "While Cato lives, his daughter has no right/ To love or hate but as his choice directs." [58]

Between letters Washington sat idly at Raystown, watching the trees on the surrounding hillsides turn in their autumn splendor. It was a brilliant contrast to the drab and uninspiring army camp. All about, the lush forest had disappeared before the redcoats' axes, giving way to a muddy plain, from which tents everywhere sprouted like summer weeds. Down the road Forbes's army was advancing slowly, as fifteen hundred men in a woodsmen brigade wrestled with the almost inpenetrable timberland and hills. Then they were through to Loyal Hannon fifty miles further west, and Washington advanced his Virginians to that post. There he lingered for another three weeks, until, abruptly, he was pushed into action. For days the British had been plagued by French and Indian raids on their livestock and baggage train; when patrols reported the approach of a large French force in mid-November, Washington was ordered to gather a thousand men and to repulse the foe. He divided his force into equal units (one under George Mercer, the other under his command) and headed into the wilderness. Hours of weary and fruitless slogging passed; then just as it appeared that the day had been wasted an enemy party was sighted. A flurry of shots rang out from both sides, but the outgunned French and Indians scattered quickly, leaving one soldier dead and three as prisoners in Washington's hands. Interrogation followed, then the three-mile trek back to camp. Both the evening light and the swirling dust stirred by so many marching feet made it difficult for men to see. Suddenly someone spotted another force. On reflex a shot was fired, then a volley; immediately cries in English to cease fire pierced the air. To the horror of everyone, Virginians had fired on Virginians. Each force had mistaken the other for a French army. Fourteen men were dead, twenty-six had been wounded.[59]

Whatever mortification Washington felt at this blunder—and it must have been considerable—he did have the satisfaction of learning that his foray had produced significant intelligence. His prisoners revealed that the Indians had returned home and that many of the French troops had been reassigned. Fort Duquesne, the captives insisted, was poorly defended.

Forbes made the decision to gamble on the veracity of the prisoners. He would dart forward, risking everything. He selected twenty-five hundred men and stripped them of all baggage save their weapons and a light backpack. This was to be as much of a blitz operation as the wilderness would permit. He divided the force into three brigades; one, consisting of the Virginia Regiment and provincials from three other colonies, was assigned to Washington.[60]

Colonel Washington's men pushed forward with gusto, throwing up jerry-built bridges and clearing a path six-to-eight miles long each day. With a week left on their enlistments everyone knew they were close to the Ohio. Scuttlebutt had it that only seven or eight miles remained. Near dusk on November 24 an Indian scout galloped into camp. Fort Duquesne had been sighted—in flames. The French had scuttled their fortress and retreated. Miles of hard hiking remained the following day, but that evening, just after darkness fell over the three great rivers that mingled below the stockade, the weary British troops reached their destination. Only a few lonely chimneys still stood. Everything else was a smoldering ruin. The land that Virginians had craved for a decade was at last in the possession of Englishmen.[61]

Washington did not stay at the point formed by those rivers long enough to reflect on the triumph. Forbes immediately dispatched him to Williamsburg to procure supplies for the provincial troops. The colonel did not require a shove. He rode to Loyal Hannon to collect his possessions, then he turned toward Winchester and, ultimately, Belvoir. Two weeks of customarily miserable winter travel brought him to the Fairfax estate, where, weary and ill with a recurrence of dysentary, he collapsed for a recuperative interlude of several days. Not until the end of the month did he feel well enough to proceed to the capital.[62]

Often during the past four years Washington had contemplated leaving the army. Now he had made up his mind to resign, though the war was not yet over. The English had gained the Ohio, but France remained a powerful foe, and two more years of hard fighting in America lay ahead before the French would agree to parley. But one of the two objectives that had excited Washington—the acquisition of the point where Fort Pitt now would be constructed atop the ruins of the French citadel—had been realized. His other great aim, that of attaining rank through a royal commission, had been dashed. Unconsciously, at least, the military's grip on Washington had begun to wane the moment he learned that his aspirations in this regard had been thwarted. After he returned from his abortive trip to entreat with Loudoun, his thoughts increasingly turned to Mount Vernon, and to matrimony. He had decided to stay in the army of Virginia through 1758, and, had Forbes's army not reached the Ohio that autumn, he might have consented to remain in the service for still another campaign. But now that Fort Duquesne had been taken, he saw no reason—no gain that could accrue—for persisting in this way of life. Thus, sometime around Christmas in 1758, while he was in Williamsburg to wheedle supplies for those men still on the Ohio, he resigned, the end for all time, he must have presumed, of his military activities.[63]

Washington had served with valor, though with meager success, for five years. Barely twenty-two when he assumed command in 1754, he simply had lacked the experience and maturity to cope with the duties for which he was accountable. One egregious mistake followed another that spring and summer, until the campaign ended ignominiously at Fort Necessity. From the late summer of 1755 until he passed under the command of Forbes and Bouquet two and one-half years later, he was charged with securing Virginia's outlying frontiers. While he sustained no such mortifying defeat as had befallen Braddock, he enjoyed little success during that thirty-month period. In truth, though, Washington was confronted with an impossible task. Even the best military leader, if furnished with the scant and poorly supplied army that was allotted young Colonel Washington, would have been unlikely to have subdued the formidable adversary that marauded in Virginia's backcountry. But another leader might have served in a more mature—even a more virtuous—manner than did the youthful commander of Virginia's forces.

Several very admirable aspects of young Washington's character were much in evidence during these years, most prominently his considerable personal courage. Indeed, his bravery simply is beyond question. In addition, he possessed a powerful and indefinable personal magnetism that enabled him to win the unabashed loyalty of his officers, a cadre that included men who were far older and far more experienced than the callow young colonel. But there was another side to Washington, a dimension far less laudable. He seemed in the grip of a disturbing and unattractive obsession with his own advancement. No amount of protestation that he soldiered only for patriotic reasons—and he made that claim regularly—is quite convincing. He cannot be blamed for having carefully weighed all the alternatives, then for having opted for this career as the one that offered the most promise. Once in command, however, he seemed unable to harness his ambition, and his lusts led him to excessive absences, to petulant outbursts, to deceitful and irresponsible conduct, to an unsavory manner that vacillated between obsequiousness and a menacing heavy-handedness, and that, at times, verged even on the treacherous.

If Washington was given to reflection during those quiet December days in 1758, even he must have been surprised at his steady ascent. Granted he had failed to win British preferment, yet only eleven years before he had been mired at Ferry Farm without much prospect of escape. Many young men would have found his situation at that time an attractive one. His inheritance of land and labor, though meager by some standards, was more than adequate for a comfortable existence. But, of course, Washington was not contented. He had seen the power and the luxuries that wealth could purchase, and he wished to possess them. And he yearned to escape the irksome restraints imposed upon him by his mother. Of the three sons born to Gus and Mary Washington, only George seems to have been so driven; it was just as well, for of the three he alone had the enormous will to realize the lofty goals that he had set for himself. Now, with five years of military service behind him, his name was known throughout—and even beyond—his province. Soon, too, by marriage he would acquire vast property holdings that would solidify his status as a planter.

Matrimony aside, what was the secret of Washington's success? Clearly he was able to move other men, to inspire their confidence. With his native genius Washington had learned a lesson only the most incisive ever grasp: how to identify his natural strengths and adapt his behavior accordingly. He comported himself so as to play on his forceful traits, attempting, meanwhile, to hide and to overcome whatever he believed could be seen as a weakness or a blemish. Those men who trusted Washington were impressed by his grave and resolute manner, by his physical prowess, and by his natural acumen. On the other hand, he was keenly aware of his shortcomings—such as his "defective education," as he put it—and these he sought to disguise.[64] With his innate intuitiveness he had discovered that a mixture of show and substance could produce success. Repeatedly, those men who were moved by him were struck by his combination of easy affability with resolution and courage.[65]

But Washington was far more than an actor. He was honest in cataloguing his deficiencies, and he set about to correct those within his reach. By a combination of keen observation and diligent study he sought to become polished and urbane. He scrutinized those at Belvoir, he learned from Lawrence, he intently observed the conversations of the powerful in Williamsburg and Barbados, in New York and Philadelphia and Boston, and he carefully studied the mannerisms of the cultivated British officers with whom he served. Eventually, he developed an air of such earnestness and strength that he was able to induce subordinates to follow his command. Likewise, he possessed an uncanny ability to convince the magistrates and the powerful that he could lead, perhaps by impressing upon them that he embodied the very traits that they longed to exhibit: strength, vigor, sobriety, tenacity, virtue, maturity, decisiveness, a steely toughness, an icy remoteness.

Washington always knew how to win the interest and favor of the powerful. He courted the Fairfax tribe assiduously. When he departed for the army he even took the precaution of urging his brother, whom he left in charge of Mount Vernon, to remain in "Harmony and good fellowship with the family at Belvoir, as it is in their power to be very serviceable . . . to us, as young beginner's. I wou'd advise your visiting often as one step toward it. . . ."[66] Following his own advice, he uxuriously beseeched aid from Dinwiddie and Shirley, from Braddock and Loudoun.

Thus, the Washington of these years was not always an attractive figure: callow, pompous at times, obsequious, and frequently self-pitying. He seems, too, to have been singularly humorless. Not only are his letters during this period devoid of wit or jocularity, but in the reminiscences of his acquaintances not one ounce of whimsicality is ever attributed to him. Instead, what appears is a figure who marshalled all his vast energies in the pursuit of one end—the realization of his fantasized goals: admiration, power, wealth. To attain these ends, he was willing to be a flatterer and an actor, and he was inclined to attribute his every failure to someone else's ineffectuality. Some, like Loudoun, were not impressed with him. Others, like Dinwiddie, may have ultimately concluded that he was merely a dishonorable ingrate.

Young Washington established few, if any, warm, companionable relationships. The handful of surviving postwar letters sent to Washington by the men who had served under him were mostly cold and businesslike. Only rarely did a hint of intimacy break through in these communications, as when Washington's former aide, George Mercer, writing from Charleston, South Carolina, complained of the "bad Shape of the Ladies [in that city], many of Them are crooked & have a very bad Air & not those enticing heaving throbing alluring plump Breasts comon with our Northern Belles." Mercer immediately apologized for his brazen manner.[67]

Washington had permitted himself to be close only to older men, perhaps unconsciously feeling that they would be more tolerant of his shortcomings. Consequently, his most unrestrained filiations were with Lawrence and with elderly Colonel Fairfax. But neither saw him as a friend: to one he was a kid brother, to the other a surrogate son. With men his own age, there is no hint of a close friendship. He drank and gambled and relaxed with many men, and while with the British army, or on surveying jobs, or in command of the Virginia Regiment, he must have sat about campfires engaged in informal conversations. Not one letter of the scores he wrote in these years bears the ring of a communication to a friend, to an equal; and, while many who knew him left behind descriptions of this young man, none ever claimed to be anything more than a follower or an admirer. He looked upon other men in terms of his superiors and his subordinates, and toward him they reciprocated in kind.

With women, too, the pattern of remoteness is similar. He made repeated attempts at a sustained and close relationship with only one person, Sally Fairfax. Yet he knew from the beginning that he could never have her. As for Martha Custis, the woman he was about to marry, whatever the relationship ultimately became, it certainly began more as a business partnership consummated through marriage than as a passionately romantic tryst.

In a sense his life during these years seems to have been empty. Later, when much older, except for an occasional fond remembrance of Sally and the delightful days he had spent at Belvoir, he seemed strikingly disinclined to reminisce about the period. It was as if his past held no special charm for him, that he was conscious only of planning for success in the future. He certainly seems to have regarded his earliest years—those before he broke away from Ferry Farm—as too painful to recollect. Nowhere in his voluminous writings is there testimony to his tenderness or affection for anyone or anything from that period; the closest he came to expressing love for his kindred was to refer to his brother John Augustine as his "intimate companion." [68] Absent, too, is any harkening to the carefree days of youth. Life seems to have begun for him only when he at last could commence his drive to rectify the omissions of those painful early years.

One can only guess at whether Washington reflected on the past decade that holiday season as he rode up the isthmus from Williamsburg to the White House, his mount cantering along effortlessly past the lonely, scraggly pines in the barren winter forests. What must certainly have been on his mind was the stupendous change that was about to occur in his life. Within days he would be a married planter. Then he and his bride would be moving to Mount Vernon where they would try to carve out a life in this "Infant Woody Country." [69]

3

The Acquisitive Planter

"My unremitting attention to every circumstance"

A two-day ride over the sandy highway that sluiced through the damp wintry forests brought Washington to Martha Custis's estate. He arrived nearly a week and a half before the scheduled date of the wedding, but he could use the time. He and his fiancee had not seen one another for more than six months, since long before he had rendezvoused the Virginia regiments with Forbes's army at Raystown. They had much to plan, from the details of the wedding ceremony to the transfer of Martha's estate and chattel to his control, the latter mandated by Virginia law, which did not permit a married woman to exercise control over property. Besides, the couple wanted to get to know one another a little better. After all, since Washington first had ridden to the White House near the end of 1757, the couple had spent only about fifteen days together. In all likelihood, too, Washington wished to become better acquainted with Martha's children, Jackie and Patsy, as everyone now called little Martha.

Nearly forty guests, friends from throughout Virginia, attended the ceremony. Weddings always were popular occasions, not just for the infectious joy communicated by the happy couple, but because in a rural society opportunities for fellowship between friends were infrequent at best. On the evening before the wedding, a bitterly cold night, winter winds nipped at the barren trees and frosted the warm, candle-lit panes of the mansion's windows, while inside partners danced far into the late hours. The next morning the guests, mostly farmers accustomed to rising early, slept late, tired from the unusual night of partying that had gone before. When the guests did slip out of their beds that morning, they must have scurried about their chilly rooms, dressing hurriedly in a mood of blithe exhilaration.

A bit after 1:00 P.M. that day, January 6, 1759, George Washington and Martha Dandridge Custis slowly, nervously, entered the drawing room of the White House, each walking to the front of the chamber, each stopping beneath a chandelier ablaze with four white candles. Martha wore a wedding gown recently ordered from London, a "grave . . . suit of clothes," as she put it. Actually, her dress was voguish though not extravagant, a gown fashioned from yellow grosgrain silk, and including both ribbons of a high-sheen pink silk as well as an aigrette of white and deep red. If she hoped to appear sedate, Washington apparently sought to strike a more celebrative chord. He, too, wore clothing ordered from London, "a coat, waistcoat and breeches" made of the "best superfine blue cotton velvet," all bedizened with silk buttons.

The ceremony was brief. An Anglican priest presided, while the many guests, among them the governor of Virginia, and a dozen or so curious servants watched, tightly packed together in the stuffy room.

Following the ceremony the guests sat down to a feast, a long banquet of epicurean delights prepared by the servants, for whom the festivities simply meant a hard day's work. Hours later, after everyone had rested and talked, another evening of dancing ensued. Not until three days later did the last visitor depart, regretfully bidding farewell and commencing the long, cold, bumpy ride home.[1]

When the last guest had departed, Washington and his bride must have tried to unwind after days of anxiety, of whirlwind entertaining. During the next six weeks the formality between the two began to lose its edge, and the outlines of a relaxed family routine took shape. Washington used the time to make arrangements for the family's move to Mount Vernon, a jaunt scheduled immediately following the adjournment of the new legislator's first session in the Burgesses; a thousand decisions had to be made, but chiefly they had to decide which possessions—including servants and slaves—would be relocated.

In mid-February the family repaired to the capital in Martha's carriage, where they lived for the next ten weeks in the house built by Martha's first husband. The Washingtons joined in the customary round of festivities, attending balls and hosting dinner parties for other legislators and their wives, including George William and Sally Fairfax.

The Burgesses convened on Washington's birthday. Just twenty-seven years old, the inexperienced, somewhat shy and uncertain young lawmaker played an inconspicuous role in these sessions. Aside from pushing for the enactment of a few purely local bills, Washington sat back, listening and learning. Accustomed as he was to giving orders he must have felt like a fish out of water during the frequent tedious committee meetings and the tiresome, legalistic parliamentary debates. By early April his impatience to return to Mount Vernon overcame his sense of obligation to his legislative duties. He supervised the loading of crates of furniture and clothing, tools and toys, then, like the baggage train of a small army, the family with its servants set out for Washington's estate. It was a long trek, more than a hundred miles from the first blossoms of spring in the everpresent forests about the capital back to the late winter dreariness that still clasped the landscape to the north. The day before their arrival at Mount Vernon, Washington sent along instructions to a servant to clean and air the house, and to procure poultry and eggs for the family's first meal on the Potomac. Late the next morning the carriage rumbled over the last mile of the journey, softly squishing through the muddy road, on and on through the unending forest, until finally the faint outlines of the white farmhouse could be seen.[2]

Washington was proud of his plantation. It was home. During the last few months he had arranged for some repairs and additional construction, and he also had purchased new furnishings in anticipation of this moment. No record has survived of Martha's initial response to her new home, but chances are it was mixed. The mansion was small and rustic compared to the White House, and the grounds were rather unkempt; moreover, the estate sat in a sparsely settled region, a district that bore the imprint of unrefined frontier coarseness. On the other hand, important people—like the Fairfaxes—lived in the neighborhood. The view, too, could be breathtaking, particularly at this time of the year when, except for the purplish-scarlet of an occasional flowering redbud or the newborn white of a fruit tree, one's gaze was unobstructed by the foliage. The terrain was more rolling than on the Pamunkey, and in the rear of the house the land sloped gently down to the wide, green-blue river that flowed past placidly.

The house that Martha first saw was little more than a country farmhouse. George had inherited a one-and-a-half-story house. The bottom floor, which covered a space of thirty-three by forty-seven feet, included four rooms, two on each side of a long central hallway; four bedrooms sat atop this space. The clapboard structure had been built about great hand-hewn oak beams, each joined by oak pins instead of nails. The living quarters stood above a cellar, whose outer walls were fashioned from sandstone while its inner partition walls consisted of brick held by oyster shell mortar. Only the previous year, as soon as he and Martha were engaged, had Washington commenced his first extensive remodeling of the house, a project that he planned without the advice of an architect. He wished not only to have the work completed quickly, but in such a manner that the essence of the structure—and its memories—would be preserved. He rebuilt the foundation (using fifteen thousand bricks made in Mount Vernon's own kiln), raised the roof so as to add a full second story, added new clapboard, which of course was freshly painted (actually, slits were cut at intervals in the board so as to resemble stone, and sand was mixed with the paint in order to give the surface a rough, granite-like texture), reglazed all the windows, built additional closets, and replaced the old staircase to the second floor with a new, but quite simple, stairway. Workmen also hurriedly replastered some rooms, then they installed a rich paneling and a new marble mantel in the west parlor. Four outbuildings, meanwhile, were connected to the house by palisades mounted on brick walls.[3]

Whatever Martha's reaction to her new home, no substantive alterations were made to the structure for fourteen years. In 1773 work began on a three-story addition; the Washingtons planned to add wings to each end of the house, but the Revolution interrupted construction after only the western side had been completed. That wing had been added for pragmatic reasons. Inundated by overnight guests, the family had sought escape. This new wing consisted of a large library on the ground floor, a bedroom (connected to the lower floor by a hidden stairway) and adjoining dressing rooms on the second level, and another room, either Patsy's or Jackie's chamber, on the third floor. But if Martha displayed little interest in redesigning the structure of the mansion, she made her presence felt in refurnishing the interior. The largely barren house soon groaned with the furniture she had brought from the Pamunkey, and to this she gradually added beds, tables, chairs, and miscellaneous objects d'art that she ordered from London.[4]

To build and furnish Mount Vernon as he wished required that Washington have considerable financial resources. His land holdings were vast. Mount Vernon consisted of about forty-five hundred acres, so divided that it really amounted to five separate farms, some of which had (or soon would have) their own overseer's house, barns, and slave cabins. Washington also owned title to Martha's Tidewater acreage, he managed Jackie's lands on the Pamunkey, and he still possessed the Bullskin tracts that he had acquired with his initial earnings as a surveyor. Before Washington could put the land to effective use, however, he had to learn something about agriculture. Although he had grown up on Ferry Farm, he had never directed its operations, and he had done precious little work in its fields. At age sixteen he had left those jaded lands, and for the past dozen years surveying and soldiering had preoccupied him. Now he would have to learn the ropes of his new vocation as he had learned his other pursuits—by observation, by reading, and by trial and error.

Like most Virginia farmers Washington planted tobacco that first year. He also rented separate portions of Mount Vernon to nine tenant families, directing each to raise the plant. Management of the crop had changed but little since early in the previous century. Nor had the uncertainties associated with this mercurial and vexatious plant vanished. At every step in the protracted cycle of producing a tobacco crop the planter faced dangers. His success depended both on good fortune and on making a series of correct decisions.

The planting process began early in the year, ideally twelve days following Christmas. At that time seeds were planted in enriched beds, manured, and covered by oak leaves or straw to protect them from the frost. Because the odds were long against a plant's survival, large planters sometimes set out a crop ten times as large as they could use. In May the burgeoning young plants were transplanted into mounds that resembled molehills, each dome situated about three feet from its nearest neighbor. A week or so later hoeing commenced, a monotonous chore, but one that each mound required every five or six days. When leaves appeared, normally about six weeks after transplanting, the plants were topped. In this operation the top of the plant literally was pinched off, leaving five to nine leaves on the stalk. Now the plant could not flower, and the vegetation's energy was free to surge into the leaves. Thereafter, the plant grew no taller, but the leaves grew larger and heavier. For the course of the growing season— about six or eight additional weeks—tobacco farmers were required to look after both the weeding and the removal of suckers, or useless sprouts that inevitably burst out.

In September the tobacco was cut. This was perhaps the most risky step in the routine. To cut too early meant the destruction of a not yet fully ripe crop, but to wait too long was to run the risk of ruination at the hands of an early frost. Once cut, the leaves were left exposed on the ground for several hours so they would wither and be less brittle. When ready, they were gathered and hung in a barn to be air-cured. Curing required several weeks, terminating with still another crucial decision by the planter, for leaves that remained too moist would rot before reaching market in Great Britain, while leaves that had been allowed to become too dry would crumble to dust during the Atlantic passage. Once cured, the leaves were stripped from the stalk, and workers began "prizing" the crop. This was the final stage, the actual layering of the leaves into large hogsheads, forty-eight by thirty inch barrels that had been constructed by coopers on the plantation. When packed, each hogshead customarily weighed close to a thousand pounds. At that point, usually in the spring about fifteen months after the cycle had begun, the tobacco at last was ready for shipment. In George Washington's case this meant that the hogsheads, secured by iron or hickory staves, were drawn by horse or oxen to the Fairfax County warehouse, where the tobacco was inspected, graded, and stored until a vessel arrived to carry it to market in Great Britain.

Washington exuberantly put in his first crop, confident of a booming trade in the plant. Prices generally had been high in the 1740s, but the market had fluctuated wildly in the 1750s, reflecting the dislocations imposed by the French and Indian War, as well as the vicissitudes of the weather. With scarcity likely because of the persistence of the war, Washington expected high prices if the weather was advantageous. He expanded his tobacco production in 1760, although, as was true with every planter, he had not yet learned how his previous year's crop had fared at market in England. In the summer of 1760 he received the bad news. The price for his first crop had been low. By the time he learned of his misfortune, he also suspected that his current crop was doomed by an overabundance of rain. Yet, the destruction of that season's yield led him to conclude that scarcity would drive prices through the roof on his 1761 crop. That was not to be the case, however, and by the end of that summer he was nearly £1900 in debt to his British factor. His problems continued. Capricious weather, damages incurred during shipping, and oversupplies in Britain's emporiums all seemed to conspire against him. So, too, did a swarm of bugs and worms, prompting him to wonder why Noah ever "suffer[ed] such a brood of vermin to get a berth in the ark." His biggest problem, however, and one that he could neither understand nor acknowledge, was that the soil at Mount Vernon simply was incapable of yielding either substantial quantities of tobacco or the best quality leaf.[5]

George Washington was mortified by his failure to produce good tobacco. In his Virginia a planter was judged by the quality of his tobacco. To fail in this endeavor was a blow to a planter's self-esteem, and to a man who required adulation and attention as much as Washington did such a failure was intolerable. He first sought to overcome his humiliation by offering a financial incentive to an overseer who could provide him with superior tobacco, but that ploy inevitably met with failure. When that and every other expedient proved ineffectual, he alleged that he had been cheated by his factors in Great Britain. He severed his ties with one company, then he carped at the purported wrongdoing of a second. His tobacco was of a superior quality, he exclaimed, yet other planters in the neighborhood netted 12d per pound for their crop and he received only 11½d. Later he railed that some planters in the Northern Neck realized 30 percent more per hogshead than he earned. His poor showing mystified him. "Certain I am no Person in Virginia takes more pains to make their Tobo. fine than I do and tis hard then [to comprehend why] I should not be well rewarded for it."[6]

Washington's greatest yields resulted from his earliest efforts. In both 1760 and 1761 he produced approximately 93,000 pounds of tobacco, but thereafter his harvests declined. A planter in his time normally realized a cash return of about 25 percent on the tobacco that he marketed, the remainder being lost to taxes, shipping and insurance costs, and the commission charged by the overseas agent. In his peak years, therefore, Washington likely made about £1200 from his tobacco crop, although from that he still had to deduct his production costs. Nevertheless, what Washington regarded as a bad showing amounted to an annual income that was perhaps tenfold that earned by an urban-based skilled artisan in the 1760s.

After 1762 Washington despaired that he could ever produce the tobacco crop that he sought. Tobacco farming might be "an Art beyond my skill," he ruefully acknowledged, and in 1764 he allowed that he might not be able to grow "even tolerable Crops." Still, he was reluctant to blame himself or Mount Vernon for the evident failures, and the notion lingered in his mind that the agents in Britain favored some Americans over others. Why continue to grow tobacco, he wondered, when the treatment accorded planters in London "only suits the Interests of a few particular Gentlemen." Thus exculpating himself for his failures, Washington by 1764 had begun to substitute a wheat crop for his tobacco, and within two years he no longer produced any tobacco. His yield in wheat, meanwhile, had leaped from a modest 257 bushels to 2331 bushels by 1766, and by the end of the decade he was reaping over 6000 bushels annually. Washington never returned to tobacco production at Mount Vernon, although his tenants continued to pay their rent with hogsheads of tobacco they had grown, and he insisted that it be planted annually on his and Jackie's lands on the Pamunkey and the York.[7]

By the mid-1760s Mount Vernon had taken on the air of a diversified industrial village. While flax and hemp sprouted in adjacent fields, the weavers hired by Washington turned out increasing quantities of homespun cloth. By early in the next decade a flour mill was in operation, permitting him to grind not only his own wheat but that of his neighbors as well. The usual farm crops (corn and turnips, for instance) were sown, but in portions just sufficient to feed the family, the labor force, and the livestock. By 1766 he launched a fishing schooner, which trolled the Potomac for shad and herring, while orchards of fruit trees lined the rolling terrain. He bred and sold horses. In addition to oxen, hogs, and sheep, he raised cattle, and before long a dairy and a smokehouse were functioning. The construction of a still and a cider press added a varied dimension to the yield of his orchards.[8]

By 1770 Washington had very nearly cut his indebtedness in half. His success as a farmer was not due to happenstance. Agricultural tracts took up a sizable portion of the shelf space in his library. Washington approached husbandry as a scientist might conduct himself in a laboratory. He experimented constantly. He tested new fertilizers, varied his planting times, tried new grasses and new seeds, grafted in the hope of growing more lush fruit, sought larger, sturdier livestock by innovative breeding practices, kept an eye out for novel, labor-saving equipment, and he even invented a more suitable plow. Unwilling to delegate too much authority to an overseer, he seemed to observe each and every occurrence at Mount Vernon. He rose each morning at 4:00 and spent the initial two hours of his day at his desk, reading, handling correspondence, and grappling with his accounts. When the others in the family had awakened, he joined them for a substantial breakfast. Regardless of the weather he was on horseback by 7:00 to make his rounds, riding about fifteen miles each day, dropping in on each section of the estate to scrutinize the previous afternoon's labor and to issue commands to the foremen for the new day.[9]

If Washington worked hard, the hands he supervised worked harder. Most of his workmen were bonded laborers, and most of the bondsmen were enslaved. Before the 1770s many in Washington's slave labor force had been acquired through purchase. At the beginning of 1759 he held just over a score of slaves. During that year he spent nearly £600 on the purchase of thirteen additional chattel. By the end of the following year his corps of slaves numbered forty-nine, many of them having reached Mount Vernon via the auction block. A census taken in 1770 showed that his slave population had risen to eighty-seven persons. Sometimes Washington personally attended the sales to purchase slaves, while on other occasions he retained George William Fairfax's brother-in-law, an Alexandria merchant, to serve as his agent. To avoid the higher Virginia duties on imported slaves, Washington and his agent often shopped on the Maryland side of the Potomac. Between 1770 and 1775 Washington's slave population more than doubled, principally the result of natural increase, for he purchased no additional slaves after 1772. By that time, however, he had spent well over £2000 on the procurement of captive labor.[10]

Washington's attitude toward blacks was typical of his time. He was a racist. No evidence exists that he was troubled by the existence of slavery at any time before the American Revolution, nor does he seem to have ever questioned the prevailing notion of white supremacy. It would have been extraordinary had he puzzled much over these matters. He had never lived in a society that frowned on slaveholding, no vocal antislavery movements existed in the colonies, and men who were far better educated and more widely read accepted the institution with no misgivings. He apparently bought and sold slaves without a second thought. Purchase "Negroes, if choice ones can be had under Forty pounds Sterl.," he instructed his agent in the West Indies, but "if not, then [buy] Rum and Sugar . . . or . . . Sugar and Molasses." On another occasion he told his agent to sell a slave for molasses, rum, limes, tamarinds, and sweetmeats. His diary entries frequently refer to "My Negroes" or to "a Wench of mine," passages that are devoid of human feelings. He was not moved to express hatred or love or empathy for his chattel. They were simply business propositions, and his comments regarding these unfortunate people were recorded with about as much passion as were his remarks on wheat rust or the efficacy of a new fertilizer.[11]

Little information exists on the conditions in which Washington's slaves lived in the period before 1775.[12] But there is no reason to suspect that Mount Vernon's slave habitations were superior to those of neighboring plantations. The quarters must have been cramped and drafty chambers, miserably cold in the winter, frightfully hot in the summer. With their earthen floors, glassless windows, and cheerless, shabby furnishings, these domiciles must have been no more hospitable than the manger in which the estate's cattle were sheltered.

If the accommodations were meager, so too was the slaves' clothing allotment. At one estate a slave received only one shirt for an entire year. In the midst of winter one year an overseer informed Washington that the "little negroes" were without clothing, and, incredibly, he inquired whether their owner "intended to give them any thing er not." On another occasion he mentioned that Washington had provided no blankets for his slaves, though he had found some "negro Cotton" for the pregnant women and small children. Letters from Washington's farm managers were filled with accounts of illness among the slaves, including the report on a man who was forced to work even though he had contracted the measles and was beset by a "Violent Pox and Vomiting." Earlier in the year the same manager had failed to call a physician to assist another ailing subject until it was too late; that child died of the mange. When slaves ran away these overseers were dumbfounded. Coachman Jamey ran off, an overseer told Washington, "without an angry word or a blow from any one." The runaways were hunted down with dogs and, when captured, were severely flogged.[13]

Washington employed other laborers in addition to the men and women he owned. He purchased a few indentured servants. Under this century-old system a person sold himself for a specified period (usually five to seven years) in return for free transportation to America. Because of his large unskilled labor force, Washington bought only servants who were skilled artisans; he acquired a joiner in 1759, for instance, and, much later, a gardener. But most of Washington's skilled artisans were hired hands, some retained on a seasonal basis, some on yearly contracts. He employed carpenters, millers, bricklayers, blacksmiths, weavers, and metal workers, and at harvest time he engaged cradlers. Their contracts stipulated salaries ranging from £25 per year to nearly double that amount. The covenants additionally called for a full measure of work; the artisan was to labor six days each week for a year, but any days lost to illness were to be made up the following year. Washington also hired overseers for his scattered farms. Some were efficient; others were indifferent. He once rode up to Bullskin to find "every thing in the utmost confusion, disorder & backwardness . . . and not half a Crop . . . prepared." His most trusted managers were John Alton, a white servant who worked for him for more than thirty years, and Lund Washington, a distant cousin whom he hired in 1764 to oversee operations at Mount Vernon.[14]

If Washington was principally a planter, he also was a businessman and a speculator. He invested in three commercial pursuits on or near his Mount Vernon property. In addition to his flour mill, he constructed a saw mill, and in 1774 he purchased a brigantine in order to expand his fishing enterprise. He contemplated investing in an iron furnace in the Shenandoah, but nothing came of it.[15] His real interest, however, was land, and following his marriage he plunged into this uncertain market with almost unbounded zeal.

His initial foray into large-scale speculation had been fruitless. The Ohio Company was to get its lands only if it had placed one hundred settlers in its allotted domain within seven years; when the deadline was reached the French and Indian War was blazing and there were no settlers on the company's lands. In 1760 Washington cooperated in an endeavor to revive the moribund company, and three years later, at the end of the war, the resuscitated Ohio Company dispatched an agent—in fact, it was Colonel Washington's former aide, George Mercer—to implore the British government to renew its grant. Mercer remained in London for five years, but ultimately he failed. In 1767 the English secretary of state announced that all of the transmontane West belonged to the king. Twenty years after its inception the Ohio Company was dead. Not one investor had made one cent off the enterprise.

Washington was not the sort to put all his eggs in one basket, however. Not when he believed that stupendous fortunes could be reaped from western land. Indeed, he told a friend that he expected wilderness investments to yield a 500 percent profit in twenty years. He bought into the Mississippi Company in 1763, an enterprise that applied to the Crown for four thousand square miles between the Wabash and the Mississippi rivers; later he employed an old military comrade, frontiersman William Crawford, to search out tracts of "rich . . . and level" land for him in western Pennsylvania, and still later he retained an agent to look for promising river land in West Florida.

But Washington's problem was not in locating good land, it was in securing clear title to such tracts. His major obstacle arose from the absence of an effective, omnipotent government capable of devising and implementing a comprehensive, unambiguous, central policy toward the newly acquired western territory. Britain commenced its control of the region with the Proclamation of 1763, a decree that prohibited settlement west of the Appalachians. That was about the only unequivocal statement that London made in regard to the West, and it was not taken too seriously in the colonies. Washington, for instance, was not in the least disturbed by the edict, passing it off as a temporary expedient to mollify the Indians; he ruminated that anyone who "neglects the present oppertunity of hunting out good Lands . . . will never again regain it." Washington was correct that this was not London's final word. What followed was an object lesson in a government's inability to formulate a coherent policy. It could not decide whether it wanted settlers pouring into the transmontane West. Some secretaries to whom responsibility for such matters fell endeavored to facilitate expansion, while others feared that western settlements would be beyond the reach of England's mercantile houses, and still other ministers preferred to settle newly acquired Canada and Florida first, then worry about the West. The result of all this was chaos. One ministry contradicted another. Royal officials in America disregarded and suppressed royal orders. Colonies accepted some treaties by which Indians ceded their hunting grounds, while they ignored other, less favorable pacts. Britain's rule was so muddled it was unable to adjudicate the complexities of the colonists' rival western claims, such as those between Pennsylvanians and Virginians over the same prized real estate. Indeed, the British government could not even determine the western boundary of Pennsylvania.

By 1773, ten years after the French and Indian War ended, Great Britain still had not decided where—or even whether—to create a new colony across the mountains. Late in the 1760s reports began to circulate that London was about to create a new colony that would encompass the general region of present-day western West Virginia and Kentucky. Yet that was the very region in which Virginia's veterans of the late war hoped to attain the bounty lands promised by Governor Dinwiddie. Alarmed, Washington warned his governor that the rumored colony would be a "fatal blow" to Virginia, meaning, of course, to himself. Typically, the issue dragged on unresolved for years, until in 1773 the Board of Trade, and then the king, granted the domain to a group of English speculators and ordered preparations to commence for the establishment of a proprietary colony. Typically, too, nothing else occurred in regard to this colony, leaving Washington in the dark as to Britain's intentions.[16] What he did know was that in the years he had watched Britain vacillate in indecision over its western policies he had grown from adolescence to middle age, and in that time his pertinacious, sometimes dangerous, pursuit of a fortune in that realm had gone largely unrewarded.

Of course he had acquired some land, although even where a clear title seemed to exist surprises had an uncanny way of occurring. Crawford had acquired some property for him in Pennsylvania, and he had purchased nearly twenty-seven hundred acres of the George Carter estate in Virginia. Moreover, during the 1760s he had become intrigued by the possibility of developing a hitherto inaccessible region known as the Great Dismal Swamp, a mélange of thickets and trees, bogs and coves, that sprawled inland from south of the Chesapeake, lapping over the Virginia border into North Carolina. Since much of the peripheral land had been cultivated with considerable success, several speculators concluded that beneath the forbidding morass of the swamp itself good, flat land suitable for farming and timbering—and within reach of the Atlantic sealanes—lay waiting to be exploited. The hitch was that the region would have to be drained before it could be of any use. Washington first visited the area early in 1763, a fact-finding excursion to determine whether investment was warranted. He concluded that the area had abundant assets. He discovered that much of the soil was rich and black, that the rivers that darted through these marshes could accommodate ocean-going vessels, and that the area had plentiful stands of timber. Pleased with the possibilities, Washington, together with several other planters, including his brothers-in-law Fielding Lewis (husband of his sister Betty) and Burwell Bassett (spouse of Martha's youngest sister), invested in a company simply named the "Adventurers for Draining the Dismal Swamp." Under its charter each member was to receive title to one thousand acres, and each was obligated to furnish cash and ten able-bodied laborers for the work force. Washington eventually made four additional trips to the site during the decade to scout for good land, and, after one trip, he and Lewis purchased over eleven hundred acres on the southern perimeter of the swamp. But the company failed to open any lands before the Revolution, although as early as 1768 Washington succeeded in marketing cypress shingles that he procured from the area.[17]

If Washington worked tirelessly to develop the swamp, he was like a man possessed in his efforts to secure the bounty land he believed he had been promised. In 1754, when Virginia raised its army to drive the French from the Ohio country, Governor Dinwiddie had proposed to divide 200,000 acres among the men who enlisted. Fifteen years after he had first donned his uniform, however, Washington had not received an acre of the land. First, the war had been unexpectedly protracted; then, the Proclamation of 1763 had prevented the fulfillment of the governor's pledge. But late in 1768 Britain and several western tribes negotiated treaties under which much of the eastern Ohio Valley was opened for colonial settlement. Washington knew the time to act had come. In fact, he realized that he had to act quickly, for not only were Virginians and Pennsylvanians certain to vie for the land, but should that be the region in which Britain chose to establish its long-rumored new colony good land would be even more difficult to attain. And Washington knew that he faced one other sticky problem. It was not at all clear that Dinwiddie had intended to give any land to the officers. The language of his proclamation, though vague, seemed to suggest that he proffered the land as an inducement for men to enlist, not for officers who accepted commissions. Washington began his quest by gathering enough of the surviving officers to draft a petition to the government requesting that the land grant at last be made, that lands be extended to officers as well as to enlisted men, and that the lands be on one or all of the following bodies of water: the Monongahela, the New River, the Great Kanawha, and Sandy Creek. A friendly aristocratic governor, Baron de Botetourt (who had arrived in Virginia only the previous year) and his council readily concurred with each point, stipulating that they hoped one satisfactory tract of 200,000 acres might be located, but agreeing to as many as twenty separate blocks. Typically, too, the government ultimately allotted 15,000 acres for each general officer, but only 400 acres per private. The government directed William and Mary College to appoint a surveyor.[18]

The claimants met in 1770 and agreed to permit Washington, a surveyor and an experienced frontiersman, to search the area for suitable tracts. That autumn Washington departed for the West, undertaking his first junket over the mountains in more than a decade. Traveling with several servants and his old army doctor, James Craik, who had set up a practice in nearby Alexandria, he arrived at the residence of William Crawford after eight days of hard walking and horseback riding. The party lodged with Crawford for three days, while Washington and the frontiersman inspected some other lands (and a coal mine) near the Youghiogheny that seemed intriguing. Another day's travel brought them to the forks of the Ohio, guarded now by Fort Pitt. Washington stayed at a tavern in the "town" of Pittsburgh, a rude village of twenty log cabins, and that evening he dined with the British officers garrisoned at the reconstructed stockade. A day or two later the men, joined now by several Indian guides, shoved off down the Ohio, beginning a month-long canoe trip that spanned over eleven hundred miles. Aside from some early season snow and the anxiety provoked by news (false news, it soon was happily learned) that Indians recently had murdered white settlers along the river, the trip was pleasant. The men stayed on the Ohio, leaving it just once for five days to explore the Great Kanawha River and the lands about it. Washington ran no surveys, but he took copious notes and he marked off two corners of "the Soldiers L[an]d (if we can get it). . . ." By mid-November they were back in Pittsburgh, and a few days later, after an absence of nine weeks, Washington was resting before his hearth at Mount Vernon.[19]

He was not idle for long. He used his influence to secure the selection of his old friend Crawford as the official surveyor of the bounty lands. Then, when the tracts were located, he utilized his persuasive powers with the veterans to attain Crawford's appointment as the surveyor to divide the general tracts into individual portions. Meanwhile, Washington set about to gently persuade some veterans to sell their shares to him; he told some men that their segments were likely to be "very hilly and broken," and he emphasized the uncertainty of ever acquiring the land, observing that should Britain create a new colony in the West it undoubtedly would include "every Inch of the Land we are expecting. . . ." He also enlisted his brother's aid, asking Charles to see some of the men without letting them know whom he represented, and "if you would (in a joking way, rather than in earnest, at first) see what value they set upon their lands." By one argument or another Washington, for a pittance, purchased lots totaling over fifty-one hundred acres. After having met twice with the surveyor, Washington next presented to the government a plan for the division of the bounty, a scheme by which he proposed to keep the best lands for himself (why not, he told a friend, for "if it had not been for my unremitting attention to every circumstance, not a single acre of Land would ever have been obtained.") The government, though ignorant of the nature of each tract, gladly accepted Washington's plan. Through grant and purchase he received 20,147 acres. At the time, no one complained, but later some of the men exploded when they actually saw their plots, venting their wrath at Crawford. They were "a good deal shagereend," the surveyor told Washington, to learn that "you in Chief of your Surveys [and Dr. Craik] have all bottom . . . Land." None of the land "in that Country is so good as your Land and his Land," he added.[20]

Only George Muse, the scapegoat for the debacle at Fort Necessity, dared to complain directly to Washington of the bilking he believed he had received. Washington's response was crude and visceral, and worth repeating:

> As I am not accustomed to receive such from any Man, nor would have taken the same language from you personally, without letting you feel some marks of my resentment; I would advise you to be cautious in writing me a second of the same tenour; for though I understand you were drunk when you did it, yet give me leave to tell you, that drunkness is no excuse for rudeness; and that, but for your stupidity and sottishness you might have known, by attending to the public Gazettes . . . that you had your full quantity of ten thousand acres of land allowed you. . . .[21]

If Muse complained openly, other men apparently protested in private, and when it was discovered in 1775 that Crawford had failed to take the oaths required of a surveyor, his measurements were disallowed by Virginia's governor. There the matter rested until three years after the Revolution began, when the House of Burgesses declared the original survey valid. Washington would get his land if America secured its independence.[22]

For all his frenetic business and speculative endeavors, Washington hardly exhausted his resources. He lived in an elegant, even opulent, manner, attended at Mount Vernon by thirteen house slaves. He poured forth a steady stream of orders to his overseas agents, purchasing guns and hunting paraphernalia, large quantities of rum and larger amounts of wine, preferring Madeira, though he also ordered other varieties by the butt (150 gallons). He frequently ordered delicacies not available in Virginia: several varieties of nuts, cheeses, candies, teas, sweetmeats, and citrus products, plus refined sugar, spices, and soap. His huge clothing purchases were staggering. He placed nine separate orders for shoes (about two dozen pairs) and boots within a decade, and he often requested gloves, trousers, hose, and suits. He acquired a new carriage ("in the newest taste, genteel and light") to replace Martha's dilapidated buggy. A fancy saddle and an elegant sword sent from London must have enabled him to cut an imposing figure. Of course, much of what he requested was for Martha—fabrics, ribbons, clothing, perfume, and snuff, for instance—and he also bought furniture, china, pewter, and silverware from abroad for the mansion.[23]

Since the goods he bought had to be transported across the Atlantic, he was forever tormented by shipping problems and other perplexities. Often the clothing fit poorly, if at all; one time the ship's crew broke into his wine and freely imbibed. The merchandise often was damaged—broken, water-stained, moth-eaten. Sometimes the company sent the wrong items. He once ordered small busts of six famous soldiers for his mantel, but his factor substituted statues of six nonmilitary figures from antiquity. The goods often arrived at the wrong river, or they never arrived at all. Once, piqued by the futility of it all, he maintained that the English merchants "palm sometimes old, sometimes very slight and Indifferent Goods upon us," and he complained to his agent that his goods were "mean in quality but not in price." Mostly, though, he seemed resigned to his fate and he quietly submitted to the inconveniences.[24]

Washington's fifteen years as a planter-entrepreneur seem to have been a period when happiness far outweighed sadness at Mount Vernon. Despite his busy schedule and frequent absences, Washington found time for recreation. He enjoyed both horse and boat racing, and like other roughhewn provincials he found cockfighting to his liking. Exotic animals intrigued him too. He once paid to see a lion and a tiger, and on another occasion he arranged to have an elk brought to Mount Vernon; he even tried, without success, to acquire buffalo for his pastures. He occasionally trekked to Alexandria to the theater, and he frequently took in plays while he was in Williamsburg. He seemed to entertain incessantly at Mount Vernon, chatting with friends over wine (he was not fond of other spirits, though he stocked whiskey for his guests), or playing cards, backgammon, and billiards. When he was in town he frequented taverns, and he seldom failed to spend some time visiting friends at the Masonic lodge hall (he had become a member of the order in 1753, quickly rising to Master Mason). Washington was a horse fancier too; he loved these elegant animals and he enjoyed trading and breeding them. Balls and wedding and dances afforded him an opportunity to visit with other farmers, but if he was displeased with the rustic's amenities he might grump to his diary, as he did after a party in Alexandria when a maladroit hostess served tea that tasted like hot water, provided an inadequate amount of food, and used pocket handkerchiefs for napkins and a tablecloth.

Washington worked vacations into his schedule when possible. He and Martha occasionally slipped away to Eltham, Burwell Bassett's estate on the Pamunkey, not far removed from the White House. At other times the family made the four-to-five-day journey across the mountains to Berkeley Springs, the warm water springs where Lawrence vainly had sought a cure. Washington found the summer heat militated by this environment, and with a cook and servants in tow he came here often, residing for up to six weeks in a cottage that George Mason, his Potomac neighbor at nearby Gunston Hall, kindly made available.

Washington loved the outdoors and his happiest moments came when he plunged off into the forests. He was fond of searching out a mountain stream and trying his luck with the fish, but more than anything he enjoyed hunting. Nothing seemed so relaxing and invigorating as a day in the fields with his dogs (to whom he gave names like Mopesy, Tarter, Jupiter, Trueman, Tiple, Truelove, Juno, Dutchess, and Sweetlips) in quest of duck, pheasant, deer, or fox, sports to which he often devoted ten full days or more a month. As with his horses, Washington took great care in the breeding of his hounds, but woe be to any offspring which through accident was not pedigree. He simply drowned those unfortunate pups.[25]

Something of Washington's attitudes and manners also are apparent in what he did *not* enjoy. He was not fond of leisure reading. He acquired many of the better books concerning scientific agriculture, but, otherwise, in these adult years he chiefly read military manuals and biographies of former martial leaders. He was familiar with important literary works like *Don Quixote* and *Tristram Shandy*, but he neither read the great works of the Enlightenment nor the principal tracts of the political theorists of his age.[26] The natural world was an important part of his life, yet his interest in nature was purely utilitarian; when he noted in his diary varieties of trees or climatological trends it always was with an eye on speculative or farming concerns. Collecting objects of art held no allure for him; and his furniture acquisitions, while tasteful, were made more with the functionalism of each piece in mind. While he loved Mount Vernon and carefully planned each addition, he remodeled only for practical reasons, never from aesthetic inclination, and he lived in the mansion for nearly twenty years before he employed a gardener to formally design the grounds.

Washington was not particularly fond of attending church. His religious interests were awakened for a time during Lawrence's protracted illness, but thereafter his faith was a rather private matter. He served for several years as a vestryman (along with eleven other men) for Truro Parish, a post concerned with collecting funds and constructing facilities. Yet he attended services only about once each month, and when he did escort Martha to worship he did not partake of the Eucharist. He was not a Deist, however. He believed in God's intervention in worldly affairs, and he anticipated a life after death.

He could be rather droll about his piety. Having learned that a friend had not attended church, Washington whimsically chided him and, very much tongue in cheek, he added: "Could you but behold with what religious zeal I hie me to church on every Lord's Day, it would do your heart good, and fill it . . . with equal fluency."[27]

Washington seemed even less eager to spend time with his mother than he was to attend church. A domineering woman, she must have nagged at her son when they were together, complaining and offering unsolicited advice that either provoked a tempest with the quick-tempered young man or left him stewing. Washington resolved the problem simply by seeing as little of her as possible. The distance between their estates (Ferry Farm was a solid day's ride away) was a good excuse for only an occasional visit, and, besides, he was genuinely busy with his farm and his own family's obligations. He apparently did not invite her to stay at Mount Vernon. Mary Washington remained at Ferry Farm until 1771, grappling with its exhausted land without much success. Four times after 1765 she called on her son for financial assistance, and each time he complied, giving her more than £25 altogether. But in 1771 George, together with his brother Charles and his sister Betty, decided the sixty-three-year-old woman could live more comfortably elsewhere. True to form, however, this tough old lady negotiated a deal: she was to be ensconced in a comfortable house on one of George's lots in Fredericksburg; George was to provide her necessities; and he was to pay her an annual rent—apparently about £30—for Ferry Farm (which, in fact, he legally owned and would now manage through an overseer). Her son agreed, but he was a shrewd chip off the block too. Shortly after his mother had moved, Washington sold the farm for £2000.[28]

If Washington scarcely saw his mother, he had plenty of other visitors. In an age when travel was slow and inns were scattered or nonexistent, wayfarers in the South expected to be lodged at the residences of others of their social class. So many pilgrims stopped by Mount Vernon that at times it seemed certain that George and Martha would never be alone, and once, in exasperation at the ubiquitous guests, he remarked in his diary: "Mrs. Possey, & some young woman whose name was unknown to any Body in this family, dined here."[29]

The Washingtons' best friends were the Bassetts and the Fairfaxes. Burwell Bassett and Martha's sister lived so far from the Potomac, however, that the families saw one another only infrequently. But Washington wrote to Bassett often, sending him gossip about mutual acquaintances and keeping him abreast of affairs at Mount Vernon. George and Martha also developed an affinity for Bryan Fairfax, George William's half brother who had emigrated to America in 1751 and settled (with Sally Fairfax's sister) on Lord Fairfax's estate in the Shenandoah. About the same age as George, yet less sober and more of a madcap, Fairfax served with Washington for years in the Burgesses and the two grew to be fast fox-hunting chums.[30]

Sally and George William Fairfax were closer than anyone else to Washington and his wife. George and young Fairfax for years had maintained a cordial, but distant, friendship. George William after all was older, a married man when

Washington still was in his teens; for several years in fact young George persisted in calling the master of Belvoir "Mister Fairfax." But after Washington matured the two men grew quite close, each admiring traits in the other which they believed were lacking in their own makeup. The one urbane, polished, well educated, something of a man of the world, the other athletic, graceful, courageous, a man equally at home in the raw wilderness or in the domesticity of his dining room. The two families had much in common: both were wealthy and powerful, and everyone was about the same age, give or take a few years. Strangely, too, for that time and place, neither family had produced any children. Yet, enough differences in temperament existed among all four to create an engaging diversity. Most importantly, Martha quickly accepted these old friends of her husband, and eventually she too grew close to the Fairfaxes. The families visited often, sometimes staying overnight at the other's mansion. The men hunted together, contemplated joint business deals, and sat side by side in the Burgesses. The women come to us in more shadowy terms, and it is more difficult to understand the bond that seemed to have developed between one who was so pert and flippant and one who was so matronly. But they did grow close, whether in spite of or because they were so different.

George and Martha had lived at Mount Vernon for only about a year when family business called the Fairfaxes to England for several months. While they were abroad George William did not write Washington, but Sally did. Yet Sally seemed to have changed when they returned to Virginia, acting for a time as if after experiencing the luster of Old World society everything about the provinces had seemed to pale by contrast. What transpired between her and George in the following decade can only be guessed at. His diary references about her were curt. For instance: "Monday Feby. 25th . . . Colo. Fx & his Lady . . . dined here. So[uther]ly Wind and remarkable fine clear day." [31] In all likelihood nothing happened between the two. If they still had tender feelings about one another, they probably communicated them silently. Each had much to lose if matters went beyond that. And Washington, shy and prudent, and inordinately proud of his virtue, was unlikely to push things too far.

In the early 1770s Sally fell ill, requiring medical attention that could only be found overseas. She and her husband sailed to England in 1773, never to return. Permanent residence abroad had not been in their plans, but when the opportunity to return to America arrived the colonies were at war with Britain, and Fairfax proclaimed his loyalty to the Crown. If they did not come back to Virginia, they were not forgotten. Washington continued to correspond with George William, often alluding to the times he had spent at Belvoir as "the happiest moments of my life." A quarter century after he last had seen Sally, and not long after he had learned of her husband's death, Washington wrote to her for the last time. In some ways it was a curious letter, alternately stiff and formal, yet breezily chatty. He seemed, too, to make a special effort to impress her, inserting a passage in French, one of the rare times he ever employed such a device. In two widely separated sections he spoke of his feelings for her. The "happiest [moments] in my life," he wrote, were those "I have enjoyed in your company." So often, he admitted, he still looked toward Belvoir and thought of her. Then, at the end of the missive, and rather obliquely, he suggested that she return to Virginia.[32]

Did his letter indicate that he had never abandoned his love for Sally? Probably. To Washington she always would be an alluring woman, beguiling, a bit mysterious, always able to ignite the emotions that he otherwise succeeded in keeping so closely controlled. Moreover, she was about the only thing that he ever had determined to pursue and attain that had eluded him.

But did his ineradicable feelings for Sally indicate unhappiness with Martha? Washington was a private person, and in nothing more so than the very personal relationship he shared with his wife. He simply was not the type to wear his feelings on his sleeve. Yet some things seem clear. Their union began as a virtual marriage of convenience. He was ready to marry, she was a widow ready to remarry; economically it was a good match. Shortly after the marriage, at a time when, as he later put it, most young men are caught up in the "transports of passion," he quaintly referred to Martha only as an "agreable Consort." But regardless of his feelings when they married, his attitude changed as he grew older. Love, he grew to believe, was too fragile a cornerstone for a marriage; "like all delicious things, it is cloying," he said, and likely to evaporate. Instead, the qualities that made for felicity in marriage, he advised his step-granddaughter, were "good sense [and] good dispostions."[33] What Washington perhaps was thinking was that he always had loved Sally Fairfax, but that with Martha he was comfortable—and quite happy.

Washington hoped to have children of his own, but year after year slipped past without issue. By the early 1770s he knew it was hopeless. Jackie and Patsy were there, and he cared for and shepherded them with all the love he would have given to his own. Jackie, without a father for half his five years before Martha married George, was a spoiled and pampered child whose manner at times utterly exasperated his stepfather. Nevertheless, Washington saw to it that the youngster had opportunities that he himself had been denied. By the time he was eight years old Jackie was studying under a tutor, and soon Washington was ordering Latin and Greek readers for the boy. When Jackie was fifteen Washington purchased nearly fifty books for him, a collection that included classics, religious tracts, histories, and the musings of contemporary philosophers. About the same time, too, George and Martha decided to pack Jackie off to school, to study under Anglican clergyman Jonathan Boucher. Washington enrolled the lad, explaining to the schoolmaster what Jackie had read, though acknowledging that he was "a little rusty" in both Latin and Greek. Otherwise, he continued, Jackie was a boy "of good genius . . . untainted in his morals, and of innocent manners." Jackie, chubby, fair, soft, departed in the summer of 1768, accompanied by his personal slave and two horses. He spent the better part of five years under

John Parke Custis ("Jackie"), by Charles Willson Peale (1772). Courtesy of the Mount Vernon Ladies' Association of the Union.

Boucher's tutelage, most of it in Maryland, first in Annapolis, then in Prince George's County. Jackie was not an impressive student. An idler to begin with, the knowledge that he would inherit a fortune when he came of age did not induce him to expend much effort on his books. Boucher found him to be one of his most exasperating pupils, calling him the most indolent and hedonistic person he had ever known, and asserting that the boy was better suited to be an "Asiatic Prince" than a scholar. Nevertheless, sniffing the boy's wealth, the rector suggested that a European tour—led, of course, by Boucher and financed by Washington—just might turn the lad around. Washington drew the line at that point, genteelly demurring on the grounds that Jackie was "by no means ripe enough for a travelling tour." (At the conclusion of his stay, Boucher maintained that the boy was deficient in the "knowledge befitting a Gentleman," and, he raged, Jackie's only interests were guns and horses.)[34]

By 1773 Jackie's parents decided the time had come for a change. He should be enrolled in college. Washington—with Boucher's accord—concluded that William and Mary College was unsatisfactory, and he opted instead for King's College (now Columbia University) in New York. Not long before he was to depart, however, eighteen-year-old Jackie dropped a bombshell. He was going to get married. The girl: Eleanor Calvert (called Nelly by her friends), the beautiful, sable-haired, dark-eyed daughter of the Benedict Calverts of Mount Airy, Maryland. Martha and George were crushed. Not only was Jackie's education jeopardized, but he had not bothered to consult his parents. Nelly, moreover, came from a more modest planting background than Washington would have preferred. Washington fretted, too, at Jackie's "fickleness," fearing that the boy might back out of his commitment and "injure the young lady." Yet, other than to argue and cajole, there was not much that could be done. With Martha's consent—and maybe after a push from her—George did write Nellie's father hoping for a postponement because of Jackie's "youth, inexperience, and unripened Education. . . . If the Affection which they have avowed for each other is fixd upon a Solid Base, it will receive no diminution in the course of two or three years. . . ." Her father agreed to "delay, not break off, the intended match." That spring Nelly, her parents, and some girl friends visited Mount Vernon, and the Washingtons later called on the Calverts. In June, as planned, Jackie matriculated at King's College. George took him to New York, along the way meeting Benjamin Franklin's son William, the governor of New Jersey, and renewing an old acquaintanceship with Sir Thomas Gage, now commander of all British troops in America. Jackie's college career lasted just six months. His stepfather wanted to force the boy to stay on, but Martha at last gave in to his importunings for her consent to an immediate marriage; Washington decided not "to push my opposition too far," and the couple were married in the winter of 1774.[35]

Martha's change of heart was prompted by a terrible tragedy. Patsy had lived a common enough life for a planter's daughter. Girlishly playful, she pampered the dolls her parents ordered for her, was tutored by her mother, and received private music lessons. Then, on a mild summer day in 1768 she suddenly fell to the floor in the grip of an epileptic seizure. Her frightened parents summoned a physician, Dr. William Rumney, a native of England and former British army surgeon who had settled in Alexandria; he bled her and prescribed *valerian,* "nerve drops." The next month he was back with more valerian and two capsules of musk oil, thought to contain an antispasmodic agent. She had a second attack in November; following this seizure Rumney administered purging pills, mercurial tablets, and a decoction, that is, warm water in which a medicinal vegetable medly had been boiled. Another seizure followed, however, and her doctor now recommended an iron ring, or a "cramp ring" as they sometimes were called; worn on the finger, these iron bands allegedly warded off fits. The next summer the family tried the baths at Berkeley Springs, but Patsy was "unwell" while undergoing this treatment. Late in 1769 her stepfather called in another physician, a University of Leyden–trained doctor who had settled in Virginia. He examined her frequently, yet in July 1770 she became seriously ill with both seizures and an "ague and fever." Dr. Rumney now showed up again, this time experimenting with various powders and with *cinchona,* or Peruvian bark, thought to be a remedy for malaria as well as for epilepsy. Six months later still another doctor was consulted, this one a graduate of the University of Edinburgh. He prescribed ether, presumed by many to be an effective antispasmodic; Washington obtained some in Annapolis, and it was administered as an oral dose.[36]

Obviously nothing had worked. By her fifteenth birthday Patsy had grown into an attractive young lady, with an altogether elegant, but friendly demeanor. Her long ebony hair accentuated her somber eyes and dark, arching brows. Her face was thin and delicate, with dainty lips, a graceful, slightly pointed nose, and beautiful, somewhat melancholy eyes. Despite her illness she seemed so full of life that neither Martha nor George were prepared for what happened. On June 19, 1773, Washington's brother John and his family were at Mount Vernon for a visit, along with Nelly and one of her girl friends. It had been an enjoyable day; Patsy felt fine—as she had for several weeks, in fact—and she was very happy to have company. Then, just as the family concluded a long Saturday afternoon meal, Patsy fell to the floor without a sound, the victim of still another seizure. She was dead in less than two minutes.[37]

George was badly shaken by the child's sudden death, and by the ineradicable recollection of the events of those final brief, horrid moments. He undertook no business for three weeks, and then it was only to write London to order mourning garments. Martha, of course, was disconsolate, wracked by grief and doubt and anger; as George put it, one could find it "an easier matter to conceive, than to describe [his wife's] distress. . . ." He postponed a trip to the West. For weeks he stayed at Mount Vernon, trying to provide solace, and seeking comfort in Martha's company as well. He and Martha took several carriage rides alone, solemn and solitary drives to nowhere in particular, something they rarely had done before, and George withdrew for lonely and unattended walks in the nearby forest. Nelly stayed on too, refusing to return with her parents when they came to pick her up three weeks after the funeral; her presence helped, for she was about Patsy's age, and she and Martha already had grown close. Except for a trip to the Calvert's home in late July, Washington did not spend a night away from Mount Vernon for three months.[38]

A jaunt to the races in Annapolis in September signaled the end of the period of mourning. Before he left, however, Washington faced the unpleasant business of the probate of Patsy's will. Her estate had accrued a value of over £16,000; Jackie received half this amount, while Martha (meaning George, of course) acquired the remainder. In November he notified his English creditors that he was using the inheritance to eliminate his long-standing debts.[39]

Although Patsy's death continued to cast a pall over the Washingtons as they traveled to Annapolis that September in their chic carriage, both George and Martha must have felt that on balance fate had smiled on them during their nearly fifteen years together. Washington had grown from a neophyte planter with potential to one of the wealthiest and most respected men in his province. Mount Vernon had been transformed, too, from a ramshackle, mismanaged farm into a grand estate. Both George and Martha, moreover, had been generally healthy. Only a brief bout with the measles in 1760 had really afflicted Martha. A year later Washington had fallen ill, the only serious medical problem (except for chronic dental problems) that he experienced for thirty years after his protracted army related ailment in 1758. Washington's troubles began with a cold, but eventually some of the maladies of his soldiering years recurred. For several months he was weak and haunted by fevers, left to worry that in this "very low and dangerous State" he might contract some even more serious ailment. By the autumn of that year, however, he once again felt fine.[40]

When he had recovered from that lone affliction, Washington joked to his brother that although he felt fine his face looked as if he was "very near my last gasp." He no longer looked like that in 1773. Early that year he hired Charles Willson Peale, a young artist (and former saddle maker) who recently had studied his new trade in Boston and London, to come to Mount Vernon and paint the family; Peale made miniatures of Martha and the children, and he completed a large oil portrait of Washington. Aged forty-one, Washington was posing for the first time. He wore the uniform he had designed for the army of Virginia; a musket was cradled jauntily in his left arm, a sword dangled at his side, written orders jutted from a waistcoat pocket. He was depicted as standing in the wilderness; the theme must have been chosen by Washington, for he was conscious that the artist was "describing to the world what manner of man I am." Peale placed Washington under dense foliage; in the background, toward the ascending western mountains, a translucent sky gave way to uncertain and morbidly opaque clouds. Washington looks paunchy, but strong and robust. His cheeks are slightly ruddy, his beard rather dark. The most striking aspect of the painting, however, is that Washington is shown to be contemplative. This may have been the way he saw

George Washington, by Charles Willson Peale (1772). Courtesy of Washington and Lee University. At age forty Washington posed for the artist in the uniform of the Virginia Regiment.

himself, or perhaps the way he wished to be seen. His eyes are looking to his right, but they do not seem to be seeing anything. Instead, he is deep in thought, the deliberative warrior, the soldier-philosopher.

Peale's representation of Washington's physical characteristics tallies with the descriptions left by many eyewitnesses, although some who saw him maintained that no portrait ever really succeeded in capturing the man. He was about 6' 3" tall (he was listed as 6' 3½" tall by those who measured him for his coffin). He must have seemed even taller to contemporaries than he would to us. For instance, not one man in fifty who had served under him stood at six feet.[41] Home cooking apparently agreed with Washington. His weight increased by 40 pounds to about 215 pounds within a few years of his marriage. Obviously Washington was a big and physically imposing man. His chest was broad and muscular, though toward the center it was indented, "caved in," the result, he believed, of a childhood respiratory illness. Undoubtedly, his waist no longer was as thin as it had been as it had been at age twenty-five, when George Mercer had referred to it as "narrow." On the other hand, according to his step-grandson, his legs, particularly his thighs, were rather slender and not nearly as thick as almost every artist tended to depict them.

Washington had large feet and quite long arms, so extended, in fact, that he was self-conscious about them. His arms were "large and sinewy," more so than ever captured on canvas, according to that same grandchild. Washington also was embarrassed by what he regarded as his abnormally large hands; they do not appear in Peale's rendering, nor would they in many subsequent portraits. Almost everyone who saw him was struck by his posture. He stood not just without a slouch but in a ramrod-straight manner, to use the metaphor of more than one soldier who observed him. Thomas Jefferson referred simply to his "erect and noble" bearing, and many who saw him commented not only on his dignified walk but on the grace and athleticism with which he moved. Historian Garry Wills has speculated that because of his long arms he was compelled to walk in an exaggeratedly erect manner; otherwise, said Wills, "he would have looked like an ape . . . about to scrape the backs of his knuckles along the ground." Then again, as a child he may simply have taken up this bearing out of mimicry of his idol Lawrence, a soldier at the time of their initial meeting.

At middle age Washington's hair still was dark brown, with no hint of greyness or baldness. His eyes were a pleasant and striking blue, yet there was a hard, penetrating glint to them as well. Pockmarks lightly dotted his face, and, though Peale concealed the fact, persistent gum problems had robbed him of some teeth and disfigured others.[42]

Two men accustomed to judging character saw a side to Washington that Peale—always his favorite artist—did not make evident. Gilbert Stuart, an artist whose livelihood depended in part on his ability to capture the true essence of his subjects, believed Washington's "features were indicative of the strongest and most ungovernable passions. Had he been born in the forests, " Stuart added, "he would have been the fiercest man among the savages." Jonathan Boucher, Jackie's tutor, thought that Washington "seems to have nothing generous or affectionate in his nature." [43]

Late in September 1773 Washington and his host in Annapolis, the governor of Maryland, played the horses in the afternoon and attended the theater in the evening. On one of those days that he relaxed and gambled, a Philadelphia newspaper carried an ominous letter. "Being a great schemer," the writer warned, the British prime minister, Lord North, had succeeded in the enactment of a bill, the Tea Act, designed to procure a revenue from the American colonists. "It is much to be wished," the herald concluded, "that the Americans will convince Lord North that they are not *yet ready* to have the yoke of slavery riveted about their necks, and [that they will] send back the tea whence it came." [44]

Events were beginning to swirl about the colonies that autumn that would change Washington's life forever, but he seemed heedless of their course. He remained preoccupied by his own small world. He managed his properties, and the Custises' too. He employed gardeners to spruce up Mount Vernon, hoping to give it a gleam that might help to ease the pain caused by the loss of Patsy. He and Martha—who was loath to stay alone at home now that both children were gone—traveled frequently. They rode to Williamsburg in October, where Washington tended to several financial matters. In November they visited the Bassetts. Later Washington dropped in on his mother, and he visited with his brother for a spell. There were visitors at Mount Vernon almost every day; sometimes his guests were good friends, but often they were people that he had never before met. Frequently he invited old cohorts to his estate for a day of hunting, and both he and Martha spent some time preparing for Jackie's imminent wedding. And on December 16, at the precise moment of the Boston Tea Party a thousand miles to the north, Washington, tired from a long day of riding and walking and inspecting two of his outlying farms, rode back home in the gloom of evening, the end of a foggy, unseasonably warm late autumn day.[45]

Throughout the fall of 1773, a tempestuous time when actions unfolded that would shape the nation's course for years to come, George Washington, typically, had expressed no interest in the politics of the British Empire. For nearly fifteen years the management of his estate and varied business interests had been very nearly his sole concerns. Throughout that warm, pleasant Virginia autumn he evinced no desire to alter his way of life. But sometimes the most important changes in one's life are neither planned nor anticipated.

4

Patrician Revolutionary

"Our lordly Masters in Great Britain"

January 19, 1774. London, bleak and sunless, lay in the grip of a damp winter's chill. Early that morning, the *Hayley,* an American three-master owned by John Hancock of Boston, dropped anchor before the British capital. Before any of the crew disembarked, the vessel's captain, pausing amidst the stack of bureaucratic papers that each entering ship's master had to complete, described to the pilots and customs people who had routinely boarded his craft the demonstration known as the Boston Tea Party which had just taken place in his native town. Like a churning wildfire, the news raced through the city. By nightfall the prime minister and most of his cabinet had learned of the events of the previous month in Boston Harbor. Three days later a London newspaper published the story, and the news began to course its way through the English hinterland. Within another week London also knew that the incident in Boston had not been an isolated event. In Charleston, South Carolina, radicals had confiscated the dutied tea rather than permit its sale, while in Philadelphia and New York the captains of the tea ships, faced by angry mobs that threatened to hold their own "tea parties," had turned for Great Britain without attempting to dock.

Ten days after the *Hayley's* arrival the ministry, having now gotten enough information to sort out a fair semblance of what had occurred during the previous month in America, held its first meeting to deal with the crisis. Thereafter, the cabinet met frequently to consider the matter, often even reassembling in one another's homes in the evenings to continue their deliberations. Slowly, they arrived at a plan of response, and by mid-March the administration had prepared four tough, unbending measures for Parliament to consider.

Frederick, Lord North, the prime minister, personally shepherded the bills through the legislature. It was hardly an exacting task. There was some opposition, of course, but North and his ministers pooh-poohed the gloomy talk of those who resisted the legislation. It was far more risky to do nothing than to act with resolve, they argued. By early spring the measures, known collectively as the Coercive Acts, were law. Despite the provocations elsewhere, only Massachusetts was to be affected. The most objectionable—intolerable, the colonists would say—portions of the acts concerned economic and political changes imposed in retaliation for the destruction of the tea. The Port Act closed Boston Harbor until restitution was made for the despoiled tea. The Massachusetts Government Act gave the provincial governor untrammeled powers to appoint members of the judiciary and the upper house of the assembly. By that act Parliament presumed to alter the charter of Massachusetts.

The North government did not want a war, but it knew that these acts raised the specter of conflict. The ministry had gambled. By singling out Massachusetts it had adopted a divide-and-conquer strategy, hoping thereby to force the other colonies into line. If the policy failed and war resulted, the government was wagering that it could win that war.[1]

Early that May, as Boston braced itself for Britain's reaction to the "tea party," George Washington, at home at Mount Vernon, was more immediately concerned with the weather than with political affairs. After a spate of warm, even sultry, days, northern Virginia suddenly had been belted by a late-season snowfall and a hard freeze. Washington had awakened on May 4 fearing the worst, and late that afternoon his suspicions were confirmed. The frost had destroyed nearly half of his one thousand acres of wheat, and it had been fatal for that year's yield from his fruit trees. That very day he was scheduled to be in Williamsburg for the opening session of the House of Burgesses, a session likely to have to deal with Britain's response to the Boston Tea Party. But he had postponed his journey until he could tend to the disaster at his farm. When he finally arrived in the capital, the legislature had been sitting for nearly two weeks.[2]

Washington's behavior in this instance was not uncharacteristic. In the six-teen years since his first election to the Burgesses, he had displayed anything but an overwhelming interest in the issues that concerned the legislators. He had continued to be repeatedly reelected, first to the Frederick County seat, then after 1765 as one of the two delegates from Fairfax County. But his legislative perfor-mance had been lackluster at best. In fact, in some years he had not bothered to attend even a single assembly session.[3]

His disinterest should not come as a surprise. He had commenced his leg-islative service without ever having enunciated his views on any public issue save for those that affected him directly. There is not much evidence that he had ex-perienced any transformation in this respect by the 1770s. What chiefly interested him was amassing and protecting his personal fortune. Western lands made up one part of that equation, but London and its colonial executives—not the House of Burgesses—largely were responsible for the policy that touched him in this realm. The legislators did deal with matters relating to slavery and farming and local taxation, but an assembly consisting almost solely of other planter-slaveowners hardly was likely to make laws inimical to his interest. The staple of a routine legislative session, the bills that proposed to tinker with county boundaries and those that licensed river pilots, held little fascination for him. More than anything else, his actions imply that he saw the legislative seat simply as another feather in the cap of the once middling planter who never tired of striving for additional confirmation of his aristocratic status, or of ways to enhance that position.

Besides, Washington must have felt like a fish out of water in this environment. He was always uncomfortable and anxious in the presence of men of learning, and there were enough college graduates and lawyers in the legislature to make him reluctant to speak out. He simply was not a loquacious person. Through his youthful experiences in the company of urbane men like Lawrence and the Fairfaxes, he had developed the custom of listening, pondering, but rarely expressing himself, so that if he did speak his utterance reflected his carefully considered best judgment. Thomas Jefferson, his colleague in the Virginia assembly for half a dozen years, once recalled that he could not remember Washington speaking on any issue for as long as ten minutes, although, he added, Washington always seemed to address "the main point which was to decide the question." Moreover, Washington must have found parliamentary debate an alien format. He was used to the military system: collect intelligence, on rare occasions summon a council of war to deliberate collectively on strategy, then issue orders. It was an arrangement that suited his disposition.[4]

Washington was only one of more than one hundred assemblymen, and for more than a decade the leadership did not treat him as a preeminent figure. They seemed to regard him as a reserved, indifferent legislator, a backbencher, to whom they ladled out piddling committee assignments, delegating him chores like looking after stray animals or overseeing ferry service. His reputation for forbearance was deserved; during his initial fourteen assembly session he seldom introduced any legislation, and unfailingly the bills that he did sponsor were local or private in scope.[5]

Nevertheless, Washington's presence in the legislature—listless as it customarily may have been—was of crucial importance. As historian Bernhard Knollenberg observed, the experience of those years taught him how to deal with men of a legislative mentality, a lesson of subsequent usefulness in dealing with the Continental Congress.[6] Moreover, his very presence in the Virginia assembly put him in a crucial spot at a crucial time, for the Boston Tea Party and the Coercive Acts were about to transform a strained Anglo-American relationship into an armed confrontation.

As recently as a decade before there had been no hint of a conflict between the colonists and the British government. Certainly differences between the two had occurred from time to time in their 150-year relationship, but nothing approaching rebellion. Even as late as 1763 there was no sign of a revolt brewing in America. Indeed, Great Britain, at last triumphant over France and Spain, had never enjoyed a warmer, more friendly connection with its colonial subjects. Its government was widely regarded as the most benevolent in Europe, and many

Americans took great pride in being part of the largest empire that had been seen in the western world since the collapse of Rome more than a thousand years earlier.

But beneath the glitter of success, problems nagged at this distended empire. Britain had acquired its vast domain through a staggering cost in blood and money; four wars had been fought in the space of seventy-five years to secure the dominion. Then, when the final triumphant march in the last victory parade had been played, Britain confronted reality. Its legacy from these chronic wars was a staggering indebtedness, running in excess of £137,000,000. Ironically, too, the last war and the splendid victory in 1763 only added to London's mistrust of its New World subjects. For years paranoid officials in London had been plagued by the fear that the Americans yearned secretly to be independent of British domination. The conduct of many colonists in the French and Indian War had only intensified those suspicions, for few colonies had supplied their quota of troops, and some provinces even had persisted in trading with the enemy while their English brethren died on American battlefields. Moreover, the peace settlement, which transferred all French and Spanish possessions east of the Mississippi River to Britain, also removed the necessity for the American colonies to rely on Great Britain for protection against the traditional foes.

In addition to these woes another difficulty existed. According to the ancient precepts of mercantilism, the colonies were to exist for the benefit of the parent state. The notion had been a byword in London's ruling circles since before Sir Walter Raleigh sent the first boatload of colonists to Roanoke Island two centuries before. Almost from the beginning of America's settlement, Britain's rulers, when permitted the luxury of peace, had tinkered with their kingdom, endeavoring to make it run as the mercantile treatises declared it should; they had meddled with crop production, sought to regulate manufacturing, tampered with trade, scrutinized the currency, pried into the operations of the provincial governments. And yet by 1763 British hegemony over its mainland colonies in America had never seemed weaker. Hence the ink was hardly dry on the Treaty of Paris before there was open talk in London of reforming the imperial relationship, fine-tuning it once again so that Britain could not only secure greater economic benefits but also tighten its grip on these allegedly recalcitrant, separatist colonists. Some printed tracts appeared in which notions like the creation of an American nobility, or the royalization of all the provinces, or even the merger of the separate colonies into one "GRAND MARITIME PROVINCE" were bruited about. More than anything else, however, the matter of the imperial indebtedness preyed on the mind of articulate Londoners, and more than one writer suggested that the debit be eliminated by taxing the colonists.

The open talk in London in 1763 only reflected what had been said there in private for two decades. As early as the 1740s the government quietly had begun to shift from a permissive to a more restrictive imperial policy, although before the new colonial policy could proceed very far King George's War had been declared in 1745, and the plans for reform had been suspended. What followed after 1763, therefore, was the crystallization of a policy that had been envisioned for years.[7]

The new colonial policy fell into three broad categories: tightening the execution of the existing trade laws; taxing the colonists; and managing the newly acquired territories. While George Washington was distracted by his recurrent vexations with tobacco production at Mount Vernon, the news of the initial measures reached the colonies. Neither the Proclamation of 1763 nor the Sugar Act of 1764 (which sought to raise a revenue from placing low duties on imported foreign sugar) produced much of a ripple in Virginia. In the northern colonies there were some minor demurrings, though nothing of the stuff of rebellion.

Then came the Stamp Act. The ministry had announced its inclination for such a tax in 1764, but the measure's final terms were deferred for a year until the colonists could be heard from. By early in 1765 they indeed had spoken. Several assemblies, including the House of Burgesses in Virginia, passed resolutions decrying the proposition, and a number of pamphlets appeared which excoriated Parliament's right to tax Americans. But the colonists had not proposed an alternative levy. Without hearing the colonists' petitions, Parliament easily passed the tax early in 1765. The duties, something like a sales tax though far more encompassing, fell on much that was sold, as well as on nearly all publicly issued documents and licenses.[8]

The ministry anticipated some colonial opposition, but nothing like that which occurred. The tone of the American protest was set in Williamsburg. The Burgesses was in session attending other business when news of the levy reached the little capital. Supposedly moved to act by the fiery rhetoric of Patrick Henry, the assembly wasted no time in responding. No one really knows what Henry said, but it is clear that George Washington said nothing on the subject. He had been in Williamsburg for a few days, then two weeks before the news of the Stamp Act arrived, he had returned to Mount Vernon. In fact, on the day the assembly acted he was at home hiring a gardener and, thus, was unable to vote on the Virginia Resolves, four resolutions that maintained that only the colonial assemblies possessed the constitutional right to impose levies upon the colonists.[9]

Had Washington remained in town he undoubtedly would have voted to support the resolves. However, he seems not to have been deeply troubled by the British legislation, seeing it as simply a mistake, an anomalous enactment, and not as the product of any conspiracy against colonial liberties. He spoke out on the act only once—in two letters penned on the same morning—and then he cast his thoughts in the language of an impartial observer. He did not portray all colonists as aggrieved by the tax; only the "speculative part of the Colonists," he suggested, looked upon the act as "a direful attack upon their liberties." The most immediate result of the legislation, he added, was that the colonists, with less money left in their pockets, would disdain British products and purchase American goods.[10]

But Washington was too busy with his farm to pay much heed to what he had referred to as this "ill judged" legislation. Elsewhere, however, a protest movement formed. Several assemblies adopted resolutions strikingly similar to the Virginia Resolves, and that autumn an intercolonial congress met in New York and protested in the same vein. In Philadelphia and Boston more violent protests occurred; in August mobs assembled in Boston, attacking the property of the stamp collectors and of those who sympathized with the act, and nearly destroying the home of Massachusetts's lieutenant governor. (At the height of these disturbances, Washington's daily diary entries read: "Sowed Turneps. . . . Began to seperate the Male from the Female hemp. . . . [P]ut some Hemp in the Rivr. to Rot. . . . Seperated my Ewes & Rams. . . . Finish'd Sowing Wheat. . . .") Sporadic boycotts of English goods also occurred, making Washington's remark that ultimately the "merchants of Great Britain trading to the Colonies will not be among the last to wish for a repeal" of the Stamp Act seem prescient. The next spring Parliament rescinded the act.[11]

Britain's imperial problems remained, however, and in 1767 a new ministry imposed still another tax. The Townshend Duties were a different sort of levy— indirect taxes placed on imports of glass, lead, paper, and tea. But these were taxes, nonetheless, and if the government had expected the colonials to acquiesce in the legislation, it once again was mistaken. Newspaper essays and pamphlets attacking the measures appeared before the end of that year. A Philadelphian, John Dickinson, a London-educated barrister, penned the most influential tract, the *Letters from a Pennsylvania Farmer* (a pamphlet that Washington purchased two years after its publication). The "Farmer's" argument was one from which the colonial radicals never deviated. The only bodies which could impose taxes on the colonists, he asserted, were the American assemblies; therefore, Parliament's taxes—whether direct or indirect assessments—were unconstitutional. Early the following year Massachusetts appealed to the other colonial legislatures to petition the Crown for repeal. The Burgesses in Virginia were the first to act, informing the king in a remonstrance that they alone were "the sole constitutional representatives of his Majesty's most dutiful and loyal subjects, the people of Virginia"; it was an act that the secretary of state for American affairs termed "more alarming than those from Massachusetts." Again the Virginia assembly acted without George Washington, however. He had remained at Mount Vernon to meet with William Crawford and complete the bargain by which the frontiersman would search out good land for him in western Pennsylvania and the Ohio country.[12]

Washington, in fact, evidently displayed no interest in the Townshend Duty crisis until more than a year after his colleagues in the Burgesses had acted. Once again he had been preoccupied by his farming and business pursuits; he had traveled extensively during those months, journeying to Fredericksburg on two occasions, and making trips to the Pamunkey, to the Great Dismal Swamp, to Williamsburg and then on to Eltham to visit the Bassetts, and finally to survey the George Carter tract on Opequon Creek.[13]

By April 1769, when he did speak out on British policies, the imperial crisis had deepened. The colonial secretary had ordered the dissolution of the Massachusetts assembly for its having protested against the Townshend Duties, and the ministry had ordered General Gage to transfer a regiment of his army to troublesome Boston. In response the three great northern port cities, New York, Philadelphia, and Boston, had joined in an economic boycott of Britain. Virginia had kept abreast of these activities through its newspaper, the *Virginia Gazette*, but it had taken no action since its resolution a year earlier. Rather suddenly, indeed quite surprisingly, Washington was among the first to suggest that the time had come to act. On April 5 he dispatched a trenchant letter to his neighbor George Mason, a missive that taken at face value reads almost like a revolutionary manifesto. The communiqué also hints strongly that Washington now believed British policy was not just ill-advised, but that it was a deliberate, concerted attack on colonial liberty.

"[O]ur lordly Masters in Great Britain," he began, "will be satisfied with nothing less than the deprication of American freedom." Something must be done, he continued. He was prepared to take up arms in defense of his liberty, he went on, but then he quickly exclaimed: "A-ms I wou'd beg leave to add, should be the last recourse, the dernier resort." Remonstrances, he said had been ineffectual. But by "starving their Trade and manufacturing," repeal perhaps could be secured—and war might be averted.[14]

Washington's letter can be read in two ways, although whichever interpretation is chosen, it is clear that this date marks a departure in his thinking. Taken literally, his strident note can be seen as the outcry of a man genuinely troubled by the constitutional tyranny of British actions. There is no evidence that he yet had read any of the popular ideological tracts spawned by the crisis—he would not purchase Dickinson's famous *Letters* until six weeks after he wrote Mason—though he must have perused a few of the somewhat similar essays that had appeared from time to time in the *Virginia Gazette*, and he surely would have heard some of his colleagues in the legislature address these points. His thinking may also have been influenced by Mason. Like Washington, Mason was a wealthy planter and land speculator, but chronic problems stemming from the gout had disabled him, forcing him into a sedentary life at Gunston Hall, a splendid Georgian brick mansion just a few miles from Mount Vernon. Mason used his enforced idleness to build an extensive library and to steep himself in the treatises of eighteenth-century Whig philosophers. Much earlier than Washington, Mason professed to see a plot in London to destroy American liberties, though he carefully confined his public denunciation of British policies to constitutional arguments. How much Mason may have influenced Washington is a matter of conjecture, but the two often met socially and it is difficult to believe that their conversations did not occasionally turn to political matters.[15]

On the other hand economic considerations seldom were far from Washington's consciousness. At least one person who knew him, Jackie Custis's tutor, Jonathan Boucher, later attributed Washington's patriotism solely to "avaricious[ness] under the most specious appearance of disinterestedness." Boucher was an exiled Tory when he reached that conclusion, and he undoubtedly was prejudiced against Washington. Nevertheless, Washington himself told Mason that there were "private as well as public advantages to result" from a boycott of English goods. The personal advantages that he alluded to were twofold: Mount Vernon's manufactured commodities might replace the boycotted English goods; moreover, with judicial proceedings suspended for the duration of the crisis, Britain's merchants would be prevented from suing planters (including Washington) for outstanding debts.[16] If Washington might gain by a boycott, it was not likely that he could be particularly harmed by a cessation of imperial trade; not only had he long since largely converted from tobacco to grain production, but Mount Vernon was virtually a self-sufficient little community.

To some it may be unpleasant to think that Washington could have acted so crassly, yet, given his profoundly acquisitive nature and his long history of tirelessly pursuing "private . . . advantage," it would be unrealistic to imagine that these forces may not have shaped his behavior. In his only reference to the Stamp Act, for example, he had spoken of the tax as unconstitutional, but he also had hinted at a crude class analysis of the legislation, obliquely identifying the principal victims of the duty as the most affluent sector of colonial society, that element with the cash in hand to consume the commodities upon which the tax was levied.[17] However, it would be overstating the case to insist that economic considerations alone motivated him. The sarcasm that dripped from his reference to "our lordly Masters" in London, and his allusion to imperiled liberty (penned, after all, in a private letter to a friend and neighbor, and hence not the sort of document that might require embellishment or false statements), suggest that he was moved by political and philosophical considerations as well.

Two aspects of Washington's outlook in 1769 often have been overlooked by historians. He already recognized that petitions to the British government were useless, a lesson that many moderates in the protest movement still had not learned five or six years later. Moreover, his statement about taking up arms is arresting. In the papers of those thought to be more radical than Washington—men like Patrick Henry, for instance, or the Adamses in Massachusetts—no reference to hostilities settling the issue can be found at such an early juncture.

A few days after his letter to Mason, the two men—together with Richard Henry Lee, the London-educated master of Chantilly plantation in Westmoreland County—prepared a draft of a nonimportation agreement for presentation at the next meeting of the Burgesses, scheduled to convene in the next few weeks. On the last day of April Washington set out for Williamsburg, pausing in Fredericksburg, then detouring to Eltham, finally arriving in the capital a few days before the assembly was galeveled to order. Lodging at Raleigh Tavern, he enjoyed several days of socializing, dining twice with the governor and as often with the speaker of the assembly, attending the annual spring horse races, and visiting friends who lived nearby. On May 16 the legislators got down to serious business. Washington was up early and rode to York County to inspect his dower lands, but he was back by 11:00 A.M. when the session began. That day the House of Burgesses adopted several resolutions, including a denunciation of the Townshend Duties. An angry Governor Botetourt immediately dissolved the legislature. "Your resolves . . . augur ill," he presciently told the assemblymen as he sent them packing. But the burgesses did not go home. They tramped down the street and conducted their official—though illegal—business at the Raleigh Tavern. For the first time Washington played a major role in legislative deliberations; he unfurled the boycott scheme and immediately was selected to a committee to prepare an embargo plan. What resulted was a far less comprehensive boycott than many northern colonies had adopted; with the exception of wine and slaves, only taxed commodities would be excluded, and no goods (certainly not tobacco) were banned from exportation. The House promptly accepted the report, then it adjourned. Washington stayed in town that night to attend a party celebrating the queen's birthday.[18]

A week before the House of Burgesses acted, the king of England had been greeted by Londoners with derisive shouts as he rode from his palace to Westminster to close a session of Parliament. London was seething, churning with fury that spring, most of it brought on by a silly clash between the Crown and John Wilkes, a scurrilous rascal who repeatedly had been denied the parliamentary seat to which he had been elected. A radical reform movement had organized too, protestors who questioned both domestic matters and the government's American policy. Under siege, the government had begun to retreat. Weeks before Whitehall learned of Virginia's resolutions or its boycott, ministers had begun to talk secretly of a partial repeal of the Townshend Duties. They did not reach an immediate decision, but on March 5, 1770—ironically the very day of the Boston Massacre—a new ministry headed by Lord North moved to rescind each of the objectionable duties, save for the tax on tea.[19]

Revocation did not occur a moment too soon for the colonial radicals. By late that summer the colonists' economic resistance was in a state of collapse; steps already were being taken in Philadelphia and New York to terminate the boycott. When the reality of deprivation (or lost sales) caused by the boycott became manifest, some—especially among the merchants and the largest consumer class—began to lose their enthusiasm for continued opposition. Some lost their zeal even earlier. George Washington, for instance, his own boycott notwithstanding, placed two orders for British commodities in July 1769 that came close to heartily violating the essence of the law he had helped to draft only two months before. Boycott or not, he ordered a powder horn, a musket, sacks ("Markd GW"), three nutcrackers, and eighty-four books for Jackie.[20]

Harmony prevailed between the colonists and the parent state during the next three years, shattered only by infrequent and always localized clashes—an assault by Rhode Island hot-heads on the *Gaspee*, a British revenue cutter, for example, or the publication by Massachusetts's radicals of purloined letters between that province's lieutenant governor and officials in London that purported to demonstrate the existence of a conspiracy to extirpate American liberties. Even the continued assessment on tea seems not to have bothered the great majority of colonists. Indeed, relations were so good that most colonists may have presumed that the tense days of the Stamp Act clash and the Townshend Duty crisis were gone forever.

Washington certainly seems to have held to this view between 1770 and 1773. At least he went about his business as if he expected the Anglo-American union to continue unabated. Even before the end of 1770 he once again exhibited enthusiasm for an effort to make the Potomac navigable from Fort Cumberland to Alexandria, a notion that he had mused over for a decade; think of the "immense advantages" to be derived by making the river the "Channel of Commerce between Great Britain and that immense Territory Tract of Country *which is* unfolding to our" west, he told an acquaintance. That August he ordered more goods from London, although they were to be shipped only if the Townshend Duties were "totally repeald." Coming more than five months after Lord North's action, it is difficult to imagine that he did not know that the taxes had been only partially rescinded; yet he evidently received the commodities that he ordered, the result perhaps of couching his directive to the London mercantile house in such artful terms. In November he arranged to purchase fifteen thousand acres in the Ohio country, if Crawford liked the looks of the tract; and it was during the next twenty months that he looked for an investment in Florida and that he expended his inexhaustible energy in pursuit of his bounty lands. By 1773 he had hired a team to build a mill on real estate that he owned on the Youghiogheny (near the present site of Perryopolis, Pennsylvania), and throughout that spring he made plans to accompany the governor of Virginia on a July land-hunting excursion into the Ohio Valley; only Patsy's death prevented him from making the trip. That autumn, when the first essays on the Tea Act appeared in colonial newspapers, Washington was looking into surveying lands below the Scioto River in the transmontane region.[21]

Indeed, that fall Washington seemed oblivious to the unrest generated by the Tea Act in South Carolina and several northern cities. Although Virginians apparently had adhered to the Townshend Duty on tea (it had paid duties on eighty thousand pounds of the beverage in 1771 and 1772), tea smuggling had become an art form in the North. The Tea Act was designed to end the contrabandage and to finally reap some real revenue from the six-year-old levy. It succeeded only in reviving the moribund protest movement, however, and in instigating a chain of events that culminated in the Boston Tea Party and the less violent responses in Philadelphia, New York, and Charleston.[22]

For weeks after Washington learned of these incidents it was business as usual at Mount Vernon. To enhance his fishing enterprise he acquired a brig for £175, and he concocted a scheme to settle a portion of his Great Kanawha lands with immigrants brought over from the Palatinate; in March 1774 he even sent out an advance party of twenty servants and hired hands to lay the groundwork. It seemed almost a carefree time for Washington. He hunted whenever business and the weather permitted (at least eight times in late December and January); he spent several nights at the theater in Alexandria, and he took in both horse and boat races. In the weeks preceeding the convening of the House of Burgesses in May— a session almost certain to deal with Britain's response to the destruction of the tea in Boston—neither his correspondence nor his diary betray the slightest evidence that he suspected that America and Britain were on the verge of momentous events. He and Martha visited the Calverts in Maryland for two days early in May, then, when he was not absorbed by his losses in the late season cold snap, his diary went on in the normal vein: "Went to a Boat Race & Barbicue. . . . We . . . went to Pohick Church. At home all day alone. . . . I contd at home all day. . . . At home all day alone. Set off with Mrs. Washington for Williamsburg. . . ." [23]

The Washingtons rode into the tiny capital on May 16, a clear and cool spring day. A serene atmosphere seemed to prevail in the city, but beneath the surface more supercharged emotions bubbled. Historically, the native gentry who dominated Virginia had been uneasy with the colony's position. Virginia's planter aristocracy traced its social, economic, and political hegemony to the vast wealth it derived from the fragile, mercurial leaves of the tobacco plant. Theirs was a one-crop economy, which gave them only a tenuous hold on wealth and power. The world tobacco market generally had boomed in the half century since the 1720s, yet there had been occasional disquieting reminders of the precariousness of the ruling class's position. For instance, episodic wars over which colonials exercised little direction had a way of playing havoc with their economic well-being, causing prices to fall, credit to tighten. But, worrisome as such circumstances may have been, so far these dislocations had always been temporary. Then came the sudden intrusion of recent British statecraft, a departure in policy that was fraught with disturbing psychological and socioeconomic implications for Virginia's ruling elite.

Since the 1750s, and especially after the Stamp Act, the substruction upon which the authority of Virginia's gentry was established increasingly had seemed to be threatened by a faraway polity over which it exerted little or no control. In the past twenty years Britain had interceded frequently to curtail Virginia's independence in economic matters, first nullifying legislation passed by the House of Burgesses to relieve provincial taxpayers (an incident in the 1750s that came to be called the "Parson's Cause"), then in 1764 forbidding the colony to put out paper money as legal tender. Those intrusions were followed by imperial taxation, the suspension of provincial assemblies by royal officials, talk of London designating a nobility for America, and prattle about arbitrary changes in colonial charters. Then, too, there had been Whitehall's muddled western land policies, dictates that blocked an additional way to wealth and only added to the burden of anxiety already borne by the gentry. That very year, in fact, authorities in London had directed the governor of Virginia to sell lands only at public auction and at a much higher minimum price than previously. Thus, when Washington's friend Richard Henry Lee spoke of the "iron hand of power" that Britain exerted over America, he expressed both the conscious and the subliminal perceptions on the part of Virginia's troubled rulers about their relation to the empire.

Britain's manifest challenge to the political and economic autonomy of the colonial ruling class threatened to further weaken, perhaps to destroy, the latter's tenuous preeminence. It was a threat that the gentry initially sought to resist by appealing to constitutional rights, an argument through which the elite meant to protect not only their class interests but what they understood to be their English— and Virginian—liberties. British actions threatened the aristocracy's self-image. The ruling elite in Virginia had presumed itself to be an aristocratic class, apeing the fashions and behavior of English noblemen, yet knowing somehow that to be a valid gentry it must have full independence, free of the taint of subordination. But now events and policies had made an impact on both the Old Dominion and its colonial brethren in such a manner as to make it all too clear that the Virginia elite's claim to gentry status was seriously threatened. For a class conditioned to think that a man must either be lord and master or a retainer, it was a revelation with potentially devastating ramifications.[24]

No one was likely to have been more aware than Washington of the potential consequences of Britain's policies to Virginia's ruling class, or of the likely impact of these acts upon individual gentrymen. More so than almost any other Virginian, this proud man already had experienced the haughty arrogance of officials who looked upon Americans as provincials, as rustic outlanders naturally inferior to their more cosmopolitan English brethren. To get his way with these officials he had been compelled to adopt the manner of a sycophant, servilely importuning other men for favors. He no longer was inclined to act in such a way. Indeed, it must always have been painful for him to play such a role, for this was the same man who had made Herculean efforts to free himself from each liability that had shackled him, from a domineering mother, from his own lack of education and his unpolished manners, from his inferiority of station compared to most elite planters, from a provincial command below that of junior officers fortunate enough—or sufficiently obsequious and parasitical—to have obtained a royal commission. Many scholars have searched in vain for signs that Washington responded to the policies of the parent state on the basis of principle or ideology. He certainly agreed with the Whig philosophy expounded by the leading American protestors, but his reaction was less that of the ideologue than of the individualist.

His response revealed his utter exasperation at foreign constraints, his sense of outrage that other men might endeavor any longer to hold him in thrall. More than almost any other statement Washington had made before 1774, his reference to those in London who would presume to be his "lordly masters" divulged the feelings of this independent man. Whatever sentiments had transported other men to this precarious moment, George Washington seems to have arrived at the precipice of rebellion by interpreting British policy in terms of his personal well-being. His path to sedition left him no less radical than other activists, however. In fact, for a man with such ardent drives, the very personalness of his perceived relationship to Great Britain may have caused him to react in terms that were far more radical than those yet embraced by most colonists. For Washington, at least, his opposition to the mother country ran far deeper than a constitutional objection to ministerial taxes.

The assembly was in session when Washington arrived in Williamsburg. Not much of consequence had occurred, nor did the legislature transact any really substantive business during the next three weeks. Its most radical step was to pass a resolution setting aside June 1 as a fast day to protest Britain's closing of the port of Boston. Had the governor, John Murray, Lord Dunmore, not responded to this innocuous resolve in an ill-advised manner, the burgesses might have returned to their homes having barely taken note of Boston's woes. But, like Governor Botetourt five years before, Dunmore responded to the fast day declaration by proroguing the assembly. The burgesses in turn reacted just as they had to Botetourt's infelicitous decision: they gathered as a rump assembly in the Apollo Room of the Raleigh Tavern and adopted resolutions threatening another economic boycott. (Washington did not let this turn of events tarnish his relations with the chief executive. On the evening of the rump assembly he attended a ball given in honor of Lady Dunmore; in fact, he had dined with the governor and his family twice—and spent the night with them once—since arriving in town, and the previous morning he had ridden with Dunmore to the governor's farm, where the two had breakfasted, then toured the property.)[25]

By May 29 most of the delegates had departed for home. Washington still was in the capital, however, tending to personal business (which for all the world appears to have been fence-mending with a governor whose good graces might be essential for attaining those elusive bounty lands). That morning Washington was up early to attend worship services. That was relatively unusual in itself; in fact, he had not been to church in three weeks, but this day he worshipped twice. Late in the afternoon a dispatch rider galloped into town; his panting, sweaty steed indicated that the rider was on a long, urgent mission. In fact, he carried an appeal from Massachusetts, a plea for a united colonial boycott of English goods. In his saddlebags, moreover, were documents showing that Philadelphia and Annapolis already had agreed to stand with Boston. The next morning the assembly's leadership rounded up the 25 percent or so of the burgesses still in town for an emergency meeting. That group considered the Bay Colony's entreaty, then ratified a vague motion to act in concert with other colonies. But it postponed a final decision until the full membership could return again in sixty days; in the interim the legislators were to ascertain the "Sense of their respective Counties" as to the wisdom of a boycott.[26]

Whatever the thoughts of others, Washington's views had crystallized. He deplored the destruction of the tea by Boston's radicals, but he felt the ministry must be shown that all America disapproved of taxation without consent. "They have no right to put their hands in my pockets," is how he put it. In addition, he regarded the Coercive Acts as "an Invasion of our Rights and Priviledges," and he was especially troubled by Britain's cavalier alterations of Massachusetts's government and charter. But how to respond to these depradations? Petitions were useless, no better than wailing and crying for relief, he counseled; on the other hand, now that he no longer was a debtor, he had concluded that it was unjust to withhold the payment of debts. Thus, it was a boycott that he favored. It had worked before, it might work again. Besides, it was morally defensible, for repeal would come only if there was "public virtue enough left among us to deny ourselves everything but the bare necessities of life to accomplish this end."[27]

Washington did not go directly home when the legislators finally adjourned. He stayed around the capital for a few days more, dining once again with Dunmore, then attending a fireworks display in honor of the colony's First Lady. When he did leave Williamsburg it was to ride to Eltham for a visit of several days, a sojourn that included a long riverboat excursion with Martha and the Bassetts to look after some land he had purchased the previous year. Washington's schedule was hectic when he finally returned to Mount Vernon. He tended to his farm, and he devoted an unusual amount of his time to political concerns. He attended two citizens' meetings in Alexandria so that he could report to and hear from his constituents; the second meeting adopted twenty-four resolves, among them a proposal for a nonimporation agreement if the Coercive Acts were not repealed. The meeting also selected Washington to head an emergency governing body for Fairfax County. In the midst of all this Washington was reelected to the Burgesses. (To celebrate he gave a party at which he was careful to offer coffee and chocolate, but not tea.) On August 1, this time accompanied by Jackie, Washington was back in the capital for the extraordinary session of the assembly, now called the Virginia Convention.[28]

By this time—about sixty days after that dispatch rider had brought Massachusetts's plea for concerted action to Williamsburg—the notion of holding a continental congress in Philadelphia in September had taken shape, and several colonies already had formally approved such a notion. Nor did Virginia hold aloof from the idea. In fact, the convention met for less than a week, concluding its business with a minimum of rancor. Almost all the assemblymen were prepared to authorize their deputies to the national congress to vote for a boycott. The only divisive issue was over whether the protest should include a nonexportation agreement as well as a nonimportation ploy. Washington and many others resisted a ban on selling goods to the mother country. If Virginia's commodities were not sold, it was said, debts could not be paid; of course, if that year's tobacco crop went unsold, many planters would suffer because of the lack of income. In the end, the members compromised. Virginia's congressmen were directed to vote for nonimportation to begin as early as November 1, but they were told that nonexportation must be postponed for one year. Before it adjourned the assembly created committees in each county to enforce the likely embargo, modeling the plan on the format outlined in the Fairfax Resolves. One of its final actions was to elect seven delegates to the congress in Phildelphia. George Washington was one of the seven.[29]

Why was Washington one of those selected? Each of the men chosen by the Burgesses had a long record of service in the legislature, and each had been vocal in his support of resistance of Britain's taxation policies, though the seven reflected a blend of ideas, some having favored a total trade stoppage while others had called for more moderate policies. Although Washington had never been a legislative leader, he was a known quantity. His colleagues evidently saw him as a moderate and level-headed man, a person of integrity, prudence, sobriety, honesty, and personal independence. His record and his great wealth certainly augured for responsible conduct in the congress. He was a soldier, too, something to be considered in this hour of crisis. Besides, he had been very active in the affairs of Virginia for twenty years. It simply was unthinkable that he could have been passed over.

One last duty—one as poignant as any he ever had faced—remained before he could set out for Philadelphia. During that eventful summer Washington had learned that George William and Sally Fairfax no longer planned to return to Virginia. At George William's request, Washington had agreed to oversee the selling of Belvoir and its furnishings. On August 15 the first of two auctions was conducted, a vendue to clear away every elegant possession in the Fairfaxes' mansion. Given his intense feelings for Belvoir and the memories it held for him, this must have been a long, painful afternoon for Washington. Strangers roamed the corridors he cherished, pawing over furniture, poking around in the rooms where for nearly twenty-five years he and his friends had shared so many joys and tragedies, where he and Sally Fairfax had talked and laughed, danced and walked, where he had said so many goodbyes to her. Washington also purchased numerous items that day. For nearly £170 he picked up curtains, a sideboard and dining room chairs, a mahogany chest of drawers, a carpet and a mirror, and, most intriguingly, the coverlets, pillows, and bolsters that had adorned Sally's bed.[30]

Late in the afternoon, as the cooling August shadows extended over the vast green lawn of Belvoir, Washington climbed upon his mount to return home. When he looked about he must have been touched by the sudden unfamiliarity of the place, by the strange faces and the trampled, unkempt landscape, by the forlorn silence even amidst the din. Then he turned to ride home to prepare for the Continental Congress, a meeting, he told a friend, that had arisen more from "the Effects of a seeming Necessity, than [from] Choice." [31] As he cantered home he may have realized that the gutting of Belvoir meant the end of a long, sweet portion of his life. But no one, and certainly not Washington, realized that the impending imperial storm was about to change everyone's life. And for no one would the change be greater than for George Washington.

For a decade and a half Washington had lived as a Virginia planter. His acquisitive manner and his fixation upon augmenting his wealth were not unique for the time and place, but in Washington's case such behavior seemed to derive from a well-established psychological pattern. Driven by his compelling need for affirmation, Washington seemed never to be contented. More and more slaves were acquired; additional indentured servants were purchased; new rooms were added to Mount Vernon; and, always, the search went on for still more land. Moreover, a certain pretentiousness characterized his life-style. He procured vast amounts of elegant clothing. He wanted to ride in the most handsome carriage. He longed to breed the best dogs. There must be no equal to his stable of horses. He seemed humiliated when Mount Vernon did not produce the best tobacco crop in the neighborhood. He wished for the very best furnishings for his estate. Washington's was a grandiose style, lived by a man who thought in grandiose terms, a man who lived in a society that admired wealth and power and who, consequently, labored tirelessly to accumulate the tokens that would result in his elevation.

The Washington of these years was not, temperamentally, a particularly appealing figure. He tended to moodiness, to what Thomas Jefferson later called periods of "gloomy apprehensions."[32] His temper was combustible and given to frequent explosions; his irascible side, furthermore, apparently was unmitigated by much of a sense of humor. But perhaps the most striking oddity about Washington was his interpersonal relationships.

With the exception of his ties to his brother-in-law, Burwell Bassett, Washington seems to have been close only to George William Fairfax, and evidence concerning his affiliation with his neighbor remains sketchy. Eight years older than Washington and the product of a formal education in England, George William likely differed considerably from his acquaintance at Mount Vernon. Yet, he seems to have regarded Washington as a friend, and there is no reason to believe that Washington felt any differently about him. Some scholars have regarded the friendship as a natural occurrence, inasmuch as the two men were neighbors and enjoyed an equally lofty status. But that is not quite true, for it confuses Washington's pre-Revolutionary status with his more exalted position of later years. In the 1760s and early 1770s George William Fairfax clearly was the wealthiest and most powerful figure in his part of Virginia, an educated and cosmopolitan descendant of the most illustrious family in the Northern Neck. He was precisely the sort of friend whom Washington always sought.

In the real sense of the word Washington had no friends among men of his own age and station. Indeed, as he once remarked in a moment of candor, he was too consumed by mistrust to have—or to want—friends. "It is easy to make acquaintances," he said, "but very difficult to shake them off, however irksome and unprofitable they are found after we have once committed ourselves to them. . . ." "Be courteous," he advised, "but become a friend only after the other person has been well tried." [33] It was the sort of advice he might have given concerning the purchase of a horse: examine it, try it out, break it in, but acquire it only if there is some profit in the endeavor. His outlook was that of the utilitarian, one who was capable of seeking others only as objects, and, in fact, his interpersonal relationships were meant to serve as a means to an end—to fulfill a grand ambition or to elicit the approval for which he yearned.

Within a few years of becoming the master of Mount Vernon, Washington again seemed to act as though something was missing in his life. His ceaseless efforts to accumulate assets were one manifestation of his emptiness, but his manner of posing for the artist Charles Willson Peale in 1772 was even more revealing. For his first portrait Washington had chosen to be seen as a warrior rather than as a planter, although he had not soldiered for fifteen years. The sense of coherence in his life had seemed to vanish when he left the Virginia Regiment in 1758. Neither the grandiosity nor the brilliance of Mount Vernon could gratify his needs any longer. Now, in the tense summer of 1774, Washington seemed to have identified his search for personal independence with his province's drive for cohesion, and he even had come to interpret Britain's new colonial policies in a very personal sense. London's actions were a threat to his "character as a man." [34] He would not submit to those who sought to become his "lordly Masters."

At dusk on August 29 the Massachusetts delegation to the Continental Congress reached Philadelphia, where they found half or more of their fellow congressmen already in their lodgings and anxious to meet and size up their colleagues. They found only two or three from Virginia's delegation, however. Washington was not among them. He still was at home at Mount Vernon, awaiting the arrival of fellow deputies with whom he would share the long ride north.

Late the next day, a blistering hot August afternoon, Patrick Henry, tall and slender, his acquiline nose and piercing grey eyes stamping his countenance with a noble, dashing air, rode up the winding trail from the Potomac to Mount Vernon, accompanied by Edmund Pendleton, a cautious veteran of more than twenty years of political warfare. They remained at the mansion that evening, dining with George and Martha, as well as with George Mason and another neighbor whom the Washingtons had invited over. The men contented themselves with small talk through the meal, but when they adjourned to a parlor they spoke with animation, discussing options and sharing information on current events in their respective counties. It was a conversation in which George must have seldom spoken, for the pedantic Mason and the flamboyant Henry, not to mention Pendleton—a tough, ambitious man whom many regarded not only as the most handsome man in Virginia but as the best debater in the province—were the sorts who naturally monopolized any gathering.[35]

After breakfast the next morning the three congressmen set out, Martha waving good-bye and, according to legend, telling her husband's colleagues: "I hope you will stand firm. I know George will." They traversed the great river by ferry, then, over the next five days they rode relentlessly until the rolling hills gave way to the flat, desolate coastal region that splayed out from the west bank of the Delaware River.

Like the party from Massachusetts, the Virginians also arrived in Philadelphia late in the day, and probably they, too, like their New England brethren, were greeted by dignitaries four or five miles outside the city. Once in town, the men stopped first at the City Tavern for a meal, then the weary travelers hurried to their lodgings. Washington stayed that night with the family of Dr. William Shippen, a University of Edinburgh–trained physician who taught at the College of Philadelphia. But rather than impose on their kindness further, he rented a room at a local inn the next day.[36]

Few congressmen knew anyone other than the members of their own delegation. Only one or two were known by reputation outside their province. Almost everyone had heard of Samuel Adams, and, because of his days as a soldier two decades before, perhaps as many also knew of Washington. He was almost the only former soldier in attendance, and no other delegate—no other resident of Philadelphia, in fact—came close to rivaling him in years of martial experience. It seems likely that he might have been quizzed by his colleagues about American prospects in the event of war with Great Britain. What he told them is not known, but that autumn he wrote a friend in the British army that "more blood [would] be spilt" in an Anglo-American war than "history has ever yet furnished instances of in the annals of North America." Washington impressed his colleagues with what Silas Deane of Connecticut called his "easy Soldierlike Air"; Deane thought him a man with a "hard . . . Countenance," but one who "speaks very Modestly, & in cool but determined Stile & Accent." Many of the delegates seem to have regarded Washington as a terribly successful soldier during the French and Indian War, and somehow the rumor was started that he had offered to pay for the creation of an entire army from his own immense fortune.[37] He did nothing to scotch either notion.

The other congressmen were unknown commodities. Indeed, Virginians knew little of the state of mind of their northern colleagues on the subject of Anglo-American difficulties. So they eagerly met one another, dining and drinking together, talking about almost nothing but politics from morning to night. If politics had a rival attraction it was the city itself, America's largest metropolis in 1774. Although Washington had been here five times before (he had passed through only a few months previously when he had taken Jackie to college), he too must have been anxious to really look at the town.

Philadelphia was big. Its twenty-five thousand inhabitants made it slightly larger than New York, about half again more populous than Boston. Yet it was a strikingly easy town to get about in. The thoroughfares in Philadelphia were straight and parallel, forming a gridiron pattern. They even had rational names, those streets running east to west designated mostly after trees, while those that intersected were numbered sequentially. These were busy byways too. There seemed to be an endless stream of activity between the town and the docks along the river, for this was the busiest harbor in America, a port that saw well over a thousand ships come and go annually. A stagecoach line also operated out of the city, funneling people and the mail to points north, and many local merchants thrived by dispatching dray after dray of commodities over these streets, then out to the large immigrant population that had flowed through Philadelphia south or west, many eventually settling on lands in the Shenandoah that Washington once had surveyed or fought for. The main streets in this city had a handsome, well-kept look about them. They were paved, all were lined by illuminated lamps as well as by trees that already had grown tall and stately. Brick sidewalks ran alongside these arteries, pathways dotted with more than five hundred public water pumps.

The city was only twelve blocks wide and twenty-five blocks long, but over six thousand houses were crowded into that space, most of them wedged into the east end of town. Few of these residences were mansions. In imitation of the English squires with whom they traded, the Philadelphia gentry had taken to the countryside, preferring to build their elegant dwellings away from the malodorous "vapors" of the city, removed from its ever-present noise and grime, its smoke and oppressive summer heat. Here and there a stroller might glimpse the town house of one who was affluent, usually a two- or three-story brick home, but it was only in the suburbs that one could see the tree-lined estates of the grandees, huge brick houses about which rolled the green, virgin acres of southeastern Pennsylvania, places with names like Woodlands and Whitby Hall, Cedar Grove and Hope Lodge.[38]

The business district squatted amidst some of the more sumptuous town-houses. Nearly three hundred mercantile establishments were bunched into the first few blocks west of the riverfront, businesses that ranged from dockside warehouses to retail shops to the work sites of the city's mechanics. Most were small businesses run by a master artisan, a workplace in which the owner labored alongside a young apprentice and one or more journeymen. Scores of craftsmen and craftswomen, each plying his or her own specialized trade, could make a go of it here. Cordwainers, coopers, tailors, and a variety of smiths (blacksmiths, tinsmiths, silversmiths, gunsmiths) operated out of their own houses, anything but elegant one- or two-story dwellings, abodes that always seemed cramped even though they were usually only sparsely furnished. Men and women who specialized in more than twenty separate crafts toiled in the ship-building industry alone, and almost as many varieties of construction tradesmen were required to erect one large house or building (and about five hundred dwellings were erected that year in this city).[39]

If Washington chose to walk west, into those neighborhoods farthest removed from the job sites, he saw a bruitish squalor that almost rivaled the loathsome conditions in his slave cabins. In fact, nearly 10 percent of Philadelphia's inhabitants were bonded laborers, slaves or indentured servants. They may not have been much worse off materially than the free but unskilled workers, the laborers who hauled goods and swept chimneys and dug ditches. Only one worker in ten could afford to purchase a house; the remainder, mostly husbands with families of six or seven or more persons, rented lodgings in dingy, drafty, wooden firetraps, tiny apartments that seldom exceeded four hundred square feet, and which were jammed side by side, abutting outhouses and even stables. Husbands and wives, and frequently their children as well, worked six days a week from sunrise to sunset, and, if lucky, the entire family earned a few pounds more than they had to spend for their food and clothing, their rent and firewood.[40]

How much of this Washington took the time to see is not known, but he did mention in his diary that he received a guided tour of the Pennsylvania Hospital. Together with John Adams and perhaps one or two other colleagues, Washington was taken out to the hospital by Dr. Shippen. A three-story T-shaped structure of brick and stone, the hospital sat in bucolic surroundings adjacent to the city's almshouse and workhouse, though it was segregated from these abhorrent institutions by white picket fence and a grove of trees. Built only twenty-five years before, this was the oldest hospital in the colonies. The facility existed for the industrious poor, as opposed to the affluent, who were treated at home, and the idle poor, who went unattended. It had been founded both by Quaker benevolence and on the supposition that it was cheaper to keep impoverished men alive and occasionally at work than it was to pay poor relief to their indigent widows and children. Washington's tour began in the basement where he looked in on the mentally ill; in reality this section was little better than a dungeon where these unfortunates were caged like criminals. Then it was upstairs to the wards, long rooms housing row after row of beds, upon which lay the lame and the ill. It was a "dreadfull Scene," Adams told his diary; the "Weakness and Languor, the Distress and Misery, of these Objects is truely a Woefull Sight." Finally, the guests were taken to Shippen's laboratory, where the physician lectured briefly on the subject of human anatomy, utilizing a plaster of paris model of the body for a guide, as well as paintings of "the Insides of a Man . . . , all the Muscles of the Belly being taken off [to reveal] the Heart, Lungs, Stomach, Gutts."[41]

Washington, who had arrived just as Congress was about to meet for the first time, soon had leisure for all the sightseeing he could wish. Congress had no more than convened before it created a committee to draft a statement of American rights. Washington was not named to the panel, thus freeing him to do as he pleased until the committee reported. For nearly two weeks he had no duties to perform, save for reporting to Carpenter's Hall each morning to learn whether Congress would meet that day. During that period he may have explored Philadelphia. Certainly he socialized with his colleagues; he probably spent some time in the evenings at the gaming table; and for a fact he did attend at least one Presbyterian worship service. He also met several Philadelphians during this period of enforced idleness. He dined at the home of Richard Penn, a former governor of Pennsylvania, and he was the guest of Thomas Mifflin, a successful young merchant, and of John Dickinson; he was hosted by the latter at Fairhill, the "Farmer's" elegant estate that overlooked the Susquehanna north of the city.[42] His most important encounter, however, was with Joseph Reed.

Ten years younger than Washington, a Princeton-educated lawyer, Reed was an opportunist. He hailed from a comfortable, but by no means wealthy family. He had struggled through years of schooling (besides his graduate degree from Princeton, he had a year of formal legal training at the Middle Temple in London) to attain a measure of prosperity and status, yet his estate was valued at only one-eighth that of Mifflin, one-seventieth that of Dickinson. Desirous of more wealth, not to mention power and recognition, Reed long since had learned that the most rapid way to the top was to hitch himself to someone already there. He had married into the family of a wealthy London merchant, then he had become something of a follower of the "Farmer" in the domestic politics of Pennsylvania. Now he was industriously courting many of the most influential congressmen, frequenting their haunts and entertaining them in his comfortable, though hardly posh home. What no one knew was that he was sending accounts of much that transpired to the American Secretary in London, playing that angle, too, in the hope that he might be offered a lucrative post in the imperial bureaucracy. Yet Reed was not a traitor. He preferred that the colonists be reconciled with Great Britain, but on terms satisfactory to the American protest movement; thus, he had been active in radical circles in Philadelphia, and he had played a major role in helping the protest movement in Pennsylvania overcome a powerful conservative resistance to the very notion of a national congress. Washington and Reed probably met frequently during those weeks. The older Virginian, now forty-two, seemed to feel comfortable with this younger man and took an immediate liking to him. Reed was friendly and outgoing, polished and intelligent. In many striking ways, in fact, his conduct was not unlike that Washington had exhibited when he too was just starting out. More striking even, Reed bore a marked physical resemblance to Washington, that is if the two paintings of him that exist—both by Peale—are reasonably accurate renditions.[43]

When the Grand Committee at last reported, Congress finally got down to business, launching a month of six-day work weeks. Washington apparently attended the meetings faithfully, but, typically, he seldom actually participated and he contributed little to the actions finally taken by the conclave. After some anxious moments in the early days of the meeting, the more radical delegates assumed control. Congress went on to adopt a declaration of rights that, though longer and more explicit, largely reiterated the stand taken by the Old Dominion in the previous decade. The delegates also quickly agreed to boycott Great Britain until the Tea Act and the Coercive Acts were repealed. Agreeing to the mechanics of the embargo proved more difficult, however, for here the selfish interests of various factions collided. Nonimportation posed few problems, but nonexporting colonies wished to immediately stop the shipment of commodities to the parent state, whereas others, principally the tobacco and rice colonies in the South, hoped to forestall a ban on the sale of their goods to England until that year's crop had been marketed. In the end the South won the clash; New England needed allies badly enough that it was willing to settle for half a loaf. It was decided to begin nonimportation in December, but to defer nonexportation for a year, and it was agreed to create an enforcement mechanism known as the Continental Association, locally elected committees to compel adherence to the boycott. The Congress then smoothed over the rough edges by drafting a soothing letter to the people of Great Britain, and, late in October, having been away from home for sixty days or more, the delegates happily voted to adjourn, pledging only to meet again the following May if the difficulties with the parent state still had not been resolved.[44]

Washington sped home (he covered the distance between Philadelphia and Virginia in a day and a half less than it had taken him to get to the Congress), arriving on a cool, sunny October afternoon, doubtless delighted to be home to witness the gaudy autumn colors the surrounding hills and forests had put on in his absence. He immediately immersed himself in his business concerns. He sought out his cousin Lund Washington, to whom he had entrusted the management of Mount Vernon, and they rode here and there, inspecting the crops and the mill, looking in on his livestock. He oversaw the auction of portions of the property of a late friend and neighbor, and he attended the final sale of the Fairfax's property at Belvoir.[45] Now and then he hunted, and hardly a day passed without a visitor appearing at his door.

Old friends and acquaintances dropped in, as did some folks that he knew only in passing. William Piercy, a Methodist minister—George referred to him as a Presbyterian in his diary—visited briefly. He was a man recently arrived from London, one whom Washington probably had just met in Philadelphia.[46] Charles Lee, styling himself as "General" though he had not risen above the rank of major in the British army, was a guest too, staying for five nights. It was the second recent meeting of the two men, for they had seen one another in Philadelphia, getting together there for the first time since they had accompanied General Braddock on his fateful trip to the Monongahela nearly twenty years before. Lee had lived a very busy life in those two decades. Despairing for advancement in Britain's peacetime army following the conclusion of the French and Indian War, he had fought as a mercenary with the Poles, commanding Russian troops against the Turks in Moldavia. (He was a general in this army, hence he had some claim to the title he used.) Late in the 1760s he was back in England, dabbling in radical politics, publishing polemics against the Crown. He also puttered with some land speculation schemes in America, and in the summer of 1773 he came for a visit and an inspection of his investments. Like a bohemian he had drifted through three or four colonies during the past year, availing himself of the hospitality of one colonist after another, pausing only long enough to write a pamphlet that argued rather convincingly that America's soldiers would be more than a match for the redcoats should war break out.

Lee had a way of offending people. Part of it was due to his unconventional life style. Not only was he prone to a nomadic existence, but there was a habitually unkempt air about him as well. According to knowledgeable contemporaries, both peculiarities were attributable to the fact that he had never married, though the reverse may have been as likely an explanation. (Actually, he had "married" and fathered a son by an Iroquois woman, but, however the Native Americans looked on the match, he thought of it simply as a matter of convenience.)

His manner was acerbic and contentious. Well educated—after early training in England he probably was schooled in France and Switzerland—and well read, he had an opinion on everything, and he was not the least reticent about expressing his views. In fact, his conversations had a way of becoming monologues, musings and dogmatic statements delivered in an odd mix of eloquence and of the salty invective of the barracks and the barroom. Then, too, there were his traveling companions. He went everywhere with a pack of dogs. Five hounds accompanied him to Mount Vernon, and, as usual, they were huge oxlike creatures, only slightly less disreputable-looking than Lee himself, though probably considerably less talkative than their master. Lee had one other unsavory habit, one that he revealed just before he departed. He talked Washington out of £15 to pay for his further travels.[47]

For the first time in fifteen years Washington's days also were taken up by military concerns that autumn. Fairfax County had organized a volunteer military company in September, even adopting as its uniform the old buff and blue design that Washington had recommended years before. By mid-January the unit had begun to drill under Washington's careful gaze, training with powder and shot purchased out of money that Washington and George Mason had lent the county. From time to time during these months Washington also assisted the drillmasters of other new companies, and he played an important role in organizing the local enforcement of the economic boycott. In March, Fairfax County elected him as its delegate to the Virginia Convention in Richmond, an *ad hoc* legislative gathering necessitated by Governor Dunmore's continued refusal to summon the Burgesses. Washington landed on the committee to oversee the colony's military preparations, and just before adjournment he was reelected as one of Virginia's delegates to the second Continental Congress.[48]

When Washington decided that war was inevitable cannot be precisely determined. His fellow congressman, Richard Henry Lee, and many other leaders as well, had left Philadelphia believing that Britain again would cave in when confronted by the boycott. Some visionaries in America even expected a revolution in England, an uprising by Old Country radicals to topple the allegedly tyrannical regime. Washington never went that far, but as late as February 1775 he still seemed to doubt that war would occur, hinting that he believed the North government would accede to the colonists' demands. When he returned from

Philadelphia, in fact, he resumed his normal speculative pursuits, making the sorts of investments that do not suggest he believed a protracted war was imminent. He secured two parcels of land, one by purchase and one in lieu of the repayment of a loan he had made years before to a neighbor. He also purchased several indentured servants.[49] But Washington's uncanny luck in business matters deserted him during these months, as he suffered one substantial setback and he was faced with the real possibility of a second loss, a stunning commercial reversal.

The previous spring Washington had sent a team of servants and hired hands to settle and commence development of his lands near the mouth of the Great Kanawha River. The venture was a fiasco. The bonded laborers escaped at the first opportunity, and the hirelings soon thereafter were driven away when the frontier again exploded in still another of its episodic bloodbaths. Washington lost over £300 on that gamble, though—in an action that admittedly bears marks of a man racing against time—he immediately bought another labor party, dispatching that team in April 1775. This group was more successful for a time, for by the next spring it had cleared and planted twenty-eight acres; then fresh hostilities with the Indians broke out and this settlement also was abandoned.[50]

At the same time that Washington was putting together his second team for the Great Kanawha, he received even more disconcerting news. Shortly after he returned from the Virginia convention sessions in Richmond, one of his old soldiers from his frontier days dropped by Mount Vernon bearing the tale that Governor Dunmore was about to disallow all the land grants previously made to the colony's veterans of the French and Indian War; supposedly, the soldier added, the surveyor of the tract, Washington's old buddy William Crawford had not been properly licensed. Washington listened with disbelief. He could lose twenty-three thousand acres! He immediately contacted the governor, adducing evidence and entreating the executive's beneficence. But Dunmore dryly responded that if Crawford was not properly certified "the patents will of consequence be declared null and void."[51]

Two days after he communicated with Lord Dunmore, Washington seemed to indicate that he now believed war would occur with Great Britain. He reported to George Mercer that he believed the people were ready to fight. One of those who thought war was certain was Horatio Gates, the former British officer with whom Washington had served on that trek to the Monongahela in 1755. Like Lee, Gates had quit the peacetime army in Britain during the 1760s; he had searched out a parcel of land in Virginia near Berkeley Springs, and he had moved there in 1773. Now that war was a possibility Gates felt the itch for his old calling, and he paid a visit to Washington in April to urge his old acquaintance to help him secure a commission in case Congress created an American army. "General" Lee dropped back by too, for another five-day stint, although whether he too was looking for a commission or simply for a roof over his head is not clear.[52]

Lee had hardly ridden away to bring his brand of cheer to some other lucky planter when Washington received ominous tidings: Governor Dunmore had directed the seizure of the colonists' powder stored in Williamsburg. Moreover, Washington learned that troops were being organized to march on the capital where, according to some, the chief executive would be confined under house arrest until the purloined powder was returned. The next day volunteer officers from Dumfries dispatched a courier to Mount Vernon to learn whether Washington would march with them. But before Washington could respond another express arrived at his door. This messenger brought even more disconcerting news. Ten days before British troops had clashed with colonial militiamen in two obscure villages in Massachusetts; there had been many casualties on both sides in the town of Lexington, as well as in a place called Concord. Everything now was altered. War with the parent state seemed a certainty. It was best to defer bellicose action in Virginia until the meeting of the second Congress, scheduled to meet in less than two weeks.[53]

Washington's last days at Mount Vernon—he would not see his treasured estate again for more than six years—were hectic. Lund Washington was to be left in charge, and he met often with the owner to plan every last detail of the farm's operations. Some sticky financial transactions also required his attention. And a plethora of visitors seemed to descend like locusts upon Washington and his wife just at this feverish moment when they most longed for privacy.[54]

One of the guests was Richard Henry Lee, Washington's congressional colleague. He arrived on May 3 to accompany Washington to Philadelphia. That afternoon, bright and hot for so early in the spring, Washington and his company—Lee and his brother Thomas, and their old friend from the Virginia assembly, Charles Carter of King George County, together with Gates, who had lingered on—sat in the shade on the veranda, thankful for each breath of cooling breeze that drifted off the great river below. They talked, in all likelihood ruminating on political strategies and on military realities, on what Congress should do and might do.[55]

That night after dinner, with the callers shown to their rooms, George and Martha at last were alone to say their private goodbyes. They faced a long separation, probably one of several months, Washington thought. But he should be home by Christmas.[56]

The next morning was intolerably hot again, the oppressive stickiness of the air adding to the unpleasantness of parting. A hurried breakfast was completed, the carriage was loaded, and the teams secured to the car. Farewells again were said. Washington and Lee clambered inside, their body servants following. The driver was in his place.

Inside Washington's baggage, just in case, were his military uniform and his sword.

PART TWO

5

Commander of America's Army

"Imbarked on a tempestuous Ocean"

During the first Congress John Adams, who already had concluded that only force could secure American rights, lashed out at his timid colleagues who "Shudder at the Prospect of Blood." As he rode from his home in Braintree, Massachusetts, to Philadelphia for the second Congress, all signs pointed to a transformation in the thinking of the overwhelming majority of his countrymen. Rhode Island was readying a force of fifteen hundred men to send to Massachusetts, he reported as he passed through that colony. When he got to Connecticut he found that colony mustering an army of six thousand. New York and New Jersey "are aroused," he discovered as he continued on. When at last he arrived in Philadelphia he found militiamen training and parading in the streets.[1] But what of Congress? Would congressmen from south of New England vote to assist their brethren? Would Congress provide men and supplies to wage war against Great Britain?

For weeks it was not clear which way Congress would lean. The more conservative congressmen, led by John Dickinson as much as anyone, were a powerful force. They desperately wanted to avoid hostilities, to once again petition the Crown in the forlorn hope that the monarch would break with his ministers and agree to the first Congress's declaration of American rights. At the outset this faction seemed to have the upper hand. It secured passage of the "Olive Branch Petition," another expression of colonial fealty, and when Adams suggested that France and Spain be sounded out for military assistance his proposal elicited looks of "horror, terror, and detestation."[2]

But the momentum of events was running against this conservative faction. Congress had hardly been gaveled into session before it learned that New England militiamen, together with a paramilitary force from Vermont, had seized Fort

Ticonderoga from a small British garrison. Then New York requested advice on how to treat the redcoats within its borders, and the New England colonies wished to know how supplies for their defense could be procured. Congress created two committees to study these thorny matters, and it appointed George Washington to chair each committee. The very act of naming this man to head the panels—a man who had not been named to a single committee at the first Congress—was indicative of the winds beginning to blow over Congress.[3]

Actually, Washington's committees made the most modest recommendations. One panel cautioned New York against provocative behavior, although it did advise that colony to raise troops for six months' service, a force that might keep open the lines of communication between New York City and the hinterland. As for supplies, the other panel simply proposed that New England alone supply the army that was drawn up before Boston.[4]

There was still another question. What of the army itself? Since that day in April when General Gage's search-and-destroy force had retreated to Boston from Lexington and Concord, the British army had remained under siege within the city. All about Boston, in an arc from north of the town swinging around the western periphery and on to the south of the Neck, the thin strip of land that connected the city to the mainland, an army of nearly twenty thousand colonists had gathered, resolved to resist any attempt by the British to leave the city. It was an intercolonial army, but all the soldiers were New Englanders, and New England was fully aware that it could not stand alone. On June 2, almost a month after Congress had reconvened, Massachusetts asked the national legislature to take command of the New England army.

By then the Adamses, John and Samuel, believed they had the votes to win congressional approval for such a move. For weeks, over dinner and ale, they and their compatriots quietly had taken soundings, and they had discovered that a majority of the southern congressmen were ready for a national army—if its commander was a southerner. They also had learned that Virginia's George Washington was their choice for the post, although a few delegates (including a Virginian, Edmund Pendleton) were "very cool about [his] Appointment." Most of the opposition apparently was due less to reservations about Washington's ability than to the fact that his selection would mean that the present commander, Artemas Ward of Massachusetts, would have to be dumped; some feared this would destroy morale in the army, and others worried that New Englanders would not serve under any commander save one from their own region.

But John Adams, the prime mover in this shadowy work, was more worried about New England's present dearth of aid. What better way was there to nationalize the struggle than to appoint a southerner as commander of the army? Besides, Adams, a most sagacious judge of men, was enthusiastic about Washington. Quiet, temperate, earnest, reserved, prudent, yet with an air of toughness about him, the Virginian seemed like the kind of man one could trust with such a burdensome responsibility; he seemed the very embodiment of those values that Adams long had prized, that he had sought to foster and to display. Adams had nothing against Ward, and he may not have even believed that Washington was a more capable soldier. It was just that Ward had to be sacrificed for the general good. So, quietly and with some effort Adams worked in private for Washington's appointment for nearly two weeks, talking and arguing primarily with others from New England. Meanwhile, Washington, who knew full well what was going on, discarded his civilian garments for his old buff and blue uniform of the Virginia Regiment, a not so subtle way of indicating his ardor for the command post.[5]

The decision to go with Washington was made sometime during the second week of June, and on June 14, a hot, sticky morning, John Adams was the first congressman to be recognized by the presiding officer. Not a very good orator, the short, stout New Englander nevertheless made a speech. The gist of his address was that the army before Boston must be nationalized by the addition of troops from outside New England. Then, after pausing for a moment, he recommended that General Ward be replaced; he had in mind a man "among Us and very well known to all of Us, a Gentleman whose Skill and Experience as an Officer, whose independent fortune, great Talents and excellent universal Character [will] command the Approbation of all America"—Colonel George Washington. John Hancock, who earlier had been elected president of the body, had presumed Adams was speaking of him. When Adams instead mentioned Washington, Hancock's face suddenly was contorted with rage; nor did Samuel Adams's second to his cousin's motion "soften the President's Phisiognomy at all," John Adams recalled years later.[6]

Washington fled the room the moment his name was mentioned, leaving Congress free to express its feelings. In all likelihood the issue was never in doubt, but the debate was fierce and protracted. After several hours of arguing it was clear that a consensus existed for Washington, although it was equally clear that Congress was deeply divided. At length the managers of the floor fight called for an adjournment until "pains [could be] taken out of doors" to procure a unanimous vote. The other portion of Adams's motion had relatively smooth sailing, and on that day Congress transformed the army at Boston into a continental force, resolving that six companies of riflemen, two each from Pennsylvania, Maryland, and Virginia, be added to the new Continental army. Congress also named Washington to chair a committee of five to prepare articles of war for the regulation of the American army, in itself virtually an act that indicated it soon would confirm him to head that army.[7]

The following day, while Washington sketched a preliminary draft of the military code in the privacy of his apartment, Congress resumed its fight over the choice of the commander of the army. During the night some of the dissidents had been won over to Washington, but not all the congressmen were in his corner, and the debate continued, sometimes acrimoniously, throughout most of the day. Finally, late in the afternoon some of Washington's friends hurried to his quarters with word of the vote. He was now General Washington, they told him, commander in chief of the Continental army.

That night one congressman after another wrote home, breaking the news of Washington's selection and explaining their decision. More than anything else they stressed the virtues of his character, pointing to qualities like modesty, amiability, bravery, generosity, sobriety, and to his long record of military experience. These attributes, they predicted, made Washington the kind of man that "youth [can] look up to ⸱ . . . as a pattern to form themselves by. . . ." But behind the rhetoric was a hard-headed pragmatism. The cause required someone from south of New England. Whom else could Congress have selected? Philip Schuyler of New York had about as much experience as Washington and he too was a congressman, yet his active support for the resistance movement had been muted, and since he had not been a delegate to the first Congress he was not as well known as the Virginian. Horatio Gates, Charles Lee, and Richard Montgomery (living now in New York) were ex-British army officers, but that fact was as much a demerit as a virtue in the minds of congressmen contemplating war with Britain. Beyond those men there was no one else with Washington's military background. Thus, as Eliphalet Dyer of Connecticut reported, Congress "Esteem[ed] him well Adapted to please A New England Army and much better Suited to the Temper & Genius of our People than any other Gent. not brought up in that Part of the Country." [8]

What went through Washington's mind during the evening of this most momentous day of his life is not known. His diary entry that night was no less mundane than for any other day: "Clear, and Cooler than Yesterday. Dined at Burn's in the Field. Spent the Eveng. on a Committee." Remembering the "Virginia Centinel," he was aware that his actions in such an exposed position could invite criticism. He even melodramatically told Patrick Henry that he expected his service to cause "the ruin of my reputation." [9] If he paused to think of what had transpired to bring him to this point, was he candid enough—or of sufficient philosophical bent—to recognize the role played by sheer luck? Though not reared in the highest stratum of Virginia society, he had had the good fortune to be born into the planter class and to parents who saw that he received some education. By the luck of the draw Lawrence had married into a rich and powerful family, thus giving George access to their influence; then, in fairly rapid succession, not only did Lawrence die at an early age, but so did his only surviving child. A middling surveyor at age sixteen, Washington had become the virtual scion of Lord Fairfax as well as the master of Mount Vernon before he was thirty. He had been lucky in other ways too, having survived several brushes with death. Smallpox felled him, twice he was struck down by camp diseases, and two years after his marriage he again fell dangerously ill. He had not only lived through each malady but recovered from each with no permanent damage. He had also escaped unhurt in his fight with Jumonville and in the attack upon Fort Necessity and, miraculously, had survived that horrible day on the Monongahela when Braddock and half his army perished. By happenstance, moreover, Washington was the right age when the French and Indian War erupted, old enough to be a soldier, but not so old as to be encumbered with a family or with physical infirmities. In retrospect he had been fortunate that Dinwiddie and Braddock, Shirley and Loudoun had been unable or unwilling to make him a British officer, and he was even luckier that his Uncle Joseph Ball had counseled against letting him join the British navy. In addition, as historian Douglas Southall Freeman observed, Washington might not have been considered for the commander's post by the second Congress had he not attended the first Congress, for his colleagues had gotten to know him, at least as much as one could become familiar with Washington in the space of a few weeks. And, finally, by chance not only was he healthy in 1775, he looked as men thought a soldier should—big, strong, robust, agile, hard.

It would be absurd, of course, to suggest that luck alone had led Washington to this moment. Other young men must have longed to soldier but had never gone to war; surely, too, other young men with similar social and educational deficiencies failed to work as assiduously as did Washington to overcome their shortcomings. Whatever the reason for his appointment as Virginia's commander in 1755, moreover, he had passed the test of responsibility and he was remembered as a good soldier. Washington had taken it upon himself, furthermore, to play an active role in the protest movement, at least from 1769 onward. Thus, although luck did play a role in the selection of Washington to command the Continental army, his lifelong yearning for recognition was of crucial importance too. And so was his vision, which extended outward to an incredible degree. Where others were content with their lot, or assumed that their ascent was impossible, Washington always seemed to believe that nothing was impossible. And once he fixed his sight on a goal he pursued it with a vigor and tenacity, almost a ruthlessness, that set him apart from most men. It was this steely resolve that most distinguished Washington from others. No obstacle, no limitation seemed too great to be overcome. So he went where others would never have dared to tread in quest of wealth and status and power, and once he gained each he wanted still more. His cravings, his resourcefulness, his uncanny ability to understand men and circumstances had brought Washington to this moment of opportunity, and those qualities in his character that made danger and struggle seem alluring compelled him to reach out for it.

On the night of his appointment, after dinner, he consulted Edmund Pendleton for assistance in drafting the acceptance speech he would have to make the following morning. He also asked Pendleton to prepare his will. That he should have turned to Pendleton was in keeping with his personality. He really required no help in the preparation of his brief remarks, and there were other lawyers among the Virginia delegates with whom he was closer. But in availing himself of the counsel of the man who had opposed his selection, Washington sought to convert Pendleton into his staunch supporter. After he left his colleague, Washington worked with his committee on the formulation of the articles of war. Only

Schuyler among the other committee members had been a soldier, so those two probably wrote most of the draft. (The committee issued its report a day or two later, though Congress did not adopt the articles until a week after Washington had departed for Boston.) At the moment, however, what most interested Washington was the selection of the other officers, and while he was anxious to see that both Lee and Gates were among those chosen, he had not forgotten the lingering ill effects that had resulted from his battle with Dinwiddie to name his subordinate officers twenty years before. Still, he believed he needed these two experienced soldiers, and he was prepared to push to assure their selection.[10]

The following morning the busy legislators made short work of the ceremony endowing Washington with his new post. Congress offered the command, and he accepted it with a brief and modest speech, one that was memorable only because he announced that he would refuse a salary, settling merely for compensation for his expenses. It was a matter of honor, he said, for he did "not wish to make any proffit" from his post. His commission came with a grant of extraordinary power. He was vested with "full power and authority" to act as he deemed necessary for the welfare of the united colonists. But he hardly was above the law. His conduct was to be guided "in every respect by the rules and discipline of war," and, what is more, he was explicitly admonished to be "careful in executing the great trust" bestowed in him.[11]

Congress spent the remainder of the day wrangling over both the suitable number of generalships to create and the appropriate pay for these positions. By evening it was agreed that two major generals, an adjutant general, and five brigadier generals would be named. Then came the difficult part—filling the new positions.[12]

The next day, a Saturday, Congress quickly named Artemas Ward as the first major general. That much was easy. Not only was Ward reputed to be an excellent soldier, but New England—and Ward—had to be mollified for the appointment of Washington. The remainder of the day was spent in a squabble over the next two positions, a protracted, petty, acrid quarrel, the most tortuous he had yet experienced as a congressman, John Adams told a correspondent.[13] What made it worse was that no one pretended that one nominee was really better qualified than another; congressmen simply wished to have favorite sons and their friends selected. In the end, after six hours of squabbling, Washington used his influence to secure Charles Lee's appointment as the other major general and Horatio Gates's selection as the adjutant general. Congress then quit for the weekend, but when it returned on Monday it was no more inclined to disinterestedly choose the best men for these posts. In fact, so many names soon were in the pot that Congress sought an escape by creating more generalships. Now there were to be four major generals and eight brigadiers. But even so, four more days of debate were needed to complete the list of thirteen general officers.

Philip Schuyler got one of the two top posts that remained. Israel Putnam of Connecticut got the other, giving New England half the major generalcies. New

England also attained seven of the eight brigadier slots. The exception was Richard Montgomery, the former British officer who now resided in New York. The other brigadier generals were Seth Pomeroy, William Heath, and John Thomas—all of Massachusetts—John Sullivan from New Hampshire, Nathanael Greene of Rhode Island, and Joseph Spencer and David Wooster from Connecticut. Most had some military experience. Indeed, Pomeroy and Wooster had served in King George's War in the 1740s. Only Greene and Sullivan had never borne arms in wartime.[14]

Once these appointments were completed—and three days after his own selection—Washington finally wrote Martha of the recent epic decisions made by Congress. (And Congressman Deane thought it odd that Washington did not first return home to visit his wife before he journeyed to Boston!) Martha must have suspected that her husband would be made an officer, although she may not have been prepared for the news that he was to be the army's commander. His letter to her was couched in a defensive, almost apologetic tone: he had not sought his new post, it had been imposed upon him by "a kind of destiny," he began. Were he to have refused the assignment, he continued in language almost identical to that he had employed twenty years earlier in telling his mother that he planned to soldier, it would have exposed "my character to such censure as would have reflected dishonor upon myself." He realized that this turn of events left Martha with the unpleasant prospect of living alone, and he encouraged her to move to Alexandria or to move in with the Bassetts at Eltham. Finally, he worried whether the job was not "a trust too great for my capacity," though all that remained was to put his reliance in God, who "has heretofore preserved and been bountiful to me."[15]

Washington remained deeply troubled over Martha. He remembered how she had suffered following the death of Patsy and the loss of Jackie through matrimony. Now she was losing him as well. The next day he wrote his brother and his stepson asking each to assist her, and he suggested that it would be wise for Jackie and Nellie to return to Mount Vernon in his absence. And just before he left Philadelphia he wrote his wife a second time, a missive in which he expressed "an unalterable affection for you, which neither time or distance can change."[16]

Washington also continued to fret over his abilities, and he turned to Burwell Bassett to pour out his misgivings. He knew his greatest shortcoming was his lack of experience, only about five years of service, all of it in command of a small force in comparison to the army besieging Boston, and most of that time he had fought Native Americans, not a professional European army. Whatever happened, Washington went on, he could promise three things—his belief in the American cause, his unwavering devotion to his responsibilities, and a wholly honest commitment to public service. He could pledge no more. He comprehended that he "now Imbarked on a tempestuous Ocean," but he would leave for the front comforted by the realization that he had "acted to the best of my judgment," and trusting that "some good to the common cause" would result from his actions.[17]

Joseph Reed, by Charles Willson Peale (c. 1776). Courtesy of the Historical Society of Pennsylvania.

Thomas Mifflin and his wife Sara Morris Mifflin, by John Singleton Copley (1773).
Courtesy of the Historical Society of Pennsylvania.

He could not leave Philadelphia, however, until two matters were out of the way. He had to await his orders, the document formally authorizing him to assume command. Moreover, Congress had voted him a stipend so that he might select two adjutants, a skelton staff that would partially ease the crushing work load he was about to bear. He knew from his days with the Virginia Regiment that there were not enough hours in the day for the commander in chief. Endless rounds of appointments, daily inspections, and a staggering amount of correspondence left a man with no time to think. He needed capable aides, men whom he could trust and with whom he could be comfortable, for the adjutants would be privy to his private thoughts and in attendance at confidential meetings. Washington pondered the matter for days, then he requested the services of Thomas Mifflin, his congressional colleague, and Joseph Reed, the young Philadelphian he had met the previous autumn. Each man was nine years younger than himself, each was well educated and quite experienced in Pennsylvania's political wars. These were men whose intellectual talents were beyond doubt, whose deft political skills might help in navigating the troubled and murky—and partisan—waters that surely lay ahead.[18]

Washington's offer came out of the blue. Mifflin accepted the post immediately, but Reed hesitated. Not only did he have no military experience, but to take the position would be to abandon a lucrative law practice, his sole source of sustenance. Still, to be an amanuensis to the general was nothing short of a breathtaking opportunity, a chance to become known, to go places. It was a difficult decision, one with which he wrestled for four days before he agreed only to accompany Washington to New York; then, he said, he would make up his mind once and for all.[19]

Washington agreed to those terms and, at last, a week after his selection, he was ready to head for the front. His final day in Philadelphia was a busy one. There were last-minute meetings with congressmen, consultations with this and that committee, farewells to new and old friends. Then, to add to this frantic milicu, a courier astride a weary mount galloped up before the State House with exciting news: another battle had been waged before Boston, an even more important clash than those at Lexington and Concord: the colonists, he said, had scored a great victory at a place called Bunker Hill.

In the weeks following the clashes at Lexington and Concord, General Gage had remained inactive, bottled up in Boston by General Ward's siege army, a force nearly seven times greater than his own. Late in May British reinforcements arrived, raising Gage's troop strength to approximately six thousand men. But the Americans still possessed a four-to-one numerical advantage. Too weak to assault the American siege lines, Gage planned instead simply to occupy the elevated points outside Boston, the heights in Dorchester to the south, Bunker Hill and Breed's Hill in Charlestown northwest of the city. Unfortunately for the British, word of Gage's scheme leaked out to the Americans, and on the night of June 16 General Ward seized the heights in Charlestown. American artillery now stared down on Boston and its lifeline to the homeland, the city's harbor. Gage was in an untenable position. He had to take the hill or relinquish Boston.

Two days after Washington was selected to replace Ward, Gage chose to assault the hill. He selected Sir William Howe, who had arrived with the British reinforcements, to lead the attack. Howe, the scion of a wealthy and influential family, had chosen a military career, and he had risen quickly, making lieutenant colonel before he was thirty. During the French and Indian War he had fought with great courage, leading the victorious assault on the Heights of Abraham during the campaign for Quebec. Tall and with an edge of toughness, callouness even, in his countenance, he looked like a soldier. And he liked to fight, impressing some in the colonial wars with his lust for battle. Besides, he liked the masculine environment of an army, its camaraderie, adventurousness, and affable forbearance toward man's profligacy.

The British took Bunker Hill, but at a frightful cost. Nearly a thousand redcoat soldiers were killed or wounded in the engagement; 42 percent of the British troops who fought that day were victims, and eighty-nine British officers were casualties. Although unscathed physically, Howe too was a victim that day. Never before had he borne responsibility in an action that resulted in such catastrophic losses. Although Howe never acknowledged that he was moved one way or another by what he subsequently would call that "unhappy day," yet he did seem to change from a daring and eager warrior to a soldier less prone to gamble with the fortunes of his men. After Bunker Hill, Howe was a man reticent to act until every ounce of intelligence had been gathered and exhaustively scrutinized, until the odds were demonstrably in his favor.[20]

It was Bunker Hill's impact on Howe that made the battle so important, for when Gage shortly thereafter was recalled by London, he was succeeded by Sir William. Thus, at perhaps the only time Britain could have won the war, the years 1775–77, a time when the Continental army still lacked military experience and before the colonists had secured foreign assistance, General Howe, now rendered irresolute and overly cautious, would be the commander of Britain's forces in America.

General Washington learned few of the details of Bunker Hill from the courier who dashed into Philadelphia. If anything, however, the news of the battle left him more eager than ever to set out for Massachusetts. At last, a week after his selection as commander, everything was ready. Washington had used his expense account to purchase a light phaeton and five new horses, sending his own carriage and dobbins back to Mount Vernon, and on June 23, just as the first rays of sun began to appear in the eastern sky, he was up to supervise the loading of the vehicle. Soon Reed and Mifflin arrived to accompany him, then Schuyler, and Charles Lee, who had come to the city to lobby for his own selection as a general officer, joined them as well. In the half-light of the early morning several local militia units assembled, prepared to lead the general's entourage out of the city.

Most of the congressmen had arisen to see them off too, as had several local and provincial officials.[21]

The horses pranced nervously. There was an air of excitement and apprehension among the men as well, a sense that Washington's imminent departure would symbolize the beginning of a change in America's relationship with the mother country. When everyone was present and all the baggage was loaded, the men said their good-byes, wishing one another well. Washington joined Lee and Schuyler on horseback. A martial band struck up a jaunty tune, and the procession slowly began to rumble forward, bouncing and clattering along the cobblestones, past the still dark stores, over the empty streets, then into the gloomy countryside. The commander of the new American army at last was on his way, off to fight a foe whose chances of victory were diminished by the events on Bunker Hill, off to take command of an uncertain colonial military force.

Rattling along in their carriages, bouncing over dust-choked roads, wearied by an oppressive June heat, Washington and his traveling mates were on the road for ten long days. When he reached the Jersey shore the general draped a purple sash over his uniform and donned a hat adorned with a vivid plume. Looking properly dashing, Washington was ferried across the Hudson River to Colonel Leonard Lispenard's spacious estate, about a mile north of New York City. Washington paused there for dinner, leaving his escort of nearly five hundred soldiers to lounge about the host's lawn in the hot sun.

While dining Washington at last received definitive word on the battle at Bunker Hill. At New Brunswick, on the first day out of Philadelphia, he had run across a courier bearing ill tidings, word that contradicted the previous messages about the engagement. Now he saw a letter from James Warren, president of the Massachusetts Provincial Congress, which described the American victory. Ominously, however, Warren also reported that the army's supply of powder was "by no means adequate" for waging war. Washington told the others, including the troops outside, of the great victory, then he rode into New York, through streets jammed with an excited, festive multitude. Three hours later Governor William Tryon, returning from fourteen months abroad, came ashore at the southern extremity of the island, greeted by a small crowd that included many fickle well-wishers who had cheered the American general earlier in the day.

Washington spent only twenty-four hours in town, much of the time in conference with Schuyler. Two matters were on the commander's mind. New York had to be safeguarded from attack by the British fleet and the royal marines who lay in the city's harbor; before he left town Washington agreed to place General Wooster in charge of the defense of the city. In addition, Washington was concerned about Canada. Capture of the St. Lawrence River not only would be an extraordinary morale-builder and negotiating tool, it would have real military benefits. The colonists' possession of Canada would close the back door to the colonies, preventing a British invasion from that direction; moreover, the fall of

Canada might be a powerful inducement to foreign powers to assist America, should that expedient ever be required. Schuyler and his commander discussed these matters far into the night, then again the following morning, sometimes conferring privately, sometimes admitting the other officers. Forty-eight hours later Congress sanctioned what the two generals had already decided, directing Schuyler to take such steps as were necessary to prevent an invasion from Canada, and, in addition, to invade Canadian soil if that step was "not . . . disagreeable to the Canadians."

Before departing the city Washington appeared at a brief ceremony before the New York Provincial Congress. Speaking quietly and concisely, as was his custom, the general assured the assemblymen that the struggle with Britain was for reconciliation, and he pledged never to forget the supremacy of civilian rulers. Those rites out of the way, he set off once again, hurrying to reach a war that already was two months old. He paused only in New Rochelle, there to meet for the first time with General Wooster (and, presumably, for the first time to hear an officer complain of his rank, for Wooster had been demoted from a major general in the Connecticut militia to brigadier general in the Continental army); from there Washington proceeded to Massachusetts, along the way spending his nights in New Haven (where he reviewed a volunteer company of Yale College students), Wethersfield, Springfield, and Marlborough, before finally reaching Cambridge on July 2. Surprisingly, for an age that loved martial pageantry, Washington's arrival to take command of the American army was accomplished without pomp. He arrived in Cambridge in the midst of a Sunday afternoon rainstorm. Only the sentries were present when the general reached the army's lines, but one of these men hurriedly rounded up a small escort to shepherd him to his new residence, the home of the president of Harvard College.[22]

General Washington soon found his accommodations to be undesirable. The college president, though shunted to a single room, was underfoot. Moreover, some of Washington's men fretted that the house was visible from the nearby Charles River, and that it might make an inviting target for British gunboats. So after less than two weeks on campus, Washington moved to the Vassall house, a larger, more opulent mansion that had been built only fifteen years before by a wealthy merchant, a man who had remained loyal to the Crown and who earlier had fled to the safety of General Gage's army. Washington paid £2 to have the house thoroughly cleaned, then toward mid-month he moved in, occupying a bedroom as well as a stark white chamber that he settled on for an office. A large retinue followed him. He employed two cooks, a maid and a washerwoman, four servants, and five slaves, one his long time body servant Billy Lee, who soon "married" one of the servants. Both food and beverages were consumed in abundance. The commander's accounts indicated an expenditure of about £35 a month for wine, including an order for over two hundred bottles for October alone.[23]

The general quickly found himself inundated with work. He spent long hours with the field officers who still were present. (Two were sulking at home, incensed at their rank.) Undoubtedly in these guarded conversations Washington probed for clues to the personality and disposition of each man. What he did find was considerable rancor. Some of the displeasure was directed at Congress, which in its wisdom had elevated a subordinate (Putnam) over his former superior officer (Spencer); in addition, in three months of service inevitable petty jealousies had arisen among these men. Between coping with these matters, Washington had to inspect the fortifications that had been thrown up by the militiamen. He was not surprised to find the facilities in good order; after all, the men were mostly healthy, robust artisans and farm boys accustomed to physical labor. But to his mortification Washington learned that no one knew the precise state of the army's manpower or its supplies. A rapid audit revealed that he had more powder than he had been led to expect, though conservation still was essential. On the other hand, instead of the twenty thousand men he thought he commanded, he found to his dismay that he had fewer than fourteen thousand troops present and fit.

At times it must have seemed to Washington that there were too few hours in the day to meet the requirements of his job. His precious time, moreover, frequently was consumed by politicians who came pleading. (The Massachusetts Provincial Congress, for instance, sent a delegation to complain about Pomeroy and Heath outranking Thomas.) Curious civilians came too. Abigail Adams was one of the earliest visitors, and she was swept off her feet by Washington. "I was struck," she gushed, by his ability to combine "Dignity with ease, and complacency." The "Gentleman and Soldier look agreeably blended in him," she added. "Modesty marks every line and feature of his face." She also met Charles Lee during her visit to headquarters, but she was not so taken by him, characterizing the shaggy General Lee as "a careless hardy Veteran." Lee was bowled over by her, however. He fetched his dogs—one so huge that a civilian guest swore he would have mistaken it for a bear had he seen it in the forest—and had them perform for Abigail, making one sit and shake hands with her, an act that this farm mistress probably found far less unpleasant than some historians have imagined.[24]

Washington soon learned that every problem, no matter how big or how small, inevitably was passed on until it stopped at his desk. His greatest immediate problems arose from the army's shortage of certain provisions. He discovered deficiences of clothing, muskets, picks, shovels, and tents. Even more alarming was the lack of money. And at the end of July he learned that he had less powder than his hurried audit had revealed. Far less, in fact. The Continental army had only ninety barrels of powder, one-third the amount he had been told was stored in the colonists' arsenals.[25]

The most painful shortage was the want of manpower. "Between you and me," Washington told a friend during that first month, "I think we are in an exceedingly dangerous situation. . . ." During his first week in Cambridge, Washington called his officers together for his initial council of war. The subject: how

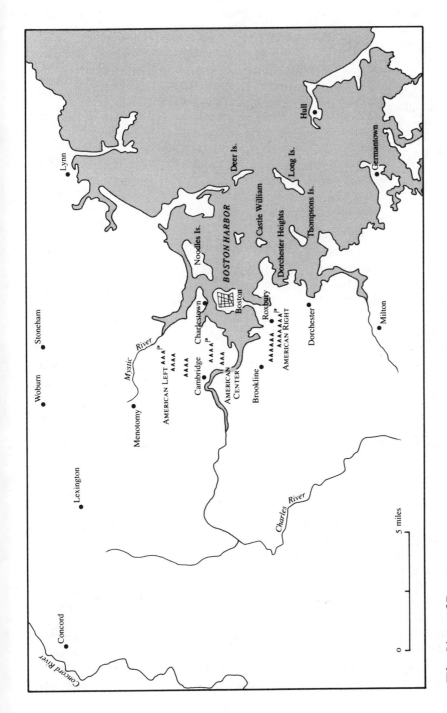

The Siege of Boston

to fill the ranks of the new army. The officers concluded that New England's contribution had about reached its optimum limit; henceforth, only "Boys, Deserters and negroes" could be induced to enlist in that picked-over region. Everyone deplored the recruitment of children and turncoats, and Washington was opposed to the use of black soldiers. He had countenanced the presence of mulatto soldiers in his Virginia Regiment, but he did not want any black men in this army. His racist outlook was not uncommon; in fact, each New England colony had forbidden black men to serve in its militia, although they had soldiered as volunteers in the colonial wars and had fought and died at Lexington-Concord and at Bunker Hill. When the siege of Boston commenced in April, blacks once again enlisted. Nevertheless, Washington thought them inherently inferior, and the sight of an armed Negro was too much for him to bear; so, with the consent of the other officers, he prohibited the recruitment of "any stroller, negro, or vagabond." (In September Congress upheld Washington's dictum, although it turned back a move by Edward Rutledge of South Carolina to expel all black soldiers already in the army.) Washington thought provincial militiamen hardly more trustworthy than blacks, though he did not yet feel free to be quite so candid; at this point he obliquely attributed the "Defficiencies in . . . their Discipline" to the allegedly long state of British oppression under which New England had groaned. Anyway, there were not many militiamen left, so the officers called on Congress to gather recruits from the colonies south of New England.[26]

Not only were there too few men, Washington was shocked by the conduct of those in camp. He found officers shaving their men, captains shining and repairing the shoes of soldiers, commanders and subordinates hailing one another on a first-name basis. He was appalled to learn that some soldiers had been browbeaten into working on their officer's farms. He discovered that soldiers came and went as they pleased, that serious offenses—cowardice at Bunker Hill, for instance, or falling asleep while on guard duty, or pillaging the property of civilians—went unpunished, that the scruffy camp where the men had lived since late April seemed devoid of measures for sanitations or hygiene. None of this should have been too surprising. Few of the men had any military experience, not even in their village militia units, for, as the French and Indian threat receded in eighteenth-century New England, local trainband companies often assumed the role more of a social than a martial organization. Moreover, these farmers and artisans who were resisting British centralization sometimes were just as loath to surrender their personal freedom and independence to an American officer.

Washington sought to counter these conditions by rigorously enforcing the Articles of War that he had helped to prepare before leaving Philadelphia. He restricted the men's mobility to and from camp. As with the Virginia Regiment, he punished swearing and drunkenness as surely as he disciplined slackers, thieves, and deserters. He ordered that the camp streets be swept daily and the barracks weekly, and he directed the disposal of "Offal and Carrion." He required attendance at worship services, certain, of course, that his frequent pronouncements would be echoed by the army's chaplains. Punishment for violators was severe—and certain. Men were made to ride the wooden horse, locked in the stockade, or forced to wear some humiliating costume; but mostly they were flogged, ten stripes for this offense, twenty for that, thirty-nine lashes for most indiscretions. In moments of petulance and exasperation during those early days in camp Washington fumed that these New Englanders were "an exceedingly dirty and nasty people," the "most indifferent kind of People I ever saw," a group characterized by the most "unaccountable kind of stupidity." But in his more dispassionate moods Washington more correctly blamed their lack of discipline on "the principles of democracy [which] so universally prevail" and on the "leveling spirit," the sense of egalitarianism, which infused the region.[27]

Washington also believed that a better solution to the problem of an intemperate and unrestrained soldiery was to create an elite and aloof officer corps. He was certain that only such a complement could command deference and fashion an orderly and disciplined fighting machine. His first step was to weed out noticeably incompetent and corrupt officers, and within two months he bragged privately of having "made a pretty good slam among such kinds of officers." In his daily orders he endeavored to educate the officers, exhorting them "to show an example of Bravery and Courage," to comport themselves with dignity and always to act with diligence. Meanwhile, he privately instructed his officers to be strict but not unreasonable, to treat their charges with impartiality, and to be vigilant. He told the officers that there must be a barrier between themselves and their men, and he advised the senior officers to be "easy and condescending in your deportment to your officers, but not too familiar, lest you subject yourself to a want of that respect, which is necessary to support a proper command." And since formal uniforms were lacking he devised what he called "Badges of Distinction" for his men of rank. Field officers were to wear red or pink cockades in their hats, captains were to sport yellow or buff, green would identify lieutenants, sergeants were to sew a stripe of red cloth on their shoulders, corporals a green stripe. Moreover, to assess his officers, as well as to heighten their sense of elitism, the commander invited each day's adjutant, officer of the guard, and officer of the day to dine with him at headquarters.[28]

Still another problem Washington discovered upon his arrival in Cambridge concerned the organization of the army. Although the force was called the "Continental army," the term was incorrect, for this still was only an army of New Englanders. In addition, since Congress had in effect decided to leave the appointment of all field grade officers to each colony in which a part of the army was stationed, the officer corps, from top to bottom, was certain to be monopolized by New Englanders. Washington had been in camp only a few days before he told Congress of the need to "new model" its three-week-old army. Principally, he hoped Congress would issue all field grade commissions, appointing meritorious men from all colonies. But Congress was in no mood to act in this fashion. Most congressmen still were confident of the army's prowess, and many were alarmed by the centralizing tendency implicit in Washington's suggestion. Congress did instruct Washington to fill certain posts, however, and after Congress selected Colonel Joseph Trumbull (another New Englander) as commissary general, the commander pointedly named Mifflin and Stephen Moylan, both Pennsylvanians, to be quartermaster general and mustermaster general respectively, and he selected two Virginians, Edmund Randolph and George Baylor, as additional aides.[29]

An army at war does not act in a vacuum. It was imperative, therefore, that Washington immediately learn as much as possible about his adversary in Boston. Using the reports of the resistance movement's spy apparatus—somewhat less trustworthy now that Boston no longer was an open city—and the carefully appraised accounts of redcoat deserters, Washington quickly got a remarkably accurate handle on Gage's problems and plans. He wildly overestimated the size of the British army (he reported it as having twelve thousand men when Gage had fewer than half that number, of which at least one-quarter were unfit for action), though he may have deliberately done so in order to pry more troops from Congress for his army. On the other hand, his knowledge of Gage's losses at Bunker Hill were extraordinarily correct, and by early August he deduced that the British were laying plans for their winter quartering needs, knowledge that led him to surmise that an attack was not imminent. Although he could ill afford to relax, Washington believed that his old friend Gage had found the American defenses too formidable to assault, preferring to await reinforcements before attacking, perhaps planning to abandon Boston and strike somewhere else.[30]

But Washington could not rely explicitly on the intelligence reports. His information might be incorrect. Thus, he continued to expand and improve the army's fortifications. For the first time, too, he began to think of a protracted siege. That meant he had to plan for his own winter quarters. He renewed his search for additional tents, made arrangements to have many of the men housed in buildings on the Harvard College campus, and directed the construction of wooden facilities; each company was left to devise its own architectural design within the limits of guidelines prepared at headquarters. (The huts were not to exceed one story, and each building was to be 108 feet in length.)[31]

Despite his manifest problems, Washington must have been pleased with the state of affairs after his first month on the job. His appointment as commander had been well received, especially by Artemas Ward, who responded to his sudden demotion without a trace of jealousy or wrath, betraying none of the prideful biliousness that had charactered Washington's behavior at his own downgrading by Dinwiddie twenty years before. Although Washington's efforts to remodel the army had made little headway, Gage's apparent inability to assault the American lines would offer time in which some changes might be made. And Washington continued to hope against hope that this would be a short war. It still was possible that he might be reunited with Martha at Mount Vernon before Christmas, although that notion was predicated on the assumption that the news of Bunker Hill would topple the North government, forcing Britain to capitulate to the colonists' demands.[32] Meanwhile, just in case, Washington's thoughts were turning to offensive operations of his own making.

Canada had been on his mind since before Congress resolved to dispatch an army into that forbidding region. With the British garrisons there startlingly under-manned, he believed that Canada might easily fall into the colonists' clutches. Having discoursed at length with General Schuyler on that topic, he presumed that an American attack was imminent. But Washington was largely ignorant of the real state of affairs on the Canadian border. Schuyler's missives, though bulging with disapproval of the rag-tag army that he commanded, conveyed the clear impression that an invasion was pending. Unfortunately, Schuyler, who was a good and brave soldier, was an inept and dilatory commander, one whose conduct bore a startling resemblance to that of young Colonel Washington on the Virginia frontier in the 1750s. Schuyler did not join his men at Fort Ticonderoga until two weeks after Washington reached his army, then he did not linger for long, preferring to run his force either from Albany or from his palatial digs in Saratoga. He detested the New England soldiers who comprised his army and complained so mawkishly of their deficiencies that an exasperated New York Congress finally told him: "It is vain to complain. . . . Use the bad troops at Ticonderoga as well as you can." But July and August dragged by and Schuyler made no use of these men. Some obstacle inevitably presented itself: the men had not been suitably trained before his arrival; the army was undersupplied; his force was too small to attack entrenched troops; his intelligence reports (which were in error) indicated that General John Burgoyne had entered Canada with a huge army of reinforcements; he could not determine from Congress's contradictory orders whether it favored an incursion under all circumstances, or whether it would sanction an attack only if the Canadians civilians welcomed the invaders; finally, he convinced himself that the Tories and Indians in New York were a greater menace than the British in Canada. In reality, Schuyler was a dawdler. Washington ever so gently prodded him to move out, but his importunings were unavailing, as were the entreaties for action both by General Montgomery, the second in command, and Governor Trumbull of Connecticut.[33]

Ultimately, Schuyler was overwhelmed by events. Since shortly after his arrival in Massachusetts, Washington had toyed with a plan of dispatching an army of his own into Canada. Several New England leaders told him that it was feasible to reach Quebec via a land and river route through the Maine wilderness, and the more Washington studied the plan, the more he liked it. A two-pronged attack— one through Maine, the other a thrust from the West commanded by Schuyler— would mean that the British commander in Canada, General Guy Carleton, would have to chose between defending only vital Quebec or dividing his already meager army. But, cleverly, Washington intended to place the burden of the final decision for such a venture on Schuyler's beleagured shoulders. Late in August he wrote his comrade, making it clear that he hoped Schuyler's army soon would act—"I am sure you will not let any Difficulties not insuperable, damp your Ardour"—but leaving the final verdict to the New Yorker.[34]

By the time Schuyler received Washington's communication, he could not refuse. While Schuyler had sat passively in Albany, General Montgomery at Fort Ticonderoga had taken matters into his own hands. He had received intelligence on August 23 which indicated that urgent action was imperative. A small British force of three hundred at Fort St. John on the Richelieu River, between the border and Montreal, was about to complete the construction of two warships; if the Americans did not act before the vessels were finished, the British would have absolute control of Lake Champlain, thus enabling them, probably forever, to prevent an American invasion, and at the same time imperiling the colonial fortresses at Ticonderoga and Crown Point. Without waiting orders, Montgomery moved out with twelve hundred men. Despite this rank insubordination, Schuyler was not angry. Perhaps his mind was of such a bent that his underling's act was necessary. At any rate, Washington's letter exhorting the army to act arrived two days later. Stirred to action at last—symbolically anyway, since he did not get around to joining Montgomery for another ten days—Schuyler agreed to Washington's scheme of a twin offensive.[35]

Washington was jubilant. Creating this new invasion force was not difficult. Gage's immobility freed the manpower. Conveyances were a bigger problem, but after much effort he acquired schooners to transport the troops from northern Massachusetts to Maine, and he arranged for the construction of *bateaux*, a kind of wilderness craft used by northern Indian traders, vessels capable of hauling six or eight men and substantial supplies. What Washington needed was a commander, and for this he turned to Benedict Arnold.[36]

Almost thirty-five, Arnold had no military experience. He had received only a miniscule formal education before he was apprenticed to two cousins to learn the apothecary trade; for a long time he ran a drugstore in New Haven, although through shrewd investments he ultimately acquired a small fleet and commenced a profitable trade (much of it illicit) with the West Indies and South America. On the eve of the war, he secured command of a New Haven militia organization, which he marched to Concord within hours of the opening shots of this conflict. Arnold could be charming and graceful, but that always seemed to be a self-serving veneer he applied to disguise his unquenchable thirst for power and wealth. Even as a child he had seemed to be aggressive and bullying, intent on achieving his goals whatever the cost. As an adult there was a faintly dubious quality to his behavior. It was difficult to pinpoint, but he gave people the impression that something of the savage predatory beast lurked just beneath his urbane surface. But societies in wartime often value brutes, finding in their normally repellent traits the qualities suited to the times. Just days after the awful scenes at Lexington-Concord, the Massachusetts Committee of Safety found in Arnold the kind of man it wanted, and he was commissioned to lead a force to capture Fort Ticonderoga. Connecticut, meanwhile, had retained a man of similar ilk, Ethan Allen, who commanded the raucous Green Mountain Boys, to lead his force against the same object. With fewer men than Allen possessed, Arnold had to play second fiddle, a role hardly suited to a man of such pride and vanity. Nor was he happy when the Green Mountain Boys got most of the credit for the victory. Humiliated, Arnold quit and returned to New Haven, sulking there until midsummer when he came to Cambridge to submit a reimbursement claim for his services. While in town, however, he secured an interview with General Gates, and he produced a plan for an invasion of Canada through the wilderness of Maine. Gates was impressed. Knowing that Washington already had begun to think in these terms, moreover, Gates passed along Arnold's scheme to headquarters.[37]

Sometime early in August Arnold was ushered in to meet Washington. The commander, who had an uncanny knack for assessing men, immediately was taken by this would-be soldier. Here was a resourceful, tough, and ruthless man, just the kind needed to lead an expedition certain to be filled with forbidding obstacles. Perhaps he saw the same qualities in Arnold that Dinwiddie had seen in him; perhaps he found in Arnold some reflection of himself. Whatever the cause, within hours of the receipt of Schuyler's letter sanctioning the mission, Arnold was named its commander. He would plunge toward Canada with two battalions totaling 1050 men, almost 10 percent of Washington's army. Among his troops would be three companies of recently arrived riflemen from Pennsylvania and Virginia.[38]

In dispatching the riflemen, Washington must have hoped that they would finally serve some good purpose. Congress quickly had voted funds for the recruitment of eight companies of these riflemen, hardy frontier types with a penchant for deadly marksmanship. These men wielded firearms with grooved or rifled barrels, weapons of far greater accuracy and range than the sturdy Brown Bess muskets carried by most American soldiers. The story made the rounds that only those who could hit the image of a human nose affixed to a board 150 yards downrange were eligible to enlist. And, in fact, there was something phenomenal about these men. En route, wherever an audience could be gathered, they provided impressive exhibitions of their skills, sometimes from a distance of sixty yards blasting the bullseye of a target that some foolhardy comrade held between his legs. And they walked—they hardly marched—from Maryland to Massachusetts in extraordinarily rapid time, one of the Virginia companies averaging an incredible thirty miles per day. Wearing Indian, or hunting, shirts, and sometimes donning war paint, they looked ferocious, and by and large they comported themselves with a callous, sinewy combativeness, as if they feared nothing. The only problem with these men was that they had little use for discipline. Some Pennsylvania riflemen paused along the way in Litchfield, Connecticut, to liberate a girl they discovered in the local jail, and a day or two later near Hartford they tarred and feathered some outspoken dimwit whom they took for a Tory. Once they were in Washington's camp, they displayed a chronic inability to obey orders, they fought endlessly with the Yankee soldiers, and they wasted Washington's precious ammunition with continual—and largely ineffectual—potshots at distant British sentries. Washington, in despair, finally admitted to General Ward that he wished they had never come, a sentiment shared by Gates and Lee, the latter calling them "dam'd riff raff—dirty, mutinous, and disaffected." But if the commander could not send them home, he could—and now he did—send them to Canada.[39]

With the Canadian expedition at last readied, and with his army beginning to take shape, Washington toyed with an offensive of his own. During the first week of September he wrote his general officers and asked them to consider the wisdom of an American attack on Boston. Three days later he called a council of war to discuss the notion. According to Joseph Reed, who sat in on the session, Washington was "very serious" about such an assault. Given the shortage of tents and lodgings, Washington began, the winter was certain to provoke enough anguish to try the mettle of veterans, much less these raw recruits. Moreover, he went on, his powder and armament shortages were not likely to be remedied by the spring, whereas Gage would then be better supplied. Finally, he said, his troops' enlistments expired in December; there was no guarantee that he would have such a large army after this year ended, and even if he had a larger army, the new force would have to be trained from scratch. A successful assault, particularly if complemented by victories in the Canadian theater, almost certainly would be a "decisive stroke," perhaps ending the war by Christmas. Contrarily, the commander acknowledged, to fail in such an attack would "be very fatal."[40] As the war later would demonstrate, there was a gambler's audacity to Washington's makeup, a willingness to run great risks by attempting bold strokes rather than waiting for his adversary to seize the initiative. Yet Washington was neither suicidal, impulsive, nor reckless. And he was not about to make such a decision unilaterally.

Only Charles Lee among the general officers supported Washington. He believed the Americans were a match for the British regulars, especially when they enjoyed a better than two-to-one numerical superiority. But the others opted for the safety of inaction, fearing, probably correctly, that an assault might result in a Bunker Hill in reverse—catastrophic colonial losses. Besides, some said, an attack might be unnecessary; North's government might have collapsed already. Washington accepted their recommendation, although two weeks later he told Reed that if the British were not defeated before reinforcements arrived from London, the consequences to America could be "dreadful." And he informed Congress that in the future he might revive the assault plan. Whether he liked it or not, the strategy he now would pursue presaged the design he largely would follow throughout the war. It was a strategy that Alexander Hamilton later succinctly summarized: "our hopes are not placed in any particular city, or spot of ground, but in preserving a good army . . . to take advantage of favorable opportunities, and waste and defeat the enemy by piecemeal."[41]

If all notions of an offensive were scrapped, Washington took satisfaction in the knowledge that his army was safe—for the time being. The British, as Reed put it, would have to be "more than madmen to think of breaking through the lines we have thrown up." Not expecting an attack, Washington told Reed that he believed the British simply hoped to fortify Boston so that it could be held by a small force. Then, he said, the redcoats "will land in different parts of the country, and lay waste as far as they dare."⁴²

In September, when the Congress resumed its monotonous sessions following a brief, late summer holiday, the delegates found the docket laden with plaintive letters from General Washington, each outlining the problems with which he had wrestled since July. The congressmen hardly had begun to grapple with these matters before still another communiqué arrived from headquarters. Now the commander ominously suggested that his army faced extinction. Given the army's chronic supply shortages, few men were likely to reenlist. If the legion's troubles were not soon rectified, he added, "the Army must absolutely break up."⁴³

Congress had heard these complaints since July, although to this point it had only coped with the problem of the powder shortage. Approximately fifteen tons of powder had been procured from New York and Pennsylvania and shipped to the army, and at Congress's urging Rhode Island provided Washington with an additional three tons of the precious commodity. These reinforcements eased the problem, yet by late August there was only enough powder on hand to provide each soldier with thirty rounds and to supply the artillery for a single day's action. So desperately short was Washington that he used his powers to dispatch an expedition to Bermuda, supposedly the site of a large powder magazine. "Enterprises which appear Chimerical, often prove successful," he forlornly told a correspondent.⁴⁴

Thoroughly alarmed by Washington's dire missive, Congress acted quickly to find a temporary solution to the army's woes. Money was sent, to be used for pay for the soldiers and to procure supplies. Clothing, pork, and flour also were sent along, and Congress appointed a committee to seek out additional amounts of powder. But the long-term solution to these myriad problems required consultation with the commander, for which Congress created a committee of three. Washington's old friend from Virginia, Benjamin Harrison, was one of the members, together with Thomas Lynch of South Carolina and Benjamin Franklin. Congress could hardly have been more proud of itself. "I doubt not," a New England congressman told Washington, "but . . . that by the opening of the next Campaign you will have the finest Army under your Command, which ever was formed in America."⁴⁵

By the time the congressional delegation reached Cambridge, the air had an autumn nip to it, and all about the army's encampment the forests had donned their red and yellow attire as if to welcome the visitors in splendor. Washington had never met the venerated Franklin. They apparently got on well enough, but the old sage, not unlike Washington, was surprisingly reserved, and the two men must have found their attempts at light conversation to be awkward. The commander had only a passing acquaintance with Lynch, having met him when they both served in Congress. But he must have been delighted at the sight of Harrison, not only a friend, but a Virginian who had just returned from a vacation in that province. Finally, the amenities out of the way, the congressmen got down to business. They opened with a bombshell. They made it clear that Congress expected Washington to assault Boston by the end of the year; if he required additional troops for the attack, they went on, he was authorized to summon as many militiamen as he needed. Congress felt strongly about this. It was not angry at Washington's inaction, but as one legislator remarked, it was "very solicitous that our Army . . . should make a resolute Attack upon the Rebels [*sic*] before a Reinforcement to them shall arrive." Then, before Washington could catch his breath, the committee unleashed another blockbuster: the pay of all officers must be reduced.[46]

General Washington must have blanched at the first directive. Whatever his feelings about the wisdom of an attack, the notion of civilians four hundred miles removed from Boston dictating strategy to the army had to be galling. But Washington had enough political acumen to know how to respond. He convened another council of war to ponder the issue, and this time, their hackles rising, the general officers unanimously rejected the notion of attacking an entrenched British army. Moreover, to cut pay, they continued, would foreclose any chance of raising another army for 1776. Their bluff called, the congressmen backed off, and during the final five days of the conference they obsequiously accepted almost every urgent request made by General Washington.[47]

Early in November Congress received the committee's report and quickly granted the commander's propositions. It was agreed that Congress would support an army of 20,372 during 1776, a force that was "intended to lie before Boston," in the curious phraseology of the legislators. Strangely, Congress had never specified the size of the army it would support in 1775, although it was presumed that Washington would inherit a force that ranged somewhere between 20,000 and 27,000 men. In fact, as Congress now realized, the army it agreed to maintain for the next year would be substantially larger than Washington's present army, containing perhaps 25 percent more troops. Salaries in the new army were to be the same as in the existing force, except for captains, lieutenants, and ensigns, who averaged raises ranging from about 25 to 30 percent. Congress also assumed responsibility for clothing the troops, and it took steps to standardize the manufacture of the army's muskets. Washington was given extraordinary powers to impress essential commodities (carriages, vessels, horses, for instance), and the Articles of War were altered, giving the commander leeway to impose even more harsh punishments upon erring soldiers.[48]

Through the initial year of war, Washington was careful to practice what he had preached to the New York Provincial Congress. He gave no hint of any inclination to undermine the authority of the civilian magistrates. That is not to say, however, that he failed to exert his delegated powers, or that he did not at times endeavor to redirect the thoughts of Congress or influential local officials. By autumn Washington had launched an unauthorized invasion into Canada, and almost alone he had succeeded in convincing Congress that the army required refabrication. The reconstruction of the army, moreover, was fraught with portentious implications for the emerging polity. In time the egalitarian army that Washington had inherited in July would give way to a force much more similar to the one with which it struggled, a military organization in which an elite, imperious officer corps commanded a soldiery increasingly composed of propertyless, long-term hirelings. But in 1775 no one could have comprehended the magnitude of the changes that had been set in motion since that rainy day in July when Washington first had arrived at headquarters.

Nor were these the only momentous changes initiated that fall. Just before he departed Philadelphia for Cambridge and the meeting with Washington, Franklin had written a friend in London that the Anglo-American crisis could be resolved if both sides would just step back and allow passions to cool. But, he predicted, that would not happen, and he added, "I see clearly we are on the high road to mutual family hatred and detestation. A separation of course will be inevitable." He was correct. That autumn some congressmen began to speak openly of American independence, and one or two provinces virtually extirpated their royal charters, substituting for them new governments which no longer expressed any allegiance to British authority. In addition, Congress renewed its year-old nonimportation agreement, and it launched a boycott of shipments from America to the parent state, a step the southern congressmen had been unwilling to take a year earlier.[49]

Moreover, to assist the war effort Congress created an American navy. Early in September Washington, desperate for supplies, had channeled funds into a small privateering venture, authorizing the use of soldiers recruited from port towns like Marblehead and Salem. Soon six craft were employed in the undertaking, a fleet that quickly was dubbed "Washington's Navy." Shortly thereafter Congress—which had no knowledge of Washington's actions—directed him to outfit two vessels to intercept a shipment of supplies from Nova Scotia to the redcoat army in Boston. From this act came the *Cabot* and the *Andrew Doria,* and the birth of the American navy. Two additional ships were authorized before the end of October, and by Christmas not only had the fleet swelled to seven vessels (with thirteen more already scheduled to be constructed), but Congress had appropriated funds for two battalions of marines and had prepared rules and regulations for the new navy. At year's end it was reported that the fleet had garnered prizes totaling £20,000, including the capture of a British ordnance brig laden with 2000 muskets, 100,000 flints, 20,000 round of shot, and 30 tons of musket balls.[50]

That fall Washington's army remained immobile; General Washington, however, was quite busy. A thousand details, some trifling, some of great moment, daily absorbed his attention. For some time he had presumed that a British attack was unlikely before the spring, if it ever came. "Our Lines are so strong, we have nothing to fear but a Surprise," as Reed put it, echoing his commander. Early in October General Washington learned that Gage had been recalled, replaced by Sir William Howe. Many in Washington's entourage believed the change in command presaged a British attack, for Howe's reputation was that of a resolute fighter. Washington took the necessary precautions, but he was inclined to believe that Howe's elevation would not alter British strategy.[51]

Sometime that autumn Washington realized that he would not be home by Christmas, that this would be a protracted war, perhaps a very long war. What changed his mind? Captured British correspondence indicated that the ministry planned to send massive reinforcements for a campaign in 1776, and, in addition, intelligence suggested that the government intended to widen the war by diverting its forces to New York, where it hoped to seize control of the Hudson River. Moreover, Washington, like others, was aware of the shift in congressional attitudes. The early aim of fighting for reconciliation was waning; a new mood of sympathy for independence was growing, a goal likely to be achieved only through a long, wearying war. Then, too, by late in the fall Washington knew that the North government had survived the news of Bunker Hill; it would remain in power, and it displayed no signs of attempting to appease the colonials.[52]

Washington spent much of his time that autumn pondering the reorganization of the army, a subject he had broached in July and which Congress had sanctioned in October. Time and again he summoned his generals to discuss the issue, but each time he discovered "so many doubts and difficulties to reconcile" that little headway was made. The troops, he was told, would serve only under a man from their own province, and until these commanders were designated the troops would refuse to reenlist. It was a double-edged sword. Without soldiers the most capable officer was helpless, but a large army commanded by incompetent officers was worthless. Caught in a bind, Washington agonized for nearly a month, then he decided to act, to "new model" the officer corps. He could not touch the general officers, for they were congressional appointees. But with their assistance he painstakingly moved to find the best men to fill the lower grades. Then he waited breathlessly to see if there would be an army left for the new officers to command.[53]

By late November the signs were ominous. Fewer than one thousand men had reenlisted in an army that was projected to exceed twenty thousand troops. The reality of this war had begun to sink in, brought home by the mounting casualty lists. First there was Bunker Hill, a costly engagement for the Americans too. Then camp diseases assaulted the army, taking a toll that the redcoats could never have exacted. Moreover, like a dark stain spreading out on a white cloth, these ailments inexorably seeped into the civilian sector, often claiming three or four victims each day in New England's once tranquil little villages. Soon the festive and patriotic spirit with which the region had greeted the onset of the war was spent, replaced, at best, by an aura of grim, sullen determination.[54]

For a time that November Washington suspected that a British assault was imminent. Surely, he reasoned, Howe would assail his rapidly thinning ranks. But Howe did not attack. Indeed, he recently had received orders from London directing him to abandon Boston. That he was still in the city was due to a lack of transports necessary to facilitate his withdrawal.[55]

Washington knew nothing of this, but he did know that if he had faced a deteriorating enemy he would have seized the initiative. He characterized the British situation as a "disgraceful confinement," hardly the words Howe would have chosen. But, then, Washington presumed his adversary had not attacked because he was "afraid of us." By mid-December Washington no longer expected an attack. In fact, he reported to Congress that the British were demolishing the paved streets of Boston in order to use the cobblestones for breastworks in expectation of an American assault.[56] Even though his judgment was based on faulty premises, Washington had fathomed much about the mettle of his foe.

Howe's inactivity may have lessened Washington's anxiety, but it did not eradicate the morose spirits that had gripped the general throughout the fall. Washington's black mood stemmed from the recruitment crisis, and, in addition, from the specter increasingly posed by signs of venality among his countrymen. The enlistments of the Connecticut troops were the first to expire, and no ploy by headquarters could induce a substantial number to reenlist. The 27th Connecticut Regiment agreed to stay until the new army was raised and in place, but the remainder marched home on December 12, quitting the encampment to a chorus of hisses and deprecatory chants by those who had to remain behind. Neither cajolery nor pleadings had availed, nor had the promise of an immediate furlough for those who agreed to stay on. Most of these men were farmers who had been away from their livelihood since April. Too poor to buy the labor of slaves or indentured servants, their farms were imperiled each day they were absent from the fields. Washington sought to plug the gaping hole caused by their departure by calling up five thousand militiamen from Massachusetts and New Hampshire, as well as various units of "Long Faces"—as the veterans promptly dubbed these less than ecstatic new warriors—marched in as Connecticut's veterans departed.[57] Later the militia would be severely criticized for its performance in this war, but without its remarkable activities at Lexington and Concord, then again at Bunker Hill, and now in perhaps saving Washington in this year-end crisis, the colonists would have commenced this long war on a very different footing.

Washington watched nervously as the recruitment process dragged on at an agonizingly slow pace. On December 4 he reported that 5900 men had reenlisted. A week and a half later the figure stood at 7100, and by December 18 it had climbed to 8500. By year's end about one-half the allotted slots in his army were filled. The remainder would have to consist of new recruits, men who would agree to enlist for only one year; Congress would authorize no other term of enlistment, apparently thinking, as did John Adams, that a hitch of any longer duration would entice only the "meanest, idlest, most intemperate and worthless" to offer their services." [58]

The reluctance of New England yeoman and artisans to reenlist perplexed and frustrated Washington. To toil at a small farm plot in order to support a family was something he had never done. Nor had he ever experienced military service from the perspective of an enlisted man; there was no wine with the foot soldier's evening meal, no cozy bed tucked under the roof of a warm, dry house. Myopically, Washington found their unwillingness to remain in the army incomprehensible. He described the conduct of those who would not stay on as "extraordinary and reprehensible," as "Scandalous." Once he even suggested that to demand pay for military service reflected "a dirty, mercenary spirit." By no means was such an attitude unique to Washington. Spokesmen for the ruling elite never seemed to tire of trumpeting the virtue of self-sacrificing courage. But not everyone was so short-sighted. General Greene, for instance, told Washington that the union was too new to expect men to serve from sentiments of patriotism alone; besides, a cash bounty would enable recruiters to select only the cream of the crop, he naively added. Strangely, Washington did not find it incongruous that officers should be paid, and that fall he wrote Congress to ask that they be given a raise. In the meantime, he granted extra rations to his officers, in effect a modest pay raise since they could draw the cash equivalent instead of the rations. Before Christmas, Congress increased the pay of officers, while it cut the salary of enlisted men by nearly 25 percent.[59]

At times during that bleak autumn Washington wished he had not taken his post. Had he forseen what he would have to endure, he confessed to Reed, "no consideration upon earth should have induced me to accept this command." Within the week, however, he counseled a similarly dejected Schuyler not to resign. In time, he reasoned, "Order and Subordination will take [the] place of Confusion, and Command [will] be rendered more agreeable.—I have met with Difficulties of the same sort . . . but they must be borne with," he went on. "The Cause we are engaged in is so just and righteous. . . ." [60]

By Christmas, Washington's spirits had brightened. This was partly due to the arrival of Martha, together with Jackie and Nelly Custis, two weeks before the holiday. "Lady Washington," as she was called at headquarters, had come by carriage from Virginia, stopping in Philadelphia to stay with—and to meet for the first time—Esther Reed. Upon reaching headquarters Martha discovered that she was treated with "great pomp as if I had been a very great some body," but it was Vallance Gates, the adjutant general's wife, who succeeded in raising eyebrows. She alighted from the carriage wearing a masculine English riding habit.[61]

Despite his brightened spirits, Washington still faced mountainous problems, not the least of which concerned the maintenance of the army's health.

Somehow, for instance, the men had to be kept warm and dry during the bitter New England winter. Incredibly, each day the army consumed 117 cords of wood, the yield of about four acres; supplies of this fuel already were growing scarce within the vicinity of the camp, meaning that green firewood now had to be transported several miles each day, often across icy or muddy roads. (The British, trapped in Boston, were in even worse shape in this regard, and they had begun to tear down wooden houses to obtain this precious commodity.) With the assistance of the Massachusetts Provincial Congress, which authorized the despoilation of Tory-owned property, Washington carefully organized the procurement of firewood, and the feared deficiencies did not materialize. The troops were fortunate, too, that it was a relatively mild winter. The season began ominously, with the first hard freeze occurring in mid-October and the initial snowfall striking just thirty days later, but generally the autumn was pleasant, though wet. Washington took no chances, however. He had some men in tents, others in handcrafted tent-like lodgings constructed of sails requisitioned from coastal villages; most of the soldiery lived in the barracks he had set the men to building while the weather still was balmy.[62]

While Washington took these steps, his army did not entirely escape the visitation of diseases. Indeed, the problem existed even before Washington arrived in Cambridge. Diarrhea, jaundice, arthritis, respiratory infections, and pleuritical disorders already had struck the camp before July. In the fall "autumnal fevers"—that generation's terminology for such maladies as dysentery, malaria, and typhus—sortied into the encampment. By October nearly 15 percent of the soldiery were on sick call. Always the unhealthiest months in New England, this September and October witnessed the arrival of the riflemen from the South, men who brought along strange viruses to disseminate among the Yankee warriors; in addition, refugees from occupied Boston also transmitted diseases, and, in fact, the situation seemed so perilous at one point that an anxious Washington even convinced himself that General Howe was endeavoring to sow illnesses within his army by dispatching sickly civilians into his midst. To keep his army fit Washington decreed that any refugee behind American lines without a pass would be jailed, an especially drastic mode of quarantine. After mid-October the threat posed by disease abated, and by year's end only about 7 percent of the soldiers were incapacitated by illness.[63]

All the while, however, Washington had prayed that his army would be spared an outbreak of smallpox, a foe that he regarded as "his most dangerous Enemy." Luck was with him. The disease made only a mild appearance. Of course, Washington's good fortune was not due entirely to luck. He had shrunk from requiring that his troops be inoculated, lest that preventive measure might actually instigate an epidemic, but he did take other steps. He sealed entree to his army to all civilians coming from infected areas, isolated those afflicted with the illness, sought to maintain proper hygienic practices within the camp, and even ordered that all letters from Boston be dipped in vinegar before they could be perused. The commander also supported the formation of an army medical corps, and by late in July Congress had more or less complied.[64]

The state of the medical art still was so primitive, however, that a citizenry or soldiery in the grip of an epidemic was in great peril. Only a few—probably less than one hundred of approximately thirty-five hundred—American physicians had any formal training. Some of these men had studied in Europe at Leyden or Utrecht, but most were graduates of the University of Edinburgh. The great majority of practicioners had studied only as apprentices, and some had no training whatsoever. However they came to hang out a shingle, most doctors employed one of two treatments both for those diseases they could identify and for those that remained undetermined. They relied either on the humoral theory (bleeding, sweating, or purging the victims) or the tension thesis (which dictated the use of stimulants and narcotics, principally the derivatives of simple herb plants and of minerals). Surgery had not progressed beyond amputation, the extraction of teeth, and the treatment of wounds.[65] While Washington would not have shared today's reservations about the medical practices of his age, he knew full well that if his army was stricken by disease his doctors would shepherd precious few of the unfortunates through their trial.

Cheered by the recent recruiting successes, the generally good health of his army, and the blithe mood at headquarters, Washington radiated an increased optimism by year's end. In his exuberance, he even told Congress that he soon expected to receive word of an American victory in Canada.[66] On that score, however, the commander was quite wrong.

General Montgomery had indeed reached Quebec, but not until the terrible Canadian winter had struck. He arrived, too, with an army depleted by disease. But Montgomery's force was in better shape than that commanded by Benedict Arnold, with which it rendezvoused early in December. Arnold's little legion had just completed a six-weeks' trek through the Maine and Canadian wilderness, a journey of almost unrelenting suffering. To no avail, the two American commanders threw up an immediate siege of the tiny British garrison overlooking the St. Lawrence. By month's end, the enlistments of most of their men due to expire within a few days, Montgomery and Arnold faced a Hobson's choice: attack Quebec, or lift the siege and retreat. They chose to storm the garrison, a gamble that quickly failed. In the first moments of the assault Montgomery was killed. Minutes later Arnold was wounded, hit in the leg by a ricocheting musket ball. He fell, rose and tried to continue, fell again, was carried forward a few steps, then, faint from shock and the loss of blood, was conveyed to the rear. The fate of the two leaders extinguished whatever spark remained in the troops. The attack began to fizzle, and before sunrise the shooting had ended.[67]

At the close of 1775 General Washington had every reason to be pleased with his performance. His errors—indiscretions really—were born of frustration, and they were both forgiveable and inconsequential. His pronouncements about the people of New England would have been better left unsaid. His venemous assault on those citizen-soldiers who refused to reenlist was short-sighted, purely and simply. His disapproval of the militiamen may not have been fair, but many of his fellow officers shared his views.

In some ways Washington had merely continued to do what General Ward had been doing, for he too maintained the siege of Boston without introducing any dramatically new strategic moves. But, in fact, he had done much more. He had displayed a certain flair for administration and organization, and the army was the better for it. He had toiled to produce better officers, he had sought to transform a motley band of patriots into something approaching an army; he had ascertained what supplies he did and did not have and had carefully, tenderly prodded Congress and the New England governments to remedy the deficiencies he uncovered. Not surprisingly for a man who had watched Virginia's armies suffer for lack of neighborly assistance, he thought in broad, national terms, pushing always to make this war a truly continental effort. The assault on Canada that he concocted was a bold and imaginative stroke, and that he had begun a navy revealed both his creativity and his intuitive understanding of the kind of war this was to be. Washington had drawn on his command experience—and perhaps on his recollection of his own history of sufferings from camp ills—to see that his army remained generally healthy. Finally, Washington had set a good example. He had remained with his army, industriously at work, maintaining a low profile and winning good will by his sober and resolute conduct in the face of multitudinous problems. Mature and self-confident, he had avoided the kind of behavior that had proved such a source of trouble to him on the frontier of Virginia.

He should have felt quite good about things, and, in fact, at year's end he did seem buoyant: "Search the vast volumes of history through, and I much question whether a case similar to ours is to be found," he jubilantly told Reed. For more than half a year, he said, the American army had faced up to "the flower of the British army," even disbanding one force and creating another in their presence. It was a breathtaking feat. But then, as if reality suddenly intruded upon his optimism, he added: "How it will end, God in his great goodness will direct. I am thankful for his protection to this time." [68]

6

At the Brink

To "run all risques"

The "French & Spaniards do not seem inclined to furnish us with military stores," Francis Lightfoot Lee of Virginia grieved in the last half of January 1776. "Their politics," he continued, "plainly tend to drive us to extremity, that we may be forced to break off all connection with G.B. and join with them, which they know nothing but hard necessity can ever effect." [1]

Hard necessity! The colonists were learning just how difficult this war would be. Within recent weeks the port towns of Falmouth, Maine, and Norfolk in Virginia had been destroyed by royal warships, and in Virginia the governor, Lord Dunmore, had promised freedom to all slaves who fled behind British lines. Moreover, the new year brought word of Montgomery's death and the American failure at Quebec. Those tidings arrived on the heels of the text of King George III's address at the opening of Parliament, a speech that seemed to strike like a sledgehammer blow, for the monarch had spoken in bellicose tones, threatening even to hire foreign mercenaries to assist in the suppression of the colonial uprising. General Washington was angered by the remarks, but he also was confident that the king's words of "rancor and resentment" would drive Congress toward independence and toward seeking foreign assistance. [2] But if the monarch's message did not have that effect, perhaps *Common Sense* would move the Congress.

Washington received a copy of Thomas Paine's brilliant tract a few days after its publication early in January. The general rejoiced at its call for independence. The pamphlet expounded "unanswerable reasoning," he thought, and one way or another he must have made certain that the troops heard Paine's ideas, especially his notion that America could win this war. *Common Sense* was like a brief stimulant for Washington, for although his army was warm and well victualed—better off than the British army in Boston in this initial winter of the war—he otherwise was laden with worries. The recruitment of his new army proceeded, but at an agonizingly languid pace; in fact, such contradictory reports reached his desk from his field officers that he was not even certain how many men were under arms. In addition, if the Continental army possessed adequate supplies of food and wood, it was woefully short of powder, and there was a need for blankets and clothing as well. An arms deficiency also emerged suddenly in January, the result of poor administration at headquarters. The commanders simply failed to confiscate the weapons of the soldiers who left the service in December, realizing too late—when only about one hundred firearms were left in store—that many of the men had departed together with their newly appropriated, government-issued muskets. To compound matters the army's treasury was depleted, so that the purchase of arms and tents (for which the high command anticipated a need when the army took the field in the spring) was out of the question. "How to get furnished I know not," Washington lamented to Reed. "The reflection on my situation, and that of this army, produces many an uneasy hour when all around me . . . are wrapped in sleep," the general confided.[3]

To these worries was added the grim news from Canada, tidings which reached his desk about mid-January. Washington immediately called a council of war, to which he invited not only his generals but some members of the Massachusetts Provincial Congress. Augmentation of the army in Canada was the first pressing issue. The officers advised against pruning any more troops from the army besieging Boston, but they recommended that Washington urge Massachusetts, New Hampshire, and Connecticut each to raise a regiment to dispatch to the north. Washington agreed, and he implemented the decision without consulting Congress. Only later did he inform the legislators of his action, adding: "do me the justice to believe that, my intentions were good, if my judgment has erred."[4]

While Washington was concerned that Congress might question his prudence in this matter, he knew full well that others—those he sardonically called "chimney corner heroes"—doubted his resolve because he had not assaulted Howe's beleaguered army. Through Reed, who had taken leave of the army during the previous autumn to return to Philadelphia, Washington knew that some of the "wise ones," as he and his young friend quite privately referred to the congressmen, were unhappy with his passiveness. That realization, together with the news of the debacle at Quebec, plunged Washington into a melancholy and sullen temper. His mood swing can be discerned in two letters to Reed, missives written ten days apart in January 1776. The commander was cautiously upbeat and even self-congratulatory in his initial letter, but in his second he spoke of his mistake in taking the command and seemed to harbor a morose presentiment of failure, even speaking of retiring to the backcountry, there to live out his life in a wigwam.[5]

Some may have seen Washington as dilatory, but in fact no one was more eager than he to strike at Howe. The backstairs questioning of his strategy perhaps played a role in his yearning to act, although he hardly needed any prodding, for he had not extinguished that impetuous streak that at times had caused him grief two decades before as a frontier warrior. After all, this was the man who had preferred to fight rather than back off at Fort Necessity, who had spoken of the sweet sound of the bullets whizzing by his head, who had chafed under Dinwiddie's defensive policies during the French and Indian War. Those qualities that led an observant painter like Stuart to think of him as a man whose features were redolent of "the most ungovernable passions" and to dub him the most fierce man among savages did at times seem to govern Washington. This barbarous undercurrent was not his most pleasant side, a fact that Washington himself realized well enough so that he struggled to keep these dark emotions reined in. But the ferocity was there nonetheless, and it was one of the elements that separated Washington from other men—and that made him the daring and remorseless soldier that he was. The situation, he had said, required that he "run all risques." Yet, he did not make such a statement as a mere rhetorical flourish. It reflected his deep inner sensibilities, and the emotions that lay behind that succinct comment revealed him to be a warrior of the kind that his adversaries could not discover to command their own armies in this war.[6]

Thus, while Washington was gathered with his officers at that council of war he once again proposed an American assault on Boston, and this time his arguments prevailed. His officers consented, but only on two conditions: such an attack was expedient, they said, only if the army obtained both more manpower and more firepower. The leaders could facilitate the acquisition of troops, and, in fact, the field officers urged Washington to call up thirteen regiments of New England militia for sixty days' service, commencing February 1. The firepower that the officers desired was additional artillery, and they knew it was on the way. The previous fall Washington had dispatched Colonel Henry Knox, his head artilleryman, to Fort Ticonderoga in quest of additional cannon and ammunition. Three days before Washington convened the council of war he learned that Knox was on the way and that he possessed substantial ordnance.[7]

The tempo of the commander's work load increased immediately. His mood soared too. At last something was happening. All brigade officers down through the rank of major were summoned to headquarters for instructions. Washington accelerated the construction of barracks, a ruse to convince Howe that he was content to sit on the outskirts of Boston. He dispatched couriers to Philadelphia in a desperate attempt to procure enough powder so that Knox's efforts would not have been in vain, and he immersed himself in the most minute details of recruitment and the arming of his men. Quickly inundated by his suddenly enlarged responsibilities, he wrote Reed on two occasions, almost pleading with him to return to Cambridge.[8]

If Reed did not immediately return to Massachusetts, Colonel Knox did. He arrived with a greater cache of weaponry than Washington had dared to expect. Looking for upwards of fifty cannon altogether, the commander was pleasantly surprised to learn that Knox had secured sixty-six pieces: fifty-two cannon of various sizes and fourteen mortars. The Continental army's park of artillery had more than doubled, and with it Washington's confidence in his ability to intuitively judge men must also have swelled, for the mission he had assigned Knox was as difficult as any he ever ordered. For nearly two months Knox had grappled with execrable weather and forbidding terrain, first dodging treacherous ice floes on the Mohawk River, then transferring the ordnance to sleighs to assail the Berkshires.[9]

By mid-February everything was in place. The artillery, which had been disassembled for its arduous trek, had been reconstructed; in addition, Washington had sixteen thousand men at hand, slightly more than half of them enlistees in the Continental army. But before he moved he called his officers together again to consider the various alternatives. The commander perceived four options. First, he could do nothing—beyond maintaining the siege. That, he said, was no longer acceptable. Or he could attack Bunker Hill, hoping to dislodge the British. Such a triumph would be "highly animating," he allowed, but to succeed the assault would have to be a carefully coordinated surprise. It would be a risky operation, he continued, and a defeat—or inordinately high casualties in a victory—could be devastating for morale. He did not recommend this tack. A third choice was to endeavor to lure Howe out of Boston, possibly by securing high ground in the Dorchester area southeast of the city, or by installing his artillery either at Lechmere Point or on Noodles Island. He rejected this option too, on the grounds that he lacked the powder and ammunition for a protracted bombardment. That left only one choice, and Washington took it: a direct assault on Boston, commencing with a one-half-mile charge across the frozen Charles River. He knew the objections to such a tactic. Such an assault was certain to result in "considerable loss." Moreover, the fate of Montgomery and his men demonstrated the folly of sending green soldiers against entrenched regulars, and even Washington was compelled to admit that his men were not likely to "march boldly up to a work, nor stand exposed in a plain." Incredibly, however, this was what he suggested should be done. Perhaps he wished only to display his bravado to his subordinates, knowing that he could count on them to reject such an idea, though such an explanation is not likely. He had too much pride and too much political sense to engage in such foolishness. It is more probable that this was a straightforward recommendation, prompted by the audacious side of Washington, the bold, almost incautious man who was willing "to run all risques." [10]

Washington's officers would not hear of such strategy. General Gates, for instance, made two crucial points: the redcoats bottled up in Boston were doing no harm; moreover, if the colonists waited long enough, Howe would be forced to attack or to abandon Boston. Why not wait and fight on the defensive? Or perhaps not have to fight at all? Regarding the chances for success in Washington's plan to be "excedingly doubtful," the generals voted not to attack Boston. But Washington prodded them to do something, and this time his officers recommended that the army invest the heights at Dorchester or some similarly suitable point. Washington demurred, then he acquiesced in their counsel. Later, however, he shot off a letter to Reed in which he aired his irritation with these men, and still later he dispatched a softer missive to Congress, one in which he explained his position. But Reed's response echoed Washington's thinking. Some "members of your council never will concur in any measure which leads to danger," he replied, and he predicted that "you will make less and less use of them every day you are with them." Congress heard Washington with a judicious silence. [11]

Despite the intense cold, the commander immediately set the army to fortifying Lechmere's Point. Meanwhile, he and his staff prepared plans for the occupation of Dorchester Heights, an operation targeted for early March. A thousand details required his attention. Endless conferences sapped his energy. At last facing imminent battle—his first in nearly twenty years—he began to feel the strain of command. If worse came to worse, he resolved, he would flee to his lands in the Ohio Country. That was not the face his soldiers saw, however. On the eve of the operation he exhorted them to act with resolution and vigor, and he issued a blunt warning: "if any Man in action shall presume to skulk, hide himself, or retreat from the enemy . . . he will be *instantly shot* down, as an example of cowardice." [12]

Washington's plans called for two, possibly three, steps. The operation would commence with three nights of bombardment by Knox's ordnance at Lechmere's Point. On the third night, while the redcoats were preoccupied with the shelling, the main force of the Continental army would steal to the ridges at Dorchester. If Howe emerged for a fight, a third act would follow: a force of four thousand under Putnam, which was to be secreted along the Charles River in Cambridge, would be rowed across to Boston where it would try to enter the west side of the city while the principal British force was fighting in Dorchester to the southeast. [13]

As always, the long wait before the operation began was the most stressful aspect of the campaign. Curiously, however, Washington seemed to grow more composed as zero hour approached. Just before the operation was to begin he took to his desk to write Reed, drafting a chatty letter in which he discoursed on horses and the sort of conveyance that he desired. Then the wait was over. In the early hours of March 2, a sharp, dark night, the evening's tranquility was shattered by the sudden thunderous whomp of a colonial cannon. Rounds were fired intermittently for several hours, then according to plan the shelling ceased. The next evening a similar pattern was followed. But on March 4, about an hour after sunset, Knox's batteries once again sprang into action, this time spewing forth ten times as many rounds as on the previous nights. Simultaneously, the men moved out for Dorchester.

Infantry and riflemen led the way, taking up positions along the waterfront. If the British discovered the American strategy and responded quickly, these men would have to protect the colonial workers-soldiers on the hill. General Thomas, with three thousand troops and about three hundred hired teamsters, came next. They proceeded up the hill, their barricades in tow.

Expecting the earth to be too frozen to yield to a shovel, these men had spent the past two weeks constructing fascines and chandeliers and parapets fashioned from bundles of hay. At preassigned points these fortifications were deployed; some men, meanwhile, were set to work felling trees from which ramparts would be made, while still other soldiers, finding the night to be felicitously mild (though the earth was frozen to a depth of eighteen inches) were ordered to dig earthworks after all. About 3:00 A.M. this stage of the operation was completed. In about seven hours six separate fortifications had been built; if nothing else it was a stupendous engineering feat. Those bone-tired troops then were evacuated, replaced by three thousand fresh, anxious men who could only await the sunrise, wondering what it would bring, aware, but not much impressed by the knowledge, that this day, March 5, was the sixth anniversary of the Boston Massacre.[14]

Washington was certain that daylight would mean a British attack. They would *have* to attack. It was unthinkable that an honorable British general would withdraw without a fight. Certainly he would attack were roles reversed.[15]

When General Howe learned of the colonists' accomplishment his first inclination was precisely as Washington had imagined it would be. He ordered an attack. But the prospect he faced was not a happy one. So extensive were the colonists' fortifications that the British presumed that Washington had more than twenty thousand men on the heights. Nevertheless, Howe was coming. He made his preparations, painstakingly, meticulously putting everything into place, moving slowly. Hour after hour crept past. The only real British action was a brief, ineffectual bombardment, all their missiles falling well short of the continentals' installations. It is not clear whether Howe planned to debouch his men that night or at flood tide the next day. Whatever the plan, they never came. By late afternoon scudding wintry clouds appeared, and before nightfall they took on a menacing black cast. That night a late winter storm hit, unleashing howling, whirling winds that churned Boston Harbor and pelted the region with a cold, drenching rain. Powder and flints temporarily were useless, all naval craft were rendered inoperative. Given time to reconsider his initial decision, Howe opted not to attack, a decision acquiesced in by a council of war that he summoned the next morning.[16] More than Washington yet realized, this was the likely choice for a man who bore a terrible remembrance of Bunker Hill. It was a wise decision, too, for an onslaught against these two fortified ridges across Dorchester Neck likely would have replicated the horror of Bunker Hill. Yet, while it was to his honor that he cancelled what surely would have been an inexpedient sortie, his immediate predicament was due largely to his own lethargy. He had had nine months to appropriate these heights. Instead, he contrived one excuse after another for inaction, leaving the prize to his more dauntless, spirited adversary.

Washington did not know of Howe's decision until late on the fourth day of the operation. In the meantime work had continued on the Dorchester installations, and by the time he discovered that Howe was not coming he was so confident of success that he already had dismissed some of his militia personnel. On March 8 word of the British intentions was communicated by a committee of Boston selectmen: Howe wished to abandon Boston, and if Washington permitted him to depart unmolested—that is, if he did not use the cannon atop Dorchester Heights to blow the British fleet out of the water—he would not harm the city; otherwise, Howe pledged to raze Boston. Washington was uncertain. Was the note official? It was signed and sent by men who had elected to remain in occupied Boston, men who might be in league with the enemy. Moreover, if the letter was genuine, was the exchange of the inviolacy of Boston for the maintenance of the redcoat army a fair bargain? The general resolved the second question first. It would be an acceptable compromise. The destruction of Boston not only would establish a frightful precedent, it was bound to strain morale in other urban centers, and this on the eve of an almost certain struggle for New York City; besides, Washington was confident that Britain would have to see Howe's evacuation as a defeat, yet with the redcoat army intact sufficient dignity might be left to the ministry that it would end hostilities. As to the veracity of the note, Washington could only take precautions, and wait.[17]

The next few days dragged slowly by. Evidence mounted that Howe did indeed plan to abandon Boston, although a week elapsed before Washington told Congress that he no longer doubted the departure of the British army. But that made the wait for the redcoats' exodus no less discomforting. March 14, then another day, and yet another, came and went. The British still were in Boston. In the more relaxed atmosphere the Continentals' discipline waned; the army was losing its fighting edge. Yet the army might have to move quickly. No one knew where the British were going. Was it to Halifax? Or to New York? To the end Washington thought it was the latter, an eventuality that would require the hasty redeployment of his army several hundred miles to the south.[13]

Shortly after sunrise on Sunday, March 17, came the sight the colonial army had awaited. The men on watch atop the highest parapets saw it first. Squinting into the low-lying, radiant sunlight, they could see British contingents in formation at the city docks; soon other British troops were spotted abandoning their posts on Bunker Hill and within the defensive perimeter about the city. After almost nine years in Boston the British exit was imminent. Once the men began to file aboard ships the operation proceeded with extraordinary speed. Before noon the fleet had begun to move, gliding slowly and gracefully away from this city that had witnessed so many Anglo-American triumphs and tragedies over the past century and a half. Twenty-four hours later General Washington laconically told Congress what it had waited long to hear: "It is with the greatest pleasure I inform you that . . . the Ministerial Army evacuated the Town of Boston, and that the Forces of the United Colonies are now in actual Possession thereof." [19]

When the last ship had weighed anchor Washington dispatched a force of five hundred men (each of whom had to verify his immunity to smallpox) under General Putnam for a look at Boston. The forward troops reached the statehouse before noon, just minutes after the last British vessel had begun to drift noiselessly toward the sea. Indeed, the British were gone, Putnam reported; moreover, the city was in better shape than anyone had dared to hope. The next day the commander crossed over from Cambridge, the first time he had set foot in Boston since he had come to implore William Shirley to secure him rank in the British army. He discovered that Howe had left behind thirty cannon and a couple of mortars, some munitions, several baggage wagons, and nearly £30,000 worth of porcelain, carpets, blankets, coal, and provender. He had not left many Loyalists, however; dozens of frightened citizens who wished to remain loyal to the British Empire had sailed off with the army. Washington prowled about for a short time, mostly inspecting the fortifications that Howe had built. Then, after only a few hours in this city that had occupied his thoughts for so many months, he was gone, hardly pausing to savor the heady delights of his bloodless conquest.[20]

Whatever ecstacy the general felt at his prize, it was balanced by his concern for Howe's destination. Most of the fleet had sailed out of sight on the 17th. Some ships had stopped at Castle William, two miles out, first to sequester its contents, then to demolish the ancient fortress. The Boston lighthouse also was razed. Other ships in the fleet endeavored to obstruct the harbor. For more than a week the flotilla sat there, stretched over nine miles, from the harbor into Nantasket Road, out beyond the clearance stations. Washington did not worry about their return; in fact, during the week after his entrance into Boston he dispatched six regiments to New York. But where would the British go? "The enemy have the best knack at puzzling people I ever met with in my life," he told Reed in exasperation on March 25.[21]

Two days later, March 27, came the word he had waited. Three weeks and a day after he sent his men up Dorchester Heights a messenger arrived with the news: the British at last were going, they were "standing out for sea," as Washington reported. The British departure from New England heralded a new phase in this war. The struggle now was about to shift to another theater. The next morning General Washington ordered contingents of the Continental army to move out for New York.[22]

The humble George Washington who had assumed command in Boston in 1775 had not been at all certain that he was equal to his task. The triumphant Washington who took leave of Boston in the spring of 1776 was less diffident. "I resolved to take possession of Dorchester" and soon "the Flower of the British Army" withdrew "in a shameful and precipitate manner out of a place the strongest by Nature on this Continent," he trumpeted to his brother shortly after his success. His victory, he added, had been accomplished against enormous odds; indeed, he went on, "I believe I may . . . affirm, that no Man perhaps since the first Institution of Armys ever commanded under more difficult circumstances." More than ever Washington now was certain that military victory was possible. Divisiveness was his greatest foe, he reckoned, although he did acknowledge that the unexceptional quality of some high officers made him uneasy. He had entirely lost confidence in Ward and Wooster; Lee and Gates were the most reliable, he still thought, but as for the others he was mostly impressed by what he regarded as their overwariness.[23]

Washington had little time to relish his victory. It was something he would muse over in his retirement years, he told a correspondent. New York now occupied his attention, as it had intermittently since January. As early as January Washington had been convinced that his adversary was about to sail for New York. How to respond? Washington still was sufficiently uncertain of his powers to find himself briefly in a quandary. While he generally was responsible for defending the colonies, his immediate charge had been to assume command of the army in Boston. Charles Lee advised him that he possessed the authority "to take any step" necessary in New York, but Washington knew his garrulous subordinate well enough to take his suggestions with a grain of salt. Luckily, John Adams still was enjoying his Christmas recess in Braintree, and the general invited him to headquarters for a pot-luck dinner. How would Congress react, asked Washington after the meal, if he sent General Lee to take command in New York? Adams did not hesitate for a moment. No friend of the resistance could question such action, he responded; besides, "it is high Time that City was secured." Of course, the two men's presumptions about an imminent British withdrawal from Boston proved illusory, though General Henry Clinton had departed with a small force for Charleston, South Carolina. Nevertheless, Lee was dispatched to Manhattan, where he spent two hectic months in a futile endeavor to disarm the local Tories and to fortify the two islands that comprised New York.[24]

As was his custom Lee seemed to be everywhere at once, blustering at the Loyalists, noisily supervising the construction of defensive works, harshly drilling his new recruits. But for all his activity Lee accomplished little with the Tories. In fact, his severe, unyielding treatment of the Loyalists only aroused the moderate Whig leaders, cautious, conservatives who resented the loss of their local authority and who feared that the small British armada lying in the harbor might retaliate against Lee's methods by shelling the city. Faced with resistance from every side, Lee ultimately backed off, having arrested and disarmed only a tiny fraction of this unfriendly group, and having resettled none among this potentially partisan corps; whenever the British arrived they would find this faction intact, ready and willing to aid and abet the royal army in its efforts to suppress the rebellion. On the other hand, Lee's work on the fortification of Manhattan and Long Island proceeded uninterrupted. A savvy professional, his choice of positions for gun emplacements and garrisons was beyond question. But even as he carried out his assignments, Lee sensed that the ramparts would be ineffectual. An island was not a easy site to defend if your assailant possessed total naval superiority. Thus, his plan was less one of saving New York than of making Britain pay dearly for its conquest.[25] Yet Lee did not recommend against fighting for the islands, leaving the historian to guess whether his silence arose from a fear of being branded a weakling or whether, given political realities, he simply acknowledged that a struggle for New York was inescapable.

The defense of New York was but one piece of the puzzle. Although Washington complained that Howe's designs were "too much behind the Curtain" to fathom, he quickly—and correctly—guessed his adversary's strategy. Britain's first goal was to secure New York; not only would that keep communication open with London, but Manhattan and Long Island would offer engaging opportunities for foraging, even for raising large herds of their own livestock. The next step would be for Howe to unite his army with a British army moving south from Canada. The two should meet somewhere along the long, curling route of the Hudson River, a linkage that would effectively isolate New England, knocking it out of the war.[26]

Although Washington did not set out from Boston until April 4, about ten days after he ordered the advance units of his army to proceed to New York, he did accompany the bulk of his troops to the south. He sent his wife and her party west to Hartford, thence to New York, reputedly the most comfortable route. Washington and the army took the fastest course, via Providence and the coastal towns of Connecticut. The movement of an army was not a small undertaking. A line of thousands of men seemed to stretch to infinity, and the baggage train appeared to be even longer. Three hundred wagons, each drawn by a team of four horses, were assembled at the Commons in Cambridge, this to transport just the ammunition and stores of the regiment of artillery; nor could these items be loaded haphazardly, for thought had to be given to placing the most essential objects in the forward vehicles. More wagons were required for hospital supplies, although, whereas Washington had carefully directed Colonel Knox's packaging activities, he told Dr. John Morgan, Director-General of medical services, that he would "refrain from giving . . . particular Directions, leaving a Latitude to your Experience and Knowledge in your Profession." The commander placed responsibility for the deliverance of each van's contents upon the shoulders of its teamster, and he appointed an overseer, or "conductor" as he called him, for every thirty wagons.[27]

Leaving behind five regiments under General Ward, Washington and the troops commenced the two-hundred-mile journey on a bitterly cold spring day. The officers traveled by horseback; the men walked. An ambush or any sort of encounter with the British was out of the question, of course, so the strict precautions that might ordinarily have attended such a trek were forsaken; moreover, unlike those European forces which characteristically posted a large rear guard— more as a means of forestalling desertion than as a safeguard against attack—the American army could afford to be less wary. A quartermaster unit moved out well in advance of the main force, spending its days searching for an agreeable site for each night's camp. The army followed, troops of dragoons, or cavalry, preceding several infantry companies, followed by more cavalry, and so on. Next came the vans bearing items for each night's bivouac, then transports laden with weaponry and accouterments; the baggage wagons followed, then came the artillery train, and finally a small guard bought up the rear. The force was divided into squads of six men, each furnished with a tent and a heavy iron pot, which the men carried by turns. The soldiers were awakened before dawn, and were on the march again before the new day's sun had climbed very high, a march that continued—with only brief rest stops—until about four o'clock in the afternoon, early enough for the latrines to be dug and the firewood gathered for that evening's use, but late enough for the army to have covered seventeen or eighteen miles during the day.[28]

General Washington accompanied the army on the first day of the march, sleeping in a tent somewhere south of Braintree. But with all going smoothly he rode on to Providence, where he established his headquarters in the mansion of Rhode Island's governor, Stephen Hopkins. Three days later he rejoined the army in Norwich, Connecticut, but after a few days he again seemed to grow weary of its sluggish pace and he hurried ahead, reaching New York in mid-April. His army marched into town three days later. It had been a cold, dreary, often wet, transit, and at journey's end almost everyone seemed plagued by "the itch," a skin disorder that arose from poor hygiene and from sleeping on the ground; a variety of home remedies were prescribed, ranging from greasing one's skin with hog lard to painting the dermis with pine tar, but not surprisingly nothing worked. Homesickness set in too. Almost to a man these were New Englanders, and the march took most of them far from their homes for the first time in their lives. In their melancholy state some soldiers lost their appetite, and many eventually experienced the physical symptoms of illness. The high morale of March receded somewhat in April as the realities of soldiering grew clear for these farm boys and village mechanics.[29]

Nor were the commander's spirits raised by what he found upon his arrival. The deployment of defensive installations had not proceeded very far before General Lee was reassigned by Congress, receiving command of the newly created Southern Department. In his absence construction had virtually stopped, leaving Washington with a problem that he had presumed to be solved. Moreover, Washington found New York's political climate far different from that in New England. John Adams once had remarked that the New England outlook toward popular resistance was ten years ahead of that in the middle colonies, and Washington must now have discovered that he had been quite correct. Compared to Boston this city overflowed with Tories and fence-sitters; besides, so much contact subsisted between city residents and the nearby British fleet that he feared his adversary knew all there was to know of his army's strength, its movements, its works, its plans. This was a new problem, and one over which he exercised little control.

The city itself presented still another problem. During the siege of Boston Washington's troops had been stationed in rural areas and in rustic villages; now they were in a city, with its fleshpots and gin joints and a thousand other forms of merriment for bored and apprehensive young men. "It should be the pride of a Soldier, to conduct himself in such a manner, as to obtain the Applause, and not the reproach of a people," the general lectured, but his speech did not halt an avalanche of discipline problems. In addition, after being relatively well supplied in Boston, his men faced a sudden dearth of many items, the result of rampant thievery as well as of a simple breakdown in the delivery system that had accompanied the recent march. Nor had the chronic shortage of arms and the periodic deficiency of payroll funds been eliminated. Yet, these were minor problems. His greatest challenge was to find a means of defending this indefensible city. Soon he had time only for work. "I give into no kind of amusements . . . but are confined from Morn' 'till Eve" to Headquarters, he told the Congress in plaintive missive in April, his unruffled calm of the previous month now sorely tested.[30]

After he dug his way from beneath these initial difficulties, Washington's mood shifted to one of assuredness. He did not despair at the obstacles to defending Manhattan and Long Island. Indeed, all along he seemed to have believed that he possessed the means to rebuff the invaders. It was a naive supposition, growing in part from his overly charitable expectation of untested troops, from his ingenuous anticipation that his shore batteries could immobilize the British navy, and from his reliance on General Lee's skill in properly locating the gun emplacements. As late as July he predicted that the redcoats "will meet a repulse," for his troops had "an agreeable Spirit and willingness for Action." He was so confident that he even detached ten regiments for the Canadian theater.[31]

Washington's plan for defending New York was based on a very optimistic reading of General Lee's report. Washington concluded that British troops might land at four possible sites: on the southwestern point of Long Island, in Gravesend or Brooklyn; somewhere along the eastern side of Manhattan; on the southern tip of Manhattan; or at the northern end of Manhattan, the King's Bridge area. He ruled out a landing on the west side. Although Lee had concluded that it was vain to believe that British men-of-war could be prevented from navigating the Hudson River, Washington believed that by the artful deployment of *chevaux de frise* (booby traps made of wire nets and spikes) and sunken ships in the stream, the enemy would find the Hudson impassable; but even if the Royal Navy could use the river, Washington doubted that Howe would order an assault up the steep, high bluffs that looked down on the Hudson. Washington believed he could defend each of the possible landfalls. The geography of western Long Island was similar to that of Bunker Hill and Dorchester Heights, providing him with a distinct advantage; moreover, even though Britain would have total naval superiority, he concluded that the colonists' shore batteries on both Long Island and Manhattan could command the East River, the estuary that sluiced between the islands, thus affording his army both a lane of supply to Brooklyn and a route of retreat off Long Island. Moreover, he believed his well-entrenched army militated against a British landing on either the eastern or the northern sides of Manhattan. Washington radiated a cocksureness, even suggesting that the only thing that could defeat his army was a shortage of entrenching tools, the spades and picks necessary to construct ramparts and parapets.[32]

After five weeks of toiling with these matters, Washington left Israel Putnam in charge and hurried to Philadelphia for consultations with Congress. The legislators had requested the meeting, but he was no less eager to see them and to press for additional troops and supplies. While there he also hoped to induce Joseph Reed to return to the army. A year earlier when Reed had accompanied the general from Philadelphia, he was uncertain whether he would serve as an aide; ultimately he remained at headquarters for four months, laboring as he seldom had before, living what he called a "jog trot life." Despite their hectic, busy schedules, Washington and Reed grew quite close. Displaying complete trust in Reed, Washington brought him into the most confidential meetings, and, late at night when the day's work at last was completed, the two men frequently relaxed and talked, the general at ease, informal, sipping a glass of wine and indulging his penchant for nuts, and revealing to Reed a side that he permitted few other men to see. Reed probably grew closer to Washington than did any other person during this war, nearer and more intimate perhaps than anyone other than George William Fairfax. A strong bond evolved between the two men, a relationship that must have mirrored Washington's earlier affiliations with Lord Fairfax and General Braddock, only this time the commander played the role of the older man of power and Reed took on the part of the surrogate son. But in the fall Reed took an indefinite leave from the army, hurrying home in the hope of saving his foundering legal practice, virtually his only source of income.[33]

Not many weeks passed before Washington was almost pleading with Reed to return. He even used his influence with Congress to secure a pay raise for the secretaries, hoping that would induce this gifted young man to hurry back to Cambridge. Reed, however, always replied evasively to Washington's entreaties, explaining that he would return when his affairs were in order, or that he would be there for the summer campaign in 1776, but never mentioning precisely when he planned to leave home. In April Washington called again. The war was shifting to New York, he said; he desperately needed Reed's political savvy to deal with the merchant-politicians in that city. This time Reed appeared ready to go, even moving his wife from Philadelphia to a safe haven in New Jersey, but at the last minute Pennsylvania's tempestuous domestic political situation bubbled over, and Reed begged off in order to serve his province. Left with no choice, Washington dropped the Pennsylvanian and named Robert Harrison as his replacement.[34]

On the eve of the commander's visit with Congress, however, another means of securing Reed's services presented itself. In mid-May Congress promoted General Gates, leaving open his post as adjutant general; Washington decided to sound out the legislators about naming Reed to that position, hoping that, if they would oblige, the young Pennsylvanian would find the higher pay and greater prestige of that post a sufficient inducement to bring him back into the service. Washington reached Philadelphia during the third week of May, and he must have immediately seen Reed at one or another social gathering; but ten days passed before he formally tendered the adjutancy. Reed was as perplexed as he was surprised by the offer, for he had neither command nor military experience. He remained an opportunist, however. A "great revolution has happened in my prospects," he told his wife. The £700 annual salary "will help to support us till these calamitous times are at an end," he assured her, adding that his sudden elevation to the rank of colonel "must put me on a respectable basis" if the war ended favorably for the colonists. As Washington expected, Reed accepted the offer.[35]

During his stay in Philadelphia, Washington appeared before the entire Congress on two occasions. He also met with two special committees that Congress empaneled after his arrival. The commander frankly told the congressmen that the pending British attack in New York, together with that summer's campaign in Canada, "will probably decide the Fate of America." He recommended the strategy that Lee earlier had proposed: make the British pay dearly for every inch of soil they secured. What he required to accomplish that objective, he said, was manpower, a two-to-one superiority if possible. He proposed that Congress fund additional enlistments—the recruits to be enticed by cash or land bounties—and that the legislators raise more than thirty thousand militiamen from the colonies for short-term service.[36]

Washington's arguments were artful and persuasive, but Congress already had been moved by news that preceded the commander to Philadelphia. Two days before his arrival word reached Congress that Great Britain had signed treaties with various German principalities to hire mercenaries. The Congress listened to Washington, then it mobilized 6000 militiamen for Canada, and 13,800—whose tour of duty was to extend until December 1—were summoned for the coming clash in New York. In addition, Congress authorized Schuyler to hire 2000 Indian allies, and it called up another 10,000 men from the middle colonies, a reserve that was to be mustered and organized into a "flying camp," a mobile force that could be summoned on short notice. Although Congress failed to approve any manner of bounty that might have facilitated recruiting, it believed it had done all that was necessary. "I am in no doubt [that] our enemies will not be able to support the war another year, said Congressman William Whipple of New Hampshire, expressing the shortsighted but prevalent view.[37]

If Washington was happy at Congress's generally obliging attitude, he must have been equally delighted by another sentiment that he discovered in Philadelphia. Most congressmen now seemed prepared to proclaim America's independence from Great Britain. Through the winter and early spring months of 1776 many legislators rather timorously had held out the forlorn hope that London was sending emissaries to negotiate a settlement. Gradually, as it became crystal clear that the ministry was unwilling to make concessions, radical strength grew; in April Congress threw open the colonial ports to trade with nations outside the Empire, and the next month the legislators directed each colony to abrogate its charters by instituting governments responsive to its own citizenry. When Washington arrived in Philadelphia, moreover, he learned that the House of Burgesses in Virginia had resolved that his province should be "absolved from all allegiance" to Britain. Just after he left to return to New York, Congress took its most decisive step. On June 11 a committee headed by Thomas Jefferson was created to draft a declaration of independence.[38]

Washington had to be gratified by these trends. Although silent on matters of independence, he gave every indication of having cut his ties with the parent state by the time he assumed command. Certainly his response to *Common Sense*,

George Washington, by Charles Willson Peale (1776). Courtesy of the Brooklyn Museum, Dick S. Ramsay Fund. Washington, age forty-four, sat for Peale during his visit to Congress in 1776.

Martha Washington, by Charles Willson Peale (1776). Courtesy of the Mount Vernon Ladies' Association of the Union. Martha Washington was forty-five when Peale made this painting.

as well as to British policies since 1774, suggests that his sympathies lay with the separatists. His amicable feelings toward his "lordly masters" in London long since had vanished, while his realization had grown that foreign assistance might be crucial for American military success. And, like Paine, he knew that certain European powers would extend a helping hand only if America altered its war aims from reconciliation to independence.

Before he left Philadelphia Washington reluctantly agreed to sit once again for Charles Willson Peale, a session commissioned and paid for by sycophantic John Hancock. Martha's portrait also was to be painted, but she refused; wan and tired from having only recently completed the ordeal of a smallpox inoculation, she was too weak to endure a protracted sitting. Rather than offend the president of Congress, George consented, but whereas in 1772 he had told Peale how he wished to be rendered, he now permitted the artist a free hand. The result was a stiff, artificial pose, fairly typical of that century, aside from the work of a more adept craftsman, someone like John Singleton Copley, for instance. With the scenes of the late siege of Boston forming a backdrop, Washington is shown with his left hand thrust inside his buff and blue waistcoat, his right arm, twisted in an awkward, affected manner, resting on a walking stick. Washington is overweight, looking every bit like a man who had just completed a tour of enforced inactivity behind a desk; his inelegant middle-age paunch endangers the buttons on his waistcoat, a noticeable double chin gropes toward his collar. His face—almost certainly drawn too long, too oval by Peale—is expressionless, characterless, betraying neither smugness nor satisfaction, neither confidence nor apprehension.[39]

Washington returned alone to New York immediately after Peale dismissed him. Martha stayed behind for a brief spell until she had recuperated fully, then she rejoined him at headquarters. Her trek to New York was pointless. On June 29, just a few days following her arrival, American officials glimpsed the lead ships in the British invasion armada, their great white sails and majestic, multicolored flags bobbing in the glistening waters off Long Island. One hundred and thirty-two sails were counted, all lapping into view within the space of five hours. This was it! The summer campaign at last was near. Washington did not hesitate. He indicated that Martha must leave immediately, and less than twenty-four hours after the first of the enemy's vessels were spotted she set out by carriage on the long, weary ride back to Philadelphia, where she intended to stay pending the course of events.[40]

With Howe's arrival Washington brimmed with fervor, giving every indication that he was keen for battle after a year of the tedium of headquarters. He knew that he occupied center stage in a stirring historical drama, and he gloried in it. The next few weeks would determine "whether Americans are to be, Freemen, or Slaves," he told his soldiers. "The fate of unborn Millions" depended on his army, he continued, sounding more like Paine than himself. The choice was stark: "conquer or die. . . . The Eyes of all our Countrymen are now upon us, and we shall have their blessings, and praises. . . ." Privately, however, Washington acknowledged that he did not believe this campaign would end the war, but he did think it probably would be the turning point, for the victor here would have a decided psychological edge over his foe.[41]

The euphoria that Washington temporarily exuded upon the British arrival soon was buried beneath a profusion of new troubles. On an almost daily basis, reports crossed his desk that must have caused him to wonder at the capability of his army. To his considerable alarm illness spread rapidly through his legion. The new militia troops brought fevers with them, touching off an epidemic of affliction.[42] But that was only the beginning of his troubles. The rate of desertion accelerated rapidly that summer, particularly after the men glimpsed the forbidding sight of the huge British fleet; week after week, with monotonous regularity, courts martial ordered thirty-nine lashes for offenders, but the punishments were as ineffective as they were repetitive.[43] Men sometimes vented their frustrations and anxieties upon one another, and at times pointed sectional differences disintegrated into open fighting as men from one part of the country fought their brethren from another region. Nor were the enlisted men the sole source of his difficulties. In violation of his orders officers repeatedly led their men on pillaging forays, stealing and plundering innocent civilians, and causing Washington to express his concern that New Yorkers soon might fear the army sent to protect them more than they feared the army about to invade them.[44]

Washington anticipated problems with the local Tories and he was not disappointed, but when evidence was uncovered of Loyalist machinations within his own army he was mortified. An alleged Loyalist plot against Washington was discovered after an imprisoned counterfeiter grew suspicious of some of his fellow jailbirds. One of the inmates in New York City's gaol was Sergeant Thomas Hickey, not only a Continental soldier but a member of Washington's guard. Incarcerated for passing bogus bills, Hickey supposedly was overheard chatting with visitors about his plans to kidnap or to assassinate the general. When Hickey's gaolmate snitched, an investigation was opened. Twenty or so presumed Tories were seized, and under heavy pressure some offered incriminating testimony against Hickey. New York buzzed with rumors of the plot. Hickey was doomed. Still in jail, that unfortunate soldier suddenly found himself charged with mutiny and sedition. In a court martial that lasted less than a morning, the defendant was confronted by a parade of frightened suspects and obsequious plea-bargaining prisoners; moreover, with a British assault imminent, some in the high command thought this the perfect opportunity to provide soldiers and civilians alike with an example of the fruits of disloyalty to America. The military tribunal found Sergeant Hickey guilty and sentenced him to death. General Washington refused to intervene. Before nearly twenty thousand spectators—most of them soldiers—Hickey was hanged. Few men ever have been convicted or put to death upon such flimsy, uncorroborated evidence. Whatever he was up to—if anything beyond passing green goods, and, in fact, he was never convicted on that charge—Hickey was the victim of a churning hysteria, a frenzy that had penetrated headquarters itself.[45]

Hickey soon was forgotten at headquarters, however. One ominous tiding after another seemed to be rolling in. On July 12 two British warships, a schooner, and two tenders blithely sailed up the Hudson, effortlessly gliding past the snares that Washington's men had labored for three months to install, and easily evading the Americans's shore batteries. Washington's cannoneers discharged nearly two hundred rounds. More might have been attempted, but at least half the artillerists failed to heed the call to arms, some because they were too intoxicated to respond, although the poor marksmanship might suggest that some inebriated gunners did report. "I am apprehensive," Washington wrote that afternoon. That was an understatement. He now knew full well how easily the British could cut off his withdrawal from Manhattan, for he had presumed all along that should worse come to worse he could escape across the Hudson or to the northeast via King's Bridge. In addition, he feared that the British could now sever his communications with Albany, and thence with the army in Canada. Three weeks later Washington was jolted by still more unfavorable news. Sir Henry Clinton, with a force of three thousand men, sailed into New York harbor. His return from the South was an eventuality that Washington had not considered. With Clinton present, together with the foreign mercenaries who were expected daily, Howe would have an army of thirty thousand, not to mention the stupendous fleet that would assist his every move. Washington reported 10,514 as present and fit for duty.[46]

On top of this portentous intelligence was a steady flow of bad news from the front in Canada. Part of the problem was Schuyler, who remained in Albany while the war was being waged far to the north; this made as much sense as if Washington had sought to direct the siege of Boston from under his rear portico at Mount Vernon. Congress was part of the problem too, for it permitted this state of affairs to continue, although the congressmen faced a predicament. The last thing Congress wished to do was offend Schuyler and his fellow New Yorkers on the eve of Britain's invasion of that province. Schuyler aside, however, the most serious problem confronting the army in Canada—as General Lee said—was simple: the Americans lacked the manpower and the heavy artillery to win that war.[47]

The manpower situation only grew worse. As soon as British reinforcements arrived in the spring, Governor Carleton took the offensive. By early June the American army had been sent reeling back toward the border. Even worse, General Sullivan, whom Washington had earlier dispatched with six regiments of reinforcements, suddenly found himself to be the ranking officer. Anything but a slacker, Sullivan counterattacked. Predictably, his move failed, and with disastrous losses. By July the "lifeless" army, as Sullivan called his force, was back at Crown Point in New York, and with nothing to show for its ten-month adventure—save for the loss of perhaps thirty-five hundred or so soldiers.[48]

The legacy of this fruitless, ugly northern war persisted, however, even after the last shot had been fired. Almost from the moment that Sullivan had assumed command in Canada, Congress had been anxious to replace him with a more experienced officer. It was a notion with which Washington concurred, for while he found Sullivan to be "useful and Good," a man of probity and knowledge, an "enterprizing genius" even, he also was aware of "his foibles." These he listed as "a little tincture of vanity, and . . . an over desire of being popular, which now and then leads him into some embarrassments." Washington favored Gates for the Canadian command, although he did not lobby for his appointment; albeit, with considerable skill Washington did use his influence to prevent Gates's appointment as the commander in Boston, thus keeping him open for the Canadian slot. It was a masterful stroke, betraying Washington's skill in bureaucratic infighting. Ultimately, too, he got what he wanted. In the spring Congress named Gates to the post in Canada. At the same time, General Ward was assigned the command in Boston, a site no longer near the military front.[49]

As early as mid-May Washington knew that the American sortie into Canada was almost over, and he dispatched no additional reinforcements to that theater. His need for troops was greater. He directed Ward to send some of the artillery-men left behind in Boston, then he issued urgent requests for state troops from Connecticut and Pennsylvania, telling the governors of those two states that "at such a time as this" he would not "scrutinize with the Terms of the Inlistment," or with much else for that matter.[50]

Washington got his troops in many ways. Some served because they were conscripted, others volunteered more for the cash bounty offered by most states than because of an overzealous sense of patriotism. Some men were bamboozled into enlisting by glib clergymen and local luminaries, others were plied with alcohol by ignoble recruiters who knew that elixir was more persuasive than they ever could be. Some men volunteered to please their fathers; some joined to defy their fathers. More than one man enlisted in the hope that some village maiden would be impressed by his pluckiness. There were those who sought adventure, and there were those who indeed were stirred by patriotic fervor.[51] One way or another General Washington's army was assembled.

And then he waited. There was nothing else he could do. General Howe would decide when the war would begin in earnest.

7

Washington's War Begins

"A Wilderness of uncertainties and Difficulty"

The "Enemy have made no movements of consequence:—They remain in the same state" as they have been in for the past month, General Washington reported to Congress in mid-August 1776. But he knew it would not be long before the blow fell. The summer was vanishing rapidly, and in a hundred days or so the British command would have to think of winter quarters.[1]

Washington had expected the attack for weeks. What he did not know was that General Howe had been ordered to postpone his strike until reinforcements arrived. The order had come down from the new colonial secretary, Lord George Germain, who had succeeded Dartmouth the previous autumn. A discredited former soldier (he had been convicted of disobeying orders on the battlefield during the Seven Years' War), Germain somehow had resuscitated his career and landed this major cabinet office. One reason he got the post, perhaps, was that he shared the prime minister's myopic view of the American rebellion. Like Lord North, Germain persisted in the belief that the great majority of colonists remained loyal to Great Britain. Get enough troops to America, they thought, and one sharp campaign ought to restore the pro-British governments to their rightful places. Thus, Germain had wheedled redcoats from various and sundry remote outposts, although the bulk of the reinforcements were to be German mercenaries, about half of whom would come from the little principality of Hessen-Kassel. The princes of that state had been in the business of hiring out their soldiers for a century; the British had been renting their services for half a century. As soon as the news of Bunker Hill reached London the government dispatched an emissary to the Continent in search of troops, and, by Christmas, Whitehall had concluded treaties that committed three German principalities to furnish seventeen thousand troops. The Hessians had agreed to contribute eight thousand of these men, and they sailed for America in the spring of 1776.[2]

While the Howe brothers awaited the arrival of these additional units, they exchanged their military headdress for peace bonnets. Appointed peace commissioners by the North government, the Howes had nothing new to offer. In fact, they even were constrained from negotiating until the colonists had surrendered and informally acknowledged the supremacy of Parliament. Nevertheless, the Howes were anxious to test the waters, and two days after the admiral arrived in New

York—and less than forty-eight hours after the men-of-war *Phoenix* and *Rose* had glided provocatively past the American batteries and the Hudson's *chevaux-de-frise*—they sought an interview with Washington. Under a flag of truce they dispatched a naval officer with their missive. Washington sent Reed to receive the gentleman.

"I have a letter, sir, from Lord Howe to Mr. Washington," the officer said, after bowing graciously to the American adjutant.

"There is no such person in the army," Reed replied coldly. "I cannot receive a letter for General Washington under such a direction."

Would he at least look at the letter? Yes, said Reed. But when he saw it was addressed to "George Washington, Esq., etc., etc., etc.," he refused to accept it for the general.

What title would be acceptable?

"You are sensible, sir, of the rank of General Washington in our Army," Reed replied with acerbity.[3]

Within the week the problem of titles was resolved (the British now referred to him as "General Washington"), and the general agreed to talk with Howe's adjutant general. Held at Knox's headquarters on Broadway, the session was cordial, though unproductive. The British officer, who throughout the interview addressed Washington as "Excellency," began with the remark that General and Admiral Howe wished to open negotiations toward a peace settlement. Washington countered those tidings with the news that he lacked the power to conduct such talks. He turned instead to the matter of American prisoners of war in Canada, but as it turned out the Howes lacked jurisdiction in that quarter. So after a few brief minutes the parley ended. Still, with Washington's sanction Reed met three times later in the week with Lord Howe's emissaries; all that came of these sessions, however, was confirmation that the British were unprepared to offer any substantive new peace proposals.[4]

Washington had never expected much to come of such talks. Now he was confident that Britain's failure to offer more than a pardon in exchange for a surrender would solidify public opinion behind the war effort. It was the second event within a week that had served as a morale-builder. On July 9 he learned officially of the Declaration of Independence, and that evening, while the still-hot sun beamed down, he summoned the army to the parade ground to hear the document read. Up and down the line brigades of men heard stentorian-voiced officers read Jefferson's stirring document; then they listened as the same officers read a somber statement by the commander in chief. Independence, Washington began, "will serve as a fresh incentive to . . . act with Fidelity and Courage." And, he cautioned, independence will depend "solely on the success of our arms."[5]

Buoyed by these developments, and hoping to strike before the mercenaries arrived, Washington briefly contemplated an assault against Howe on Staten Island. Manpower shortages and a lack of naval craft soon forced him to abandon such thoughts, however. But if it was action that he hungered for, Washington knew that he would not have a long wait. Early in August, Clinton's army returned from South Carolina, and a week later the initial batch of Hessians dropped anchor below Long Island. Now Howe's blow could not be far away.[6]

When a week passed without an attack, Washington attributed Howe's inaction to the chronically inclement weather of that August. In reality, the British had delayed their assault because nearly eight hundred of their German auxilliaries were afflicted with various ills, ranging from dysentery to fevers to scurvy, the legacy of a baneful nine-week voyage to the New World.[7] These problems were not unique to Washington's adversaries. By mid-August he was complaining of the "Sickly condition" of his own men, including an alarming number of field officers. One of the most seriously ill was Nathanael Greene, in command of the Continental troops in the Brooklyn sector; stricken by fever and nausea on August 15, he still was bedridden five days later when all signs pointed to an imminent attack, and one now almost certain to commence in the vicinity of Brooklyn. Greene had to be replaced. But by whom?

The two highest-ranking officers present were John Sullivan and Israel Putnam. It was an impossible as far as Washington was concerned. So certain was he of Sullivan's liabilities that he had taken the highly unusual step of divulging to Congress his sentiments about the New Englander's "foibles"; on the other hand, despite the facts that "Old Put" was a veteran of the French and Indian War who had commanded with valor and success atop Bunker Hill and that he was familiar with the terrain of Long Island, Washington was not comfortable with him. Finally, the commander leaned toward Sullivan, perhaps because he was younger and because he burned with a desire to erase the stigma of his recent setbacks in Canada.[8]

That same day Washington told his army to expect the British assault as soon as the wind and tide were favorable. It was not an idle guess. Stirrings had been detected in the British fleet lying at anchor in The Narrows. Forty-eight hours later, at sunrise on August 22, the Americans could count an armada of four hundred transport and thirty-seven men-of-war in Gravesend Bay south of Brooklyn. This was it![9]

During the day vessel after vessel brought British and German troops to Long Island. They came ashore unopposed. Inasmuch as Washington based his plan of defense on the model prepared in the spring by General Lee, he never had intended to challenge the British landing. Since April his men had been digging an arcing line of five interconnected forts and entrenchments in the hilly Brooklyn Heights area, a district about six miles inland from Gravesend Bay. The site was ideal, for forward of these works, in the region where the British had moved into Long Island, the topography was table-top flat (thus the name of villages like Flatbush in that sector); immediately before the American lines a thick, virgin forest posed a forbidding obstacle to men and an impenetrable barrier to horse-drawn artillery. Hence, if the British reached these elevated abatis, they still could look forward to assaulting a Bunker Hill–like parapet. Keeping the adversary from this string of forts, however, meant controlling the many roads that radiated from the beach toward the hills. Lee and Washington believed they had planned for this too, and throughout that hot, dry summer troops had toiled to scratch earthworks out of the rock-hard soil in the zone where the littoral flatlands yielded to rolling woodlands. Washington's plan, therefore, was to fight where he could use the terrain as an ally, and that was not on the beach.[10]

Throughout the long day of the landing Washington's headquarters was kept abreast of every British endeavor. The commander, however, did not cross over to Brooklyn, for it was possible that Howe's landing was merely a feint. Indeed, Washington's suspicions soon grew. For one thing, his agents told him that the British had landed just eight thousand men on Long Island, too few, he reasoned, to be their principal assault force. Daylight on the 23rd brought no strike. The day passed, and the next as well; other than some small arms fire around Flatbush Pass, the British remained inactive. By noon on the third day Washington was virtually certain that the landing was a ruse, although he now decided to cross to Long Island for a first-hand look. What he saw when he rode down to the earthworks south of the heights was staggering: his intelligence network had made a stupendous error: instead of eight thousand British and German troops, nearly twice that many adversaries had come ashore.

Shaken by his discovery, Washington summoned reinforcements. He also was seized by a fit of indecision, choosing this moment to second-guess himself. With an attack likely at any moment, he removed Sullivan from command on Long Island, placing Putnam in control. He moved Sullivan over to command the left in the Continentals' most forward line; Lord Stirling remained in charge of the right. Stirling was a New Jersey grandee who claimed a Scottish earldom, pretentiously affixing the title "Lord" to his more commonplace name—William Alexander; Stirling had served as an aide to Governor Shirley in the French and Indian War, but he had not become militarily active in the Revolution until months after Bunker Hill, and even then his chief claim to fame was that he had led the corps that captured New Jersey's governor, William Franklin.[11]

Washington returned to Manhattan and waited. Two more days and still Howe had not moved! But on August 26 information seeped into headquarters that indicated the attack was imminent. Late that afternoon he returned to Long Island. This time he did not have long to wait. That night, while Washington slept, his war finally began.

About midnight a British column—ten thousand men strong—quietly moved out. Led by three local Tories, they took a circuitous route to the front; swinging far to the east of the Continental lines, their objective was the Jamaica Road, which would convey them behind America's most forward emplacements. It was easier than ever they had dared imagine it could be. By 3:00 A.M. they had overpowered the lone American guards on the highway—five men who surrendered without firing a shot. At daybreak the British force back at The Narrows opened up on the Americans, though their attack, of course, was a diversion to

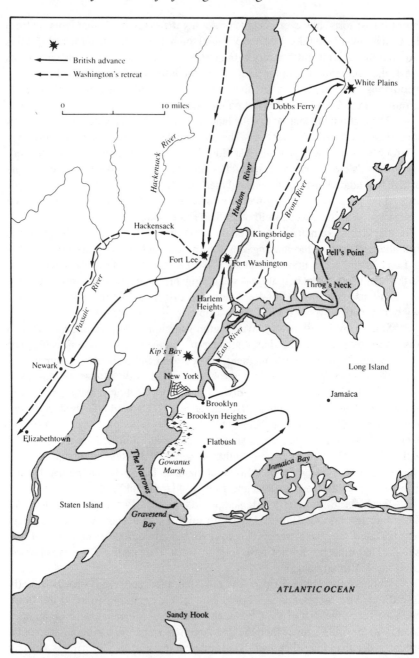

The New York Campaign

draw attention away from the flanking brigades about to march down the Jamaica Road. The callow American command fell into the snare, however, and in mid-morning the trap slammed shut. Just as the Continentals were congratulating themselves for their steely conduct in the face of this initial British attack, the main British army waylaid them from the rear. It was worse even than the ambush of Braddock twenty years before! How could ten thousand men, marching in a column two miles long and felling trees along the way to clear a path for their cannon, arrive unnoticed?

Sullivan took the worst of it. Attacked from the rear while simultaneously under assault in front by blue-coated Hessians, his men had no chance. Their lines collapsed. Soldiers fled into the woods or along the roads that led to the principal American redoubts three miles away in Brooklyn Heights. Meanwhile, the British sledge hammer methodically fell upon the American right under Stirling. Some of his men fled the moment they saw a blue coat, so fierce was the reputation of the Hessians. But generally he held his troops together longer than Sullivan, then these men also broke and raced pell-mell to the rear; for many the only escape route was through a swampy salt marsh, then across Gowanus Creek, deep and more than a hundred yards wide. Scores did not make it to safety. In a half day of fighting more than three hundred Americans were killed, and three times that many were taken prisoner. Both Stirling and Sullivan were among the captives, the latter apprehended as he hid in a cornfield.[12]

It was a long, stressful day for General Washington. With Reed always at his side, he had ridden here and there seeking accurate information, dispatching orders. That hard day was followed by a difficult night. The commander expected a British assault that evening, and he stayed up until early morning before he finally gave in to a few hours of fitful sleep. He awakened to find that there had been no attack. Indeed, the attack never came. Howe decided instead on a siege, overruling several of his battalion commanders who were eager to immediately storm the American redoubt. A siege would take longer, Howe knew, but he was confident that the result would be the same, and without the heavy losses that inevitably would accompany an attack. While he vainly sought sleep through much of that long, troubled night, Washington had guessed that Howe would opt for a siege operation. Sunrise brought confirmation. A British siege line was visible only six hundred yards away.[13]

Washington was in a box. Half his army was on Long Island, trapped there, in fact, so long as his adversary's navy patrolled the East River, his one conduit to safety. Yet, incredibly, Washington ordered still more men over.[14]

Luckily for Washington a cold, dreary rain fell all the next day, silencing the guns. It still was raining the following day as well, when the commander summoned seven generals to a war council. At last he had made up his mind. Long Island had to be abandoned. Somehow the men had to be moved back to Manhattan. He had no difficulty convincing his officers of the wisdom of retreating.[15]

He moved that night. The weather was favorable for that, if for nothing else. Late in the afternoon the rain had tapered off, then quit, jeopardizing the operation; at the mercy of the elements, Washington had waited anxiously. But the murky, clouds had persisted, and as evening turned to night a fog stole in, dropping a thin white curtain about the redoubt and the Brooklyn beach. It was then that the operation commenced, a move to get twelve thousand men off Long Island in about eight hours. And without being discovered.

The men were assembled and prepared to march. Sternly, they were ordered not to speak, not even to cough. They treked mutely to the beach, there to wait in silence for the vessels that would transport them across the broad river.[16]

The maneuver was a stupendous accomplishment. Little went wrong. Boats were found. The men were moved stealthily, without panic. Meanwhile, Putnam had some Native Americans in his detachment set about wailing and bellowing war chants, which, in turn, seemed to induce every dog on Long Island to yowl and yammer until such a clamor resulted that the British could not hear the sounds made by their retreating foe.[17] Howe awakened the following morning to discover that his bagged quarry had fled. Bunker Hill had paid still another dividend.

The Continental army had survived its first battle, but its problems had not disappeared. Disillusioned troops, fearing that the debacle on Long Island might only be a cataclysmic preview of what was to come, deserted in droves. Moreover, discipline verged on collapse among the men who remained in camp. Soldiers seemed to come and go at will, the lawless plundering of civilians increased, and an extraordinary degree of pilfering erupted within the army. (Someone even took the opportunity of Lord Stirling's captivity to burglarize his headquarters.) Washington threatened and cajoled, but his position was so tenuous that he was compelled to punish offenders in private, fearing that public floggings would provoke further defections.[18]

Washington attributed these problems to the example set by the militiamen, and he was partially correct. But he was all too willing to overlook the possibility that the errors committed by the officers might have shaken the confidence of the men. He dumped some blame on Sullivan's failure to secure the Jamaica Road, although that was as far as he was willing to go. He did not reproach himself.[19]

Still, Washington had learned from his distasteful experience with Dinwiddie two decades before. This setback was not followed by a string of whining, complaining letters. Though his rancor toward the militiamen remained unaltered, he now took pains to be tactful, almost magnanimous, in explaining their shortcomings. In addition, despite his feelings toward certain officers, not to mention his exasperation at chronic supply shortages, he refrained from the irritation that he had exhibited while he was the callow commander of Virginia's army.

Defending Manhattan was his most pressing problem. An island just like the one he so recently had fled, Manhattan presented Washington with the same problems he had faced on Long Island. In fact, said Reed, it was akin to being "cooped up . . . between hawk and buzzard" all over again.[20] If things went badly there were few escape routes to the mainland. One could cross King's Bridge at Spuyten Duyvil on the northern tip of the island, or one could traverse the Hudson into New Jersey; then again, with Britain's naval predominance egress through either artery was problematic. The commander had known since April of the adversities inherent in defending the place, yet he had remained the optimist, even in the face of the successful voyages of the *Rose* and *Phoenix*. However, the performance of his army on Long Island finally encouraged him to rethink the matter, as did a steady stream of advice, particularly from Reed and General Greene. Nevertheless, his views on strategy that September appear to have been muddled and confused, his thinking perhaps disjointed from fatigue and his bewilderingly hectic schedule.

On the one hand Washington favored abandoning New York, then razing the city in order to prevent his adversary from using it for winter quarters. On the other hand, he denounced the notion of evacuating New York as likely to "dispirit the Troops and enfeeble our Cause." At the same moment, however, an addled and uncertain—and obviously amateurish—General Washington spoke of the need to "avoid a general Action, or [to] put anything to the Risque." Instead, he seemed to hint, he favored a Fabian strategy of cutting and running, of avoiding a direct clash. "On our Side," he remarked, "the War should be defensive. It has even been called a War of Posts." On September 7 the matter appeared to have been resolved. Having learned that Congress expected the city to be defended, a council of war voted to fight for New York.[21]

Washington accepted his generals' recommendation, only to reverse himself five days later and summon a second council of war. He now urged the evacuation of New York, but he continued to believe that he could win a pitched battle with Howe—if his men "would behave with tolerable resolution." He had "never spared the Spade and Pick Ax," he said, nor had he in the construction of the installations in the hills of Harlem above the city. "We are a strong Post," he added. Harlem, not New York, was the place to fight.

The council agreed with Washington. General Greene, who had worked tirelessly to convince both the commander and his colleagues to reconsider the decision to defend New York, was partially responsible. In addition, just after the initial meeting the British occupied Montressor's Island at Hell's Gate, thus permitting their navy to seal off the escape routes east of the city. Most importantly, however, word arrived that Congress had clarified its position. It now authorized the abandonment, if not the destruction, of New York.[22] There was only one problem. The decision to quit the city was made too late.

Actually, the languid Howe brothers had given Washington ample time to act, but in this instance it was the American commander who was indecisive and sluggish. Two weeks elapsed between the American escape from Brooklyn and

Sir William's next move, a period the British utilized to launch additional peace talks, nudging them into life by paroling General Sullivan, who agreed in turn to ride to Philadelphia and urge the Congress to negotiate. In the end, nothing came of the episode except that Stirling and Sullivan were exchanged and rejoined Washington—and, of course, Howe lost fifteen days of good weather.

Finally, on September 15, Howe was ready. His plan was to invade Manhattan at Kip's Bay, about a third of the way up the east side of the island and well north of the city. Washington had expected the British to land about four miles further north, on the Plains of Harlem, but he did have men entrenched at Howe's projected landing site. Howe anticipated a difficult fight. His men would have to wade ashore, struggling slowly through waist-deep water, all the while braving the fire of the Americans. Once on the beach, moreover, the invaders still would be faced with surmounting a steep, rocky eminence before they actually reached the entrenched defenders. The British knew that success was not guaranteed, and on the eve of the attack anxious Hessian *Jägers*, the cream of the assault force, huddled together in the holds of the invasion armada quietly singing hymns.

The assault began on a Sunday, an unusually hot, muggy day for so late in September. Just after daybreak five British warships—one of them the hyperactive *Phoenix*—opened up on the coastal installations. The shelling did its work. Convinced that no one could survive the awesome bombardment, America's green officers ordered a retreat. Soon, panic set in. No longer was anyone in control, as the terrified soldiers rushed pell-mell for the apparent safety of a nearby, dark forest. A few minutes later the *Jägers* landed unopposed. "This on the whole was an unfortunate Day to the American States," a soldier from North Haven, Connecticut, noted in his journal that night.[23]

Washington was several miles away in Harlem when the muffled blasts of the flotilla were heard. He sped to the scene immediately, but by the time he arrived the American panic was in full swing. No words could describe the towering, purple rage that gripped Washington when he saw the troops—officers as well as men—racing for safety. He rode among them, screaming, cursing, pummeling the frightened men with his riding crop, but nothing could stem the blind terror of the soldiers. Suddenly an aide spotted a party of seventy or so Hessians approaching; in their preoccupation with stopping the rout, the general and his men had forgotten the enemy. The aide shouted an alarm, but Washington, stupefied, immobilized by his seething fury, was heedless. One of his men grabbed the reins of his horse and hurried Washington to a safer place.[24]

The Continental army's second major battle in New York was a second debacle. Still, the Americans were fortunate that the morning's disaster was not followed by an even more egregious calamity. With luck, and greater resolution, the British might have immediately severed the island, isolating the Continental force still in New York City. Certainly the British had the capability to do just that, for there was nothing to prevent the invasion force from driving all the way across Manhattan to the Hudson. But Howe, expecting stiff resistance, had ordered Sir

Henry Clinton, the commander of the incursionary force to secure the beachhead and await reinforcements before moving inland. A daring, intrepid general might have seen the opportunity and seized it. Not Clinton. He followed orders. Within two hours of the initial landing the British had four thousand men ashore, but none were more than a few thousand yards inland; by that time Putnam had evacuated the city and was using a seldom-traveled road—thanks to a tip from his aide, Aaron Burr—to retreat to Harlem. He brought out five thousand men and a considerable portion of the Continental army's artillery.[25]

The gloom that General Washington experienced that night probably was unmatched on any other day of this long war. In less than twenty-four hours, however, he was dramatically "inspirited," as he put it. The commander spent a busy night shoring up his lines on Harlem Heights, and early the next morning— at almost the same moment that the redcoats paraded down Broadway to take possession of New York—he dispatched patrols to discover what Howe had been up to. Garbled reports of British movements soon filtered back to headquarters. Reed, frustrated by his desk job amid all the action, volunteered to lead a party in quest of definitive intelligence. Washington consented. Not long thereafter the commander also rode out for a look. A few minutes later a contingent of Continentals on the left encountered a British advance party of three hundred, and a sharp fire fight erupted. Washington, joined now by Reed, hurried toward the sound of the shooting, arriving in time to hear an insolent redcoat bugler blow the call to a fox hunt. Reed was both enraged and embarrassed. The British impertinence "seemed to crown our disgrace," he said of their effrontery. But if Washington was piqued, he did not show it. Instead, he reacted by busily hurling reinforcements into the skirmish, and he watched with grim satisfaction as his men stood and fought, and eventually compelled their foe to retreat. It had been a small, insignificant encounter, but its effect on Washington was like a magic elixir. At last, he thought, his untrained men had "persevered . . . with the greatest Resolution."[26]

Reed, too, had fought well in his first taste of combat. He had thrown himself into the fray, hoping—he later said—that his example would inspire the troops. He was lucky to escape unharmed. His horse took a hit in its shoulder, the bullet missing his leg by only an inch or two. But his closest call came in a confrontation with an American soldier. In the course of the battle Reed ran upon a Connecticut private who was heading for the rear. When Reed drew in front of him to block his retreat, the soldier turned his musket on his interceptor and from a distance of only about five yards attempted to shoot. His piece misfired. Reed, in turn, tried to shoot him, but his weapon also failed; Reed then unsheathed his sword, slashing his assailant about the head, even cutting off his thumb, before arresting him. Later that unhappy soldier was court martialed and sentenced to die, a judgment that aroused a fury of indignation among the troops; they were convinced that the soldier had been ordered from the front in quest of additional ammunition. Headquarters learned of "secret and open threats" to mutiny if the death sentence was carried out, and, at the last moment, with the soldier before the firing squad, Washington ordered a reprieve, claiming he had done so because Reed had intervened to spare the man.[27]

The elevation of Washington's morale that resulted from the Battle of Harlem Heights nearly proved fatal. The events that followed Britain's Kip's Bay landing made for a compelling argument to abandon Manhattan, lest Howe plug all the avenues of escape. Washington, however, refused to consider such a step. Instead, he chose to remain in his bastion at Harlem Heights with half his army, while he stationed the remainder at King's Bridge. He seemed mesmerized by his craggy fortress, ever mindful of Bunker Hill, seemingly heedless of the lessons of Brooklyn and of the potential scope of British naval predominance. Nor did he seem to recall his recent dictum of avoiding a general action. Convinced that his men would fight, the commander sat back and waited Howe's assault.

But Howe had no intention of attacking these lines. Dorchester Heights and Brooklyn Heights had demonstrated that he had no stomach for such a blood-letting; besides, in this instance there was no need to send his men on such a mission. His plan, instead, was twofold: he would land a force on the mainland above Long Island Sound, cutting off Washington's lane of retreat to the north-east; meanwhile, his men-of-war would secure the Hudson north of Manhattan, blockading the flow of supplies to the Continentals. Washington would be snared, besieged in a giant trap fashioned by his own improvidence. Howe did nothing quickly, however. A month disappeared while he awaited reinforcements and secured New York City, his quarters for the coming winter.[28]

On October 8 Washington received a hint of the flaws in his strategy. The British ran another batch of men-of-war up the Hudson, shutting that river to the Continental army on Manhattan. Four days later Howe landed his army at Throg's Neck on the northern shore of Long Island Sound, about five miles southeast of King's Bridge. His operation to envelop Washington had commenced. Washington now was in greater peril than he had faced six weeks before in Brooklyn, if for no other reason than that he seemed unconvinced of the scope of his predicament. His entire army stood on the precipice of entrapment, yet he was certain that it could not happen. He did not think the redcoats could fight their way to King's Bridge. The ground between Throg's Neck and King's Bridge, he blithely told Congress, was defensible—it was "full of Stonefences . . . which will render it difficult for . . . a large Body of foot soldiers to advance"—and, besides, his men were in "good spirits." [29]

British ineptitude rescued Washington from the scrape. The landing at Throg's Neck was a monument to poor planning. In reality, the Neck was a small island from which the mainland could be reached only by traversing both a long stretch of marsh and a wide creek. It was a nasty undertaking under any con-ditions; it was murderous to ask a soldier to slowly wade through this exposed swamp in the face of enemy fire. So deadly was such an undertaking, in fact, that twenty-five Pennsylvania riflemen, the entire American force posted in the sector, stopped the redcoats cold, leaving Howe puzzled and inert for the next six days. Then he reloaded his army and conveyed it to Pell's Point—or Pelham—three miles away on the mainland, the landing site he should have chosen in the first place.

By then Washington had sent reinforcements to aid those Pennsylvania sharpshooters at Throg's Neck, but until four days after the initial landing he took no additional action. Then he called a council of war. One new face was in attendance—General Lee, back from his southern command. The officers conjectured that Howe planned to drive to White Plains, about seventeen miles north of Pell's Point, thence west to the Hudson. If he succeeded he would have possession of the high ground, from which he could block Washington's northward advance while the navy inhibited his escape in every other direction. At last the officers voted to abandon Manhattan, with the exception of Fort Washington, which still would be garrisoned.[30]

Had Howe moved quickly and resolutely he still might have scored a decisive victory—perhaps the pivotal triumph. But that would not have been Howe. Sir William was slow, so slow. By October 22 Washington was at White Plains. Howe arrived six days later. True, his force had encountered tenacious resistance en route, enough at times to thwart the redcoats' huge numerical superiority. At one point, in fact, 4000 of the enemy were paralyzed for days by just 750 Yankees. Chiefly, though, Howe himself was the problem. He continued to fight by the maxims of European warfare, unmindful that his adversary was not a European force, and seemingly oblivious to the fact that this was not a conventional war. Thus, when he reached New Rochelle he paused for three days. When he got to Mamaroneck, only two miles up the road, he stopped for four more days. As a disgusted British historian later observed, in the sixty days since he first had deployed his army on Long Island, Howe had progressed exactly thirty-five miles.[31]

The long-awaited collision of the two armies finally occurred at the end of October, but it was a relatively small-scale clash involving only about 15 percent of each force. Washington placed the bulk of his army in the hilly region behind White Plains, detaching about fifteen hundred men behind stone walls at the foot of these heights and another force of about equal size atop Chatterton's Hill, which overlooked his right wing. The British assault began in early morning, just as the sun peeked over the ridges. To their surprise, these Americans did not panic. They fought ferociously, stopping several Hessian charges before falling back. Howe then turned his gaze on Chatterton's Hill, an eminence that could imperil Washington's position. With tilled green fields and pastoral stone walls ranging about the summit of the knoll, this bucolic rise seemed too idyllic for the grim business at hand. The British opened with an artillery barrage that soon shrouded the ridge with a layer of dust and smoke, the latter curling from fires ignited in the dry forests by the cannonade. The assault came in mid-afternoon. Again the American forces fought well. Only when the British unleashed their dragoons, or cavalry, did some panic set in, and the hill was lost.

Washington moved out his wounded—about 175 Continentals had been killed or disabled in the long day of fighting—and laid plans for a further retreat, if necessary. For the time being, though, he was prepared to fight again in this spot. Few options existed. The British stood in front of him, and they quickly sealed off his exists on the right and left. He still could fall back to the north, unless Howe turned his flank and swept behind him, of course, though the terrain rendered such a British maneuver highly unlikely.

A day passed. Then two more. From time to time intelligence of an imminent attack reached American headquarters, harrying Washington, exacerbating the crushing strain under which he already labored. By November 1 Howe had received reinforcements. He had twenty thousand men, more than a four-to-three superiority. But he did not move. Four more anxious days passed. Nothing from the redcoats. After dark on November 4 a messenger arrived at headquarters. The British were moving; the Americans had heard the unmistakeable sounds of mobile wagons and the clattering rattlebang of marching soldiers. The commander ordered an alert. An attack was likely at any moment. At headquarters men strained to hear, awaiting the thunderous boom of artillery, the muffled clap of distant musket fire. Nothing. Minutes dragged past. No gunfire was heard. More minutes slowly ticked away. Then an unexpected sound, that of another courier. He brought puzzling news. The British had broken camp. They were returning to Manhattan.

The British have "made a Sudden and unexpected movement," Washington reported immediately to Congress. "The design of this Manoeuvre is a matter of much conjecture and speculation," he added laconically. The joy of their deliverance, thus, was muted only by their uncertainty at Howe's intentions. Some officers believed the British were retiring to their winter quarters; some anticipated a strike up the Hudson, northward toward the Highland passes. A few of Washington's advisors believed Britain was about to shift the war to the southern states. Still others guessed that the British soon would attack Fort Washington on Manhattan Island, then follow with an invasion of New Jersey. Washington thought the latter option was the most likely, but no one could be certain. All he could do was divide his army, a portion to protect the North, the remainder to defend a more southerly sector. The commander posted Heath at Peekskill with 4000 men, and he left Lee at White Plains with another 7000. He took 2000 men—less than 20 percent of the Continental army—to New Jersey, but he expected to be reinforced by 3500 men from the Flying Camp, and he had been assured that he could expect considerable assistance from the New Jersey militia.[32]

Before departing Washington reconnoitered the Highlands, then he rode south to Fort Lee, on the Jersey side of the Hudson and almost directly across from Fort Washington. He arrived on November 13, and immediately met with Nathanael Greene, the commander of the two posts. The bastion on Mount Washington was a pentagonal fortress, constructed entirely of earth. Defended by more than twenty-five hundred men, thirty-four cannon, and two howitzers, it sat atop very high, rocky ground; an attacker would have to surmount a steep incline, all the while exposed to the fire of the defenders. But the citadel was flawed, too. The British repeatedly had demonstrated their ability to navigate the Hudson, from whence their vessels could pound the installation. In addition, a protracted siege seemed certain to succeed. Fort Washington had no well. In fact, its commander, Colonel Robert Magaw, already had reported that the unavailability of water meant that he could not survive a siege of more than six or seven weeks. Washington knew all this, and, additionally, he knew that Reed, whom he trusted, advised against its retention.

On the other hand, General Greene, whom he also had grown to trust, counseled that Fort Washington could be held, that the British could be kept even from implementing a siege. Congress, furthermore, had unequivocally expressed its desire that the Hudson should be obstructed; Fort Washington offered about the last hope of answering Congress's wishes.

Defend the bastion or abandon it? Washington vacillated indecisively. To fight for the fort was to risk the loss of an army half as large as the one he would employ in New Jersey, while to jettison the place was to enhance the size of his army during the coming struggle in New Jersey. But to defend the fort and enmesh Howe in a protracted fight would mean that Howe might have to forgo any other offensives until the next summer.

Washington grappled irresolutely with these matters for three days, then he made a decision of sorts. He would cross to the fortress for a first-hand inspection. But it was too late. As his party was being transported across the river Howe launched his attack. The decision had been made for Washington.[33]

For once Howe had shaken loose from the unsettling remembrance of Bunker Hill, and with spectacular results. Within an hour or so of the opening shots Washington realized his error, but nothing now could be done. Howe was not even obliged to institute a siege. The supposedly impregnable bastion was taken on the very day the assault was launched. The Continental army lost 2818 men, almost all as prisoners of war.[34]

The episode was not Washington's brightest hour. Nor did his explanation for the catastrophe do him honor. He refused to bear the blame for the decision to defend the post, although the final responsibility was his alone. He had arrived at Fort Lee more than forty-eight hours before the attack, ample time to have ordered Magaw's withdrawal. Moreover, as the commander under whose guidance the fortress had been completed, he should have been familiar with its very real liabilities. Instead, Washington reproached General Greene for the disaster.[35]

For two months Washington had survived largely by fortuity. But his providential luck deserted him in the debacle at Fort Washington, an utterly unnecessary disaster that left many Americans with an uneasy sense of imminent doom. No one knew that better than Washington. "The situation of our Affairs is truly critical and such as requires uncommon exertions on our part," he accurately reported. Then he braced for Britain's pending invasion of New Jersey, falling back into the province, bent on putting a river between his meager force and his advancing adversary.[36]

Weeks of setbacks inevitably had sowed doubts, though the doubters were careful to keep their dissatisfactions hidden. Sounding like the "Virginia Centinel" of an earlier crisis, John Adams privately railed at the highest officers' negligence, indolence, and ineptitude. While he never suggested that Washington should be removed, he wished out loud that fall that Charles Lee were at headquarters; would his presence "not give a flow of Spirits to our Army," he wondered.[37]

Nor was Adams the only observer who questioned the army's leadership that autumn. The debacle at Fort Washington plunged Joseph Reed into hopeless despair, shaking his trust in some leaders, reawakening both his fear that the contest was lost and his inveterate opportunism. He too looked to General Lee. That loquacious entity had breezily surfaced in the northern theater only within the last few weeks; his star had never shown more brightly. As soon as Congress learned that he had thwarted Clinton's invasion of Charleston, he was summoned northward. By the time he reached New York—he had paused en route in Philadelphia to beguile Congress out of enough money to pay off the mortgage on his Virginia farm—the American armies had suffered the two mortifying defeats at Brooklyn and Kip's Bay. Lee had taken the lead in encouraging the relinquishment of Manhattan, and subsequently he performed capably in encounters with Howe above Pell's Point and at White Plains. He inspired confidence. Congressmen and local politicians were taken with him, a view shared by some of the younger officers. Lee did nothing to discourage such thoughts (who would have?), but he also was in no way disloyal or maleficent toward Washington.[38]

Reed found Lee to be a man with an opinion on everything, and no hesitancy about airing his beliefs. Such a man seemed to radiate decisiveness. Moreover, when Reed learned that Lee had counseled the abandonment of Fort Washington, that only confirmed his view of the wisdom of this ex-professional soldier. Five days after the disaster on Mount Washington, on the day the army crossed to the west side of the Passaic River, Reed, no babe in the woods when it came to playing both sides of the fence, wrote to this meteor: "I do not mean to flatter or praise you at the expense of any other," he said in a manner that could only be seen as approbatory, "but I confess I do think it is entirely owing to you that this army . . . is not totally cut off. You have decision, a quality often wanted in minds otherwise valuable." Had you been here to advise Washington, Reed continued, there could be no doubt that the calamity would have been averted.

Instead, Washington had listened to Greene. "Oh! General," Reed concluded his obsequious communiqué, "an indecisive mind is one of the greatest misfortunes that can befall an army; how often have I lamented it this campaign." [39]

Washington's retreating army reached Newark the day after Reed penned that letter. Desperate for assistance, the commander dispatched Thomas Mifflin to Philadelphia and Reed to Burlington, New Jersey, each to plead with a state governor for reinforcements. Colonel Reed still was absent when Lee's reply arrived late in November. Although the letter was addressed to Reed, Washington tore it open. Lee had been ordered to fetch his army to the south so he could rendezvous with Washington; the commander was anxious to learn of his subordinate's whereabouts. What Washington read stopped him in his tracks: "I received your most obliging flattering letter," Lee began his missive, troublingly written at the same headquarters near White Plains that he had occupied for nearly a month. That he had not moved at all was cause for concern. What followed, however, was mortifying. General Lee acknowledged his agreement with Reed that a "fatal indecision of mind . . . in war is a much greater disqualification that stupidity or even want of personal courage—accident may put a decisive Blunderer in the right—but eternal defeat and miscarriage must attend the man of the best parts if curs'd with indecision." He would be coming south shortly, Lee closed, adding with his usual modesty, "for to confess a truth I really think my Chief will do better with me than without me." [40]

Washington could not have been unaware of complaints behind his back. He was hardly a novice to the politics of command; besides, with the pernicious setbacks of the past ninety days, it was too much to hope that the doubters and the quick-fix artists would not be set in motion. But Reed? The man he had repeatedly beseeched to join him? This young man whom he had looked upon almost as a son? The man whose rise he had overseen from the status of an amanuensis to a colonel? This bright, garrulous young man with whom he had been so uncharacteristically informal during those long evenings outside Boston? If not Reed, whom could he trust? Was a conspiracy afoot? Was Lee, the hyperactive warrior now given so suddenly to immobility, part of a plot? He long since had concluded that Lee was fickle. But Reed? [41] More hurt than angry, he forwarded Lee's letter to Reed, accompanying it with a note of his own that must have been devastating for what was left unsaid:

> The enclosed was put into my hands by an Express from White Plains. Having no Idea of its being a Private Letter, much less suspecting the tendency of the correspondence, I opened it, as I have done all other Letters to you, from the same place. . . .
>
> This, as it is the truth, must be my excuse for seeing the contents of a Letter, which neither my inclination or intention would have prompted my to.
>
> I thank you for the trouble and fatigue you have undergone in your Journey to Burlington.[42]

Dissatisfied with the nature of his post and desperately lonely for his wife, Reed had planned an imminent retirement from the army, vowing, in fact, to quit when that autumn's campaign ended. But now it no longer appeared that the British would retire to winter quarters any time soon. Late in November the Earl of Cornwallis moved out in pursuit of the Continental army, and at Newark he nearly caught up with his prey, for the British army entered the north side of the village while Washington was exiting on the south side. The American commander reeled backwards, passing through New Brunswick and on to the south side of still another river, the Raritan. Reed did not wish to quit while fighting persisted. Moreover, to resign at the moment that his disingenuous and ambiguous behavior had been discovered, a time when Washington probably looked upon him as a blackguard, would constitute political suicide.[43]

Thus, as soon as his business in Burlington was completed, Reed hurried north to see Washington. It must have been an awkward, painful meeting for both men, the one both embarrassed and heartsick at his unmasking, the other a proud but insecure man. Washington welcomed Reed back, yet the relationship was no longer the same. One man seemed too submissive, the other too wary. But Reed was only a part, a small part, of Washington's troubles that December.[44]

"The movements and designs of the Enemy are not yet understood," General Washington reported to Congress a few hours before the assault on Fort Washington. Two weeks later he informed the legislators that the redcoats had crossed the Passaic and were "advancing this way," that is, in the general direction of Philadelphia and the Congress. Necessity had compelled him to retreat, he added, as his force was "by no means sufficient to make a stand against the Enemy"; besides, his army was devoid of entrenching tools, a deficiency that would make a fight on this "dead Flat" terrain suicidal.[45]

Whatever he had suggested in September after the debacle on Long Island, Washington's decision to pursue a Fabian strategy of cautious retreat was made only after the collapse of the fortress on Mount Washington. He did not abandon Fort Lee and retreat quickly enough to avoid still another calamity, however. Nearly a week after the loss of the first bastion overlooking the Hudson, the British seized the second fort as well, taking that one without a fight; the Americans had removed some of their equipment before their adversary arrived, but still they lost all but two cannon, nearly three hundred precious blankets, and a huge quantity of flour.[46]

Washington's first step thereafter had been to cross the Passaic, lest he be caught between that stream and the Hackensack. At Brunswick he united his exiguous force with that under Lord Stirling. Almost every step of the way he had been appealing for militia reinforcements. And he had ordered Lee to move to the south. Again and again, in fact, he directed that capricious warrior to move out. "I confess I expected you would have been sooner in motion," he wrote a week after sending his initial orders. Four days later: "I must entreat you to hasten your march." After another forty-eight hours: "You will readily agree that I have sufficient cause for my anxiety and to wish your arrival as early as possible." A week later: "Genl. Howe is pressing forward. . . . I cannot but request and entreat you . . . to march and join me . . . with all possible expedition." The next day: "I must therefore entreat you to push on with every possible succor you can bring." Three days later: "it is painful to me to add [another] Word upon the Subject. Let me once more request and entreat you to march immediately. . . ." [47] Where was this indolent, torpid soldier?

Washington can be excused if he suspected the worst in Lee's behavior. Given his discovery of Lee's contentious comments to Reed, and now his apparent dalliance, it would not have been surprising had he believed some sinister motive lay behind his behavior. Yet, if he did think such dark thoughts he did not share them with anyone, and to Congress he simply, coolly, remarked on Lee's absence, letting just a hint of his agitation show through. Actually, Lee's failure to join Washington was innocent enough—up to a point. Some confusion initially occurred over Washington's orders, not an uncommon phenomenon when commands had to be relayed by courier over hundreds of miles; then a shortage of shoes and blankets delayed Lee. Even so, his men were marching within five days of the receipt of Washington's first directive. But when Lee entered New Jersey he took matters in his own hands, preferring to assault the rear of the pursuing redcoat army. There was logic to his idea, inasmuch as he hoped to induce the British to abandon the chase; if trouble occurred, moreover, he easily could reach the security of the Jersey highlands to the west. There was one problem, however. He was disobeying the orders of his commander.

On December 13—Friday the 13th—matters were resolved. The night before, not wishing to remain with his army, Lee opted to sojourn in a tavern at Basking Ridge. He took along fifteen men to serve as his personal guard, but they were not enough. A British scouting party of twenty-five, tipped off to Lee's whereabouts by some captured American sentries, surrounded the inn, overpowered his guard, and at 10:00 A.M.—two hours after his army had begun its daily march—captured the uncharacteristically stationary general. For good or ill Washington had not only lost Lee but was left with no choice but to elevate Lee's second in command, General Sullivan. At least that officer brought his new army to Washington within a week.[48]

If the mercurial Lee had moved slowly, Washington's salvation may have been that his British pursuers acted with almost equal sluggishness. Cornwallis had been sent after Washington on November 18 with forty-five hundred men. Formally trained at the military academy in Turin, a man with considerable battlefield experience in the Seven Years' War, Cornwallis seemed the perfect choice to shadow the elusive American general. Upon entering New Jersey his first target had been Fort Lee, and once it was taken he had moved out with dispatch in pursuit of Washington. It was a game of chase. Washington actually had more troops than his foe when Cornwallis's stalking began; but many of the American soldiers looked forward to the expiration of their enlistments within only four or five days, and numerous others were untested militiamen. For a week Cornwallis pushed his men to the point of exhaustion, often marching them twenty or more miles a day; by then even his horses were weary, and without his equine corps he would be devoid of artillery and dragoons. On December 1 he reached New Brunswick just as Washington quit the town; the American's destination now was Trenton.

Cornwallis went no further. Not only did everyone need a breather, his orders were to break off the hunt at this point. The British force bivouacked in the little village for nearly a week, until Howe joined them, then they again set out after Washington. They almost bagged two American brigades at Princeton, but the Continentals barely slithered away just before the British arrived. Howe and Cornwallis entered Princeton, and, incredibly, they paused there; even more amazingly, they did not even resume their march until after 9:00 the following morning. Obviously Howe was back in command. When they finally got started the redcoats moved very slowly, partly because they feared an ambush, partly because the retreating Americans had laid waste to every bridge along the way. Howe finally arrived in Trenton at 2:00 P.M., just in time to see the last of his adversary escape across the Delaware River.[49]

For the moment Washington's army was safe. He posted brigades at the four most likely river crossings; in addition, his men had secured or destroyed every vessel in sight, and every bridge across the river had been blown up. But Washington was not sanguine. He suspected that Howe planned to march on Philadelphia, and he told Lund Washington back at Mount Vernon that he had "no idea of being able to make a stand" to stop him. Howe could easily obtain vessels—there were plenty of boats left on the Raritan for British use, one generally reliable Loyalist later wrote, adding that there was enough wire and planks in Trenton to build a whole flotilla—and cross the river upstream. Or Howe could await a hard freeze and simply send his men over that natural bridge. "[W]e wander in a Wilderness of uncertainties and difficulty," General Washington lamented, straits made even more troublesome by still another year-end recruiting crisis.[50]

In the space of two weeks between late November and early December Washington's force shrank by almost one quarter. The arrival of Sullivan helped somewhat, but it did not solve the problem. The commander summoned General Heath and his army from the Highlands; the Flying Camp also had been brought forward, and he requisitioned General Gates and some of the contingents that he had sent to Schuyler some months before. Congress sought to help too by offering bounties to those who enlisted in the Continental army. Mostly, however, the militia would have to be used to augment his army. Washington was not optimistic. Already he had called for help from New Jersey's trainbandsmen, and the results had been spectacularly unsuccessful. In fact, he charged that if that state's militia had turned out in adequate numbers he could have made a stand against the British advance either at the Hackensack or the Raritan. Nevertheless,

Mifflin had garnered several Pennsylvania units totaling about two thousand men. Yet these actions were merely stopgap measures. In "10 days more . . . an end to the existence of our Army" will occur, he reported on December 20, alluding to the end-of-the-year expiration date for most enlistments. Thereafter—if not before—Howe would take Philadelphia ("in truth I do not see what is to hinder him," the general predicted). Surely, too, Washington conjectured, Howe would actively harass the Continentals, breaking down their supply lines and disrupting recruiting for 1777.[51] This is what he would have done had he commanded the British army. But not Howe! Washington again had overestimated his adversary's verve.

At almost the same moment that the American commander meditated on the breakup of his army, Howe decided to end the campaign and order his army to winter quarters. To secure New Jersey he stationed troops in a line of seven cantonments stretching from Fort Lee to the Delaware; oddly, he assigned the fewest troops to the posts nearest Washington's army. Howe placed a Hessian brigade of fifteen hundred in Trenton and about the same number at nearby Bordentown and Black Horse. Then he hurried back to New York, where he learned that a delighted George III had knighted him for his victory on Long Island.[52]

Since the first week in December the Continentals had been strung along a twenty-five-mile line south of the Delaware, awaiting Howe's attack. Gradually, however, Washington began to toy with the idea of seizing the initiative. From time to time since his retreat began in mid-November he vaguely had alluded to wheeling about and striking his pursuers. In fact, as events before Boston had indicated, such notions never were far from his mind, and in this instance he well may have remembered the success the Native Americans had enjoyed against his undermanned string of forts on the Virginia frontier twenty years earlier. Moreover, better than anyone else Washington could have deduced imperative reasons for launching a surprise attack. Civilian morale had sagged with each backward step he had taken especially since the ruinous hiding the army had suffered at Fort Washington. By now, in fact, even one signer of the Declaration of Independence had defected to the British. A vigorous action on his part might additionally impress potential allies in Europe, and it could not but help secure recruits for the campaign of 1777. Then there was Congress. Some members, he knew, had grown restless during the months of American retreats and defeats. That Congress had fled Philadelphia for Baltimore in mid-December was not likely to have won him any friends.[53]

But there was more, too. If his urge to act was born somewhat of desperation—"I think the game is pretty near up," he had remarked—it also grew from a temperament that boiled with rage and mortification. To have been "pushed . . . from place to place," to have been "obliged to retire before the Enemy," as he delicately put it, to have been compelled to act with "fatal supiness" rankled to the marrow. All his life he had prided himself on his enterprise and his pluck, and he had looked with favor on men of "Activity and Spirit"; yet, the recent humbling events had evoked a specter of possible vanquishment and lost esteem. He had endured a swift series of reproachful episodes, and he could sit still no longer. This man of pride would act, but he would not act capriciously. Venturesome he might be; suicidal he was not.[54]

If he could use the element of surprise he would have an advantage over his adversary. Moreover, in contrast to those Hessian cantonments across the Delaware, he would have manpower superiority. But what of his troops, by now mostly militiamen? Scholars are familiar with Washington's ceaseless grumbling about his soldiery, especially his militiamen. Even while he planned to act during that cold December he groused about his "want of good Troops," and he predicted that the militiamen would "prove the downfall of our cause." What often is overlooked, however, is that he used these men, not with timidity, and not because he had no choice, but in a manner that signaled more confidence in their abilities than his pronouncements implied. He concocted intricate plans for these inexperienced soldiers, and he threw them at his foe when there were safer, more cautious avenues he could have taken. And he was profoundly certain of his own abilities, as only one who once had grappled with and overcome his innate sense of worthlessness could be. (In his subsequent report to Congress on the action he now was contemplating, he used the pronoun "I" thirteen times in two brief paragraphs, in phrases such as: "an enterprize which I had formed," "I ordered," "I threw," "I well knew," "I determined.")[55]

One of Washington's officers later remembered that the commander had spoken of attacking Trenton as early as December 10 or 11. It seems reasonable. Even though Howe did not leave that Jersey village until December 15—a fact that Washington learned that very day, thanks to his efficient and generally reliable intelligence network—he had told Gates the day before that if he could "draw our forces together . . . we may yet effect an important stroke. . . ." And that same day he wrote Connecticut's Governor Trumbull that if he secured adequate reinforcements he might "attempt a Stroke upon the Forces of the Enemy, who lay a good deal scattered," and who he knew, thanks again to his spies, had lowered their guard. During the next week the general quietly discussed the idea with his men; day after day his field officers arrived at headquarters, a thirteen-year-old stone farmhouse about four miles back from the river, to mull over the plan. One visitor found the commander moody and depressed, and he noticed that Washington was doodling as his officers debated the wisdom of an attack; upon a closer look the visitor found what Washington had scribbled on his notepad: "Victory or Death." By the time Reed wrote Washington on December 22 urging that "something must be attempted to . . . give our Cause some degree of Reputation," the commander's plan had taken shape. Like Reed, he believed that "even a Failure cannot be more fatal" than inaction.[56]

Washington's plan was put into motion three days before Christmas. Six hundred men of the Flying Camp crossed into Burlington County, New Jersey, hoping to harass and distract the Hessians at Black Horse and Bordentown. Their activity did get the Germans's attention, but it also attracted the notice of the British posted to the north, very nearly wrecking the remainder of Washington's scheme; fortunately for the American commander, the British high command did nothing more than dispatch orders exhorting their allies to greater vigilance.

On Christmas afternoon Washington began to implement the heart of his plan. He divided his army into three contingents: he posted a detachment of Pennsylvania and New Jersey militia under Brigadier General James Ewing directly across the river from Trenton; Colonel John Cadwalader took a second force, which included both Continentals and state troops, down river, a bit south of Bordentown; Washington took command of the remaining twenty-four hundred men, all Continentals, and began to move upstream. Washington planned to cross the Delaware about nine miles above the little village; he would wait until night had fallen before he crossed, then he would strike out for Trenton. If all went well he would be in position to launch an attack at 5:00 A.M. The timing was crucial, he thought. "They make a great deal of Christmas in Germany," one of his aides noted in his diary that night; surely the Hessians would be sleeping off "a great deal of beer" at that early hour, he added. While Washington was on the march, Ewing and Cadwalader were also to be active. Ewing was to cross later in the evening, then he was to march toward Trenton and endeavor to plug the mercenaries' exits on the south side of town; Cadwalader, likewise, was to cross into New Jersey, his objective being to tie up the Hessians southeast of Trenton.[57]

The object of all this surreptitious planning was a Hessian brigade of fifteen hundred men under Colonel Johann Rall, stationed for the past week and a half at Trenton. An able warrior, Rall had soldiered all his adult life, winning commendations for his valor in earlier wars and serving with distinction both at Long Island and at White Plains. But he was in over his head at Trenton. An inexperienced colonel, he unexpectedly found himself in command of a brigade only because of the simultaneous death or incapacitation of four more senior officers. And his problems were exacerbated when fatigue, then illness, descended on his men, the legacy of nine consecutive months of sailing and marching and fighting, and, more recently, of ten days of constant alarms and vigilance against an American attack. If Rall erred that Christmas evening, he was not the only one who blundered. A week earlier General James Grant, the British commander of all the Jersey posts, had instructed the German leaders along the Delaware that Washington could hardly be expected to try to cross that river; Grant even pooh-poohed some of Rall's precautions, once claiming that he "could keep the peace in New Jersey with a corporal's guard." Nevertheless, on Christmas Eve Grant reversed himself, advising Rall "to be on your guard against a surprise Attack." Rall was. On Christmas Eve! He was not particularly vigilant after midnight, however. A bleak, terribly cold night, and a holiday to boot, he permitted the soldiery to relax in their comfortable barracks, even canceling the customary dawn patrol.

Washington's men, meanwhile, were in the elements. Obscured by low-lying hills, the men had begun to move out in mid-afternoon, each division marching to its designated spot on the river. There was no holiday spirit in any sector. A light dusting snow already was falling, accompanied by a piercing wind, the sort that can numb a man yet leave his face stinging and aching. Men sought to shield themselves by walking close in the shadow of their companions, but there was little shelter for men garbed mostly in summer clothing, and certainly none for the shoeless. Nor was there any refuge from the gnawing anxiety that attended the thought of coming combat. The men were kept away from the river—and the sight of sentries that might be lurking on the Jersey side—until darkness enveloped the countryside. Then they were ordered to move quickly to the water's edge, where they found Durham boats awaiting them—large, bulky river craft (about fifty to sixty feet in length, eight feet wide) ordinarily used to ship iron ore and agricultural staples. Those men who got to sit were fortunate, for they had been standing or marching for about four hours; besides, the hull helped block off some of the wind. Other men had to load the eighteen field cannon that went across, grueling, wearying labor. While they toiled the snow began to fall more heavily. Finally, about three hours behind schedule, everything was ready, and the army started across, conveyed by the Marblehead sailor-soldiers who had gotten Washington's army off Long Island four months earlier. This time their assignment was even more difficult, for they had to grapple with a swift current that swirled and swept huge chunks of ice perilously about each craft.

Washington was at headquarters until after nightfall, remaining at this more or less central command post in case difficulties arose with any of the three scattered divisions. Shortly after 7:00 P.M., satisfied that all still was well, he rode forward to join the principal contingent of his force at McKonkey's Ferry. The unanticipated delays in loading that he soon discovered must have dismayed him. The planned assault at sunrise now was out of the question. By midnight, moreover, the snow had turned to a cutting sleet; the dampness could render his muskets inoperative. In that event, he decreed, the attack would be by bayonct.

Washington was one of the first to cross the Delaware. He stood on the Jersey shore for nearly an hour directing the operation, looking "calm and collected, but very determined" to one of his aides. By 4:00 A.M. the men and cannon had been unloaded. No enemy sentries, no patrols had appeared. But a nine-mile trek lay ahead, and the first rays of light would extinguish this pitch black night in about three hours. From experience Washington knew his army—no army—could traverse the distance in less than four hours. But he ruled out a retreat now. Such a move would be spotted, negating a second chance for such an attack. Besides, there had been enough retreating. They moved out. No one spoke. The division stopped once to eat, the men's first food in eighteen or more hours, but it was only a brief stop. When they started again the force had been divided. Greene led one group down the Pennington Road toward the north side of the village; General Sullivan took the River Road that led to the south side of Trenton, a move designed to cut off the German's exit across the Assunpink Bridge. Washington accompanied Greene.

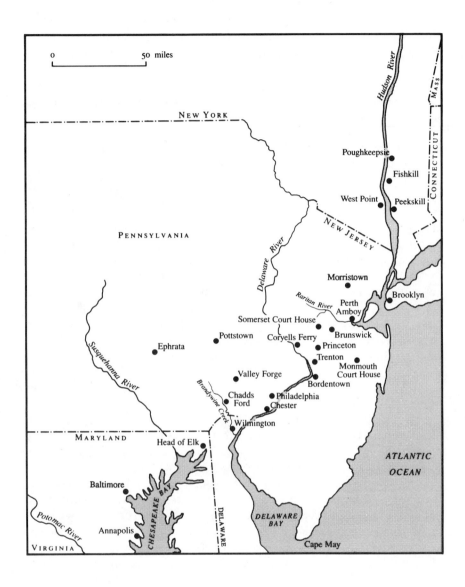

The Pennsylvania–New Jersey Theater

Inside Trenton the Hessians were none the wiser. At 8:00 A.M., forty-five minutes after the daylight first had pierced the blackness, many of the mercenaries still slept contentedly, some, like Colonel Rall, slumbering deeply after losing a struggle to a bottle of spirits on the previous evening.

Finally, only a few hundred yards from the village, pickets on the Pennington Road discovered the advancing Americans. Almost simultaneously Sullivan spotted the pickets on the south side of town, easily overpowering them. In a few minutes the sleepy-eyed Germans were falling out, alerted at last by the not-too-distant sound of musket fire. But it was too late. All but one road out of town already had been sealed off by the attackers. Rall hurriedly tried to rally a defense; some of his units fought well, others seemed confused, almost paralyzed, by this sudden onslaught, for they were being assailed from every direction, by cannon from the forests, by men who huddled behind walls or who fired from the open windows of houses. It did not take long for the Germans to realize the immensity of their dilemma, that "they must inevitably be cut to pieces if they made any further Resistance," as Washington later put it. Individual units began to submit, until surrender fed surrender and the battle was over. One who did not quit soon enough was Rall; he was gunned down in the street and died a day and a half later. Three Hessian regiments capitulated. After a thirty-minute clash, 20 Hessians were dead (compared to 4 Americans who died and 8 who were wounded), and 919 were prisoners of war. The victory could have been even greater. Neither Ewing nor Cadwalader made it across the Delaware; the former did not even attempt to cross, the latter gave up after an arguable effort, with the result that more than 500 Hessians escaped into the very areas in which the two were to have operated.[58]

It was a stupendous victory, nevertheless, the capstone to an ingenious and perilous operation executed by a man with the genius to see, then to seize, every opportunity that fell his way. There were enough dangers to the plan to have forestalled a less intrepid commander than Washington. Still, while attended by risks (as is virtually every wartime undertaking), the hazards that accompanied the mission often have been overemphasized. Washington's knowledge of his enemy's activities was considerable; in fact, he knew far more about them than they seem to have known about him. The Americans, moreover, had a numerical superiority of better than two to one. And if the plan went awry—if the element of surprise was foiled, or if his adversary surprised him—he had good reason to believe he still could get back across the river to safety, for not only did he have manpower superiority, he had a colossal artillery advantage, perhaps five times as many cannon as Rall had in his possession. Washington could have lost heavily, but the odds were better that either he would gain nothing or that he would gain everything.

If Cadwalader had not made it across the dangerously swirling river on Christmas night, he got over the next morning, and his belated trek opened the possibility for still more action by Washington. Actually, the commander's initial reaction to Cadwalader's belated move probably was one of anxiety, for he now was all alone in New Jersey. If the Hessians at Bordentown bottled up this American division, or if British forces rushed to the Delaware and crushed Cadwalader, the loss would nullify the gains secured the night before. Yet there was something refreshing about the way this Pennsylvania officer spoke. Washington received a letter from him on the day after Trenton, a missive in which he talked of action, of linking with Putnam's troops in Philadelphia in order to create a diversion that would permit the commander to act. Washington immediately summoned a council of war. Should the army recross the Delaware? No—not immediately anyway, his officers advised. Rations were depleted, and the men already were tired and hungry; besides, many men's enlistments expired in just four days. Washington must have been disappointed by their answer, for he already had answered Cadwalader with a letter that pulsated with his new zeal for action. He was "extremely ready" to move out, he had said.[59] But once again he refused to overrule his generals.

By the following morning the situation had changed. The Americans learned that the Hessians at Bordentown and Black Horse were gone; fearing a repeat of the Christmas night debacle, their commander had retreated to Princeton, leaving Cadwalader, joined at last by Ewing and a large contingent of militiamen under Mifflin, to prowl about their recent haunts. That same day Washington decided to cross back into New Jersey; he acted without convening another war council. "Reinforcements are coming in" that "will make our force very respectable," he told a correspondent. More militia units were on the way, and, in addition, he had ordered up some units that he had posted before Philadelphia on the eve of the holiday foray. His plan now was growing more grandiose. When he addressed his generals the day before he apparently had thought only of flushing out the remaining Hessians near the Delaware. Now he spoke of fording the river "for the purpose of attempting a recovery of that Country [all of New Jersey, that is] from the Enemy." One more stunning success, he reasoned, and Howe might be compelled to abandon the entire state.[60]

Washington's thinking was audacious. To have caught a regiment in its cups after a holiday revelry was one thing. To march into the lion's den against a large enemy force that only recently had run him off Long Island and Manhattan, that had chased him across New Jersey in the weeks following its pulverizing victory at Fort Washington, was the act of a daredevil, a gambler who was willing to hazard every advantage he had won at Trenton on another roll of the dice. It was a side that Washington had divulged many times in the past eighteen months, although before Trenton he always had permitted himself to be restrained by his general officers. At Trenton, however, he had pursued his instincts—and he had won, just as he had at Dorchester Heights. Now his instincts guided him once again. He believed in his own capabilities, and he knew that the size of the rival forces would be more evenly balanced than had been the case during the summer campaign. Besides, the customary British naval superiority was of no consequence in Jersey.[61]

Washington tried to cross the Delaware on December 29, but the icy river was in worse shape than it had been on Christmas Eve. He went over the following day, however, accompanied by startling news from Baltimore. Congress had voted to make him a virtual military dictator for six months. He was given "full, ample, and complete powers" in almost every matter pertaining to the conduct of the war. Once he got his men across, moreover, he assembled them and in a rare speech he proffered a ten-dollar bounty to every soldier who would remain on for another six weeks; enough men responded that he could continue to harbor thoughts of action.[62]

Meanwhile, the commander established his headquarters in Trenton, posting his army on a slight ridge on the south side of the Assunpink. His adversary would have to get across that deep stream to get to him. On the other hand, his army's back was against the Delaware, a river whose mercurial, uncooperative temperament had been frequently shown during the past week. Before he moved any further Washington sent patrols north to garner information on British activities. One party, the group he sent to Princeton, was led by Joseph Reed. On New Year's Day it reported: the British were massing their forces in that little college town; soon, it appeared, they would be on their way toward Trenton.[63]

The Earl of Cornwallis was back in command. Howe was pulling duty at headquarters in New York. Cornwallis rounded up eight thousand troops—giving him a three-to-two numerical advantage over Washington—and started for Trenton on January 2. It was not a pleasant march. A Continental brigade had been posted at Maidenhead, about a third of the way toward Trenton, and from that point on the redcoats were compelled to gingerly pick their way south, their every step dogged by the fire of American riflemen; in addition, a January thaw had set in, sending the temperature to early spring records for warmth and transforming the compact, frozen highway into an oozy, sticky bog. Under ordinary circumstances Cornwallis would have reached Trenton by mid-morning. This day he got into town at 5:00 P.M., only a few precious minutes before daylight was extinguished.

To his delight Cornwallis discovered that the American commander awaited him, still nestled south of the deep, vertiginous creek. Why Washington had remained there, hemmed between this coursing stream and the Delaware, has troubled historians. It has been suggested that he was mentally fatigued from the constant strain of command, although neither his action at Trenton nor his behavior immediately thereafter support such a conjecture. Did he know all along that he could escape? Perhaps. Yet there is no evidence to lend credence to that notion. Nor is there any real evidence that he was misled by his subordinates, as some writers have maintained. Could his intelligence network have broken down so completely that Cornwallis's arrival was a surprise? Not very likely. Indeed, Reed had returned from Princeton with word that Cornwallis shortly would be on the way. Maybe the simplest explanation—though the most difficult for many historians to accept—is that Washington erred. For weeks he had spoken longingly of making a stand. Here was his chance. The terrain was hilly, and thus favorable for a defensive stand; in addition, the Americans had massed more artillery in one place than at any previous time in the war. Washington seemed to feel that Cornwallis could never get to him, and that the British army would be bled white in its futile endeavor.[64] It might have worked out that way, too, but given time to reconsider Washington evidently concluded that he had erred, that he did not wish to have to fight with his back pinioned against the Delaware River.

When Cornwallis marched into town, however, he was looking at his army's best chance of making a cornered Washington fight since Howe had backed the Continental army against the East River in August. More diligent— and experienced—than Howe, Cornwallis did not wait to attack. He immediately hurled two columns at the creek. Furious fights developed; if the British reached the stream Washington would be in terrible peril. In the barely visible twilight, clouded even more by the low-hanging smoke discharged by a score or more of cannon, by thousands of muskets, the two forces grappled. First one, then the other assault column, was repulsed. But Cornwallis came again. And again the Continentals' deadly fire drove the British back. About thirty minutes had elapsed. Darkness had descended. Cornwallis had to make a simple choice: attack now, or wait until sunrise. He made the wrong choice. He opted to wait, apparently be- cause at that moment his men were too tired even to fight a ragged inexperienced, half-starved army. When he awakened the next morning Washington was gone.

Like an artful, cornered cat, Washington suddenly had bounded out of Cornwallis's grasp. The American commander had not had much choice, as Corn- wallis should immediately have realized. Washington could stand and fight against a numerically superior professional army; he could attempt to pull out, retreat- ing south of the Delaware; or he could try to slither away to the north, behind Cornwallis. Those were his grim alternatives. He rejected a further stand on the Assunpink, but he was too full of fight to fall back into Pennsylvania. Shortly after sunset, after Cornwallis called off his propulsive assaults, Washington made his decision, perhaps unilaterally, although he did hold another council of war. He would sally deeper into the enemy's lair. Moving his army across the blood- ied creek, skirting wide around the left flank of the slumbering redcoat army and moving northward in his greatest gamble of the war, he would strike behind Cornwallis.

Several lures pulled Washington into this hazardous venture. New Bruns- wick housed Britain's principal supply depot in this theater, and its capture or destruction was an enticing thought. Furthermore, any victory, however slight, might help in the recruitment of next year's army. Washington, moreover, always had been given to grandiloquent plans, and this was no exception. A stupendous victory, he dreamed, might compel the British to abandon the entire state, for- feiting their every stinging victory of those bleak days of November and early December.

The troops moved out just after midnight, a huge operation that required the uprooting of an army whose lines stretched for more than four miles behind the watery buttress. Men were left behind to tend four hundred campfires, while others toiled to dig earthworks that would never be used, the flickering light and the ringing clatter of metal against rock designed to reassure the British that the Americans indeed remained nearby. While those soldiers excavated a soon-to-be-abandoned slope, Reed rendered his greatest service to Washington. Since the commander had stumbled onto his confidential remarks to Lee six weeks earlier, Reed had acted with boundless energy. Having already resigned his adjutancy, he made an about-face early in December and asked Congress to permit him to stay on. During the next thirty days he worked tirelessly to raise and organize troops, he ran a small-scale intelligence operation in the Bordentown and Trenton areas, he joined those at headquarters to help plan the attack on Rall's Hessians, and he crossed into New Jersey with Cadwalader on the day after Christmas, personally leading dangerous scouting parties to compile information for Washington, including his foray as far north as Princeton on New Year's Eve, a mission upon which he captured a dozen British dragoons. Reed, of course, knew this region intimately; he was a native of Trenton and a graduate of the College of New Jersey at Princeton. Now, despite whatever lingering hurt or animosity Washington still might have harbored toward Reed, he turned to the young man for help. Indeed, it may even have been Reed who put the notion of striking north into Washington's mind; at least that was the claim made later by one of his friends. Whatever the case, with the British front only 150 yards ahead, Reed moved the army over the Assunpink, then down a labyrinth of country roads. No one spoke, and to further guarantee quiet the rattle of the wagons and artillery carriages was muffled by wrapping their great wheels with cloth. Washington's army completed its circuitous Trenton-Princeton journey in half the time it had taken Cornwallis to traverse a shorter route, although the Continentals were unopposed and the muck and mire of Jersey's inhospitable roads had refrozen by the late night hour when the march commenced.[65]

The men were exhausted when they reached Princeton. None had slept for twenty-four hours, and many had fought or marched for a good portion of that period. Still they proceeded, reaching the southern periphery of the little village just as the sun's rays first began to sparkle on the hard, icy road. Using a map drawn from memory by Cadwalader, Washington watched intently for a fork in the Quaker Road that he was traveling. Finally, it was visible. He divided his army at this juncture. He took the main body along the road that skirted the east side of Princeton, then looped about behind—or on the north side—of the hamlet. He sent 350 men down the road that crooked to the left, charging them with securing the stone bridge on the main Trenton-Princeton highway, a possession that would forestall any escape from Princeton while, at the same time, it would deny Cornwallis immediate access to the village when he arrived. Washington placed an old friend from Virginia, Brigadier General Hugh Mercer, in charge of this division. The two men had known one another since they had served under Braddock in 1755. Subsequently, Mercer, a Scottish immigrant and a physician, had moved to Virginia, and in 1774, following one of his occasional visits to Mount Vernon, he had purchased Ferry Farm from his friend. A planter and respected doctor for the past fifteen years, he nevertheless had a long military record, having fought in the French and Indian War and, before that, for Bonnie Prince Charlie at Culloden.[66]

The two columns parted, each pressing toward its objective. But they hardly were out of one another's sight before a hitch developed. Most of the men in the three British regiments posted in Princeton had been ordered to Trenton, and by happenstance they were lumbering down the Trenton highway at that very moment. The redcoats spotted their adversary first, but only seconds later Mercer glimpsed the scarlet uniforms of his foe. He quickly led his men off the road and into an orchard atop a slight rise; from there, positioned behind hedges and a fence, they looked down on the massing British. The fight that followed was brief. Following a few volleys, the British commander, Colonel Charles Mawhood, ordered a bayonet charge. The sight of these gleaming steel knives was too much. A panic set in. Soldiers raced back through the orchard, abandoning their wounded brethren; many Americans left in that orchard perished, including Mercer who had remained trying to rally his men. (He was bayoneted seven times, and died a British prisoner the following day.)

Hearing the shots Washington galloped to the ridge in time to see his men in pell-mell flight. Exposing himself to the gunsights of the British professionals only thirty yards away, he rode here and there desperately trying to stem the retreat and restore order. He must have presented an inviting target, a large man on a white steed. But his luck held. Order was recovered, although more because reinforcements from the main army arrived. Now it was the Continentals who attacked, Washington at the very front of the line. The British fell back. The battle seesawed for a time. Both sides fought resolutely, but Washington had superior numbers on his side, and he pushed Mawhood back to the Trenton Road. He was unable to corner him, however. The British slipped over the bridge that had been Mercer's destination when the contest erupted. Mawhood was safe, yet his losses had been heavy. It was a "glorious day," a Pennsylvania volunteer wrote his wife, and especially because of Washington's courageous conduct. "I saw him brave all the dangers of the field and his important life hanging as it were a single hair with a thousand deaths flying around him." [67]

With Mawhood out of the way Washington turned toward Princeton itself, defended now by only a tiny British force. Some fighting raged about the lone building of the diminutive college campus, although this fight was but a skirmish compared to the battle that had gone before. In a matter of minutes the operation had ended. It had been another miserable day for the British. About a hundred of the king's men were killed, wounded, or captured.[68]

The casualty list at Princeton was not extensive, not when compared to the

Washington at the Battle of Princeton, by Charles Willson Peale (1784).
Courtesy of Princeton University.

wars of Europe, or even by contrast to the engagements of the last six months. But what Washington had wrought in the space of just nine days was staggering. The two victories, prizes secured through daring and resourceful attacks made upon one of the western world's preeminent armies, raised American morale just when it had begun to appear to many that all was lost. In addition, the great victory at Trenton exploded the myth of Hessian invincibility. Washington's venturousness and his success—above all his success—shut down those questions about his capabilities that had been whispered behind his back. A British traveler sojourning in the unlikely spot of Loudoun County in Virginia heard the news of Trenton and Princeton from his host, a Leesburg planter who had been lambasting Washington's "want of skill and experience" just before the tidings arrived. "But now the scale is turned and Washington's name is extolled to the clouds," the Englishman ruefully noted in his journal. Just a few days earlier the folks he met "had given up the cause for lost. . . . This has given them new spirits, got them fresh succours and will prolong the War, perhaps for two years," he added.[69]

Nor was the significance of Washington's stroke lost on the heads of state in Europe. The news of his victories made its way across the Atlantic and into the thoughts of important men who watched this war with considerable interest. The consensus view was that Washington had proven himself to be an adroit and competent commander. Oddly, the British government seemed to attach less importance to their misfortunes than anyone else. Certainly the heady optimism which had blazed in London since Howe's landing at Gravesend Bay was diluted by the arrival of the news of the engagements at Trenton and Princeton; moreover, the opposition press, which always had lamented the use of mercenaries, had a field day with the news of the Hessian failure. But North and his men, although conceding that these defeats signified a longer, more costly war, nevertheless took the position that 1776 had been an excellent year. Canada and New York had been taken, the British losses were but a token of the American losses at Fort Washington, and nearly forty thousand colonists had affirmed their loyalty to the Empire by receiving pardons from Howe. Indeed, the prevailing wisdom in London was that the navy's inability to institute an effective blockade was a greater failure than the two recent losses to Washington. Nor did General Howe initially seem to regard the vanquishments as irreversible disasters. He was not happy, of course, but he already had concluded that one more campaign would be necessary before the rebels could be subdued.[70]

General Washington had envisioned Princeton as only his first step, and two hours after the shooting stopped, his army was on the road for New Brunswick, seventeen miles away. Even so, the commander had begun to reconsider his plans even before he left the little college town. For one thing his men were dead tired; subsequently he told Congress that he would have proceeded on had he had six to eight hundred fresh troops. But he could not wait for his men to rest. Cornwallis had wheeled about and was coming north. Washington did not wish to be squeezed between that army and the British contingents at New Brunswick and Amboy.[71]

On second thought Washington scuttled his notion of continuing the expedition, and the army veered away from New Brunswick. Forty-eight hours later, six days into 1777, the campaign of 1776 finally ended. The Continental army had marched wearily into western New Jersey, there to make camp under the guardianship of the lush rolling hills at Morristown.

8

The Campaign of 1777

"Outdone by their northern Brethren"

After weeks of retreat, of campaigning in mud and slush, Washington's tired men must have found Morristown charming and cozy looking. But the place had not been selected for the army's winter quarters because of its beauty. The surrounding hills and rolling terrain, an undulating topography that offered security against attack, especially against surprise attack, was the compelling reason for wintering in this diminutive village. Then, too, this was known to be a lush, fertile region, an area suitable for good foraging, one aspect of an armed force's existence that the Continental army could hardly afford to ignore.

Otherwise, there was not much to distinguish the little farm town from scores of other hamlets. The customary village common sat in the heart of the town, a plot of land whose normal cheery green vista had given way to the dreariness of dead winter. The Green lay under a mantle of snow when the troops arrived, though from time to time in January and February patches of withered brown grass were visible, a complement to the barren, colorless trees. A church and a cemetery stood nearby, as did a long frame tavern, a place that Washington claimed for his lodging and office. He needed the space. He had eight, sometimes ten, aides now, and he wanted at least some of them to have rooms near his quarters, partly for convenience's sake when work was required, partly because he could relax in the presence of most of these young men. The space in the tavern also was convenient for Martha, who joined him in mid-March and stayed for eight weeks. There was a kitchen and dining room downstairs, facilities that could be useful both for conferences and for entertainment. Another house or two stood near the Green, but most of the forty to fifty dwellings spread out from the town, remote from one another in the manner of little farming communities.

The more accommodating among the prosperous families volunteered rooms in these dwellings to the highest-ranking officers; otherwise, men lived in tents, or in hurriedly constructed log cabins. From a security standpoint Morristown was a good choice, although the comforts of the previous winter outside Boston were not likely to be available to most of the soldiers.[1]

The first decision that Washington made following his arrival was to have his army inoculated against smallpox. Since it was a process that would debilitate many of his soldiers for several weeks (the ordeal included a few days of preparatory dieting, then up to two weeks of discomfort, including days of headaches and nausea), he evidently discounted the likelihood of any British movement. But he could not be certain, and during the next few weeks he puzzled and fretted over Howe's intentions while he toyed with plans of his own. All he knew was that the British command had assembled a large force of redcoats at New Brunswick; whether it was for offensive or defensive purposes he had no idea. To rid himself of this adversary was his first aim, although he soon began to think along more grandiose lines. He ordered General Heath to make a feint at New York from his base in the Highlands, a ploy that he hoped might compel the recently burned British to summon virtually every soldier in New Jersey to Manhattan. Washington pleaded with the officials in New England to provide Heath with militia personnel, then he told the general to act as though he was about to fall on the city. If the British responded as he hoped, Washington planned to swoop down on the city with most of the disparate Continental forces and whatever militia he could scrape together; he presumed that the British had not had time to stockpile adequate provisions, and if that were the case the redcoats would have to fight their way through the American siege lines or face starvation. Thus, only a week after Princeton, Washington again was dreaming of seizing the initiative.[2]

Not much came of this enterprising scheme, however. In mid-January Heath, who had only trainbandsmen under his command, marched to Fort Independence, the British installation that guarded the Kingsbridge entrance to Manhattan Island; once there he desultorily fired a few artillery rounds at the garrison, then he produced a rather grandiloquent document demanding that the British surrender. But when the British refused to comply, Heath simply withdrew and the operation fizzled. Indeed, all that came of the planning was that Heath's conduct propelled Washington into a rage—feelings that he hardly tried to hide, for he told Heath straight away that his retreat after issuing a surrender summons not only invited the ridicule of the adversary but insured that the British in New York remained unhindered in their foraging endeavors.[3]

Even though that opportunity was gone, Washington continued to harass British food-gathering activities throughout the winter. He repeatedly ordered American detachments of five hundred or more men into the field to impede the enemy, a tactic that compelled Howe to send out quite large foraging parties, units that often exceeded two thousand men. Washington's plan was simple: render the adversary's horses so weak that they would be unable to take the field in the spring, and in the meantime provoke as much distress as possible within the redcoats' ranks. To a remarkable degree Washington's strategy worked, although, inexplicably, the significance of the achievement often has been overlooked. Perhaps it has been largely ignored by historians because the British troops quartered in New York had few problems with their food supply, having wisely stockpiled enough comestibles to see them through the winter and spring. Neither their horses nor their comrades in New Jersey fared so well, however. Long Island, which the British had thought would supply fodder for their horses, proved a disappointment, whereas the Continentals' vexing raids became a real hindrance to the supplying of both men and beasts in the camps from New Brunswick to Amboy. But these were only part of their difficulties. When Britain's transatlantic supply train failed to arrive before the army entered its winter quarters, Howe's problems were exacerbated, and when his logistical deficiencies grew evident, America's perspicacious Yankee farmers quickly increased the prices of their precious commodities. By late spring the redcoats were being bled white through a continual series of Lexington-Concord type firefights with the Continentals' flying columns as well as with swarms of militiamen, losing perhaps more men in these operations than they had lost in all the combined battles since August. Moreover, the undependability of an American food supply eventually forced Howe to revise his thinking; thereafter, he was compelled to rely largely on the government at home for certain items, even though the American navy and privateers at times threatened to render that source untrustworthy as well.[4]

The victualing requirements of an eighteenth-century army were enormous. The British soldier was supposed to have a daily ration of one pound of bread and either one pound of beef or nine ounces of pork; in addition, oatmeal, cheese, peas, rice, butter, molasses, rum, and porter (a dark beer made from browned malt) were supposed to be a regular part of his diet, and all this might be supplemented by vinegar, sauerkraut, or various fresh vegetables when available. Multiply these per capita requirements by an army that normally exceeded twenty thousand men, and it is obvious that Britain's logistical problems would have been considerable even if the American forces had not attempted to impede its operation. While Washington's harassing activity did not immediately end the war, it did make the redcoats dependent on London for the barest necessities. Thereafter, Britain would have to ship approximately 20 million pounds of bread, flour, and rice to America each year, as well as 2 million pounds of salt beef and 10 million pounds of salt pork, plus still more incredible quantities of additional staples. And that was just to feed the men. About 28 million pounds of hay and 12 million pounds of oats were required each year for the horses. Then came munitions and weapons, uniforms and tents, cooking utensils and medical supplies, skilled artisans and replacements for dead and wounded soldiers and the equine corps, even coal and wood had to be shipped across the Atlantic, and all this had to compete for space on the British ships that plied the trade lanes of the Empire. Coordinated by a bureaucracy that was anything but streamlined, it was all Britain could do to keep an army the size of Howe's in the middle states and Carleton's in Canada well supplied; to raise and supply sizable legions of Loyalists was out of the question.[5]

While this war for supplies proceeded unheralded and often unreported, Washington wondered at his adversary's winter intentions, even speculating that "a Storm will burst soon, somewhere." He remained alert in case Howe should plan a strike at his army, or for the remote possibility that the British might either assail New England or march on Philadelphia. Six weeks after his arrival in Morristown he better understood his indolent foe, and, because Howe had elected not to fall on America's debilitated army in the hills of New Jersey, Washington now characterized the general as a "Man of no enterprize."[6]

What was Howe up to that winter? That he had abundant problems is clear. Finding housing for his men was a gigantic burden, for a large section of New York City had been consumed by fire soon after the Americans' hurried escape in September. Looking after considerable numbers of American prisoners of war, not to mention having to care for the Tories that besieged his army for protection, also were full-time jobs. And there was the constant worry over supplies. But, in truth, it was not simply these perplexities that impeded General Howe. His torpor was nothing new. What was new was that whereas Sir William had had good reasons for his inertia during the previous winter, there no longer was much justification for his languor and his excessive caution. His army had a huge numerical advantage over Washington's shrunken little force, an edge that was all the greater in that during those months the American army principally consisted of trainbandsmen. Supplying his troops over America's muddy winter roads would have been difficult, but if he could have made Washington abandon Morristown the American commander then would have faced the same supply problems with which the British grappled. Washington also had the advantage of terrain at Morristown, but his position was not unassailable; indeed, the Continental army's emplacement lacked the topographical barriers that supposedly had made Fort Washington impregnable. But Howe made no move, and, in fact, he seems never to have seriously considered such a step.

Howe remained in New York that winter, luxuriating in the company— and in the bed—of the wife of the British commissary of prisoners, pleasures from which he occasionally tore himself in order to draft ambitious plans for the coming season of campaigning. His initial notion, which he composed in November while Washington was in retreat across New Jersey, was for a three-pronged attack on the northeastern states: one army would drive toward Boston, a second would ascend the Hudson toward Albany, where it would meet the third force, the Canadian army, over which he had no jurisdiction, but which he hoped would be advancing simultaneously to the south. Once things were mopped up in this sector, probably in September or October, the three forces would plunge into the southern states. All resistance, he projected, would be crushed by Christmas.

Three weeks later Howe inexplicably scrubbed that plan and postulated a different enterprise. Now he proposed to use his army to seize Philadelphia. His army, he wrote, would march from New York to the Delaware, presumably combating the Continental army en route. This plan arrived in London just as the king approved a scheme concocted by General John Burgoyne, a design that provided for the Canadian army to march on Albany, where it would rendezvous with Howe's legions. Incredibly, even though the plans of Howe and Burgoyne hardly coincided, Lord Germain gave his enthusiastic endorsement to the notion of an attack on Philadelphia.

As if sufficient confusion did not already exist within the British high command, Howe, in mid-January, drafted still another plan for 1777. Now he asked for twenty thousand additional troops—a 100 percent augmentation of his army— so that he might make a joint naval and overland trek to Philadelphia, and so that some troops might be placed in Rhode Island, from whence they could make forays into Connecticut and Massachusetts. Why a campaign to take Philadelphia? Evidently it did not occur to anyone in a position of authority in London to ask that question, and even today no one knows exactly what logic lay behind Howe's thinking. However, he probably believed that the terrain was more suitable for a fight in eastern Pennsylvania—less like Bunker Hill, that is—than in New Jersey or above Manhattan; then, too, he almost certainly guessed that the number of militiamen in a place like Pennsylvania would be fewer than in the New England states. Still, what gain would Howe realize by taking Philadelphia? Even a non-military man like John Adams sagaciously concluded that Howe's "Possession of this Town . . . would be the worst Situation he could be in, because it would employ the whole Force by Sea and Land to keep it, and the Command of the [Delaware] River." Whatever his thinking, Howe proposed this plan just after he learned of the setbacks at Trenton and Princeton, and the effects of those losses showed through. His upbeat tone had vanished, and, in fact, he now told London for the first time that he no longer believed that one more campaign would end the war.[7]

Whatever Howe decided to do, Washington's most urgent need was for additional troops. For the second consecutive year he faced the task of raising a new army, then of training it from scratch. This time, however, there would be a difference. After working closely with Washington, Congress in September 1776 had resolved to reorganize the army. It called for eighty-eight regiments, including three in artillery, a three-thousand-man cavalry force, and a small corps of engineers. To eliminate the uncertainty of having to recruit a new army at the end of each year, Congress also provided lucrative bounties of cash and land for enlistees. The result was the emergence of a different army. In 1775–76 the ranks had been filled chiefly with zealous republican patriots, men who never doubted that sturdy, virtuous citizens could fight and lick professional soldiers. Howe's campaign in New York demonstrated the folly of such a notion. At the end of the year these earliest Revolutionary soldiers went home and did not come back.

In their stead came men who were lured by the promises of money and land. The new soldiers, thus, were drawn from the ranks of America's very poorest inhabitants. The landless and the unemployed, indentured servants as well as free blacks and slaves, now flowed into Washington's army, some serving because they had volunteered, others because they had been conscripted.[8]

Reorganization on paper was not quite the same as actually fleshing out an army, however. Predictably, recruiting proceeded with agonizing slowness. Two months after the process began four Connecticut regiments that should have totaled approximately three thousand men had secured only about fourteen hundred enlistees, whereas Massachusetts had garnered only about 25 percent of its quota. A month later ten states had yet to get a single new recruit to Morristown. That same month, with the campaign of 1777 presumably imminent, Connecticut and Massachusetts resorted to conscription, although both states permitted a draftee to buy an exemption—for £5, roughly a month's wages for an unskilled laborer—and, oddly, Connecticut even paid a bounty to conscriptees. On the last day of May Washington wrote to Governor Henry to complain that his own state had not met its quota, and about the same time he lamented that for most Americans it was "almost a matter of moonshine" whether the ranks ever were filled. If some way to get men into the army was not soon discovered, he added five months after the recruiting drive commenced, it was unlikely that he could offer "any effectual opposition" to the British that summer. Of the seventy-five thousand men Congress had dreamt of, Washington had fewer than nine thousand with him at the dawn of the summer. For the second consecutive year the militia had seen him through the crisis, for as late as mid-March two of every three soldiers at Morristown were trainbandsmen.[9]

Obtaining adequate numbers of men was just one of Washington's manpower problems. He continued to face a chronic problem of ineptitude within his officer corps. From the beginning the selection process had been shot through with politics, as congressmen simmered and quarreled in their efforts to name old chums and favorite sons to every vacancy, a practice also routinely followed by state officials who named those officers holding rank beneath the level of general officers. By early 1777 most congressmen probably regarded Schuyler, Putnam, Spencer, and Heath as less than competent for the posts they held, although there was nothing to do but "wish they would all resign," as a disgusted John Adams put it that winter. These four men had plenty of company, although the incessant carping that one heard about the general officers was not entirely justified. Impatient critics wanted a well-trained, well-oiled, skilled fighting army—and they wanted it immediately. When their army all too frequently performed ineffectually, the general officers were blamed. Some of the criticism was justified. It was difficult to be a good officer. "Many qualities, independent of personal Courage, are requisite to form the good Officer," Washington advised. The best officer, he said, would be an active, steady, diligent gentleman, one who was willing to make sacrifices, one who could inspire confidence. Few men possessed all these virtuous traits, and under the system of selection that prevailed fewer still were being appointed and promoted. Instead, a distressing number of lower grade officers were slothful and negligent. Some were drunks or thieves or somehow on the take, too many were disobedient or took a cavalier attitude toward their duties, and some seemed constitutionally unable to maintain a discreet distance between themselves and the enlisted men.[10]

If Washington hoped for anything better in February 1777 when Congress announced its intention of electing five additional major generals and ten more brigadiers, he soon must have been disappointed. Congress evidently hoped to accomplish two things: get better officers, and bring an end to the incessant wrangling over rank that had characterized this army. Before it acted Congress debated several criteria for promoting men from lower grades to general officers, but in the end the legislators decided to give as much weight to the number of troops raised by each state as it did to merit and the line of succession. The result was that good officers—like Benedict Arnold, who saw five junior officers promoted in his stead—were passed over, and in one instance a New Hampshire colonel even watched with incredulity as a subordinate was advanced and became his superior. Rather than solving an acute problem Congress's shameless particularistic decision only exacerbated matters. On the eve of the congressional action John Adams had remarked that the officers "Quarrel like Cats and Dogs. They worry one another like Mastiffs, scrambling for Rank and Pay like Apes for Nutts." Nothing had changed in the aftermath of Congress's reform. Washington endeavored to pacify the sensitive and irascible Arnold by telling him that he deserved better for his many "honest exertions," but such a bromide provided little comfort.[11]

Amidst the gloom of recruitment adversities, some good news trickled into Washington's morose headquarters that spring. The United States reaped the first real benefit of French friendship—or at least of Versailles' anti-British sentiments—when more than two hundred artillery pieces from Gallic supply depots reached these shores; soon additional French ships arrived bearing nearly twenty-five thousand muskets and vast quantities of flints and powder. Moreover, although nothing had come of it yet, Congress, after much prodding by Washington, established a foundry at Philadelphia and laboratories at Carlisle, Pennsylvania, and Springfield, Massachusetts, for the production of ordnance.[12]

Washington seldom had the opportunity to savor good news in this war. Either bad news or a fresh crisis—or both—seemed always to lurk just around the bend. Late in March distressing news from New York reached headquarters, tidings that later would seem a fitting prelude for the series of unpleasant communiqués that would reach the commander in chief during the next one hundred or so days. About March 26 Washington learned that the British had successfully assaulted the American post at Peekskill, an installation that was supposed to guard the Highlands between Albany and New York; about five hundred redcoats not only destroyed the village, they seized or torched large quantities of the Continental army's desperately needed stores. What made the debacle even more bitter to take was that it need never have occurred; earlier Washington had pleaded with Massachusetts to send more than three thousand men to the post, yet on the day of the assault a force of only two hundred fifty was quartered there. Washington feared that this was only the first act of a new British policy, and he worried that by year's end all the United States' installations on the Hudson might be gone. He was wrong. The British made no more sallies into the Highlands, although the next month a raiding party organized by Governor Tryon struck at Danbury, Connecticut, killing, wounding, or capturing more than four hundred Americans. This second raid was even more disquieting because the foe had landed, then marched unopposed for a considerable distance before it reached the depot. Once alerted, a Continental force under General Wooster had fallen on the retreating redcoats, killing or wounding 154 of the raiders, a bloody skirmish in which Wooster himself perished, the third (after Montgomery and Thomas) of the original thirteen general officers to die in this war.[13]

In April, with New Yorkers already enjoying their spring flowers and an occasional balmy day, Howe decided to draft still another plan for the coming campaign, this one presumably necessitated by London's refusal to provide more troops than he had possessed in 1776. Now he proposed to abandon the projected assault on New England and to withdraw all redcoats from New Jersey; his only recommendation for action was that he sail with his army for Philadelphia.

And that was it. Plan after plan had been written and accepted, then discarded. Now no time was left. The British high command had lurched from one idea to another, until finally, insensibly, it had at last arrived at a notion of what it would do in 1777. The ministry had had no hand in concocting the plan, nor had Howe made any attempt to coordinate his operations with those of the British army in Canada. In a separate missive to Quebec, Sir William merely suggested that the goal of the northern army should be to seize Fort Ticonderoga and Albany. Ultimately, London more or less accepted Howe's final plan, although Germain did advise him to send a diversionary force against the coasts of Massachusetts and New Hampshire while he was invading Pennsylvania, and the secretary additionally reported that the king expected that he would cooperate with the army coming from Canada. Howe chose to ignore both recommendations.[14]

Not only Washington but many within the British army in New York had expected Howe to open the campaign of 1777 early in the year, perhaps even in March. But it was mid-June before he left New York, and then, contrary to every plan he had submitted, Howe marched into New Jersey. Later he insisted that his aim had been to lure Washington into an engagement. It was as good an explanation as any other for what rapidly was becoming an addled campaign.[15]

By early May Washington still did not know what Howe might do that year. Until about the time of his victories at Trenton and Princeton he had presumed that Howe would strike at Philadelphia, but during the winter and early spring he seems to have leaned toward the view that his adversary would drive north from New York. In the middle of the month Washington's ideas changed again; his intelligence network reported that Howe planned to evacuate New Jersey and Rhode Island, then to assail Pennsylvania. Washington immediately developed plans for occupying any Jersey post that Britain might relinquish, and by the end of the month he had broken winter quarters. The American commander assembled his force at Middlebrook, a relatively safe, protected site about seven miles from the British post at New Brunswick, while he stationed another force under Sullivan near the Delaware. His plan was to keep an eye on Howe, shadowing and harassing his army as it marched toward Philadelphia. Day after day Washington waited, all the while perplexed by contradictory surveillance reports, some of which indicated that Howe was about to embark by sea while others advised of land operations.[16]

On June 14 Washington had his answer. Howe had plunged into New Jersey, heading for Somerset Court House, a tiny village on the road from Middlebrook to Princeton, thence to Trenton and the Delaware. At first glance Washington believed the British would turn left and bolt for Philadelphia, but in time he deduced that Howe had no intention of crossing into Pennsylvania; he was traveling without the boats and portable bridges needed to ford the Delaware. What he must have in mind, Washington conjectured, was one of three ends: either he hoped to draw the American forces from the Highlands passes so that another redcoat army might strike there; or he sought to entice Washington from his lair and onto terrain more favorable for a general battle; or he planned to slice between Middlebrook and Trenton, dividing the American forces so that he could fall upon Sullivan's weaker, isolated army, pinioning it against the Delaware and repaying the colonists in kind for the mortifying defeat of the Hessians on Christmas night. Fearing the latter Washington moved Sullivan to safety, then he sat tight. Now it was Howe's move. The British commander in chief did nothing for five days, then he retreated to New Brunswick.[17]

Furious firefights developed along the line of retreat as Washington ordered Greene's division, together with Anthony Wayne's brigade and Daniel Morgan's riflemen, to attack the rear of the British army. Although he "got a pretty good peppering," Howe fought his way to safety on the east side of the Raritan, from which, still bothered but not endangered, he fell back to Amboy. To that point it appeared as though Washington had made Howe look foolish; he had been in the field for eleven days, and he had absolutely nothing to show for it. A blunder by Washington, however, nearly made a masterstroke of Howe's meanderings.[18]

On June 25, thinking that Howe was about to sail from Amboy to New York, Washington descended from his hilly refuge. His intention, he told Congress, was to be "nearer the Enemy [in order to] act according to circumstances." It was a dangerous, perhaps useless, foray, for Washington's presence was unlikely to produce any beneficial results. After months of witnessing Howe's chronic lethargy and excessive caution, Washington apparently misjudged his foe; or, possibly, Howe for once acted out of character. Seizing the opportunity the British general cast aside his thoughts of sailing and, in the dead of night, sallied out of the Jersey port town. His extemporaneous plan was well conceived. Two columns plunged west from the coast, moving parallel to one another. Their goals: simultaneously envelop Lord Stirling's two brigades at Metuchen and close off Washington's lane of retreat toward Middlebrook. Washington at last would be made to stand and fight—and Howe possessed better than a two-to-one numerical superiority.[19]

But little came of Howe's suddenly venturesome behavior. His right wing, a column led by Cornwallis, did assault Stirling, inflicting moderate losses (about a dozen Americans killed and perhaps sixty wounded, in addition to the capture of several valuable field pieces). Had Stirling pulled back quickly his casualties might have been lighter; instead, his men stood and fought, and they fought well, delaying Cornwallis's advance long enough for Washington to learn what was afoot—he originally seemed to think that Howe was a "little disgrac'd" and merely "wanted to flourish off a little"—and to fall back to Middlebrook, seven miles to the west. That was it. With Washington once again safe in the rolling hills, Howe pulled back to Amboy, this time to return to New York. His trek across New Jersey had been next to pointless, a fact that Washington believed must have caused him "much chagreen." If Howe was not mortified, he should have been. Many of his officers were dispirited at the recent useless roving, and their disappointment eddied into the ranks of the Tories. After all, two months or more of the summer were gone with nothing to show for it. Even more, after two years of war the British could hardly point to a single gain south of Canada, save the occupation of Manhattan and Long Island, and that was counterbalanced by the loss first of Boston and now New Jersey. "All men appear dissatisfied," Howe's usually cheerful secretary noted a day or two after the redcoats had departed New Jersey. All were "full of Regret that the Cause of our King & Country does not proceed so quick as our Desires"; "much dejected," "very melancholy," "pensive," he added on succeeding days.[20]

General Washington was able to relish Howe's failure for only about a week before a dispatch rider reached headquarters with alarming news. Fort Ticonderoga had fallen to a British army led by Burgoyne.[21] Never before had the threat been so great that Howe and the Canadian army might be able to unite along the Hudson River, severing all ties between the New England states and their compatriots to the south.

The campaign that resulted in the collapse of that bastion actually had begun the previous autumn. Following the debacle under Sullivan in June 1776, the American army had retreated south of the Canadian border, abandoning the rotten, tumbledown fort at Crown Point at the head of Lake Champlain, and had taken up residence at Ticonderoga. A brilliant delaying action during the previous fall—under the oversight of Colonel Arnold—had stymied an immediate British invasion, but by the summer of 1777 the king's forces again were ready to march. John Burgoyne, who earlier that year had been placed in command of Britain's

Canadian army, led the invasion army, and with initial success. He envisioned a protracted siege of Ticonderoga, but the Americans abandoned the bastion without a fight. By the time Washington learned of Burgoyne's easy victory, the redcoat army was deep in the New York wilderness, headed for Albany and the Hudson River. When London learned of Burgoyne's achievement, the ministry promoted its hero, while the king was said to have reacted to the news by rushing gleefully into the queen's bedchamber shouting, "I have beat them! I have beat all the Americans!" [22]

Not quite. Indeed, if anyone noticed, Burgoyne was on his own in the wilds of New York, in command of an expedition that, as events ultimately would demonstrate, was badly flawed. Burgoyne had neglected to equip his army with a proper supply of transport vehicles and horses, an oversight that perhaps arose because he failed to grasp the reality of campaigning in America. Even more reflective of Burgoyne's ignorance of America was his decision to eschew passage via Lake George in favor of a wilderness land route. Moreover, although he soon learned that he would be outnumbered by his American adversary, he pushed on. And that Burgoyne would have to face a numerically superior foe was due, of course, to the muddled nature of Britain's plans for 1777. In March Germain had stressed the need for Burgoyne and Howe to rendezvous their forces. In May, however, Germain seemed to endorse Howe's fourth strategic plan for that year (the one that called for his army to sail for Philadelphia), although he implied that his acceptance was conditioned on Sir William's ability to complete operations in Pennsylvania in time to cooperate with Burgoyne. Inasmuch as Howe could not know before late June that his plan for 1777 had been condoned, and considering the characteristically languid manner in which the general did things, Germain's reference to a junction of Burgoyne's army with Howe's army smacks less of a resolute order than of an attempt by the secretary—and an empty one at that—to protect his political backside. At any rate Howe did not interpret it as a command. By mid-July, a week after learning of the seizure of Ticonderoga, he began loading his army onto vessels of the British navy. Unless Washington moved north to assist against Burgoyne, Howe was headed for Philadelphia.[23]

Washington's initial reaction to the news from the North was disbelief. Like Burgoyne, he had expected a long siege of Ticonderoga, if the British could even get into position for that tact. But what if the news was correct? The militia must be called out in force, he suggested, and he proposed General Arnold as a commander for these men. "He is active, judicious and brave, and an Officer in whom the Militia will repose great confidence," he added. Presuming the news surely would cause Howe to abandon all intentions of trying to take Philadelphia, Washington additionally planned to unite his army with the Continental units already stationed in the Highlands.[24]

The day after he learned of Ticonderoga's collapse, the American commander had his army on the move—headed north. The army traveled for five days. On the second day of the trek he received definitive word of the fortress's surrender, but it was another forty-eight hours before he learned that Arthur St. Clair's army had not been captured in battle, that, in fact, there had been no battle. A cold fury moving his hand, Washington sought to discover what had occurred. "The evacuation . . . is an event of Chagrine and Surprise, not apprehended, nor within the compass of my reasoning," he told Schuyler, and he hinted broadly of court martial proceedings. Five days into his march Washington received more perplexing news. Howe's army was boarding naval craft off Staten Island. Washington ordered an abrupt halt to the march. What was Howe's destination? The American commander still suspected that Howe would go north. General Howe "certainly ought in good policy to endeavor to Cooperate with Genl. Burgoyne," he reasoned, but until he knew in which direction Howe had sailed he would advance no further. A day passed, then another, then several. Eight days after being informed of Howe's embarkation, he learned that his adversary had sailed, though he still could only guess at the redcoats' destination. Initially, all signs pointed toward a northern campaign, and he detached some units for that sector; then it appeared that Howe was en route to Philadelphia, and he dispatched some of his force in that direction. Three more days passed, by which time the evidence seemed clear that Pennsylvania was Howe's destination. Washington hesitantly moved south, convinced that it was too preposterous to be true that Howe really was "abandoning Genl. Burgoyne." But it was true. By late July the British fleet had been sighted below Delaware Bay; now Washington and his army stepped up their march, the hot, weary soldiers once again traversing the Delaware, crossing at the very spot the commander had selected for his Christmas Night sortie half a year before.[25]

However, just when it seemed that the three-week-old mystery of Howe's intentions had been solved, the British fleet of some two hundred sixty vessels turned from the entrance to Delaware Bay and promptly disappeared. What could that mean? Had Howe's southward voyage merely been a "deep feint" to throw the American army off guard? Was he indeed going back to Burgoyne? Was he sailing for the Carolina or Georgia coast? What a "very irksome State of Suspense," Washington complained. Three additional weeks of uncertainty lay ahead. But despite the aggravation caused by Howe's tergiversation, the British commander was being considerably less foxy than Washington assumed. All along he had been undecided over whether to approach Philadelphia from the Delaware Bay or the Chesapeake Bay. When the fleet reached the Delaware Capes, Howe chose to enter that estuary, only to discover shortly that Washington had crossed at Trenton and was in a position to contest a landing south of Philadelphia. In addition, the Americans had prepared strong defenses along the river south of the city; and, besides, to land in the vicinity of Wilmington would preclude Howe's ability to close Washington's safety hatch across the Susquehanna and on to the West. Howe considered all these factors, then he ordered the fleet to turn for the Chesapeake.[26]

Washington set up camp midway between Trenton and Philadelphia. And he waited "in the most perfect ignorance, and disagreeable state of Suspence," thinking all the while that the unseen armada was returning to the North or sailing for Charleston. He was not inactive, however. While his weary army rested, he inspected the gun emplacements and fortifications south of Philadelphia, looked in on the construction of booby traps in the Delaware River, and prepared his intelligence network. By the third week in August Washington was certain that all this work had been in vain, for if Howe had been headed for the Chesapeake he should already have arrived. (Actually, unfavorable winds off the Virginia Capes had delayed the flotilla.) That morning the commander summoned a council of war to consider the options. Everyone agreed that Charleston must be Howe's objective, and all agreed, too, that a protracted summer march from Pennsylvania to South Carolina would debilitate the army; therefore, the officers voted unanimously to return to New York, there to resist Burgoyne's invasion or to fall on the meager force of defenders left on Manhattan Island.[27]

Everything was set for a 5:00 march the next morning when a courier galloped into camp. The missing fleet had been sighted—in the Chesapeake. At last Howe's intention was clear.[28] The battle for Philadelphia which had been expected as early as the previous December at last was about to begin.

Within thirty-six hours General Washington was prepared to move his army between Philadelphia and the Chesapeake, passing through the capital city en route. Most congressmen had never seen Washington's army, and the general carefully oversaw even the most minute aspects of the parade. He arranged the organization of the march, ordered the officers to be especially vigilant for any sign of straggling or loafing, had the men wash their clothes and/or uniforms and insert a green sprig (emblematic of hope, he said) in their hats, and made it very clear that he did not want any of the female camp followers to be seen with the army from the moment the Continentals entered one side of town until they exited from the other side. It was a public-relations pageant, and a generally successful one at that. Stationed at the head of the army, Washington's steed briskly cantered into town early on the morning of August 29, a bright, delightfully cool day following a night of heavy thunderstorms. It took two hours for the army to file past, a slow, steady caravan of soldiery doing what it was supposed to do—buck up morale on the home front. They marched with "a lively smart step," one congressman thought, while John Adams concluded that the units were well provided for and "tolerably disciplined." Adams additionally noted the warriors lack of precision, their absence of jauntiness, of pride, all of which led him to judge that "our soldiers have not yet quite the Air of Soldiers."[29]

By mid-morning the following day the American army was south of Philadelphia, about fifty miles from Head of Elk, the point at the top of Chesapeake Bay where the British flotilla was just landing. As Howe's men filed off the creaking, yawing vessels for the welcome earth, it was clear that his army was not in good shape. The navy's square-rigged accommodations had been home to these landlubbers for almost nine weeks. Jammed like sardines into their floating lodgings, the men, all garbed in heavy wool uniforms, had sweltered and baked in the merciless American summer, respites from the murderous heat coming only when perilous storms flayed their craft. Some men were ill from the moment the armada had weighed anchor back in New York, and many were too weak to think about fighting for the next few days. If the men fared poorly, the horses had a worse time; scores of the beasts had perished or were thrown overboard for lack of water to give them when the anticipated short voyage persisted seemingly without end. The cruise would have been worthwhile had it been necessary or had it presented Howe with a strategic edge. But the whole notion of a campaign against Philadelphia made little sense, especially when another British force was descending from Canada. Howe once had possessed Boston and he presently held New York, yet the occupation of these cities had done nothing to shorten the war. There was little doubt that he could take Philadelphia, but he might have to pay a stiff price to get it, and when he got it what would he have accomplished? Moreover, if after two years of war, not to mention the supposed suppression of the rebellion in New Jersey during the previous autumn, the only safe way of getting from New York to Philadelphia was via an arduous naval expedition, it should have dawned on Howe—or London—that the war was not proceeding very well. Besides, once Howe landed at Head of Elk he still was no closer to Philadelphia than he had been in June when he sallied out to New Brunswick.[30] Only now the summer was almost over.

Although plagued by a thousand and one details that required attention in order to prepare for the British advance, Washington's concentration frequently was diverted by reports on the course of the war in other theaters. Not all the news was good, and as usual much of the bad news concerned irascible and fallible General Sullivan. His problems with Sullivan had begun early that year. The New Hampshire officer had exploded when he learned that he had not received command of Ticonderoga, and he had written Washington an angry, petulant letter. Out of patience, Washington had responded in as ill-tempered and direct a manner as he dared: "No other officer of rank, in the whole army," he began, "has so often conceived himself neglected, Slighted, and ill treated, as you have done, and none I am sure has had less cause than yourself to entertain such Ideas." You are haunted by imaginary demons, the commander went on, suspicions that only spoil your own happiness and cause torment for others. Washington's sharp retort quieted Sullivan, and thereafter the two had little contact until after Howe moved into New Jersey in June; when that foray ended Washington left Sullivan posted in Jersey, south of New York, while he moved well to the south toward Philadelphia. Sullivan's orders were to remain in this central location, from which he could move north or south depending on Howe's intentions; in addition, he was to endeavor to discover the size of the redcoat force left behind by Howe in New York. In mid-August Washington received dismaying news. Sullivan, apparently without explicit orders, had launched a raid on the British and Loyalists on Staten Island. The raid failed, and American casualties loomed near 150. Once again that "little tincture of vanity . . . which now and then leads him into some embarassment," and to which Washington had attested a year earlier, had led Sullivan astray. Curiously, however, Washington seems not to have been angry, although he did order an inquiry into the causes of the failure. Maybe his bland reaction was due to an awareness that the overweening pride that propelled Sullivan was not unlike his own; or, perhaps, in the wake of the Ticonderoga affair he may have found it inexpedient to criticize an officer with the gumption to act.[31]

From further north more felicitous news trickled into headquarters that month. The exaggerated fears that had followed the news of the loss of Ticonderoga soon proved unfounded. A month after the collapse of that bastion, Burgoyne had advanced only about thirty miles, less than half the distance between Albany and Ticonderoga. It already had been an arduous trek for the redcoats, a journey through primeval forests and interminable swamps, a march made more difficult by Schuyler's axemen who worked assiduously to fell ponderous trees in the path of the advancing army. Nor did Burgoyne make matters easy for himself. At times it seemed as though he had brought along everyone in Canada. Women, children, dogs, cats, a 138-piece artillery train, and a never-ending baggage caravan (Burgoyne's wardrobe and stock of wine alone took up thirty wagons) slogged beside the six thousand soldiers. Nor was Burgoyne helped by Congress's decision to appoint a more resolute commander of its northern army. On August 1 Schuyler finally was recalled and—when Washington begged off naming his successor—Congress selected Horatio Gates as the new head of the Northern Department.

Early in August Burgoyne began to experience problems. His initial difficulty arose from a bare pantry, cleaned out by his distended retinue. He was compelled to pause, and to detach a force of German mercenaries to Bennington, Vermont, in search of victuals, footwear, and horses. Burgoyne's first disaster resulted. More than nine hundred men never returned from the food-gathering foray, all the victims of New England militia under General John Stark of New Hampshire. Soon, too, it was clear that Burgoyne faced still another problem. The several hundred Loyalists and Indians under Barry St. Leger had been contained by swarms of New York militia in the Mohawk Valley; they would not be joining the main invasion army. And that was only the beginning. Undermanned now, Burgoyne next learned that Gates was in possession of favorable terrain astride the British army's route. Burgoyne was in real trouble. In fact, on the day the British fleet reached Head of Elk, General Washington was able to report to his troops on a "signal victory obtained at the northward" by Gates, and by September 1 the commander was able to believe with some confidence that he might not have to fear the invasion from Canada.[32]

Late in August Howe was on Pennsylvania soil, moving ever so slowly toward Philadelphia with an army of 16,500 men, his advance delayed by a lack of maps, a want of horses, and the necessity to forage along the way. Washington, meanwhile, set up headquarters in Wilmington, and for the next two weeks he watched Howe's leisurely, at times erratic, progress. On the 5th the commander published a ringing speech to his men, a pronouncement in which he suggested that a great victory might break Britain's will to resist and could definitely "free the land from rapine, devastations and burnings, and female innocence from brutal lust and violence." Two days later Washington stripped his army of all items that might encumber a hasty retreat; other than their arms, the men could carry only one shirt, one blanket, and one coat, while the officers could keep those items as well as "three or four shifts of under clothes." In another forty-eight hours he had his army in place on the sloping terrain to the east of Brandywine Creek.[33]

With about eleven thousand men at his disposal, the commander's tactics were simple. Washington envisioned a general engagement, granting Howe his best shot at the American army since Brooklyn a year before. Washington stationed Maryland militia units below Howe's right, a force that could nip at the British rear; Pennsylvania militia were posted at the most southerly ford across the Brandywine, the crossing that he believed Howe was least likely to use. Greene was given command of the center at Chad's Ford, while he put Sullivan, who had joined him following the Staten Island raid, in charge of his right wing up the creek at Brinton's Ford. Why did Washington place Sullivan, whose record was anything but spotless and who at the moment was awaiting an inquiry into his most recent failure, in command of nearly half the American army, a half that was on one of the flanks to boot? The commander had few other options. He could have taken charge of one portion of the army himself, leaving the remainder to Greene; but his custom was to farm out such duty, freeing himself to observe the overall flow of events. Or, he could have placed someone subordinate to Sullivan in command, perhaps using the pending inquiry as his excuse. That tack had political liabilities, however, for Sullivan's friends in Congress were certain to howl; in addition, such a move might antagonize many officers, a corps of hypersensitive men—as, indeed, Washington had been in the 1750s—when it came to rank and seniority. To replace Sullivan, moreover, was to invite that temperamental officer to resign, an eventuality that Washington apparently did not wish to face. Therefore, he put Sullivan in command of one wing, but he placed him in charge of a sector that he believed to be safe, for his intelligence service had advised him that the British could not possibly cross the Brandywine except at Chad's Ford, and he had put the more trustworthy Greene in control there.

On the morning of the 11th, a warm, still, late summer day, a dense fog shrouded the bucolic landscape of rustic Chester County. That cover burned off as the day went along, but its slow dissipation, together with the thick smoke coughed out by cannon and musket fire, would impede visibility throughout this long day. At 8:00 A.M. the British unloosed a terrific artillery barrage, the usual prelude to an assault. It was "the grandest scene I ever saw," exclaimed a New

Jersey captain, but most of the Continentals were less impressed; they simply dug in and tried to remain hidden behind tall earthworks, all the while anxiously awaiting word that the redcoats were coming, and hoping they would survive until then. In the meantime, they listened as Knox's gunners answered the shelling. For most of the morning the two sides implacably—and purposelessly—thumped and thundered at one another. Then these blasts died away. The attack must be imminent. But minutes passed, then an hour, then still another, with no sign of Howe.

About 11:00 A.M. information arrived that a five-thousand-man redcoat detachment was moving north, presumably intent on turning the American right under Sullivan. Washington's first impulse was to discount the report, and at least two witnesses later reported that he laughed at the tidings. There was no place in that sector where Howe could cross! As the minutes passed Washington was seized with a second impulse: to strike, to launch an assault of his own on what was left of the redcoat center across from Chad's Ford. He ordered Greene out, and he sent word to Sullivan to wheel about and lash at the left flank of the British west of Chad's Ford. Greene started forward, but as his men were splashing across the creek word arrived from Sullivan that discounted the earlier communication about a British move to the north. Sullivan must be correct, Washington reasoned. Why would the redcoats be engaged in a feckless march to the north, away from the American army? Washington abandoned his plan to strike, and he waited.

Another hour passed. Then at 2:00 P.M. a neighborhood farmer, followed shortly by an official dispatch rider, brought the word he had awaited. The British were on the move! But there was more—ominously more. Cornwallis, accompanied by Howe, had been moving north and he had gone undetected; or, at least, when he evidently had been spotted Washington had been induced to ignore the reports after he received Sullivan's contradictory communication. Washington now learned that the British had slipped around Sullivan. The man who had been outflanked on the Jamaica Road once again had been surprised. A very large British force (an entire division of seven thousand men, in fact) had gotten well to Sullivan's right. At about 3:30, from atop Osborne's Hill, Cornwallis commenced an artillery pounding, followed by a charge against the far right of Sullivan's lines, a point under the command of Lord Stirling. If the British broke through, Washington's army would be enveloped. For the moment, the very survival of the American army hinged on the performance of the two generals who had been captured at Brooklyn a year earlier.

Washington, meanwhile, remained three miles away, and very much in the dark. He could hear the strident boom of a great many cannon. But how many? Enough to destroy Sullivan? Was this merely a gambit to lure him away from Chad's Ford so the bulk of the British army could swarm across and strike at a weakened American center?

The thunderous sound of Cornwallis's artillery that roared past Chad's Ford was the signal for the British center to open up. Greene again was under fire, but from whom? Washington was confused. Contradictory reports in battle were expected, but this was worse. What was happening? Washington waited, sought more information, waited some more. At first he was certain that the attack on Sullivan was a feint, and, indeed, for two hours after the attacks on the two fronts commenced, he still refused to believe that his center was not the real British target. Only about 5:30 P.M. did Washington think differently. Leaving a few Continentals and Pennsylvania militiamen at Chad's Ford, he detached the bulk of Greene's army from the center and started for the furious battle raging near Birmingham Meeting House to the northwest. While Greene's men double-timed through the thick woods and across the verdant corn fields, Washington and his staff galloped ahead.

The commander had almost waited too long, but finally, after hours had dragged by, he had become convinced that the attack on Sullivan had to be his adversary's principal move. Had he waited much longer it is likely he would have faced a real disaster. Fortunately for Washington, Sullivan had performed well. He wisely had placed his forces atop Meeting House Hill, and when the action began he called in the reserves commanded by Stirling and Colonel Adam Stephen. Stirling, in particular, had made effective use of his artillery in countering Cornwallis's thrusts. Moreover, the men had fought very well. Early in the battle Sullivan's left wing had buckled in the face of a Hessian bayonet charge. "We broke and Rallied and Rallied & broke," one of the participants put it. But other men had stood firm, even though some veterans of European wars later said they had never witnessed such "Close & Severe" fighting. The conduct of the Americans was even more noteworthy considering that their foe outnumbered them two to one. Nevertheless, that British superiority had carried the day, and the American front was collapsing when Washington arrived. Exposed to enemy gunners for thirty minutes or more, Washington rode here and there exhorting the men to fight (he emerged untouched, though another officer riding beside him was shot through the leg), but the best he could do was plug Greene's force into the weakest holes. That did not stop the retreat, though it did keep it orderly, and the presence of these reinforcements—as well as the enveloping darkness at the end of this long, hot day—forestalled British pursuit. Washington, in fact, may never have seen such a welcome sight as the setting sun which closed that day, for it ended a battle that had gone badly on both fronts for the Americans. Shortly after Greene had been pulled out from Chad's Ford, British and Germans had attacked with considerable success, taking the field and a large prize of Continental artillery; but it had grown too dark by then for those men to link up with Howe. Another hour of daylight, Sir William later remarked, might have resulted in the "total overthrow" of Washington's army—an exaggeration, although in this instance Howe may not have been too far from the truth.[34]

In his report to Congress that night Washington labeled the encounter a "misfortune." That was an understatement. The British lost 583 killed, wounded, and captured, but the Americans lost at least twice that number. Washington could be thankful that Howe had not been in a position to attack until barely two hours of daylight remained, but there was little else over which to rejoice, save that the much-maligned soldiers—Continentals and trainbandsmen—had performed reasonably well. But things had not gone well. Washington later endeavored to pass off the defeat as the result of a series of "unlucky incidents." In fact, he bore more responsibility for the events than he ever acknowledged. Despite the luxury of ample time before the battle commenced, he had done an unsatisfactory job of reconnoitering the area. Two days before the battle Washington assured Sullivan that the British could not cross the Brandywine anywhere near his position, when, in fact, several fords existed just north of his army; moreover, when the commander rode from his headquarters—a farmhouse a mile behind Chad's Ford—to join Sullivan during the battle, he did not even know the way, and a frightened local farmer had to be commandeered and compelled at knife point to lead him. In addition, for members of an army that was two years old, Washington's intelligence network performed in an inexcusably lackluster manner. At one point misinformation nearly led him to launch what could have been a disastrous attack, while later "uncertain and contradictory" intelligence almost caused him to ignore Sullivan's plight until it was too late to be of assistance. In between these blunders, Washington was led to believe that the British were nowhere near Sullivan's position when, in fact, they were on the verge of fording the Brandywine and falling on the rear of one-half of the Continental army.

Even so, had Washington done everything correctly he probably could not have defeated Howe or stopped his advance. The British outnumbered the Americans, an advantage that was even greater when it is remembered that most of Washington's force consisted of untested regulars and short-term militiamen. Moreover, Washington's greatest successes hitherto had come from surprise raids and from his adherence to Fabian tactics, whereas his strategy at the Brandywine featured neither of these ploys. Undoubtedly his shortcomings lost him the opportunity of making Howe pay even more dearly in his campaign to take Philadelphia, but more than anything else what the events of that day—not to mention the late occurrences at Fort Ticonderoga—seemed to demonstrate was that a tenacious British pursuit of this war against America's inexperienced commanders might well have produced a British victory long before the autumn of 1777.[35]

By the next sunrise Washington had moved his army back to Chester, and soon thereafter he crossed to the east side of the Schuylkill in order to regroup. Howe had chosen not to pursue; his army had marched seventeen miles, then fought for three hours during that long day on the Brandywine. Still they were professionals, and Washington's army, if not on the ropes, also was tired and somewhat disarrayed. But Howe remained Howe, unenterprising and cautious, and Washington once again slipped away. The British remained at Chad's Ford for five days, stirring themselves only to send a regiment to seize Wilmington. While Howe took his time, Washington prepared for another clash. He still stood between Howe and Philadelphia. If the abandoned capital fell, he intended to see that the British earned it.

Washington did not recross the Schuylkill until Howe at last resumed his march, then he hurried toward the Lancaster Pike, ready again for another confrontation. Nature intruded on his plans, however. Two days after Brandywine an early season cold front banished the September heat that had gripped eastern Pennsylvania, and on the 16th, with the two armies facing one another near the White Horse Tavern, the autumn crispness gave way to a genuine williwaw. It rained for more than twenty-four hours, causing many in Washington's army who had cursed the searing heat a few days earlier to pray for its speedy return, for these were campaigners without tents or blankets, without a change of clothes or socks. They also were without dry cartridges, Washington discovered to his horror on the second day of the deluge. The blowing rain, together with flimsy, unlined cartouche boxes, had resulted in the destruction of more than four hundred thousand cartridges. Not only could the Americans not attack, they could not defend themselves if the British struck. Washington pulled out precipitately, beginning a long circuitous march (fifty miles in three days, twenty-nine of it during the final day) in search of supplies, until finally almost all the army again was east of the Schulykill; only General William Smallwood and Anthony Wayne, the latter with fifteen hundred men and four cannon, had been left to the west, stationed near Paoli Tavern, from whence they could fall on the rear of Howe's advancing legion.[36]

Suddenly the British acted with resolution. On the 18th Cornwallis discovered a rebel supply depot at Valley Forge and seized a congeries of much-needed foodstuffs and tools. More importantly Howe was tipped off to Wayne's outpost by local Tories, and after midnight on the 21st this American division was surprised and overrun, with the loss of more than 10 percent of its men.

No longer worried about his rear, Howe pushed off. For the next few hours he looked like a consummate professional, and Washington appeared quite amateurish. Howe, already northwest of Philadelphia, moved out in a northeastward direction, that is away from the capital and toward a major American supply depot at Reading Furnace (Warwick). Washington fell for the ploy. He rushed about half his army in this direction, whereupon Howe deftly reversed himself and streaked for a lightly held ford at Fatland, twelve miles south of Washington's headquarters. He made it easily. On September 26 the advance units of the British army entered Philadelphia, the difficult and uncertain—and likely quite bloody—crossing of a major river in the face of an entrenched foe overcome by Howe's unexpected adroitness. Characteristically, Washington refused to credit Howe or to take the blame. "I could not derive the least intelligence," he explained to Congress, since the countryside about Philadelphia was "to a man" inhabited only by uncooperative Loyalists.[37]

In the past, failure—or the appearance of having failed—only seemed to stoke Washington's zeal to act, whether as when he lobbied Forbes to act in the aftermath of the debacle of Virginians killing Virginians near Raystown, or urgently assailed Boston after months of unspectacular inactivity, or yearned to fight on Manhattan Island after the dénouements at Brooklyn and Kip's Bay. After Brandywine and the British crossing of the Schuylkill, his passion to strike burned at a fever pitch, equally fueled by his own lack of success and the American triumph to the north.

Eight days after the battle on the Brandywine, Burgoyne's and Gates's forces clashed for the first time. Burgoyne nearly met total disaster in that initial action; as it was he lost six hundred men—twice the American losses—at Free-man's Farm, as the scene of battle was called. But if Burgoyne's army was intact at the end of the clash, it was doomed. Gentleman Johnny's beleagured force was too weak to fight its way out of its predicament, and Sir Henry Clinton, left by Howe in command of New York, was too undermanned to fight through to its rescue; Clinton did send about two thousand troops up the Hudson to create a diversion in the American rear, but to no avail. By late September General Washington knew that "our Northern affairs [are] extremely pleasing" inasmuch as Burgoyne had fallen into "circumstances that threaten his ruin." [38]

Anxious to move, Washington called in reinforcements from Virginia and even from General Gates. ("This Army had not been able to oppose Genl. Howe's with the success that was wished and needs a Reinforcement," he tersely wrote the northern commander.) He additionally summoned twenty-five hundred men from the Highlands, a move that might have backfired. Learning that Clinton recently had been reinforced by British and Hessian forces, General Putnam at Peekskill pleaded with Washington not to take his men, lest their recall enable the foe to strike up the Hudson and spring Burgoyne from his trap. Washington pooh-poohed Old Put's alarms. If "Genl. Clinton moves at all, it will be thro' Jersey to form a junction with Genl. Howe," he predicted. Two days later Clinton moved north and captured the southernmost American installation in the Highlands. Fortunately for Washington, Clinton resembled Howe in many ways, and never more so than in this instance, for having concluded that he never could reach Burgoyne he made only a desultory attempt to drive through to Saratoga.[39]

Washington next summoned a council of war to solicit views concerning an immediate attack. What position Washington took cannot be known, but he probably preferred to await the arrival of reinforcements, and that ultimately was the unanimous recommendation of his subordinates. Three days later he called the officers together again. The situation had changed. More than thirteen hundred regulars had arrived, mostly from Peekskill, together with sizable contingents of militiamen from Pennsylvania, New Jersey, and Maryland; in all, he had eleven thousand men, nearly three-fourths of whom were Continentals, and more might arrive from the North shortly. Although Washington's position cannot precisely be determined, his papers convey the impression that he favored an attack, but when he polled the officers the vote was ten to five against an immediate assault. The commander assented, although with their blessing he moved the army nearer to Germantown. By October 2 Howe's force was just a dozen miles away.[40]

A day or two later Washington's intelligence operatives recaptured a bit of their tarnished credibility by intercepting two priceless letters forwarded by Howe. Through these documents Washington learned that the British force was badly divided. Some redcoats had been dispatched to assist in the eradication of rebel donjons along the Delaware, others were in Philadelphia, and still others were employed in fetching supplies from Head of Elk. That left Howe with eight or nine thousand troops at most at Germantown. There can be no question that Washington now was eager to strike, but having been rebuffed by a council of war once—maybe twice—in the past few days, he shied away from that vehicle as an instrument for making policy. This time he consulted with each general officer privately, individually. And he got what he wanted—authorization for an immediate attack on Germantown.[41]

The operation that Washington planned was complex. Knowing that Howe occupied emplacements on the southern periphery of the little village, Washington's plan was to divide his army into four columns, each entering Germantown via a different road. The two approaching from the north were to assail the opposite flanks of the defenders, the other two were to strike from the south at the British rear, and all four were to open the attack with a bayonet charge at precisely 5:00 A.M. Sullivan was placed in command of the American right, although Washington pointedly accompanied him. Greene commanded the left, John Armstrong and Smallwood those units attacking from the rear.

To be in place for this operation required a long march beginning about sunset, commencing then so that each column would have time to reach its destination and to relax for a spell during the last hours of darkness. To succeed, the men (about 10 percent of whom lacked shoes) had to traverse unfamiliar roads at night, then attack in an environment dotted with houses and fences behind which the British could hide. The men shoved off with a message from General Washington ringing in their ears: in the Northern Department "every thing wears the most favourable aspect . . . and promises success," he began; this "surely must animate every man. . . . This army . . . will certainly not suffer itself to be out done by their northern Brethren; they will never endure such disgrace. . . . Covet! my Countrymen, and fellow soldiers! Covet! a share of the glory due to heroic deeds!"[42]

Problems soon arose. Poor maps and a heavy fog that crept in during the early morning hours hindered the march, causing most units to arrive late. One who reached Germantown later than expected was Greene, and he had two-thirds of the American army; he did not reach the village until forty-five minutes after the battle had begun. Moreover, the British were not surprised by the arrival of the Americans. Their pickets opened fire before the bayonet charge materialized, then the main contingents rushed forward to the north side of the hamlet to contest the attackers. But despite the initial difficulties the Americans did not break. It was a vicious fight, and in time British units were the first to begin falling back, retreating through buckwheat fields toward the center of town. Visibility, however, was cut to thirty yards by the fog and smoke, and the American pursuers could only grope after their prey. Soon they could not move at all. A small number of redcoat light infantry commandeered the Benjamin Chew house, the residence of Pennsylvania's chief justice, a bulky, two-story, stone mansion that sat along the thoroughfare upon which Sullivan's men were traveling; that abode became a castle, a fortress, from which the deadly fire of a few British troops pinned down an entire American division for sixty minutes. Knox tried to no avail to blow down the dwelling with his cannon. It would not collapse. Washington then ordered that it be burned out. That failed too, and it ultimately was taken only by repeated methodical assaults.

It was during that fray that Greene—whose guide had taken him four miles in the wrong direction—finally arrived and joined the fight. At first it seemed that his appearance would turn the day. The British right sagged. All across the line the adversary was falling back. But two occurrences reversed the tide. British units on the left regrouped and attacked; Sullivan's men had walked into a bayonet charge, a sudden terrifying moment when, as if in an apparition men in red burst through the fog, screaming, running, light glistening off the cold steel knives attached to their muskets. There were few times in this war when America's green soldiery stood resolutely in the face of a bayonet attack. This was not one of them. At almost the same moment another disaster struck. Adam Stephen, Washington's old lieutenant colonel in the Virginia Regiment, now a general assigned to Greene's column, disobeyed orders, igniting an unfortunate incident. Contrary to his directions, he broke away from Greene to assist in the attack on the Chew House; en route his men stumbled into fog-shrouded troops whom he believed to be redcoats. They were not. They were Continentals under Anthony Wayne, scurrying to catch up with Sullivan. The two units fired on each other, then a frenzied, unaccountable panic set in that seemed to unnerve tired, overwrought men in other units. Men in some outfits raced pell-mell for safety, although more often than not these spent, disconcerted soldiers simply drifted away. Exposing himself once again to great danger, Washington rode here and there in a futile attempt to stop this curious retreat, and his example may have bucked up other officers who likewise displayed great valor in slowing the fallback and preventing a complete rout. But the fight was over. Three hours after entering Germantown the American troops departed, facing another twelve-mile march on weary feet and stomachs that had not been fed for eighteen hours or more.[43]

With 152 killed (57 at the Chew House alone), the Americans suffered about twice as many fatalities as their adversary. About 100 more Americans than British were wounded (521 to 450), but 400 of Washington's soldiers were captured, whereas the Continentals took no prisoners. From Washington's view, however, the most egregious disappointment was the American failure to score the stunning victory that was within its grasp. It is not likely that Germantown ever could have become a second Trenton, but for a few precious minutes another Princeton seemed conceivable. And such a victory, coupled with events in the northern theater, might have ended the conflict by breaking the British will to continue. Yet victory had eluded them, although this time Washington hardly was to blame, save perhaps for his not ordering that the Chew House be bypassed altogether. His repeated assaults on that inconsequential bastion only squandered time and men, and permitted a few stalwart redcoats to become an unnecessary impediment; besides, it seems absurd to believe that these few British infantrymen could have done any harm to the American rear—if for no other reason than that a handful of Americans could have contained them within that scarred mansion. In reality, no one really caused the attack to fail. By necessity victory hinged on the implementation of a complicated plan executed by a callow army that operated under difficult conditions, including the need to fight a professional army. Given the impediments to success, it is more surprising that Washington's army came so near to victory than that it failed.

The British held Philadelphia. But the struggle for that municipality had not ended. Washington believed that he could besiege the town and inhibit British foraging activities as he had done at Boston two years earlier. If he could simultaneously thwart Britain's access to the sea, Howe's taking of the city could "prove his Ruin," the commander told Congress.[44] The army and the militia had a good record when it came to sitting on British foraging parties, but obstructing Howe's maritime lifeline was a different matter. The booby traps and fortifications along the Hudson had been spectacularly unsuccessful summer before last. Could they succeed now?

General Washington first raised that question on the day he passed through Philadelphia en route to the Brandywine. Greene, Knox, Reed, and Philippe Charles Tronson du Coudray, a French officer who had surfaced at Morristown in the spring, studied the problem and counseled that the British could be denied the use of the Delaware. Various traps and snares had been in place for nearly two years; in addition, each added, the river was long and narrow, and the ingenious utilization of fire rafts, together with the careful selection of gun emplacements, could render the waterway too perilous for use. Washington was won over, and in August work commenced on the defenses.[45]

The plan was to fortify and otherwise obstruct a five-mile stretch of the river below Philadelphia. Not only were three forts constructed, but six sets of *chevaux de frise*, heavy timbers laced together by wire and studded with iron spikes, were submerged in the space between the islands and the sandbars that dotted the river. Any British vessel that sought to reach the capital would have a gauntlet to run.[46]

It sounded impregnable. It was not, although several bloody weeks of fighting passed before Howe secured the river. Not until late November, with casualties above four hundred on each side, did the first British vessel reach Philadelphia.[47]

This is the situation, Washington wrote his younger brother Samuel three weeks after the clash at Germantown: "The Enemy are in Phila., and we are hovering round them, to distress and retard their operations as much as possible." [48]

Ten days after Germantown, Howe fell back into Philadelphia with his principal army; there, behind fourteen redoubts constructed in a giant arc spanning from the Schuylkill to the Delaware on the north side of the city, he took up quarters in relative safety. Washington, meanwhile, oddly—uselessly, too, it would appear—moved his army from pillar to post during October, before lighting at White Marsh, ten or twelve miles north of Philadelphia.

That was indeed the situation. But there was more, too, which Washington did not mention. Above Albany the trapped redcoats in Burgoyne's army had flailed and struggled for sixteen days to extricate themselves from Gates's web. They did not succeed. With little food or water left, and no hope of being rescued by Clinton, Burgoyne surrendered his entire army on October 17. In the space of a one-hundred-day campaign Great Britain had lost a six-thousand-man army. Washington immediately sent his congratulations, trumpeting this "Event that does the highest honor to American Arms." However, on the same day he churlishly admonished Gates for having failed to keep him informed of his activities at Saratoga.[49]

Late in October the commander summoned a council of war to consider an attack on Howe in Philadelphia. In all likelihood Washington knew the answer before he raised the question. No, the generals responded. Howe was too strongly entrenched to be challenged, they said, and, besides, the enervated American army was too tired and too inadequately supplied to contemplate any move. Most of the meeting was consumed by a discussion of administrative problems (promotions and rewards, for instance), concerns that predominate when a year's campaign is at an end. But the Continental army did not immediately enter winter quarters. Instead, it remained at White Marsh through the struggle for the Delaware River, although Washington continued to consider undertaking a more active role. When Howe began to pound the Delaware River forts, Washington toyed with the notion of a strike by about fifteen-hundred men against the British gunners. Ultimately he abandoned the idea as too dangerous. Later, when Cornwallis was ordered out to complete the sequestration of the river bastions, Washington directed Greene to counter the advancing redcoats.

It was not the best idea that the commander ever hatched. Greene's force was only about 60 percent the size of his adversary's army, and he would have to fight on terrain that was boggy and difficult to traverse, and in a region that was lined with winding streams and branches. In short, it was the sort of place in which an army easily could find itself trapped. Greene delicately explained these problems to his commander, but he also knew the reason for Washington's order: the commander was under heavy pressure to act, some of it self-imposed, but much of it, in Greene's words, the result of criticism from "an ignorant and impatient populace." Greene's response, thus, was one of the most remarkable missives sent by any subordinate to this thin-skinned general. Not to act, he advised Washington, would be the wise option militarily, yet it would result in additional censure by civilians; to act would be unwise, and if the action failed

Washington would be "condemned . . . by all military Gentlemen of Experience." Do not commit "a lasting Evil," Greene counseled. "The Cause is too important to be trifled with to shew our Courage, and your Character [is] too deeply interested to sport away upon unmilitary Principles." Washington knew that Greene was correct, and the next day, without acknowledging the Rhode Islander's advice, he withdrew his orders and, in fact, summoned that force to White Marsh.[50]

What suddenly concerned Washington at the end of November was that every sign indicated that Howe might make one last sally against his army. This time Washington's intelligence was correct. Certain that his actions would be questioned even more severely than were Washington's, Howe at last was anxious to make Washington fight, and with the American army split between Pennsylvania and New Jersey, the time seemed propitious to act. Howe moved out of Philadelphia, although, typically, he advanced with the speed of a sluggish tortoise. American headquarters got the first hint of British intentions on November 26. Howe debouched at midnight seven days later. By then not only Green's force but some of Gates's men had joined Washington; the American commander monitored every step of Howe's advance, and, ironically, he even struck the first blow. Washington sent six hundred Pennsylvania militia forward to attack one of Howe's advance posts. The attack failed, although it did stop the British in their tracks for forty-eight hours. On the 7th Howe moved to within a mile of the American left, then under cover of darkness he tried an ingenious ploy: he staged a flanking movement similar to that which had succeeded at Long Island and Brandywine, sending a large force toward Washington's right; this time, however, it was a feint, for he planned to make his principal assault on the American left. It was a clever stratagem. But Washington did not rise to the bait, and Howe, flustered that he would not be able to score a cheap victory through chicanery, simply withdrew to Philadelphia. After nothing more than a brief skirmish Howe had abandoned his final opportunity for a clash with Washington. As at Dorchester and Brooklyn, Harlem and Somerset Court House, White Plains and now at White Marsh, Howe had shrunk from an attack because he believed his adversary was too well entrenched in unfavorable terrain.[51] It was a familiar excuse, a plaintive lament that served as Sir William's valediction.

Washington probably had hoped to get his men into winter quarters as soon as the last Delaware fort fell to the British. His army was tired and battered, and with its meager furnishings any sort of offensive was out of the question. Sometime after the middle of November the high command began to discuss and debate various sites at which to winter, centering on a variety of places between Reading and Lancaster to the north and west of Philadelphia, and somewhere near Wilmington to the southwest. All the general officers favored an immediate retirement to winter quarters, but some in Congress were of a different mind. Many legislators, principally delegates from New Jersey and Pennsylvania who feared that their states would be plundered if the army did not stay on the heels of the redcoats, carped against any thought of the Continentals retreating to winter quarters. Whatever the clout of this faction, Congress resolved unanimously to send a committee to White Marsh to plump for a cold-weather campaign. It was the first time since the army lay before Boston that Congress had meddled to the extent of sending representatives to headquarters in order to influence strategy, and Washington handled these men as easily as he had handled their predecessors two years before. Bolstering his position with testimony written by his officers, Washington pleaded that nothing could be done without militia assistance, and such units could not be procured during the winter months; moreover, if train-bandsmen could be made to come to camp, there would not be enough food for them and the Continentals too. The legislative committee was convinced. It reported that a winter campaign was inexpedient, and it even was induced to propose improving officer's benefits as a means of ending the chronic "discontents" in the army.[52]

If Washington won that round Congress nevertheless pressured him to find quarters near Philadelphia. The congressmen conveyed their wishes to the commander after receiving a somewhat hysterical appeal from the Pennsylvania Assembly, a remonstrance that predicted that Howe's legions would commit the most hideous excesses if Washington's army was not nearby. Unwilling to buck Congress, Washington broke camp at White Marsh on December 11. He still was not quite certain where he would lodge for the winter, only that he wished to be on the west side of the Schuylkill. He spent the next week looking for suitable quarters, moving west, then south, then west again, dogged much of the time by Cornwallis; meanwhile, his army camped without tents and suffered first through a cold dreary rain, then through an early winter snow storm.

All the while Washington seethed and simmered at what was happening, until he could no longer restrain himself from penning two bitter, sardonic letters to Congress. "I can assure those Gentlemen" who had resisted the army's plans to take up quarters before the winter descended, he wrote in one of the missives, "that it is a much easier and less distressing thing to draw remonstrances in a comfortable room by a good fire side than to occupy a cold bleak hill and sleep under frost and Snow without Cloaths or Blankets."[53]

Finally, upon the advice of some of his Pennsylvania officers, Washington settled on a gently rolling area flanked by the Valley Creek and the west bank of the Schuylkill, a site eighteen to twenty miles from Philadelphia.

On December 19 the army splashed through the mud and the lingering slush of a recent storm to the rustic locale that had been selected for their winter home, a place the locals called Valley Forge.

9

The New Continental Army

"Long Live General Washington"

Washington had good reason to feel that the campaign of 1777 had been a success. Not only had he preserved his army, he had made the British pay dearly for their sole acquisition—Philadelphia. And his accomplishments had come in the face of a numerically superior adversary. As for Howe's capture of Philadelphia, Washington concluded that "but for the eclat it is attended with," the possession of the city "brings no solid advantage to their arms." Then, too, there was the American victory over Burgoyne in the North. So splendid had been his and Gates's campaigns, in fact, that almost everyone now suspected that France, and perhaps Spain as well, would openly enter the war in 1778 as America's ally. Ironically, however, at the very peak of its military achievements, America's fortunes ebbed to an unprecedented low point. Much later Washington would find it impossible to forget the pain his men faced that winter, and he would tell a historian that "you might have tracked the army from White Marsh to Valley Forge by the blood of their feet." [1]

Valley Forge! Words that would come to symbolize the suffering of the fighting men in that war, a place, a time, of ineffable and needless anguish, the moment when America came nearest to witnessing the extirpation of its army.

The commander's first object at Valley Forge was to get his men into some kind of shelter. The soldiers were divided into work parties of a dozen men each and directed to build fourteen-by-sixteen-foot log cabins, abodes in which "to *stay* . . . not to live," as one soldier put it. The Marquis de Lafayette thought them "scarcely gayer than dungeon cells," but they did provide some shelter. Washington and his very highest officers lived more commodiously, usually finding quarters in private residences. In Washington's case, headquarters was established in a nearby two-story stone farmhouse. The commander and Martha, who arrived at Valley Forge early in February, used the upstairs for their private habitation; the downstairs rooms—including a large dining room which was added to the house that winter—were set aside for official business. [2]

Washington found it more difficult to supply his army than to house it. Nearly one-third of the soldiers were without shoes, and even larger numbers had neither blankets nor adequate clothing. Victuals were almost as scarce. Washington ordered a bakehouse constructed, but flour was in such short supply that the structure more frequently was used as a courtroom to hear court martial proceedings. Fresh meat and vegetables never were available, and even salt-pork or salt-beef was a rare treat for the men. The highest ranking officers fared better, however, though some were heard to complain that they had "nothing but bread and beef to eat morning, noon, and night." Whenever food was available, these soldiers were not inclined to share it with anyone or anything, and certainly not with the army's horses. While there is no record of any soldier having starved to death during that terrible winter, more than five hundred horses perished of malnutrition.[3]

Illness was the inevitable offspring of deprivation. Early on Washington ordered the construction of two log-cabin infirmaries for each brigade, but soon these facilities proved inadequate, and men were hospitalized in nearby Lutheran and German Reformed churches. Even taverns were made to serve as sick bays. Continental army returns for February show that nearly 7000 men were ill and that 290 died. The next month the number of sick declined to 600, but the death rate rose by one-third, to 424.[4]

Washington escaped affliction at Valley Forge, in all likelihood because he barely experienced the deprivations that gripped his men. He too lived in a tent until every soldier was hutted, then he moved into the warm and dry farmhouse, a dwelling in which he could sleep in his own bed—literally his own bed, for he had it dismantled and moved each time he changed quarters. Washington did not dine sumptuously during those months, but he never seems to have gone without food, nor does he appear to have suffered any shortage of tea or coffee. In addition, his wife lived with him during most of his stay at Valley Forge, a solace denied the soldiery. The commander, in fact, took a dim view of having any women in camp, unless they were in the company of officers; "care is to be taken to prevent a number of women from following your Regiment," he ordered his colonels, "as they. . . ." Intriguingly, he did not complete the sentence, although a month later he maintained that female visitors enticed the soldiers to desert.[5]

If Washington did not think it improper for officers to live comfortably while the soldiery suffered, he had plenty of company. It was as if two armies wintered at Valley Forge, one composed of the highest officers, and a second made up of the rank and file and their lowest ranking officers—a woeful, vexed company upon whom few of the amenities of their superiors ever devolved. But, curiously, the common soldier seemed more inclined than the officers to stoically—virtuously, Washington might have said a year or two earlier—accept the hardships. Enlisted men did desert and there may even have been one brief, isolated instance of mutiny, but in comparison to their officers these men exhibited a quiet, stout patriotism that is as astonishing today as it was then to the foreign officers who were present; a European army, they agreed, would have disintegrated in rebellion or flight under similar conditions.

Many officers, on the other hand, whined and complained with an insensitiveness that is difficult to imagine, grumbling principally about the alleged financial ruin that they faced for serving for low pay, and, while already living grandly by the standards of their men, pleaded for even more largess. (General Greene, for instance, once proposed that about forty gallons of recently discovered liquor be given to each regiment for the use of the officers; he did not recommend that any be given to the men.) Because of such officers' overweening self-indulgence, the very existence of the Continental army was placed in jeopardy. In mid-March Washington told Congress that many officers were threatening to resign. In fact, upwards of three hundred officers had quit during the past ninety days, fifty from General Greene's division walking out on the same day in December. Washington acted to minimize the crisis by granting extended furloughs to his officers, so that many hardly were present to experience the vexations of Valley Forge. But, chiefly, he served as their principal lobbyist with Congress, pleading and arm-twisting for the financial demands his officers made.[6]

What the officers wanted from the legislators was a guarantee of half-pay for life upon their involuntary retirement at the end of the war. The English, these officers argued, compensated their officers in this manner, as well as by permitting them to sell their commissions. For a variety of reasons Washington had no difficulty supporting the officers' demands. Not only did he fear the loss of his army if the officers were unappeased, he had jettisoned his earlier idealistic sentiments about virtuous, sacrificial service. Self-interest, he now said, was mankind's predominant passion; public virtue briefly might take precedence, but eventually man's private interest would assert itself and win out. His officers were no exception to this universal maxim. For a time they gladly had risked death for a meager salary, yet those days were gone. Now the half-pay measure was essential to keep good men in the service, good men who would be made into better officers by this reform, "because when an officer's commission is made valuable to him, and he fears to lose it, you then may exact obedience from him."[7]

Many in Congress forcefully resisted the half-pay scheme. Some feared it would lead to a standing army, others saw this special dispensation as contrary to the virtuous ideals of the Revolution. Moreover, pragmatists found Washington's argument to be based on a flimsy foundation. If officers were so financially strapped that they could not remain in the army, they asked, how would a pension that would not commence for perhaps five years, maybe even ten years, be of any help? But Congress was in a jam. Not to act was to court trouble, and in the end, in May 1778 the legislators voted a compromise that the officers found acceptable: half-pay for a seven-year period following retirement. (The enlisted men—about whose severance pay Washington had remained silent—were to receive a one-shot bonus of eighty dollars if they enlisted for the duration of the war.)[8] The officers within the Continental army had blackmailed the Congress of the United States and secured their own ransom.

If Washington ever contemplated the double-standard at Valley Forge, he did not bother to record his thoughts. However, he was concerned about the implications of his soldiers' torments. Unless supplies quickly were found, he told Congress in his first hours at Valley Forge, "this Army must dissolve" totally, or it must break up into small, ineffectual units. He did not have "a single hoof of any kind to Slaughter, and not more than 25 Barls. of Flour!" He needed four thousand blankets, three thousand pairs of shoes and an equal number of stockings, he added. He had nine thousand men with him when he entered the encampment, a third of whom were too ill-equipped to be fit for duty, and still more who were ailing and hospitalized.[9]

Washington had foreseen the problems and had begun to take steps to meet them six weeks before he entered his winter quarters. Early in November he urged Congress to institute legal means by which goods could be confiscated from Tories, and he urged the legislators to commission agents who could purchase articles from patriotic Americans. From the army's war chest, moreover, he found funds by which he could send forth officers to purchase needed commodities. And, of course, he had foraging parties in the field, although he knew that the seizure of goods would alienate civilians. (As a precaution, he issued explicit orders directing his search gangs to buy, not steal, items from the citizenry.) He also pleaded with governors in neighboring states to find and ship food and clothing to his army. "No pains, no efforts can be too great for this purpose," he implored. Once at Valley Forge he took adequate steps to get the men housed quickly, he furloughed as many men as he could spare in order to conserve his precious stockpile of food, he endeavored to regulate the prices that sutlers could charge for scarce goods, and he refused to allow his general officers to keep horses—even at their own expense—because the beasts would consume essential provender. Yet the crisis persisted as if his efforts had never been undertaken. So baffled was Washington that he acknowledged that he did "not know from what cause, this alarming deficiency or rather total failure of Supplies arises." [10]

Indeed, what was the cause of this disaster? Many in Congress believed that Washington was partly to blame. The general was reluctant to impress commodities which belonged to civilians, fearing that the practice would result in "the most pernicious consequences." Ultimately, Congress ordered him to seize the goods of farmers who would not sell their goods to the army.[11]

However, the army's supply problems ran far deeper than General Washington's unwillingness to risk the eclipse of morale on the home front.[12] Administrative inefficiency and incompetence, as well as rampant graft and corruption within the quartermaster service, took its toll during this winter. In addition, the vicissitudes of war contributed to the suffering. For instance, Howe's occupation of Philadelphia closed the lanes of supply between Pennsylvania and the South. Nor can the climate be overlooked. While the winter of 1777–78 was not unusual for southeastern Pennsylvania, heavy snows and frequent winter rains often closed the roads to the army's supply wagons, leaving Valley Forge a scene of destitution in the midst of plenty.[13]

The logistical difficulties that occupied much of Washington's time at Valley Forge were not his only problem. He came to believe that his position as commander in chief was jeopardized. At first it was just an instinctive feeling, but he was concerned and his worry surfaced in the defensive tone he suddenly adopted in his correspondence. Never, he began to tell some correspondents, had his troop strength been the equal of Howe's army. Besides, he had been compelled to fight the British in a region that teemed with Loyalists. "How different the case in the Northern department!" There, he said, thousands of militiamen had turned out to help Gates, and they had been joined by detachments of regulars which he had sent north. Considering his disadvantages, Washington went on, he had done well, confining Howe's acquisitions to Philadelphia, a questionable prize. Exculpatory expressions were not uncommon to his manner, although up to this point in the war Washington had never seemed so inclined to seek excuses. In light of Gates's magisterial victory and his own setbacks at Brandywine and Germantown, common sense led him to conclude that questions inevitably would be raised about his performance. After all, if a person like Reed with whom he had been close had questioned his capabilities a year earlier, what would others now say? He got an inkling on November 8. Among the items in that morning's mail was a missive from Lord Stirling. "The enclosed was communicated by Colonl. Wilkinson to Majr. McWilliams," Stirling tattled. "In a letter from Genl. Conway to Genl. Gates he says: 'Heaven has been determined to save your Country; or a weak General and bad Councellors would have ruind it.' " [14]

Washington was not too surprised that others were whispering about his abilities. But the revelation that Gates might be acting in league with the doubters was sufficient to arouse the deepest anxiety within the commander's wary, uneasy mind. Gates had revealed himself to be an intensely political person, one with many friends in Congress. He also had just won that victory at Saratoga, a triumph certain to garner more friends.

Washington's relationship with Gates already was strained. Their friendship and mutual respect appears to have begun to cool as early as the spring of 1776, although the reasons can only be guessed at. During the siege of Boston it appears to have been an open secret that Gates assiduously was courting the more radical congressmen, particularly influential New England legislators like John and Samuel Adams. Washington, who also had been wooed by Gates before the Second Continental Congress, may have come to see the man as too wily, too ambitious to be completely trustworthy. The next spring Gates became miffed at Washington; almost openly soliciting the Canadian command following the demise of Montgomery and Thomas, Gates seems to have concluded—unfairly it would appear—that he did not have Washington's support for that post. He got that command, but it initiated a protracted controversy in Congress between his supporters and Schuyler's defenders, a bitter quarrel that still was in full swing when the commander, reeling across New Jersey in the late fall of 1776, summoned Gates's assistance against Cornwallis. Gates did hurry south, and three days before Christmas he parked his force with Washington's army across the river from Trenton. But Gates was not present on the day of Washington's famous attack on the Hessian cantonment. He had gone to Baltimore, where Congress then was meeting. The next summer Gates's intriguing paid off. Congress recalled Schuyler and asked Washington to choose a new commander for the Northern Department, but unwilling to risk antagonizing one faction or another in Congress, the commander declined to act. Congress ultimately placed Major General Gates in command of that department, but by then he may have concluded—for the second time—that he did not have Washington's support.

By the fall of 1777 Washington already had begun to have sleepless nights on account of Thomas Conway, the author of that cryptic missive to Gates. An Irish-born French officer whom Silas Deane had recruited, Conway had arrived at headquarters during Washington's final days at Morristown the previous spring. The commander welcomed him as an experienced officer who could be of help, and his effusive support induced Congress to appoint Conway as a brigadier general. Washington's acumen seemed justified when Conway fought superbly in New Jersey, then again at Brandywine and Germantown. No one was higher on Conway than Conway himself, however, and in October 1777 he commenced an active lobbying campaign with Congress to win a promotion to the rank of major general. Vain and opinionated, Conway loudly interspersed his exalted views of his own talents with his cynical judgment of Washington; the Virginian was a gentleman, he thought, but to put him in charge of the Continental army was to put him out of his league. In the meantime, Washington had begun a campaign of his own to block Conway's promotion. It is likely that Washington had gotten wind of this Gallic officer's imputations, but in this case the commander did not act out of personal spite. He quite rightly feared that Conway's advancement over many with longer American service records would have disastrous results, perhaps provoking some who had expressed their rancor over pay and deplorable conditions to quit. The issue was hanging fire on November 8 when Stirling snitched on Conway.

Washington's initial reaction probably mingled alarm and relief, for if the correspondence hinted at a conspiracy against him it also afforded a possible means of embarrassing Conway and preventing his promotion. Washington dealt with Conway first, immediately writing him a terse note penned in the same vein as his ominously curt letter to Reed a year earlier:

> Sir: A Letter which I received last Night, containd the following paragraph. In a Letter from Genl. Conway to Genl. Gates he says: "Heaven has been determined to save your Country; or a weak General and bad Councellors would have ruined it."
>
> I am Sir Yr. Hble Servt.[15]

He did not have long to wait for a reply. Within hours Conway responded. He admitted having criticized the army and some of its policies, and he confessed that he had aired these views to Gates and others, including former Quartermaster General Mifflin; however, he denied having attacked Washington. "My opinion of you, sir, without flattery or envy is . . . that You are a brave man, an honest man, a patriot and a man of good sense . . . [but that] you have often been influenced by men who were not equal to you in point of experience, knowledge or judgment." Less than a week later Conway submitted a letter of resignation to Congress.

Whatever veracity Washington might have attached to Conway's reply, he gleaned one kernel of information from it: Mifflin as well as Gates appeared to be close to Conway. Moreover, on the day before Stirling's communication arrived, Congress had reorganized the Board of War, replacing the congressional members with permanent members and naming Mifflin as the president of the reconstituted body. Two weeks later Gates was added to the Board, and two weeks after that the first fruits of this new complement became evident. Congress—which initially had referred Conway's letter of resignation to the Board of War—reversed itself in mid-December, naming the Frenchman to a new post, inspector-general, and promoting him to major general. This was precisely the moment, too, when Congress virtually ordered Washington's army to take up winter quarters around Philadelphia, Mifflin's hometown.

Washington, always overly sensitive to criticism, now tired and overworked from the anguish and constant strain of six consecutive months of life-and-death decisions, exaggerated the extent of those who reproached his leadership. He imagined the existence of a conspiracy to overthrow him, a plot that some historians have called the "Conway Cabal." Conway, Gates, and Mifflin were but the tip of the iceberg, Washington believed, concluding that others in Congress and on the Board of War also had united against him. It is not difficult to imagine the gossip and the half-truths that must have been passed on to him by well-meaning aides and friends, as well as by sycophants and those whose own future was intimately linked to Washington's survival as commander. Even his old friend Dr. Craik wrote from home to inform him that he had been told on good authority that a "Strong Faction [is] forming Against you"; "Eastern and Southern Members [of Congress] are at the bottom of it," he related. Washington seems to have credulously accepted most of the tales, as if no tattle was too fanciful for him to believe.[16]

There is no question that doubts and harsh judgments about Washington were uttered that fall and winter. His intelligence network was reprehensible, it was charged. It was alleged that his army was undisciplined. Another imputation had it that Washington was too much under the "pernicious influence" of Knox and Greene. Washington plainly was inept, said some accusers. Major General Johann de Kalb, a Bavarian-born soldier of fortune who joined Washington in 1777, even suggested that the commander was sluggish, indeed, lazy. "We want a General," said Jonathan Dickinson Sergeant, a former New Jersey congressman, now the attorney general of Pennsylvania.[17] But to grumble about Washington and to question the wisdom of some of his decisions was a far cry from actually conspiring to bring about his downfall.

It is too much to believe that some did not wish to depose Washington. It is known that Dr. Benjamin Rush, the medical director of the Middle Department, urged Washington's removal and proposed that Gates or Lee or Conway supplant him. Yet with the possible exception of William Duer, a congressman from New York who once was alleged by a colleague to be part of a cabal to dump the commander, there is no hard evidence that anyone else sought to oust Washington. Certainly there is no evidence that Gates or Mifflin—or even Conway—endeavored to remove Washington, nor is there much likelihood that they could have succeeded had they been part of such a conspiracy. The hard, cold fact of the matter was that once Congress selected Washington it was stuck with him—at least until he suffered a cataclysmic beating, some defeat that went beyond anything that had occurred through the campaign of 1777. Barring that, or some sort of illicit behavior on his part, Washington virtually had to be kept, for otherwise to have ousted him would have been to expose the Revolution and the fledgling nation to incalculable dangers. Not only is it difficult to conceive of his proud fellow Virginians watching patiently and quietly while Congress dumped the commander without sufficient reason, but for many Washington already had come to symbolize the sacrifice of the Revolution. Scuttle him, said one of the alleged plotters, and "American will lose perhaps her only prop." [18]

But it was not as though Washington remained in power simply because Congress was stuck with him. Many congressmen genuinely admired the commander, and the great majority were fair enough to realize that the army's shortcomings at Brandywine and Germantown were not due to his ineptitude. Henry Laurens, the president of Congress, thought him to be "the first of the Age," and Robert Morris, a Pennsylvania congressman and later a financial agent for Congress, spoke of Washington as the "*first* Man in this World." "I love him to a Degree of Adoration," wrote Richard Peters, a member of the board of war and supposedly a member of the anti-Washington cabal. John Adams was typical of those who recognized that Washington had fought the cream of the British army, whereas Gates had been blessed with advantages unavailable to the commander. Even so, he was not uncritical of Washington, and, in fact, he was somewhat apprehensive of the idolatrous tendencies that he perceived people held toward him. Once Adams even expressed some relief that the army had not succeeded at Philadelphia, lest the "Adulation would have been unbounded, so excessive as to endanger our Liberties." Still, he was satisfied with Washington's abilities, and he chided Dr. Rush: "You are daily looking out for some great military Character.—Have you found none?" Heroes are all about, he went on, and they included Washington and Gates, as well as other officers and the common soldier. How many other countries would have displayed enough "Examples of Fortitude, Valour, and Skill" to have fought Great Britain so successfully for three years? Then he added: the "Idea that any one Man, alone can Save Us, is too Silly . . . to harbour for a Moment." [19]

No one could have convinced Washington that there was not a conspiracy. He spent most of that dreary winter engaged in a futile, often malevolent, correspondence with Gates. Actually, Gates initiated communications. Roughly a month after Washington first had written Conway, Gates learned through Mifflin that his correspondence with the French officer had been made public. In his first letter to Washington he said nothing about his views toward the commander, only fulminating that someone—"a Wretch, who may betray me"—had rifled through his private papers. He also told Washington that he was sending a copy of this letter to Congress. The commander's reply was masterfully concocted, a reminder that he was anything but inept in the nice art of infighting. All along he had presumed, he now claimed, that Gates himself was behind the revelation of Conway's "infidelity," a friendly gesture by a colleague in arms to forewarn him of another's "intrieguing dispositions." "I have found myself mistaken," he concluded.[20]

It was not until late January 1778 that Gates got around to commenting on his correspondence with Conway. He defended the inspector-general, referred to Conway's missive as "harmless," one that contained only some justified criticism of the lack of discipline among American soldiers, and he alleged that the quotation which had been passed on to Washington was a forgery concocted by some personal enemy, perhaps, he said in a left-handed way, by Alexander Hamilton, one of the commander's aides. He did not send along a copy of Conway's epistle, however, and Washington's response played on this omission. Washington also meanly ridiculed Conway's capabilities, only to close with the sarcastic caveat that perhaps he was wrong and Gates was correct about the French officer's talents, since Gates had a "better acquaintance with him, than I [previously had] reason to think you have had."[21]

Washington was too skilled at infighting for Gates, as that outmatched officer now realized. He sent one last missive in which he apologized to the commander for whatever unpleasantness had occurred and pledged that he had never been part of any cabal. Gates also pleaded for an end to this rancorous affair. By late February, when that final letter arrived, Washington felt safe, and he, too, was ready to put the incident to rest. "My temper leads me to peace and harmony with all Men," he wrote unconvincingly.[22]

One thing that had eased Washington's mind was that he had masterfully rid himself of Inspector-General Conway by that time. When the two men were forced together by official business, Washington had treated Conway with a cold formality that did nothing to hide his impenetrable loathing for the man. His manner drove Conway to write Washington, protesting such treatment and defending his action. Eventually, however, Conway destroyed himself. On the last day of December he sent the commander a missive that dripped with sarcasm. He charged that Washington demanded standards for promotion that were too high; perhaps he did not measure up, but he had served for thirty years and he believed that he had learned his craft better than those Americans who had been officers for only a few months. Otherwise, few men could ever attain the "universal merit" that the commander desired, perhaps only "frederick [the Great] in europe, and the great Washington in this continent. I certainly never was so rash as to pretend to such a prodigious height."[23]

The day after Washington received this remarkable letter, he dumped all his correspondence with Conway into the lap of Congress. It was clear that the legislators had to do something, lest the army's already sagging morale be further eroded by this clash. Given a choice between Washington and Conway there never was a doubt which way the Congress would lean. Nor was there any question about which man Washington's most ambitious subordinates would choose. A truckler like the Marquis de Lafayette, who earlier had offered warm praise for Conway, now characterized his colleague as "cunning" and "dangerous," while Washington's young aide Hamilton, himself no stranger to the arts of lickspittle, quickly denounced the French officer as "vermin" and a "villainous calumniator and incendiary." General Greene used almost identical language when he appraised Conway, as did Washington himself, who now openly called the inspector-general "a secret enemy; or, in other words, a dangerous incendiary."

Once the Washington-Conway tempest became public knowledge Congress moved quickly, transferring the French officer to the remote North. A few months later, with little to do but watch the snow fall endlessly in this theater, Conway resigned, an option that Congress was only too happy to see exercised. Before he could sail for France, however, Conway became involved in a war of words with Brigadier General John Cadwalader, a foolish altercation that resulted in a duel. Conway was shot in the face during the clash, but he survived the painful wound and returned to France, where he served with distinction for several more years. His final act as an American officer was to write Washington a gracious letter begging forgiveness for any "grief" he may have caused and wishing the commander the best, as "You are in my eyes the great and good man." General Washington never responded.[24]

Conway was not the only foreign volunteer to give Washington fits. Since early in 1777 a growing number of foreign soldiers had arrived in America, and while their expertise and experience was valued, Washington soon discovered that their presence was a mixed blessing. When the war was about a year old Congress happily learned that many professional soldiers in Europe were anxious to fight under America's banners; some were adventurers in quest of a war, some saw this as a chance to gain experience and promotion upon their return to their own army, and some—Frenchmen anyway—interpreted America's fight against Britain as a service to their native land. Without considering all the ramifications of the move, Congress quickly authorized its agent in Paris to sign on some of the volunteers, especially those with engineering or artillery backgrounds. The result often was disappointing, however. Some who came were untalented imposters, and others, although skilled, were unable to express their specialized knowledge in understandable English. Congress sadly discovered, too, that one of its agents, Silas Deane, had dispatched some of those officers with commissions that bestowed very high rank in the Continental Army.

One such case involved Philippe du Coudray, a colonel in the French army whom Deane commissioned as a major general. Since his commission was dated

August 1, 1776, he was to be the head of the Continental army's artillery, supplanting Knox and outranking Sullivan and Greene. All three American officers were properly outraged, huffing and pledging to resign before submitting to such an insult. Congress would have faced an impossible quandary had not du Coudray's horse solved matters for the legislators. With the Frenchman on its back, the beast clumsily fell off a ferry into the Schuylkill River, whereupon both it and its rider drowned.[25]

Experiences with other imported officers turned out more happily for all involved. Louis le Bégue de Presle Duportail, a French technician, was placed in command of all American engineers, and he skillfully planned both the Delaware River defences and the layout of the encampment at Valley Forge. Johannes de Kalb, a self-styled Bavarian aristocrat, served valiantly as an infantry officer until his death on a southern battlefield in 1780. Colonel Andrew Thaddeus Kosciuszko, a captain in the army of Poland, also served with distinction as an engineer, as did another Pole, Casimir Pulaski, a cavalry officer who died in the Battle of Savannah in 1779.

Two of the foreign officers perhaps are even better known today than are many American officers. Gilbert du Motier, officially the Marquis de Lafayette, arrived in America in 1777. Born into the French aristocracy, he was the son of an army captain who died in battle when the boy was just two years old. Young Lafayette was married by age sixteen—an arranged marriage with the fourteen-year-old daughter of another blueblood. A rather bashful, awkward youth, he easily was overlooked in the heady social swirl of Versailles, and perhaps for this reason he latched onto the army as a means of gaining attention. America, however, was the only place in the western world where one could find a war in progress. He closely watched the conflict for eighteen months, then, just nineteen years old and only a captain in the French reserves, Lafayette talked Deane into a commission as a major general. In the summer of 1777 he arrived in America, and on the same day Washington and his army paraded through Philadelphia en route to the Brandywine, Congress formally commissioned Lafayette. Like the commander, Lafayette agreed to serve without pay. Indeed, in many ways he resembled a young Washington. Wealthy, demure, shy, eager to learn, he also was courageous under fire. (At Brandywine, his first combat experience ever, he continued to fight after sustaining a gunshot wound below the calf, and a few weeks later, even though his leg still was too painful to wear a boot, he again was in action about Philadelphia.)

Already fed up with foreign officers when Lafayette arrived, Washington nevertheless soon took this young Frenchman under his wing. Still almost a boy at twenty, Lafayette seemed to embody every virtue that Washington most prized; for the Frenchman, on the other hand, the commander evidently represented the sobriety and the unselfish commitment to the public good that he thought was required of the citizen and nobleman. In a sense, the relationship that developed between these two was not unlike that which had existed between young Washington and Lord Fairfax, a closeness facilitated by Lafayette's ability to play the role of son, just as the man who now became his "father" once had done. Still, the filiation that developed between these two was genuinely close, a bonding that grew from mutual respect, trust, and love.[26]

Frederick Steube, self-styled as Frederick Wilhelm August Heinrich Ferdinand, and still better known as Baron von Steuben, was one of the last foreigner volunteers to arrive, reaching Valley Forge only in February 1778. Never more than a captain in his native Prussia, he fibbed that he had been a lieutenant general, and his gullible hosts in America swallowed his story. He was not a Teutonic aristocrat either. Nor did he own a vast estate in Swabia, as he claimed. His allegations were bogus through and through—except that he was indeed a soldier. He came strictly as a volunteer, initially serving without rank in the Continental army and reporting directly to Washington (though he shortly was made a major general and he succeeded Conway as inspector-general). Without any sign of the bluster that had been the hallmark of so many European volunteers, "the Baron" allowed as how he would like to train the troops. Impressed by what seemed to be his candor, Washington additionally realized all too well that his army could not get too much training. He immediately put the German to work. First von Steuben drilled a squad while a hand-picked company watched, then he drilled the company while a regiment watched. And instead of sergeants training the men, he prescribed that officers drill the soldiery. Short and stocky, with thick, powerful arms, von Steuben looked a little like a well-dressed blacksmith; his air of toughness was augmented by his gutteral commands and his favorite Germanic invectives. He was the sort of officer who inspired both fear and respect, not the least because he, too, was on the drill field marching with the men. A month after his arrival he had the entire army at Valley Forge practicing his drill program, a streamlined version of the Prussian system. By the time the spring buds had burst into their radiant hues, the Continental army had begun to look more like a real army, at least on the parade ground, and the leadership had reason to hope that there was some truth in von Steuben's once sarcastic observation that in the "European armies a man who has been drilled for three months is called a recruit, here in two months . . . a soldier." [27]

Von Steuben's labors to train the soldiery were only part of a concerted effort to remodel the Continental army. Washington still was residing in his tent at Valley Forge when he informed Congress of his desire to initiate major administrative reforms—to "rectifie mistakes and bring things to order," as he put it—before fighting once again commenced. "We have not more than 3 months to prepare a great deal of business in," he told Congress; "if we let these slip, or waste, we shall be labouring under the same difficulties all next Campaign as we have done this. . . ." Would Congress send a committee to camp to work with him in the preparation of the "most perfect plan" possible for the army's reorganization? The legislators responded immediately, sending a committee of four to Valley Forge, a panel that included Joseph Reed, a recent addition to Pennsylvania's congressional delegation. The congressmen remained with Washington for seven weeks, scrutinizing changes made during the past summer, considering new ideas.[28]

By the summer of 1778 the army had a somewhat different look. A more formally instituted engineer corps existed, as did companies of sappers and miners, that is combat engineers, men who specialized in digging entrenchments and tunnels. Troops of light dragoons patterned after European partisan corps had come into being, as had mounted police units (the Marechaussee Corps) and special forces (the Corps of Invalids) responsible for guarding prisoners. Units of work crews had been constituted, and responsibility for the maintenance, storage, and transportation of all the cannoneers' tools had been consolidated in the new Artillery Artificer Regiment. Some minor administrative tinkering was undertaken to improve the accessibility of food and drugs within the Medical Department, and more drastic mending led both infantry and artillery regiments to be reconstituted along the lines of the British model (additional companies, but fewer officers). Of course, all the reorganizing would be useless if there were no men in the army. To hold on to its disgruntled officers, Congress took two steps: it was at this point that it hit upon the half-pay compromise; and, it also voted to refuse the services of additional foreign volunteers, excepting only those men of extraordinary merit. Enlisted men had to be gathered too, and Congress urged each state to institute conscription as a means of replacing those soldiers whose tour of duty had ended.[29]

The destitution all about them at Valley Forge made it clear that reform of the army's logistical departments was the congressional committee's most pressing problem, although by spring only minor changes had occurred. The committee and Washington proposed to improve the commissary system by curtailing its bureaucracy, reducing, as the committee report stated, the "number of little piddling pilfering Plunderers" who operated within this network. But other than stating that intention, little actual reform took place. The one substantive change occurred when the committee, and especially Washington, induced a reluctant Nathanael Greene to accept the vacant post of quartermaster general; in addition, two assistant quartermasters general—both relatives of Reed—were named, one to be responsible for all acquisitions and issues, the other a comptroller. Congress accepted the recommendations in March, and, incredibly, it voted to allow Greene and each assistant a one-third of one percent commission on all the money they spent.[30]

General Greene's transference to a desk was not that winter's only major change in the line-up of officers about Washington. Before the army abandoned Valley Forge the commander moved General Sullivan to a distant post. In October Sullivan had been cleared by a court of inquiry that studied his raid on Staten Island; six months later, when Joseph Spencer resigned his commission, the way was open for the commander to appoint Sullivan as his replacement in command of the American army in Rhode Island.[31]

Another general was not as fortunate. Adam Stephen, an old acquaintance of the commander, the second in command under Washington in the Virginia Regiment twenty years earlier, was convicted by a military tribunal of chronic drunkenness, as well as of malfeasance during the retreat from Germantown. It was left to the commander to accept or reject the court's findings. If Washington had known Stephen for years, the two never had been close. Young Washington had thought him a less than fit officer in the 1750s, and after the French and Indian War, when Stephen had challenged the master of Mount Vernon for his seat in the Burgesses, their relationship had grown especially cool. Stephen, moreover, had made it his business to keep a particularly close eye on Washington's land hunting for the Virginia Regiment veterans, as though he had not quite trusted George's honesty. Nor had this war brought them any closer. Indeed, on Christmas night in 1776 Washington had loudly accused Stephen of nearly wrecking his planned attack on Trenton, for without orders he had sent a patrol to that Jersey village just hours before the scheduled assault. The court's recommendation was the final straw. Without a word to his one-time comrade, Washington approved the verdict and dismissed General Stephen from the Continental army. Lafayette was given his command.[32]

If Washington rid himself of two officers whom he thought to be frequent sources of affliction, he was compelled to receive Charles Lee back into the fold. For sixteen months after his capture at Basking Ridge, Lee had been a British prisoner. At first he had feared that as an ex-redcoat officer he might be hanged as a traitor, but Congress had made it quite clear to Howe that if anything happened to Lee reprisals would be carried out against British prisoners in American hands. Thereafter Lee lived well, sumptuously even, in captivity, residing with his dogs in the council chambers of the city hall in New York, then aboard a vessel in the city's harbor, and finally in a comfortable apartment in town. From the moment of his capture Congress had worked diligently to secure his release. Finally, in April 1778 its efforts paid off, and Lee was exchanged for a British general held by the United States. Needless to say Lee was delighted, and he presumed that Washington would share his exhilaration; "considering how [Washington] is surrounded" by inept advisors, Lee told the president of Congress, "he cannot do without me." Accompanied by his usual retinue of canines, as well as by the wife of a British sergeant ("a miserable dirty hussy," according to America's commissary general of prisoners), Lee breezed into Valley Forge.[33] Whatever Washington privately felt about this man who had joined Reed in criticizing his generalship back in the dark days of 1776, he welcomed him with the grace and ceremony that might have been accorded a conquering hero.

According to one officer the coldest period of the winter hit during the first week of March. It may only have seemed colder, because on one or two fleeting occasions the men had been teased with springlike days. The troops also had been misled into believing that the other hardships of that awful winter were at an end. Before the end of January the stow of food improved a bit. The supply departments finally got some victuals into camp, while foraging parties rounded up supplementary fare. In addition, beginning in mid-month Washington countenanced the establishment of a public market on the camp's periphery, enabling those with the wherewithal (primarily officers, since the men had not been paid for two months) to purchase comestibles. The shortage of clothing and blankets remained chronic however. What made the situation even more maddening to Washington was that he was aware of a generous supply of apparel stockpiled in the Highlands, but confusion and ineptitude among wagoners and within the department of military stores prevented its arrival. The army did procure one considerable cache of livery. At the beginning of January the British brig *Symetry* ran aground above Wilmington and was captured by the United States. Its cargo included forty terrified women, the wives of British officers, General Howe's personal silver service, and a hold laden with cloth, hats, shoes, boots, and stockings. After being held for two months, Washington directed that the women and Sir William's silver be delivered to Philadelphia; he ordered that the raiment be sold among the officers, a somewhat shortsighted step for a commander who prided himself "the common Guardian of the Rights of every man in this Army." [34]

A few mild days early in February unclogged the Schuylkill south of Reading, enabling the commissariat to funnel in stores of much-needed supplies. For a moment conditions improved, then another howling winter storm swept through. The miseries of this loathsome place returned in earnest. On February 1 Washington had depicted the army merely as "uncomfortably provided" for; a week later he described its state as "most Melancholy." For four days there was no meat to allocate, and almost every other commodity was in perilously short supply as well. Desertions increased, averaging ten to fifteen each day, and Washington grew anxious at the prospect of a "general mutiny." A "fatal Crisis" had set in, warned the commander, whose communiqués reassumed the same desperate air that had characterized his letters to Congress during the first days at Valley Forge. [35]

It seemed as though Washington's proverbial good fortune had taken a holiday. He sent Anthony Wayne with over five hundred men into southern New Jersey on a foraging mission, and the party succeeded splendidly in locating cattle and other precious commodities, but the sudden appearance of British cruisers south of Philadelphia prohibited their recrossing the Delaware for an immediate return to Valley Forge. Wayne was compelled to drive the livestock and forage wagons all the way to the vicinity of Trenton before he could cross, and it was nearly March before he returned with his viands, by which time some men had been without meat for seven days. Washington learned, too, that 130 beeves were en route from New England, but unfortunately for him the British also got wind of the cattle drive; incredibly the cowpunchers had not been provided with military guards, and when the British were the first to get to the herd the American army lost what would have made several days of succulent dining.[36]

With all his other worries Washington at least generally was unencumbered about the likelihood that Howe might assail Valley Forge. Duportail had laid out strong defenses for the camp, and it seemed likely that if Howe had shrunk from an onslaught against the more primitive ramparts at places like Dorchester Heights and White Plains, he would not be inclined to attack here. In fact, although Washington was unaware of it, General Howe's war was all but at an end. Back in mid-November, at the moment he succeeded in opening the Delaware, he had offered his resignation; that winter Sir William was far busier preparing a defense of his conduct during the past two years—inadequate supplies and too few troops, would be the kernel of his plea—than in contemplating an attack on Washington's ragged army.[37]

Could an attack on Valley Forge have succeeded? The Loyalists thought so. Joseph Galloway, a Pennsylvania Tory, was the most vocal proponent of an assault. Formerly an American congressman, he had defected to the British just after Howe's victory at Fort Washington, and in the fall of 1777 he became the superintendent of occupied Philadelphia and a chief operative in the redcoats' intelligence network. He kept the high command very well informed about the misery and desertion at Valley Forge; it seemed to him that cold, hungry soldiers were not likely to fight too well. In this assessment Galloway had company. Much later George Washington agreed that Howe had been unwise not to have assaulted the encampment. However, for once Howe may have been correct. Washington outnumbered Howe eleven thousand to ten thousand, and had a battle loomed the Americans could have gotten enough additional militia to have inflated the odds to considerably more satisfactory levels. The roads were in such poor condition that the transportation of the redcoats' artillery and support systems was problematical. Furthermore, Howe would have had to cross—then recross—the Schuylkill, never an easy task in the face of the enemy. And all this to attack a well-entrenched foe that occupied hilly terrain.[38]

Under the circumstances Howe seems to have given no thought to an attack. His inactivity further estranged him from the Loyalists, now an increasingly desperate group who, behind his back that winter, sang a bitter doggerel:

> Awake, arouse, Sir Billy,
> There's forage in the plain,
> Ah, leave your little Filly,
> And open the campaign.[39]

That caustic verse was Sir William's swan song. Late in the spring he was relieved of command.

While the British idled away the winter, plans for the new year were being discussed in American staterooms. One notion that germinated that season called

for still another invasion of Canada. Several factors made a Canadian operation seem attractive. Now that Burgoyne's army had been destroyed and the
domain was only weakly defended, Canada might easily be taken. Moreover,
some thought that America had failed in its earlier endeavors in Canada largely
because it had not secured the support of the French-Canadian citizenry, but an
invasion force that consisted of a large number of the French volunteers serving the Continental army might rouse those recalcitrant British subjects. It was
observed that the acquisition of Canada would close the door to any future British
notions of invading the United States through that portal. It might even topple
the North government, ending the war immediately. The thoughts of some also
turned to postwar territorial considerations, leading them to conclude that unless
Canada was won on the battlefield, it would not be won at all.

Washington, however, was not among those mesmerized by still another
Canadian adventure. America's bleak record of failure in that faraway domain left
him unenthusiastic about still another try. Furthermore, he wondered, why squander troops in what now was likely to be a backwater sector of the war? Certainly
Britain would not attempt another invasion from Canada. Washington, therefore,
denounced the thought of invading Canada as "folly" and "not practicable." [40]

But others were hopeful of success, and in January Gates prevailed on
Congress to endorse an "irruption into Canada," as the notion was labeled.
Lafayette was named as the expedition's commander; Thomas Conway was made
the second in command. Then the Board of War informed the commander in chief
of its plans and asked him to lop off one of his regiments to help flesh out the
invasion army.[41]

There can be no doubt that Washington felt humiliated, proudly believing
that he had been subjected to shabby treatment. There also is no doubt that he
interpreted the episode as the work of the "Conway Cabal." He seems to have
viewed the adventure as nothing more than a ploy by the Board of War to erode
his authority, while at the same time the prestige of Gates, Mifflin, and company
would be enhanced. (Some historians even have seen the proposed expedition as a
device through which the alleged plotters could lure Lafayette from Washington,
and by which the Frenchmen could be used as a tool to bring France into the war.)
In fact, it seems certain that the increasingly suspicious commander overreacted.
Indeed, a good case can be made for the soundness of the plan to invade Canada at
that moment. An attack launched in February or March, before Lake Champlain
thawed and restored Britain's total naval superiority, just might have succeeded.
Moreover, if the attackers reached Quebec and once again besieged that fortress
city there was a reasonable chance for success. Certainly by January 1778 the
evidence was strong that France was about to enter the war, an event that probably
would have prevented Great Britain from sending a relief force to rescue Quebec.
As to who most favored the endeavor, there can be little question that New
Englanders were the strongest backers of the "irruption"; and there also can be
little doubt that they were less concerned about overthrowing Washington than

about securing regional security, hardly a sinister motive for a people who had fought five wars in the past seventy-five years against armies descending from Canada.[42]

In the end the project failed, a victim of the politics of command that simmered that winter. Washington's young friend Lafayette, who was unwilling to offend his sullen commander by participating alongside Conway in any campaign, Canadian or otherwise, helped its demise. Whether because of his political acumen or because of a genuine love for Washington, or both, Lafayette spent two precious winter weeks dickering with Congress over his command. Conway must be dropped, he insisted, and Washington must be permitted to name his successor. In addition, he dictated, he must remain subject to Washington and report to him. If these terms were not met, he would resign his commission and return to France, accompanied, he promised, by several of his countrymen presently in America's service. The legislators caved in. But valuable time had been lost. Lafayette did not reach Albany until late in February, and there he quickly discovered a multitude of problems that soured him on the venture. Only half the promised twenty-five hundred men were present and fit for duty, and he learned that several Canadian veterans, including Arnold and Schuyler, had counseled against the invasion under such conditions. Early in March he decreed that the expedition must be "thrown down," the victim, he said, of a "hell of blunders, madness, and deception."[43] By the beginning of April he once again was at Washington's side at Valley Forge.

The ceaseless onslaught of military problems that confronted Washington that winter was not his only quandary. As a citizen-soldier, a warrior who took no salary and who expected to leave the army for Mount Vernon at the end of the struggle, General Washington could ill afford to ignore his planting and business concerns for the duration of the Anglo-American conflict. While at times it must have seemed that the war would never end, Washington realistically could expect to return home while still only about fifty years of age. During his initial months as commander in chief, he had tried to direct affairs at Mount Vernon over long distance, averaging a communication every ten days to Lund Washington, his cousin from Chotank who had assisted in the management of the estate since 1764. But early in 1776 the anxious owner and his cousin reached an agreement: Lund would remain at Mount Vernon as Washington's manager until the war ended, and, in return, he was to be guaranteed good wages, a salary that never was to be lower than the highest annual compensation he had received during his first eleven years with Washington. Both men were happy. The salary gave Lund hope that someday he could purchase a home of his own, while Washington was confident that his affairs remained in competent hands. "[N]othing but your having the charge of my business, and the entire confidence I repose in you, could make me tolerable easy [while away] from home for such a length of time," the general confessed.[44]

The arrangement hardly prevented the busy general from communicating his wishes to "Doctor Lund," as he joshingly called his superintendent following the receipt of some unsolicited medical advice from his cousin. The "New Chimneys are not to smoke," he carefully instructed; plant a grove of hardwoods at each end of the house, using "all the clever kind of Trees," that is, flowering varieties such as crabapples and dogwoods; install a window at the gable end of the cellar; stay on the lookout for available land in the Northern Neck, acreage for which he would pay "(almost) any price," even exchanging his slaves—"of whom I every day long more and more to get clear of"—or certain of his livestock, but not his cash.[45]

During this morose winter at Valley Forge Washington grew fearful that Lund would desert him, lured away perhaps by the prospect of receiving a land bounty in return for his enlistment in the Continental army. To assure his continued service, the general proposed to increase his salary, but it was a ploy that outraged Lund. "I hope for the future you will entertain a better opinion of me," he shot back, "than to beleive that while you are encountering every danger and difficulty, at the hazard of your life and repose . . . I would attempt to take advantage of you by screwing up my wages or leaving your estate to the care of a stranger." But Washington hiked his salary anyway, a necessary action, he explained, because of the potentially ruinous inflation that had befallen the colonies.[46]

Running Washington's business affairs was a full-time job. Lund oversaw the spinners who labored with flax and wool, directed the operations of the mill that ground corn and wheat, looked after the livestock, and tended to the ongoing construction of the gardens and the expansion of the house that Washington had begun just before the Continental Congress first convened in 1774. In addition, he supervised the agricultural operations of Washington's vast empire, five separate farms at Mount Vernon that totaled thousands of acres worked by approximately 250 slaves, indentured servants, and free skilled artisans, as well as his dower farmholds and those he had purchased as a young man. And on top of all this he was responsible for the safety of Martha and Mount Vernon. Mrs. Washington probably was safe enough, but the estate and its slaves were owned by a traitor—at least in the eyes of Virginia's last royal governor, Lord Dunmore. Lund expected to see a royal fleet ascend the Potomac, burning farms and liberating slaves in its path, and he took what precautions he could; he packed many of the general's most precious items so they could be moved on a moment's notice, and he arranged to store Washington's wine in a neighbor's cellar. Lund was prescient. Dunmore's fleet did sally upriver in August 1776, hoping to raze Mount Vernon and other plantations along the way, but it was stopped twenty-five miles short of Washington's home. It was Dunmore's only such foray, and three months later he was en route to England, gone forever from Virginia.[47]

Mount Vernon was not Washington's only financial concern during these years. The inflation that led him to increase Lund's wages ate away at his investments. Not only did Virginia debtors retire their obligations to him in currency that was worth only a fraction of its original value, but he had to watch helplessly as bonds worth perhaps £7000 in 1775 depreciated until three years later they were worth only about one-tenth their earlier value. Nor did he realize any monetary gain from his western lands. His properties across the mountains continued to stand idle and unsold, a condition certain to persist as long as the war continued. The war undoubtedly had still another impact on him: given the collapse of the English market, less of the produce of Mount Vernon could be sold. There were times when Washington longed for liquid capital, but none was available, not even an officer's salary, for he had asked that he be compensated only for his expenses. So worried was the general that he once predicted that he might "come home with empty pockets whenever Peace shall take place." [48]

But Washington exaggerated his financial plight. His concern for the depreciation of his investments was justified, as was his anguish at the inevitable and persistent visits of the tax collector; moreover, he had good reason to fret over his income, inasmuch as the revenue produced by Mount Vernon apparently declined steadily during the initial years of the war. On the other hand, creditors had no cause to hound him and, while the overhead cost of operating his estate was huge, the expense was manageable, for a considerable portion of the outlay went into feeding—not paying—his labor force, hardly an impossible requirement for an agrarian operation. Still, Washington's shrill reaction was natural. Not only was he absent and largely in the dark about the state of affairs at home, but these were new problems for him. In reality, he faced a period of unaccustomed austerity, although he never was so impecunious as to be unable to consider the purchase of additional property or to actually invest in a privateering venture in 1777. [49]

One means existed by which he could have converted his assets into ready cash. He could have sold his slave property, a prospect he seemed to find intriguing. His thinking on this matter was strictly pragmatic. Slavery, he had come to realize, was a notoriously inefficient labor system for a wheat farmer like himself. Unlike tobacco, wheat not only required little labor during its growing season, but at harvest time the permanent work force could be supplemented by temporarily retained hired hands; Mount Vernon, he concluded, had a surplus of labor. Washington calculated that by selling his bondsmen he might realize as much as £15,000, and he deduced that the interest that might accrue from the wise investment of that sum would yield far more than the annual merchandising of Mount Vernon's slave-grown produce. But Washington only thought of this course. He had no scruples about selling these people, provided that families were not sundered, yet he was too reluctant to exchange his slaves for continually depreciating money ever to take such a step. [50]

By the third week in April 1778 the gloom that for months had shrouded headquarters was beginning to lift. The snow was gone, the sun now beamed warm and radiant, and the first signs of spring had begun to transform Valley Forge from its winter dreariness to a bucolic wonderland. But better weather was not the only source of rising spirits. Washington was certain that he had smashed the cabal that had threatened his power, and he knew that he enjoyed more support than ever within Congress. Moreover, although at the first sign of winter's demise, the commander briefly had worried that Howe might strike his sickly, undermanned army, the attack never came. Soon Washington spoke of a future "big with events of the most interesting importance," alluding to rumors that swirled about York and Valley Forge like a biting March wind. France must seize upon Britain's misfortune, some said, and declare war upon its ancient rival, perhaps even formally entering into an alliance with the United States. To forestall that, others hoped, Britain would seek to avoid a two-front war by offering acceptable peace terms to America. Washington's position was clear. "Nothing short of Independence . . . can possibly do." Never again could he accede to British dominion. "Our Character as Men, are opposed to a coalition with them as subjects, but in case of the last extremity." In his mind there was but one choice. If Britain refused to recognize American independence, the war must continue, waged now alongside France.[51]

Whatever fears Washington might have harbored that Congress would opt to end the war by reconciling America to Great Britain soon were alleviated. At the end of April news reached America—brought by an aptly named brig, *La Sensible*—that France indeed had recognized the independence of the United States, and that emissaries of the two nations had concluded treaties of alliance and commerce, subject, of course, to congressional approval. The commander promptly let Congress know his feelings about these "good tidings," and the day after the legislators ratified the covenants Washington ordered a celebration at Valley Forge.[52]

He appointed May 6 for a *feu de joie,* a day of exultation. This army had never experienced anything quite like this; indeed, it had not had much to celebrate since its remarkable triumphs at Trenton and Princeton a year and a half earlier.

It was warm, hot even for so early in the spring, when the festivities commenced at 9:00 A.M. First the chaplains of each brigade read summaries of the treaties, then they preached for the better part of ninety minutes; Martha and George Washington listened to the sermon offered by New Jersey's chaplain. At 10:30 a single cannon blast rumbled across the rolling green hills, the signal to begin the inspection of the troops. An hour later another cannon's roar was the sign to commence the next phase. General Washington rode out first, trailed by his aides and his guard. Slowly he rode past the massed soldiery, until he reached a reviewing station atop a knoll, and there he paused to review the troops. After the last man had paraded past, another cannon barked—and another, and still another. Thirteen in all, each fired three times, each accompanied by two running fires of musketry, begun by the commander's guard then spreading systematically from brigade to brigade. Following the initial artillery explosions the troops shouted: "Long live the King of France." Another whomp of cannonery and the men cheered: "And long live the friendly European Powers." The final report from the artillery park evoked the last cheer: "To the American States." For the men the celebration was over. For the officers it had only begun. They rode to tents erected before the smoking cannon, where they dismounted and in knots of thirteen each, linked arm-in-arm, marched to the shade of the canopies to partake of an elegant buffet of cold meats and flowing wine and liquor, a repast made all the more enjoyable by the presence of several young women from nearby villages who had been invited to the spectacle. The party still was in swing when the long shadows of late afternoon crept over this once dreary camp. Washington was first to take his leave, and as he ascended his steed to ride away a spontaneous applause began. Men hurled their hats into the air and cheered: "Long live General Washington."[53]

It had been a grand day, a fitting crown to a "season of General Joy," as Washington called it. (So moved was he, in fact, that he pardoned and released every prisoner in the army's stockade.) A measure of prosperity had returned to this once forlorn cantonment. The "martial appearance of the troops [had given] sensible pleasure to every one present"; the commander's popularity had been visibly confirmed; and, like many others, Washington believed the coming Gallic presence would "chalk out a plain and easy road to independence."[54]

During those balmy vernal days, Washington's time began to be taken up less by frantic searches for supplies and more with thoughts of the coming summer campaign. He knew that about 15,000 men were in the Continental army; he had 12,000 at Valley Forge, roughly 2000 were in the Highlands, the remainder were stationed in Wilmington. The British were thought to have 17,000, nearly two-thirds of whom were in Philadelphia. Washington could envision only three options for his army: attack Howe's army in Philadelphia; attack the small British force holding New York; or remain at Valley Forge, where the army could continue to be trained. He elicited the written views of his officers, then two days after the grand *feu de joie* he summoned them to a council of war. The response was unanimous—sit tight. Both Philadelphia and New York were too heavily fortified to be attacked, and the army would require triple its present manpower capabilities before it could even think of a siege. Besides, with the French entering the war there seemed little need to act in haste, if for no other reason than it was unlikely the ministry would be able to send reinforcements across the Atlantic any time soon.[55]

Ten days after the officers met, the first hint of British intentions unfolded. Spies in Philadelphia began to report that Britain planned to evacuate Philadelphia. The next day the commander's intelligence network reported that the redcoats were returning to New York. His secret agents could not have been more correct. The French treaty with America, tantamount to a Gallic declaration of war against Britain, had compelled Whitehall to reappraise its strategy. Its naval blockade would have to be relaxed so that more of the fleet could be used for the defense of the home islands. The ministry also opted to attack the French island of St. Lucia in the West Indies, a much-contested spot in Anglo-French warfare, because British control of the island hindered the French fleet's use of its more northern Leeward Islands. The operation in the Caribbean, however, would not leave Sir Henry Clinton, Howe's successor as commander of the British army in America, with enough troops to hold Philadelphia, New York, and Rhode Island simultaneously. Since New York was demonstrably the most important—and the most easily defended—of the two cities, London in effect decreed that the Pennsylvania metropolis would have to be jettisoned.[56] Clinton arrived in town on May 8 to relieve Howe. The next day a vessel arrived from London with orders for him to transfer the army to New York.

In many ways Clinton did not strike visitors as a battle-hardened veteran soldier. His features were soft, and his eyes seemed to radiate good will and compassion. He enjoyed hikes and canoe trips that permitted him to study flowers and bird life, but his passion was the violin, one of several musical instruments that he played in an accomplished manner. Visitors also found him to be a difficult person to know. Painfully timid and retiring ("I am a shy bitch," he once said of himself), Clinton was happiest when left to his solitary pursuits.

The son of an army officer who also once served as the royal governor of New York, young Henry spent eight of his early years in America. At nineteen he entered the British army, and he served during both King George's War and the Seven Years' War, seeing considerable action—and suffering a serious wound—in the latter conflict. By the 1770s he not only had attained the rank of major general, he sat in the House of Commons. But the most important event for Clinton during these years was a personal tragedy. He lost his wife to complications from childbirth. Grief-stricken and disconsolate, he fell into a deep, lengthy depression, in the course of which he seemed to further isolate himself from others.

Clinton accompanied Howe and Burgoyne to America in 1775, and for the next thirty months he was the second in command in the British army. He served capably, though without flamboyance, and when Howe resigned he was not London's first choice to take control of their forces. Lord North preferred General Jeffrey Amherst for the post, but he declined the offer. Carleton, the Canadian governor, also could have had the position, but he refused to serve under Germain. One or two others likewise had an inside track, only to turn their backs on the opportunity. So it was Clinton, a man who had never stirred intense devotion among his fellow officers, a man with little political clout in Whitehall, who became the commander of the British army in America.[57]

Whether Clinton chose to return his army to New York by land or by sea would dictate Washington's response, and for weeks the American commander was unable to get a handle on his counterpart's intentions. Of one thing only was Washington certain: he would surrender none of his troops to the Continental units in the Northeast, for he wished to have a large enough army to assail Clinton in the event that the British journeyed by land. By early in June he believed the overland option almost certainly would be Clinton's choice, but it was not until June 18 that he knew for certain. The redcoats left their barracks that morning at 3:00 A.M., rattling and stomping about the cobblestone streets while they organized. Then they set forth—on foot. Behind them they left the smoldering ruins of every bridge into the city, as well as several ships that had been scuttled; they took with them almost all the Philadelphia Loyalists, thoroughly discouraged folk who, in the words of a civilian aide to Lord Howe, now were but "a ruined Enemy [to the rebels], & to us an inefficient Friend." [58] After only nine months in Philadelphia, the Howe brothers' great prize, was yielded up.

Forty-eight hours after the last British soldier had passed from the city into New Jersey, Washington's soldiery was on the move—out of Valley Forge. The Americans headed almost due north toward the Delaware River, a few days later crossing that now-familiar stream at Coryel's Ferry. Time was not a particular problem. Conveying an army that included a twelve-mile-long baggage train, Clinton was not moving any too quickly; besides, the redcoats were compelled to pause every so often to remove trees from their path, obstacles felled by Washington's ancillary forces, and to reconstruct bridges that the Americans had demolished. [59]

Washington was in a good position. He had nearly 13,000 men, counting nearly 2000 militiamen and various Continental units posted here and there in New Jersey; against this force, Clinton had barely 10,000 men. By June 23 the British army reached Allentown, almost due east of Trenton. Washington must have hoped they would continue on a northerly course, for that would have compelled them to hurdle the Raritan at New Brunswick, no mean feat with an adversary breathing down their neck. Instead, Clinton turned right at Allentown, taking a narrow road that led northeast toward Raritan Bay and the threshold of Staten Island. For two days the British and their mercenary allies trugged on, covering only five or six miles each day, though it must have seemed like far more to these men. A June heat wave had set in. By noon each day the temperature climbed to near 100 degrees; later each afternoon thunderstorms raged, but by the following morning it always was clear and hot again, the sort of humid, steamy kind of heat that, for men marching in woolen uniforms and carrying heavy backpacks, must have been nearly unbearable. Heatstrokes were not uncommon. [60]

At Monmouth Court House Clinton called a temporary halt. Throughout the 26th, then again the next day, he waited, hoping for more seasonal temperatures. The American army, which had been shadowing Clinton's every step, was brought forward and parked just to the northwest of the redcoats' lines. Washington faced a difficult decision. Evidently he yearned to assail his adversary, but three times in the past six weeks, twice during the march of the past week, he had been advised by unanimous votes of councils of war not to risk a full-scale attack; at best, his generals urged only a limited, harassing foray. Yet Washington knew that if he did not strike now he would not have another chance before Clinton reached the coast, barely fifteen miles away. He wrestled with the problem until intelligence arrived that Clinton planned to move out again the next morning, then, egged on by Knox, Wayne, Lafayette, and Greene, he decided to strike. Still, it was Washington's decision, one entirely in keeping with the instinct for daring that he always had manifested, one that now was hastened perhaps as much by the past winter's criticism of his alleged passivity and overwariness as by his yearning to test the results of von Steuben's season of training his army. His plan was to send out an advance force of nearly fifty-five hundred men, about 80 percent of whom were Continentals. The main army would follow, remaining close by in case its assistance was needed.[61] But who would command?

Washington had little choice but to offer Charles Lee the opportunity to lead the advance units. After all, he was the senior American general beneath the commander. Whether Washington was troubled by the prospect of placing Lee in charge of a crucial operation is not clear. As thin-skinned as was Washington concerning the alleged plots against him, he might have had misgivings about placing someone as fickle—and, in some quarters anyway, as popular—as Lee in a position to reap the rewards of victory. More troubling, however, would have been the fact that since his return from captivity, Lee consistently had counseled against attacking the British, at one point even recommending that the American army adopt the tactics of a guerrilla force. Lee seems to have believed that with the French entrance into the war the Americans simply had to persevere to win their objectives; to hazard heavy losses in an unnecessary attack seemed to him a poor strategy to pursue. Washington must have wondered whether a man of such temperament could lead an attack force, but in the end he offered him the opportunity to do just that. To Washington's amazement, and probably his infinite relief, Lee refused the honor, indicating that the thought of commanding such a small force was too undignified to be considered by someone of his rank.[62]

General Washington then turned to Lafayette, bypassing both Greene and Stirling. In all likelihood it was not a popular choice, but in the aftermath of the hysteria at headquarters during the past winter no one was inclined to challenge the commander's thinking. It clearly was a curious choice. Lafayette was not quite twenty-one years old, and he had never commanded an army of this size. A month earlier Washington had put him in charge of a division—about twenty-two hundred men—and sent him on an utterly useless mission into the no man's land between the Schuylkill and the Delaware. Ostensibly he was to harass the British in Philadelphia, but in the end he narrowly escaped a drubbing at Barren Hill, midway between the city and Valley Forge. Now, seemingly mesmerized by this young man, Washington turned to him again, certain that he would win the laurels he so much lusted after.[63]

Once in command Lafayette performed poorly. Ordered to "attack the rear of the enemy" at the earliest opportunity, he planned a night march followed by an assault at daybreak on June 27. But during that night he lost contact with Washington. Indeed, he soon had no idea of the whereabouts of Washington and the main army. For that matter, he no longer was certain of the location of his foe.

Alone, isolated, and seemingly confused, Lafayette was in a vulnerable position, one that Clinton might have exploited had he not been preoccupied by his own problems. In the end Lafayette was saved by the commander. As intelligence gradually drifted into headquarters, Washington discovered the truth: Lafayette had succeeded in getting into an extraordinarily precarious position. Washington ordered the young Frenchman to fall back so that he could be supported by the main army, and his directive reached Lafayette just in time. His advance units already had stumbled to within less than a mile of the enemy's lines.[64]

With the clash averted for the moment, Lee now stepped forward and requested the command he previously had brushed aside. He had decided, he said, that leading such a large corps was "undoubtedly the most honorable command next to the Commander-in-Chief." [65] Having witnessed Lafayette's performance, some of Lee's colleagues may have impressed upon him the need for such a request. If so, he probably did not require much coaxing.

Washington may even have been relieved by Lee's entreaty. At any rate, he acceded to his wishes, seemingly perturbed only by the possibility that his vain young protégé might be offended by his sudden loss of power. Late in the afternoon of June 27 Lee supplanted Lafayette, taking command of the corps at Englishtown. Washington and the main army remained at Cranbury, about four miles to the rear, but separated from Lee by deep ravines, topography hardly ideal for rapid deployment; about nine hundred New Jersey militia were posted a similar distance on the opposite side of Englishtown. Washington's army was ready to fight. But so was Clinton's army. The British commander easily could have moved northeast to the more hilly ground of Middletown, there escaping a clash. Obviously, he had no desire to duck an action. The redcoats were on tabletop-flat terrain, the sort of environment in which they normally fought best.

Lee's orders were to engage the British the next morning. But what Washington really intended has been the subject of endless dispute. On the morning of the Battle of Monmouth Court House he wrote that he meant only "to harass" his foe, and his earlier directives to Lafayette had directed him merely to annoy the redcoats. However, Washington subsequently characterized his aims as those of a commander bent on attacking Clinton's army and provoking a full-scale battle.[66]

At 7:00 A.M. on June 28, the morning still and already hot, Lee moved forward. In no time he was bedeviled by an intelligence breakdown. Told first that Clinton had not moved, then informed that he had moved, Lee had to pause to await definitive word. Thirty minutes or more passed before he proceeded, crossing two ravines en route, the first—or the "west ravine"—spanned by a narrow bridge, the next one—the "middle ravine"—traversed by an equally narrow causeway. Lee had to be worried by what he was discovering. This terrain—which Washington had not troubled to reconnoiter—was not conducive to a battle; indeed, he already had entered a sector from which a hurried retreat would be impossible. However, not only did Lee fail to inform Washington of the perplexities that he faced, but when he discovered that the British were moving he confidently informed the commander that he could ravage their rear guard. Lee pushed on past the court house at Monmouth, then angled north, taking a position just east of still another morass, the "east ravine." Now he was ready to strike. What he did not know—or what he ignored, depending on whose subsequent account one chose to believe—was that Clinton had rushed units back to protect his endangered rear. The British also planned a strike. And Clinton was first to get his men in motion.

In no time the American left wing buckled under the British assault. Immediately thereafter, moreover, three regiments on the American right commanded by Lafayette pulled back. The Frenchman apparently acted on his own initiative; Lee certainly did not order his retreat, and Wayne, in command of the center, counseled against his action, imploring him to stay so they could jointly counterattack. With both the right and left collapsing, Wayne was left with no choice but to fall back too, and that, in turn, compelled Lee, who still was full of fight, to order a retreat to a point behind Monmouth. Inexplicably, however, Lee once again failed to inform Washington of the course of events.

Lee sent Duportail ahead to select the best site behind the east ravine, the place where he would make his second stand. But when Lee arrived with his army, he discovered that the French engineer had chosen a poor location for a fight. Duportail had picked a spot which exposed the American right to the enemy, while its center was beneath an eminence that the redcoats surely would command. At the same moment that Lee discovered Duportail's unaccountable error, he also learned that Washington and the main army still were more than two miles away, too far removed to provide immediate aid. Most importantly, however, Lee now realized that his force of about 2500 men faced a reinforced adversary that consisted of "the whole flowr of the British Army, Grenadiers, Light Infantry, Cavalry & Artillery, amounting in all to 7,000 men." [67] He ordered yet another retreat, this one across the two remaining bottoms and onto the high ground beyond the west ravine.

The initial retreat had been orderly, and so, in all likelihood, was the second withdrawal, although subsequent eyewitness accounts varied. All that now is clear is that sometime around noon Washington learned that Lee was retreating, and he hurried forward to discover the reason for this action. Along the way he encountered squads and companies, even entire regiments, falling back. Passing through part of a light infantry unit that had gone out with Lee that morning, Washington paused to ask who had ordered the retreat. When told that Lee was responsible, he was heard to mutter: "d——n him." [68]

By the time Washington and Lee met just beyond the west ravine, each man still astride his thirsty, sweaty mount, the commander had worked himself into a rage. His first words to Lee were uttered in an irate, contemptuous tone, and (depending on the eyewitness) were something along the lines of: "I desire to know, sir, what is the reason, whence arises all this confusion?," or "My God, General Lee, What are you about?" Some recollected that Washington swore at him. Lafayette claimed that Washington called Lee a "damned poltroon." Whatever he said it certainly was not what Lee had expected to hear; indeed, Lee was so stunned that for once in his life he was speechless. He could only stammer, "Sir, sir——." Some thought it evidence that Lee had lost control of himself, and of his army. Washington acerbically repeated his question, adding that he believed Lee had fled from an insignificant British "covering party." Now Lee responded. He denied that there was any confusion. The retreat was orderly and it was justified, he insisted. Washington was unmoved. He in effect denounced Lee for having taken the command, considering his aversion all along to an attack. Then he assumed command.[69]

Interestingly, among Washington's first orders was a directive to fall back to the very spot for which Lee had been heading when their tête-à-tête had occurred, and by all accounts the commander performed an extraordinary feat in quickly getting the men in place. Yet, by the time everyone again was ready to fight, Washington must have realized that he had erred in accusing Lee of retreating before a small British force. In a rare gesture of magnanimity Washington rode back to Lee and asked him to take command of all the troops in the rear, and a bit later that afternoon the commander observed that the American difficulties had occurred because the British had been able to effectively utilize their cavalry, an implicit admission that Lee had done as well as could have been expected inasmuch as his force lacked such a wing.

A few minutes later the first British assault came. The fighting raged for an hour—and it was in this action that "Molly Pitcher" (probably Mary Ludwig Hayes, in reality) allegedly took over the cannon her fallen husband had helped to operate—before Washington was able to bring up the main army. That hour was probably the most crucial of the day, for the danger of a British breakthrough was very real. The Americans largely fought defensively, often at very close quarters. But the American line held, and in the end it was the British army that disengaged and began to fall back. Washington responded by ordering his army to advance, but the men were too spent from the torrid heat and the long, hot fight to continue.

The battle had hardly been the sort of fight that General Washington had envisioned that morning. Yet, one of his prayers had been answered. Throughout the ordeal the American soldiery had performed capably, a tribute in considerable measure to the lessons taught by von Steuben at Valley Forge. Still, no one had been a victor on this bloody day. The British had lost at least 350, killed and wounded, the Americans about 60 percent of that number. For all that, the clash had resolved nothing.[70]

By 6:00 the battle was over, save for a relatively futile and harmless artillery duel, the last gasp of two armies spent from the searing heat and the long strain of combat. After an hour or so that too ceased, and men watched with satisfaction as the cooling shadows lengthened and ultimately night fell, a happy intermission in the bloodletting, albeit only a temporary one. Or so the men believed. They slept on the battlefield that evening, their commander with them, likewise slumbering fitfully on the hard earth, waiting to renew the battle at sunrise.

But this fight was indeed over. The army awakened the next morning to discover that the British were gone. Clinton had stolen away for Sandy Hook on the Jersey coast, departing as stealthily as his foe once had left Long Island and the Assunpink.

George Washington must have fairly beamed that morning as he rode about the battlefield, inspecting this, looking into that. His army had survived, from the icy, hungry weeks at Valley Forge to that unbearable high summer day at Monmouth. Philadelphia was in American hands, and, for a change, it was his adversary who had broken off the fight on this sandy littoral in New Jersey. If the doubters had not previously been silenced, this campaign surely would hush their protests. And, if all that was not enough, the future had never looked so rosy. Soon the French would arrive and the course of the war would change.

In fact, the nature of this struggle already had changed. General Washington simply had no way of knowing how different the war henceforth would be.

IO

The Character of General Washington

"The strictest rectitude"

George Washington was honest with himself—up to a point at any rate. Early in life he had circumspectly catalogued his faults and set about to correct them. One of his "foibles," he had discovered, was his temper. It was not as though he was a surly, irascible sort, but when it seemed to him that his integrity was being questioned, his temper was certain to flare. And he had learned early on that the only safeguard against behavior that he might later regret was to stifle his passions.

It was an elementary lesson, but that Washington had learned it and Charles Lee had not was only one of a multitude of differences between these two men. At Monmouth Washington had failed to keep a rein on his temper, but later in the afternoon of that battle his passion had cooled and he had come as close to apologizing to Lee as he ever was likely to come. That he took no adverse action against General Lee during the next three days would seem to be tantamount to his silent approbation of his subordinate's conduct. During that same period, however, Lee had stewed over Washington's behavior until he no longer could restrain himself. Then he wrote his commander a remarkable letter. He alternately seemed to blame Washington and the sycophants ("dirty earwigs," he called them) at headquarters for the harsh words uttered on the battlefield. Whoever was responsible, he said, he believed his conduct and his courage had been questioned, and he requested that Washington either apologize or formally press charges so that he could defend himself. Whatever his previous feelings toward his voluble subordinate, Washington now made no attempt to restrain his fury. He sent guards to place Lee under arrest pending an inquiry, and he accused him of acting with "disrespect to the commander in chief," as well as of having disobeyed orders and of having made "an unnecessary, disorderly, and shameful retreat" at Monmouth.[1]

General Washington easily could have chosen to mollify Lee. He might have spoken with him privately; he might have sent him a carefully worded letter designed to placate, the sort of missive he had learned to master in three years of dealing with other volatile personalities. He might even have apologized. Instead, he acted in the manner of one who could brook no questioning of his actions. Perhaps, too, he simply took the opportunity to scuttle Lee, a troublesome subordinate whose performance too often had been lackadaisical and questionable. But it also is possible that Washington responded viscerally and not as a result of calculation. What now is clear is that Washington's victimization of Lee was but part of a pattern of edgy, often hostile behavior which he exhibited toward those officers who possessed the power to constitute a potential threat to his position.

By 1778 half the original thirteen general officers were gone, including Montgomery and Wooster, who had been killed in combat, and Pomeroy and Thomas, who had perished from diseases. Three others among the thirteen had quit the service by then. Almost everyone quickly concluded that Joseph Spencer had been miscast; indeed, his nickname, "Granny," spoke volumes about the impression he gave. Washington undoubtedly reached a similar conclusion about his fitness, and from the outset he managed to keep him on the sidelines. Spencer finally resigned in 1778. Schuyler also was gone by 1778, but he had never served directly under Washington. The commander had treated him cordially and had offered every possible aid to ensure his success. Nevertheless, Schuyler had been terribly unpopular with many in Congress, and he was replaced in 1777, prompting his resignation; while Lee's hearing was being prepared, Schuyler awaited trial on a charge of incompetence. Artemas Ward was the third of the original general officers to resign. From the very beginning Washington had depicted Ward as fat, lazy, and incompetent, and as too inert to remove himself "from the smoke of his own chimney," the same allegations—in virtually identical language—that he had made against General Joshua Fry, his commander in the Virginia Regiment in 1754. It is far from certain, however, that Ward really was as useless as Washington suggested. The authorities in Massachusetts, a colony with more military tradition than any other American polity, had thought enough of Ward to make him their commander in 1775, and he had overseen the successful operation at Bunker Hill. Nevertheless, Washington quickly established a pattern of granting him only inconsequential assignments, and after two years the first American commander left the service.[2]

On the other hand, from the outset Washington had placed some trust in Putnam, Heath, and Sullivan, three men whom he could never have considered a personal threat. Although Putnam had been the only major general unanimously selected by Congress, no one could have imagined him as commander in chief. At fifty-seven, he was thought by many to be too old, but mostly he lacked the polish for such a post; a farmer and former tavern owner, "Old Put" never overcame his humble beginnings, even impressing one Philadelphian as "much fitter to head a band of sickle-men or ditchers, than musketeers."[3] Washington gave Putnam a shot at glory, but after witnessing a string of ineffectual performances the commander rebuked him and assigned him to the lackluster task of recruiting in Connecticut. Heath had been the tenth of the thirteen selected, almost an afterthought. He had little military experience, no combat experience, and he was unknown outside Massachusetts. Still, Washington bestowed upon him several important commands, until he, too, was reprimanded for his indifferent leadership in the Highlands; thereafter, he was used only for staff work, and by 1778 he was in command of Boston, now safely in the backwater of things. Washington was most tolerant of Sullivan among these three. As inexperienced and powerless as Heath, Sullivan owed his appointment to Congress's whim that New Hampshire should not be left without a general. His actions on the battlefield in 1776 and 1777 had won him few friends in high places, while his willingness to serve as Howe's errand boy in transmitting British peace feelers to Congress had gained him the lasting enmity of many. Yet Washington stuck with him through failure after failure, and a few weeks before Monmouth he placed him in command in Rhode Island, a very active theater.

There can be no doubt that Washington was closer to Nathanael Greene than to any of the original thirteen. The commander took to him from the beginning, impressed that his men were the best-disciplined soldiers within the ragtag army he inherited in 1775. A year later he pushed for Greene's elevation to major general, then he put him in charge of the defense of Brooklyn. Washington's confidence in him could not be sundered, not even by Greene's egregious blunder at Fort Washington. But what was the source of the commander's unshakeable trust?

Washington generally was a good judge of men, and intuitively he may have recognized Greene's talents. If so, Greene's conduct as quartermaster general, and later as commander of the American forces in the South, certainly confirmed Washington's judgment. In addition, Washington may have been drawn to Greene for reasons that he could not fully understand. While ambitious, and rather bold, impetuous even, in action, Greene was inclined to be respectful, almost obsequious to those in authority. His behavior toward Washington was nothing if not ingratiating—just as it earlier had been toward Artemas Ward. Dominated by a father who still ordered him about when he was nearly thirty years old, Greene long had been accustomed to deferential conduct. On the eve of the Revolution, in fact, he had helped organize a volunteer infantry company, but when his candidacy for rank was turned down because of his slight limp, he stayed on as a private.[4] It is unimaginable that Washington—or virtually any other of the original offiers, for that matter—would have acquiesced in such an affront. It was equally unimaginable that a person of such temperament ever could have posed a threat to Washington's leadership, and this may have increased Greene's attractiveness.

The same could not be said of Gates or Lee, however. Before leaving Philadelphia in 1775 Washington had supported both men's appointments, confident that each was experienced and capable, and almost certainly trusting in their loyalty to him. It took only a year or so for his relations with each man to cool. Later Washington expressed his belief that Gates first had exhibited "symptoms of coldness and constraint" toward him. In a sense he probably was correct. While a visitor at Mount Vernon, Gates undoubtedly had been friendly and relaxed with his host, a man he more or less must have regarded as an equal; but when Gates once again donned his uniform, years of military service would have caused him instinctively to adopt a formal demeanor toward his commander. His coldness "increased as he rose into greater consequence," the commander added, until he allegedly became openly malevolent. The problem with Washington's account is that it lacks substantiation. No hint of ill will toward Washington is present in Gates's voluminous correspondence, nor did any of his aides or officers, men who must have heard him air his views in private, ever come forward with such a claim. What *is* clear is that Washington's communiqués to Gates grew cold, especially as it became evident that the northern army might score a great victory over Burgoyne in 1777. When the victory was won, Washington's congratulatory note seemed forced, and he even took that occasion to admonish Gates for his failure to keep him adequately informed of events. Moreover, instead of rejoicing at the victory of Saratoga, Washington's aides hurriedly spread the tale that Gates had feared to step on the battlefield, that he "hug himself at a distance [to] leave an Arnold to win laurels for him." Shortly thereafter, upon learning that Conway had spoken critically about the army to Gates, Washington seized the opening to attenuate the power of the conqueror of Burgoyne. Contrast Washington's behavior in this instance with his reaction to learning that Reed had written—not received—a letter which, however murkily, seemed to question Washington's ability to command. The young, powerless Pennsylvanian ultimately was restored to Washington's good graces, but the victor at Saratoga was vilified as an inveterate fomenter of "little underhand intrigues."[5]

Of the original leaders who had enjoyed considerable political backing, Lee alone remained relatively unscathed by the summer of 1778. He had fought well at Charleston in repulsing Clinton's invasion in 1776, and his performance at White Plains had been commendable. Neither the doubtful conduct that had resulted in his capture, nor his behavior as a prisoner had caused him any harm. (No one was aware that while a prisoner Lee had drafted a remarkable document that purported to coach Howe on the best means of suppressing the revolt. His motives in counseling the British remain mysterious; treason has been alleged by some, although his best biographer, John Alden, doubts that charge and hints that Lee merely had endeavored to mislead the British commander by telling him all the wrong things to do.) It is impossible to know Washington's real attitude toward Lee upon his release, but within the commander's entourage great concern was expressed about this eccentric soldier's loyalty to his chief. Greene, whose views so replicated those of Washington that some even thought him responsible for planting ideas in his leader's brain, marked Lee's return by expressing his "hope [that] he may of use," continuing, "but I apprehend no great good, as the junto will endeavor to debauch and poison his mind with prejudice. . . . [H]e is not a little unhappy in his temper." Greene also quipped that he believed things had gone better during Lee's fifteen-month absence than when he had been present.[6]

Washington's attitude toward Lee remained obscure until he ordered his arrest. The evidence suggests, however, that Lee's letter was more responsible for subsequent events than were his actions on the battlefield. It is apparent that Washington regarded Lee's questionable language and the charges he brought against the staff at headquarters as a threat to Washington's very position. The commander seldom required any help to get into this frame of mind, but in this instance his emotions probably had been played on by some of those close to him. Anthony Wayne and Brigadier General Charles Scott already had filed written criticisms of Lee's conduct by the time his heated letter reached Washington, and at least one of the commander's aides is known to have pressed the silly idea that Lee's actions may have been treasonous—that is, that he had tried to lose the battle.[7]

Moreover, when Washington moved against Lee, he acted in a wholly characteristic manner. Two patterns of behavior were habitual to Washington's conduct as a leader. For one thing, he seemed unable to take responsibility for failure. Nearly a quarter-century earlier his second in command at Fort Necessity had been made to take the blame for that disaster, while his translator had been held responsible for having accepted odious surrender terms. In this war it was Sullivan who became the culprit for the debacle at Brooklyn; the militia was faulted for the loss at Kip's Bay; Greene quietly took the heat for Fort Washington; Sullivan again responded mutely to the notion that he was responsible for the losses at Brandywine; and Adam Stephen was made something of a scapegoat for Germantown. Now it was Monmouth, and it was Lee's turn. In fact, after this battle Washington's supporters had it both ways. Lee was blamed for every shortcoming that occurred in the course of the battle, while Washington was credited with having reversed the tide and secured a great American victory.[8] No mean trick considering that Monmouth at best had been a draw.

In addition, Washington always seemed driven to eliminate any man who might pose a threat to his power. Lee saw that aspect of Washington's character, and, however dimly, so too did Lafayette, who ultimately came close to acknowledging in public that Washington's actions after Monmouth had been prompted by a desire to obliterate a rival for power. That was the ultimate end of the affair, for soon Lee was gone, first convicted by the court martial and suspended from the army for one year, then banished forever from the Continental army by Congress.[9] Washington now was safe, and so were those who had hitched their chariots to his star.

With the exception of Gates, who now exercised command in the Highlands above New York, Washington could turn to a new generation of general officers. Young men mostly, all seemed to owe their advancement to him. A few months before Washington arrived in Cambridge in 1775 Henry Knox had been a twenty-four-year-old bookseller with no military experience; the new commander made him the head of the army artillery corps. His performance at Boston and Trenton, as well as on the Assunpink, makes it difficult to quarrel with Washington's judgment. Benedict Arnold had been restored to the service by Washington, and his brilliant, valorous conduct once again demonstrated the commander's skill in judging men. Washington had less to do with the early stages of Anthony Wayne's career. The Pennsylvanian cut his martial teeth in the northern theater, not joining Washington until after the winter at Morristown. He fought well when Howe poked his head out of New York that summer, and he gave a good performance at Brandywine. His defeat at Paoli was more humiliating, and unnecessary, than anything that had flowed from Lee's alleged errors at Monmouth, but Washington stuck with Wayne and was rewarded by the Pennsylvanian's zealous action at Germantown and in the clash with Clinton at Monmouth.

Together with Lafayette, these were the general officers whom Washington had grown to trust above all others. Three of the five resembled young Washington in that they were headstrong, eager and daring in battle, thirsting for glory, if they erred, likely to do so on the side of impetuosity. Knox and Greene were different. Calmer, more pragmatic, more students of military science, these two nevertheless were bold and sturdy. All five had two important things in common. By 1778 each had demonstrated his mettle on the battlefield. And none had displayed any sign of disloyalty to his commander in chief.[10]

Just as the composition of Washington's principal officers had changed after three years of warfare, so had his official "family," the young men who served as his aides. Reed and Mifflin, the first in a long line of Washington's military secretaries (more than thirty young men served in this capacity during the eight-year conflict), long since had gone on to other pursuits. By 1777 the number of his aides had risen to seven, and even then they were taxed to keep pace with the commander's extraordinary work load; one aide complained of continual working dinners, of rising very early, laboring all day, and finally, in the still early hours of evening, of collapsing from exhaustion. Mostly the job consisted of taking dictation from Washington, then penning the final draft of his correspondence, although with sufficient experience came the priviledge of actually composing some of the general's letters. These men also acted as file clerks, and sometimes Washington used them as emissaries, dispatching them on long journeys to communicate with another commander, or to elicit information from political leaders. They even interrogated deserters and prisoners of war, and some served as intelligence gatherers. In short, Washington saw them as jacks-of-all-trades, but chiefly as "persons that can think for me, as well as execute orders." [11]

Naturally, Washington surrounded himself with talented young men with whom he felt comfortable. After all, these men spent several hours each day in his company, customarily even sleeping in the same house with him. At Morristown four of his seven aides were young Virginians, and a fifth hailed from Maryland, not far from Mount Vernon. Almost all of his aides were from socially and economically prominent families. John Laurens was the son of the president of the Continental Congress, for instance, while others were sons of important state officials, prosperous lawyers, and well-heeled merchants. In an age when less than 1 percent of all males attended college, an extraordinary number of these men were college graduates, and at least two had studied outside the mainland colonies. Of all the men who served him in this capacity, Washington was closest to Robert Hanson Harrison of Alexandria, Virginia, an old friend who literally had accompanied the commander to war. Thirteen years younger than Washington, Harrison—a lawyer by training—was a frequent guest at Mount Vernon during the half dozen years before the war commenced. Aside from him, none ever got closer to Washington than Joseph Reed and Alexander Hamilton, young men with strikingly similar characters. [12]

If a man's friends are a measure of his character, Washington's choice of intimate associates is revealing. Lafayette immediately noticed that the commander had surrounded himself with flatterers, and he fell right into step as he inched closer to Washington. Nor can there be much doubt that both Reed and Hamilton played the courtier. Like Reed—and Washington, for that matter—Hamilton was not favored by birth into society's most elite stratum. In fact, in his case the obstacles to his rise were truly mountainous. He began life as an illegitimate child, born in Nevis in the West Indies. Left a penniless orphan at age thirteen when his mother died, a bleak future of penury, or, at best, of obscure struggle within the commonality, seemed his fate. To rise above that lot required not only considerable skill and intelligence but a personality that was possessed by an all-consuming will to succeed. He also needed luck. "I wish there was a War," he wrote while still an adolescent, recognizing such an event as a potentially fast route to bigger and better things. He got his wish, and in this respect he was even more fortunate than Washington had been. Washington had been compelled to wait until he was twenty-two before his war commenced; Hamilton's war began when he was twenty.

By 1775 Hamilton had come a long way. Beginning as a clerk on St. Croix, he had caught the attention of his employers, rising steadily in the ranks of the employees, and eventually having his education at King's College in New York paid for through the largess of one of the company's owners. Only a few weeks after he matriculated he published two well-received pamphlets that defended the actions of the First Continental Congress. His polemics brought him into contact with Whig leaders such as John Jay and Alexander McDougall, men who pulled strings to secure his appointment in 1776 as a captain in a New York artillery company. In all likelihood he saw no action until he joined Washington's retreating army in those last grim weeks before Trenton. No one knows how he came to Washington's attention, but with Reed and Mifflin both gone on missions to procure more troops, Washington may have passed the word among his officers to be on the lookout for a person with clerking skills; someone probably knew of Hamilton's background and recommended him to headquarters. At any rate Hamilton joined Washington's "family" at Morristown on March 1, 1777.[13]

An incident that occurred four years later between the general and his aide revealed much about the two men. One morning Hamilton was slow to respond to Washington's request for a meeting. When Hamilton finally arrived he received a dressing down: "Colonel Hamilton, you have kept me waiting . . . these ten minutes," Washington angrily charged, adding that "I must tell you Sir you treat me with disrespect." Hamilton neither blanched nor hesitated: "I am not conscious of it Sir but since you have thought it necessary to tell me so we part." Taken aback, Washington merely replied, "Very well. . . ." But later that morning when he had collected himself, the commander apologized, an act of contrition that Washington would have performed for few men. That did not end the matter, however. Hamilton refused to accept the general's apology. Privately he remarked that he never had felt any friendship for Washington; how could he feel affinity for a man who was extraordinarily vain and "neither remarkable for delicacy nor good temper." Hamilton finally patched up his relationship with the commander, largely because his father-in-law, former General Schuyler (like Washington and Lafayette, Reed and Arnold, Hamilton had courted and married a lady with rich and powerful ties) impressed upon him the wisdom of keeping the general happy. However much he disliked Washington, Hamilton took Schuyler's advice, but it was clear, as he privately admitted, that the commander was nothing more than "an aegis very essential" to his success. The incident laid open the young man's penchant for deceit and cunning, the Janus-faced persona that had germinated out of his life of lonely struggle.[14]

In that moment of candor Hamilton had alluded to a dark side of Washington, and he pledged at war's end to "say many things" about the general's character. For the time being, however, prudence required an "inviolable silence." Whatever Hamilton's intentions, he never publicly unburdened himself about Washington. Nor did very many men who had served with Washington publicly criticize his character. Forbearance must have seemed the wisest course considering Washington's extraordinary stature, yet the almost total dearth even of private expressions of adverse opinion might also be taken to indicate that few contemporaries discovered iniquitous traits in the man's makeup. Of course, there were a few who perceived unsavory qualities in his temperament. Some discerned a hard, violent side to him, and one observer thought his features betrayed toughness and insensitivity; on the other hand a French officer described his countenance as expressing no distinguishing traits. Others thought him vain, and still others believed him to be vindictive and petty, at least in his dealings with Charles Lee. The brother of one of his aides described him as somber and coarse, "better endowed by nature in habit for an Eastern monarch, than a republican general." [15]

Washington's most discussed trait was his reserved, formal, and aloof manner. He was not depicted as inhospitable or belligerent, but as someone with whom it was difficult to feel at ease, to get close to, or to understand. Some simply pointed out that he was cautious and wary in the presence of others. Some were put off by his behavior, as was the English visitor who was struck by his "repulsive coldness . . . under a courteous demeanour." To someone like Aaron Burr, Washington merely was a boring, colorless person.[16]

General Washington's brighter side was more often alluded to by those who knew him better. His "virtue" was his most striking trait, said witness after witness. To that age "virtue" meant many things, but chiefly it involved traits such as selflessness, courage, honesty, and dedication. In addition, Washington frequently was labeled as "noble," and his "integrity" often was noted. Others were impressed by his calmness and firmness, as well as by his penchant for hard work. Virtually every observer was struck by his "*stately* bearing" and his "mild gravity." Some who knew of his temper commented on his extraordinary self-discipline. Two foreign volunteers were amazed at his uncanny ability to win the love of most with whom he dealt, while another lauded the commander for the Spartan manner in which he chose to live. More than one witness was impressed by his ability to function under extraordinary pressure, as well as by his talent for rebounding from terrible disappointments. None who knew him regarded Washington as a genius, but some ascribed to him a quality that perhaps was even more desirable. He realized his limitations, they said; he had learned to elicit advice, sifting and sorting and weighing the counsel until, with great deliberateness, he made up his mind. His painstaking manner of making decisions caused some mistakenly to think him lazy. Two who also had to make many crucial decisions, and who were more gifted intellectually than Washington, were more charitable. John Adams thought him "slow, but sure." Thomas Jefferson took a little longer to say the same thing. Washington's mind, he observed, was "slow in operation, being aided little by invention or imagination, but sure in conclusion." [17]

A man must be judged both by the traits he possesses and by those he does not. Thus it is revealing that no one thought to characterize Washington as convivial or carefree, for example; no one thought him loquacious or irresponsible. No one ever described him as moved or shaken by the carnage of the battlefield, nor did anyone claim to know that he was troubled by the brutal punishments, including the occasional death sentences, meted out to his soldiery. No one ever kidded himself into believing that he had become a close friend of the commander.

Washington's manner aroused very different responses. Foreign observers were more likely than American acquaintances to think him "amiable," and women saw in him quite different qualities from those perceived by men. Quite sophisticated women such as Abigail Adams and Mercy Otis Warren, the latter a playwright and historian as well as the wife of the president of the Massachusetts Provincial Congress, considered him friendly, gracious, and charming, while he impressed the wife of Colonel Theodore Bland as being bold, even a bit pert. Mrs. Bland also seemed to think him unlike most other men in that he listened attentively and seriously when women spoke.[18]

The trait most often referred to by those describing Washington's manner was his aloofness. Yet the commander was not isolated at headquarters from civil authorities or from other general officers, and he apparently made no attempt to seclude himself. Just the opposite. Daily he was surrounded by numerous aides and advisors, and he met frequently—too often, he sometimes complained—with congressmen, state officials, and, most irksomely, with ubiquitous local dignitaries who merely wished to be permitted to meet such an esteemed figure. So busy was he, the commander was heard to grumble, that he had little time for reflection and contemplation, and he sometimes had to apologize for letters that he feared would appear to be "crude, and undigested." To keep pace with his duties he rose early, as had been his habit on the farm. Normally, he was up and busy by 5:00 A.M., usually working alone in his bedchamber or a separate study, and generally devoting these first hours to his correspondence. After three or four hours he emerged to join his entourage for a long, brisk ride on his favorite mount. In mid-morning he returned to headquarters for breakfast, usually a hurried affair. Several hours of work followed. In mid-afternoon, about three o'clock, all labor stopped and the day's principal meal commenced, a repast that customarily lasted for about two hours. Several people joined him at this mess, including the young officer of the day, a practice he had begun at Cambridge and was to continue with mixed success throughout the war. The fare at the meals varied from the adequate but unspectacular cuisine at Valley Forge to sumptuous feasts featuring eight to ten separate dishes of meat and poultry, numerous vegetables, and a variety of pastries and pies and puddings, all of which was capped by huge bowls of assorted nuts. At the conclusion of this lengthy meal, work was resumed, continuing until about 7:30 or 8:00 P.M., when the commander returned to the dining room for a light supper. One meat and a variety of fruit, accompanied by claret or Madeira, usually constituted this meal, which, like the earlier gathering, tended to be a relaxed and protracted affair. During these meals Washington customarily said little, merely listening contentedly while his more loquacious aides and generals bantered, a practice he continued when the entourage adjourned from the dining room table to a parlor or living room in the commander's residence for another hour or so of conversation over coffee and tea.[19]

What appears at first glance to have been a comfortable, if busy, life, often, in fact, was the very opposite. Throughout the war Washington labored under great adversity, often facing brief periods of extraordinary stress. Inevitably, he experienced moments of despair and hopelessness, times when sleep came with difficulty, when he snapped angrily at those about him, even when, as occurred on one or two instances, he acknowledged his unhappiness with his position as supreme commander. What was far more remarkable, however, was his facility for coping with his burdens. For eight years he made decisions upon which hung the well-being of his men, the life of the nation, and, as he well knew, his own life and fortune, yet there is no indication that he was harmed physically or emotionally by the weight he bore. Consider his contemporary John Adams, so overwhelmed by the stress and anxiety that accompanied power that he collapsed on at least two occasions during the Revolution, or subsequent statesmen like Abraham Lincoln or Franklin Roosevelt, both gaunt, lined, emaciated, exhausted, seemingly aging by quantum leaps under the strain of leadership. But, aside from graying and lining, the only sign of major physical change that Washington exhibited in these years was that he eventually was compelled to wear reading glasses, hardly an abnormal development for a person progressing from age forty-three in 1775 to age fifty at war's end. He seems not to have grown stooped or frail or enfeebled, he suffered no apparent gastrointestinal debilities, and the many portraits made of him during these years unfailingly depict his appearance about as one would expect a healthy man at that stage of life to look.

Washington was aware of the health hazards that accompanied his job, and he sought to protect himself through daily exercise. Each morning, rain or shine, he rode fifteen miles, a trek that consumed about forty-five minutes to an hour. When the press of business permitted he also sought to relax through some amusing diversion. As a Virginia planter he often had taken his pleasure in taverns, where he played cards and shot billiards, but as commander in chief he eschewed such recreation, undoubtedly fearing the example it might set. More surprisingly he also abandoned fox hunting, which had been his principal sport at Mount Vernon, apparently riding the hounds only once during the war years. Occasionally he tossed a ball or played wickets with the younger officers, and during the long days of summer he sometimes accompanied riding parties after the evening meal had been completed. In addition, he attended plays and visited local landmarks, and from time to time he took a picnic lunch to the restful banks of some nearby stream.[20]

Something evidently kept him fit, for he experienced only three minor illnesses in these eight years. In each of these three instances he seems to have suffered nothing more serious than a two- or three-day bout with some form of infectious viral disease. Otherwise, his only physical malady was his persistent dental problem, a disorder that set in at least twenty years before the Revolution. Washington already was using some false teeth when he took command in 1775 (in fact, at one point he wrote home to request that some teeth he had left behind at Mount Vernon be mailed to him). He wore sets made from wood and ivory, but since England was the source of the latter dentures he was unable to replace some broken and defective plates until the war ended. His teeth or gum problems aside, he was more than fit. At the end of the conflict he weighed 209 pounds, certainly an appropriate weight for a 53-year-old man who was 6' 3" in height.[21]

By then the extra weight visible in Peale's 1776 portrait obviously had been shed. Indeed, his 1779 painting of Washington, one commissioned by the executive council of Pennsylvania to commemorate his victories at Trenton and Princeton, depicted Washington as he must have looked during the last several years of the war. He is shown in a jaunty pose, his left hand leaning on a field piece, his right arm cocked on his hip, his left leg crossing his right. His hair had grayed since Peale first had met him at Mount Vernon seven years before, and, while the artist omitted the lines around the subject's features, Washington nevertheless seemed older. But the aura of the man was what really seemed to have changed. Now, in fact, Washington seemed different from other men. In 1772 he had almost the appearance of an actor, a man who sought to convince others to accept his view of himself. Even so, in that earliest painting Washington's countenance had been bland and inscrutable. In 1779, however, he reeked of poise and of success, of fearlessness, of assurance that he would inevitably triumph. Tall, ramrod-straight, thinner than after his first winter of war, although still not thin, his features a bit softer and more animated than in the previous portraits, the commander appeared to be relaxed and cocksure, yet detached and alone. Well removed from the soldierly ranks that paraded in the background, Washington seemed an Olympian personage, remote and unapproachable.

What manner of military commander was General Washington? Moreover, what was the relationship between Washington's character and his leadership? Was he the man that Charles Lee saw, a "puffed up charlatan . . . extremely prodigal of other men's blood and a great oeconomist of his own." Was he the man that one of his young officers saw, the "last stage of perfection to which human nature is capable of attaining."[22] Or, with more information and greater detachment, can the historian see still a different Washington?

In most respects it is difficult to imagine Washington pursuing alternative military strategies. Not only did his army's tactics generally conform to the martial wisdom of the age, his decisions normally reflected the collective wisdom of his general officers as expressed in the frequent councils of war. Yet the manner in which he longed to act can be revealing, as can be those episodes when he shook loose of the counsel of his officers and struck out on his own path. Always Washington seemed to view a conservative, defensive strategy with disdain. During the siege of Boston he yearned to assail Howe. He fretted over losing the "esteem of mankind" if he remained inactive, and even though he acknowledged that to attack might be "to undertake more than could be warranted by prudence," he nevertheless sought to secure his officers' backing for an assault. Washington similarly exhibited a penchant for standing and fighting on Long Island and Manhattan, and once again in the contest for Fort Washington. Only at Long Island, where congressional pressure probably hectored Washington into a duel with the British and Hessian forces, did he lack a free hand; in the other instances there were compelling reasons to have retreated and fought a "war of posts," a strategy which he had articulated but infrequently pursued. In the year and a half that followed the debacle at Fort Washington, he again and again lashed out at his adversary, making dangerous assaults at Trenton and Princeton, at Germantown and Monmouth. Once again, safer, more cautious courses might have been embraced, yet he always seemed to equate retreat with personal weakness. He seemed mesmerized by the "honor of making a brave defense," by which, curiously, he meant resolutely fighting his foe in a pitched battle. On the other hand, he feared he would be subject to "reproach" if he adopted a Fabian strategy. "I see the impossibility of serving with reputation," he remarked in frustration, often speaking of the certainty that he would "lose my Character" in this war, sometimes seeming to equate the destruction of his reputation with the policy of inaction which circumstances often made unavoidable. Thus to preserve his honor he leaned toward defiant action, toward bold and vigorous conduct, and when he succeeded in the pursuit of a daring and grandiose plan his response was relief, not just for the victory but because "my reputation stands firm." [23]

His conduct in this war was not uncharacteristic. This was the same man who had stood at Fort Necessity, who repeatedly had urged an assault on Fort Duquesne, who had carped incessantly at the "string of forts" concept. Always he longed to execute a brilliant stroke, always he thought in terms of the grand and audacious gesture. To imagine George Washington thinking any other way is not only to fail to understand the man but to fail to comprehend that it was his inescapable quest for esteem that governed and dictated the life-and-death choices he made.

What of his relations with his principal officers? When Charles Lee remarked that Washington was a "dark designing" man bent upon the destruction of every man whom he considered to be a threat to his station, he may have come closer to the truth than most historians have cared to admit. Washington perhaps put it most succinctly. While he sought talent and dedication in his officers, he also wanted "attachment" and the "purest affection" from those about him. He valued the sort of behavior perhaps best exemplified by Lafayette, who acted, in the commander's opinion, "upon very different principles" from those of men like Lee and Gates. But one did not have to be servile to win Washington's support. Lafayette and Reed, and, one suspects, Greene and probably Hamilton, among others, were not above playing that role. A man like Arnold was not so inclined, however, and Washington respected him. Washington's relationships with his general officers worked on several levels. Some men provided the adoration and support that he required. Some officers—Lafayette and Arnold, and probably Sullivan, Hamilton, and Reed—served almost as models, embodying the virtues that Washington longed to manifest, whether it was intelligence, education, urbanity, eloquence, courage, or daring. But finally, and most importantly, General Washington had to be in total control, or, at least, he needed to believe that his powers of control were in no way jeopardized. From the very outset his control over Ward, for example, was questionable, and Washington immediately was cool, even hostile, toward him. When he discovered that Reed had questioned his judgment, he turned implacably cold. When he grew to believe that his control of Gates and Lee had diminished, he ruthlessly turned against them.[24]

Washington's personality and temperament were that of a self-centered and self-absorbed man, one who since youth had exhibited a fragile self-esteem. His need for admiration and affirmation was considerable, for only thus could his nagging doubts about his capabilities and his competence be overcome. Lest his imagined inadequacies be discovered, he adopted an aloof and formal manner. The result was that he had no friends in the real sense of the word, and he was at ease with—and closest to—only those who accommodated his needs, principally aspiring young men who basked in his presence and women who, in the custom of the times, treated him with deference. His attitude was a prescription for judging all men as either threatening or amicable.

Many contemporaries seemed unable to understand Washington. Some observers ascribed almost superhuman virtues to him, and they fretted over America's fate should his presence be lost. He came to be regarded as the indispensable man of the War of Independence, the one person upon whom the success—indeed, the very continuation—of the war depended. Washington's absence would lead to "the ruin of our Cause," the president of Congress, Henry Laurens, told his son, whereas the commander's "magnanimity, his patience, will save the Country. . . ." Lafayette, more characteristically, expressed the same thoughts directly to Washington. If "you were lost for America, there is nobody who could keep the army and the Revolution [intact] for six months."[25] But was General Washington truly the linchpin of the Revolution?

Washington's continued presence as commander of the Continental army was important, if only for symbolic reasons. By 1778, as Laurens and Lafayette had said, Washington already had come to symbolize the Revolution. To a degree that was unrivaled, Washington continued to embody those noble traits that had comprised the Revolutionary outlook at the outset of the war. His honesty, courage, and selfless service seemed beyond question, and even after three years as the commander of the Continental army, he continued to be seen, not as a hardened soldier, but as a trustworthy civilian who had been called to arms. In addition, it was crucial for the success of the war effort that no attempt be made to remove Washington from command. Had Congress deposed Washington in 1777 or 1778—or had that body even attempted to remove him—the act surely would have been seen as venal and narrowly factious, indeed as an antirevolutionary blow. Any move against Washington would have resulted in an atmosphere of ill-feeling and uncertainty that would surely have jeopardized the war effort.

But was Washington's continued presence essential only for symbolic and political reasons? The Washington who had ridden to Cambridge to assume command was a man of many talents. His earlier soldiering had helped prepare him for the administrative responsibilities he would bear, no small matter when it is remembered that the management of the military machine was a constant concern, whereas the army actually was thrust into battlefield situations only infrequently. Washington's years as a Virginia soldier also provided him with valuable experience in dealing with politicians, teaching him how to get his way, when to push and when it was expedient to let matters lie. He was wise enough not to ally himself with one faction in Congress, and he knew that it would be counterproductive to appeal over that body's head to the general public. He additionally knew better than to revert to the whining, petulant behavior that had tarnished his relationship with Dinwiddie, and after his experience with Forbes and Bouquet he was careful to avoid the folly of pushing for ends that were narrowly self-serving. Since boyhood Washington had been a careful student of behavior, watching to see what fashion dictated, then striving to shape his own conduct to conform. By the war years his plain, sober, vigilant, hard-working life style was too deeply rooted in his temperament to have been superficial or contrived. Even so, he understood the public temper in a way that leaders such as Schuyler or Lee could never have fathomed, and that intuitive genius led him to disdain a salary, to jettison certain pastimes—hunting and gaming, for instance—that long had been his habit as a Virginia planter, and scrupulously to avoid the public appearance of indulgences that smacked of intemperance or indifference toward his responsibilities.

On the other hand, there was little in Washington's background to prepare him for the strategic and tactical decisions he would have to make, and he was even more a greenhorn when it came to commanding under fire. As a Virginia soldier he never had commanded more than a thousand men, nor had he ever led his men against a professional European army. His combat experience consisted of three engagements: the ten-minute ambush of Jumonville, and the one-day fights at Fort Necessity and alongside Braddock on the Monongahela.

Nevertheless, by 1778 he had survived—and succeeded—on the battlefield. In part, Washington's achievements were due to luck. Four times in 1776 his inexperience, his penchant for standing and fighting, and his early inability to resist the demands of powerful politicians, led him into nearly fatal traps. On Long Island, at Manhattan, at Fort Washington, and when Cornwallis had him pinioned between the Assunpink and the Delaware, Washington seemingly had blundered into fighting in areas from which retreat would be difficult, perhaps impossible. But only at Fort Washington did he suffer for his errors. From the other traps he escaped, largely through fortuitous occurrences: sudden rainstorms, unanticipated fog, felicitous nightfalls that seemed to come on when he most needed them, although Washington was also sufficiently resourceful to seize the good fortune that fate offered. Between 1775 and 1778, however, his best stroke of luck was not only to have had an adversary such as the indolent, cautious

Howe, but to have been fighting an enemy that entered the conflict unprepared for the kind of war this was certain to be, a struggle that would require a huge commitment of manpower, men that would have to be supplied against almost insurmountable obstacles.

But Washington's accomplishments transcended luck. Essentially he understood this struggle. He knew what could win the war, as well as what might lose it. He could be cautious, resorting to the Fabian tactics that ran counter to his grain, retreating to preserve his army for another day, all the while protracting the conflict, buying time for war weariness to set in and eat away at Britain, time that would eventually induce America's friends in Europe to intervene. But he could be—he longed to be—unpredictably daring as well. At Dorchester Heights and again at Trenton and Princeton, at Germantown and still again at Monmouth, he lashed out in hazardous undertakings that so bore the imprint of his militant, activist, venturesome character that it is difficult to conceive of many other high American officers even contemplating such steps. Indeed, he alone seems to have planned the Trenton-Princeton operations; he had to nudge his general officers repeatedly to gain their consent to act at Dorchester; he obtained their approval for the strike at Germantown through what amounted to outright trickery; and he acted at Monmouth despite almost everyone's advice to remain inert. It was his nature to think in grandiose terms and to act in a daring manner. In fact, he was driven toward this behavior, for to act otherwise was to raise the specter of inadequacy and self-contempt. It was his good fortune to escape the blunders into which his temperament might have led him, but it was due to these same compelling drives that he had reaped for America its greatest victories in this war.

The insecurities that led Washington to his quest for self-esteem, as well as to his venturesome proclivities, his remoteness, and his suspicious, distrusting nature were not always endearing qualities. Nor did they always serve him well. His search for self cohesion led him into clashes with good general officers, perhaps even to the ruination of men like Ward and Lee; it prompted him to tolerate a essential mediocrity such as Sullivan, while blinding him to the inexperience and failures of a lad like Lafayette, and it almost certainly influenced his negative reaction to the plan to invade Canada, a strategy with considerable potential merit. But at the same time his makeup helped him find daring and capable officers like Arnold and Wayne and Knox. Indeed, qualities that might have been deleterious in almost any other pursuit became virtues when exercised by the commander of an army, for his character steeled him for difficult decisions, drove him to action, and even isolated him, contributing to his larger-than-life aura.

Lee and Hamilton saw the dark side of George Washington. But those who esteemed this man also were correct, for he exhibited many admirable qualities. He combined courage with diligence. The first came naturally, but industry and perseverence were traits that he had been compelled to learn in his long ascent from Ferry Farm. In many ways, as historian Bernard Mayo observed, he was a man of unexceptional endowments who through "human effort"—not by "mythic magic"—had attained one objective after another.[26] Now, an amateur soldier confronted by a professional adversary, Washington once again called upon those strategies that always had served him so well. To compensate for his inexperience he studiously read the best military manuals. Realizing his own inadequacies, he sought and listened to advice. He worked hard, putting in one long day after another. He learned from his mistakes, and, above all, he learned the folly of indecision.

Washington's greatest asset, a French officer once noted, was his faculty for understanding "the art of making himself beloved." Not only did Washington seem untainted by the corruptibility that his countrymen perceived as the inevitable accompaniment of royalty, but, even more, his actions seemed to manifest the greatest virtues of republicanism. Again, his refusal of a salary, his eschewing of a sumptuous life style, his sacrifice in the public cause, his willingness as commander to abide by the general will of his civilian governors, his very embodiment of what John Adams once called the "great, manly, warlike virtues" captured the popular imagination.[27] He knew what was expected of him. His office, he once said, required that he behave with "the strictest rectitude, and most scrupulous exactness." As usual in such matters he was correct. Perhaps, as some scholars have suggested, his grasp of what was required of him arose from some innate genius.[28] Yet Washington was a man well practiced in the art of understanding others. At the core of his being lay the compelling drive that led to his search for self-enhancement, and all his life Washington had sought to learn the techniques that would facilitate his yearnings.

Perhaps it would have been preferable for another man to have commanded the Continental army, but few contemporaries—and still fewer historians—would have hazarded that opinion. To swap Washington for an elderly Ward, an indolent Schuyler, a rustic Putnam, a temperamental and acerbic Lee hardly seems a bargain. What if Gates had supplanted Washington? He was ambitious, political, vain, and manipulative, but so was Washington. Gates also was more experienced militarily, he too was a good administrator, his compassion for his men was at least equal to that of Washington, and his commitment to the principles of the Revolution was above question. Thus, he was a reasonable candidate for the job, though we cannot know how Gates would have performed as the commander of the Continental army any more than we can know how Washington would have acted had he initially been appointed to serve under Gates.

By 1778, Washington had lived up to his countrymen's expectations, and by 1778 he had come to symbolize the Revolution, embodying the republican virtues of courage and selfless public service. On the other hand, his generalship was laudatory, but not brilliant. While his leadership had resulted in one extraordinary triumph (Trenton-Princeton), as well as one estimable maneuver that produced an apparent victory (Dorchester Heights), he was also largely responsible for one crushing defeat (Fort Washington). His daring almost led to another sensational victory at Germantown, but by the same token his risk-taking nearly had resulted in losses both in the New York and the Monmouth engagements, and his shoddy attention to military intelligence contributed to his army's losses at Brandywine.

By 1778, therefore, it is difficult to disagree with John Adams's assessment. The Revolution was too big to hang on the performance of one man, he had told Dr. Rush. Washington's contributions to the war effort were obvious and crucial, but Adams was correct to suggest that success or failure hinged on many men and many variables. Moreover, given his own genius at understanding the events of his time, Adams realized what many have been unable to accept: through the summer of 1778 Britain itself was more responsible for its own military woes than was any American leader.

II

The Forgotten Years, 1778–1780

"I have almost ceased to hope"

Washington had made the journey many times. Out of the rolling hills about Middlebrook, across the Delaware River, now a familiar friend, on through the undulating countryside of rural Pennsylvania, and into Philadelphia. This time he was traveling because Congress had called him to consider plans for the coming campaign. Washington must have felt good in December 1778—better, anyway, than he had at the same time the previous year when he had just taken his army into Valley Forge. France now was a belligerent, officially at war with Great Britain since the past spring, and there was talk that Spain, too, might soon enter the war. For the first time, moreover, Washington even indulged in the hope that the British army might abandon America, that "the enemys continuance among us" would end as the ministry opted to pull out in order to concentrate on fighting its traditional European foes.

The commander reached Philadelphia about Christmas, the first time he had been in the capital since he had paraded through en route to the Brandywine Creek sixteen months before. Then the atmosphere had been grim, tense. Congressmen packing to leave as Howe neared the city had expected much of Washington, and—at least in Washington's imagination—some were skulking and plotting to find another general to lead America's forces. Now he discovered a much different spirit abroad in the city. The general was warmly received, fêted each night at a sumptuous banquet, respected, deferred to as the warrior to whom the nation inextricably had tethered its military fortunes.

But as gratified as he must have been at his reception, Washington also discovered a new, disturbing aura round the capital. The war seemed a million miles away, remote from the lives of most Philadelphians. Nor was Philadelphia unique, and that was what concerned Washington. A "general lax of public virtue" seemed to have come over the land, he thought. Able leaders had deserted the public cause in the pursuit of private gain; in their stead power had passed to lesser men, politicos who often "horribly conducted" the affairs of state. He feared that venality and corruption had spread to a degree that imperiled the war effort, that the Revolution might collapse in a "general wreck," the victim of "our own folly . . . or perhaps of living in ease and tranquility." In a sense, he came to think, America had reached its most serious crisis yet in this war, worse even than those black, uncertain weeks late in 1776 or the desperate days at Valley Forge. The nation's very spirit seemed now to be "mouldering and sinking," in danger of extirpation through the "idleness, dissipation and extravagence" of its citizenry and its leaders. Indeed, he felt Britain's continued presence in this war was owing to these new circumstances. London had discovered new hope, he thought, an expectation based less on its chances for military victory than on its belief that America must collapse from war weariness, from its venal spirit, from its foundering, inflation-ridden economy. The commander comforted himself with the thought that in earlier dark moments "Providence has . . . taken us up when all other means and hope" had vanished.[1] There was not much else that he could do.

But what about the military situation? What would Britain do? Never had his adversary's intentions been more difficult to fathom. Had Washington been possessed of modern communications he would have had a better idea, for in the final days of 1778, at the very moment he was recording his morose thoughts in a letter to a friend in Virginia, British troops were landing far from Philadelphia— on the flat, sandy littoral of south Georgia, at the fifty-year-old city of Savannah. If the spirit and leadership of the Revolution had altered, its war was also about to change.

Britain's new solution to suppressing the rebellion, its southern strategy, had begun. Despairing ever of subduing New England, the war had been shifted south, to states that allegedly teemed with Loyalists. Clinton inaugurated the plan by sending an army of 3500 to Georgia, there to rendezvous with 2000 redcoats up from bases in Florida; simultaneously, he sent 5000 men to St. Lucia. Meanwhile, he waited with about 8000 men in New York. His diminutive force at Manhattan was too meager to do much with, but it was large enough to tie Washington's hands. If the American general abandoned the cusp of New York to aid his southern brethren, Clinton could take his little army up the Hudson and, on the cheap, accomplish what Howe had failed to achieve in two bloody, frustrating summers. Washington's war, therefore, had entered a very different phase, a period of protracted immobility.

The commander could not have known it, but when he awakened that muggy June morning to find that Clinton had stolen away from Monmouth in the dead of the night he had inherited a new war. Given his inclination for action, this would be a frustrating period for Washington, although initially his disappointment stemmed more from missed opportunities than from a dearth of fighting. Early in July 1778, America witnessed the first visible fruits of the French alliance when a Gallic fleet of sixteen vessels carrying four thousand soldiers magestically glided up to Sandy Hook in New Jersey. Commanded by Vice Admiral Count d'Estaing, a favorite of Marie Antoinette's, the flotilla arrived on July 11, six days after Clinton's army had boarded transports bound for New York. A matter of a few days only had perhaps prevented Washington from trapping the British army on the Jersey coast. Nevertheless, if that opening was lost, Washington believed that a combined naval and land operation against New York was possible. But, no. D'Estaing's pilots warned that the channel was too shallow for his vessels, and the French admiral instead turned for Rhode Island, hoping to cooperate with the American army stationed near Providence—the force that Washington had placed under General Sullivan back in March.

Britain had seized Newport in December 1776. Situated near the southern tip of a ten-mile-long, ink-blot-shaped island in Narragansett Bay, the British navy apparently relished the spot as a good winter port, although, in truth, the installation had been of no real help to the redcoats. Now the British were faced with defending the base or relinquishing their one tiny toehold in New England, for Congress had instructed Washington to make a probe at taking Newport, by "which possession of a safe port may be gained."

The choice of a commander would be crucial. Sullivan had the post, but as the campaign loomed General Gates hinted that he coveted the assignment. Washington refused. He did not wish to remove "an officer of distinguished merit to gratify unjustly a doubtful friend," or so Nathanael Greene said. The last portion of Greene's analysis seems beyond dispute, but whatever Washington's opinion of Sullivan he rushed Greene and Lafayette to Rhode Island to serve under him. Meanwhile, every New England state contributed militia units (commanded by John Hancock, of all people), and, by August, Sullivan's force was one-third again as large as that of his adversary. Yet while the allies possessed manpower superiority, the British knew they could garner a larger fleet, one with 10 percent more guns than d'Estaing had. That advantage convinced the British to defend Newport.[2]

It was a wise decision, for the Franco-American operation soon proved a fiasco. Before it could act, the French fleet was immobilized—nearly wrecked, in fact—by a large Atlantic storm. Sullivan was left ensconced on an island, his army dwindling rapidly as militiamen deserted in droves. By the end of August Sullivan was left with an army about one-half the size of the redcoat force now in Newport, and he hurriedly withdrew to the mainland, an operation that might not have succeeded had the British moved quickly to stop him.[3] Indeed, Clinton soon appeared to be no more anxious for a fight than Howe had been. For a time he contemplated a *coup de main* against Boston, knowing that the French fleet was penned up in its harbor, having limped there for repairs. Washington spent several days in "an awkward and disagreeable state of suspense," but ultimately Clinton overcame his sudden urge for action. Instead, he further divided his army, dispatching even more men to St. Lucia and the South. For the last time the British command had contemplated its four-year-old dream of a major offensive into the northern states.[4]

The British soon were busy in the South, however, and with seemingly favorable results. At year's end, 1778, British and Hessian troops, accompanied for the first time in this war by Loyalist regiments, landed in Georgia, sloshing ashore through a coastal rice field a few miles from Savannah. Before sunset of that day Savannah was back in Great Britain's grasp. The Americans lost more than 550 men in the engagement, as well as over 70 precious cannon and artillery pieces. British losses were just 7 dead and 19 wounded.[5]

Following this auspicious beginning, British operations soon returned to a more normal gait. During the entirety of 1779 Britain's most substantive acquisition in the South was Augusta, an important little outpost on the Savannah River. The redcoats, however, did repulse a Franco-American attempt to recover Savannah, once again inflicting heavy losses. But, as General Washington understood, the British victory was of little real significance. The "Enemy's invasion of Georgia, and possession of its capitol," he predicted, will "add some thing to their supplies" but it "will contribute very little to the brilliancy of their arms."[6]

Nevertheless, General Washington waited with "impatience and anxiety" for word of "the effectual deliverance of the Southern States," only to receive instead the customary tidings of failure.[7] Yet if the operation to retake Savannah was a disappointment, 1779 brought some small accomplishments in the North, and even greater success might have occurred had Washington been capable of overcoming his antipathy toward Gates.

Late in the summer of 1778 Congress once again raised the possibility of another Canadian expedition, a scheme whose principal proponents continued to be Gates and his New England friends. A thrust into Canada was not without potential merit. The advocates of the plan believed the "iruption" could kill three birds with one stone: this vast domain, with its fisheries and fur trade, could be acquired for the United States; the expulsion of the British would bring peace to the nation's smoldering frontiers in the northwest, for Great Britain clearly was the chief arms supplier of the western Loyalists and Native Americans; finally, the invasion of Canada would divert Britain from its own invasion of the South, thus leaving the armies to fight on someone else's soil. Nor were Gates and his congressional friends the only advocates of such a venture. Benjamin Franklin, one of America's envoys in Paris, drew up a battle plan for such an undertaking, urging a Franco-American operation that would feature a three-pronged attack from western Pennsylvania across to the Massachusetts boundary, followed by campaigns against Quebec and Halifax.[8]

But Washington chose to use his influence to thwart such a course. His objections were reasonable, but it is difficult to believe that the fact of Gates's support for such a campaign did not contribute to his own demurral. The commander argued that so long as Britain held New York and Rhode Island, America would lack the manpower for the operation. While the acquisition of Canada was desirable, he went on, it was not crucial to the war effort, and a military setback in that region could decimate American morale. Moreover, the very factors that had stymied American efforts in Canada in 1775 and 1776—manpower and material shortages, the lack of an American fleet, the vastness of the country—would work against success this time as well. Finally, he added, he did not quite trust the French, whom, he feared, might seek to use American men to regain their old imperial possession. Washington carried the issue. Congress mulled over his thoughts, then vetoed the project.[9]

Although Washington's arguments were cogent, they nevertheless rang rather hollow. Canada was but weakly defended, and it was wildly unlikely that the British army ever again would be numerically superior—much less possess a five-to-one superiority as it had in 1776. Washington could not have known that Britain's defenses were inadequate (as the redcoat commander was reporting by 1778), but he must have known that with France in the war the British no longer could depend on the loyalty of the French-Canadian populace. Had Washington by nature been timid and reluctant to run risks, his objections to a Canadian venture would have been more understandable. But his sudden caution was an uncharacteristic posture, as was his unwillingness to listen to Lafayette, an ardent proponent of such a course. What is most arresting, however, is that two years later he suddenly was converted to the notion of invading Canada, and in 1780 and again in 1782 he proposed such an operation. To deny that Washington's about-face had nothing to do with Gates's almost simultaneous fall from grace in 1780, or to believe that the commander's sudden support for a Canadian campaign was unrelated to the fact that Gates was left without the slightest prospect of leading an invasion army, was a leap to faith that not all contemporaries were willing to make.[10]

With another Canadian invasion repudiated, Washington met with a committee of Congress in January 1779 to plan other options. More than anything else he favored a campaign against the British in New York, although he knew that the resources, including French maritime assistance, were uncertain. He did think that a successful assault on Staten Island might demoralize Clinton, and he seemed to feel that still another attack on Newport might compel the redcoats to abandon that outpost. But at the very least Washington wanted a force large enough simultaneously to keep Clinton bottled up in New York and to leave him free to deal with his Indian and Loyalist adversaries on the frontier. Whatever plan was adopted, something must be done, he pleaded, lest America's inactivity nourish the reconciliationists at home while it lessened France's zeal to commit its navy to America's cause.[11]

The fact of the matter, however, was that Washington's plans were merely contingencies. Everything really hinged on French intentions, and the path that France trod depended on many circumstances, including the course of the war in Europe. Early that year Washington learned that the war in Europe was broadening. Spain, he discovered, had entered the war against Britain, news that at once pleased and troubled him. On the one hand he was delighted, for he was certain that the French and Spanish navies would be more than a match for the royal fleet; yet he feared that Spain's entry would provoke Russia and other continental powers to enter the conflict as allies of Britain, events that might compel France to ignore the American theater.[12]

It was May before Washington got his first inkling of French plans, and he learned of his ally's intentions not from correspondence with Versailles but through word conveyed by the new Spanish minister to the United States. D'Estaing was contemplating an assault on Halifax and Newfoundland. First, however, he wanted to know whether the United States could maintain these posts after they were taken.

Canada again! And once again Washington did his best to scuttle such an operation. He lacked the manpower for garrisoning those bases, he replied. Instead, he hearkened back to his plan for a joint attack on Clinton in New York.[13] Then he waited, a long interminable wait for the French reply.

In the meantime the commander was pushed into an operation in which he was only mildly interested. For at least a year bloody fighting had raged in the Wyoming Valley of Pennsylvania and at Cherry Valley in New York, deadly clashes between rebel settlers and loyalist raiders who had allied with Indians of the Six Nations. The worst incident occurred in the summer of 1778, just after the larger clash at Monmouth. Early in July a Tory-Indian force of nine hundred extirpated a rebel militia contingent at Forty Fort in Pennsylvania, killing three hundred. Panic-stricken residents poured from the region, their stories of atrocities filling American newspapers and fanning the flames for a campaign against these British allies. Despite the public outcry Washington was lukewarm at best about sending any of his army to the frontier. His reservations were not ill founded. Should d'Estaing suddenly arrive in northern waters, he wished to have an adequate army with which to act in concert with the new ally; to be rendered unable to cooperate would prolong the war and perhaps antagonize the French. Washington resisted the public's entreaties for six months, but in the end he had to act, for Congress made it clear that it wished him to pacify the frontiers.[14]

Washington's first choice of a commander for the expedition was curious. He turned to Gates, a decision, he said, that was based solely on matters of seniority. Gates, however, believed that Washington meant to embarrass him.

Everyone knew that he was too old and infirm to undertake such a campaign, he charged; it was revealing, he added huffily, that "your Exly should offer me the only command to which I am entirely unequal." There was something to Gates's acrimonious suggestion, for despite having begun his search on the basis of seniority, Washington then proceeded to bypass Putnam, the next in line, and offered the post to Sullivan instead. It was a position that would afford him the "flattering prospect of acquiring more credit than can be expected by any other officer this year," the commander told him. Sullivan, of course, accepted without hesitation, much to the chagrin of some in Congress who howled at Washington's selection of a man whose record was one of repeated failure. "I have a hard time of it," Washington responded defensively. "To please everybody is impossible," he added, and he further maintained that Sullivan was more than equal to the task.[15]

And for once Sullivan almost succeeded. His mission, according to Washington's orders, was to destroy every Indian settlement he could find. In addition, he was to seize Fort Niagara, the funnel through which British supplies trickled south from Canada.[16] What ensued has been called the "most ruthless application of a scorched earth policy in American history." It was that, but for all the destruction and suffering wrought by Sullivan the expedition still might have produced greater military benefits.[17]

The Indians in Sullivan's path simply chose to pull back, leaving village after village undefended and an inviting target for the invaders. After a trek of nearly 150 miles Sullivan's army had obliterated 40 villages, killed and scalped a handful of Indians, raped some captive squaws, burned 160,000 bushels of corn, and pillaged huge amounts of other commodities. Fewer than 40 of his men had perished. Then he decided to return home, although it still was in September and the weather was mild and dry. A lack of supplies prevented him from proceeding to Niagara, he asserted, and, considering the swollen size of his force, perhaps he was correct. He had done great damage to the Indians, but he had not brought peace to the frontier. "The nests are destroyed, but the birds are still on the wing," one of the expedition's officers wryly observed that autumn, and, indeed, the Indians still were able to launch episodic raids the following summer.[18]

On the eve of Sullivan's campaign unsettling news trickled into Washington's headquarters. A few weeks before, it was learned, Clinton had dispatched a small flotilla to the Chesapeake. Landing near Portsmouth, Virginia, on the Elizabeth River, the fleet had destroyed considerable amounts of rebel shipping and supplies; the enterprise was completed within two weeks, and the marines returning to New York laden with the spoils of their easy conquest. That action was a minor episode in this war, but Clinton followed it with what seemed to be a more ominous undertaking. On June 1, 1779, he sent six thousand grenadiers and jägers against Stony Point and Verplanck's Point on the Hudson, sites of the two southernmost American installations on that important concourse. The uncompleted fort at Stony Point fell without opposition, while Fort Lafayette directly across the river at Verplanck's surrendered almost as swiftly.

General Washington was not certain what Clinton intended. Since the redcoats' possession of these two bastions moved them to within about a dozen miles of West Point, this could mean the commencement of operations to seize the Hudson. But that was unlikely, considering the diminutive size of the British army in New York. Washington guessed that Clinton merely wished to increase his foraging area, while at the same time he inconvenienced the Americans, for the loss of these bases added about ninety miles to the communications link between New England and New Jersey. Washington's guess was essentially correct, although Clinton's actions also had been guided by two considerations that the American commander did not address. The British high command hoped their operations would compel Washington to try to retake the fortresses. Moreover, Clinton was confident that reinforcements were speeding across the Atlantic, enough additional men, in fact, to permit him to contemplate further raids into the Highlands, either against West Point or its lines of communication.[19]

Washington's initial reaction to the loss of the forts was to do nothing. "All we can do is to lament what we cannot remedy," he said. But in a couple of weeks his penchant for action persuaded him to consider an assault. By early July the general and his staff had succeeded in getting a spy into the post at Stony Point, while Washington personally reconnoitered the surrounding area. His endeavors convinced him that success was possible, and he concocted a complicated, risky plan for assailing the post. He proposed that a special light infantry unit of about two hundred men be constituted. Striking at midnight on the darkest possible night, these crack troops were to advance from three directions; each party was to be led by a cadre of "prudent and determined" men, volunteers who were to proceed with fixed bayonets, but unloaded muskets, and whose job it would be to silently overpower all sentries and guards. He placed Anthony Wayne in command.[20]

Wayne struck on July 16, a night when low, scudding clouds obliterated every beam of moonlight. His men hacked their way inside the fort, then fought doggedly against British soldiers who resisted with bayonets and knives, even with their fists. Nearly half the attackers were killed or wounded, but the British suffered 133 casualties, 543 captured, and the loss of Stony Point.[21]

Washington did not hold his new possession for long, however, for he suddenly realized that it would require an enormous force to defend the installation. There was another compelling reason for abandoning the place, one dictated by the commander's experience at Fort Washington and the Delaware River forts. To abandon Stony Point was to invite inconvenience. To attempt to hold it was to court disaster. He razed the compound. Still, Washington realized what he really had hoped for from the daring venture. The successful action was a morale-builder, something uncommon in the twelve months since Monmouth. It was, he thought, a much needed tonic for the flagging spirits of his countrymen, a people whose commitment to this protracted war, if not to independence, was languishing under the stress of economic despair.[22]

Buoyed by this victory, Washington soon approved a similar mission against the British fort at Paulus Hook. This time he placed Henry Lee—Light Horse Harry Lee, as he thereafter would be known—in command. Barely twenty-four, Major Lee was the sort of man to whom Washington was attracted. He once described Lee as zealous, prudent, and brave; everyone seemed to agree that he was bold and daring. At Valley Forge Washington had invited Lee to join his staff as an aide, but the young Virginian rebuffed his commander. "I am wedded to my sword," he had responded. His air of truculence toward headquarters life appealed to Washington. Here was a man who embodied those qualities that the commander hoped would be visible in himself. In the summer of 1779, when Washington received intelligence that the British were neglecting Paulus Hook, he turned to Lee to make a reconnaissance, then to lead the attack. It was an extraordinary appointment. Lee was a cavalry officer, yet he was to lead infantry-men; in addition, he was not a member of the division that he was given to lead, nor had he any experience in commanding the number of men he would have for this operation.[23]

Considering the paucity of booty that might be taken, this was a risky, perhaps foolhardy, venture. Washington understood from the outset that he was incapable of holding this fort. Moreover, while a successful strike would boost morale, the commander knew that America could "lose more in case of failure than we could gain in case of success." Lee's men lashed out on August 18, and in a few minutes they killed 50 defenders and took 158 prisoners. But the attack was only a partial success. The likelihood that nearby redcoat installations would dispatch relief parties compelled Lee to abandon the fort before he could put it to the torch.[24]

The two victories seemed to lift a burden that Washington long had borne. Four days after Lee's daring raid he chose to make amends with Joseph Reed, terminating the chill in their relationship that had begun in the aftermath of the disaster at Fort Washington. Washington confessed that he was "at a loss myself to tell" why he chose this moment to rehabilitate the friendship, nor could he explain why, for the first time, he felt compelled to offer a lengthy explanation for his conduct in the Hudson Fort episode. It is not likely that he ever could have understood the reasons for his gesture toward Reed, for the answer to his curious behavior—as well, perhaps, to why he launched these hazardous attacks at Stony Point and Paulus Hook—lay in Washington's psyche. It was as though his "Spirit of enterprize" in inflicting these "instances of disgrace to the British arms" had exonerated him of responsibility for his earlier debacle on the Hudson. That he selected Wayne and Lee to lead the assaults—the one, in his view, a "brave gallant and Sensible Officers," the other "the Gentleman and the Soldier"—was as close as he could come to leading the attacks himself. Gallant, prudent, enterprising, and brave were the terms he used to describe his two young officers, the very qualities he always had sought to embody. In effect he demanded that Wayne and Lee bring him glory, and each met his demand, restoring his shaken self-image, the very esteem that Reed had helped to shatter by doubting Washington's decisiveness.[25]

Washington was certain that his two surprise attacks would make the British "feel sore" and cause them to seek vengeance. He was partially correct. Henry Clinton's "temper from these two unlucky blows of fortune become[s] much soured," noted an officer at British headquarters. But he did not retaliate. Indeed, Clinton soon learned that the reinforcements he had anticipated would not be coming that year, and by the end of October he had jettisoned not only his Hudson River bases above Manhattan but Newport as well. The British leader anticipated a Franco-American campaign against New York, and he was digging in.[26] But he was wrong. d'Estaing instead had sailed south, ending a year of small-scale actions about New York.

When Washington learned that d'Estaing would winter in the Caribbean in 1779–80, his own thoughts turned to winter quarters. He had spent the previous winter in New Jersey, and he returned there—to Morristown, where he had gone after Trenton-Princeton—for this season too, summoning his legions from the southern and middle states to sites previously selected by Quartermaster General Greene. The prior winter had been a far cry from those dismal months at Valley Forge. The men had been well clothed, better than in any winter since the siege of Boston; their good fortune was due to the French alliance, for ships bearing the news of the partnership barely had cleared ports in New England before other vessels arrived laden with heavy, winter livery. Some men had suffered a dearth of blankets and shoes, but there were ample tents and, ultimately, enough huts for shelter. And the food supply was adequate, due in part to a more streamlined supply service, as well as to the fact that the troops were divided among several cantonments, each conveniently situated near a supply depot.[27]

Washington was in high spirits as the campaign of 1779 ended, not only because of his own successes, but on account of his adversary's failures. Great Britain had "wasted another Campaign," he believed, frittering away precious weeks in the Caribbean, a theater of secondary importance, while in New York and Pennsylvania a relatively small Continental army was permitted without opposition to destroy the homelands of their "good and faithful Allies," the Native Americans. Only a few days at Morristown, however, extinguished his cheer.[28]

Hard times returned that winter, and before that vexatious season ended Washington called this period "the most distressing of any we have experienced since the beginning of the War." What he did not realize was that the longest and bleakest—and in some ways the most dangerous—period of the war had commenced. The travail of Morristown was the first blow. The commander lived comfortably that winter, setting up headquarters in the spacious, two-year-old Ford Mansion, an eight-room, white clapboard Georgia dwelling located half a mile out of town on the Newark and Whippany Road. The soldiery spent a less luxurious season. Often, the men went ten days or more without meat and, on occasion, almost as long without bread. Private Joseph Plumb Martin once went four days without food of any kind, and he reported that some famished officers had killed and roasted their pet dogs in a vain attempt to assuage their hunger. Early in January the situation grew so desperate that half-starved soldiers fled camp to beg food from nearby farmers. The general officers and Washington's "family," meanwhile, seem to have fared better. During the three weeks in December that Washington lived in Morristown, headquarters procured the following comestibles: 116 fowl, 13 rabbits, 12 geese, 12 turkeys, 32 pounds of ham butts, 56 quail, 10 pigeons, 15 bushels of potatoes, 9 dozen eggs, 36 head of cabbage, 13 bushels of turnips, and 10 pounds of butter.

Uniforms and blankets, as well as shoes and hats, also were in short supply at the Morristown cantonment. Private Martin, who was posted close by at Basking Ridge, remembered weeks of sleeping in a tent on a bed of buckwheat straw. In fact, he moved into a hut only after he and a few comrades stole enough tools from local farmers to construct such a facility. As at Valley Forge, illness soon was the companion of ill-clothed, famished soldiers who, like Martin, "had now got beyond hunger" to a point of being "faint & weak." Fevers and pulmonary disorders struck the men. Colds became as commonplace as the raw biting wind that never seemed to abate, and at one point not only was General Washington afflicted, but eighteen of his aides as well.[29]

"The great man is confounded" as to the cause of the army's misfortunes, General Greene advised a friend that winter. In fact, however, Washington had a pretty good idea of what was responsible. In part, he blamed the misery on fraud and mismanagement within the supply service, chicanery that left the army with eleven thousand tons less hay and three-quarters of a million fewer bushels of grain than it had requisitioned. He also attributed his woes to the shortcomings of Congress. The national legislature, he charged, not only did not devote sufficient attention to the chronic enigma of provisioning its army, it lacked the executive personnel to administer such a program. He might have been reminded of what he had concluded during his first winter in this place two years before; Congress, he had fumed, "think it is but to say Presto begone, and everything is done." Washington and everyone else also knew that the awful weather that roared in just before Christmas exacerbated each other defect in the supply system. This winter was worse than any that even the oldest Morristown resident could remember. Nearly twenty inches of snow was dumped on the camp during the holiday period, and before the snowbound soldiery could dig out another blizzard howled across New Jersey. By early January four feet of snow lay like a canopy over the army; by February the camps were buried beneath twelve-foot-high drifts, choking off all river and road access to the outer world. To make matters worse, when a thaw set in around the 10th of January, and again in February, the highways leading to Morristown quickly turned to impassable quagmires.[30]

Washington never mentioned his own culpability in contributing to the shortages, but some of the responsibility was his. Early in October, despite a lack of convincing evidence that d'Estaing might return to the northern theater, Washington summoned twelve thousand militiamen to active duty. Thirty days later he countermanded his order, certain at last that the French fleet would not appear. But by then the trainbandsmen had helped reduce the army's precious stockpile of supplies.[31]

Whatever the cause, Washington knew that something must be done. "We can no longer drudge on in the same way," he warned. Some high officers had a solution. They whispered about the need for a military dictatorship, an expedient that some civilians also found palatable. That winter a conclave of New England states endorsed such a remedy, inasmuch as it formally recommended that Washington be given dictatorial powers for the purpose of supplying the army.[32]

Congress had a more modest solution in mind. It believed the problem stemmed from the economic malaise that gripped the nation. By the time Washington's army entered winter quarters the depreciation of Continental paper stood at thirty-nine to one, leaving the general and his suppliers to watch in wonder as farmers refused to sell their beef and grain despite steadily rising prices. No one was interested in the nearly worthless currency. The government borrowed money, raised revenues by the expedient of seizing and selling the property of the Loyalists, printed more and more paper, and, finally, revalued the debt. In the end the army muddled through. For the most part the soldiers simply endured, displaying that same persistent fortitude that had gotten them through Valley Forge. The only break came late in May when two regiments of hungry Connecticut men mutinied, hoping to escape the privation by hurrying home. The rising was quelled in short order, both by promises and by cajolery, but Washington recognized the incident for what it was—still another sign of the war weariness that clutched soldiers and civilians alike. The "patience of the soldiery" is "worn out," he acknowledged; "we see in every line in the army, the most serious features of mutiny and sedition," the general added. Then, ominously, he told Joseph Reed: "I have almost ceased to hope. The country in general is in such a state of insensibility and indifference to its interests, that I dare not flatter myself with any change for the better."[33]

Washington must have believed that his spirits had reached their nadir when he poured out his despondency to his former aide. But only twenty-four hours later, near dusk on May 29, 1780, a courier arrived at headquarters with even more lamentable tidings. Charleston had fallen to the adversary. An American army of fifty-five hundred men had been lost.[34]

In 1780 Clinton at last had launched his southern strategy in earnest. It was a policy born of desperation. Temporarily writing off the North, Britain now sought to push the rebels from each southern state, leaving it to their Loyalist allies—organized now into auxiliary units—to secure what they had gained.[35]

With Savannah in hand, Clinton struck first at Charleston, South Carolina, a city defended by Major General Benjamin Lincoln, the commander of America's southern army. Lincoln committed every error that Washington had made in his Brooklyn campaign, but with more devastating results. Soon trapped by a superior force, Lincoln surrendered his entire army. In its worst defeat during this war, America lost 5466 men, 6000 weapons, nearly 400 barrels of powder, and a huge cache of military stores.[36]

By the end of June British forces had swept into the interior, occupying a string of forts across the South Carolina frontier. All that remained of the Continental forces in the South was about 1400 men in North Carolina under Baron de Kalb, a contingent that Washington had dispatched in April to augment Lincoln's forces. Their trek from Morristown had met with one delay after another, fortunate hindrances as it turned out, for otherwise these men would have arrived just in time to be captured. Now, deep in North Carolina, de Kalb paused for orders, and, since he was a foreigner, the likely notification of his replacement. Word arrived in July. Congress had appointed Horatio Gates.[37]

General Gates had lobbied hard for the post, writing southern politicians, even visiting Congress to urge his case. Washington favored Greene for the command, but he did not press the matter, and in mid-June, without consulting Washington, Congress awarded the post to Gates. It was late July before he finally reached de Kalb and his meager army. What he found was not encouraging: a few ragged soldiers, a commissary in a "deplorable state," a "Deficiency of Magazines." On the other hand, his intelligence service reported that the foe had divided its army, that Cornwallis, who had been placed in command when Clinton returned to New York following the collapse of Charleston, had marched to Savannah, leaving only a small British force in northeast South Carolina. Despite the ill-prepared state of his own army, Gates opted to fight.

It was a disastrous decision. Gates ran upon the British at Camden, and to his horror he found that his intelligence reports had been faulty. This was a large British force, one led by Cornwallis. Gates outnumbered his adversary, but Cornwallis's army consisted largely of regulars, and it would have the only cavalrymen on the field. The result perhaps was predictable. Gates's army was overrun. De Kalb was killed, as were at least six hundred others, but most just fled into the wilderness, there to hide and, eventually, simply to melt away, so that only about one-third of those with Gates that day ever were accounted for. Gates, too, was one of those who dashed for safety, he and his staff madly riding for sixty miles across the South's bleached dust and shallow, russet streams before they finally stopped in Charlotte.[38]

The general's frantic dash from the scene proved his ruination. His defeat at Camden was complete, but it might have been forgiven; after all, Washington had survived three similarly disastrous thrashings in 1776, just as St. Clair was not made to suffer for losing Ticonderoga or Lincoln for his defeat at Charleston. But Gates's dismaying flight, however pragmatic, was deemed unpardonable, a verdict encouraged by those who had a score to settle with him. Such a harsh judgment seemed necessary to others, however, simply in order to restore morale. Congress relieved him of command pending an inquiry and directed Washington to appoint his successor. The commander named Nathanael Greene.[39]

Throughout the summer of 1780 Washington had been on pins and needles, not just because of the portentous news from the South, but over the role his army should play during that campaign. He feared that it would be unable to do a thing. Some men still were without shirts or shoes, and well into July many continued to endure five or six consecutive meatless days. In the midst of plenty, the soldiery experienced frequent scarcities even of bread. In addition, there was a dearth of salt and of rum, tents could not be found, hospitals lacked medical supplies, and by early summer the troops had not been paid for two months. Nor did Washington have the manpower he had anticipated. The "bitterness of my soul" knows no bounds, he confessed sardonically to his brother-in-law that July. Not only could the war have been ended successfully many years earlier, he went on, but now victory was imperiled as never before. And all for "want of System." The national government was too weak, the states too strong. America had created "a many headed Monster . . . that never will or can, steer to the same point," for each state was moved only to consider its local interests. "The contest among the different States *now,* is not which shall do the most for the common cause, but which shall do least. . . ."[40]

So weak was the army that Washington feared that he could not act defensively, much less offensively. He doubted that he could protect the supplies at Morristown should the British endeavor to raid that post, and, more importantly, he was not certain whether West Point could be successfully defended. As for a siege of New York, the insufficiency of stores seemed to rule out such a venture. And this summer was—perhaps it had to be—"the time for America by one great exertion to put an end to the war."[41]

But Washington was not without hope. Early in May he received the tidings that he had longed to hear for two years: a French army was en route to the United States. He first learned of the French action via a Tory newspaper. Lafayette, who had sailed to France following the battle for Newport, brought the news with him when he returned to America that spring; but he dallied in Boston and along the way to Morristown, so it was a Loyalist publisher in New York who broke the story. Whatever the source, Washington could hardly have been more delighted. Escorted by a half dozen ships of the line, French transports containing six thousand professional soldiers were ploughing across the Atlantic, all due in Rhode Island sometime in June. Their instructions, Lafayette told Washington when he finally arrived at headquarters, were to permit Washington to plan strategy. There was talk at Versailles of a campaign against Halifax, yet there was equal sentiment for striking at the British in the South or for besieging New York. But it would be Washington's task to recommend a course of action.[42]

It was not until mid-July, a month later than expected, that the white sails and the colorful banners of the Gallic flotilla at last were spotted in waters off Newport. On board, clad in their traditional white uniforms, were crack soldiers, many of whom had come topside for a first glimpse of the New World. The Compte de Rochambeau was the general in command of the army. Rochambeau's appearance was friendly and avuncular, more that of a Paris shopkeeper than of a soldier. But looks were deceiving: he had soldiered for thirty-seven of his fifty-five years, and when one looked more closely the legacy of his trade could be discerned. A long scar extended from his hairline onto his face, and he walked with a slight limp—both the result of battle wounds. Cold without being supercilious, he came with neither much respect for his ally nor with much enthusiasm for helping them in their struggle against imperial and monarchical domination. The naval commander (d'Estaing had returned to France on crutches, nursing wounds he had received at Savannah) was Chevalier de Ternay, an old salt with three years more service than Rochambeau. In poor health and unhappy with duty in America, Ternay, a naturally ill-humored man, was particularly out of sorts when he arrived, not least because he feared an immediate British strike.[43]

Rochambeau hurried his men ashore and sat about constructing his defenses, yet for ten days the French army was exposed and vulnerable to attack. It was an anxious time for the French commander. But the British made no move. Indeed, Clinton did not even know that his adversary had reached Rhode Island until more than a week after the French fleet dropped anchor. British intelligence had failed miserably. Had Clinton quickly attacked, one young French officer later remarked, the British army "would have met with but feeble resistance."[44]

Some American leaders also believed that a turning point had been reached, but the uncommonly upbeat atmosphere at headquarters soon vanished. In the weeks before the French arrival Washington and his closest advisors had determined to recommend joint operations against New York; Lafayette had proposed an assault on the city, but Washington wisely brushed that foolhardy notion aside, favoring a plan by Knox to besiege the adversary. The idea was to strike simultaneously at Staten Island and Morrissania, fanning out thereafter until the redcoats' contact with the outside world was severed, its ability to forage impeded by the American army, its Atlantic lifeline severed by the French fleet.

The French were hardly ashore in Rhode Island before the American commander dispatched Lafayette to test his countrymen's response to the American plan. Their answer was not promising. Until naval reinforcements arrived, they would not act. Moreover, the Franco-American land force would total only about fourteen thousand men, roughly the equivalent of Clinton's army. European military textbooks, they reminded Lafayette, stipulated that to succeed the siege army must have a two-to-one numerical superiority. In addition, many of Washington's men would be militiamen, and he could not guarantee their presence after December 31, a date certain to be reached before siege operations could be concluded. Besides, they went on, the wagons necessary to move the French army to New York had not yet even begun to be gathered. Behind these sound arguments lay still another factor: the French were uneasy with their new ally. Rochambeau, already dismayed by the Americans's capitulation at Charleston, was shocked by the Continental soldiers that he had seen; no doubt, too, he found Washington's supply problems to be worse than he had been led to believe by Versailles. Still, Rochambeau told Lafayette, if Washington could get more men, if Ternay's flotilla could obtain reinforcements from the West Indies, and if the French Second Division arrived from France, a siege might be possible.[45]

There the issue hung for a month, until Rochambeau learned that reinforcements might arrive in October. He immediately wished to speak directly with Washington. He had taken an instant dislike to Lafayette, whom he found to be foolish and so ill-informed on military matters as to be difficult to converse with when planning strategy. Besides, he was anxious to meet and appraise his counterpart. One needed to know his ally as well as his adversary before the shooting commenced. He proposed a conference with the American commander, and Washington agreed. It was set for mid-September in Hartford, a midway point between the two generals' headquarters.[46]

In the sixty days between the arrival of Rochambeau and Washington's meeting with him, the latter's spirits sagged to perhaps their lowest ebb since the first weeks at Valley Forge. Week by week he had watched helplessly while the hopes of midsummer "vanish[ed] like Morning Dew." While Lafayette was holding his first meeting in Newport, Washington was buoyed by "a well grounded hope of putting a speedy and happy termination to the war." Then came the news of his ally's intransigent refusal to act without naval superiority. That was a blow, but it was understandable, he noted early in August, and he advised against pressuring the French into action. "Should they yield to importunity and an accident happen . . . they would lay the consequences to us." Two weeks later he learned that the French naval reinforcements were coming, yet that news only heightened his frustration. Now he feared that he lacked the manpower to act in concert with his ally. By August 15 he had gotten only about 40 percent of the men he had requested. "[O]ur prospects of operating diminish," he had to tell Congress. In fact, not only was the army undersized, he could barely feed the men who were on duty. "It is a most mortifying reflexion," he told Reed. "Should we . . . be found, after all our promises of a cooperating force, deficient in Men, provision, and every other essential," the consequences surely would be catastrophic. By late August he feared that if the siege of New York was cancelled due to America's infirmities, one of two occurrences virtually was certain: either the army would dissolve before 1781, for "the hope which has hitherto supported them of a change for the better" would have been dashed; or, France would abandon the United States. Yet late in August, just as Washington's spirits hit bottom, came word of a reprieve. News arrived that both the French naval reinforcements and the Second Division had been delayed by British squadrons. Neither would be coming in 1780. At least the onus for inaction was not entirely on America's shoulders.[47]

Washington's mood had brightened when he—together with his aides, a few advisors, and the Commander's Guard—set out for Hartford in mid-September. Still, his spirits hardly were soaring as they had been the last time he had been in New England—when he had recaptured Boston early in 1776. He arrived in Hartford on the 22nd, entering town about the same time as Rochambeau and Ternay. A prim and rustic little village like Hartford didn't offer much in the way of amusements, but Washington made amends by providing a lavish dinner. A superficial air of camaraderie prevailed at the table; as a brotherly gesture Washington's men had added white to the black cockades they wore, and the French had touched their white cockades with black to reciprocate. Animated discussions accompanied by plentiful toasts must have run around the table, while the three leaders, all reticent men, talked stiffly. The French were impressed by Washington, finding him cold and standoffish like their own general, yet businesslike and competent. Even Count Rochambeau was pleased with Washington's skills, and the meeting removed the doubts with which he had crossed the Atlantic, reservations that for a time had seemed to be borne out by the fact that the American commander had been so taken in by the likes of Lafayette. Washington seemed equally impressed by his counterpart. Late that afternoon the table was cleared and the leaders got down to business.[48]

Washington had come prepared to offer four plans. First priority, he told the French, must be placed on taking New York, for he believed its capture would end the war. He suggested a siege if and when French naval reinforcements arrived, but barring that he proposed that the two armies move to the very periphery of Manhattan; at least that would prevent Clinton from sending reinforcements to Cornwallis in the South. While his allies mulled over those possibilities, he suggested two alternative courses of action: a joint expedition to the South, a venture that would compel Clinton to assist Cornwallis and which might produce the first major clash of the adversaries in the two years since Monmouth; curiously, he also suggested a joint expedition into Canada, the sort of enterprise he had found abhorrent as long as Gates was plumping for such a strategy. Rochambeau listened patiently to what must have been a dreadfully long presentation for Washington, then he replied in kind. His speech threw cold water all over Washington's planning. A siege of New York he agreed to, but only in the unlikely event that enough French ships of war slipped through to America. He vetoed the other notions, apparently asserting that his orders were to use the army only in concert with the navy, and that Ternay's fleet was too small to consider a thrust either to the southward or into Canada. With that the meeting ended. One thing only seemed to have been decided. There would be no further action in 1780, and next summer's campaign would depend on the mood in Versailles as well as on the willingness of thirteen American states to prosecute the war. The future, which had "appeared pregnant with events of a favourable complexn" in July, had "prov'd delosury," Washington lamented in September. "I see nothing before us but accumulating distress," he now maintained.[49]

The next morning Washington was up early and on his way out of Hartford.

If he could not take the offensive, he had to be certain that his defenses in the Highlands were adequate. His destination was West Point on the Hudson, where he planned to confer with its commander, Major General Benedict Arnold.

Arnold's career had followed a twisted, tortuous path since his heroics three years earlier in the Saratoga campaign. Seriously wounded in the leg during that fray, he spent six months recuperating, returning to active duty only just before Washington departed Valley Forge. He was still in pain and limping badly, however, and a battlefield post was out of the question. Hence, upon Clinton's withdrawal from Philadelphia that summer, Washington named Arnold to command the army in that city. It turned out to be a more dangerous theater for Arnold than any battlefield upon which he had fought.

His policies, his expensive habits, his open friendliness with many prominent neutralist—some said Tory—families, and his eventual marriage to Peggy Shippen, a member of one of those suspect families, angered many Philadelphians. Today, Arnold's behavior in these instances seems perfectly innocent. Some of his financial dealings probably were not, however. Arnold always had lusted after money and the status he believed it would fetch, and during his stint in Philadelphia he engaged in several shady financial transactions, maneuverings in which he seems to have misused public property for his own private ends. Ultimately, the Council of Pennsylvania drew up a list of eight charges against him. Arnold immediately asked Washington to convene a court martial. It was his only hope of exoneration.

While he awaited word of his fate, Arnold's anger swelled. Already passed over by Congress for a promotion that he believed he deserved, Arnold seethed at this new affront. Even before the court convened to hear his case, Arnold, bitter and frustrated, initiated clandestine talks with the British high command. If the price was right, he suggested, he might engage in a treasonous act.

Ultimately, Clinton's headquarters made clear what it hoped to procure from Arnold: West Point. He remained interested, more so, in fact, following the verdict of the panel that heard his court martial. He was acquitted on seven charges, but convicted of mishandling public property. While his sentence was light—merely a reprimand from General Washington—Arnold could only look on the conviction as a dark stain upon his honor. He continued to talk with the British, haggling over the fee that his betrayal would bring. Meanwhile, he stumped to gain command of that vital post. He wrote influential friends, and he called on Washington at Morristown early in June. The commander's response was disappointing, for he planned to garrison West Point with invalids. Washington indicated that he preferred to give Arnold a field command instead.[50]

A few weeks later Washington formally announced that if a Franco-American campaign against New York occurred, Arnold would command the American left in the siege army. The appointment was meant to confirm Arnold's vindication, at least in Washington's eyes, but Arnold's bitterness toward the United

States evidently was immutable. Arnold hurried to headquarters as soon as he read the orders. He wished to decline the post, he told Washington, pleading that his slowly mending wounds precluded his assumption of a field command. Once again, he asked to be given command of West Point. Later Washington realized that Arnold's requests should have aroused his suspicions. At the time, however, he took Arnold's excuse at face value. Early in August, Arnold was granted command of the Highlands post.

Soon Arnold had everything he wanted, for the turncoat shortly struck a deal with Clinton. He would exchange West Point and its entire garrison for twenty thousand dollars. He sped north to take command, and he established his headquarters nearby in the Robinson house, a dwelling once owned by Beverley Robinson, the friend with whom Washington had stayed during his journey to Boston in 1756.[51]

Much work had to be done to prepare for the sell-out, but for Arnold all went well until September 22, the very day that Washington was meeting with the French leaders a hundred or so miles to the east of West Point. Arnold, too, had a meeting that day. His was with a young British officer, Major John André. They rendezvoused in a grove of firs near the Hudson, there to complete the arrangements for the transferral of West Point. Following the meeting André started back to Manhattan. He did not make it. After traveling several miles, he was stopped by sentries. A search uncovered suspicious papers concealed in his boot. The guards ushered André to North Castle, the site of the nearest Continental army post, where he was detained; meanwhile, his papers were sent to Washington, while simultaneously word was sent to Arnold—until now, ignorant of the events of the past thirty-six hours—of André's detention. It now was September 23, and General Washington was departing Hartford for his return to West Point at almost that very moment.

When Arnold awakened that Monday morning he still did not know of André's difficulties. Nor did Washington. The courier sent with the captured papers had been unable to locate the commander, and he had been rerouted to West Point. In the earliest hours of the day, hence, three men were proceeding toward the Robinson house from different directions: Washington, ignorant of any of the recent curious occurrences; the messenger instructed to tell Arnold of André's arrest; and the dispatch-rider bearing the incriminating documents for Washington's perusal. Members of General Washington's staff were the first to arrive at Arnold's residence. The commander had been delayed, aides to Lafayette and Knox told Arnold; Washington, they added had urged everyone to begin breakfast without him. Sometime during the meal the messenger looking for Arnold arrived. Without evident emotion Arnold read the letter from North Castle, asked his guests to excuse him for a moment, went upstairs to speak with his wife, then returned to the dining room to announce that he had been summoned to West Point. He would be back within thirty minutes, he said. Instead, spurring his horse on at breakneck speed, he raced to the Hudson and to the barge that normally carried him across to West Point. This time, however, he ordered the vessel to proceed downriver.[52]

A few minutes after Arnold's departure Washington arrived. Hungry after his own long ride, he ate without waiting for Arnold to return. But when the meal ended and Arnold still had not returned, Washington and his retinue rode to the fort. Perhaps there was an emergency. Perplexingly, Arnold was not there either. For that matter, neither had he come to West Point that morning nor had anyone summoned him. Washington inspected the outpost, then he was rowed back to the Robinson House. It was about 3:30. Arnold still was unaccounted for. But soon the mystery was resolved. The emissary whose saddlebags contained André's incriminating papers finally arrived just before 4:00.

The commander did not have to read the documents twice to deduce what Arnold was about, and he immediately dispatched a party led by Hamilton to stop the traitor before he escaped. Washington quickly interrogated Arnold's principal officers and aides, then, with Lafayette in tow, he entered Mrs. Arnold's bedchamber and tried to speak with her. It was hopeless. Disheveled, clad only in a rumpled nightgown, her eyes red and swollen from a day of weeping, she paced the floor throughout the interview, crying and raving about this and that, none of it very comprehensible. She did not even recognize Washington. He excused himself after a few minutes, anxious to escape a scene that he found embarrassing. All about Washington people seemed to have been transported into a frenzy, but he remained calm, issuing his initial orders with an icy calm that had become habitual after encountering one crisis after another for so many years. When all his commands were given, however, he lowered his guard, and his real emotions poured out. Lafayette, whose imagination was too vivid to be very trustworthy, later alleged that Washington wept like a baby. The man who owned the house where André had slept on the twenty-first told a different story. Washington, he said, shrieked in a black fury, denouncing Arnold and expressing his distrust of each and every one of his officers. This version sounds more probable, and, indeed, a month later Washington urged the Board of War to pursue every lead it came upon that might suggest perfidious conduct by any officer.[53]

Strangely, the commander hesitated for more than three hours before issuing orders to put his army on full alert. Fortunately, Clinton was not coming, but Washington was finally certain of that only after he spent a long, tense, vigilant evening. During the night he learned that Arnold, with his seven-hour head start, had escaped onto a British ship of war. In fact, before dawn Washington even received a brief note from the traitor, but it was too confusing and contradictory to shed much light on his actions. Arnold seemed to attribute his behavior to patriotism and to revanchism, to his desire to settle the score for the "ingratitude of my country." [54]

Washington kept the army on the ready for seventy-two hours, all the while seeing to it that both André and the people who had served Arnold were questioned relentlessly. He also had his aides go through Peggy Arnold's correspondence, and he even directed them to search her quarters for clues to her husband's treachery. With that finally done, he concluded that Arnold had acted alone, that his grandiose plot had been foiled.

All that was left was to deal with André. Caught behind American lines in civilian attire, he could be treated as a spy. Whatever Washington thought of him, he felt that American security required that an example had to be made of this unfortunate young man. A military tribunal recommended capital punishment, and the commander consented, postponing the execution for a day to receive the emissaries of Clinton. The British commander desperately bargained for the officer's release, but he would not consent to the one demand made by Washington that instantly would have liberated André: a swap of Arnold for the British major. On October 2, nine days after his capture, Major André was hanged.[55]

The public was shaken by Arnold's apostasy, but not just because of the "deadly wound if not a fatal stab" that would have resulted from the loss of West Point. As one scholar has demonstrated, contemporaries feared that Arnold's venality was the final, cataclysmic symbol of the loss of America's virtue. From the outset the nation seemed unanimous in its belief that independence could only be attained—and, indeed, that it would only be desirable—if the citizenry was virtuous, if men fought and risked their lives and estates, if the populace eschewed self-indulgence. Some grew concerned for American virtue as early as 1776 when enlistments fell off, but the citizenry generally had remained confident through the best and worst of times. Yet the events of 1780 nearly extinguished all cause for optimism. First the inhabitants of South Carolina had failed to rally behind Lincoln at Charleston, while at Camden militiamen and their officers had fled in a panic, leaving the South almost undefended. Now Arnold—literally selling out, a turncoat's act that seemed to symbolize the eclipse of the public's virtue. Washington recognized the danger, and in public he endeavored to paper over the event. He told Rochambeau, for instance, that "traitors are the growth of every country" and a commonplace ingredient of civil wars. The wonder is, he added, that their numbers were so few. In private, however, he seethed with anger. "The world are disappointed at not seeing Arnold in Gibbets," he told a young aide six months later. That Arnold was never punished was not due to lack of effort on the part of Washington. He churned with a lust to seize the traitor, once even sending an intrepid young Virginian, a sergeant under Light Horse Harry Lee, into New York on a mission to kidnap Arnold, as if the turncoat's blood would cleanse the nation of its impurity. Of course the enterprise to take Arnold failed, and Washington was left to reflect aloud that if virtuous men did not emerge "to rescue our affairs" all might be lost "in the general Wreck."[56]

One thing came of Arnold's treachery. Since sometime in 1779 Continental army officers had resumed their hue and cry about pensions. They barely had secured the national government's commitment of half-pay for seven years before they began to beseech Congress to grant them half-pay for life at the end of the war. For a year the financially strapped Congress rebuffed their every entreaty.

Now, suddenly, things were different. Arnold's act seemed to be at least partially attributable to his financial woes. If he had stabbed the nation in the back for that reason, what was to keep other officers from similarly selling out? Late in 1780, with Arnold's treachery sticking like a bone in its craw, Congress pledged half-pay for life to the army's officers. It pledged nothing to the common soldiery.[57]

What more could 1780 bring to this beleagured nation? Within a few days of Arnold's treason some good news trickled into headquarters at Preakness. At King's Mountain in South Carolina a force of militiamen had drubbed an enemy army consisting mostly of Loyalists. At about the same time Congress reorganized the Continental army more or less along the lines that Washington had recommended. During the summer Washington had proposed to a congressional committee that men be conscripted for three-year hitches. Congress would not go quite that far. Instead, it passed legislation that assigned a manpower quota to each state. Men were to sign on or be drafted for varying periods, and in September of each year each state was to be apprised of any shortfall in its recruitment; on January 1, if the errant state had not made up its deficiency, an appropriate number of veteran soldiers from that state, men whose service should be ending, would be detained in the ranks. Not only would Washington be assured of his troop strength, but the new plan would save money by reducing the incredible loss of supplies that resulted when thousands of men annually were mustered into the army in the stead of thousands who departed. There might be an immediate benefit as well. Washington was convinced that Britain had remained at war in part because it thought each American army surely would be its last army. Now with an army assured for 1781, and with French troops still here too, Britain might reconsider its commitment.[58]

In a letter that rang with his ebullience at the army's reorganization, Washington noted: "The history of the war is a history of false hopes and temporary expedients. Would to God they were to end here!" Such was not the case. Three days into 1781 came the news that Washington had feared since that very first winter—mutiny had erupted within the ranks, a contagion born of anguish and frustration, and potentially more deadly to the war effort than the blackest treason.[59]

Washington had entered winter quarters in the late fall of 1780, scattering his troops from New Jersey to West Point, while his French allies cantoned in abandoned houses in Newport. In no time the Continental army was afflicted by the familiar problems of the season, and its commander's letters read like carbon copies of the plaintive messages he had written three winters before at Valley Forge. Once again there was a "scarcity of provision," a "want of Cloathing," inadequate supplies of coats and blankets, much "distress for want of flour," too few hours to forage and too little provender for the horses that conveyed the men who looked for food, breeds of livestock that were too poor and thin to provide much meat, a dearth of supplies for the army's hospitals, and insufficient funds with which to pay the troops.[60]

"Our soldiers are not devoid of reasoning faculties," Pennsylvania's General Wayne observed that December, and some Pennsylvania troops soon reasoned that the best means of getting the attention of officialdom was to protest. Their principal grievances concerned the length of their service. They had signed on for three years or the duration, but they had been told that "duration" meant that they would be discharged if the war lasted less than three years. Having come aboard during that winter at Valley Forge, their service obligation ended on January 1, 1781—or so they concluded. But the authorities reached a different conclusion. They believed the soldiers were compelled to serve for the duration—that is, until the war ended. The ingredients were in place for a confrontation. The explosion occurred about 9:00 P.M. on New Year's Day.[61]

Nearly one thousand men—fully 15 percent of Washington's army—mutinied, commencing a march on Congress from their cantonment at Mount Kemble, near Morristown. General Wayne, the commander of the post, was powerless to stop them, for his non-mutinous troops balked at fighting other Continental soldiers. He tried to cajole them, then he sought to bargain. Nothing worked. By mid-afternoon on January 2 the mutineers, armed now with six cannon, were marching—literally marching, for they were a well-disciplined outfit —on Philadelphia.

These disgruntled soldiers had trekked about fifteen miles when Washington learned of the uprising. There was not much he could do other than to direct his officers to endeavor to talk to these men. Indeed, he was so alarmed at the temper of the soldiery at West Point that he did not dare leave his post to assist Wayne.

At Princeton, almost five years to the day following Washington's great victory in the little college town, a settlement was reached. Joseph Reed, now the president of Pennsylvania, arrived and engaged in an amicable but spirited parley that resolved the matter. Those men who had volunteered before 1778 were to be discharged. Otherwise, commissioners were to be appointed to hear the case of each disputed enlistment.[62]

That scare was over, but through the spring the threat of mutiny hung in the air like a heavy, pungent fragrance. Two weeks after the insurgents in the Pennsylvania Line returned to the fold, rioting broke out among New Jersey troops. This time Washington's response was ruthless. He sent General Robert Howe with troops from West Point to suppress the uprising, ordering him not to negotiate and to "instantly execute a few of the most active and most incendiary leaders." Howe did just that, eventually compelling twelve arrested mutineers to serve as a firing squad that executed two ringleaders. The mutiny was suppressed before January ended.[63]

"[E]very thing is now quiet," Washington could report at the beginning of the next month. But a sense of profound uneasiness had settled in at headquarters. Two campaigns had come and gone since Monmouth, since France had entered the war, and each year the allies had failed to score the sort of decisive victory that might have compelled Britain to recognize American independence. Despite the sanguinity of the commander when he had emerged from Valley Forge, these years had been more devastating to the United States than to the enemy. Enervated, its economy in shambles, its spirit strained, its troops restless and disgruntled, its armies battered in the South, the nation's future seemed bleak. For Washington, moreover, the war suddenly had struck home even harder, for on January 3 redcoat forces under their new brigadier general, Benedict Arnold, invaded Virginia.[64]

In public Washington strove to remain optimistic, to exhort his men to further sacrifice. "We began a Contest for Liberty and Independence . . . relying on our Patriotism" to see us through. It remains "our duty to bear present Evils with Fortitude." But in private he was more candid, and more atrabilious. He could not "count on a speedy end to the War," nor could he put much faith in the staying power of France or Spain, inasmuch as the "change or caprice of a single Minister is capable of altering the whole system of Europe." His mood was one of funereal gloom, for he sensed that the United States began 1781 on the "verge of ruin," near to the point that "we must once more return to the Government of G: Britain, and be made to kiss the rod preparing for our correction. . . ." Washington's pessimism was matched by Britain's glee. "No resistance on their part is to be apprehended that can materially obstruct the progress of the King's arms in the speedy suppression of the rebellion," trumpeted a blithe Germain at Whitehall. And even the taciturn Clinton thought victory was at hand. "I have all to hope," he exulted early in 1781, "and Washington all to fear."[65]

12

Victory and Retirement

"Cornwallis must fall into our hands"

Early in 1781, for the first time since the war began, General Washington embarked on a new year certain that America's cause was lost if his army was not active and victorious before the next winter. Fiscal chaos was the culprit. The people were no less zealous for independence, but they were exasperated with the nation's feebleness, with the inertia that grew from its bewildering economic miseries. Still another year of missed opportunities would sap the citizenry's will to persist, he predicted; nor could he guarantee the survival of the army if conditions went unimproved. The "patience of the army . . . is now nearly exhausted," he had to admit.[1]

Three changes could save the Revolution, Washington wrote that January.

A foreign loan was the most essential ingredient in advancing America's ability to prosecute the war. French naval superiority was nearly as important. Finally, he and Rochambeau agreed that fifteen thousand additional French troops would provide the allies with strategic options that presently did not exist.[2]

As bleak as conditions appeared, there was hope. Rochambeau had dispatched his son to Versailles to beg for money for the United States, and Congress had sent John Laurens, the son of its president, to the same source to plead for a loan, for reinforcements, and for supplies for the Continental army. At the same time, Congress finally ratified a national constitution, the Articles of Confederation. For four years that document had gathered dust, the hostage of conflicting western land claims and of factions who feared relinquishing even a particle of state sovereignty to a national government. At last, however, the war crisis had provoked the foot-draggers to act. After all, if General Washington's gloomy predictions about the floundering war effort were correct, there soon would be no United States, much less a constitutional issue with which to be concerned. Virginia's change of heart—which occurred when Benedict Arnold and his new friends invaded the state—was perhaps the most crucial turning point, for the Old Dominion's wilderness land holdings were enormous. When Maryland followed suit at the beginning of March, the United States had a written constitution that outlined Congress's powers.

The charter did not really give Congress much power. Indeed, real power was reserved to the states. Yet the new government created federal departments, including a centralized war department that was to direct the war effort. Moreover, even with its inherent shortcomings the new constitution could only aid young Rochambeau and Laurens in their quest for assistance at the French court.

At the beginning of 1781 it seemed that all planning for the annual campaign would have to await the decisions of the royal court at Versailles. But early in January Washington learned that Arnold had led a British force into Virginia. That altered matters. The landing of the redcoat force of sixteen hundred was opposed by only fifty Virginia militiamen, and forty-eight hours after disembarking, without the loss of a man, Arnold's troops had driven well up the James River to claim possession of Richmond. Shortly thereafter Arnold went into winter quarters, but his presence in Virginia compelled Washington to reconsider his options.[3]

Since late in November the principal American army in the South had belonged to Nathanael Greene. Appointed by Washington after Gate's failure at Camden, Greene had taken command at Charlotte thirty days before Arnold's landing in Virginia. Heavily outnumbered, Greene envisaged a war of posts, his army sustained by shipments of essential goods by—and through—Virginia. Arnold's abrupt appearance, therefore, constituted a potentially serious threat, for if the redcoats succeeded in cutting the supply routes that linked the northern and southern states, the British could block all succor to Greene.

Strangely, Washington initial reaction to the incursion into Virginia was muted. He seemed to think that Arnold soon would abandon the state, as the British had done following the raid at Portsmouth in 1778. A month after Arnold's landing Washington still was exhorting Thomas Jefferson, now the governor of the province, to forget the redcoats in Virginia and to aid Greene. But early in February the commander's views changed. He learned that the British fleet which had blockaded the French navy at Rhode Island had suffered heavy damage during a winter storm; miraculously, the French fleet, tethered at Newport, had survived unscathed. Perhaps now Rochambeau would consent to act. If he would send a large fleet to the Chesapeake, Arnold could be bottled up, prey for a combined Franco-American army that the two commanders might send after him. Washington hurriedly sent a courier to Rhode Island to inquire, hoping that this was the break that was needed to destroy Britain's will to continue.[4]

While he waited the French response good news reached headquarters, tidings that he quickly shared with his allies at Newport. An American force under Daniel Morgan had defeated a larger British army at a place called Cowpens in South Carolina. Indeed, it was not just a victory, but America's first success in the southern war, and a major triumph at that, for the redcoats had suffered over eight hundred casualties, while Morgan lost just twelve, with sixty wounded.[5]

The day after Washington learned of Morgan's "most decisive victory," he received disappointing word from Rhode Island. The new commander of the French squadron, Chevalier Destouches, successor to Ternay who had died in December, agreed to act in the Chesapeake, but he planned to send only four warships to that theater. Washington was dismayed. His European allies were beginning to seem as cautious as the British commanders. This would be still another missed opportunity, he exclaimed, unless Destouches sent his entire fleet, and unless Rochambeau sent at least a thousand men to act in concert with the twelve hundred Americans he could detach. Do that, he said, and the Chesapeake could be blocked, sealing Arnold's egress. But the French would not budge. Even so, Washington's mind had changed. He now saw Virginia as crucial to Greene's survival, and he spoke of Arnold's destruction as something of "immense importance." With or without French help, Washington planned to send an American force into Virginia.[6]

While he readied an expedition, Washington waited impatiently for word on the fate of the diminutive fleet that Destouches had sent to the Chesapeake. First came good news. The little Gallic fleet had met with some success. Commanded by Captain le Gardeur de Tilly, the French flotilla had caught their adversary off guard; four British transports had been destroyed, and a large frigate, four additional transports, two privateers, and five hundred royal seamen had been captured. On March 1 even better news reached Washington. A courier sent by Rochambeau galloped up to headquarters at New Windsor with the word Washington had longed to hear. Flushed with success, Destouches had experienced a change of heart. The entire French fleet at Newport was sailing for the Chesapeake, and on board would be eleven hundred soldiers. Washington immediately matched the French infantry commitment. He gave Lafayette command of America's soldiery, directing that officer to march from Peekskill and to rendezvous with his countrymen on the beach of the Chesapeake. And he set out for Newport for a second meeting with Rochambeau, this one "to level all difficulties" in preparing for the campaign.[7]

General Washington reached Newport early in March, just in time to learn that the French army already had departed and that Destouches had all but sailed. He stayed a week nevertheless, meeting with Rochambeau, and from time to time speaking with New England dignitaries. By the third week in March he was back at headquarters near West Point, there to wait with "anxious solicitude" for news from the South. Given all the false hopes of the past half dozen years he must have been steeled for the worst, although he tried to cheer himself with the reminder of God's "many remarkable interpositions . . . in the hours of our deepest distress and darkness." Once again, he added, he could only trust "in our deliverance" from the present "awful crisis" by that "hand of Providence."[8]

At the end of the month bad news arrived, though it was not as dreadful as it might have been. For weeks Washington had feared the destruction of the French fleet, an expectation that left him on tenterhooks. His anxiety had been heightened because the French had procrastinated in agreeing to his plan until the British navy had repaired the damage sustained in the February storm; now, he knew, Destouches's armada would be "unquestionably inferior" to the royal fleet it would find at the Chesapeake. Thus, although he learned that the mission had failed, it was with great relief that he discovered that Destouches had returned safely to Rhode Island.[9]

Hoping to outwit the English, Destouches had sailed directly east from Newport, gliding a hundred miles into the Atlantic before turning south. His ploy did not work. The British fleet was waiting at the entrance to the Chesapeake when its adversary arrived. A short, brisk engagement ensued, and both sides sustained some damage, enough to dampen Destouches's appetite for further combat. He turned tail for Rhode Island. Americans "could only console ourselves in the thought of having done everything practicable," Washington intoned, trying to put the best face on the episode. In fact, more could be done, and Congress did it. For public consumption it lauded and trumpeted the French action, even throwing a victory party in Philadelphia when Destouches sent the *Hermione*, his flagship, to the capital on a good-will junket. Given the possible blow to morale that the truth might have brought, Congress's action was wise. It also was necessary for another reason. A letter in which General Washington had injudiciously criticized the French failure to listen to his plans fell into Tory hands and was published by the royalist *New York Gazette*.[10]

Essential as was the public-relations gimmickry, it hardly altered the military situation. Arnold remained unscathed; Lafayette was left alone in Virginia to contend with the British, though he had only half as many troops as his adversary;

and Greene's predicament remained as sticky as ever. Yet, almost unnoticed at headquarters, the war in the South was changing. Grimly, quietly, a deadly partisan war had begun to rage in this sector, an almost hidden conflict that steadily took its toll on the British supply lines and manpower lists. Led by men like Francis Marion and Thomas Sumter, both former regulars, and by Andrew Pickens, still a militia officer, these guerrilla fighters darted out of swamps and forests periodically to make their strikes, scourging Britain's river traffic, plundering its supply waggons, sniping at foraging parties, cutting lines of communication.[11]

Meanwhile, alongside this nasty struggle, Morgan had rejoined forces with Greene, and the diminutive American army commenced a retreat to the Dan River, a blue-green stream that wound about the Virginia–North Carolina border. Too weak to fight, Greene's strategy was not unlike that which Washington had adopted in 1776: fall back, draw the foe on, save his own meager force, wear down Cornwallis. The British general seized the bait that dangled before his eyes, and set out after Greene.

In March 1781 the two armies collided at Guilford Court House, a wooded, rolling site that Greene had selected for the confrontation. Cornwallis finally had his shot, and at day's end he owned the battlefield. He must have wondered at what cost though, for he had lost one-quarter of his army.[12]

That night, while a steady rain smacked his tent, and while the forlorn cries of the unattended wounded pierced his ears, Cornwallis decided to jettison the Carolinas. He would take his army to Wilmington on the coast to be reoutfitted, then he would strike into Virginia. It was not an unwise decision, for it afforded the best hope of winning the war in the South. Cornwallis knew that the Carolinas had been denuded of supplies. Take Virginia, he reasoned, and the funnel could be plugged through which the Americans slipped provisions into the lower South. The Carolinas then could easily be squeezed to death. In a year or so the British flag would fly from the Potomac to the Savannah River, and Cornwallis could link his army with Clinton's to resume the war in the North. By late spring, without Clinton's consent, Cornwallis had begun his incursion into Virginia.

Washington followed these events closely, and he immediately understood their significance. The events at Guilford Court House would "retard and injure" Cornwallis's mobility in the Carolinas, he wrote, and he expressed no surprise when the British swept into Virginia. Nor did he find Cornwallis's action to be as befuddled as have many historians. Indeed, he thought the move was "exceedingly alarming." His consternation soon proved well founded. The British "are marching thro' the State almost without controul," he reported, for Lafayette's army was too small to offer an effective resistance.[13]

Still, Washington's gaze remained fixed on New York. After the war he sought to foster the notion that his posturing before Manhattan had been a bluff, that all along Virginia and Cornwallis were his real concern. But the evidence does not support his claim. With the summer almost on them, he and Rochambeau— together with Comte de Barras, who only days before had arrived in America and supplanted Destouches—met at Wethersfield, Connecticut, to map their plans for the year. Familiar with one another, each quite respectful of the other's talents, these two reserved men found this to be their easiest session yet. Rochambeau opened the meeting with important news: Comte de Grasse had cleared Brest with a large French armada and with six hundred fresh reinforcements for the army; the flotilla was headed for the West Indies, though the troops were to be detached and transported to Newport. It was possible, he went on, that de Grasse might be able to sail for the American mainland at a later date that year. Washington had hardly digested those tidings before Rochambeau divulged additional news. He was sorry to report that Versailles had decided not to send his Second Division to America; in its place, however, 6 million livres worth of supplies and credit would be provided. Rochambeau had considered all these details. He had a recommendation. He proposed that the allies shift the war to the South during the summer of 1781.[14]

As happy as Washington must have been with most of his counterpart's presentation, he persisted in his argument that New York must remain the allies' principal target. As much as he yearned to fight in Virginia, "where all my property and Connexion's are," New York still was a more important object. Besides, a long land march—450 miles from the Hudson, over 600 miles from Newport—seemed the only way to get to Virginia. It would be expensive and time-consuming, and to make the trek in the course of the summer was to risk the loss to disease of perhaps a fourth of the soldiery. In addition, if the two armies took up positions outside New York, Clinton almost certainly would recall some, perhaps all of his forces in Virginia, for he was believed to have only about 7500 troops scattered about the city's environs; if Clinton declined to augment his forces, the allies would possess "a favourable opportunity" to assail him and reclaim the city. As to whether de Grasse should be instructed to sail to New York or to the Chesapeake, Washington proposed that the decision be postponed pending events of the next several weeks.[15]

The French listened to Washington's arguments, and they agreed to pursue his recommendations. At the close of the meeting Rochambeau pledged to move out to join Washington within a few weeks. At last, almost a year after the French army had arrived, it was about to be linked to the Continental army for a joint operation. And for the first time since that day at Monmouth three years before, a chance existed for a general engagement.[16]

Throughout June 1781, Washington waited impatiently for the French to arrive, alternately urging them to hasten their march, then cautioning them not to move too far, too fast, in the summer heat. Washington clearly was on pins and needles. The commander had begun to sense a chance for success for the first time since 1778. If everything worked just right, both Cornwallis and Clinton might be defeated. Yet that eventuality depended on the arrival of de Grasse's fleet. If it did not come, or if it arrived at the wrong time, nothing would be accomplished; moreover, if Washington sat immobile, fearing to move before that phantom flotilla arrived, he might let a golden opportunity slip through his fingers. Until the end of the month he seemed uncertain of what he might attempt, but then intelligence reports flooded headquarters with word that Clinton had sent a large foraging party into New Jersey. The redcoats' garrison was reduced by about 20 percent. Seizing upon this "most favorable opportunity," Washington drew up plans for a strike.[17]

The operation he planned resembled his tactics at Germantown, and it was easily as complicated. He envisioned a three-pronged attack, one American wing crossing the Hudson and assailing the British forts near Spuyten Duyvil, the main army falling straight down the Hudson to Kingsbridge, and the French attacking from the east. His object was to seize Britain's perimeter forts, enabling the allies to launch siege operations against New York's inner defenses. Washington hurriedly put his plan into motion in the dead of night on July 2. The scheme was sound, but the mission quickly fizzled nonetheless. Clinton's men were vigilant and learned of their opponents' moves almost as soon as they began, causing the planned assault to be aborted after only a handful of the attackers had swung into action. One reason, in fact, for the British command's wariness was that it had captured still more of Washington's correspondence, letters which indiscreetly discussed the Weathersfield agreement to someday attack New York.[18]

For a siege to have any chance of success the French navy had to be present in force. As there was no guarantee when—or if—that would occur, the Franco-American armies simply sat outside New York throughout July, engaged in little more than harassing and reconnoitering activities. Officially, Washington remained committed to that strategy, but there were signs that he had begun to waver. De Grasse's arrival was problematical; then, too, he might prove as reluctant as had d'Estaing to utilize his fleet in the waters about New York. But if de Grasse sailed into the Chesapeake instead, Cornwallis might be bagged. In mid-June the commander hinted that such a course might be "more practicable [than a siege of New York] and equally advisable," and a month later he broached the idea directly to de Grasse, although he indicated clearly that it still was his second choice.[19]

All the while Washington kept a close watch on events in the South. Indeed, he now had another reason for following events in that theater. That summer one increasingly heard talk of an armistice based on the notion of *uti possidetis*, that is, that each nation would possess what its armies held at the moment of the truce. In such an event, America's claim to the transmontane West would be tenuous. Even worse, with a British army in Virginia at that very moment, the fate of his own province would be uncertain.[20]

Already Washington had experienced a scare over Mount Vernon. In April a small British fleet had ascended the Potomac to Mount Vernon. Although Washington lost a twenty-four-foot river craft and eighteen of his slaves to the little flotilla, his estate had been unscathed, perhaps because his cousin Lund had boarded the English flagship and almost pleaded with its commander to prevent any further plundering. Washington rebuked his farm manager for his conduct, but his estate was intact—for the moment. Subsequent British actions, he had to know, could imperil his access to his very home.[21]

Soon, however, the situation in Virginia improved. For all his haste to get into the state, Cornwallis had done little other than launch an occasional raid on his adversary's magazines. By July these forays were at an end, for Clinton had ordered him to take coastal Portsmouth, from which raids could be carried out to interdict American supply lines. Late in June Cornwallis withdrew his army to Williamsburg, then to Yorktown. Washington was delighted, for he was certain that Cornwallis's withdrawal to the coast signaled the first step in Britain's abandonment of Virginia. Surely, he thought, Cornwallis had been summoned to New York to augment Clinton's army, and he even speculated that the recall had resulted from the information Clinton had gleaned from captured American correspondence. But decisions were not made quite so simply in Britain's high command.[22]

British strategy seemed as muddled as it had been for the fateful campaign of 1777. Clinton's letters to Cornwallis during the summer of 1781 read like those of a man who had lost touch with reality. He started out well enough by ordering to New York a large portion of the British army in Virginia, but in July, with the men already loaded aboard transports, Clinton changed his mind and directed Cornwallis to keep his entire army on Williamsburg Neck. What is so damning about Clinton's thinking was that from intercepted French messages he could be fairly certain that de Grasse would be coming north within a few weeks. Weak and indecisive, Clinton in the end apparently decided to leave Cornwallis where he was because he knew that Germain favored British action in the Chesapeake. Thus in midsummer of the seventh year at war, Clinton remained in the grip of paralysis in New York, leaving to molder in Virginia the reinforcements that might have given him some leverage against his foes. Britain's strategy had sunk to the point of merely trying to outlast the rebels, of holding on until America collapsed from its myriad difficulties, then of picking up some of what was left at a peace conference.[23]

But if British planning had stagnated, Washington's thoughts were aswirl. Since early in July he had been wavering in his determination to besiege New York. Under optimum conditions the odds against success in such a complicated operation were astronomical; besides, it had not been his good fortune to experience optimum conditions very often in this war. By the first week of August, moreover, some new dimensions had been added to the puzzle. Clinton had been reinforced by another batch of German mercenaries, as well as by redcoats fleeing from Pensacola, a garrison recently seized by the Spanish; altogether, Clinton's army had swelled by about 2000–2500 men, not enough to permit the British commander to contemplate an offensive, but perhaps sufficient numbers to permit him to repulse the contemplated joint attack on New York. Indeed, on July 27 Washington had received Duportail's plan for the siege of New York, a gloomy document that suggested that success was possible, but only if the allies had twice as many men as were under arms at that moment.[24]

As late as the first week in August Washington still expected Cornwallis to rejoin Clinton, but he also knew that those British troops in Virginia had not yet been withdrawn. With its back pinioned against the Chesapeake, that redcoat army increasingly looked like an inviting target. A smashing victory over either Clinton or Cornwallis might break Britain's will to persist, and, at the very least, the subjugation of Britain's army in Virginia would doom Whitehall's hopes of holding that state—and probably North Carolina as well—if the war ended with a negotiated settlement. In July, pending a decision of whether to fight in the North or in the South, Washington terminated shipments of artillery pieces from Philadelphia to New York. On August 1 he confessed to his diary—which he recently had begun to keep once again after a lapse of six years—that he had begun to lean more toward making a foray against Cornwallis. Two weeks later his choice was made for him.[25]

On August 14 word reached headquarters at Dobb's Ferry that de Grasse was sailing for the Chesapeake. He was bringing twenty-eight warships and three thousand troops, and he would remain off the coast of Virginia until mid-October. Through the spring both Washington and Rochambeau had made it clear that they hoped the fleet would sail to New York, but, luckily, Chevalier la Luzerne, the French minister to the United States, had made it equally clear to de Grasse that Virginia constituted the more pressing problem—and the most promising site for scoring a great victory. Once he discovered that de Grasse was coming, Washington wasted little time. Five days after he learned of the destination of the Gallic fleet, he too was on his way to Virginia, his first trip to his home state since that suffocatingly hot day in May 1775 when his carriage had pulled away from Mount Vernon for Philadelphia. He brought with him twenty-five hundred American troops and virtually every French soldier in America.[26]

Time and secrecy were crucial to the success of the march. If Clinton intercepted the allied armies in New Jersey or Pennsylvania, he might prevent them from reaching the Chesapeake until after de Grasse had departed. Washington worried and fretted, but ironically the gravest impediment to haste arose from his own planning of the operation. The commander set out to make Clinton believe the army's destination was the vicinity of Sandy Hook, where it might cooperate with de Grasse against New York; but so secret was Washington that even his quartermaster personnel were taken by surprise. Washington's plan called for both armies to make an overland trek to Trenton, where boats would be waiting to speed them to the Chesapeake. Yet when Rochambeau reached that little Jersey town there were no vessels to be seen. Improvisation was required. The French army marched to Head of Elk. These problems aside, however, Clinton was kept off guard.[27]

The British commander immediately learned that the two armies and the small French naval squadron at Newport had moved out, but despite good intelligence reports he persistently doubted that Washington and de Grasse planned to rendezvous. He seems to have seen these maneuvers as a feint. Besides, he was preoccupied with a scheme of his own. Clinton had begun to chew over the possibility of a strike at Newport, now all but abandoned by Rochambeau. Those ambitious thoughts soon vanished. On August 31 Cornwallis peered from his window at Yorktown to see a ship of the line flying the flag of France; it was de Grasse's flotilla, the largest armada this war had witnessed since the Howe brothers arrived off Long Island in 1776. Cornwallis immediately wrote Clinton, his letter crossing a belated warning note penned by his commander. The British high command finally had deduced Washington's plans. But on the day that Clinton unraveled the mystery, the American army was parading through Philadelphia, just hours away from the Chesapeake.[28]

While he proceeded south, Washington remained unaware of the progress of de Grasse's fleet, and he was nagged by the worry that the British navy at New York might reach the Chesapeake before their French counterparts. But this time luck was with him. On September 5 word arrived that de Grasse was off the coast of Virginia; two days later the American army began to board southbound transports. Washington's happiest moment, however, must have come on the 9th. Early that morning he awakened in Baltimore, and while the first streaks of light pierced the night's blackness he and his party set out—for Mount Vernon. It was a long day's ride over familiar terrain, past old landmarks, until late on that warm summer day he finally glimpsed it, his first sight of the estate in more than six years, his first view ever of the additions to the house that had begun to be constructed just before he left for the war.[29]

Washington remained at home for seventy-two hours, and after years of commanding out of other peoples' homes he must have luxuriated in making Mount Vernon his headquarters. Rochambeau and his entourage arrived the next day, a day of relaxation, of feasting on the opulent bounty of this plantation, of sightseeing. On the 11th the reality of the war, almost but never quite forgotten during the past few hours, returned, forcing Washington into conferences and back to his desk to catch up with his correspondence. At sunrise on September 12 he again was on his mount, headed for Williamsburg and, ultimately, Yorktown.

General Washington reached the Virginia capital late on the 14th. Good news greeted him. From Mount Vernon Washington had written Lafayette of his "hope [that] you will keep Lord Cornwallis safe, without Provisions or Forage untill we arrive." That much the young Frenchman had done, though Cornwallis's quandary largely was due to other factors. He had not known of de Grasse's descent on the Chesapeake until he actually spotted the armada, nor, thanks to Clinton, had he known that Washington and Rochambeau were coming until mid-September, nearly twenty-five days after the Franco-American armies had begun their southward advance. By the time he learned what was happening it was probably too late to fight his way off the peninsula. Had he acted hurriedly in the first moments after he discovered de Grasse's presence, he might have escaped. But he would have had to move quickly, for within only a few hours of his arrival de Grasse had sent forty small transports containing three thousand French soldiers to join with Lafayette; in fact, two days before Washington put his men on board ships at Head of Elk the allies already outnumbered Cornwallis. All the British commander at Yorktown could do was wait, hoping against hope for reinforcements from New York—which Clinton had promised—and for the timely arrival of a long-anticipated royal naval squadron from London.[30]

At Williamsburg, meanwhile, Washington also learned that the advance units of Rochambeau's army had begun to arrive. But the best tidings came from de Grasse. The French and British fleets had clashed off the Virginia Capes on September 5. It had been a sharp, although not very conclusive engagement. Two days of maneuvering followed as the two navies drifted as far south as Cape Hatteras, then the fleets separated and the outnumbered British squadron returned to New York. When de Grasse returned he discovered that the French flotilla out of Rhode Island had arrived in his absence, an armada laden with siege artillery and provisions. Daily Washington watched as the allied armies swelled with the addition of Frenchmen at last arriving on the bay, together with fresh, raw units of American militia that marched in over the worn, dusty roads of the peninsula. Only time now seemed to be a real enemy. To succeed the operation had to be completed before the French fleet sailed away, and in a September 17 meeting with Washington aboard the flagship *Ville de Paris*, de Grasse agreed to stay until the end of October, two weeks longer than he had initially planned to linger in these waters. Thereafter, Washington exuded optimism. "What may be in the Womb of Fate is very uncertain," he admitted, "but we anticipate the Reduction of Ld Cornwallis with his army. . . ."[31]

There "are reports that we are in a very bad situation," a young German mercenary in Yorktown observed in his diary about this time. It was one of the more sagacious observations made within British lines that year. There seemed little doubt of allied success. Six, maybe seven, weeks were left before de Grasse would sail; furthermore, Washington and Rochambeau had more than twice as many troops, ample artillery (more than forty heavy siege cannon, in addition to the customary field pieces), and more than adequate amounts of provender, trenching tools, and a thousand and one other items required by a siege army.[32]

At the end of September the two armies advanced from Williamsburg, the Americans taking up posts on the right before the little hamlet of Yorktown, the French on the west. On the last day of the month fighting began for control of the outermost approaches, a struggle waged as much with pick and shovel as with musket and cannon, for the armies had to dig their implacements, redoubts from which the British hoped to stave off the allied advance, parallels from which the attacker's batteries would endeavor to pound the redcoats into submission.

By the end of the first week in October the allied soldiers had moved close enough to begin digging their first parallel, a deep trench in which siege guns

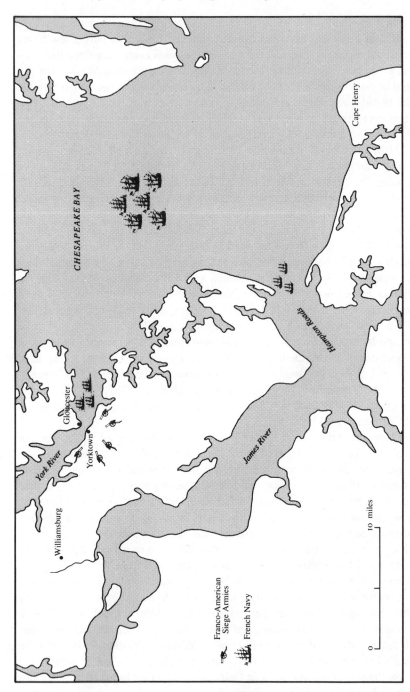

The Siege of Yorktown

could be placed only a few hundred yards from the defender's lines. Laboring under a hot sun (Rochambeau likened Virginia's climate to that of Algiers), these sappers and miners worked in the open while missiles fired from their comrades' field artillery tore over their heads and smashed into the British redoubts. A part of this corps since 1780, Private Joseph Plumb Martin was one of those assigned to this construction project. On the first night of the excavation a strange officer approached his squad, asked a few questions, made some small talk, and departed. Later Martin learned that the man had been General Washington. After six years of soldiering for him, Private Martin at last had been in his presence and he had not recognized him. But he saw him again the next evening. Washington returned to the same area and struck a couple of ceremonial first blows with a pick.[33]

When the parallel was completed and siege guns had been brought forward, Washington was given the honor of firing the first round. The men watched expectantly, straining to see the damage this projectile would cause, listening as the ball whistled across the terrain, gloating, perhaps, as they heard it tear through house after house. Later it was learned that the shell had collapsed the roof of one dwelling, the debris and heavy rafters falling upon a clatch of unsuspecting British officers dining inside; rumor had it that one man had been killed.[34]

By the 10th, two additional batteries were operational, the site for one of the installations having been taken in a charge led by Colonel Hamilton, who had pleaded with his chief for this one last opportunity to gain noteriety in battle. With over a hundred allied cannon hurling hot metal upon Yorktown's defenders, the toll within the redcoat lines was devastating. Cornwallis lost thirty men in the first five hours of shelling, and five hundred additional troops were killed, wounded, or fell ill in the next five days. Fewer and fewer British field pieces remained operational, and food stocks shrank to below the meager level. On the 15th, Cornwallis emerged from the underground bunker that had become his headquarters and launched his own assault, but it was merely a gesture of éclat that the European warriors knew as the *baroud d'honneur*, a practice by which proud officers endeavored to save face; that a few lives were squandered seemed not to matter. The attack was easily repulsed, of course, in this instance by French soldiers who shouted what their American allies must have found an incongruous cheer—"Vive le Roi."

The next night Cornwallis made his only real attempt to escape. He tried to get his army across the York River to Gloucester, from whence—minus stores and artillery—he might make a run for it. He almost succeeded. As it was he got about one-quarter of his men across before a howling storm arose that compelled him to cease operations. Cornwallis now admitted what he long had known, that there was no hope. The campaign that had seemed so promising a year before when Gates and America's southern army lay crushed and dispersed at Camden, that still had seemed to be on the cusp of a magnificent success only six months earlier when both Arnold and Cornwallis moved at will about Virginia, now was over.

Ignominiously over. At 10:00 A.M. on October 17 Cornwallis initiated surrender talks.[35]

Washington's role in the twenty-one days of actual campaigning at Yorktown was strangely unlike his conduct in earlier engagements. He spoke of the assistance which his allies rendered, but, in fact, he deferred to their expertise. This was a siege operation, a "regular Operation," as he called it, a form of war common in Europe; as it was the fourteenth siege of which Rochambeau had been a part, moreover, Washington concluded that it was best left to the European professionals and specialists who could assure that Cornwallis's defeat was "reducible to calculation," and that it would be brought about with haste. His frequent meetings with Rochambeau during the investment, sessions usually held in the Frenchman's tent, must have had an air of unreality about them, at least to Washington's aides, for if the American commander ever had been consistent it was in his insistence that he be fully in charge of every detail of every deployment. As if to compensate, Washington fell into the habit of issuing orders that covered the most minute aspects of supply and weaponry. His instructed the soldiery on hurdles and gabions, on pickets and trenches, on saps and batteries, on angles and avenues.[36] For instance, he told his men that the fascines were

> to be six feet long and six inches through, to be made of branches, the twigs of which are to be crossed, to be bound with Withs at each end and in the middle, to each fascine [were to be added] three pickets of three feet long and two or three inches diameter.[37]

In still another way Washington's life was quite different during this campaign. Never had he lived so comfortably during the course of an engagement. The list of food purchased for his "household" for October alone was staggering: 62 turkeys, 39 ducks, 102 chickens, 4 dozen trout, 3 dozen perch, 29 bushels of oysters, 1 goose, 1 lamb, 138 pounds of pork, 54 pounds of ham, 261 pounds of mutton, 36 pounds of veal, 3 pigs, and 2 sheep. And all this was augmented by a stunning variety of fruit and fresh vegetables.[38]

Despite his material comforts, Washington remained under enormous pressure. He knew he would not have another chance to crush a British army. Fail here, and the opportunity would never come again. Not only would the British command not repeat the mistakes that had led its army into this trap, but France was unlikely ever again to commit so much naval and land power simultaneously. In addition, disappointment in the face of "these brillant prospects" would certainly result in "disgrace," not to mention the thorough destruction of American morale.[39]

Absorbed as was Washington by events at Yorktown, he nevertheless kept an eye on Greene's war further to the south. The news was good there too, capped by word in September that in an engagement at Eutaw Springs the redcoats had outfought Greene's army, only to score still another pyrrhic victory. The British lost nine hundred men in the battle, the Americans about one-half that number.

From that point on Washington sought to induce de Grasse to fall on Charleston as soon as his siege of Cornwallis ended, hoping that such an action would replicate the Yorktown campaign. But de Grasse refused to be swayed by Washington's pleas, for his orders were to be gone from mainland America by late October.[40]

From the moment he arrived on the peninsula Washington was confident of success. A week into the siege, buoyed by the progress of the sappers, he exclaimed that "in all probability Lord Cornwallis must fall into our hands." His one nagging worry was that the beleaguered Cornwallis might turn the tables on him and escape in the night, as Washington had done on the Assunpink when Cornwallis seemed to have pinioned him. As late as the day before Cornwallis in fact tried that tack, Washington warned that the British might endeavor to slip across the York, then use the Pamunkey as the shield that would enable them to hasten northward out of harm's way. Only de Grasse could close that escape hatch, however, and no amount of importuning by Washington could convince him to station vessels on the York above Yorktown; the danger from fire rafts was too great, the Frenchman always insisted. Washington's final appeal to the admiral involved a scheme in which 150 militiamen would be posted in small boats, vessels that they could paddle about to divert each fire raft launched by the British.[41] Whatever de Grasse thought of this notion, he was spared a reply by the rapid pace of events.

On the morning of the 17th, cooler and clear now that the storm of the previous night had blown out, Washington was at his desk preparing still another appeal to de Grasse when a messenger arrived with a one-sentence epistle from Cornwallis. The note requested a meeting "to settle terms of the surrender of the posts at York and Gloucester." [42]

Never before had Washington negotiated a surrender, except for his own vanquishment at Fort Necessity. Strangely, he acted as if Cornwallis's appeal had come as a surprise. He did not respond with written demands of his own, but merely inquired into what Cornwallis was willing to concede. For the next forty-eight hours the two sides parleyed under a flag of truce, a time that Cornwallis used to scuttle a couple of his naval craft rather than see them fall to de Grasse. Some time was required to translate the British replies for the French, and Washington and Rochambeau—and an emissary from de Grasse's fleet—conferred at length after each proposal and counterproposal. Moreover, having been badly burned by the agreement he negotiated at Great Meadows twenty-seven years before, Washington must have wished now to be very certain of what he signed. All the while, as if by magic, the milieu of Yorktown changed as the generals talked. Where only hours before men had sought to make themselves invisible behind fascines and earthen walls, now they ambled about freely, some exercising and playing, others listening to concerts offered by the surviving bagpipers within Britain's lines.

By the 19th, only two issues were left unresolved, and Washington made concessions on both matters in order to wrap up the proceedings. Initially, he had not only demanded the surrender of all British soldiers and vessels at Yorktown but also insisted that Cornwallis hand over all Tories and American deserters who had taken refuge behind British lines. Now, however, he agreed that Cornwallis could send the H.M.S. *Bonetta* to New York. Ostensibly it was only to transmit letters to the British High Command, but, as Washington waived the right to inspect the craft before it sailed, all expected its cargo to consist of turntails and Loyalists.[43] Otherwise, the surrender was complete, with Cornwallis even consenting to yield up the American slaves who had fled to his protection. By noon everything was finalized, save for the actual ceremony of surrender.

That afternoon, bright and sunny and pleasantly warm, the three armies gathered for one last time. Early in the day, while French and American military bands played, the two victorious armies marched out to line Yorktown Road, Gallic soldiers on one side, Americans on the other. They waited three hours for the British and Hessian troops to appear and parade between them. At 2:00 P.M. their foes finally arrived, marching and wheeling into formation. Soon high-ranking British officers appeared, riding slowly to a point where Washington and Rochambeau sat on horseback with their principal subordinates. Cornwallis, it was noticed, was not among the redcoats. Pleading illness, he had remained behind, sending an Irishman, Brigadier General Charles O'Hara in his stead. The proceedings were swift and uneventful, except that O'Hara mistook Rochambeau for Washington and had to be rerouted to the proper party. Off in another corner of this plain—at least according to tradition—British musicians had begun to play a march. It was "The World Turned Upside Down." Some British officers wept as they watched and listened; it struck Private Martin that the Germans did not much care. Soon all that remained was for the defeated soldiery to march out, company by company, and lay down their arms. And by the time that was concluded the long shadows of late afternoon had begun to creep over the killing ground, for on this day Cornwallis surrendered 7241 men.[44]

Washington referred to his victory as "an important success" and a "glorious event," but like other contemporaries he could not be certain of its full meaning. Clinton, for instance, initially expressed an interest in continuing in command as if nothing had happened, planning still another campaign for still another year. Britain's admirals did go on with the business of war, and, in fact, when de Grasse sailed from North America at the end of the month the suzerainty of the Royal British Navy once again was magically restored. What Washington was certain of were the opportunities and the dangers of the moment. He continued to plead with de Grasse to fall upon Charleston or Wilmington in North Carolina, but the French commander was equally recalcitrant. Orders were orders, he always replied. Washington soon sent Wayne, St. Clair, and Lafayette with about two thousand men to reinforce Greene, but that was as much as he could do, for he felt compelled to return the bulk of his army to the defense of

General Washington, the Marquis de Lafayette, and Tench Tilghman at Yorktown, by Charles Willson Peale (1784). Courtesy of the Maryland Commission on Artistic Property. Lafayette is in the center.

the Highland passes. Indeed, within two weeks of Cornwallis's capitulation his thoughts had returned to his old notion of a siege of New York. He also preached the need for a firm, resolute commitment to the war; nothing, he repeated, would so discourage the British or so impress the European powers, who might yet have to settle America's boundaries by arbitration, as to gaze across the Atlantic and see that the United States had maintained its war footing. But he feared that just the opposite would occur. Thinking the war now was as good as over, the weary public would let down, prompting Whitehall to continue the war.[45]

That last concern was his "only apprehension," however. He remained at Yorktown for two weeks following Cornwallis's surrender, overseeing the removal of the prisoners and meeting with the French commanders. Once those duties were tended to he planned to hurry to Mount Vernon for a few days' rest, then rejoin the army above New York. But on the eve of his planned departure grievous news arrived. It was a summons from his old friend Burwell Bassett: Jackie Custis lay dying at his estate. Come at once.

Although still recuperating from an illness that had stricken him early in the fall, Jackie had come to Yorktown in the course of the siege, anxious to contribute something to the war effort. He spent several days at headquarters serving as an aide to his stepfather. Sometime after mid-month, probably after the British capitulation, he fell ill with a camp disease and was moved to Eltham, the Bassett estate, about thirty miles away. Little is known of his illness, but it was not uncommon for complications to set in, often after one's recovery seemed certain. This must have happened in this instance, as Washington was not called until at least two weeks after the young man was taken ill.

The commander left immediately, covering the long distance in one day's hard ride. He arrived just after dark. Martha and Nelly were at Jackie's bedside, he discovered, and as each woman was grieving and deeply anguished he must have known instantly that the end was near. And, in fact, death came only moments after the general entered the mansion. Jackie had lived for just twenty-seven years, and he had forfeited his life needlessly.[46]

Washington left behind no account of his inner feelings at this tragedy, although a contemporary characterized him as "uncommonly affected."[47] He must have been shaken as he had been by Patsy's death, although Jackie was older and Washington had seen him only infrequently during the past six years. Revealingly, Washington abruptly discontinued his diary, his final entry ending in mid-sentence on the day that Bassett's message arrived, probably at the moment it reached his hands. It was if in his pain and despair he might record unmanly thoughts.

Washington remained at Eltham for five days for the wake and the funeral, then he stopped over at Mount Vernon for a week, resting and meeting daily with Lund to plan the business of the estate. By late in November he was in Philadelphia, closeted with Congress to plan the next campaign—if there was to be another campaign. Washington's sojourn in Philadelphia was not brief. He remained in the capital for five months, by far his longest absence from the army since this war began.

Washington's itinerary was indicative that the war had changed, although, to be sure, the military situation could not have seemed more murky. Now Britain might opt for peace. Or, it might press the war, seeking to redress its humiliating loss at Yorktown and still hoping to outlast its war-weary adversary. Or, it might eschew mainland America and contend for bargaining chips in the Caribbean or elsewhere. Washington believed that everything depended on France. If America's ally maintained its military commitment, he suggested, the war would end quickly and "honourably." Given the uncertainty, however, what should he do? To act boldly by seizing the initiative was to risk defeat and the negation of every gain procured by the victory at Yorktown. To do nothing was to encourage the French to lose interest in America's war. In the end Washington and Congress chose merely to assure that the army would be prepared for any eventuality in the next campaign, and Congress voted to maintain the same troop strength of the previous year. That would be adequate for "all the purposes of the American War," the commander reported. But would the states furnish the men, and would the troops be supplied? That he could not answer, but he knew that if the states failed the army the nation would continue "wasting ourselves in a lingering ineffectual War." [48]

As autumn gradually faded from the Delaware Valley, it became obvious that Britain planned no immediate action in the wintry North. Likewise, within a couple weeks of Christmas, it was clear that the foe had no plans for the South. Whitehall replaced Clinton with Sir Guy Carleton, but otherwise Britain's inaction hinted that the ministry was embroiled in a protracted reexamination of the war. Indeed, at the beginning of the next summer Washington still reported that "the Enemy continue in the same state as they have been in for some time past." Technically, that was not quite accurate. Signs abounded that Carleton planned to abandon the garrison in Charleston, and at the very moment that Washington penned his observation royal transports were en route to Savannah with orders to gather up every redcoat cantoned at that outpost. [49]

Ten weeks into 1782 Washington seemed to radiate confidence. The news from Europe convinced him that London was "done with all thoughts of an excursive War." In fact, the news that eddied across the Atlantic that winter and spring must have been music to his ears, for it was clear that word of Cornwallis's surrender had hit Great Britain like "a ball in the breast," to use the metaphor that occurred to Germain as he observed Lord North's reaction to word of Yorktown. Early in February Germain resigned, and a month later North's ministry collapsed, succeeded by a government put together by Marquis Rockingham, long a foe of the coercion of America. North's demise had been expected, for the reprints of the parliamentary debates that ran in the American press had made it clear that for a substantial number of legislators the luster had worn off this war. [50]

But Washington's exultation was shattered by two unrelated events. In April, after a winter of frenetic campaigning in the Caribbean, the British navy inflicted a serious defeat on the French, repulsing a Gallic attack on Jamaica, destroying nearly a fifth of their adversary's fleet (including the *Ville de Paris*), and even capturing de Grasse. At the least Washington knew that the engagement doomed any hope for French naval assistance in 1782, and he feared that the Royal Navy's victory would tantalize Whitehall to persevere in this war. A few weeks later came the news that Rockingham was dead. A new ministry headed by the Earl of Shelburne, an unknown quantity, was in power. "Events have shewn, that [America's] Hopes have risen too high," Washington noted despondently. "We now begin again to reflect upon . . . a probable Continuance of our present Trouble." [51]

Washington's fears of a resumption of the war on the mainland proved unfounded, however. Outside of the Caribbean, the year 1782 came and went like a lamb. The French army remained in Virginia for six months after their victory at Yorktown, wintering in that happy, sunny climate, positioned to move toward New York or South Carolina as events dictated, but doing neither until midsummer. In July Rochambeau brought his soldiery north, although when he at last moved it was less to begin an action than to deter Carleton from sending succor to the redcoats in the Caribbean. [52]

Rochambeau and Washington did not even confer about any concerted action in 1782 until the year was half gone, then at a brief conference in Philadelphia they decided against taking any initiative. Curiously, Washington had opened the meeting with a proposal to launch a joint offensive "into the Bowels of Canada," but Rochambeau expressed no interest in such a venture, and in the end the two agreed to simply camp on the doorstep of New York at least until Versailles was heard from. By September the ministry had made up its mind. Presuming the war on the mainland to be over, its interest had shifted to the West Indies, where France might recoup some of its losses from the Seven Years' War. [53] At a final meeting between the two allied commanders, this one at Verplanck's Point north of New York, Rochambeau informed Washington of his government's decision, and he revealed that his army soon would be transported to the Caribbean. [54]

For the first time in more than two years the armed forces of the United States would have to stand alone, although such a turn of events no longer was as alarming as it would have been only a few weeks earlier. Many signs now suggested that Great Britain had decided to end its war for North America. Everyone knew that peace talks were underway in Paris, and in August General Carleton even had proposed to Washington that all prisoners be exchanged, a step he was anxious to take, he said, inasmuch as he had suspended his military activities and his government had decided to recognize "the independency of the thirteen Provinces." Washington remained a skeptic, however, and he continued to warn that the peace talks might only be a ruse to lull America from its vigilant posture. Yet even Washington sensed that if Whitehall persisted with the war it was likely to be largely a naval conflict, and as the autumn progressed his hopes grew that perhaps the end really was near. Since he first had heard that the diplomats were talking, he had presumed that the issue would be resolved by early in 1783; either peace would be agreed to, or the talks would end in time to undertake a campaign in the summer of 1783. And all signs pointed toward peace. The American intelligence network reported that Carleton not only planned to end the occupation of Charleston, but that shortly he would reduce the size of his garrison in New York. It was difficult not to be optimistic.[55]

Still, headquarters seldom took a holiday from vexation, and even amid all the felicitous signs—because of them, actually—Washington was tormented by a crisis prompted by the action of some of his own officers. During the fall of 1782, with the war seemingly all but over, apprehension grew in some circles that with peace Congress would disband the army, and that it would neither compensate the officers for the back pay that was their due nor honor the half-pay-for-life pledge that it had made two years before. On at least seven occasions that fall Washington advised the civilian authorities of the officers' problems, and he warned that an ugly mood was growing, that the patience of men "soured by penury and . . . the ingratitude of the Public" was nearing its end. The commander had not exaggerated. Soon after the army went into winter quarters at Newburgh north of New York, some officers decided to act. Just after Christmas they sent a petition to Congress, a memorial written by Henry Knox, that outlined their grievances in regard to pay, and which for the first time expressed their willingness to forego the half-pay scheme in return for an equivalent one-shot cash payment at war's end.[56]

The officers' petition was like manna from heaven to those legislators who had been struggling against insuperable odds to enlarge the powers of the central government. To meet the officers' demands would require additional revenue, and that could be garnered only through a new funding system. Some nationalists, men like Alexander Hamilton and the Morrises—Robert and Gouverneur—instantly saw that they might use the threat of unrest within the army to augment the powers of the national government. This faction quickly introduced a bill to substitute commutation, or the lump-sum cash payment, for half-pay for life; Congress debated the issue for thirty days, but twice, once in January and again early in February, it rejected such a course.

What followed during the next month is shrouded in mystery, but there can be little doubt that some nationalists in Congress encouraged some officers at Newburgh to threaten action tantamount to mutiny against civil authority. Cleverly, the plotters in Philadelphia also saw to it that Washington was forewarned, thus enabling him to take the steps necessary to control his army. Thus, the officers' menacing posturing would frighten Congress into acting to augment the powers of the national government, while the commander would keep the Continental army from actually doing any real harm.

How much Washington knew of the plotting will never be ascertained. It is known, however, that late in February he received a remarkable letter from one of the conspirators, his former aide Hamilton. Now a New York congressman, Hamilton's motive in confiding in Washington is cloudy, but it probably stemmed from his desire to coach the commander on how to handle the coming crisis; after all, if Washington was his engine to achieve bigger things, he would not have wished to see the general's reputation sullied by a political blunder. Hamilton began his missive with the claim that by June the nation would be broke. There would be no money with which to wage the war, he warned, nor would there be funds for pensions if peace had been negotiated by then. A dearth of "wisdom and decision" in Congress prevented that body from acting to meet the crisis, he went on. However, if the army once again urged Congress to act, such a tack might sway "those weak minds which are influenced by their apprehensions more than their judgments." The difficulty inherent in such a move was "to keep a *complaining* and *suffering army* within the bounds of moderation." This was where Washington came in. From behind the scenes he could see that "prudent persons" directed the army's petitioning. If matters got out of hand, he then could come forward and "bring order perhaps even good, out of confusion." [57]

Leaving nothing to chance the plotters sent emissaries to the Hudson to appeal to those "prudent persons" of whom Hamilton had spoken. They must have approached Knox—undoubtedly the person to whom Hamilton expected Washington to turn—but he apparently rebuffed their entreaties, probably on the advice of the commander, who clearly wished to have no part in these machinations. Some historians think the nationalists elicited the participation of Gates, a man who still was quite popular with many of the congressional foes of a stronger national government; but that can not be proven. What does seem clear, however, is that Gates, deeply in debt and in dire and immediate need of cash, became enmeshed in the rampant intriguing and that he encouraged and aided those who protested. What also seems obvious is that the real heart of the cabal at Newburgh lay within the ranks of the middle-grade officers, young men who had spent most or all of their adult life in the army and who harbored an abiding contempt for the Congress that had treated the soldiery so wretchedly. Many of these young zealots were close to Gates, but it can not be determined whether they brought him into their campaign, or vice versa.

The officers' protest burst into the open on March 10, 1783. That morning the plotters published an unsigned statement that urged a general meeting on the next day. Secretly written by Major John Armstrong, a former aide to Gates, the Newburgh Address demanded a redress of grievances, and pointed the way to bludgeon Congress into action. On the morrow, the address proclaimed, the officers must resolve to resign en masse if the war continued, or they must indicate their intention not to disband the army if peace occurred.[58]

Washington immediately deduced what was afoot. The conspiracy "was not only planned, but also digested and matured in Philadelphia," he declared; congressional plotters—chiefly "public creditors"—had sought to use the army as tool to gain their selfish ends. Although he shared the ideology of the nationalists in Congress and also agreed that the officers had not received their due, yet he would not countenance a revolt against civilian jurisdiction, and he moved to head off the protest. He issued general orders that suggested that the officers "pay very little attention to [the] irregular invitation" to the proposed meeting. Instead, he summoned the officers to an official meeting four days hence. It was a shrewd move. He would attend the conclave that he had called, and his presence might deter the hotheads from a radical course.[59]

A second address was issued by the plotters during the four-day interim between Washington's orders and the formal meeting, but its design was merely to buck up morale.[60] Then came Saturday, the day Washington had set for the meeting. The officers crammed into the Temple of Virtue, a wooden facility they had thrown up just after Christmas, a place for worship on Sunday and for social occasions during the week. Everyone was present and in his seat a few minutes early. It was sweltering inside the crowded Temple, the heat mixing unpleasantly with the heavy, semisweet fragrance of fresh-cut wood, with the pervasive reek of the tobacco users, with the atmosphere of supercharged tension.

Precisely at noon Washington strode into the hall. He walked briskly to the front where, from behind a rustic pulpit, he slowly began to speak. Initially he fumbled nervously. Then, more calmly, he read on, plowing through a carefully prepared address. Speaking softly, now flawlessly, he required only about fifteen minutes to deliver a message that minced no words. The recent anonymous remarks of a few officers, he said, had been "unmilitary" and "subversive." He knew the problems faced by the officers; after all, he had been with the army from the beginning. But how to solve those problems? Is it to be by "deserting our Country in the extremest hour of her distress, or [by] turning our Arms against it . . . ?" Had Great Britain sent an emissary into their midst to sow such ideas?

Congress would redress their grievances, he continued, but the officers must have faith and remember that by nature legislative bodies acted slowly. As proof that Congress had not forgotten, he paused to read from a private letter he recently had received from a friend in Virginia's delegation to the national legislature. As he began reading he stumbled a bit over the foreign hand. Pausing, he reached into his pocket for his reading glasses. "Gentlemen, you must pardon me," he said looking up. "I have grown gray in your service and now find myself growing blind." Then on with the missive and, finally, back to the conclusion of his speech. To carry out the threat proposed in the Newburgh Address was to court the detestation of the citizenry and to "open the flood Gates of Civil discord, and deluge our rising Empire in Blood." To reject the appeal of the intriguers would be "one more distinguished proof of unexampled patriotism and patient virtue." Choose the latter course, he added in the same flat, calm tone, and posterity would say of them: " 'had this day been wanting, the World had never seen the last stage of perfection to which human nature is capable of attaining.' "[61]

With that Washington slowly folded his speech, removed his spectacles, and strode from the hall. The meeting continued, but the commander's moving address had defused the plotters, leaving many officers, if one or two eyewitness accounts can be believed, in tears. Men close to Washington dominated the remaining minutes of the conclave, pushing through a statement of loyalty to Congress, one obviously prepared during the four-day lull that Washington had secured when he deferred the unofficial meeting. It was all over in twenty or thirty minutes, and not one word was uttered by any officer known to have been active in the intrigue.[62]

Washington had acted from principle. A civilian who had taken up arms, he had no stomach for a mutiny—or even the appearance of such—against civilian authority. He knew, too that the army was not the vehicle to use to pursue the end for which both he and the nationalists in Congress yearned. Pragmatic where Hamilton was Machiavellian, politically shrewder than business moguls like the Morrises who comprehended how to get their way chiefly by the application of money or by deceit or brute force, Washington thoroughly understood the public temperament, and he realized full well the contempt with which such a radical step would be held by this republican people. It was a ploy almost certain to backfire, to assure the maintenance of state sovereignty; and for that reason too, he said, he had acted to thwart the conspirators. And that he had done, humbling and quieting the officers' cabal not just with his words but with the drama of his staged performance as well. This man who early on had learned how to read and assess other men, this man who possessed what Garry Wills referred to as a "theatrical sense of audience," had measured his quarry and scored another easy victory.[63]

That done Washington proceeded to lobby tirelessly with Congress on behalf of his officers. Either because of his efforts, or because of the Newburgh Address, Congress was moved. Within a few days of the dramatic events in the northern cantonment, the legislators voted for commutation, an act that granted officers full pay for five years following the war's end.[64] Washington's action in facing down the army's conspirators has resulted in almost universal praise from historians. What often seems to be forgotten, however, is that he acted almost precisely as Hamilton hoped he would, and that in record time the plotters within the army achieved exactly what they had set out to get.

Although no one knew it, even as Washington addressed his officers that tense day in the Temple of Virtue peace already had been agreed to. Thirty days before the country had learned through George III's annual speech to Parliament that the Crown was inclined toward peace; from that moment on the burning question as to British intentions had been answered. Afterwards only the details of the peace treaty were awaited, and that information reached Washington's headquarters three days after his moving speech.[65]

The document had been signed in Paris more than three months before. It was an incomplete pact in that final details awaited the conclusion of negotiations of the separate Anglo-French treaty. But this compact nevertheless proclaimed an end to hostilities, it recognized the independence of the United States, and it stipulated that prisoners were to be exchanged. The army would have to remain intact until the definitive treaty arrived, probably within a few weeks or months at most, but the long-awaited moment finally had arrived. On April 9, nearly eight years to the day since shots had shattered the morning stillness at Lexington and Concord, Generals Carleton and Washington almost simultaneously issued orders for a cease fire.[66]

Desirous as was Washington to hurry to the ease and beauty of Mount Vernon, the period from April 9 until noon, November 25, the moment when the last redcoat in New York stepped off American soil and onto the gangplank of his out-bound ship, must have seemed an eternity. For the most part the nature of his work remained as it had since Cornwallis's surrender—repetitious, meticulous administrative drudgery. But the work load was lighter, and the strain that had accompanied life-and-death decisions at last was gone too, a fact that prompted one eyewitness who first had observed the commander in 1775 to remark now that the general's formerly "contracted, pensive phiz, betokening deep thought and much care" had given way to an "uncommonly open and pleasant" demeanor.[67]

During these last months of the war two matters took up most of Washington's time. Working from an office in the Hasbrouck House in Newburgh, a two-story stone farmhouse that stood elegantly atop a knoll overlooking the Hudson, he presided over the final exchange of the prisoners of war and the breaking up of his army.

Negotiating prisoner releases was not a new undertaking for Washington. Beginning in 1776 when large numbers of Arnold's and Montgomery's armies fell into British hands at Quebec, he had been pressed by congressional inaction—as well as by the potential chaos that would have resulted from thirteen states attempting to regain its captive sons—into taking over this responsibility. The following year Congress created a Commissary of Prisoners, but this official was only to carry out the prisoner swaps negotiated by the commander, and it fell to Washington to disentangle a myriad of thorny questions that arose from taking captives in a civil war. Were Continental army captives rebels or military prisoners? What of America's Tory internees? And what of United States privateers captured on the high seas? How should the women and children who were captured along with the redcoat soldiery be treated? Should prisoners be swapped straight up, or, as the British proposed, should there be a tariff of exchange providing that officers carried more weight than did the men? Compared to the thicket of problems that always had attended prisoner negotiations, Washington's task in 1783 was not too difficult. The capture of Cornwallis and his army gave him the bargaining chips to facilitate the final transfer, as did a congressional act passed in 1782 that bestowed upon him plenipotentiary powers to reach any accord on this matter with the British high command. Nevertheless, matters dragged until General Carleton knew for certain that the war was about to end; then terms for the final exchange were worked out, much of it actually negotiated by Washington's emissaries, Knox and Gouverneur Morris.[68]

While the prisoner exchanges proceeded, Congress first authorized, then ordered, the commander to furlough many of his troops, a money-saving expedient that the legislators hit upon, for a smaller army would consume smaller amounts of food. Soon, too, those who had signed on for the duration were formally discharged.[69]

As happy as was Washington to see these men depart—it meant that his own "retirement to the placid Walks of domestic life" could not be too far removed—he knew that the veterans were marching home under a cloud. Unpaid for months, the men expected to leave camp with at least three months' back pay jingling in their pockets, for Washington was known to have pleaded with Congress to find and distribute at least that meager amount. But the Congress did not provide the money. Although the legislators presumably would leave no stone unturned to make a more than generous settlement with the officers, Congress provided the soldiery only with back-pay certificates that could not be redeemed before January 1784, and then only for three months' overdue wages. "Ingratitude has been experienced in all Ages, and Republics in particular have even been famed for the exercise of that unnatural and Sordid Vice," Washington suggested, as if in comfort. Strikingly, though, his correspondence conveys little empathy for the plight of the common soldier. The nation's niggardly treatment of these poor souls might tarnish the "future reputation, tranquility, happiness and glory of this . . . *Union,*" he feared, but it was "particularly to the officers" that his heart bled for any potential "consequences or distresses of the most cruel nature." [70]

Unburdened of campaign responsibilities, Washington undertook a business and pleasure trip that summer. Bored with the "distressing Taedium" of headquarters life, he longed to get away for a couple of weeks, and in mid-July he and a few aides and officers set out on a nineteen-day sojourn through New York's northern wilderness. It was his first trek into such an environment in nearly fifteen years, but he took right to it, displaying the stamina of a young man—or of a man of his age who had worked to remain fit. Indeed, Washington seemed to find solace in long hours on horseback, many of them spent thrashing through dense woods, or in awkwardly steering a mount across a cold, swift stream. He traveled up the east bank of the Hudson to Albany, then to Saratoga, and ultimately to Ticonderoga and Crown Point, to places where his armies had been posted and had fought, but that he had never seen, to faraway donjons of which he had heard tales when he was only a child. He inspected installations and took mental notes of the terrain, filing away the data for who-knew-what subsequent eventuality. Aside from whatever rest and relaxation a fifty-one-year-old man could derive from such a strenuous jaunt, the only concrete result that stemmed from the journey came later when Washington, together with Governor George Clinton of New York, purchased a lush tract of upstate real estate at Oriskany, near Fort Stanwix.[71]

Bored before his trip, Washington had even less to do when he returned. Indeed, he already had begun to say his goodbyes. Even before his junket Washington had issued a somber farewell to the citizenry. In this "Circular Letter," as Washington called his epistle, the commander offered a few perfunctory comments on public sacrifice before getting down to cases, for the heart of the address was a four-thousand-word admonition on popular policy. It was a curious undertaking for a military commander in chief, and, in fact, Washington apologized for "stepping out of the proper line of duty" to make his remarks. But he made them anyway. At its core his address was a refrain that he had uttered in private during the previous three years: there must be "adequate authority in the Supreme Power," the federal government, and "unless the States will suffer Congress to exercise" its constitutional powers "the Union cannot be of long duration," for its central government would be so weak as to rob it of its very reason for existence.[72]

Washington had hardly returned to Newburgh from upstate New York when Congress summoned him for consultation. Some legislators characterized the invitation as merely an opportunity for him to escape the tedium of headquarters, but others had some important matters in mind. Chiefly, these men wished to talk with him about the postwar army and about future United States policy toward the Native Americans. Washington welcomed Congress's call, as much to escape the routine of camp as to air some of his ideas. For one thing, if the United States acquired the transmontane West in the final peace treaty, he hoped to convince Congress to maintain garrisons in the region. Moreover, there still was lobbying to undertake on behalf of his officers, principally in securing promotions for this and that worthy, advancements that could boost a man's severance pay quite handsomely.[73]

Washington's departure from Newburgh was delayed by an illness that had stricken Martha—he found her in the grip of a fever when he returned from his frontier trek—but he finally set out on the 19th. It was the beginning of what would become a three month's absence from the army. His route was thoroughly familiar, although this time his destination was Princeton, not Philadelphia. In June still another army mutiny had flared, and though short and inconsequential, the event had induced Congress—which briefly had been encircled by the rebellious soldiery—to abandon Philadelphia for the third time in this war. The legislators moved up to the sleepy little college town in New Jersey, a place where not much had occurred since Washington fought his battle in and about the place seven years before.[74]

Washington and his wife set up residence in a country farmhouse just outside of town, a dwelling that had been pretentiously christened "Rocky Hill." In the midst of a 320-acre estate, much of it given to orchards of apple, pear, plum, peach, and cherry trees, the new headquarters perched atop a steep knoll above the Millstone River. A two-story white clapboard dwelling, Rocky Hill was comfortable, and the guests settled in for an extended stay. If Washington was anxious to get home to his own farm, this nevertheless was a comfortable period. The pace was slow and easy, the weather was sunny and Indian-summer mild, and the autumn foliage in this bucolic setting was unsurpassed for its beauty.

The commander had no sooner arrived than he addressed both Congress and the faculty of the College of New Jersey. Then, beginning about two weeks after he reached the little hamlet, he met on occasion with the proper congressional committees. The commander had some quite definite ideas about the West, the "New Country," as he alluded to it. Peace in that region was essential. The nation needed peace just now, but common decency also dictated policies that might prevent another blood bath, while common sense suggested that prudent restraint would more rapidly open the area for settlement. Washington hinted at something like a federal territorial policy, an expedient that would control the flow of population into this region, making it conform to the national interest; in addition, he proposed the return of all Indian prisoners of war and the creation of an office to supervise trade with the Native Americans.[75]

He was no less opinionated about the postwar army. A standing army was "indispensably necessary," he told Congress, not because of a threat from Europe but to protect the citizenry in the "New Country." Once established, however, the army's existence would assure that the nation would never again be as unprepared for war as it had been in 1775. He proposed a modest army—2631 men, about three-fourths in infantry units, the remainder in one artillery regiment. Initially, the soldiery would be comprised of the three-year enlistees already in the army, men whose term had not yet expired when the War for Independence ended; in time, many veterans would reenlist "upon almost any Terms," for they would be put off by the "hard labour" of their civilian pursuits. In another generation or so, he went on, conscription would be necessary. To see that a trained officer corps existed, he advocated the creation of national military academies at certain artillery bases. The army that he envisioned would garrison bases on the Great Lakes and at West Point, as well as on the Ohio, Susquehanna, and Potomac rivers, and it would be augmented by a uniform militia system throughout the states, one in which each male between eighteen and fifty would be compelled to serve, and whose original officers would be required to have officered in the Continental army.[76]

Congress considered Washington's advice, but it took no action. Now that he had made his pitch, the general's stay in Princeton—indeed, in the army— must have begun to seem irksome to him, especially as he watched Martha ride off for Mount Vernon early in October, a journey she was anxious to complete before the onset of cold, inclement weather. He devoted a good bit of his time to the details of supplying the army during the coming winter, but increasingly his thoughts roamed back to his farm. It was "in a deranged state, and very much impaired," he thought, so much so that he could "form no plan for my future" until he had actually overseen operations at Mount Vernon for a spell. And as he waited and waited for news of the treaty, he relaxed and caught up on his correspondence—some of which he actually got through the mails, no thanks to the postmaster of Princeton, a lazy, stupid oaf, if Washington is to be believed.[77]

Finally, early November brought the tidings everyone had awaited since the spring. The definitive peace treaty, inked two months earlier in Paris, at last arrived. Officially, the war was at an end, the pact signed almost seven years to the day after the commencement of that dark, dreadful campaign for New York. Now all that remained for Washington was to reoccupy that city and bid farewell to his army.

The general left immediately for West Point. His joy must have known no bounds. He had no quarrel with the peace treaty, and he simply characterized the document's promulgation as a "glorious" and "happy Event." Moreover, he had the satisfaction of knowing that he had presided over the victorious prosecution of the war. Already the "distresses" he had experienced were fading, overcome by remembrances of the "uncommon scenes," the "astonishing events . . . which seldom if ever before [had] taken place on the stage of human action," and of which he had been a part. He must have remembered those grim weeks after Brandywine when he came to believe that a plot existed in Congress to relieve him of his command, and perhaps now as he made the long ride back to the Hudson he reflected on his triumphant generalship. Obviously, too, the renown that he had pursued relentlessly as a young man had been realized to a degree that he would never have thought possible. Wherever he went he was fêted and cheered; folks struggled for a glimpse of this man, and already poets and scribblers referred to him as "the father of His Country," or as "the Father of the People."[78]

Whatever Washington may have thought, he carefully guarded his inner self. If he ever gave much thought to the reasons for victory, he did not record it. At various times he maintained that the war had been won because of the "patronage of Heaven," or because of the populace's commitment to the Revolutionary ideology and idealism. The turning point, he once said, came with his victories at Trenton and Princeton, but he also noted that the presence of the French navy "rendered practicable . . . enterprizes which without it could not . . . have been attempted." Many capable general officers assisted him, he added, and he also noted that the perseverence of the soldiery was crucial to success, especially after 1778 when his army was built on long-term service. He did not mention Britain's shortcomings as a factor, nor did he make an attempt to evaluate his own role in the triumph.[79]

With the obvious exception of his Yorktown engagement, Washington's performance in the years after Monmouth has often been slighted by historians. After all, during those three years he was involved in only that single general engagement on the Virginia peninsula, and it could be argued that America's success owed more to the French presence than to Washington's generalship. Of course, Washington's dearth of action between 1779 and 1781 arose principally from factors beyond his control. Britain altered its strategy, France entered the war, and Washington simply adapted to the new situation, choosing to remain virtually immobile until he could act in concert with a French fleet. Still, he might have pursued alternative courses of action. An invasion of Canada or an attack on the British in New York—the sort of action he repeatedly had urged against Howe in Boston—were possibilities. That he chose not to undertake such risks usually has been attributed to his greater experience; he was pushed about early in the war, it often has been said, but in the process he learned valuable lessons, and after 1778 he no longer was the bumbling amateur. No one would quibble with such an assessment, though it does ignore an additional factor—Washington's personality.

After 1779 Washington evinced a great deal of caution that previously had been absent from his generalship. While the new military conditions contributed to his altered deportment, so too perhaps did personality factors. The demise of Lee, as well as Congress's tacit reconfirmation of the commander's superiority over Gates in 1778, left Washington in a far more secure position than he believed he previously had enjoyed. Surrounded now by devoted officers and lauded by domestic politicians, not to mention fawning foreign emissaries and warriors, he had acquired that complete control that his disposition required, a turn that fulfilled the self-enhancement for which he had striven. Those inner needs that had driven him to feats of daring before 1778 now were met. Indeed, his only daring acts as commander were to sanction the raids on Britain's two Hudson outposts, and those decisions came hard on the heels of his only real setback, the loss of Stony Point in 1779. Otherwise, his very tone seemed different.

Once so eager to act that he was willing to manipulate balky subordinates into consenting to his wishes, Washington now found reasons for inaction, though chiefly he attributed his inertia to the nation's economic woes and its political chaos. He longed to act, he said repeatedly, but "the object of my Wishes [is] not within the compass of my powers." He understood the danger of his course, and in 1780 he even told Congress: "If we fail for want of proper exertions . . . I trust the responsibility will fall where it ought and that I shall stand justified to Congress, to my Country, and to the World." Still, when he seriously contemplated acting, a note of hesitancy was there that had not been present earlier, and repeatedly he spoke of fighting only when there was "a moral certainty of victory" for "should we fail . . . it would be a real disgrace," leaving "us in a state of relaxation and debility, from which it will be difficult if not impracticable to recover." [80]

How then to evaluate Washington's leadership in these last years of the war? His generalship is open to criticism, much of it owing to the attitudes he harbored toward his subordinates. His decisions to leave Sullivan in command in Rhode Island, then to select him to lead the expedition to the frontier in 1779, were misguided, nearly resulting in disastrous defeat in the first instance, and leading to an incomplete conquest in the second. Moreover, the idea of launching another campaign into Canada had real merit, but it was a dead letter with Washington so long as Gates was certain to command the invasion army. What Washington did focus on in these years was a prospective Franco-American siege of New York; indeed, he embraced this notion until it seemed to become a fixed idea virtually to the exclusion of every other possibility. A victory there would have been magnificent, surely ending the war in one fell swoop. But the odds against success were considerable, for the French and American armies would have been barely larger than Clinton's force, while the French navy— assuming it would have been able to act in these waters—was not likely ever to have been vastly superior to its adversary. Even a friend like Jefferson eventually criticized Washington's obsession with New York, comparing the likely futility of such an enterprise to the doomed attempt by France and Spain to besiege Gibraltor.[81] In a sense Washington's fascination with besieging New York was in keeping with his proclivity for the grandiose, for the most bold, resolute design. Curiously, however, while such a gamble was filled with risks for the United States—to fail might extirpate American morale and erode French willingness to persevere—it would have been a relatively safe undertaking for Washington, for failure was more likely to be attributed to his ally's maritime shortcomings, or to the very magnitude of the endeavor, than to his errors. And, of course, just as the successful assaults on Stony Point and Paulus Hook seemed in Washington's mind to remove the stigma of his failure at Fort Washington, a victory over Clinton in New York might have eradicated the memory of the egregious losses that he had sustained on these islands in 1776.

On the other hand, there is much in Washington's performance to praise, particularly in the contributions he made away from the battlefield. He worked well with the French, an important fact that often is overlooked. Much could have gone wrong in the relationship between temperamental, savvy professionals and an insecure, inexperienced, amateur soldier, as Sullivan demonstrated in his own plaintive dealings with d'Estaing. Yet Washington's relations with Rochambeau and three successive naval commanders were proper, amicable in some instances, and always characterized by mutual respect. Anything less might have jeopardized the 1781 campaign that ultimately resulted in the victory at Yorktown.

In fact, Washington's principal contribution in these years stemmed from his demeanor and his temperament. After 1778 his character became a weapon in the war, more powerful in some ways than his regiments. The commander had been popular from the beginning of his appointment, but after Valley Forge and the alleged machinations of the cabal his stature grew until it transcended just being reputable. Washington thereafter was admired, even beloved. In 1779 his countrymen began to celebrate his birthday, and throughout this dark period sermons and essays, speeches and songs applauded him. For a society that feared it was witnessing the inexorable sapping of its revolutionary virtue by the vicissitudes of war, Washington had come to be seen as one of the last virtuous men. He became, according to historian Charles Royster, the "exemplar of the qualities that would achieve the continent's promised future." [82]

Others used public life for private gain, or abandoned office altogether to seek greater rewards in private endeavors, but Washington, serving without a salary, was constant. Come pain or travail or disappointment, he was there. The public thought him above the improbity and the treachery it perceived in others, and in him it saw a man whose character matched the ideals of the American revolutionary identity. In these years he grew larger than life, "godlike" even, according to a popular song. He may not have been indispensable, but he had come to seem so in those buoyant early years of the conflict, for his persona had come to symbolize the preservation both of the army and the Revolution, and he was seen both by officers and political leaders as the unbending guardian of the revolutionary credo. Never more than in the long, difficult span from late 1778 until Yorktown did the new nation need a man with a felicitous genius for understanding what the nation expected of its commander in chief.

That November, as Washington returned for the final time to West Point, the encomiums continued to roll in. Along the way he paused frequently to be honored, and in return to address the local citizenry. In mid-month he reached the outpost, where he remained only for a week, tending to a few administrative chores and issuing a farewell address to his soldiery. Then, learning that the redcoats were about to depart New York City, he rode south, across Kingsbridge, already abandoned by Carleton, then on along the rustic environs of northern Manhattan until he reached Harlem. Finally, at noon on the 25th, the last British soldier stepped off New York soil, and Washington and his entourage, led by a suburban militia outfit, paraded into the city. It was a chilly day, but the late fall cold had kept few people at home. Citizens lined the streets, cheering the elegant little procession as it passed, craning for a glimpse of the large man most had come to see. At Cape's Tavern on lower Broadway the parade ended. Washington alighted from his mount, inspected his militia escort, listened to still another round of panegyric addresses, then simply went inside for a private banquet.[83]

From this moment everything must have seemed anticlimactic to Washington. New York, the scene of his worst defeats in this war, a recurrent subject in his thoughts for seven long years, had been restored to American control. At last the war really was over.

He remained in town until the weather permitted Carleton to sail. At times it must have seemed that the town would not let him leave even then, for dinners and congratulatory affairs crowded in on him. But finally, on December 4, all was clear. He summoned his officers for the final time, now for a luncheon of cold meats, wine, and brandy at Fraunces's Tavern. The men gathered at noon. Four general officers, perhaps a score from the lower grades, were present; among these men only Knox had been with the commander since that first day at Cambridge. The meeting was fraught with emotion, and with an intense consciousness of the past and the future, for these men knew that they were witnesses to the end of an epoch, and that their lives would never again be the same. Washington made no speech. What was left to say? At the end of the meal he simply asked each man to come up and say goodbye individually. Many recalled later that the commander wept.[84]

Then he was gone. Accompanied now by just one aide, David Humphreys, he was conveyed by barge to New Jersey, then he began the long, familiar ride home, alternately traveling on horseback and in a carriage. Another wagon brought along his wartime possessions, his uniforms, his bed, his eating utensils, and packed with those items were gifts, some that he had received, some that he had purchased during a brief trip to Philadelphia in October or while in New York. For Martha he brought lockets and sashes, hats and hose and an umbrella; there were books and a fiddle and a whirligig for the grandchildren. And for himself there was a new pair of reading glasses, some books to use the spectacles on, a hunting rifle, a few bottles of good wine, and the delicacies that he loved—walnuts and brazil nuts, capers and olives, anchovies and raisins.[85]

Four days out of New York the general reached Philadelphia, where, for him anyway, the war had begun. Business detained him for a week, then he was off again. He paused briefly in Baltimore before riding on toward his next-to-last stop, Annapolis, where Congress had moved in November.

Washington had one last piece of public business to transact. Quietly he submitted his expense account (which Congress scrutinized into 1784 before it reported that the general had made an error; he had shortchanged himself by one dollar, they declared, and they awarded him $64, 355.30 in paper securities), then at noon on the 23rd the legislators formally received him. The session was gaveled to order by the president, Thomas Mifflin, once his aide, then his quartermaster general. When the unusually large gathering of lawmakers and onlookers fell quiet, he called General Washington forward. Slowly, almost faintly, the general read his final address as commander in chief, this one his resignation, an act that was in order, he said, because the United States, now independent and sovereign, had become "a respectable Nation." In closing, he said, he "resign[ed] with satisfaction the Appointment I accepted with diffidence."[86]

It was a brief ceremony, mercifully. He had promised his wife that he would enjoy Christmas dinner with her at home. He kept his promise. In the last lingering rays of light on Christmas Eve he spotted Mount Vernon. Perhaps he reined his huge gray mount to a slower pace so he could fully enjoy the sight. Certainly there no longer was any hurry. It had been ten years and five days since the Boston Tea Party set in motion the tumultuous events over which he had presided. But now they were over. At last he was home—to stay. As he had told Congress the previous day: "I retire from the great theater of Action."

PART THREE

13

A Brief Retirement

"I have had my day"

Mount Vernon. At last. A place where the retired general could be "under the shadow of my own Vine and my own Fig-tree, free from the bustle of a camp and the busy scenes of public life." [1]

The Mount Vernon to which Washington returned differed in many ways from the estate he had left behind that humid morning in 1775 when he had set out with Richard Henry Lee for Philadelphia and the Continental Congress. Almost a year before his departure he had initiated a program of extensive alterations on the estate, hiring a master builder, ordering the necessary materials, and then in the spring of 1774 seeing work commence. The plan was to transform his handsome country farmhouse into a larger, more opulent estate befitting the status of a Virginia planter, adding to one side a section that included a study or library on the ground floor and a bedchamber above, and to the other side a high-ceilinged banquet room; alterations to the ceiling and the fireplace in the old dining room also went forward, while outside a piazza was planned for the back of the house and a cupola was proposed for the roof. The grounds continued to be improved too, work that had begun shortly after Patsy's death. This landscaping project soon grew quite ambitious, as Washington came to envision not only gardens but the addition of a palisade, either a formal fence or an arcaded wall that connected the main house to the two front buildings. [2] Construction had not proceeded very far before the war lured Washington away, but the workmen's toil continued in his absence, overseen, of course, by Lund Washington and orchestrated through occasional letters from the owner to his manager.

For years after 1774 scaffolding obscured portions of the exterior of Mount Vernon, and sections of the rich, green lawn that had rolled out from the house were transformed into trampled, dusty marl in the summer, to an unsightly bog in other months. Progress was slow. At the start of the project it had taken the sharp-eyed owner only a few days to learn that the work "goes on better whilst I am present, than in my absence from the workmen," and his eight years away from the estate had done nothing to hasten the job's completion.[3] But undertakings of this sort always proceeded at a crawl, regardless of the workers. Wood had to be cut and hauled to the building site. Before nailing it into place, it was wise to give the lumber, especially the heavy beams, a prolonged exposure to the sun; otherwise, warping was certain to result. Artisans worked by hand, moreover, using a vast array of tools whose very names today sound quaint: the ripping chisel, whip saw, frame saw, pit saw, gouge, piercer, gimlet, and the jack.

Before Washington departed for the war, the south wing—the library addition—had been raised. By late 1776, thirty months after work began, the exterior of the north addition also was completed, and the following year the piazza was erected. But in the next two years little was accomplished. In 1778 the chief builder, together with one assistant, were the sole workers, and in 1779 all labor was left to an assistant, a sad development that arose because—in Lund's view— the head of the endeavor was a "worthless" sort. The last really major undertaking carried out before the general's return had been the erection of the rear portico, and that had been in 1777. Nearly a hundred feet in length and almost thirty feet high—this airy back porch was supported by eight massive wooden pillars. But the most striking feature of this addition was that it was without precedent in the Virginia of that day, an innovation by a man who, though he seldom sought to be different, evidently took to heart his plan to sit "under the shadow" of his mythical fig.[4]

The completion of these alterations occupied much of Washington's attention upon his return, that and the replacement of Mount Vernon's roof, the gradual impairment of which Lund earlier had warned, as well as the mending of chronic leaks about his new cupola. He also had to oversee what had not been finished in his absence. The doors, windows, and floors were in place in his banquet room, but work had not begun on the interior walls; he wished to have the walls stuccoed, as that was the "present taste in England," but he had not decided on the best color ("plain blew or green" were his preferences), and he had no idea whether stucco should be painted or whether it was fashionable to install this cement-based material below the chair rail. Likewise, while the roof was up on his rear piazza, nothing had been done about the floor of this porch, and that set the general to investigating tile, black and white flagstone, and similarly colored marble. (He finally settled on imported white flagstone cut to uniform size, each no less than twelve inches square.[5]

Even before the arrival of the first hot days in the summer of 1784, Washington discovered that a new ice house built following his return was next to worthless, although he was uncertain whether it was due to shoddy workmanship or because he had packed it with snow, not ice. On the other hand, although he had intended to have several chimneys rebuilt and to replace some existing mantels, close inspection convinced him that they were unlikely to be improved. If he saved his money in that instance, he had been home for only a few months before he hit upon the need for a greenhouse, and he set his skilled servants to building one, only to discover that it would be too small. He wrote Tench Tilghman, his former aide, to request that he learn the dimensions of a hothouse he remembered seeing on a plantation in Maryland. By 1786 most of the remodeling was complete, though Washington soon learned what homeowners with a passion for puttering eventually discover—that work on a house never ends; in that year he was searching for copper gutters and downspouts, as well as for a more solid pavement for his serpentine stone driveways.[6]

As concerned as was Washington with the buildings at Mount Vernon, he devoted almost as much attention to the grounds of his estate. He procured flowers and shrubs from many parts of America and looked for grass seed that would enable him to have the "best turf" possible. The variety of trees that he sought was almost limitless: he wanted balsams and white pines, spruces, hemlocks, magnolias, live oaks, aspens, locusts, redbuds, and even palmettoes, and he succeeded in acquiring some of each species, planting them adjacent to his existing peach orchard and amongst this or that coppice of cherry and plum, pear and apple. He returned from one of his journeys with pecan seedlings, and by the 1790s he had a small grove that annually bore several bushels for its delighted owner. Many of his trees came as gifts from friends. Governor Clinton sent lindens and limes (as well as sprigs of ivy), other acquaintances dispatched lilacs and mock orange and paw paw trees, and "Light Horse Harry" Lee had buckeye nuts delivered to Mount Vernon.[7]

Washington also sought to grace his estate with exotic animals. He imported pheasants and partridges, but the birds soon died. (He sent the carcasses of two of the ill-fated fowls to Charles Willson Peale, who stuffed and exhibited them in his museum in Philadelphia.) He had better luck in his endeavors to create a deer park, all the rage in fashionable English circles. He acquired a buck doe, and six fawns of the "best English deer," which he confined until they were tame, and he additionally procured six American deer. By 1787 he gleefully reported that his little drove at last had begun to multiply. However, what would really set Mount Vernon apart, he thought, was a buffalo herd, and Washington set out to acquire some of this species, but in this quest he came up empty-handed.[8]

Each of Washington's endeavors—interior and exterior—proceeded at a snail's pace, slowed by the unavailability of skilled workmen, especially joiners and bricklayers. Although many styled themselves tradesmen, he discovered that few really were journeymen artisans. In one instance he evidently hired a "brick-layer," only to discover that the man really was experienced only in mixing mortar. Find some workers, he beseeched Tench Tilghman; if they were good, it mattered not whether they were Africans or Asians, "Mahometans, Jews or Christians of any Sect, or . . . Atheists." In fact, despite his antipathy toward acquiring additional slaves, he even purchased one bondsman presumed to be an

Mount Vernon, East Front, overlooking the Potomac River, by an unknown artist (ca. 1792). Courtesy of the Mount Vernon Ladies' Association of the Union.

Mount Vernon, West Front, by an unknown artist (ca. 1792). Courtesy of the Mount Vernon Ladies' Association of the Union.

artisan with a skill that his building project required. Mostly, however, he sought to find his workers among the pool of German redemptioners who entered Virginia, or among free laborers. But he was not always successful. He had been home for eighteen months before he located a joiner, and more than two years after returning to Mount Vernon he still was looking for a bricklayer.[9]

Those workers whom Washington owned or hired could have attested that time had not mellowed the master of Mount Vernon. He remained the exacting taskmaster he had been before the war, expecting his labor force to be at work from daylight to dark. He carefully planned the myriad operations of his estate a year in advance, this to assure that his workers would not be left with "nothing to do." Moreover, he expected the managers of his properties to be virtual efficiency engineers, but in case they lacked that talent he prepared meticulous instructions, directions—he called them "head work"—designed to "guard against the misapplication of labour. . . ." His free workers were lectured "to avoid bad Company" and to shun the bottle, the "ruin of half the workers in this Country," for the "aching head and trembling limbs which are inevitable effects of drinking disincline the hands from work," leading first to laziness, then to indifference, and finally to total inactivity. But the dearth of skilled artisans left Washington with little clout over these employees, and he was compelled to forego some of his principles to retain their labor. For years he tolerated a chronically besotted miller, and in a contract with a gardner he not only consented to permit the man to be drunk four days and four nights both at Christmas and Easter, and for two days and two nights at Whitsuntide, but he sanctioned his daily intake of a dram (one-half ounce) of rum each morning and a grog of spirits with dinner.[10]

One of the workmen with whom Washington first had to deal was his cousin Lund. Late in the war the general had discovered he was deeply in debt to his estate manager, as Lund had taken no pay since 1778, a course he quietly and voluntarily had pursued because of Mount Vernon's economic woes. Not only did he have to be paid but, immediately upon his boss's return, Lund had expressed a desire to leave the estate; he had married in 1779, and he now hoped to realize his long-standing dream of acquiring his own farm. The two evidently struck a deal during the owner's first year back in Virginia. Beginning the next year, Washington undertook to remunerate Lund for his back wages, a process that required five years of annual payments. Moreover, in 1783 or 1784 Washington permitted Lund and his wife to set up residence on a 450-acre tract that he owned about five miles south of Alexandria, real estate that the young planter had acquired a few years before. In 1785 the tract was deeded formally to Lund, who by then had christened the place "Hayfield," undoubtedly after the role the area had played while part of Washington's property. Late that same year Lund ended his tenure as Mount Vernon's manager, and the general proclaimed himself to be his own director. Lund's last official act at Mount Vernon was to train George Augustine Washington, the general's nephew, to become the assistant manager of the place, although during the remainder of the decade he occasionally acted as an agent in the marketing of Washington's livestock, flour, and fish.[11]

If Washington's attention was absorbed by the problems of his workers and the alterations on his estate, he did not lose sight of his principal pursuit. When he came home from Newburgh he once again became a farmer. But try as he might, Washington never excelled—at least not to his own exacting standards—in this capacity. Soon after Lund's departure, in fact, he felt compelled to find "a thorough bred *practical* english Farmer" to run his enterprises. A year-long search was required before he retained James Bloxham of Gloucestershire, a specialist recommended by George William Fairfax, who still lived abroad in Bath. Washington paid Bloxham sixty guineas a year, gave him free and "comfortable" room and board, a horse, and a stipend with which he could bring his family to America. The general promptly liked his English yeoman, finding him to be polite and industrious, as well as a pleasant conversationalist. But there also were immediate problems. Bloxham was chagrined to find that the war had taken a heavy toll on the estate, and that the farm implements that one took for granted in England were nonexistent in Virginia; for his part, Washington soon discovered that his employee had never run such a huge operation, nor was he at all certain that Bloxham was up to it. Things worked out, nevertheless. The two renewed their contract the following year, and in 1788 Washington pronounced that Bloxham and his family "appear to be contented with the country." Apparently he was correct, for the Englishmen managed Mount Vernon for five years.[12]

Bloxham faced a difficult assignment. If not useless, Mount Vernon's soil was at best indifferent, its nutrients depleted through too many years of wasteful cultivation. This tract of land had never been superlative, as Washington had discovered two decades before when the estate's tobacco crops had been incapable of matching that of its neighbors either in quality or in quantity. The owner's recent protracted absence and the indifferent, perfunctory forced labor performed by the farm's hands must have increased the odds against the estate's agricultural success. Nor did the weather cooperate. Too much rain was followed by too little, and that in turn was succeeded by another round of torrential downpours. Conditions were so bad, in fact, that in 1786 Washington had to purchase corn, supposedly one of his two principal crops, in order to feed his laborers and livestock.[13]

Strangely, despite his dismal record in husbandry, Washington was an energetic farmer, one who, by American standards, was ahead of his time in his enthusiasm both for scientific agriculture and for experimentation. He bought and read the treatises of Arthur Young, the great English agrarian, and he even took up a correspondence with him in these years. As a result he shifted his methods to those advocated by Young, chiefly a procedure by which he sowed his fields in grasses rather than permitting them to lie fallow between the harvest and the next planting. Washington was one of the first farmers in his region to use a

mechanical seed spreader, having one built at Mount Vernon from plans that he
had seen in an agricultural manual. In fact, he was nothing if not innovative. He
tried numerous varieties of wheat, planted potatoes with and without manure,
sowed and harvested at varying times to gauge the seasonal impact, experimented
with plaster of paris as a fertilizer, and would have used mud from the bottom
of the Potomac as dressing had he solved the problem of how to extract it. One
of his more ingenious ideas was to turn Mount Vernon's undulating lands into a
vineyard, making the estate into the wine-producing center of America. He knew
that the familiar European grapes would not do, for experiments by others had
demonstrated that when grown in Virginia these fruits resulted in an acidic taste.
Hence, he raised native vines and also imported exotic varieties. But, typically,
that experiment failed too, and following his fourth summer back in Virginia he
remorsefully acknowledged the continued failure of Mount Vernon to produce
bountiful outputs of any plant.[14]

Washington was a rancher as well as a farmer. He owned over 600 head of
cattle, in addition to 135 horses, and it was as a stockman that he embarked on
one of his most novel experiments. Beginning in 1785, when he received a gift
of a jackass from the king of Spain, he set out to "stock the Country" with these
beasts. Sturdy and long-lived, and inexpensive to maintain when compared to
horses and cattle, asses, Washington believed, not only would supplant all other
livestock as the principal laboring animal on America's farms but would take the
place of horses in matters of conveyance. His original scheme was to put "Royal
Gift," as he named his new possession, out to stud with his mares. That did not
work. The ass could not have been less interested. Evidently he was "too full of
Royalty, to have any thing to do with a plebian race," Washington cracked, as he
led him from the horse pen; eventually, he borrowed a jenny from a neighbor and
introduced her to Royal Gift. Nature immediately took its course. The jenny acted
"like a true female," Washington reported, for she had been undaunted by the
royal ass's huge personal parts. Lafayette soon thereafter presented Washington
with another jack and two jennies, and the great experiment began in earnest.
But like so many of his other agricultural endeavors this, too, failed, resulting
in nothing more than whatever pride Washington took in owning a few of these
striking and still exotic creatures. He undoubtedly put the jacks to work, but there
is no evidence that he ever rode to the hounds on the back of an ass, nor did he
replace his traditional carriage teams with pairs of jennies.[15]

Washington also expressed a willingness to experiment when it came to
liberating slaves. The institution should be abolished, he admitted shortly after
the war. His reasoning, moreover, had taken a new twist since the late 1770s
when he had confessed that slavery had become an economic burden. Now he
seemed to feel that slavery was a moral wrong. Before leaving Mount Vernon for
the war he seemed never to have given the matter any thought, but during the
long conflict something changed his outlook. Perhaps it was because thousands
of blacks from the North, given the chance to soldier during the late war, had

performed as capably as their white counterparts; maybe it was due to the zeal with which southern blacks had denounced slavery by fleeing behind British lines. It could have been the impact of Whig ideology which reverberated about the land, for notions such as the equality of men and mankind's innate rights to life, liberty, and the pursuit of happiness were difficult to square with human bondage. In addition, animated discussions on the issue of slavery must have occurred at headquarters, and inasmuch as two of his favorites, Lafayette and John Laurens, were outspoken foes of the institution, Washington must have been moved to reconsider his predispositions.

At best, however, the issue remained an abstract philosophical matter for him, as he would support abolition only if slavery was set aside very, very gradually. Someone should concoct a scheme to abolish the institution, he once said, but he had no intention of being that someone. Nor did he make an effort to aid the struggling young abolitionist movement born during the Revolution. In fact, when he learned that some Philadelphia Quakers had sought by court action to attain a slave's freedom, he denounced their endeavor. He spoke out for property rights, not human rights, crying that it amounted to "oppression" of the slaveowner when "happy and contented" slaves were "tampered with" by outside agitators.[16] And, of course, he took no steps to manumit his own chattel during the 1780s. Indeed, he sold nine slaves in 1786, for which he realized nearly a thousand dollars, and he acquired two additional slaves while he remained at Mount Vernon during that decade.[17]

After Washington returned to Virginia in 1783 he often lamented his financial plight, sometimes painting a picture of a man on the precipice of economic disaster. He was barely home before a nephew and a brother called with their hands out, each hoping for a loan. Washington refused both men (though he asked George Mason to lend his brother $500). He had not made a cent off Mount Vernon in nearly a decade, he said, adding that he faced the prospect of selling portions of his estate to raise cash. Taxes had to be paid, he went on, and then there was the matter of paying off both Lund and the workmen who had labored on his house; he faced several other encumbrances as well, he might have added, the largest being the retirement of a $6000 loan he had received to purchase the Oriskany lands in upstate New York. In fact, by 1785 he also was in debt to Governor Clinton, who lent him the funds to meet his first note on this tract. Washington confessed that he was "ashamed" of his condition. The "fact is that I am *really* in want of money," he claimed.[18]

The general's obligations were real, and his concern at his financial situation was both genuine and warranted. But his cries of imminent insolvency appear to have been exaggerated. At first glance he seemed harried. He called in loans (he was due in excess of £4000, mostly in varied settlements of Patsy's and Jackie's estates, as well as that of Martha's first husband), he put some of his land on the market, and he sold almost all the securities he had received from Congress upon submitting his wartime expense account, even maintaining that he was forced to sell those notes for only one-twentieth of their face value. That he resorted to all these expedients might seem to indicate he was in desperate straits. In all likelihood, however, that was not the case. To demand that his debtors meet their obligations was hardly a new ploy for him, and there is no evidence to suggest that he acted any more assiduously in these endeavors in the 1780s than he had during the fifteen years before the Revolution. His land-sale scheme was designed to raise cash so that he could make payments on his New York lands, tracts that he concluded were likely to turn a profit more rapidly than were his western Pennsylvania and western Virginia holdings, as "the Yankees will delay no time" in opening ties between New York and the site of his lands. Confirmation that his Pennsylvania and Virginia lands for the moment were useless came when he was unable to find a buyer for that domain. As for selling his securities, the value of all certificates was depreciating almost by the moment in the 1780s, in itself a powerful inducement for selling immediately. In addition, Washington's claim to have sold his securities at twenty to one seems unlikely, as the notes never declined to such a low level in Virginia.[19] For the most part, in fact, his lamentations of woe were forthcoming when he was approached by acquaintances hoping to dun him of his wealth. Otherwise, his actions were less those of a man faced with the likelihood of ruin than those of a person compelled to substitute a measure of austerity for his customarily acquisitive life style. In fact, within two or three years of returning home he had begun to realize a healthy cash flow, and during the next fifteen years he annually took in anywhere between $4500 and $15,000 from the varied enterprises of Mount Vernon alone; even more wealth rolled in from the vast and profitable Custis properties.[20]

However financially troubled he may have been, Washington never abandoned his materialistic or speculative pursuits. Aside from the costly alterations to his estate, Washington was engaged in three expensive endeavors in the 1780s. He barely was home before his gaze fell again on the Dismal Swamp. The company he had helped to establish two decades earlier to develop that boggy wilderness largely had ceased to function during the war, but with an assist from Washington it cranked up again in the spring of 1784. What Washington hoped to facilitate was the linking via canal of the Virginia–North Carolina backcountry to the Atlantic. The watercourse that he had in mind would shoot out from the swamp to the Elizabeth River in Virginia and the Albemarle in North Carolina, waterways that stretched like craggy fingers from the coast to the piedmont. As usual, Washington's vision was grandiose. By means of the canal "the whole trade of [the western] Territory . . . is now unfolding to . . . view," he wrote, proffering a vista of wealth that will "exceed the most sanguine imagination." At its initial postwar meeting the company's board rubber-stamped Washington's views, agreeing to advertise in Europe both for additional investors and for a source of cheap labor. The following year Washington summoned the entrepreneurs to Richmond for another meeting, and this time the directors agreed—again at the general's behest—to seek Virginia's aid by promising to surrender to the state all profits from the canal's tolls. But at the end of the decade the canal remained only a project on paper, the beginning of construction repeatedly frustrated by rivalries among Virginia's varied interest groups, as well as by fears in North Carolina that the channel would only serve to divert its trade to the Old Dominion.[21]

Washington was even more interested in another canal scheme. Like Lawrence Washington before him, he also long had envisioned the further extension of the Potomac River into the western hinterlands, opening the 287-mile-long river to its headwaters on the North Branch. To accomplish this feat a colossal undertaking would be required. Nearly 175 miles of the river above tidewater would need be cleared, minor rapids at three points would have to be surmounted, and the impediments posed by both the Little Falls and the Great Falls would somehow have to be overcome; moreover, work on these obstructions would have to be performed in the face of episodic summer droughts that reduced the water to uncommonly low levels, and despite seasonal snowmelts that transformed the tranquil river into a rampaging monster. Washington initially ruminated on this scheme during his initial year as commander of the Virginia Regiment, proposing in 1754 that work be undertaken to clear out some of the rock in the river, thus opening channels through which vessels could sail. Such an operation would have facilitated the supply of his army deep in western Virginia. In the 1760s, then as a member of the Virginia assembly, he resurrected the project. By then his motives were more pecuniary, as he realized that a successful Potomac canal would improve his chances of selling his vast frontier holdings. Normally mute inside the halls of the legislature, Washington had pushed hard for provincial funding of the enterprise. He almost succeeded. Virginia agreed to the project, and to a similar undertaking on the James River. But Maryland, which under Lord Baltimore's colonial charter had sole possession of the river, refused to sanction the plan.[22]

Washington hardly had laid down his sword in 1783 before he resumed his dream. Much as he had seen a symbiosis between private gain and public weal in the affairs of the Ohio Company three decades before, he now squared personal profit and patriotism in this scheme. Washington acknowledged that he was "not . . . disinterested" economically in his plans to make the Potomac into the West's highway to the Chesapeake, and he confided that the value of his "Lands in that Country . . . would be enhanced, by the adoption of such a Scheme." But a nationalistic impetus also guided the general. He feared that if the West was not linked economically to the East, separatist sentiments would burgeon in the transmontane region. Again, typically, the vision he beheld was grandiose. Work on a Potomac canal was to begin at the falls above Georgetown, an undertaking designed to tame the raging stream and render it navigable. Further west, additional canals and other improvements would elongate the river, and at its western terminus wilderness roads would be blazed to other rivers that flowed still further to the west. These, in turn, would be adjoined to the Ohio, which would be tied by still more roads and canals to the Great Lakes. The inhabitants of the West would be bound to the East by economic connections, the new American union would be solidified, and every western commodity would flow through Virginia en route to market, creating a metropolis within the state—almost certainly at nearby Alexandria, where the goods would have to be shifted from river craft to ocean vessels—that someday would dwarf Philadelphia and New York.[23]

Throughout 1784 Washington and like-minded nationalists and investors in Virginia worked behind the scenes to secure a public commitment for their grand scheme. At the end of the year their tireless labor was rewarded. That autumn the Virginia assembly asked the general and his old rival Horatio Gates to meet with a delegation from Maryland to plan the venture, and almost simultaneously in December the two states enacted legislation based on the recommendations of Washington and his fellow panelists. Virginia and Maryland chartered the Potomac Company. Each state, moreover, subscribed fifty shares and voted money to cut roads from the Potomac to the Cheat and the Monongahela rivers. The states' funding amounted to one-third of the company's operating capital. Stockholders provided the rest. Washington invested over $2200 and agreed to serve as the company's president.

The job cut into his time. He attended board meetings, lobbied politicians in Richmond and Annapolis, importuned wealthy acquaintances to buy into the endeavor, solicited workers, and made inspection trips along the great river. He seemed to be racing against time. Not only was New York likely to pursue a similar goal, Pennsylvania and Maryland already had designs on the Susquehanna River for a comparable venture. Like others, Washington was optimistic. After all, a company report issued in 1783 characterized the Great Falls, the most considerable obstacle to navigation on the river, as a "trifling impediment." Within five years, the report continued, the project would be completed. At Washington's behest the firm hired an engineer—an inventor, really, a man from Berkeley Springs who once had contrived a steam-propelled river boat, but who had no experience in the construction of canals. Within two years the company appeared to be headed for success. Before the end of 1785 the Potomac Company had raised forty thousand dollars. Work was proceeding. Washington began to sound like a cheerleader. He had "no doubt" of success. The "work will not prove more arduous than we had conceived," he predicted. The difficulties rather vanish than increase as we proceed," he told those who would listen.[24]

However, it soon was obvious that neither Washington's optimism nor the air of haste would produce success. Two teams of fifty laborers had been put to work on the first phase of the project, clearing the river near Georgetown. That work was supposed to be completed by the end of 1787, but by then barely a dent had been made in taming the falls. An overabundance of rain from late 1785 to the end of 1786 often left the river too swollen to work, and, besides, the company provided too few hands for the amount of labor required. In addition, the engineer hired by Washington soon proved to be ignorant of hydrodynamics.

In a few years he had departed, to be followed by a succession of engineers—the company hired seven such technicians in a span of fifteen years—none of whom possessed the skills to surmount the adversities posed by the Potomac. In 1787 Virginia and Maryland extended the deadline for the fulfillment of the first phase of the undertaking to 1790, leading Washington to continue to paint a rosy picture of the company's prospects. But in private he had grown more skeptical, though even there he tried to sound upbeat, claiming that overcoming that first great obstacle would be "the *most* doubtful part of our Work." In reality, the entire scheme was beginning to look doubtful. Stockholders had begun to default on their assessments, and the company's attempt to auction off their shares yielded little capital. Toward the end of the decade, moreover, it became apparent that the adversities posed by this river might be too great for that generation's engineering know-how, and as with his Dismal Swamp venture Washington did not realize a single cent from this speculative gambit during the 1780s.[25]

Washington's third major enterprise in these years was the oldest and closest to his heart: land speculation. He purchased 376 acres on Hunting Creek, a tract adjacent to Mount Vernon, and he contracted to pay an annual sum of £136 in rent for the use of lands and slaves belonging to a widowed neighbor. In addition, he purchased the lease to a plantation in the Clifton Neck region of Fairfax County, and he acquired a modest tract in Maryland.[26]

Mostly, however, the frontier lands he had gained before the Revolution were his chief concern. Now that independence was won and Lord Dunmore, the royal governor who had cast doubts on the legitimacy of Washington's frontier claims, was long gone, there was nothing to dispute the general's right to nearly sixty thousand acres in the West. But for all his frenetic scrambling to secure this domain, he had yet to realize any profit from these holdings. With peace, however, settlers were expected to push west as never before, so Washington hardly had made himself at home at Mount Vernon before he began to plan a trip into the wilderness. The trek would have many objectives, not all of which were related to business, for Washington soon was so plain bored by his new, more sedentary life style that he appeared to look with relish on an arduous, perhaps even dangerous, journey. In fact, even before he resigned from the army he had concocted plans for an expedition from Virginia north to Canada, thence west to the Mississippi, down that artery to the Gulf of Mexico, across to Pensacola, and home via Georgia and the Carolinas. However, the "deranged state" of his finances compelled him to forego that jaunt, while encouraging him to look in on his trans-Appalachian properties. He wished to survey and stake out his lands, and he also planned to look in on the squatters who allegedly were roosting on his realty. Then, too, he was more than anxious to see Gilbert Simpson, the settler in whose trust he had left the expensive grist mill he had built on the Youghiogheny in 1774. "I ought to have a good deal of wealth in your hands, arising from the produce" of the mill, Washington had written him at the end of the war, for he had been told that his was the best and busiest mill operating west of the mountains. Strangely, though, he had seen none of the profit turned up by the mill. "I expect something very handsome therefore from that quarter," Washington told Simpson, unless, as rumor had it, he was something other than the "honest, industrious and frugal man" the general had taken him to be. Whatever he thought of Simpson, Washington already had decided to sell the mill; he published notices of his intention to conduct a public auction at the site of the mill, a vendue he planned to attend just to be certain that everything was run on the up and up.[27]

Washington pieced together a small party that included his nephew Bushrod Washington and his old friend and neighbor Dr. Craik, as well as a bevy of servants, three of whom were to wait on him. His bags stocked with silver cups and spoons, two kegs of spirits, Madeira, Port, "cherry bounce" (cherries steeped in brandy and sugar), oil, vinegar, mustard, "Spices of all sorts," tea, seven pounds of sugar, fishing equipment, canteens, bedding, and an assortment of pots, pans, and kettles, the party set out late in the summer of 1784. Within three days the expedition had reached what now is West Virginia, still a lush, green primitive region. There Washington paused to visit his brother Charles. Once the proprietor of the Rising Sun Tavern in Fredericksburg, Charles had headed west about 1780, moving into the Shenandoah Valley. Always the entrepreneur, he established a town, Charles Town, immodestly naming it for himself, and calling its streets after various members of the Washington clan. The general looked upon this stop as more than just a social call. While in town he called on several tenants who were in arrears in their obligations to him, netting £90 for his trouble. From this rustic village the party clambered up the road that Braddock's men had opened in 1755, to and beyond Fort Cumberland, past the "shades of death," gloomy, sunless mountain regions shielded behind the wilderness canopy, on to the Great Meadows, where Washington owned more than two hundred acres, and, finally, on the thirteenth day to Simpson's place in southwestern Pennsylvania, rich and fertile lowland, a site known locally as "Washington's bottom."[28]

The news in this quarter was not pleasant. The general discovered that Simpson owed him £600. He also learned that Simpson had only £30 in cash, although the mill manager was willing to throw in a female slave and a few bushels of wheat as a part payment on his debt. Washington took it all, only to learn a few weeks later that Simpson had deceived him on this trade too, for the "slave" he had acquired was legally a free person. While still with Simpson, moreover, he found that his mill had been so poorly maintained that it was not even operative. His investment of £1200 on this facility would continue to be worthless. Not surprisingly there were no takers when the auction was conducted.

From Simpson's homestead, Washington sped north to his lands at Miller's Run on Chartier's Creek, about twenty-five miles west of Fort Pitt. He doubtless was overjoyed at leaving Simpson's company, but what he found in Washington County, as Pennsylvania had named the area in which his property was located, was just as disturbing, perhaps more so. He discovered squatters everywhere, families that had moved in and appropriated his lands. What ensued in the next day or two must have been quite a scene. His mood already black and surly after a couple of days in "Washington's bottom," Washington evidently had little difficulty working himself into one of his towering rages. At a general meeting he railed at these people, and they answered him in kind. Accustomed to deference, Washington must have been taken aback by their response. Of Scotch-Irish descent, these folk had pluck. They had cleared this land, lavishing love and labor on these rolling acres for the past several years; that should count for something, they reckoned. When Washington hauled out the papers that demonstrated his ownership of this domain, their bewilderment might have been excused. How, they might have wondered, could a people be asked to bleed in a war against British tyranny, yet now be asked to acquiesce in a land deed stamped in 1770 with the royal seal? Nevertheless, they offered to purchase the property they worked. At first he refused, then he relented. But he struck a hard bargain. He would not sell individual plots. The squatters could jointly purchase his entire claim for twenty-five shillings an acre, dividing it as they pleased, or each family could rent the parcel it inhabited. No! By God, he could sue them, they retorted. That was just what he would do—and just what he did, winning his suit two years later, then endeavoring to sell this domain as "improved Lands."[29]

From Chartier's Creek Washington headed home, canceling a trip further west when he learned of Indian unrest on down the Ohio. But he returned to Mount Vernon along a new route. He dropped back into his native state near present-day Morgantown, West Virginia, just below the point where the Monongahela divided, one flank of that cool, green stream becoming the Cheat River. Washington's object was to explore this meandering stream, as well as the rugged wilderness between it and the North Branch of the Potomac. He plunged into this gnarled landscape, conversing with the settlers he encountered, studying the river, slogging through the forests until, finally, he had an answer to what he was searching for: this was the best route to the Ohio for the Potomac Company to pursue. At last something had come of this desultory trip, and armed with that knowledge he hurried home, reaching his estate five weeks after he had set out.[30]

Washington's western excursion in 1784 was one of many journeys that he made during his initial years back from the war. He had been home less than four months before he returned to Philadephia to meet with some of his former officers, and before the year ended business had taken him to Richmond and Fredericksburg and Annapolis. Thereafter, however, with the exception of brief peregrinations to attend board meetings, he did not leave Mount Vernon for more than two years.

Although seldom a day passed during which one or more guests were not housed at Mount Vernon, Washington did not permit their presence to interfere with his customary pursuits. A creature of habit, he soon fell into a daily routine not unlike that he had followed as a young planter. He arose about 5:00 A.M., and thereafter for an hour or so his correspondence—he wrote four to five letters each week on average—and his financial ledgers laid first claim to his attention.

About 6:00 he shaved himself and donned the clothing a servant had laid out for him, rather plain work garments. Each morning before breakfast he looked in on his nearby stables, ascertaining that his favorite horses—at least two of whom had soldiered with him for the entirety of the war—were fine. Soon he returned for a light meal, usually Indian cakes, honey, and tea. About 7:30 or so he left his guests with books and papers, and rode off to look into his plantation's myriad activities.

For Washington the ride was an opportunity to combine business with his penchant for exercise. (In inclement weather he frequently substituted walks for these rides, each step of his hike taken under the shelter of his rear portico, pacing ninety feet to the north, then ninety feet to the south, on and on until in this tedious manner he had logged several miles.) He visited one field after another, often scrutinizing the work on all five farms on the same day, a circuit that required a ride of about fifteen miles. He rode unattended, in the warm weather sitting beneath an umbrella that he had attached to his saddle, while, for extra protection against the sun, he wore a broad-brimmed white hat. Frequently he stopped to question a worker or a supervisor, sometimes he dismounted and worked a bit himself, repairing a fence, toiling with livestock, whatever seemed to beckon. Shortly before 3:00 he returned home, changed to more formal attire, and attended the day's principal meal, a sumptuous repast that he and Martha invariably took in the company of guests. Washington apparently liked almost every sort of food, but he was especially fond of fish, and on Sundays he demanded that salt codfish be served. He seldom ate desserts, but when engrossed by the dinner table conversation he was known to absent-mindedly nibble on walnuts and hazelnuts for as long as two hours at a stretch. Once the table was cleared Washington enjoyed sending "the bottle about pretty freely," as a guest recalled, and he seems to have completed each meal with four or five glasses—and, at times, even as much as a pint—of Madeira.

If his guests expected wit or wisdom at Washington's table they were disappointed, as conversation during these meals seldom rose above the level of banality. Either the general said little, expressing himself only on the most "indifferent subjects," as one visitor recalled, or, as another guest experienced, he droned on and on about some mundanity—mileage distances along the Potomac in this instance—that aroused only boredom. If it still was daylight when the meal was completed, Washington sometimes escorted his guests about a part of his estate, and on occasion he even returned to the fields or the mill or the shops to look into the completion of some task. But usually he retired to his library, where he looked at the day's mail, made his diary entries, perhaps read a bit, and tended whatever business matters might have arisen. In the early evening he reemerged to entertain his callers. A light supper was served; Washington seldom ate, though he sometimes drank tea and frequently he imbibed more wine. Once when an English diarist was present Washington drank several glasses of champagne and "got quite merry." If there were no visitors—which was seldom, although the

Washingtons discouraged company on Sundays—he read to his family, and especially to his grandchildren, from books and newspapers. Nothing was likely to keep him up very late, however, and precisely at 9:00 each evening he retired.[31]

Washington must have found the nearly ceaseless appearance of visitors at his door to be terribly distracting. In eighteenth-century Virginia, rural and almost devoid of inns, planters were expected to take in travelers for a night or two, but in Washington's case visitors came to the state especially to see him, anxious to reach Mount Vernon and to say they had met the great man, certain they could divine the qualities that separated the general from other men. "No pilgrim ever approached mecca with deeper enthusiasm," one wayfarer noted of his ascent to Washington's home, a sentiment that many other callers might have echoed. Many visitors were unknown to the Washingtons, and the host simply chronicled their visitations with diary entries that "a Mr. Clare," "a Mr. Stephens," "a Doctr. Graham here & stayed all Night"; his inscription for May 19, 1785, noted that "a Mr. Noah Webster came here," and still others seemed to remain anonymous even to the general, as with his simple attestation that "two reverend Gentlemen . . . dined and lodged here." [32]

Other callers were connected to his business concerns, and many important figures in Virginia's public life, men like Richard Henry Lee and James Madison and young James Monroe, also dropped in. Old wartime comrades showed up too, officers such as Benjamin Lincoln and John Cadwalader. Another guest was the Reverend William Gordon of Roxbury, Massachusetts. An early activist in the colonies' protest movement, Gordon soon developed an itch to write a history of the rebellion; he began to collect documents almost as soon as the war broke out, and during the conflict he often wrote Washington about this or that point. After clearing matters, he came to Mount Vernon for two weeks in 1784, intent on digging through Washington's papers, the first in a long line of historians to plumb this massive correspondence. His labors were rewarded, and four years later he published a four-volume study under the ponderous title, *History of the Rise, Progress, and Establishment of Independence of the United States of America*.[33] Of course, neighbors such as George Mason or Robert Harrison, Washington's former aide, often were invited to Mount Vernon, but the biggest commotion must have come when really special guests appeared.

Undoubtedly Washington drew the greatest satisfaction from a visit by Lafayette. Having sailed home shortly after Yorktown, the young Frenchman returned to America in 1784 and almost immediately called on his friend. He tarried at Mount Vernon for two weeks, and still later in the year, when the general had completed his western tour, the two men—by prearrangement—met once again, this time in Richmond, where business matters had drawn Washington. It was a melancholy meeting. Lafayette was about to return home, and, although the Washingtons had spoken of a vacation in France, in his heart the general knew that he probably never again would see his friend. Reluctant to part company, Washington rode almost to Baltimore with him before, in the grip of an early winter storm, he bade farewell and turned toward his own home. "In the moment of our separation . . . and every hour since," the general confessed in an epistle penned upon his return to Mount Vernon, "I felt all that love, respect and attachment for you, with which . . . your merits have inspired me." [34]

In mid-1785 he was honored by a very different kind of guest. Catherine Macaulay Graham, the English political activist and historian, and from the beginning of the late American protest a friend of the colonial Whigs, insisted on meeting Washington while she was visiting the states. Her political activities alone would have made men in the eighteenth century look upon her as an eccentric. Graham's personal appearance and habits only confirmed that she marched to a different drummer, from her gaudy, overpainted exterior to the fact that while in her fifties she was married to a man not quite half her age. She talked loudly and nonstop, ideas gushing out in such full-throated sonority that listeners were frequently overwhelmed. But Washington could not have been more flattered by her visit. It was one thing to have the adulation of politicians and quite another to be sought out by a *littérateur*. He invited some neighbors over to meet his famous visitor, carefully, delicately, warning them of her maverick demeanor, and firmly explaining that he wished "to shew them [the Grahams] all the respect I can." [35] It is difficult to imagine two more different personalities than those of this shy, conventional man and this verbose, eccentric woman, yet they seemed to hit it off well enough, much as Washington and nonconformist Charles Lee got on until the latter was fancied to be a threat.

Among the other visitors to Mount Vernon were at least one painter and two sculptors. The three artists arrived within a six-month period of one another in 1785, each hoping to capture the true essence of their famous subject. Seven members of the family sat for Robert Pine, an English portraitist whom Washington referred to as a "Historian Painter," because much of his previous work had been renderings of epic events. His visit came on the heels of that of an obscure American sculptor, Joseph Wright, whose life mask of the general was marred because Washington laughed in the midst of the setting. The best-known artist to lug his tools to Mount Vernon was the French sculptor, Jean Antoine Houdon. Virginia had provided the money for his labors, and Jefferson and Franklin, diplomats in Paris, had undertaken to put him under contract to sculpt their famous countryman. To say that Houdon was excited at the prospect of interpreting Washington would be an understatement, for he turned down the opportunity to cast Catherine the Great—and for a higher fee—in order to come to Virginia. Not long before midnight one evening in the fall of 1785 he arrived and beat on the front door of Mount Vernon, rousing the master of the estate from a deep sleep. The next morning, aided by three Parisian assistants, he got right to work, and for the next two weeks he toiled assiduously at his trade, laboring to make a life mask and to complete what he could of two busts of the general while still on the Potomac, though it would require much work in France to finish the project. [36]

Within a fortnight Houdon had concluded what he could and had set out for Philadelphia. The completion of his major enterprise, a life-size statue of Washington, was years away; it would not be put into stone for about five years, and a decade would pass before it would be erected in Richmond. However, he did execute a terra cotta bust of the general. Washington must have liked what he saw. He had hoped to be depicted in modern garments, not in the classical toga that many contemporary artists adopted for statesmen. He need not have worried. Houdon did not clothe Washington at all, so that the thick, muscular structure of the general's neck and chest were apparent, more so than in any other representation of the man. Indeed, Houdon succeeded where almost every other artist failed, for his Washington was a sinewy man of action, a leader whose tough, resolute, indomitable appearance served as a clarion call to others to follow his command. The bust suggests the intrepidity of the man who fought Indians, gambled at Trenton, and lashed out at Monmouth, and the power of the personality that moved congressmen to appoint him to command in 1775, that reduced officers to tears at Newburgh in 1783.

Among all the guests he entertained, Washington did not find the two people he would most have loved to see—George William and Sally Fairfax. During the war, correspondence between these old friends had declined, and in some years no letters were exchanged, though the lapses were due to logistical problems, not to altered feelings. When the wartime obstacles to communication vanished, Washington once again wrote frequently, usually every three to four months, and he mildly scolded George William for not writing more often. Now that the war had ended he hoped the Fairfaxes would return to Virginia, and he looked forward to the two families becoming "intimate Companions of our old Age." But George William and Sally were happy in England, something they could not count on in Virginia inasmuch as they would certainly be adjudged to have been Tories during the rebellion. Then, too, Belvoir no longer existed. It had been destroyed by fire in 1783, perhaps the target of vandals, but more likely the victim of lightning. As late as 1785 Washington still rode there from time to time, and always he was struck by the same soulful melancholy when he gazed upon the ruins. "I could not trace a room in the house (now all rubbish)," he wrote after one visit, "that did not bring to my mind the recollection of pleasing scenes." The wistful sight, he went on, caused him to hurry home "with painful sensations, and sorrowing for the contrast." Washington offered to house his former neighbors for as long as it took them to rebuild their plantation house, but George William declined.[37] Virginia no longer offered him much, save an increasingly alien culture. The Fairfaxes never returned, not even for a visit, and the Washingtons never again saw their old friends.

Late in 1787 the sad tidings of George William's death at the age of sixty-three reached Mount Vernon. If Washington and his wife sent their condolences to the widow, no record of their letter has survived. In fact, there is no evidence that Washington wrote Sally Fairfax until eleven years later. Some historians have made much of that letter because Washington invited her to consider returning to Virginia. But it was the first—indeed, the only—letter he had written her since she departed America more than a quarter-century before. Besides, Martha appended a note of her own to her husband's missive, then the packet was taken to England by the Washingtons' old friend and Sally's in-law, Bryan Fairfax.[38] In all likelihood, had Fairfax not been traveling to England, the Washingtons would not have written. Sally seems not to have bothered to have answered their letter. Despite the heroic attempts to the contrary by some scholars, it is difficult to attach much significance to this one rather stiff communication.

As occupied as was Washington with his many business pursuits, he found ample time to enjoy his leisure. He obviously delighted in entertaining, especially as those who came to Mount Vernon were "people of the first distinction," as he put it, and they came to pay homage to him, fulfilling his need to be esteemed. For the most part, however, his tastes were not unlike those of most other planters. Periodically he attended the theater in nearby Alexandria, and on one of his two trips to Philadelphia he escorted Robert Morris's wife, Mary, to concerts, where for the first time he heard works of Joseph Haydn and Johann Sebastian Bach performed. He frequented the race track at Annapolis, a pastime that he also permitted his slaves to enjoy. He also laid out a bowling green on his lawn at Mount Vernon, and on occasion he sought the solace of a nearby stream for an afternoon of fishing. His delight in breeding and raising his horses and hounds persisted, but, inexplicably, his ardor for hunting waned about a year after his return from the war. In 1784 he frequently was on the hunt, often in quest of the fox as many as three times each week. Garbed in the costume of the age—blue coat, scarlet waistcoat, buckskin pants, top boots, a velvet cap, and carrying a whip—Washington rode on with his guests, happy in this deadly pursuit. When Lafayette presented him with several ferocious dogs, breeds trained in hunting boar and deer and wolves, Washington plunged deeper back into the forests in search of larger game. But then he quit the pursuit, and for the next fifteen years he did not even allow hunting on his estate, a tradition he broke only in 1799 when he authorized a deer hunt, and then he carefully stipulated that only one stag could be taken. Although in good health, he did not accompany the hunters on that occasion.[39]

Whatever led him to abandon hunting, it was not due to reasons of health. He was home for three years before he experienced any illness whatever, and then he appears to have been afflicted with nothing more serious than a brief, though unpleasant, bout with some viral adversary. Later, however, rheumatic pains were his frequent companion. At times he ached so badly that he could turn his head only with difficulty, and he complained that a continuous night's sleep was impossible, for he awakened in agony each time that he tossed and turned. During these years, too, Washington began to experience a gradual decline in his hearing, until by 1787 one overnight visitor at Mount Vernon was moved to exclaim that he believed the general was so deaf that he barely had heard the mealtime conversation. Washington's physical ills and the unmistakable signs of decline left him painfully aware that he was "descending the hill" he "had been 52 years climbing." So, too, did the occasional tidings of the demise of this or that Revolutionary comrade. The war had hardly ended, it seemed before he learned that General Greene was gone, taken at his retirement estate in Georgia, news that came in the wake of word that Joseph Reed, still in his early forties, also was dead. But more than anything, Washington knew that he "was of a short lived family."[40]

That many Washingtons died young was a maxim repeatedly demonstrated. George's father, Gus, had died while still in his forties. Lawrence had not reached even that age; while George's other half-brother, Augustine, had lived only forty-two years. In the 1780s two of these three younger brothers also died. Samuel, who had inherited a six-hundred-acre tract near Chotank, and who ultimately moved from the Tidewater to "Harewood," an estate he built on Evitts Run in present-day West Virginia, died of tuberculosis in 1781. Six years later John Augustine died at "Bushfield," the family home of his wife, on Nomini Bay overlooking the Potomac. Both died at the age of forty-seven.[41] Charles and Betty still were alive, however, and so was his mother.

Mary Ball Washington was seventy-eight years old when her son returned from the war. He had not seen her when he came to Virginia for the fight with Cornwallis in 1781, but he had been home only three weeks in 1784 before he rode to Fredericksburg for a visit, calling at the little one-story house he had acquired for her, in which she lived behind constantly shut and barred windows. It was a trip that he characterized as a "duty." A more apt description Washington never offered, for while he always honored her, he also remembered that extended contact between the two of them—both independent, strong-willed people—inevitably produced friction. As an adolescent he had escaped her presence at the first opportunity, and as a young man he took pains to be in her company only occasionally, and then for the shortest possible period. He did not see her at all between 1775 and 1781, but he certainly heard of her activities. As the war dragged on she repeatedly—and eventually publicly—pleaded for money; on at least nine occasions she badgered Lund for financial relief, altogether obtaining over £260, and she must have leaned even more heavily on Betty and John Augustine, who lived nearby. There also is evidence that she received handouts from some outside the family. "I never lived so pore in my life," she railed, her protestations finally becoming an acute embarrassment, especially when she additionally was moved to utter some remarks with Tory overtones. Some Virginia politician got the bright idea of shutting her up by providing her with a state pension, but when her son, the general, heard of it he immediately told the authorities to mind their own business. She "has an ample income of her own," he wrote from headquarters in 1781, and if she ever wanted he would divide his "last sixpence to relieve her from any *real* distress." But the commander shied away from confronting her; instead, he asked John Augustine "to represent to her in delicate terms the impropriety of her complaints."[42]

John evidently had little success in quieting her. In his first three years back at Mount Vernon, George paid her £50 out of pocket, yet early in 1787 she once again was begging outside the immediate family. George sent her fifteen guineas in hush money, accompanied by a long letter in which he claimed—none too convincingly—that he was giving her the last bit of cash in his possession. "This is really and truely" all my money, he wrote, adding that he would suffer for giving it to her as he was so deeply in debt. "I know not where or when, I shall receive one shilling with which to pay it," he added, but for good measure he told her that "whilst I have a shilling left, you shall have part, if it is wanted, whatever my own distress may be."

The solution to her woes, he went on, would be for her to sell her house in Fredericksburg and move in with one of her three children. Charles and Betty would be the best candidates, he added, for Mount Vernon, chronically overrun with visitors, was noisy and lacking in privacy. The revenue from the sale of her property would "answer all your wants and make ample amends" to Charles or Betty; "if it did not, I would most cheerfully contribute more," he concluded, not bothering to explain where, in his penurious state, he would find the funds. Within days of receiving his letter Mary Washington fell ill, stricken with cancer. She sank rapidly and in April 1787 her doctors believed her death was imminent. Washington hurried to see her, finding her already "reduced . . . to a Skeleton." But the disease evidently went into remission, and she lived for another thirty months, finally succumbing in September 1789. When her will was opened it revealed that she had left the lion's share of her estate to her favorite child, by then the President of the United States.[43]

When Washington cautioned his mother of the noise at Mount Vernon, he had not exaggerated. Although the Washingtons were childless, the mansion seemed to teem with young people. The grandchildren—three daughters and a son from Jackie's marriage to Nelly—seemed always to be present, even though their mother continued to live at her own home above Alexandria. Some doubted that Nelly ever would remarry, but Washington expected it, and, in fact, after waiting a suitable interval following her husband's death she began to attend balls, then to keep company with Dr. David Stuart, a Fairfax County physician. Early in 1784 the couple were married. Strangely, two of her children, five-year-old Eleanor Custis, or Nelly, and three-year-old George Washington Parke Custis, remained with their grandparents. They joined Harriet Washington, the daughter of George's brother Sam, who had come to live at Mount Vernon three years before. Subsequently two other nieces joined the Washingtons. Patty Dandridge, the daughter of Martha's brother, was taken in upon her father's death in 1785; and Burwell Bassett's daughter Frances—Fanny, everyone called her—moved in on Christmas Eve in 1784, sent there by her father who felt unable to care for her after his wife, Martha's sister, died. Besides, she was a sickly young girl, and her father hoped that Mount Vernon's proximity to the sea might rejuvenate her. Something did restore her health. Within four months of being transplanted to this clime she was engaged to George Augustine Washington, the general's nephew and assistant farm manager. That autumn the two were married, an unusual match in that she was the daughter of Martha's sister, he the son of George's brother.[44]

Fanny barely had moved in amidst the three younger, romping, boisterous children before still another newcomer settled in. Still saddled with the demands of a heavy correspondence a full year after his retirement, Washington quietly began to advertise for a clerical assistant. He wanted more than just an amanuensis, however. He wanted someone who also could "keep accounts; examine, arrange and properly methodize my papers. . . ; ride, at my expence, to do such business as I may have in different parts of this, or the other States," and tutor his two grandchildren who lived at Mount Vernon.[45]

That summer he hired a young Canadian, William Shaw, for the post, selecting him over Noah Webster, who had applied in person. Washington agreed to pay Shaw £50 per year, in addition to free room and board. The young man lasted the full year, a considerably longer period than his employer came to wish. He was not without talent, but, young and unsettled, he gave his work less than the full attention that Washington expected. The general groused and complained about his repeated absences due to jaunts to Alexandria, but, in fact, Shaw left Mount Vernon infrequently, only eight times in the last eight months of his tenure, and he remained away from the estate overnight on only one of these occasions. At any rate, when Washington noted without further comment that "Mr. Shaw quitted this family to day," there was an air of relief in his diary inscription.[46]

Whether Shaw knew it or not, about halfway through his tenure at Mount Vernon, Washington arranged to hire his successor. Before Shaw was retained Washington had asked General Lincoln to be on the lookout for someone suitable for the position. It took Lincoln nearly a year, but in January 1786 he wrote that he had located a young man with the "character of a Gentleman and a schooler." The man was Tobias Lear, twenty-four years old, a graduate of Harvard College, and recently returned from a year's travels in Europe. Washington hired him sight unseen, agreeing to pay him an annual salary of two hundred dollars, but stipulating that the appointment be renewed from year to year. Lear arrived three months before Shaw departed, and if it was an awkward arrangement for the young men, Washington seems only to have been delighted by Lincoln's judgment. An enterprising and indefatigable worker, Lear was just what Washington had been looking for, a responsible and trustworthy aide, one who—even more than Lund—could be counted on when the master of Mount Vernon was away.[47]

Not that Washington had any expectation of once again being away for an extended period—and certainly not for additional public service. Washington made no attempt to seek reelection to the House of Burgesses, and he was far too much the nationalist to find the governor's chair in Richmond to be very alluring. Never one to function too well in a corporate setting, he could not have looked upon a seat in the United States Congress with any enthusiasm, nor could he imagine any sort of crisis that might induce him "to draw my sword again." [48]

Still, Washington found the transition back to civilian pursuits to be difficult, inasmuch as he had spent many years listening to "the clangor of arms and the bustle of a camp." During his first several weeks at home letter after letter to former general officers and high public officials left Mount Vernon, each tinged with that aura of authority that had become his habit. He was home for nearly ten weeks before he even claimed that he was adapting to his prewar life style, and more than a year passed before he endeavored to speak with any enthusiasm about the "tranquility and rural amusements" of the pastoral life. He was determined, he said, "to make the remainder of my life easy, [and to] let the world or the affairs of it go as they may." His public life was over, he told Lafayette in 1784. "I have had my day." [49]

But he was having a difficult time convincing himself. Indeed, Washington faced a dilemma that stemmed in part from his public image. An adoring populace had come to see Washington as a modern Cincinnatus, equating him with the ancient legend of Cincinnatus, the Roman who was summoned from his plow to save his country. Having served and then surrendered his power, Washington, like the first Cincinnatus, perhaps felt compelled to remain at his plow. Yet Washington was less happy at Mount Vernon than many historians have realized. He missed the bustle and excitement and, certainly, the flattery and acclaim that had accompanied his public service. For a time he sought to find some of those same rewards in the attempt to remake Mount Vernon into a showplace; he tried so hard, in fact, that one visitor remarked that the general had paid more attention to turning the estate into an exposition than he had to simply enjoying the place. Next, he sought to "spend the remainder of my Days in cultivating the affections of good Men." There were drawbacks to that endeavor too. Still, Washington was reluctant to lay aside his plow. As Garry Wills discerned, he had a "heavy emotional investment in the symbol of his resignation." His was the ultimate act of the Revolution, the great virtuous gesture to accommodate republican idealism; whatever acclaim he had received for his military feats, he had drawn even more praise for his breathtaking act of having resigned his power in 1783. [50]

Thus, he could not abandon his vine and fig tree. Not unless danger lurked and he again was summoned from Mount Vernon. And by 1786 he was convinced that a critical period once again had dawned.

14

An End to Retirement

"There exists not a power to check"

Having "assisted in bringing the Ship into Port, and having been fairly discharged," Washington wrote about thirty months after returning to Mount Vernon, "it is not my business to embark again on a sea of troubles." Perhaps not, but that metaphorically studded sentence immediately followed a line in which he remarked that he could not "feel myself an unconcerned spectator" to public affairs.[1]

As he watched from the sidelines, Washington was most concerned by the jealousy between the states, a covetousness and mistrust which resulted in their refusal "to yield competent powers to . . . the Federal Government." Obviously, this was not a new concern. Through the war years he had repeatedly echoed these sentiments in private, while in his farewell remarks as commander in chief he had aired his views publicly. Yet once he returned home he really was a spectator. Removed from the day-to-day cares of office, the immediacy of the problem largely vanished for him, surfacing only infrequently in 1784 and 1785, principally when political decentralization threatened to adversely affect his interests. The simmering sectional rivalries, for instance, posed a constant menace to his Potomac navigation plans, and because, as he observed, he was "not so disinterested in this matter," he was moved to complain about the several states' "short sighted politics." The impotent central government's inability to compel Spain "to open the avenues of trade" in the transmontane region was another side to the same coin, for it impeded the flow of population into the West. Still, diverted by his own pursuits, and deeply content now that the war had ended victoriously, Washington betrayed no sense of the presence of an urgent national crisis during his first two years back at Mount Vernon. On into 1786 he remained confident that everything would be worked out. In fact, he predicted that America's lagging foreign trade eventually would compel the states—all Atlantic seaboard entities—to vest the central government with adequate powers in "all matters of common concern."[2]

During his first two years back in Virginia the only public matter in which Washington displayed much activity occurred during the tempest over the Society of the Cincinnati. Founded in 1783, the organization evidently was meant to be a fraternal order for former Revolutionary officers who had served for three years or who were in the army when the war ended; their brethren in the French officer corps also were eligible for membership. But among a people with an abiding distrust of standing armies, it probably was inevitable that some citizens would be apprehensive over such a federation. When the society limited future membership to certain descendants of the original initiates, protest was certain, for the former officers appeared to have created a blue-blooded aristocratic order. Nor were the critics mere cranks. Thomas Jefferson wrote Washington expressing his fear that if left intact the society ultimately would "produce an hereditary aristocracy which will change the form of our governments from the best to the worst in the world." Franklin voiced similar fears, and John Adams denounced the order as anti-egalitarian and as the perfect vehicle for saddling America someday with a military dictatorship.[3] By the spring of 1784 the society's existence had spawned a white-hot furor, the very sort of commotion that could besmirch the reputation of its president-general, George Washington.

The general was caught off guard by the uproar. He had endorsed the society with enthusiasm, seeing it as a harmless fraternal entity and as a vehicle for providing assistance to comrades who had fallen on hard times. He must also have relished the thought that at the society's meetings he would be "treated with . . . uncommon marks of attention and attachment," as he put it. His initial reaction to the public outcry against the society was merely to suggest that the people were ill informed. As public protest mounted, however, he contemplated reforms for the Cincinnati's charter. He journeyed to Philadelphia in the spring of 1784 to preside over the first convention of the organization, and once there he bluntly told the stunned membership that its charter needed to be drastically revised, specifying in particular that the "hereditary part in all its connexions, absolutely" must be discontinued. The national conference promptly rubber-stamped his proposals, but over the next two years several state chapters dragged their feet, and some adamantly refused to endorse his suggestions. Thereafter, Washington's position toward the society was ambivalent. He stopped wearing the order's eagle emblem, told its members that he would not again accept the presidency of the organizations, and announced that he would not attend their convention scheduled to be held in Philadelphia in 1787. The last pledge he kept, even though he was in the city attending the Constitutional Convention when the Cincinnati assembled. On the other hand, when the order reelected him as president he accepted the post and continued in office until his death.[4]

"Things cannot go on in the same train forever," Washington prophesied repeatedly during the summer and fall of 1786. This was a new refrain for Washington, one uttered with a sudden urgency. What he most feared was a counter-revolution staged by the "better kind of people." Already many "respectable characters speak of a monarchical form of Government without horror," he noted, perhaps remembering that in 1782 the head of the invalid corps in the Continental army had proposed that he, Washington, become the king of America. He thought a rebellion by the "minor part," the commonality, was less likely, but should such an insurgency occur it could snowball until its "weight is too great and irrestible to be stopped." Nevertheless, whether the unrest came from the right or the left, the result would be the same: chaos, then despotism, the very fate the Loyalists had foreseen when the Revolutionaries of 1776 had spoken of self-government.[5]

Whatever the Tories had predicted, the problem, as Washington saw it, arose neither from his countrymen's inherent inability to govern themselves nor from innate imperfections in republican governance. Disorder and tyranny were conceivable, he had concluded, because the constitution was flawed. Just as his army had been left nearly unarmed and certainly underfed by an impotent national government, now the same defect threatened stability, perhaps even the existence of the Union. Something must be done. His solution: "the reins of government [must] be braced and held with a steady hand, and every violation of the Constitution be . . . amended."

Washington was prone to hyperbole. For years he had argued incessantly that without reform the war could not be won, yet victory had been secured; in 1784 and 1785 he had warned of fiscal anarchy, but by 1786 economic recovery was in the air and his own state again was exporting as much tobacco as it had on the eve of its Townshend Duty boycott in 1769. From time to time, too, he had seemed forlorn about national affairs, but his tone in 1786 was new. Before he had seen the national government's weakness only as a potential future menace to the public weal. In 1786 he came to see the crisis as real and present.[6]

Others also believed that a serious crisis was at hand. The central government remained too weak to remove British troops from the string of old royal forts that guarded the wilderness frontier, installations through which arms allegedly continued to flow to the Native Americans and from which British traders supposedly monopolized the northwestern fur trade. Nor could the United States do anything to coerce Spain into opening the Mississippi River to the commerce of America's western farmers, without which these yeomen could not rise above a subsistence level. If Britain and Spain could not be brought to terms, moreover, few husbandrymen would hazard a move across the mountains, a fact that would do nothing for land speculators who hoped to sell frontier acreage, nor would it aid the nation's burgeoning manufacturering class, who dreamed of selling their wares to prosperous sodbusters in the Ohio Valley and beyond. In fact, without access to the Mississippi the United States probably could not even retain the West, for as Washington reported upon his return from western Pennsylvania in 1784 "the touch of a feather, would turn" those who already had settled in the West into the arms of Spain.[7]

However, it was the United States' commercial difficulties with Great Britain that instigated the first concrete step toward real constitutional change. Some American leaders evidently had expected that the War for Independence soon would be followed by a treaty of commerce between the two former belligerents. Great Britain had other ideas. While it dumped huge quantities of goods on the American market, Whitehall also enacted a series of navigation acts that prohibited trade between its West Indian colonies and the United States. As Congress had no power to regulate trade, the new nation had no way of fighting back, with the consequence that between 1783 and 1789 America's annual sales to Britain were only about 50 percent of what they had been during the last six years before the war. Of course, Britain was not the only nation with ports. The United States continued the commerce with France that had begun in 1788, business that resulted in a felicitous balance of trade for the new nation, despite a disappointing traffic with the French West Indies. The high seas also witnessed a brisk, though diminutive, commerce between American merchants and their counterparts in the Netherlands, Prussia, Sweden, and even China. Virginia was one of the states that seemed to do all right; by 1790 one-third again as much tonnage was clearing its ports each year as had been the case on the eve of the Revolution. Still, some men wanted even more, something that would not be realized while the national government was too weak to offer much help.[8]

Since 1784 some in Congress had sought to augment the national government's commercial powers. Their plan was to amend the Articles of Confederation so that Congress might impose duties on imports and exports, a step that might bludgeon Great Britain into countenancing a freer trade with the United States. But southern opposition foiled the plan, for many great planters fretted lest a northern-dominated Congress might use its new power to slap imposts on rice and tobacco exports.[9]

Amid whispers of northern secession, the issue from time to time bobbed to the surface in Congress, but without resolution.[10] Two occurrences in the second half of 1786, however, changed that.

The Mississippi question flared up again that summer, ignited when Spain sent an envoy to the United States to discuss opening commercial relations between the two countries. But trade was of secondary importance to Madrid, inasmuch as it would agree to a treaty of commerce only if the United States relinquished its claim to free navigation of the Mississippi River. The northern maritime states were willing to embrace such a deal. The South, however, feared that the loss of the Mississippi would trigger secessionist movements all along the frontier, propelling the inhabitants of the West into the arms of the Spanish, or even back under the aegis of Great Britain. In addition, the South knew that the loss of the West would insure northeastern hegemony in the diminutive confederation of states east of the mountains. In the end nothing was resolved, for the North lacked the votes to ratify such a treaty. But this rancorous battle clearly demonstrated that without sectional compromise the Union was in great peril.[11]

Only weeks after this imbroglio a violent outburst occurred in Massachusetts. The ink was hardly dry on the Treaty of Paris before it was obvious that many farmers in New England faced a more sinister foe that King George's regiments ever could have been. Hard times ushered in by the postwar depression soon left many farmers deeply in debt. From time to time in 1784 and 1785 farmers in the Bay State collectively beseeched their elected officials to inflate the currency and to reduce taxes. The creditors that ran the state acted otherwise, of course, and by harvest time in 1786 the court dockets in the hinterland counties had begun to groan under foreclosure cases. Hardened by war and infused with the Revolution's spirit of activism, farmers gathered in county seats to prevent courts from sitting. In Springfield their leader was Daniel Shays, a farm boy who had risen to the rank of captain in the late war and who now marched his "company" in front of the courthouse. For three months or so the farmers were amazingly successful, often intimidating magistrates into not convening courts, seeing that impartial jurors could not be found, convincing the local militia units that it would be unwise to try to enforce the law. Then Massachusetts acted. It raised an army of four thousand men, and sent them west under General Benjamin Lincoln. The general had far better luck against the "army" of cold, hungry, and thoroughly terrified yeomen than he had experienced at Charleston in 1780, and by February 1787 the dissenters were in flight or in jail.[12] Less than a month after Massachusetts crushed the rebellion, Congress approved a national convention to reform the Articles of Confederation.

The call for that national conclave first had been issued in September 1786 by the Annapolis Convention, a parley that Virginia had urged to treat commercial problems. Only five states had sent delegates, but the small gathering in Annapolis issued a call for a convention to meet in Philadelphia in May, a conference that might recommend those changes "as shall appear . . . necessary to render the constitution of the Federal Government adequate to the exigencies of the Union." [13]

Congress received the address in October, but it took no action until early in 1787. By then Shays's Rebellion had created alarm in some circles well beyond Massachusetts, and several states had elected delegates to the proposed convention. Virginia was one of those states. In the fall it had chosen a seven-man delegation to go to Philadelphia. George Washington's name was at the top of its list.[14]

Before the fall of 1786 Washington had consistently regarded the weaknesses of the national government only as a source of possible future trouble. Throughout this period he had consistently depicted domestic America in idyllic terms. Tranquility prevailed, he wrote, and "justice is well adminstered; robbery, violence or murder is not heard of from New Hampshire to Georgia"; moreover, prosperity was returning and the "ravages of war are repaired." Besides, "our internal Governments are daily acquiring strength" and are "tolerably well administered." In time, he went on, the impotence of the national government would be corrected. "Democratical States must always *feel* before they can *see*," he reflected; "it is this that makes their Government slow, but the people will be right at last." [15] But as news of Shays's Rebellion trickled down to Mount Vernon, mostly related in frenzied tones by Henry Knox and David Humphries, the general's outlook changed. Both men painted the most lurid picture of events in

Massachusetts, leading Washington to believe that "a formidable rebellion against reason [and] the principles of all government" was under way. In one breath Knox depicted the "desperate and unprincipled men" under Shays as levelers, in the next, incongruously, he suggested that they might even wish to "return [America] to great Britain." Whichever was the case, it was his conclusion that because of the Shaysites "we are forced to see our national humiliation." Each of these old comrades told Washington that the upheaval arose from the same malady. In the absence of a strong central government, a "licencious spirit" had seized the people. "The machine works miserably," said Knox. Either there is change, intoned Humphreys, or "we cannot remain as a nation much longer. . . ." [16]

"Good God!" Washington wailed. Maybe the Tories had been correct about the Revolution. He feared that a "critical moment" had arrived. Perhaps "we are fast verging to anarchy and confusion," he conjectured. What was it about the activism of the Massachusetts farmers that so alarmed Washington? Thanks to Knox—whose descriptions of the conduct of the Shaysites he quoted in his correspondence to others, something he was not in the habit of doing—Washington worked himself into a lather over the report that these dissenters regarded the lands of America "to be the *common property* of all." The seeming inability of Massachusetts to protect realty, and the certainty that the infirm national government could not be relied on for assistance in such an emergency, also frightened him. "If there exists not a power to check" these "desperate characters," he asked, what "security has a man for life, liberty, or property." [17]

But Washington had more than property rights on his mind. His very identity was interlaced with the existence of the new nation, and in a moment of candor he acknowledged that the "end of Foederal union . . . would be a disagreeable circumstance . . . [and] particularly so for a person in my situation." This man, whose search for renown had been the central business of his life, had achieved his self-esteem in the course of years of travail and sacrifice to create the nation. In the four corners of the land his birthday was celebrated; like a patron saint he already was regarded as the father of the new nation. Visitors filed up to his estate as if it were a holy shrine. On patriotic holidays his name was hallowed above all others. But now the Union was imperiled, and if it ceased to exist his achievements inevitably would be forgotten, a relic of the ancient past, as forgotten as the memory of the short-lived nation he had helped to create. Unable to envision himself apart from the nation, he saw disunion as death. It was akin to a virulent, fatal storm that "enveloped in darkness" all that it touched; it was to be "so fallen! so lost!" Disunion would "bury us"; worse, it would be an insult and a disgrace. [18]

Washington's concerns, however, hardly were limited to matters of self-esteem. He was one of the oldest and most persistent critics of the Articles's shortcomings, first decrying the national government's weaknesses about thirty months before the war ended. But it took the Shaysite disorders and the simultaneous sectional split of the Mississippi question to convert him from a concerned optimist into an alarmed and anguished pessimist, for the one crisis threatened chaos and anarchy while the other posed a threat to the Union itself. The solution, he thought, must be the establishment of a strong central government. Only such a polity could maintain order and protect property, and only such a government could hope to force Britain's withdrawal from the West while it pressured Spain into opening the Mississippi, the steps necessary to prevent the Union from foundering over the sectional discord wrought by rival trans-Appalachian interests.[19]

Almost to a person those men whom Washington most admired were among the noisiest proponents of constitutional change. Generals Sullivan and Knox, David Humphreys and Henry Lee, and especially Hamilton, the Morrises, and young James Madison had been preaching for a stronger central government for years. Their activism may have influenced Washington, and their ideological reservations about the Articles of Confederation may have helped shape his views.

Within that circle some had come to despair for republicanism. Some feared that America's Revolutionary virtues, particularly the ideal of noble, selfless sacrifice which had enthralled the public in 1775, had disappeared, rendering republicanism unsuitable for the new nation; others believed republicanism to be a form of government unworkable in a huge country such as America, a nation whose sprawl encompassed faction upon faction. Most, however, thought the problem was more mechanical. The new government must be a republican government, said Henry Knox, but the polity must be "modified and wrought together" in such a manner as to be "durable & efficient." Many concluded that the problem had arisen because the Revolution had gone too far. The revulsion sparked by the English monarch and his royal governors had led the early revolutionaries to attenuate the executive authority throughout America, to make its legislative bodies too strong, to render its judiciaries too dependent on momentary popular whim, to leave its central government virtually powerless. By 1786 and 1787 voices increasingly were heard that called for a rigorous separation of powers at the national level, for bicameralism, for an independent judiciary, and for a more powerful executive official. Could the convention in Philadelphia accomplish all this? No, said Knox, who saw the meeting as but "a stage in the business" of altering the Articles of Confederation. But the step must be taken, he told Washington. "To attempt less will be to hazard the existence of republicanism, and to subject us either to a division of the European powers, or to a despotism arising from high handed commotions." His next prediction was even more chilling. The meeting in Philadelphia was the nationalists' last hope for bloodless change. Washington's friends, therefore, envisioned the Philadelphia convention as the first step toward ending the American Revolution. They proposed nothing less than constitutional alterations that were designed to save the Revolution from itself. Washington agreed with their prescription, and he viewed the changes they advanced as "radical cures," as revolutionary—or, perhaps, counterrevolutionary—in their own right, something he could not countenance before the events of late 1786.[20]

Washington's friends had not troubled to invite him to the Annapolis Convention, but sensing that the Philadelphia meeting in all likelihood would be their last hope for success the extreme nationalists wanted Washington's prestige added to the conclave. After all, as an Englishmen who toured the States that year noted about Washington, "the people have no confidence in any other man." Besides, the nationalists knew that Washington shared their convictions. The only problem was that for four months following his election to the Virginia delegation, General Washington disclaimed any intention of attending the meeting. His hesitancy did not stem from any quarrel over amending the Articles, for now he was convinced that "the superstructure we have been seven years raising . . . must fall" unless "some alteration in our political creed" was fashioned.[21] Why then was Washington so reluctant to be a part of the convention?

He attributed his temporizing to the fact that he had fibbed himself into an embarrassing corner. In declining to attend the meeting of the Cincinnati set for May in Philadelphia, he had pleaded that the demands of his business would not permit a prolonged absence. To attend the constitutional conclave would expose him. But other factors also weighed on his mind. If this meeting was poorly attended and resulted in a fiasco as had its predecessor at Annapolis, Washington would appear a fool. If the movement for constitutional reform failed, his reputation would suffer for having embraced an unpopular cause. "I should not like to be a sharer in this business," he said. Of even greater importance, however, was his concern about the legality of the Philadelphia meeting. John Jay, in fact, had confessed to Washington that the legitimacy of the convention was "questionable," that is, illegal; moreover, the general knew that Patrick Henry had announced that he would not attend allegedly because he "smelt a rat." While the Articles were vague about the lawful amending process, Washington had good reason for wondering about the origin of the proposed meeting, inasmuch as it had been called by the Annapolis Convention, itself an unofficial gathering of men from fewer than one-half the states. What is clear is that Washington worried that the Philadelphia convention might be illicit business. "A Convention so holden," he said in an oddly quaint manner, "may not be legal." Neither the importunings of Madison nor those of Governor Edmund Randolph, not to mention the pleas of various legislators, could budge him. Only in the final week of March, barely six weeks before the meeting was to start, did he consent to attend, his change of heart coming only forty-eight hours after he learned that Congress had approved the meeting.[22]

When Washington left the army he believed his public service was at an end. He doubtless hoped it was, too, for crowned with glory he aspired to fill the role of Cincinnatus. Now he must have looked with mixed emotion on being swept "back into the tide of public affairs." A man of Washington's temperament had to be elated at his countrymen's summons, and the prospect of an exciting respite from retirement must also have been alluring. Yet against those gains he had to weigh the potential risks to his reputation, not to mention the danger his absence might pose for his business concerns. Nor could he have been human had he not wondered if the Philadelphia meeting was not but the first step in a renewed round of public service. He was aware of the talk of creating a separate executive official; presuming the reformers succeeded, could he not have wondered who might be selected to hold that office?[23]

Washington was late setting out for Philadelphia. On the eve of his planned departure late in April word arrived of his mother's serious illness. He rushed to her bedside in Fredericksburg. Still later heavy rains forced him to postpone his journey, but just after sunrise on May 9 his carriage pulled away from Mount Vernon. His apprehension at leaving must have been considerable, and, indeed, before that day ended he had been seized by a violent headache, symtomatic perhaps of a severe case of raw nerves. As Martha had become "too domestic, and too attentive to two little Grand Children" to tear herself away, the general rode alone—that is, with only his customary retinue of body servants and coachmen—for most of the journey, a bumpy, lonely, five-day trek. Only on the fourth day was the monotony broken, for near Head of Elk he ran into an acquaintance, a Virginia planter-legislator en route to Philadelphia on private business, and the two men continued on together over the final forty or so miles. Along the way Washington spent two evenings at the residences of friends and two others in inns; on the 13th, punctual as usual, for the Convention was slated to begin the next morning, he rode on in from Wilmington. Philadelphia rolled out the red carpet for him. At the Schuylkill he was met by the city's light horse and artillery companies and escorted across the river, crossing on a bridge constructed by the British during their occupation in 1777–78. Late in the afternoon he reached Philadelphia, where tolling bells announced his arrival and a cheering throng along the sidewalks ecstatically greeted him.[24]

The general may have been prompt, but few other delegates were so inclined. In fact, aside from some of the host state's representatives, only one other delegate was in town. James Madison had arrived more than a week earlier, left with nothing to do but stew and fret that this conclave surely would end as had its predecessor unless the representatives came quickly. Washington seemed more annoyed than worried by the lack of delegates, although as day after day passed without a quorum he, too, became concerned. Nevertheless, unlike Madison he managed to enjoy himself while he waited. He lodged with Robert Morris's family, often dining with them in "a family way," and once escorting the financier's wife, Mary White, to a charity lecture on eloquence; when he did not dine with the Morrises during his first nights in Philadelphia, he usually was entertained by some other locally prominent person. Franklin was his host one evening; John Penn, the grandson of the founder of Pennsylvania, another; on subsequent nights Jared Ingersoll, the son of a Connecticut Tory, Dr. John Ross, a former Continental army doctor, now a Philadelphia physician, and Thomas Willing, the mercantile magnate, entertained the famous general. One evening he attended a wedding reception, and one Sunday he worshipped at a Roman Catholic mass; on the 23rd he accepted a gracious invitation to breakfast at the residence of Governor Thomas Mifflin, whose complicity in the "Conway Cabal" he had suspected in 1778. Almost daily during this interim delegates arrived in town, until, finally, on May 25 seven states—a majority—were represented. That morning twenty-nine delegates (only one of which was from New England) sloshed through cool spring showers to the Pennsylvania State House, where they brought themselves to order and proceeded to organize. Their initial act of substance was to elect a presiding officer, and in the very room where a dozen years earlier he had been chosen to command the Continental army, Washington, to no one's great surprise, was elected without a dissenting vote.[25]

Washington had come expecting a long meeting, but he probably never dreamed that this conclave would drag on for four tedious months. With the exception of a ten-day hiatus late in July, the delegates worked almost every day, Monday through Saturday, usually from early morning until 4:00 P.M., throughout that hot, sticky summer. Typically, much of the work was done in committee, and a considerable amount of buttonholing and politicking took place around dinner tables or from roughhewn tavern benches. Three days after the Convention began nine more delegates had arrived, and the remainder trickled in during the next two weeks. Eventually fifty-five men from every state but Rhode Island surfaced at the meeting. Twenty-nine were there from the first session to the last, while ten others were in town for all but a few days that summer; on the other hand, a dozen delegates missed 50 percent or more of the sessions, and four men attended so infrequently that they were hardly worthy of being considered working members. Three representatives who had been elected and agreed to attend never arrived. On any given day about thirty delegates bothered to get out of bed and stroll down to the State House, there to meet in the tall-ceilinged, richly paneled little chamber where so much history had been made since the time of that fateful morning at Lexington and Concord a bit more than a decade before. Washington was one of those who attended regularly, not missing a single session between May and September.[26]

The delegates to this Convention would not have been looked upon by their contemporaries as typical or commonplace Americans. None was poor. Without question at least ten were very rich, and only a quibbler would have argued that another fifteen or so were anything but wealthy men. Virtually all the others, save for four or five men of quite modest standing, two of whom hovered at the edge of insolvency, would have been classed by the general population as men of means. Nineteen delegates were slaveowners, their holdings varying from those who possessed two or three domestic slaves to the two hundred or more slaves owned by each of two South Carolinians. Thirty-four men were lawyers, sixteen were planters, two were more modest farmers, fifteen were engaged in some form of mercantile activity, two were physicians, and three have been classed as pensioners. Just over half the men owned public securities, but their investments ranged from Elbridge Gerry's $50,000 down to David Brearly's $15. (Washington still owned $500 in securities, though their actual value in 1787 was only about $75.) Twelve men were creditors in the sense that they had invested in banking capital; three had investments in manufacturing; twelve were land speculators.[27]

At age fifty-five Washington was an elder among these men. The average age was forty-three, a fact that suggested that most of the delegates had come of age during the years of the colonial protest and rebellion. As a result many had served the national government far more than their state government, leading them almost inevitably toward a nationalistic inclination. Three had served in the Stamp Act Congress twenty-two years before, forty-two had sat in Congress—where eight had signed the Declaration of Independence—and thirty had borne arms in the War of independence, ten for enough years to be considered real warriors, not "summer soldiers." In an age when only about 1 percent of the male population attended college, twenty-five of these men were college graduates (eight were from Princeton alone), and six had completed post-graduate degrees, mostly by studying abroad.[28]

Whether their political views differed from those of the "common man" is a matter that has divided scholars. On one count their ideas certainly were different. Virtually every one of the delegates thought America was in crisis, and, in fact, as historian Forrest McDonald has observed, this was "a critical moment . . . for the United States as United States."[29] Not all their countrymen would have agreed that the United States was worth saving, but quite obviously the men who came to this Convention believed the salvation of the Union was in their interest.

Washington always thought of political activists in terms of the interests they represented, and his correspondence is studded with references to the "financial interest," the "mercantile interests," the "local interest," the "interested views of desperate characters," the "minor part" and the "better kind of people," "men of consequence" as well as those who were "actuated by ambitious motives," and, finally, among the varied "classes of people" he discerned the "self-interested designing disaffected." With such an outlook he would have had far less difficulty than have some historians in seeing this Convention as a assemblage of various interest groups intent on altering the national charter in such a way as to protect and further their own factional considerations. Indeed, he ultimately characterized the delegates as representing a "diversity of interests." In one sense there was only one interest group here: private property owners from the most privileged economic stratum. But within that class there were subspecies, men whose concerns ranged from exporting to importing, from large-scale farming to manufacturing to mercantile endeavors, from slaveholding to nonslaveholding, and from land speculation to investments in securities and other negotiables. And since each man was part of a state delegation, consideration had to be given to the state's size and its well-being.[30]

Whatever their interest almost everyone at the Convention shared certain ideas. Views about government were derived from the colonial experience, from the successes and failures of writing state constitutions, and from both the pens of Europe's great minds and the rich vein of political theory composed by American activists over the past twenty years. In the abstract all believed it essential to protect minorities from majorities; there was absolutely unanimous agreement on the necessity of securing private property. Almost everyone also would have agreed with Edmund Randolph, the governor of Virginia, who opened the Convention by proclaiming that the "chief danger arises from the democratic parts" of the state constitutions. That "chief danger," it went unsaid, was the menace to the man of wealth; his private property, as well as his pursuit of additional riches through the channels of finance, commerce, and foreign and western policy, was jeopardized because the "democracy," the mass of the citizenry, was not sufficiently restrained. The state constitutions had failed to "provide . . . sufficient checks," Randolph had suggested, and, given the enfeebled nature of the Articles government, the states were virtually sovereign. A year earlier Washington had said more or less the same thing when he had remarked that "we have probably had too good an opinion of human nature in forming our confederation." [31] Checks were needed because it was human nature to act according to selfish interests.

Unanimity disappeared, however, when it came to discovering a solution to these woes, although a majority of the delegates generally agreed with the notion of still another Virginian, James Madison. The national government, he said, must be "clearly paramount" over the states, which, in turn, should be left in a "subordinately useful" position, whatever that meant. Certainly Washington agreed with that view, even though he might have been struck by the irony of events. Thirteen years before, while attending the First Continental Congress, he had heard Joseph Galloway tell the legislators the same thing, only then he had voted against such a concept. Of course Galloway was speaking of the necessity for having a sovereign government within the British Empire. Now Washington and his young friend in the Virginia delegation were expressing the same general philosophy as Tory Galloway, who now resided in impecunious straits in exile far away in London.[32]

If unanimity was absent from this chamber, greed and idealism comingled, enough to keep the meeting going until these men had produced what one scholar called "a virtual revolution in American politics," a revolution to save a revolution by preventing a revolution. These men realized that the American Revolution had unleashed profound—and unexpected—change. New men, often from previously unrepresented strata of society, were in power, or they were jostling for influence. Some had succeeded the vanquished Loyalists; others were thrust into prominence when elections became commonplace, or when the electorate was expanded, or when legislatures were enlarged. Change—and its constant companion, uncertainty—also flowed from the Revolution's disruption of established trade patterns, as well as from the fiscal chaos and the profiteering that accompanied the war and its immediate aftermath. Like an undertow that drags an unsuspecting swimmer deeper into danger, the Revolution, it now was held in some circles, unwittingly had deposited power "into the Hands of those whose ability or situation in Life does not intitle them to it." Social chaos was the result, a menace that threatened total anarchy—and with it the very extirpation of the Revolution. Thus, the men of the Convention saw their mission as nothing less than the preservation of the American Revolution. They would create a continental republic, one in which republicanism could be saved from itself.[33]

Washington, too, feared that this Convention might be the last hope of the Revolution, and he likewise thought "radical cures" were necessary in order to save the liberties and opportunities won by independence. But his views differed from those of many delegates. A near victim of Hamilton's and "the financier's" machinations while at the Newburgh cantonment, he was almost as suspicious of their motives as he was fearful of the Shaysites and other "incendiaries." He had heard and alluded to the suggestions of men in august circles who speculated that America required a monarchical government, an expedient that he found as displeasing as the leveling ideas of Massachusetts's protesting yeomen; what other designs of "wickedness" were harbored by some reformers he could only guess at. Eight years as commander in chief had left him with a cynical view of America's "boasted virtue." His countrymen—regardless of their economic class—were no more virtuous than men from the Old World; all men, he believed, were actuated by selfish interests. Unlike some of his colleagues, however, he did not conclude from this that republicanism could not work. Instead, the conclusion he reached was that a system of curbs and counterchecks was necessary—a central government composed of several branches, a national government indisputably sovereign over the states.

As was his custom in such a body, Washington was reluctant to speak out during the Convention's wearying sessions. In fact, he addressed only one issue. At the conclave's final meeting he announced his belief that members of the lower house should represent thirty thousand inhabitants, not forty thousand as the delegates earlier had agreed. (The delegates immediately reversed themselves and accepted his suggestion.) What role, if any, Washington played "out of doors" is not clear, but as he believed that "his situation [as presiding officer] . . . restricted him from offering his sentiments" indoors, he probably engaged in little if any politicking in the evening. He obviously felt ill suited for such behavior, and besides there was no real need for him to assume such a role. On the third day of the Convention, Governor Edmund Randolph introduced the Virginia Plan, a scheme prepared by Madison that called for far more than mere amendments to the Articles. Madison's idea was to draft a new constitution, one that would provide for a sovereign national government that included executive, judicial, and bicameral legislative branches. Manifestly, Washington agreed with the basic outline of the Virginia Plan. Moreover, as the next four months largely were spent in debating and amending that scheme, and as Madison was more than equal to marshalling a defense of his own design, there was little cause for Washington to enter the debates.[34]

Washington did little but listen and occasionally gavel querulous delegates to order. And there were enough differences among these men to produce rancorous moments. Big-state interests clashed with small-state concerns, slaveowners collided with those who owned no chattel, and there were differences over such issues as taxation and representation. But the amount of bickering has been overstated. As historian Edmund S. Morgan has observed, there "was never any serious doubt about the main features" of the Virginia Plan. Various interest groups battled over the details of Madison's scheme, but in the end expediency and the delegates' shared concerns led them into one compromise after another.[35]

The daily immobility brought on by these long, tedious sessions must ultimately have made the Convention an ordeal to a man of action such as Washington. Still he was careful to get his daily exercise, and his social calender was booked as solidly as it would have been at Mount Vernon. He began each day with his customary horseback ride, but by mid-morning he was at his desk in the State House, there to face a meeting that never lasted fewer than five hours and often exceeded six or even seven hours. Throughout the summer he dined out several evenings each week, sometimes in the company of other delegates at a local tavern, and once with the members attending the Society of Cincinnati gathering. Usually, however, he was a dinner guest in the home of some Philadelphia notable, occasions when he must have been offered a sumptuous repast in comparison to the customarily Spartan evening meals served at Mount Vernon. On at least five occasions he ventured into Philadelphia's balmy nights to attend plays or concerts, and he often filled his free time with sightseeing forays. On two occasions he visited the botanical gardens of William Bartram, the famed naturalist, and once he slipped out of town to call on a farmer renowned in those parts for his innovative use of fertilizers in the production of wheat. He dropped in on the "Anatomical Museum" of wax figures operated by the surgeon Abraham Chovet; he looked in Charles Willson Peale's partly completed museum that opened during the Convention (where, perhaps, he saw the stuffed and mounted pheasants he had sent the artist); and he attended a demonstration of Franklin's newest invention, the "mangle," a clothes-press. A nostalgic Washington once rode out to examine the battlefield at Germantown, a visit that came on the heels of a junket to White Marsh, where his army had camped in that dismal late autumn of 1777. During the ten-day adjournment that began late in July, Washington departed with Robert Morris on a fishing excursion that led them to the vicinities of Trenton and Valley Forge. Morris seems to have been the more interested of the two in the angling endeavors, for Washington excused himself to make side trips to the two historical sites. Whatever he expected to find, his laconic diary entry while at Valley Forge betrayed a feeling of melancholy, for he discovered that his former cantonment was "in Ruins" and overgrown with weeds.[36]

As always on a trip to the big city Washington was an extraordinary consumer. In addition to razors and hair ribbons, soap, powder, and powder puffs, he purchased a leather chair and even a dog while in Philadelphia. As is the lot of the traveler in every age, he had to pay for services that the homebody takes for granted. Among other things he paid for his baths, which he took but once a week.[37]

For weeks before leaving home Washington had been tormented by a painful rheumatic condition, and until the very eve of his trip he had worn a sling to alleviate the distress. But if he worried about suffering from that or some other affliction while he was away from the care of his family and his customary physician, he need not have concerned himself. By the time he got to Philadelphia his rheumatism was "much abated" and did not interfere with his physical activities. Certainly it was inclination, not health, that dictated his Sunday schedules. He attended church services on only two of his eighteen Sundays in Philadelphia, and not at all between June 17 and his departure on September 18. Mostly he relaxed at Morris's residence on Sundays, though that was the day he usually devoted to keeping abreast of his correspondence. Some of his free time was given to Charles Willson Peale, who asked to be permitted to make a mezzotint of this famous man. Peale had hopes that a Washington picture would sell like hotcakes, lifting him out of debt; instead, it sold so poorly that he had to cut the purchase price by one-third to find a market for still another depiction of the general. It may have been just as well, as his 1787 representation of Washington was in all probability not a very good likeness. Peale always seemed to have difficulty with this man. George Washington Parke Custis, who lived with the general during the last half dozen years of the decade, generally did not fancy Peale's renditions of his renowned stepgrandfather, and even the artist's son, Rembrandt Peale, criticized some of his father's work on Washington. The Washington of this instance seems marred by a misrepresentation of his eyes; the general's eyes are made to exude a soft, merry, pleasing quality, a characterization that does not tally with what other portraitists or eyewitnesses saw in this man.[38]

"The Constitution that is submitted is not free from imperfections," Washington acknowledged at the end of the Convention's work. He was just as certain that its defects could not be attributed to hasty or reckless craftsmanship. For about fifteen weeks Washington watched and listened as his fellow delegates hammered out the document. Early on they agreed to write a new constitution, not merely to amend the Articles, the "sole and express purpose" for which they had been sent to Philadelphia. Thereafter, working in secrecy, these men argued and bargained and compromised until they had a completed document. As historian Merrill Jensen has written, three broad groups slugged it out during these weeks. One group, with which Washington undoubtedly sympathized, favored a powerful national government freed of all state controls, a polity that would include a strong executive official; at the opposite extreme were those who wished to strengthen the national government, but to do so without undercutting the states or totally destroying the Articles of Confederation. Between the poles was the largest group, a faction that possessed the votes to determine the outcome. These men favored a strong central government, but one whose powers—and limits—would be defined, a polity divided into separate legislative, executive, and judicial branches. Above all, they believed the new government must have powers that the government under the Articles had never dreamed of possessing. It must be capable of regulating foreign and domestic commerce, raising revenues, suppressing rebellions, and when so requested by state legislatures of intervening to subdue local insurrections. They also longed for an extraordinarily powerful president, a chief executive who would boast a degree of authority and power held by no other comparable constitutional figure in America since royal officialdom had been turned out in 1775–76, an office of such potential magnitude that some delegates even worried that it was but the "foetus of a monarchy." [39]

If philosophical divisions over sovereignty and state power, over executive and legislative puissance, divided these delegates, so did economic considerations between the various sections. Until those matters of jarring contention were resolved the document could not be completed. To some degree the Convention proceeded in two phases. During the initial two months the delegates sought to determine the powers of the national government and its several branches; after the late July recess the Convention wrestled with the issues of sectionalism. Not surprisingly the result was a series of compromises. The South secured protection against outside interference with slavery, a ban on Congress's power to levy export duties, and the easy admission of new western states on an equal footing with the original states. The commercial states obtained the right to levy navigation acts by a simple majority vote. [40]

Washington had to have been happy with the work of the Convention, but he took his vow of secrecy so seriously that he refused to record his thoughts even in his diary. During the long meeting he wrote only one letter in which he commented on the progress of constitution making, a missive to Hamilton six weeks into the conclave in which he despaired for the chances of erecting a "strong and energetic [central] government." Yet when the work was at an end he gazed upon a document that called for the very sort of central government he long had hoped to see. Some provisions would "never . . . obtain my *cordial* approbation," he told an acquaintance, yet "in the aggregate, it is the best Constitution that can be obtained." [41]

Of all the components of this document Washington must have watched most closely as the office of chief executive was pieced together. Whatever else happened, Benjamin Franklin remarked during the first week of the Convention, "the first man put at the helm [as president] will be a good one." No one required a translator to understand that he meant that the initial president was certain to be George Washington. Indeed, one delegate later even claimed that the office was designed with Washington in mind. Many "members cast their eyes toward

George Washington at the time of the Constitutional Convention, by Charles Willson Peale (1787). Courtesy of the Pennsylvania Academy of the Fine Arts, Joseph and Sarah Harrison Collection.

General Washington as President," Pierce Butler of South Carolina reflected, "and shaped their ideas of the powers to be given to a President, by their opinions of his virtue." [42]

The presidency came together in stages. The Virginia Plan proposed an executive elected by the national legislature to serve one fixed term and possessed of "general authority" to administer the laws. By mid-June the Convention had agreed to an executive elected by Congress to serve one seven-year term, and to be ineligible for reelection. The New Jersey Plan introduced on June 15 recommended a plural executive. It got nowhere. Nor did Hamilton and the Morrises, among others, who—with Washington in mind—sought tenure for life, as well as an absolute veto, for the president. By early August the Convention had decided that the executive should be elected independently of Congress and that the president should be eligible for reelection to a six-year term. Moreover, it had decided that the chief executive would have broad powers with which to enforce the law, considerable appointive capacities, the lead role in the making of foreign policy, and command of the nation's armed forces. All that was left was a little tinkering. The president's term eventually was reduced to four years, and the contrivance known as the Electoral College was created for the election of the chief executive. [43]

Three and one-half months after it began the Convention appointed a committee of style to spruce things up in a clean, final draft, and when it reported on September 12 only four days were required for the delegates to comb through the committee's report. The last day business ran on until 6:00 P.M., later than any other session all summer, but it was a Saturday and everyone was anxious to get home. When work was completed that day all that remained was for the document to be engrossed and for the delegates to cast their final vote for acceptance or rejection. On Sunday Washington tended to his correspondence, and in one remarkably candid letter he offered a clue to the private motives that had combined with his nationalistic concerns to bring him to Philadelphia. He instructed his land agent in western Pennsylvania not to sell his property for a meager two dollars per acre, advising that if the new constitution was ratified he had "no doubt of obtaining the price I have fixed on the land, and that in a short time." (He was correct. He eventually sold the land for more than seven dollars an acre.) Monday morning the Convention met for the final time. It was a brief session, one highlighted by Washington's sole utterance during the entire meeting, as well as by the unanimous vote of the states in favor of the document. But if all the states approved the constitution, unanimity was lacking among the delegates. Both Governor Randolph and George Mason refused to sign the document, acts of protest in which Elbridge Gerry of Massachusetts also participated. Nevertheless, each state delegation had given its approval. The charter was ready to be sent to the states for their consideration. While the men were gathering their papers for the last time, Franklin, typically, got in the final word. Throughout those often tiresome weeks, he said, he had puzzled over the painting of the sun which adorned the back of the chair occupied daily by Washington; at last, the old sage went on, he happily knew "that it is a rising and not a setting sun." With that, the meeting ended.[44]

That evening a somber Washington kept to himself in his chambers, "meditat[ing] on the momentous wk. which had been executed." On Tuesday, after a noon meal with the Morris family, he set out along the familiar path that led home. Those delegates who had planned the presidency for Washington almost saw their efforts made vain during the course of his journey. Crossing an ancient and rotten bridge near Head of Elk, one member of his team of horses fell, nearly pulling his carriage off the span, a spill that would have provoked a fifteen-foot plunge into the dangerous waters below. But no other horse was pulled over, and Washington's servants, assisted by several bystanders, swiftly disengaged the team from the vehicle. Shaken but uninjured, Washington continued, stopping in Baltimore on the 21st, and finally reaching Mount Vernon about 6:00 P.M. on Saturday, "after an absence of four Months and 14 days," as he wearily noted.[45]

It still looked like summer on the Potomac, but moderating temperatures indicated that autumn had commenced, just as the calendar reported. That dictated an accelerated work schedule, and Washington immediately plunged back into his farm activities, overseeing the harvest, looking into some second season planting, and supervising the labor of his "Negro ditche[r]s" and other chattel. Like a man who soon expected to leave again, he fell to taking a census of his various holdings—it showed that he owned more than 100 horses, 19 oxen, 311 cows, and 389 head of sheep. No matter seemed too small to command his attention.[46]

Through the early fall relatively few visitors rapped on Mount Vernon's door, a pleasing turn of affairs after his prolonged absence. In his free time Washington closely watched the process of ratification of the proposed constitution. Congress had received a report on the Convention's work even before Washington got back to Virginia, and by the end of September it sent the projected charter to the states. It was clear that the document's proponents faced a fight. Already its foes in Congress had endeavored without success to amend the plan, or even to hold a second convention. Washington was not surprised at the opposition. Ratification, he told his former aide David Humphreys, would be an uphill battle, inasmuch as many interests "will be affected by the change." Success, he thought, hinged upon the "literary abilities" of the Federalists, as the champions of the document were being called, and he hoped they would inundate the newspapers with their essays. But that was not the sort of role he wished to play.[47]

In fact, he did not play much of a public role in this struggle. He made clear his convictions to Patrick Henry, certain to be a pivotal figure in Virginia's decision, and he indicated that he had no objection to having his name bandied about as a supporter of the document. On the other hand, he neither authored any essays in support of the constitution nor did he seek election to his state's ratification convention. Save for brief trips to Alexandria, Georgetown, and Fredericksburg, Washington did not leave Mount Vernon during the course of the ratification struggle. During those months his only resolute step came when Maryland's Anti-Federalists endeavored to postpone a vote in their convention until Virginia had acted. Washington intervened—"meddled," he said—to the point of rallying his Federalist acquaintances to call the vote. They did, and the state endorsed the constitution by a lopsided margin.[48]

Throughout the nine-month ratification campaign the Federalists did indeed use Washington's name—and Franklin's too—as a selling point. Some who were more zealous than veracious depicted Washington as having played a major role at the Convention, and one artful Federalist penman even composed a stirring speech that the general allegedly made when he voted for the document, a harangue in which he supposedly predicted that blood would flow if the constitution was not approved. It sounded credible. His farewell remarks as commander also had contained a warning of likely disorder. Besides, late in 1787 some conniving Federalist had latched onto and printed one of Washington's recent letters, a missive in which he had written: "My decided opinion . . . is that there is no alternative between the adoption of [the proposed constitution] and anarchy." His style of campaigning—or lack of it—was in keeping with his temper, but his low-key approach also arose from a fear that some might attribute his support for ratification to a desire to be the first president under the new charter. He knew, of course, that his election was a "probability," although he claimed that the office held no charms for him that could equal his "growing love of retirement." [49]

By the time his private letter was surreptitiously published, the Federalists seemed assured of success. Five states had ratified the proposed constitution by early in January 1788, and by then all but one state had called conventions to consider the matter. For weeks, thereafter, however, the juggernaut slowed to a creep. Only one state affirmed the document in February, and two additional months elapsed before the seventh state consented; another month dragged by before the eighth state acted. Thus, on June 2, when Virginia's convention at last assembled, the Federalists were only one state short of victory.

"A few short weeks will determine the political fate of America for . . . a long succession of ages to come," Washington predicted as Richmond began to swell with the arriving delegates. He was ecstatic. Ratification seemed a certainty, if not by Virginia's vote, then perhaps by that of New York, where Hamilton would play a leading role, or in New Hampshire, where John Sullivan would be a dominant force. Of course, Washington realized that a victory without the compliance of powerful entities such as Virginia and New York would be a hollow triumph, yet success seemed to loom in the Old Dominion. More Federalists than Anti-Federalists had been elected to the convention, though about 7 percent of the delegates were uncommitted. They would decide the issue.[50]

The fight in Virginia was similar to the battle elsewhere, for here, too, men of the Anti-Federalist persuasion saw themselves as old-line Whigs battling to protect the people's liberties from hegemonic government. They disapproved of the absence of a bill of rights from the proposed constitution, and they warned that the states would be imperiled by the powerful new national government. In addition, they predicted that both the House and Senate would be dominated by aristocrats, and they argued that the limitations on the national government's power were too inexplicit. George Mason denounced the charter as undemocratic. The people never would elect the president, he complained. Moreover, the branches were not adequately divided to suit him; he believed the "Constitution has *married* the President and Senate" by giving the two such coequal powers. Unlike their comrades elsewhere, Virginia's Anti-Federalists were beset by two gnawing fears. Mason and others fretted that the northern majority would barter away the Mississippi River, as the Yankee merchants had tried to do two years earlier, and some worried that Congress's commercial powers would make the state's tobacco exporters mere slaves of northern carriers, as "ill-fated Ireland" had been to England, according to one delegate. But on the 25th, when the issue was decided, the Federalists had the votes—narrowly. The tally was eighty-nine to seventy-nine. A switch of six votes, just one-quarter of the uncommitted delegates, and the Constitution would have been rejected by Virginia.[51]

On the day the vote was cast, an unusually cool, windy June day, Washington rode about his farms, looking after the planting of Irish potatoes in one sector, watching his slaves hoe corn in another, and in still another area dropping in to visit his kiln where more brick was about to be fashioned. Two days passed before news of the ratification vote eddied this far inland, and only a few hours after the courier arrived bearing those tidings another dispatch rider galloped by with more news: New Hampshire likewise had affirmed the Constitution. Ten states now had acted positively. The new compact was over the top. All that remained was to elect the officials. The momentous vote in Richmond had come almost twelve years to the day after Congress had voted independence, but Washington noted that the victory celebration he attended in Alexandria on the 28th came on the tenth anniversary of the battle at Monmouth. Perhaps it was not strange for him to think now of that engagement, for his "victory" that day, as well as the subsequent excision of General Lee that resulted from the events of that chaotic afternoon, had, he believed, been his real day of independence.[52]

If Washington ever had doubted that he might be his countrymen's first choice—only choice, really—to be the nation's initial president, such notions had to have evaporated within a few days of the crucial votes in Virginia and New Hampshire. At July 4th celebrations in various states his name was mentioned in that regard, and soon, too, newspaper essayists were alluding to him almost as if he already was the chief executive. He disavowed any interest in the post. There was his "increasing love of retirement," he said. It was his "sincerest wish" merely to live and die a private citizen at Mount Vernon. Washington's disclaimers usually have been taken at face value by historians. In fact, his protestations were not terribly convincing. All his life Washington had sought recognition and acclaim; granted he now had renown aplenty, enough to satisfy most men many times over. But he was not Everyman. His inner need to expand his identity was never likely to be fully satisfied. True, he must have relished the leisure of retirement and been loath to once again shoulder the burdens of public office. Yet he must also have missed the stimulation and acclaim that went with activism. His return to the sites of his military adventures, to Germantown and White Marsh, to Trenton and Valley Forge, his telling recollection of Monmouth, disclosed a yearning for a time of activity and glory. In 1788, while he disavowed an interest in leaving Mount Vernon, he was rehearsing what he had done previously. Until he was called, he would not leave his estate to resume command of the Virginia Regiment in 1755, nor would he take an active role in the colonists' protest movement, nor, indeed, would he attend the Constitutional Convention. Now he awaited still another call. And there could not have been much doubt about his final decision on this matter. Despite his disclaimers, he was careful never to unequivocally close the door to serving. What he really said—and on more than one occasion—was that he did not wish to appear to be soliciting the office, and that he fretted, in light of his ballyhooed retirement, that to accept the post might expose him to the charge of *"inconsistency* and *ambition."* [53]

Hamilton was one to whom he conveyed such views, certain that the young New Yorker would find a way to banish his worries. His former aide was up to the task: "The absolute retreat [from public life] which you meditated at the close of the late war was natural and proper," he began. Now, however, "the crisis" leaves "you no alternative but to comply" with the "unanimous wish of your country" to lead the new government. There could be no censure for abandoning retirement, Hamilton went on, inasmuch as the "necessity of your filling the station in question is so universal that you can run no risk of any uncandid imputation, by submitting to it." But to fail to serve, he added, would be to venture "greater hazard to that fame, which must be and ought to be dear to you," for if the new Constitution should fail—and well it might if he refused to serve—he, as one of the framers, might be brought into "disrepute," since by his actions at the Convention he had "pulled down one Utopia . . . to build up another." Washington must have read Hamilton's missive closely. Shortly after receiving it he announced that he would accept the position if he was convinced that "the partiality of my Countrymen had made my services absolutely necessary." He even began to reflect on how he would cooperate with the vice president.[54]

By early January 1789, when the members of the Electoral College were selected, Washington had been beseeched to accept the presidency so often that he could not mistake the country's mood. He was mentioned frequently in public discourses, and Federalist devotees such as Madison and Robert and Gouverneur Morris came to Mount Vernon to urge him to serve. At month's end he spoke of accepting the presidency, albeit with "unfeigned reluctance." [55]

The electors from the eleven ratifying states—Rhode Island and North Carolina had refused to sanction the charter—met in their respective state capitals on February 4 to vote for a president and vice president. Although the results would not be official for about thirty days, Washington received reports during the period that left no doubt that he was the unanimous choice for the presidency. He began to speak of it being his "inevitable fate to administer the government," and early in March when he called on his ailing mother he seemed certain that he never again would see her, an indication that in his own mind he already had decided to abide by the electors' choice. Within three weeks or so, in fact, he not only was concerning himself with the question of accomodations in New York, but with the necessary arrangements for the relatives who would be left behind at Mount Vernon.[56]

When Charles Thomson, still the secretary of Congress, as he had been since the first day the Continental Congress had gathered back in 1774, arrived at Mount Vernon on April 14 with the official Electoral College results, Washington's acceptance was a mere formality. Indeed, when Thomson informed him that his selection had been unanimous and that John Adams had been elected to the vice presidency, Washington responded with a letter of acceptance that he had written days before. The vote "scarcely leaves me the alternative for an option," he had written. To the very end he felt the need to convince himself that, like Cincinnatus, he was serving only because he had been summoned to do his duty.[57]

Scarely forty-eight hours later, following a farewell dinner in Alexandria and a last round of superintendency at his estate, Washington was on his way to New York. Receptions in Baltimore, Wilmington, and Philadelphia slowed the journey, but not by much; traveling by carriage, accompanied by Thomson and his former aide David Humphreys, he completed the trek in six days, roughly two days faster than on his 1756 and 1773 trips along more or less the same route. At times this journey took on the overtones of a royal procession at least insofar as a fiercely republican people would permit themselves to indulge in such festivities. In each metropolis bells and booming field artillery, parading militia companies and flag-bedecked streets and harbors greeted him, and in Philadelphia twenty thousand inhabitants lined the sidewalks to catch a glimpse of this man. In many small towns, too, his carriage paused for simpler ceremonies, stays that must have been quite brief, for on days when he halted for as many as five such festivities the party still advanced about forty miles. At Trenton, crossing the bridge that spanned Assunpink Creek, his carriage passed under a sign that proclaimed him the "Mighty Chief! once more," and in New Brunswick and Elizabeth Town, in Bridgetown and Rahway, he was serenaded by trainbandsmen with fife and drum. Then on the 23rd he crossed onto Manhattan Island, his first time back since his real farewell to his officers on that cold December day six years before. There the greatest of all celebrations was held. Luncheons followed parades, speeches followed banquets, and a throng of thirty thousand turned out to once again salute the man who had tried so hard and for so long to secure this city's liberation.[58]

New York must have outdone itself that day, for the Inauguration Day fes-

George Washington, by Joseph Wright (1790). Courtesy of the Cleveland Museum, Henry B. Hurlbut Collection. Washington was fifty-eight and had been president for only about one year when this portrait was made.

tivities a week later were simple by contrast. Indeed, even though this age loved pomp and ceremony, the rites of April 30 seldom have been surpassed in simplicity or brevity by any subsequent inaugural observance.

The citizenry was awakened at dawn by festive blasts from artillery posted at the Battery. Three hours later, at 9:00 A.M., church bells summoned New Yorkers to prayer services. At noon Congress assembled, and each house dispatched a delegation to Washington's residence to fetch him to the capitol; thirty minutes later the procession rumbled over the city's cobblestone streets, returning to Federal Hall. Five military companies marched at its head, followed in turn by the mayor and sheriff of New York, each on horseback. The Senate committee, squeezed into one carriage, came next. Then came Washington, seated alone in a large coach drawn by four dobbins. He was followed by the House committee, then by John Jay and Henry Knox, the two executive department heads under the Articles government; Chancellor Robert Livingston of New York and assorted local notables brought up the rear. At about 1:00 P.M. they arrived at their destination, Congress's partially completed new quarters just south of Wall Street. Accompanied now by a committee of legislators, Washington was ushered before the two houses, where he was greeted by John Adams, whose duties included presiding over joint sessions of Congress.

They were in the Senate's chamber, a modest, forty-by-thirty-foot room. Portraits of Christopher Columbus, Washington, and various Revolutionary heroes decorated the walls; another painting, this one of a sun and thirteen stars, looked down on the room's occupants from a tall, arched ceiling. Washington was escorted to a canopy-draped platform in the front of the hall. He looked out on the members of the House, sitting to his right, and on diplomats and senators to his left. Behind him were three doors which led onto a balcony.

The vice president, nervous and trembling so badly that he could speak only with difficulty, opened the festivities with a few remarks. The swearing-in followed. A problem had arisen over who could administer the oath of office, for until the president was in office there would be no federal judges. In the end it was agreed that Chancellor Livingston, a state official, would have to do. He and Washington stepped through the doors and onto the balcony above Broad and Wall streets. There, standing beneath a red-and-white-striped canopy and behind a red velvet draped table, and in full view both of Congress and the citizenry below, he took the oath.

It was over in seconds. Outside the crowd surged and cheered, and ships in the nearby harbor boomed their salutations, even the *Galveston*, a Spanish sloop-of-war moored in these waters, joining in with a deafening greeting; inside the congressmen applauded politely.

What Washington must have reckoned the least pleasant part of the day followed—his Inaugural Address. Dressed in a simple American-made brown broadcloth suit, white stockings, and white gloves, his sword strapped to his side, the president reentered the Senate chamber and mounted the low platform to read his speech. Mercifully, he had discarded an oration prepared by David Humphreys, a seventy-three-page manuscript; instead, he proceeded with an address of only seven paragraphs. With one hand plunged into his pocket, he slowly read his remarks. He was almost inaudible. Characteristically, he spoke in a low voice, and on this day it also was "a little tremulous." some witnesses thought him embarrassed. One thought he was "grave, almost to sadness." Surely he was uneasy. What his audience heard was not particularly memorable. One of Pennsylvania's senators thought it a "heavy, dull, stupid" speech, and, indeed, not one ringing, enduring phrase emerged from his remarks.

He began by reiterating that he had not sought his office, that he was there "in obedience to the public summons." As for public matters, he hoped his term would be free of "party animosities," and he exhorted his countrymen to behave virtuously, for liberty and republicanism were at stake. Perhaps to the surprise of his audience, he declined to accept a salary, an offer which Congress soon would refuse.

In less than twenty minutes it was over. Washington and the members of Congress, together with other notables, walked nearly half a mile to St. Paul's Chapel, an Anglican church, for a brief service, and that evening they were regaled with a fireworks show.[59]

Once again George Washington was at the throbbing heart of public affairs, but then he had been there already for a full three years. Only he had refused to acknowledge that fact.

PART FOUR ❧

15

The Early Presidency

"All things . . . seem to succeed"

If George Washington sensed that change was in the air in the 1780s he did not record those thoughts. Of course, he was aware of the changes that he had helped to make. British authority, with its titled aristocracy, its class prerogatives, its royal governors and other "lordly masters," not to mention its convenient commercial ties and its generous subsidies, was gone, and with it had gone about 250,000 inhabitants of America who had chosen to remain loyal to the Crown. From the sidelines he had watched as other changes occurred. Every northern state had taken steps to abolish slavery, and all thirteen states had elected to stop the importation of African slaves. There were written constitutions and more elected officials than ever before, and the legislatures were more broadly representative than in the colonial days. Now, too, there was a new national government. Upon its success, Washington believed, hung the fate both of the American political union and the American Revolution.

Momentous as were these changes, there remained a sense of continuity with the past, so much so in fact that contemporaries at times seemed almost ready to shrug off the departures ushered in by the Revolution. During his ride north from Mount Vernon, for instance, much of what Washington glimpsed must have appeared as it had thirty-five years before when he first rode along this very route. Today change is so pervasive, so continuous, that a period of thirty-five years seems almost a millennium, a period during which customs and popular culture and society's artifacts can be altered and extirpated many times over. But for Washington and his contemporaries the hum of daily life must have seemed unchanged. In 1789, for example, the means of land travel remained what it had been all his life: people and things moved by horseback or horse-drawn carriage—a slow, wearying transit across dusty (or muddy or frozen) country roads, fording rivers and streams by ferry or by rustic, hazardous wooden bridges. Nor had men's and women's clothing fashions changed substantially in the course of Washington's fifty-seven years. The dances and amusements that he first had enjoyed three decades earlier were no less popular in 1789, and they remained unchallenged by new conventions. Newspapers and pamphlets and books looked no different than at mid-century, furniture styles had hardly changed, and the architecture of the newly erected houses and buildings that Washington gazed upon as he passed through Baltimore and Wilmington and Philadelphia that spring still resembled the forms used in edifices constructed decades before. People's day-to-day lives, from the moment they rose at dawn until they snuffed out the evening's last candle upon returning to bed seemed to vary little from year to year.

Nor had conditions abroad seemed to change appreciably since the end of the War for Independence. George III still was the king of England, though he was so plagued by mental disorders that until a few weeks before Washington's inauguration he had to be confined in a straitjacket. A Pitt—William Pitt the Younger—again was the prime minister in London, and Lord Cornwallis, Washington's victim at Yorktown, had risen to be governor general of Britain's dominion in India. Prussia and Austria still were preoccupied with Poland, hapless nation which they initially had partitioned in the year when the Continental Congress first met; and Russia once again was at war with Turkey. Moreover, for all the negotiating and all the killing of the last three decades, the French and Spanish empires looked about as they had since 1763.

But on that April 30 when Washington's simple little inaugural took place, the western world was on the threshold of great change. Already French legislators were gathering at Versailles for the opening session of the Estates-General, the first time the nation's parliament had met since 1614; within weeks that body would set in motion events that would forever alter the political face of Europe. Yet an even greater transformation already had begun, a process that has been termed a "deep change," a course of modernization that in the next few decades would modify virtually every aspect of the world that Washington knew, from the size of its families to its understanding of technology to the environment in which people lived and worked, until, finally, in its wake, the eighteenth century would come to seem but a relic of some enigmatic, ancient past.[1] Ironically, however, while Washington's administration came at the tag end of a dying age, the decisions it made would have an enormous impact on the destiny of America's political future, leaving virtually every subsequent generation of the nation's political and constitutional leaders in its debt.

Washington had taken up residence in a newly furnished house on the East Side, a privately owned dwelling that had been a home to the last several presidents of Congress. Built on the eve of the Revolution by a prosperous merchant, it was large and comfortable, and situated just a block from the East River, so that on warm summer evenings its occupants delighted in the pleasingly cool breezes that swept in from the waters. The New York City of this era still was rebuilding from the war years, during which two disastrous fires and a seven-year occupation by the British army had beset this metropolis. Yet the place bore the earmarks of prosperity. Its inhabitants now numbered between twenty-five and thirty thousand. New streets were being laid out to handle the population surge (up about 20 percent in fifteen years), and new street lamps were being installed everywhere.[2]

For a time Washington had toyed with the notion of holding the presidency only briefly, perhaps for a year or two. Once the new government was established, once it had a revenue and was functioning in an orderly manner, he would step aside. John Adams and others then could have the task of continuing what he had begun.[3] The thought was not an idle pipe dream. Such a step would have been fully in keeping with Washington's psychological pattern, for he once again would have acted out the Cincinnatus role that he cherished. Having laid aside his plow in order to save the public from chaos, he would return to his farm, although not before he had endured what seemed to be great personal sacrifice. It was, as Garry Wills has observed, a notion that amounted to a secular variation of the concept of divine intervention.[4]

His first weeks in office must have convinced him of the wisdom of an early resignation. He soon seemed to harbor doubts about his ability to perform his job. "I greatly apprehend that my Countrymen will expect too much from me," he confided. "I feel an insuperable diffidence in my own abilities," he added, and he admitted his fear that the public's "extravagent . . . praises" would be turned into "extravagent . . . censures." Suddenly he had been seized by the same anxiety that had accompanied him on the ride from Philadelphia to the siege lines at Cambridge in 1775. He feared that from the day of his inauguration he had begun to court "my fall, and the ruin of my reputation." [5]

Washington's concern in part was triggered by the sudden onslaught of office seekers that hammered at his front door. This was a new experience for him. Congress had appointed the general officers beneath him at the outset of the war, and, in turn, the states had named the lesser field officers. Now Washington bore the responsibility of filling the important offices. Facing the supplicants was a "delicate," "unpleasing," even an embarrassing task, he thought. It also was a losing proposition. Even though he acted without partiality in most instances, yet those who were rebuffed were certain to be angry.[6]

The president also was troubled over the proper style required by his new office. He had had sufficient military experience before 1775 so that the manner of his conduct as commander had not vexed him. But how should he comport himself as president? What suited the office? What did a republican people desire? Aware that his actions would become a model for those who followed, and wishing to be certain that "these precedents may be fixed on true principles," he sought the advice of those about him, in particular the vice president, but especially Hamilton, Madison, and Jay, the triumvirate responsible for the *Federalist* essays in defense of the new Constitution.

Washington bombarded them with questions. Should he seclude himself from the public? How often should he meet the public? Should he open his office for business at 8:00 A.M. each day? Should he periodically dine with members of the Congress? Should he host state dinners? Would it be improper for him to call upon private acquaintances? Should he make a tour of the United States? In short, was he to shape the presidency in the image of a monarchical court, or should this become a more popular office? Or should the office be sculpted into something in between those two poles?[7]

Not surprisingly, considering that he regarded the British government as the world's best, Hamilton recommended that the office be shrouded at once with a royal "dignity," a feat to be accomplished by distancing the president from his subjects. Only department chiefs, diplomats, and members of the Senate, he counseled, should be privileged to have free access to the chief executive. Otherwise, "Your Excellency," as he now referred to Washington, might conduct a "levee" no more than once each week, and then he should admit only invited guests; the president, moreover, should appear at these sessions for exactly thirty minutes, no more and no less, and he should be careful to speak in the most concise manner. Up to four annual state dinners would be acceptable, Hamilton went on, but the president must never call on anyone, nor should he submit to being entertained by anyone.[8]

Vice President Adams wished for a "dignified and respectable government." Shortly he would campaign in the Senate to impose a pompous, officious title upon the presidency, yet his recommendations were less stiff than those of Hamilton. Despite the suspicions of many contemporaries that he longed to establish aristocratic institutions in America, including rule by a monarch, Adams envisioned a genuinely republican presidency, one that the people could esteem because they would realize that the office holder was, like themselves, a citizen. He thought two levees per week would be acceptable, and, more importantly, he proposed that these gatherings should be more or less open to the general public; he evidently thought it too republican for the president to give large and formal dinners, and he told Washington that he should feel free to entertain and to call upon whomever he pleased.[9] Whatever Madison and Jay advised—their suggestions have been lost—it is clear that President Washington blended the proposals of Hamilton and Adams.

Already Washington had decided that he would accept what he quaintly called "visits of compliment" on only two afternoons each week, and then for just an hour at a time. And he had decided not to venture from his abode to be a dinner guest at any private residence. Otherwise, he would hold a levee for suitably dressed males during one hour every Tuesday afternoon, a public tea party for both sexes each Friday night, and a small dinner—by invitation only—at 4:00

P.M. each Wednesday. A creature of habit, President Washington hardly altered this ritual during the next eight years. If his taste was starchy and sober, and if his levees soon were seen by some as unrepublican, aristocratic affairs, Congress at least stripped away some of the marble veneer that seemed about to encase the presidency. While Washington fretted over style, the legislators, as if they had nothing better to do, squandered several days in a debate over the best title for the occupant of the office. They kicked around everything from "Honourable" to "His Elective Highness" (or "Majesty") to the unctuous-sounding mouthful that John Adams fancied, "His Highness the President of the United States and Protector of the Rights of the Same." Finally, thanks in large measure to the obstinacy of a few former Anti-Federalists such as Patrick Henry, the legislators decided on the exquisitely simple denomination: "The President of the United States." [10]

The truth of the matter was that Washington had more time on his hands during the first several weeks of his tenure than has any subsequent chief executive. Congress was busy—it is equally doubtful that any of its successors ever was confronted by so many major decisions in such a brief time—but Washington largely chose not to become involved. As he was neither a lawyer nor a political philosopher, he was unsure of his relationship with Congress. The Constitution gave him a veto and administrative responsibilities; otherwise its provisions were murky. He could draw on his recollection of how a succession of Virginia's governors had acted toward the Burgesses, or his own relationship with Congress during the war might serve him as a model. Yet no previous relation really offered much guidance. Washington knew that he clearly possessed the constitutional power to initiate United States foreign policy, but there was no one with whom to work, no foreign minister, no ministers abroad. (Thomas Jefferson, minister to France since 1784, had been granted leave to return to America; otherwise, the United States had only a chargé d'affairs in Madrid.) Nor had the federal departments or the national judiciary been created. So he simply waited, in the interim gradually meeting with office seekers and piecing together his clerical staff, naming about one-third as many secretaries as he had utilized a year or two into the war. David Humphreys, who had been one of those military aides, returned to Washington's side, and Tobias Lear was summoned from Mount Vernon; Thomas Nelson, scion of Virginia's wartime governor, and Robert Lewis, Betty Washington Lewis's son, joined William Jackson, recently the official secretary of the Constitutional Convention, to round out the team. With so little to do, the president must have been delighted when Lewis arrived, for alighting from the carriage with him, garbed in homespun as Washington himself had been when he had taken office, was the First Lady. After six weeks alone, and forced to entertain both officials and curiosity seekers by himself, Washington must have found Martha's presence especially welcome.[11]

It was late summer before Congress created the federal departments and the court system, at last giving the new chief executive something with which to work. Actually Congress's delay probably was fortuitous, inasmuch as Washington was ill and unable to work for several weeks during that summer. He fell sick in mid-June, stricken with an ailment that many feared might be fatal. A couple of weeks after his wife's arrival, Washington began to run a high fever and feel indisposed; within two or three days a slight pain developed in his thigh, and in another day or two a growth was discernable at the site of the discomfort. A leading New York physician was called in, but he only watched the tumor grow, until Washington refered to it as "very large." Unable to move without considerable distress, he was forced to bed and compelled by the pain to spend each day lying only on his right side; his sickness exacerbated by anxiety, Washington seemed to be dangerously ill. Suspicions grew that he was a victim of cancer; rumor also coursed through the capital that he had an anthrax infection, what contemporaries called the "wool sorters disease." While his doctors debated what steps to take, Cherry Street was blocked to traffic to spare the president its distressing noise. Then, suddenly, the growth abscessed and the doctor lanced and drained the lesion. Ever so gradually Washington's strength returned. Two weeks following the surgery Washington complained that "a feebleness still hangs upon me," and for a month much of his correspondence was handled by his secretaries. Almost seven weeks elapsed from the moment of the onset of the earliest symptoms until he finally, fully, resumed his duties, although even then he still was compelled to spend much of his time reclining on soft pillows as he worked. Three months later the still-recumbent chief executive wrote his old friend Dr. Craik that the "wound given by the incision is not yet closed." Even then the tumescent growth remained the size of a barley corn.[12]

While Washington languished on his sickbed, Congress painstakingly created three executive departments—state, war, and treasury—and two federal agencies with less exalted status, the offices of attorney general and postmaster general. And by early autumn a national court system was established, as Congress fashioned thirteen district courts as the "inferior tribunals" beneath the six-member Supreme Court. At last Washington had some places to put a few of the horde of office seekers that had been inveigling appointments from him since even before he left Mount Vernon. Indeed, he had more than one thousand posts to fill.[13]

The tough part was turning down men with whom he had long been close. Financially pressed Benjamin Lincoln sought to head a department, but, instead, Washington sent him to Georgia to help negotiate a treaty normalizing relations with the Creek Indians. The president's nephew, Bushrod Washington, longed to be appointed United States district attorney for Virginia; Washington refused, telling him bluntly that his "standing at the bar" would not justify his nomination. By contrast, picking the key men was easy. He intended to go with men whom he knew and trusted, and for the most part he planned to chose only from among those who had been demonstrable advocates of the new Constitution.[14]

The war department was easiest. Henry Knox had been the last director of this jurisdiction under the Articles of Confederation, and though the department technically ceased to exist with the ratification of the new Constitution, Washington had asked him to continue in the interim. To no one's great surprise the president designated his loyal general as the initial director of military matters.

Nor was it particularly startling when Hamilton was offered the post of secretary of the treasury. That brilliant young New Yorker had been busy since the day at Yorktown when he had persuaded his leader to permit him to lead an assault on the redcoats' lines. Shortly after Cornwallis's surrender he had left the army, returning to New York and gaining admittance to the bar—after but three months' study. Soon thereafter he was elected to Congress. He served only eight months, just long enough to become embroiled in the Newburgh Conspiracy. Hamilton, who at the age of fourteen had wished for a war in order to extricate himself from the miasma of his West Indian childhood, had made the most of the War of Independence. When peace returned he was a lawyer with a Wall Street address, a well-known public figure, a man of wealth with connections both to the Schuyler family and to George Washington. And he still was ten years younger than Washington had been when he had taken command of the Continental army.

Immediately after the war Hamilton no longer seemed to have time for Washington, as if the old general at Mount Vernon was unlikely ever again to serve as his "aegis" to bigger and better things. For three years the two men had almost no contact. Hamilton did not even visit Mount Vernon when he attended the Annapolis Convention in 1786, and he wrote to Washington only twice in those years, once to transmit some data from a New York business that might have been relevant to the general's wartime expense account and once to discuss the Order of the Cincinnati. The campaign to strengthen the national government, as well as his leading role in the creation of the Bank of New York, thrust Hamilton back into public affairs, leading first to his election to the New York legislature in 1786 and subsequently to his important role in drafting and ratifying the Constitution. His latter activities made him the indispensable leader of his state's Federalist faction. He also spent some of his time after early 1787 cozying up to Washington again. In the year that followed the Constitutional Convention he wrote three times as many letters to his former benefactor as he had in the three years preceding the Philadelphia meeting. One missive was dispatched for the purpose of requesting that Washington assist him in refuting public charges that he had "*palmed* myself upon you." Washington obliged him.[15]

In Washington's mind the treasury department was the key post, at least until the new government was secured. The nation's revenue problems had served as the catalyst that had activated many bystanders to think of a new constitution; moreover, the president knew that the new government's very ability to survive hinged on the success of this department. The secretary must be a wily politician, for money matters were certain to divide men; shepherding revenue bills through Congress might be as difficult as pushing that proverbial camel through the eye of

Alexander Hamilton, from an original miniature by Archibald Robertson, engraved by John F.E. Prud'homme (c. 1790). Courtesy of the New-York Historical Society.

a needle. Although Washington never divulged his reasons for selecting Hamilton, that young man obviously seemed to fit every requirement for the job. Not only was he experienced in the boggy landscape of finance, but Washington explicitly trusted his acumen, having already turned to him for advice concerning accepting the presidency and the style he should set for the office. Furthermore, there could be no doubt that the New Yorker was unrivaled in guile and political dexterity. Thus, less than a week after the department was created, and without bothering to seek any advice, Washington nominated Hamilton.

The state department was the next most important office. In fact, if Hamilton quickly resolved the national government's financial ills, state in the long run would be the principal office. Washington initially leaned toward John Jay, the last head of foreign affairs under the Articles, but Jay longed for the Supreme Court and the president acceded to his wishes. The next offer was extended to Thomas Jefferson. It was a logical move. Not only did Washington know him and feel that he could work with him, but few men had as much diplomatic experience. In fact, Jefferson was unaware of his nomination until he disembarked in Norfolk in November 1789 at the completion of a four-year stretch as the United States minister to France. Obviously he was well versed in the affairs of that important nation, a country that Washington now knew was experiencing the "first paroxysm"—and probably not the last—of a great revolution.[16]

Washington named Samuel Osgood of Massachusetts (the owner of his Cherry Street residence) as his postmaster general. Edmund Randolph, who had introduced the Virginia Plan at the Constitutional Convention, was nominated to be attorney general. After Jay was nominated as chief justice of the United States, Washington sent the Senate the names of five men to be considered for the remaining seats on the High Court. He was close to three of the five: James Wilson, an old loyal supporter from Pennsylvania; fellow Virginian John Blair; and his former wartime aide Robert Harrison. John Rutledge of South Carolina and William Cushing of Massachusetts also were named, and a few weeks later when Harrison declined the post—he was ill and died early in 1790—Washington nominated James Iredell of North Carolina.

Even though dispirited from his surgery, to which in September was added the melancholy news of his mother's death, President Washington continued to wrestle with the long list of appointments yet to be made. By early fall he had filled nearly 125 vacant office, ranging in importance from federal judgeships to ministerial posts to fairly trifling provincial postal offices. The more weighty selections were consented to by the Senate with little fanfare, but the president was flabbergasted to learn that his appointee to be the naval officer of the port of Savannah was rejected; Georgia's two senators objected, and their colleagues in Federal Hall fell in step to thwart Washington. Their action established the precedent that came to be known as "senatorial courtesy," a practice that in reality virtually entrusted minor local appointments to each state's two senators.[17]

During that initial session of Congress, one additional item of business occupied the legislators. Nine states had ratified the Constitution with the under-standing that a bill of rights soon would be amended to that charter, and, in fact, more than two hundred amendments containing about eighty substantive changes had been proposed by the ratifying conventions. Principally the Anti-Federalists had feared that a strong central government might encroach on individual liber-ties, although some feared that the Constitution might bestow rights on some folk whose liberties presently were restrained; hence one New England state longed for an emendation that would prevent "Jews, Turks and infidels" from holding office. Clearly Congress had to do something. In fact, the Federalist leadership was anxious to act hurriedly, if for no other reason than to head off the opposi-tion's calls for a second Constitutional Convention, something the framers looked upon—to quote Washington—as an "insidious" plot to destroy the national gov-ernment by "set[ting] every thing afloat again." [18]

Madison, as much of a Federalist kingpin as existed in a remarkably leader-less House of Representatives, wasted no time that spring. Using the recom-mendations of his home state's ratifying convention as a guide, he distilled the multitude of disparate proposals from the various states down to a workable num-ber and hurried them to a committee. In August the full House took up the issue, by September it was in the hands of the Senate, and three weeks later twelve amendments were on their way to the states for ratification. Two years later ten of the twelve had been added to the Constitution. In the inaugural address that he wrote but never delivered, President Washington had planned to recommend that it would not be prudent to immediately alter the Constitution in any manner. It seems unlikely, therefore, that he had anything to do with Madison's decision to initiate the process, and there is no evidence that he played any role in the course of Congress's consideration of the proposed amendments. [19]

By early autumn 1789, Washington, longing for a break from the tedium of his job, began to plan his initial presidential trip. Since boyhood he had been convinced that travel was a formative and educational activity; it was good exercise too, something he now could use to regain his vitality. Before setting out he tested his strength with periodic walks and horseback rides, and on one occasion he and Vice President Adams, together with a few congressmen and Chancellor Livingston, undertook a long trek out to Long Island to inspect a fifty-year-old botanical garden. By mid-october he felt fine once again, and when Congress voted to adjourn until after Christmas, the way was clear for his departure. New England seemed the logical place to go. Aside from his brief meetings with Rochambeau in 1780 and 1781, he had not been in that section since his first year as commander fourteen years before, and he had never been north of Boston. Hurrying to beat the onset of winter in that quadrant, he set out in mid-month, his second long journey that year, for in April he had traveled more than two hundred miles in riding from Mount Vernon to the capital. [20]

Once again he proceeded without his wife, for she preferred to remain at home with the grandchildren. A three-day ride, during which time he seems to have been chiefly absorbed by the state of the farming he observed ("their hogs large but rather long legged," and "all the Farmers busily employed in gathering, grinding, and expressing the Juice of their Apples," were typical of his diary entries), carried him through northern Manhattan's forests, into Connecticut, and finally to New Haven. He spent a Sunday in that little college town, attending an Episcopal church in the morning and Congregational services in the afternoon. A couple of days later he reached Hartford, where he had come once before to confer with the French military leaders, and nine days after he left the capital he entered Cambridge, there to find Lieutenant Governor Samuel Adams at the head of a delegation sent to greet him and to escort him across the Charles River. In each village he had been greeted warmly, fêted, serenaded, paraded, saluted, and ushered about by the ubiquitous trainbandsmen.[21]

Boston was no different. A large and festive crowd turned out, oddly grouped by professions, each species of craftsman standing beneath a banner that identified its skill. Washington rode under an arch inscribed "To the Man who unites all hearts," and on past a sign that announced "Boston relieved March 17, 1776." It was gracious and charming, except for one thing. The governor of Massachusetts, John Hancock, had not bothered to welcome the president, nor had he offered his residence as a lodging. The President of the United States found quarters at the widow Ingersoll's boarding house at Court and Tremont.[22]

The episode set Washington fuming. Not only did he feel slighted, but he perceived a constitutional issue in this absurd affair. He reasoned that protocol demanded that a lowly governor must call upon the president before the nation's chief executive paid his respects to the state official. Under the circumstances Washington refused an invitation to dine at the governor's mansion, taking his meal instead at Mrs. Ingersoll's residence. When Samuel Adams dropped in during the meal to wanly plead that Hancock had been too ill to welcome the president, Washington remained obdurate, asseverating that he "should not see the Govr. unless it was at my own lodgings." The next day things were straightened out. Alleging that he had been laid low by the gout, the governor had himself carried on a stretcher to Washington's domicile, where he officially and complaisantly greeted the province's guest.[23]

The following morning Washington awakened ill with a cold and an inflammation in his left eye, one of the first victims of an influenza epidemic about to sweep over Boston, an outbreak the citizenry soon would dub the "Washington flu," as if he had brought it to town. Nevertheless, he went to tea at Hancock's that afternoon, and he spent almost all of the following day attending state ceremonies. Departing Boston on the 29th he visited Harvard College, where he seemed to be astonished at the magnitude of its thirteen-thousand-volume library. Marblehead, whose sons had been indispensable in his escape from Brooklyn and his attack on Trenton in 1776, was next on his itinerary. The president had insisted on coming to this seaport town, but he was depressed at what he found, noting in his diary that the village's "streets [are] dirty—and the common people not very clean." During the next several days he called on a bevy of burgeoning little manufacturing towns, places like Lynn and Salem and Newburyport, where he lingered to watch the production of shoes and textiles and ships. Accompanied by John Adams he took his leave of Massachusetts at the end of the month, riding into the gaudy autumn splendor offered by New Hampshire. There he called on John Sullivan, the fiery general he had so trusted, fished a bit, visited several municipalities, and inspected still more textile mills.[24]

Washington journeyed as far north as Kittery, Maine, before turning back. He had planned to cross through Vermont to Albany, returning to New York City along the Hudson path that he knew so well. However, a heavy early-season snow in the mountains induced him to return by a more direct route. That was a lucky break in a way. During his stay in Boston he had hoped to visit Lexington, the little hamlet where the war had begun in 1775, but the junket had been postponed because of his brief illness. Now he took the opportunity to pass through the village, remaining just long enough to sightsee for a few minutes and to have dinner. Although he never seemed to weary of the populace's surfeit of good will, Washington found the return trip tedious and often unpleasant. His lodgings frequently were poor (widow Collidge's house in Watertown being "indifferent" and Perkins's Tavern in Pomfret, Connecticut, "by the bye is not a good one"), faulty directions provided by "blind & ignorant" farmers more than once caused him to go out of his way, and a detour to see "Old Put," Israel Putnam, backfired inasmuch as he discovered that his former general did not live where he thought he did. Twenty-eight days after he set out, the president returned to New York, happy to find Martha and the grandchildren well, probably not so pleased to find that the First Lady had scheduled a levee and that he barely had time to change from his dusty traveling attire before he had to begin greeting the guests.[25]

The president had almost two months to rest before Congress returned in January 1790. In fact, the new government was forming so slowly that there was little work to undertake; that air of urgency that had driven the Federalists in 1786–87 seemed to have disappeared like an early morning fog under a hot sun. By year's end only about 10 percent of the federal bureaucracy had been appointed. Moreover, Jefferson did not even learn of his appointment until ten days after Washington returned from his New England excursion, and he did not reach the capital until the first day of spring in 1790, nearly a year after the president's inauguration. Randolph arrived even later.[26]

Washington relaxed while he awaited the new year. When the fall weather cooperated he walked or rode, and he particularly liked to make the "14 Miles round," a long circuitous carriage ride about a portion of Manhattan Island, a journey he enjoyed in the company of Martha and sprightly Nelly and George Washington Parke Custis, or Wash, for "little Washington," as Martha called him. These jaunts were undertaken as much for Martha's serenity as for his own. She missed Mount Vernon terribly, and she seemed to feel cheated by Washington's decision to quit his life of retirement. After the war, she said, the "dearest wish of my heart" had been that she and her husband could "grow old in solitude and tranquility together" in Virginia. Were she younger, she conceded, she might enjoy being First Lady. But she was too old even to partake of "the innocent gaities" of public life. Not only that, she was treated "like a prisoner," tied down to her Cherry Street residence and unaware of what was happening in the city. Hers was "a very dull life here," she told a relative. The rides helped her adjust to public life, and though she never overcame her homesickness she did come to appreciate New York both as a consumer's paradise and for the educational opportunities it offered her grandchildren. During that fall the Washingtons attended the theater and a ball; the president sat for the artist Edward Savage; and, of course, the First Family entertained frequently. One of their parties almost ended disastrously. The ostrich feathers in the headdress worn by one of the guests brushed against a chandelier and caught fire, but one of the president's young aides acted quickly and intrepidly, extinguishing the flames with his bare hands before the lady or anyone else was injured.[27]

During these weeks Washington's behavior changed in only one way. After years of seldom attending church services, he once again regularly dropped in on Sunday devotions. He missed only one Sabbath worship service (and then because the weather was atrocious) during the last twelve weeks of the year, and he proclaimed the final Thursday in November a day of national thanksgiving.[28]

On January 7 his wait for the return of Congress ended. The following morning he rode to Federal Hall to deliver the first State of the Union Address. Dressed gravely in a blue-black suit, and speaking not only to the legislators and department heads but to a large number of citizens who pushed into the chamber, Washington, in the words of one of the senators, "read his speech well." It was brief and innocuous in content, though couched in an upbeat tone. Washington announced that he sensed an "increasing good will" toward the new government, inasmuch as North Carolina at last had ratified the Constitution, leaving only recalcitrant Rhode Island outside the fold. Otherwise, he gave no hint of an administrative program, save for a few general remarks about "providing for the common defense."

A week later Congress learned what the administration wished to do in the financial realm. Pursuing an earlier House of Representatives directive to prepare a plan for retiring the national debt, Secretary Hamilton unveiled his answer.[29] Although poor record-keeping resulted in much confusion over specific accounts, there was not much question about the basic nature of the public debt in 1790. Totaling about $75 million, it fell into three classes: a foreign debt of about $12 million, about three-quarters of which arose from wartime loans made by France; about $40 million in debts and interest accrued by the pre-1789 Congress, once again most of it resulting from the war years when the national legislature had issued bonds (called "loan office certificates") and promissory notes to obtain supplies and pay wages; and, finally, around $25 million in state debts that had arisen primarily after 1780 when a vitiated national government virtually had asked the states to pay for the conduct of the war.

Together with the roughly thirty-five other employees in the treasury department (its personnel ledger was about seven times greater than that of either of the other departments), Hamilton had spent the autumn and early winter hard at work on meeting the House's instructions. Toiling in his chilly, sparsely furnished little office—all the furniture in the room would not have cost ten dollars a French visitor clucked—Hamilton quickly learned a few things.[30] Almost everyone, he discovered, favored retiring the foreign debt and Congress's indebtedness. The states' debt was a different matter entirely, inasmuch as four or five states already had virtually met their obligations. In addition, there was not likely to be anything resembling unanimity on a proposal to redeem the Continental securities at their present value, nor would everyone favor recompensing the current owners at the original value of paper. Considering the magnitude of the problem, Hamilton worked with stunning swiftness. Within one hundred days he completed his labors, setting forth his conclusions and plans in an abstruse and ponderous forty-thousand-word Report Relative to a Provision for the Support of Public Credit. Almost hidden within the recondite language of the secretary's account was a disclosure of the Federalist's first step toward a planned revolution to save the Revolution.

The full debt easily could have been retired through a revenue tariff and public land sales. Hamilton, however, had far more on his mind. Inspired by Great Britain's financial practices during the past half century, the secretary proposed not just to adopt the methods of the former parent state, but through those means to see that republican America was recast as nearly as was possible along the lines that had existed in the pre-Revolutionary, pre-republican days of the colonial era. As such the British political system would be recapitulated in an American guise. The new Constitution already had done much of the work. It afforded the government a means of "vigorous execution," something that many in 1776 had believed was incompatible with a republican system. Moreover, the new charter made centralized governance in America a real possibility for the first time since the colonials had taken to the streets in 1765 to resist such a notion. Hamilton's plan was to bring both concepts into full play, in the process establishing the powerful and sovereign national government of which he and Washington had dreamed since the time when they had looked out on cold, hungry, unpaid, and potentially unwilling soldiers in Revolutionary cantonments. But there was another ingredient too. Hamilton sought a safeguard against what he had referred to at the Constitutional Convention as the "caprice and contumacy" of America's inhabitants. The Constitution he had helped to write and ratify already had made a start, for it had isolated the election of the president from popular stridency, it had denied the electorate a direct vote in the selection of senators to their lengthy terms, and it had erected myriad checks to forestall the House should it act in too democratic a manner. All that remained was to elevate America's lords of commerce and manufacturing, its financial barons and landed nabobs, to a peerage standing; while that certainly was impossible, the propertied elite could be firmly attached to the new government, its unswerving allegiance a guarantee of stability and an assurance that the refractory among the privileged would be kept in its proper place.

Hamilton proposed that the full indebtedness, principal and interest, on the foreign, national, and state debts be paid, and that this be accomplished by the federal government's funding the entire obligation. In a nutshell, his plan was that the old chits be liquidated through a brand new indebtedness. A new loan would be issued by the United States, subscribers to the new securities generally realizing about 5 to 6 percent interest (and in some instances western land as well), depending on which of several plans they bought into. With this revenue the old indebtedness would be retired. By this process Hamilton hoped to do two things. Assuming naturally that almost all the "stockholders" in the new national government would be drawn from among the most privileged class of the citizenry, his plan would bond that important element, with its power and prestige, to the new government, for redemption of their investment would hinge on the very survival of that government. Moreover, not only would the state creditors be brought under the aegis of the national government, but the states, left with no reason to raise taxes, and, in fact, almost stripped by the United States Constitution of access to the best sources of taxable wealth, would simply atrophy, becoming little more than unnecessary appendages to the body politic. As in England, where the national government had only counties with which to contend, the new United States government would be truly sovereign and unimpeded, in theory guided by the general will of the people, but in actuality drawing its sustenance from the "better kind of people," as Washington had labeled the privileged class on the eve of the Constitutional Convention.[31]

The secretary's Report ignited a firestorm in Federal Hall, but not because his adversaries found the plan's elitism to be repugnant. As historian John C. Miller pointed out, this was "a quarrel within the house of capitalism," one that would pit section against section, not class against class. Most of the opposition rolled up from the planter-dominated South. With over four-fifths of the national debt owed to inhabitants of northern states, with the majority of southern states already out from under their former indebtedness, and with Hamilton's plan certain to strengthen northern businessmen at the expense of southern agrarians, disapproval of the plan chiefly came from among congressmen hailing from below the Mason and Dixon Line. Added to these ranks were others who balked at the prospect of payment at face value to the present holders of the national securities. To Hamilton's astonishment, James Madison, his old colleague from the ratification fight days, took the lead in organizing the resistance. It was a battle that would consume the three quarters of 1790.[32]

Madison responded in mid-February with an alternative plan. On the certificate question his scheme was to pay the full value of the securities only to those original holders who never had sold their notes; otherwise, speculators would receive an amount equal to the highest market rate (plus interest) attained by the securities between acquisition and January 1790, while the difference between face value and the compensation received by the speculator would be paid to each original holder who had sold his note. As for the assumption of state debts, the young Virginian proposed that the national government merely take on the debts that had existed as of the end of the war in 1783.[33]

His was hardly a radical alternative to Hamilton's schemes. Madison had not recommended that the debt be scuttled, as it still was to be paid. Nor had he complained of the size of the federal outlay, for, in fact, his plan would have required an even greater national expenditure. His contrivance did seem more fair in many ways. Soldiers, some of whom had been drafted and others who had volunteered for lengthy service, finally would be paid more or less what their government had promised them when they were enticed—or coerced—into making a sacrifice for their nation. Moreover, those states which had been sufficiently responsible to meet their obligations, would not now have to bear an extreme burden to help out their more feckless neighbors. But moderate and fair as were his views, Madison's notions about the domestic debt faced absolutely no prospect of enactment by a Congress composed largely of capitalist businessmen and investors who were disinclined to set such a precedent when it came to financial speculation. The problem of the state debts was a different matter altogether, however, and as the first signs of triumphed over New York's winter, and even when June's warmer days arrived, the battle still dragged on, leaving Congress prostrate in its wake.

President Washington did not play a direct role in this protracted battle, although no one doubted that he supported the position taken by his treasury secretary. He was content to leave the issue to the legislators, for his task, as he saw it, was to make recommendations, then to execute whatever Congress decided. During the first weeks of the congressional fray he occupied himself with the never-ending chore of filling the ubiquitous new offices of the new government. He also seems to have devoted almost as much time and attention to acquiring a new residence, the Macomb House on Broadway, for which he paid nearly $100 a month in rent. New and expensive, the squarish four-story dwelling was described by a visitor as the "grandest" house in the city, perhaps in America. That, in fact, seemed to be the principal reason for Washington's sudden interest in abandoning his Cherry Street quarters. Once he secured this mansion, the president immediately spent more than $3000 of his salary on new furniture and wallpaper for the place; still not satisfied, he spent another $400 to construct stables and a wash house in the rear of the house, and a few weeks later, at an additional expense of $75, he had a small dairy in operation behind the presidential mansion. On his fifty-eighth birthday he and Martha and the grandchildren began the move into their new dwelling.[34]

Washington's move into such a high-rent district seemed to put an end to his continual complaints of financial hardship. There can be little doubt that his lack of liquid assets did present a problem, and, in fact, he was compelled to borrow a large sum at 6 percent per annum—an excessive rate of interest, he charged—before leaving Virginia for New York. But he had no sooner taken the oath of office before Congress voted him a generous salary. Actually, Washington had proposed that he be compensated only for his expenses, a tactic that had actually served him quite well financially during the inflationary surge that accompanied the war. But the legislators refused the proposal this time, instead providing him with a salary of $25,000 per year, five times the amount it voted for the vice president, about one hundred times what a skilled artisan in New York City might earn in 1789. From that amount, however, Washington was expected to meet both his private needs and his public responsibilities, including the entertainment, labor, and even the travel expenses occasioned by his office. The salary was ample to permit a comfortable, almost regal, style of living, although one could not live in a princely manner and expect to save any of the earnings.[35]

Given his taste for elegance, President Washington probably lived in a more sumptuous manner than have any of his successors. Certainly he demonstrated that he could outspend his salary. During 1790 Hamilton's treasury granted him nearly $7000 more than he was due, although in the previous year he had been underpaid by about $4000, and in his last year in office he would receive approximately $3000 less than his stipulated salary. Washington spent much of his salary on the kinds of things that any ordinary middle- or upper-class citizen would have indulged in. He had to purchase his own firewood (eight cords in September, an additional twenty in December, at a cost of about $4.00 per cord). Schooling for ten-year-old Nelly and "Little Washington" had to be paid for. Washington's doctors charged $210 to treat his illness in 1789 and $200 to attend him the following year. Washington's ever-recurring dental work resulted in another outlay, this time for the purchase of a set of teeth made of hippopotamus ivory. Both President Washington and the First Lady—as well as the grandchildren, who usually went with Lear—frequently attended the theater, tickets running about $3.00 per person. On the other hand, some of his expenditures were more due to the nature of his office. He faced a staggering liquor bill, expending 7 percent of his salary on spirits, chiefly wine. Early in 1790 he purchased over $450 worth of the beverage, and twelve months later he spent more than $1000 in acquiring two pipes of wine. The Washingtons also sought out the best cook they could find, hiring a chef for $15 per month. But it is difficult to determine the dividing line between the requirements of the office and Washington's expensive tastes. For instance, his service staff—he referred to it as his "family"—was huge. He brought seven slaves along from Mount Vernon, all body servants and house slaves, and to their number he added fourteen white servants. In addition, he kept twelve to sixteen horses in his new stables at an expense of more than a thousand dollars annually; when he rode about in public, moreover, he sat on a gaudy new saddle, while his horses only appeared after they were draped in specially purchased showy leopardskin housings. For that matter, the President and Mrs. Washington often wore fur coats, for which he had paid more than $100. Indeed, Martha had her indulgences, spending $50 a year at the hairdresser's and $150 in 1790 on jewelry. All in all, it cost about $115 a week—a year's income for an unskilled laborer—to run the president's house, and for his first term Washington's expenses exceeded $100,000.[36]

Throughout March and April, while the wrangle over Hamilton's Report continued, the president was not overly taxed with work. To be sure there were frequent meetings with his advisors, but there also was ample time for exercising and sightseeing, and even for sitting to artist John Trumbull. Certainly no physical problems—save for a brief but painful toothache in January—had plagued Washington. He long since had recovered from his protracted disability of the previous year, and the rheumatic discomforts that had bedeviled him in 1786 and 1787 appear to have vanished by the early years of his presidency. By May 1790, well free of the supposed dangers of winter, Washington was in fine fettle. Suddenly, however, he was struck down by another serious illness. Influenza, perhaps the same strain that had swept Boston the previous autumn, descended on New York that spring. Either that malady or pneumonia—his physician thought it the latter—felled him on May 9. Once again his life was despaired of, and even his principal doctor characterized his condition as so serious that he feared for the worst. For six days Washington seemed to linger on the edge of death, each day his breathing growing more labored, more shallow. One shaman after another was summoned to the Macomb House until finally, and surprisingly, late on the afternoon of May 16, just as suddenly as when the disease first had struck, an abrupt, dramatic reversal set in. Washington broke into a heavy sweat, his breathing and pulse rate seemed to improve; some hope began to spread through the mansion, though four more anxious days passed before the doctors pronounced him out of danger. For a week and a half he had lain near death, more desperately ill than he had been in nearly thirty years. A full month of recuperation awaited him before he possessed the strength to once again appear in public. In an age that believed each serious ailment stole away some of the patient's fighting reserve, Washington presumed that another such forbidding sickness probably would be his last, putting "me to sleep with my fathers." Perhaps he was correct. At any rate, many of his friends believed that he never again displayed the vigor that he had before this terrible illness.[37]

During Washington's recovery period word arrived that Rhode Island at last had ratified the Constitution. All thirteen states now were under its canopy. Equally cheering news reached the president a month later. He learned that some movement toward resolving the deadlock over Hamilton's fiscal plan at last had begun.

By June, six months after its introduction, Hamilton's assumption scheme still languished in Congress. In February Madison's plan to discriminate between the original and current holders of securities had been soundly defeated, while Hamilton's expedient likewise had failed in April. The secretary's plan had been defeated narrowly, however, raising the prospect of some sort of compromise solution, something that was being discussed openly throughout the spring. The issue to which assumption most often was linked was the enduring debate over the site of the national capital. By 1790 the residence issue had kicked around the halls of Congress for seven years, with Philadelphia, New York, Baltimore, Pittsburgh, Annapolis, Williamsburg, even Nottingham, New Jersey, and Kingston, New York, in addition to various sites on the Susquehanna, the Scioto, and the Potomac having been mentioned as desirable locations. Agrarians wanted their legislators removed from the influence of big city financial moguls; southerners worried about keeping their slaves in a nonslave state; and everybody also saw the ultimate site in terms of a potential economic bonanza that they would just as soon have within their reach. During that first month of summer in 1790 renewed stirrings toward a resolution of the two issues seemed to crystallize, arising perhaps from Hamilton's threats to resign if Congress rejected his program, or perhaps from the fact that some order had begun to take shape within the "leaderless herd" that had been the Congress. Jefferson's recent arrival in New York may have been important too, as perhaps was the sixth sense of legislators who finally determined that at last the time to deal had arrived.[38]

Four days before President Washington took his first halting ride following his recent illness, Jefferson brought Hamilton and Madison together for dinner at his house. By then the two Virginians knew they had the votes in the House to pass a bill that would move the capital temporarily to Philadelphia while a permanent seat was under construction at a site on the Potomac. They did not have the votes to get the bill through the Senate, however, and that was where Hamilton came in. If the treasury secretary would use his influence to block any attempt by northeastern senators to permanently base the capital in Pennsylvania or New York, Jefferson and Madison proposed, they would seek to change enough votes within the Virginia and Maryland delegations to enact Hamilton's economic program.

How successful these three bargainers were has been the subject of considerable recent debate among scholars. Yet it is clear that while a majority of southern legislators continued to resist Hamilton's assumption bill, four representatives— two from Virginia and two from Maryland, all four from districts on the Potomac —made an about-face between the April roll call and the final vote in July. Moreover, Massachusetts's senators suddenly opted not to endeavor to undermine the Philadelphia-Potomac residence proposition. Hamilton also apparently facilitated matters by making some adjustments on the details of his economic package, compromising on the rate of interest carried by the new debt and conceding to some states an increase in the amount of their credit. Virginia and Maryland also offered enticements to facilitate the deal. Each state promised grants of land and cash if Congress voted to locate the new capital on the Potomac. Even Washington, who had remained in the background thus far, pitched in. It is clear that he brought considerable pressure on Robert Morris to accept the bargain, and he probably subtly courted other congressmen.

The dark, labyrinthian ways of legislators make it impossible to recapture all the dickering and dragooning that must have occurred that June and July, but by midsummer funding and assumption were the law of the land. It also had been agreed to transfer the seat of government to Philadelphia for ten years, then, in 1800, to move it to the banks of the Potomac. Congress directed that the federal district be located somewhere between the eastern branch of the Potomac (now called the Anacostia) and the Conogocheague Creek far to the west, a stream that enters the Potomac above present-day Harper's Ferry, West Virginia.[39]

A few days after these historic votes Congress adjourned. It would next assemble in Philadelphia. President Washington also was packing, planning to say goodbye, probably forever, to New York City, a city so remote in so many ways from his rural Virginia, but a place where he had spent nearly 5 percent of his adult life. First, however, he crossed Long Island Sound by packet to pay a state visit to Rhode Island, a place omitted from his itinerary during the past autumn because it had not then ratified the Constitution. The round trip was brief, taking less than a week. Upon his return to Manhattan his stay at the Macomb House was almost as short. For weeks, at least since his spring illness, Washington had planned an excursion to Mount Vernon, his first journey home in almost a year and a half. He felt good again, and he was buoyant at the prospects of the new government. Sixteen months into his presidency he still could report that "public sentiment runs with us, and all things hitherto seem to succeed according to our wishes."[40]

The same day in all likelihood that he penned those thoughts a little box bearing a Paris postmark arrived at the Macomb House. It was from Lafayette. Always impatient to hear from his dear young friend, Washington must have eagerly torn open the parcel. Inside, of all things, he discovered a key and a picture. The one was the jailor's key to the Bastille, the other a likeness of the prison being dismantled by a Parisian mob. The one symbolized the despotism of the Ancient Regime, the other, the etching, captured the notion that a great European power had commenced its own "leap into the dark."[41]

Based on what little information he could get from the Continent, Washington knew that the sweeping revolution at Versailles and Paris was likely to be "stupendous in its consequences."[42] As he and his family rode to the New Jersey ferry on August 30, President Washington must have wondered what those consequences would mean for his own nation.

16

The End of the First Term

"Internal dissensions . . . tearing our vitals"

The president deliberately kept his travel plans secret. He hoped to avoid the "fatiguing and oftentimes painful" ceremonies that each village along his route felt compelled to conduct in his honor. Mostly, though, he just hoped to save time, to hasten his journey to Mount Vernon and perhaps to get in a couple additional days of relaxation. His strategy worked, although the authorities of Philadelphia could not resist sending out its trainband honor guard to greet him, pealing the city's bells, and proclaiming a "Day of Joy" upon his arrival.[1]

The newly ordained temporary capital held Washington for four days. That was pretty much as he had planned. Philadelphia's authorities had rented Robert Morris's town villa on Market Street for the president, and he wished to inspect it closely, perhaps with an eye to recommending some alterations to suit his needs. This was the same house General Howe had utilized during his occupation of the city, the same dwelling in which Washington had resided during the Constitutional Convention. It was a three-story brick structure, though two dormers facing the street announced the presence of a capacious fourth-floor attic. The house set only a few feet from its neighbor on the east, while to the other side a generous garden lay hidden behind a five-foot-high brick wall. Washington remembered it as "the best *single House* in the City," but upon seeing it now he found it inadequate to the *commodious* accommodation of my family." He wished to have a small building constructed in the rear to serve as an abode for some of his servants, while the others would be crammed into quarters above the wash house and the stable or beneath the kitchen, and some unfortunate would be put up in the smoke house. Inside the main residence, he proposed the ingenious use of partitions to carve out a private study and a dressing room for himself and two new "public Rooms" for entertaining. Washington summoned Lear to superintend the repairs, and on September 6, 1790, a day or two later than he had hoped, the First Family resumed its journey back to Virginia.[2]

Mount Vernon enveloped the president and his homesick wife for nearly twelve weeks, long enough for them to watch the foliage magically undertake its ritual transformation from greens to resplendent reds and yellows, then to disappear altogether. He hardly could have had a more relaxing vacation. Conditions at his farm apparently pleased him, and the bliss which that induced went uninterrupted by public crises. So tranquil were the times that the president did not receive even a single diplomatic packet from his secretary of state. During those serene weeks only one item of public business faced Washington. He had to select the site on the Potomac for the new federal district. Actually, the Residence Act implied that a presidentially appointed commission was to fix the site, but Washington ignored the spirit of the law and made the decision unilaterally. Indeed, it now appears that he had made his choice even before leaving New York. He wished the federal district to be located from "just above the commencement of the [Potomac River Company] canal" to "the lower end of Alexandria," and the "Federal city," as he had begun to call it, constructed somewhere between the little village of Georgetown, on Rock Creek, and Carrollsburg, a "town" (it existed on paper only) at the junction of the Potomac and the Eastern branch of the great river.

He could not immediately reveal his intentions, however, lest he antagonize the Congress, for the legislators expected the eighty-mile span between Carrollsburg and Williamsport to be scrutinized seriously; besides, pursuing Madison's suggestion he concluded that an apparent inspection tour of the long stretch would induce rival aspirants "to bid against each other in offers of land or money." Thus, he nosed about Georgetown a bit, where he found the drooling landowners willing to ante up four hundred free acres to the national government, then he journeyed seventy miles upriver to look over the region about the Conococheague. The inhabitants of that area outbid their eastern brethren. Antietam offered 475 acres and a grant of $4800, while Shepherdstown pledged over $20,000. There was no way they could have known that their furious endeavors to impress Washington were exercises in futility.[3]

Other than the permanent site of the capital, his pending move to Philadelphia was the matter that seemed to weigh most heavily on Washington's mind during these months. He wrote letter after letter to Lear, each a long and exhaustive compendium of assignments for his aide to oversee, some concerning the renovation of the Morris House, others given to intricate instructions about packing his furniture, and a few discoursing on the proper schooling for his grandchildren and his niece Harriet. Then, late in November, with the normally dry autumn soon due to give way to the customary seasonal rains, Washington and his family set out for the temporary capital. It must have been gloomy enough to be ending such an idyllic vacation, but a thoroughly unpleasant return trip conspired to make matters even worse. The President of the United States and his family were driven by an unskilled, habitually intoxicated coachman, a man who had to be removed from the presidential carriage to a wagon laden with trunks, then ultimately replaced altogether when, in his stupor, he succeeded in twice overturning that vehicle.[4]

That frightful trip was an augury of what lay ahead. The final two years of his term would prove to be far less pleasant than the months that had gone before. The president barely had reached Philadelphia and made a start at trying to settle in amidst the carpenters and joiners who continued to toil inside his new residence before Congress reconvened. Persisting in the practice begun by the English monarch, America's chief executive addressed the legislators at the opening of their session. Reading a speech drafted largely by Madison and Hamilton, he touched briefly on frontier issues, foreign policy concerns, and fiscal matters— the three problems that would dominate the remainder of his term. A day or two later Secretary Hamilton got the first crack at the legislators.[5]

Two weeks before Christmas the treasury secretary sent up a report containing recommendations that fleshed out his venturesome economic program. Working assiduously in the library of the house he had rented, a dwelling that once had belonged to Dr. Benjamin Rush, Hamilton completed his lengthy fiscal blueprint. The report urged the creation of a national bank capitalized at $10 million, four-fifths of the total provided by private investors, the remainder by the government. The existence of such an institution would serve several ends. It would be a source for the accumulation of capital and a means of providing a greater accessibility of credit. It also would further wed the merchant-financial classes to the new national polity. The bank, therefore, would join with other devices to become a source of revenue for that government. Congress already had enacted a nondiscriminatory tariff, that is one whose burden fell equally on the merchandise of all nations. In addition, in his initial report earlier that year Hamilton had proposed that excise taxes be levied on certain commodities, but principally on distilled spirits. In a sense, the proposal was a sop to the South, for two-thirds of the nation's distillers were in New York and New England, the rest out on the frontier. Previously Congress had balked at these duties, but now the so-called Whiskey Tax passed, and by the third week in February the Bank Bill also had been enacted.[6]

Although the Bank Bill got through Congress with little difficulty, southerners in that body hoisted a red warning flag that troubled the president. Harboring the eighteenth-century farmer's inherent antipathy toward banks, and assuming— correctly—that their region would realize few direct benefits from the proposed institution, most southern congressmen had opposed the bill, fighting its passage on the only terrain that might lead to victory. Introducing a whole new element into the simmering national factionalism, Madison raised the question of the scope of Congress's power. Recanting the position he had taken at the Constitutional Convention, he now contended that the fundamental charter was a "grant of particular powers only." For Congress to arrogate to itself a power not specifically delegated was not just unconstitutional, he said, but dangerous to the whole precept of limited government. President Washington, he implied, must veto the bill.[7]

The president had no idea what to do. Jefferson, who sided with the bank's foes, thought him "unready, short and embarrassed," but, if so, the chief executive can be excused. Questions of this sort would divide constitutional experts in every subsequent generation. Actually, Washington responded as he often did when confronted by an abstruse problem. He sought advice. He elicited the opinions of Jefferson, Madison, and Attorney General Randolph, and after studying their strict constructionist views he asked Hamilton to submit a written opinion. A bit put off by the president's doubts, the secretary nevertheless spent a week recording his ideas, and the result was a masterpiece of constitutional as well as pragmatic logic. The national government was sovereign, he began, and it possessed the "*means*" to do whatever was not specifically forbidden. For instance, everyone agreed that under its right to regulate trade Congress could expend money for the construction of lighthouses and buoys, although the Constitution did not explicitly spell out the legislature's power to build these navigational devices. Moreover, a bank had considerable utilitarian value; through its resources, government would have immediate access to funds in the event of a national emergency, and even in the pursuit of its frontier military policies. If the Constitution was to endure, he went on, it must be flexible. If it was interpreted inflexibly, Congress's authority would be suffocated and the new government would collapse as surely as had its impotent predecessor. Washington received Hamilton's thoughts on the day after his fifty-ninth birthday. Two days later he signed the bill into law.[8]

Hamilton's cogent argument was not the only factor that induced Washington to sign the Bank Bill. Immediately after the Senate passed that legislation Washington revealed the site he had selected for the new capital. The district, he reported, would be a diamond-shaped area that included acreage both in Virginia and in Maryland, and it would run from just below the Great Falls of the Potomac through Alexandria. Some in Congress were annoyed that he had taken on himself the sole responsibility for making the selection and others were provoked at his sleight of hand, but so considerable was the president's prestige that his critics confined their grumbling to private letters and diaries. Nevertheless, Washington's inclusion of Alexandria, which lay south of the Eastern Branch and thus outside the parameters that Congress had designated for the site of the district, clearly transgressed the legislator's intentions. Washington's decision was risky, too, inasmuch as it would require Congress's consent, and that would reopen the entire residency question. The president realized the danger, and beginning several days before he announced his decision he undertook to court and flatter some legislators who earlier had openly resisted situating the district against the Potomac. If his artful tactics helped discourage the rekindling of the long, vexatious capital-site battle, so, too, did some political horsetrading. One senator thought a deal was struck so that in return for certain legislators' consent, Washington would appoint Gouverneur Morris as America's envoy to Britain, from whence he would be advantageously placed to peddle Robert Morris's Scottish realty. In addition, other wily congressmen simply sat on the bill to amend the Residence Act until Washington saw fit to sign the Bank Bill. When the president agreed to Congress's act, the legislators consented immediately to Washington's decision regarding the district. What amounted to a second capital-fiscal compromise had occurred.[9]

Washington never displayed more mysterious behavior than in the course of selecting the site of the federal district. He disregarded sound arguments for locating the district well up the Potomac. Defense considerations, particularly in light of Congress's frequent peregrinations in the recent war, were a persuasive argument in behalf of a more inland site. Moreover, in its cession of lands for a district Virginia clearly had demonstrated its preference for a location at or above the Great Falls northwest of Georgetown. What is more, generous pledges of money and land had been made by hamlets near the Conococheague. Yet Washington had ignored all these considerations, ultimately even choosing a site lying outside the region designated by Congress.

Some friends of the president endeavored to explain his behavior by suggesting that his choice was dictated by the handsome, scenic vistas alongside the Potomac. Such an explanation was palpable nonsense. It also has been proposed that the president's decision grew from his concern about partisan politics in Virginia. According to this logic, he acted out of a desire to win over his neighbor, George Mason, a leading Virginia Anti-Federalist, who additionally was the owner of considerable property within the region Washington selected. The principal problem with such a hypothesis is that it, too, lacks substantiation; besides, Washington would have known that, while such a step might have assuaged Mason, it was bound to antagonize others, and as such it could not—and, indeed, did not—end the partisan wars that raged in his home state.[10]

Better explanations exist for Washington's behavior. Most historians agree that a part of the assumption-capital bargain in 1790 was that two Virginia congressmen would switch their vote to assure passage of Hamilton's credit legislation. The two congressmen in question, Richard Bland Lee and Alexander White, each owned land about Georgetown. The selection of the area surrounding Georgetown to be the seat of the new Federal City was the political payoff of the capital bargain, and Washington, a skilled and worldly politician, simply was the instrument through which the final detail of the deal was consummated. Why did Washington and Jefferson turn to Lee and White? After all, other congressmen must have been equally willing to change their vote in return for a similar prize. Surely the answer must be that Washington's interests dovetailed with those of Lee and White. There can be no doubt that Washington concluded that a Potomac site, one embracing both Georgetown and Alexandria, the two principal ports on that river, would cement both Virginia's and the West's shaky ties to the Union. At this moment, before the railroad, before the steamboat, before the Erie Canal, Washington continued to believe that the Potomac would be America's highway to the frontier. Settling the capital on its blue-green waters must have seemed not only to assure the river's ascendancy over all rivals but to guarantee that the economic and political center of the United States would be one and the same—and it would repose on what amounted to the soil of Maryland and Virginia.

Was there still another motive? Did Washington seek personal gain through his selection of the Potomac site? Some contemporary politicians believed that he did, although none were so courageous as to publicly make such a charge. It is unlikely, however, that the directors of the Potomac Company were terribly disappointed in the conduct of their chairman of the board, George Washington.[11] For the past two years they had undertaken a publicity campaign aimed at making Georgetown-Alexandria the site of the new capital, and once the decision was announced Washington confessed to them that his actions had been dictated by self-interest. His motives, he said, had been divided between "an intimate connection in political and pecuniary considerations." In his behavior, he added, "Public and private motives combine. . . ."[12]

Few public figures in American history could match Washington's record of virtuous and selfless service, but even he stumbled when the vast potential of the frontier West was at stake. This was the man who had exhorted Forbes and Bouquet to cut a wilderness road through a route that would be of benefit to him, the man whose attentive amassing of the best bounty lands available to the Virginia Regiment bore the stench of scandal. That personal considerations, from the potential enhancement of his Mount Vernon properties to the added value that would accrue to the real estate he owned in Alexandria, should now have entered his thoughts can hardly come as a surprise. As always, he convinced himself that the nation was the chief beneficiary of his actions. If that was not quite the case, it nevertheless would be difficult to argue that the national interest was in any way harmed by his conduct.

Within thirty days of the resolution of the Bank Bill and the federal district issue, Washington took his leave of Philadelphia, the commencement of a three-month absence from the capital. His first stop was on the banks of the Potomac, where he hoped to visit with the landowners of Georgetown and Carrollsburg. The president was anxious to clear away all impediments to the construction of the new capital city. The chief obstacle was that Congress had appropriated no money with which to construct the Federal buildings. Virginia and Maryland had pledged $200,000 for that purpose, but it would not go far. Washington needed land to sell; from the resulting revenue the new capital could be constructed. Three days of intense meetings between the president and landowners were required before he could announce that the haggling was "happily finished." More than a little bit experienced in the art of landjobbing, Washington took a characteristically tough stance with these men. Make a deal or risk losing everything, he told them bluntly, reminding them that there were men in Philadelphia who would just as soon not let the national capital escape their city. In the end a fair deal was struck. All land between Georgetown and Carrollsburg (a length of one and one-half miles and a depth of one mile) was ceded to the national government. The United States would survey the region, divide it into lots, and return alternate lots to the original owners. In fact, even before this bargain was struck Washington was shepherding the venture toward actuality. He finally had named people to the three-member commission that Congress had created to oversee the undertaking, and he quietly had hired an engineer to lay out the new city.[13]

During his first month as president, Washington had pledged to visit every state during his tenure in office, and since the beginning of the year he had planned an official trip into the South. He had never been to Georgia or South Carolina, and the only part of North Carolina that he had visited was the tiny segment where the Dismal Swamp lapped across the Virginia boundary. Everything hinged on getting away early enough, however, for in the wake of his two recent illnesses the president was determined not to face the miasmic southern climate after late May. When Congress adjourned early and he wrapped up the Potomac land transactions at the very end of March, the way was cleared for his journey. First he hurried from Georgetown to Mount Vernon to rest himself and his horses, and to look into the operation of his farms, then early in April 1791, he started south.[14]

As with his last exit from Mount Vernon, this trip began badly. Crossing Occoquan Creek at Colchester, Washington's lead horse stumbled off the ferry, dragging his three terrified teammates with him into the cold, swirling water. Fortunately, the quick-thinking driver succeeded in disengaging the animals before the carriage could also be pulled over. Miraculously all the horses rescued themselves by swimming safely to the shore, where they were restrained and re-hitched to the president's vehicle. Within a few minutes Washington again was on his way. He spent two nights at his sister's house in Fredericksburg, stopped the coach one afternoon to fish for a spell, inspected the progress of canal building on the James River, and everywhere, it seemed, he faced "a salute from cannon & an Escort of Horse." So weary of the latter did he grow, in fact, that he fibbed to the commander of Petersburg's trainband company, telling him that he would depart at 8:00 A.M., only to sneak out in serene privacy before sunrise.[15]

"[T]ravelling in a continued cloud of dust" across Virginia's primitive roads, Washington pressed into North Carolina on the ninth day of his trip, somewhat startled at the "few good Houses" and the "small appearances of wealth" that he observed as he proceeded. Yet everywhere he found the citizenry "orderly and Civil," not to mention "happy, contented and satisfied." Down now in the region where the armies of Greene and Cornwallis had struggled a decade earlier, he crossed the Roanoke River at Halifax, watched the marketing of tar at Greenville (recently named for the late general) on the Tar River, stopped and breakfasted one morning at what he thought was a tavern, only to learn later—to his considerable embarrassment—that it was the private residence of a member of the North Carolina legislature, attended a dance in New Bern, and near the end of the month arrived at Wilmington on the Cape Fear River.[16]

By now the tobacco lands had given way to the moist green rice fields of the coast. A couple of days out of Wilmington he crossed the Waccamaw and entered Georgetown, South Carolina, a town of about five hundred that still was struggling to recover from the ravages of the British occupation ten years earlier. There he attended a tea party at which he was entertained by several belles dressed in flowing skirts and wearing headdresses upon which were printed such tributes as "Long life to the President," and "Welcome to the hero." On the road to Charleston he lodged with a rancher who raised cattle and razorback hogs, thence to Snee Farm, the rice plantation of Governor Charles Pinckney. On May 2 he was rowed across to Charleston, where he paused for a week. Washington's itinerary was so crowded that he probably got only a bit of the rest that he needed. Dinners and concerts and balls took up each evening, affairs always made all the more enjoyable by the presence of several of South Carolina's lovely maidens, young women whom Washington pronounced to be the most attractive creatures he had ever seen. By day he inspected the city's sites, its forts and warehouses and homes, one day even visiting an orphanage, something he never before had seen.[17]

From Charleston, Washington headed for the southernmost point of his excursion. The heat of May already upon him, the President hurried over the sandy coastal littoral. Finding no public inns along his route, he lodged in carefully selected private homes each night, bypassing the log cabins with chimneys fashioned from "Split sticks filled with dirt between them," that he discovered comprised the residences of most of the inhabitants of this region. Along the way he stopped at Mulberry Grove to visit Catherine Greene, the widow of his loyal general, then he proceeded to Savannah, arriving just as the last rays of the day's sun bathed the town in splendor. As he alighted in St. James Square, cannon boomed from vessels on the Savannah River, the Chatham County Artillery Company went through its paces, and a band played "He comes, the Hero comes." Washington lingered three full days in this tranquil southern town, spending one night with the state's Order of the Cincinnati and its commander, Anthony Wayne, who like Greene had moved to Georgia following the war, and another evening at a dance attended by nearly one hundred "handsome" Georgia damsels.[18]

In mid-May Washington started home, a twenty-eight-day trek over a different route. It began with a long, difficult ride through the Georgia pine barrens, across roads so sandy that his horses tired quickly and the traveler fretted that at this rate he would not see Mount Vernon before Christmas. After pausing to pay his respects to Mrs. Greene once again, he continued on to Augusta; there, apparently for the first time during this trip, he was compelled to conduct public business, for the governor of Georgia wished to plead with the president for more federal assistance in obtaining runaway slaves. The next day Washington was back in South Carolina, visiting Columbia and, subsequently, Camden, where Gates had been compelled to flee for his life in 1780, and where he visited the gravesite of Baron de Kalb. From there he proceeded to Charlotte, up to Salisbury, then across the Yadkin to Salem, a fifteen-year-old Moravian settlement that was conspicuous for welcoming him with music—trumpets, French horns, trombones—not with gunfire. He had hoped to be home by June 1, but on that day he and the governor of North Carolina attended a *singstunde,* a song service provided by the German immigrants who inhabited this tiny village. The next morning he was on his way to Guilford Court House, where he inspected the site of Cornwallis's Pyrrhic victory over Greene, the battle that sent the British army reeling to the coast and ultimately into Virginia in 1781. Two days later the president, too, was in Virginia, and a week later he reached Mount Vernon, arriving in time for his customary mid-afternoon dinner, a meal to celebrate the completion of a round trip of 1887 miles.[19]

The president enjoyed the lush, warm, green vista of Mount Vernon in summer for only two weeks before departing for the capital. Never would he take a more circuitous route back to Philadelphia. His first stop was in Georgetown to meet with the three commissioners for the federal district. But it was the project engineer, thirty-seven-year-old Major Pierre Charles L'Enfant, a former officer in the Continental army, a survivor of the clash at Savannah, with whom he most wished to talk. "Langfang," as Washington persisted in calling the Frenchman, had a good track record, one that included the design of several buildings in New York—most importantly, the Federal Hall—which Washington had admired. L'Enfant seemed to display a mind that comingled order and art, one with a bent toward the grandiose and ostentatious, the "en grande," as he put it. Thus, when he appealed to Washington for the opportunity to design the new capital, the president was interested, and when Hamilton, Knox, and Robert Morris endorsed him, Washington was certain that L'Enfant was his man.[20]

From the outset, however, the president and the secretary of state had conflicting views about the engineer's duties. Jefferson seemed to think L'Enfant was only to pick the sites for the various buildings, while he designed the layout of the city and chose the proper architectural mode for its structures. In fact, Jefferson did prepare a schematic drawing for the city, one in which the new capital was to be arranged in a rectangular gridiron pattern, its buildings closely bunched and nearly every vestige of the bucolic countryside eradicated.[21] L'Enfant characterized such a notion as "tiresome and insipid," envisioning instead a city in which nature and art were intertwined. He preferred to leave much of the natural topography intact, planning streets around hillocks and creeks, with circles and wide boulevards intermingling with smaller thoroughfares, and minor streets abutting major arteries that coursed along at a slight angle, as if the designer had carelessly dropped an overlay atop his initial conception. Whether the president also thought Jefferson's design was mundane cannot be known, but he did direct L'Enfant to prepare a plan.[22]

When Washington reached Georgetown on his return to Philadelphia, his first day was consumed by meetings with the commissioners and landowners. Several of the latter, having gotten wind of L'Enfant's thinking, now were grumbling about the distended size of the planned city, fearing the sprawl might reduce their property values. The president once again quieted them with tough talk, and the next day he and his engineer rode about the area. L'Enfant still had not committed a final draft to paper, but his rough sketches were clear enough for Washington to grasp. The Frenchman also showed his visitor to the sites where the president's house, the capitol, and the various department buildings would be located, waxing eloquent about parks and gardens and "grand fountains . . . with a constant spout of water," and he may even have pointed out the site for the "Grand Equestrian" monument that Congress had voted in 1783 to erect in honor of General Washington. L'Enfant expounded a bit about the style of each building. Washington must have listened closely when he spoke of the president's dwelling, a structure that the Frenchman thought should combine the "sumptuousness of a palace, the convenience of a house and the agreeableness of a country seat." After an inspection that could not have lasted more than three or four hours, Washington gave his sanction to L'Enfant's ideas. By the middle of the next week a journalist broke the news of what the new capital would look like. That was how Jefferson learned of the shape of the proposed city.[23]

By then the president was back in the temporary capital, having gotten there via a mini-tour that ranged from Georgetown to Frederick, Maryland, then up the Susquehanna to York (where he attended a worship service conducted entirely in German), east through Lancaster, and eventually to Philadelphia.[24] Back in his office he found his desk laden with papers and reports that had accumulated during his four-month absence. Many concerned frontier issues and America's relations with the principal European powers, matters that often were interrelated. These concerns had provoked much rhetoric and anxiety in the Articles of Confederation era, but in the first two years of the Washington administration other problems had forced them into the background. For the remainder of his term, however, neither matter ever would be far from the president's thoughts.

Soon after the war with Britain ended, the national government, acting under the Ordinance of 1785, began to survey parts of the Ohio Country. Meanwhile, a succession of treaties negotiated by the Articles government with the Iroquois, Ottawa, Delaware, and other tribes opened to settlement an area that extended to the falls of the Ohio. United States citizens once again began to push west. Soon the flow of humanity into this region resembled an avalanche, as each month hundreds of adventurous settlers coursed down the Ohio into the newly acquired lands. Soon, too, land-hungry farmers crossed the river and squatted on lands which the Indians had not ceded, territory as far west as the present boundary of Indiana-Illinois. In fact, the Native Americans not only had never surrendered these lands, they saw no reason to recognize the Treaty of Paris, by which Great Britain had so magnanimously presented the trans-Appalachian West to the United States. Instead, the tribesmen in the Northwest took the position that the Ohio River was to be the outer boundary of the United States. Supported by the British, who continued to hold the old royal forts in this area, the Indians were far from powerless.

When negotiations in the mid-1780s failed to resolve the stalemate, it seemed to many that force alone would facilitate the ambitions of the new nation's land-hungry citizenry. Unpropitiously, however, the United States was virtually without an army. In the final weeks of the War of Independence, while he lived at Rocky Hill outside Princeton, General Washington had testified before a congressional committee that an army of about 2000 men should be maintained; the committee, a panel chaired by Hamilton, eventually requested a standing force of 2500.[25] But Congress did nothing, and six months after Washington's retirement the United States had an army of only 80 men, 25 soldiers at Fort Pitt, the remainder at West Point; none held rank above captain. When relations with the Native Americans grew tense the following year, Congress enlarged the army to 700 men. On paper, anyway, it remained at that strength throughout the decade, although when Washington was inaugurated only 694 men actually were in uniform. The new president, a man with a long and deep interest in the West, envisioned a vigorous role for the new national government in the pacification of the frontier. He quickly prevailed on Congress to enlarge the United States army to over 1200 men.[26]

Even so, Washington was not unalterably committed to the use of force to resolve the problems in the West. Indeed, for the foreseeable future he believed that peace was imperative for the security of the United States. In this "still *very early* stage of our affairs," he reasoned, a vast conflagration along the frontier might prove to be catastrophic. A conflict that was costly both in blood and in dollars was likely to erode support for the new federal union. In addition, a war in the Northwest with the Native Americans could escalate into a second war with Great Britain, this time, perhaps, with disastrous results.[27]

Of course, the president never contemplated an abrogation of what he conceived as the nation's interests in the West. If for no other reason, the United States must control the West to keep Great Britain from establishing its suzerainty over the region. He dreamed of wresting control of the Indian trade, and he even spoke of American dominion as a means of putting an end to the area's potential as a haven for fugitive slaves. The West was essential, too, for the preservation of America's "primoeval simplicity." The regenerative qualities of the frontier, he said, would serve as a counterpoise against the "luxury, dissipation, and corruption" likely to be endemic in the urbanizing, commercial East. Mostly, however, Washington portrayed the West as the "cement" of the Union, for he envisioned the transmontane region as a virtual colony of the North and the South, the lucrative bond that would make it worthwhile for the two very different sections to remain united.[28]

When Washington took office he sought to avoid the annihilation of the western Indians, both from humanitarian reasons and because he feared that rapid destruction of these people would open the West more quickly than he thought advisable. Washington believed that the United States should carefully control the flow of population onto the frontier. You "cannot stop the road," he once told

Congress, but you can "mark the way." A West that grew too quickly, he feared, might go its own way, perhaps even separating from the United States. The West must be controlled and shaped, so that it would complement the interests of the existing states. Consequently, the Washington administration would keep western land prices at exorbitant levels, nearly fifteen times higher than they would be twenty years later. That policy would bind East and West, while it minimized the likelihood of a frontier war.[29]

In some respects Washington's views toward the Native Americans were far ahead of those of his contemporaries. He had overcome much of his youthful prejudice, and now he could even envision the assimilation of the tribesmen into the society of the white settlers. As the frontiersmen slowly seeped into the West, Washington reasoned, the Native Americans's hunting grounds would be destroyed. But this might be a gradual process, affording the Indians the opportunity to convert to Euro-American's farming habits. He happily pledged federal assistance to aid the Indians in this conversion. If the Indians refused to acquiesce, there remained a simple and peaceful means by which the United States could obtain their lands. The Indian's domain could be bought, he said, and it "can be had by purchase at less expense" than by the use of force.[30]

Events in the Northwest on the eve of Washington's inauguration made it evident that urgent action was required of his administration. Recurrent clashes between settlers and Indians indicated that the frontier was tumbling quickly toward full-scale warfare. There was ample blame to spread about for this dismaying state of affairs. In part, said Washington, "incursions . . . by certain banditti" among the Indians were responsible for the conflicts, a statement which signified that he believed only some tribes, perhaps even only some elements among the tribesmen, were to blame. Yet, if Washington reproached some Indians, he held the frontiersmen even more accountable. He spoke of the settlers "disorderly conduct," and he acknowledged that the frontiersmen had crossed into Indian territory, "alienating their lands." That, he charged, was the "main source of discontent and war."[31]

Fearing that these border clashes might escalate until the frontier was everywhere ablaze, Washington acted quickly during his first year in office. It was at this point that he induced Congress to enlarge the regular army, and he additionally secured the legislators' assent to authorize Arthur St. Clair, the governor of the Northwest Territory, to mobilize fifteen hundred militiamen from Pennsylvania and Virginia. At the same time, Washington directed St. Clair to parley with the leaders of the Wabash and Illinois tribes.[32]

It was a muddled policy. The army's chief mission was to restrain the frontiersmen, in Washington's eyes the principal culprits in instigating the mayhem in the West. Yet, he made it clear that it was the behavior of the Indians that would determine whether the United States used force. If he concluded that the "security of the frontier inhabitants, the security of the troops, and the national dignity" were imperiled, his government would "be constrained to punish [the Indians] with severity."[33]

Opposition to Washington's policy was immediate. Some in Congress suspected that the president's course was but a pretext for the fulfillment of the nationalists' long-standing aim of establishing a permanent army. Others feared that the Washington administration, given an army to play with, would blunder into war. It had been wrong to create a department of war "when we were at peace," complained Senator William Maclay of Pennsylvania. "Give Knox his army," Maclay now added, and "he . . . will have a war in less than six months." New England objected for other reasons. Many in that section were notably unenthusiastic about paying for a war to open a remote frontier. But Washington did not hear only from those who criticized his apparently truculent policies. Some frontier leaders, land speculators, and even some high army officers, carped at the administration for not taking forthright military action against the Indians.[34]

These critics did not have long to wait before the administration took a much tougher stance. In the spring of 1790 Washington concluded that St. Clair's diplomatic endeavors had failed. By now the president was convinced that Great Britain was provoking and arming the Native Americans. Under such circumstances, he believed, it "will be in vain I fear to expect peace with the Indians." Eschewing the essentially defensive policies it hitherto had pursued, the Washington government ordered an expedition into the troubled territory. However the Indians may have viewed the invasion, Washington saw the campaign as limited in scope. He sought to pacify the entire Northwest by authorizing a punitive expedition against the recalcitrant Native American "banditti" along the banks of the Maumee and the Wabash.[35]

Colonel Josiah Harmar, a brave commander but one with little experience in fighting Indians, and a man allegedly wont to nip too heavily at the brown jug, was selected to lead the frontier army. It was largely to be a militia operation, for Washington, fearing that the frontier soon might explode from the Lakes to the Southwest, doubted that he had time to raise and train a regular army. With fifteen hundred militiamen and about three hundred regulars under his command, therefore, Harmar debouched from near present-day Cincinnati into the Ohio wilderness.[36]

For three weeks the campaign appeared to be a replay of the Sullivan Expedition of 1779. The soldiers found nothing along the Maumee except deserted villages, which, together with stores of foodstuffs, were put to the torch. In mid-October, however, things began to go awry. First, a large unit of Kentucky trainbandsmen succeeded in walking into an ambush, which resulted in heavy losses. Two days later a similar fate befell Harmar's regulars, and he was compelled to withdraw. The foray had resulted in the considerable destruction of Indian lives and property, yet, in return, the United States forfeited more than two hundred, killed and wounded, including the loss of nearly one in three men in its regular army. What is more, the expedition had failed to bring peace to the frontier.[37]

Behind closed doors President Washington railed at Harmar as one cause of the failure. "I expected *little* from the moment I heard he was a *drunkard*," he raged. Harmar's conduct in the field had been "disgraceful," he told Knox.

But the real reason for the thrashing, Washington and his secretary of war agreed in private, stemmed from the inherent liabilities of a militia force. Reports had reached the president's office that the militiamen had been disorderly and undisciplined, and that they had broken under fire. Given their inveterate hostility toward trainband units, Washington and Knox seized upon such accounts and promptly made the decision to urge a second Northwestern campaign.[38]

Their conduct reeked with duplicity. In public the administration spoke of the campaign as necessary to force the Indians to listen to the "humane overtures" of the United States. In private, however, Knox admitted that the government's end was to "extirpate, totally if possible," the Miami tribes in the Ohio Country; anything less, he argued, might stimulate separatist aspirations among the frontiers settlers. In addition, whereas Washington privately held the expansive, lawless Kentuckians at least as responsible as the Indians for the onset of frontier hostilities, he publicly enumerated only the "provocations" of the Indian "aggressors." The proposed new campaign also provided a golden opportunity for the Washington government to augment the United States army, an end that the nationalists had cherished since the end of the War of Independence. Soon after learning of Harmar's misfortune, the president proposed that the ranks of the army be doubled.

The regular army now would exceed two thousand men, but many soldiers would be unavailable for a renewed offensive in the Ohio Country. About half the men would be stationed elsewhere, many garrisoning a string of forts that the war department planned throughout the vast frontier. Thus, Washington proposed that the regulars be augmented by "levies," volunteers who would enlist for the duration of this mission. In January 1791, Congress assented to Washington's design. Sometimes, the president reflected, "acts of force . . . [were] the safest means of compelling . . . an amicable settlement." Besides, if full-scale war was to engulf the frontier, better for it to result from "a deliberate plan, not . . . an accidental collision." [39]

Governor St. Clair, a former Revolutionary War general, was appointed to command the operation. By the fall he had a force one-third again as large as Harmar had possessed, but recruiting problems had foiled Washington's hopes for a largely regular force. Three quarters of this army would consist of semi-trained or untrained militiamen and volunteers. Naturally, that troubled the president, as did his selection of St. Clair to lead the force. Not only did the governor have even less experience as an Indian fighter than had the ill-prepared Harmar, he—like Braddock—was an ex-British officer, trained more for Europe's wars than for America's wilderness battles.[40] Washington's fears were not ill founded.

St. Clair pursued a strategy somewhat akin to that which young Colonel Washington had followed on the Virginia frontier in the 1750s. He, too, set about building a string of forts, his line of garrisons running northward up the Miami River. St. Clair had completed only two of the installations when disaster struck. A swelling Indian force led by Little Turtle attacked, catching the invading army off guard and sending its poorly trained volunteers fleeing southward in a panic. St. Clair was not able to restore order and reassemble his army until he reached a point twenty miles above the Ohio. There to his horror, he learned that over six hundred of his men had been killed; another three hundred had been wounded. He had suffered a calamity nearly as great as that which had befallen Braddock almost thirty years before, and greater even than that which would strike General George Custer at the Little Big Horn a century later.[41]

The news of the latest tragedy provoked a wave of criticism of the administration's bellicose policies, yet as with virtually every preceding debacle for which he had borne some responsibility, Washington escaped unscathed. Critics blasted the cost of the war and the loss of human life, but the president was not openly attacked. The failure, many now said, was due to the abysmal quality of the men raised through the levies. These recruits had been dragged from "the prisons[,] wheelbarrows and brothels of the nation," as a Northwest Territory judge put it.[42]

Be that as it may, after three years Washington's Northwest policy could only be judged a failure. To make matters worse, he now faced the task of securing Congress's approval for still another frontier expedition. The administration, not about to give up, staged an artful public-relations campaign, promising that fresh negotiations would be attempted. Indeed, Washington sent out a new team of commissioners to treat with the Indians, emissaries who took along the president's pledge that he would "be gratified with the opportunity of imparting to you all the blessings of civilized life. . . ." Privately, however, Washington noted that there were "strong evidences" that the Indians would not agree to peaceably surrender any territory, and he ordered Knox to "proceed as if war was inevitable." [43]

Meanwhile, the administration called for the creation of a huge regular army, one that would be five times the size of the force it had shepherded into being in its initial year in power, an army ten times larger than that which had existed at the time of the Constitutional Convention. Washington and Knox wanted an army of five thousand men, a force that would cost three times as much to raise as had St. Clair's legion. Debating the issue in secret sessions, a sectionally divided Congress consented, authorizing the creation of an army of five regiments, the soldiery enlisting for three-year hitches. Washington finally had attained what he had sought almost since the moment of his arrival in Cambridge in July 1775 to take command of the Continental army: he had fashioned a large standing army and had achieved the simultaneous downgrading of the militia. It was a victory which "Congress and the public gave the administration," historian Richard Kohn has observed, "in order to restore the peace to the frontier which many felt the administration had bungled away." [44]

The new army required a new commander, but while there were plenty of candidates Washington faced a difficult choice. He thought only two of the nine major generals possessed the necessary qualities to lead such an army. Benjamin Lincoln was the best of the lot, he believed, but he was too infirm for frontier duty. Steuben was nearly his equal, yet he was a foreigner and perhaps a bit too impetuous. Interestingly, given his zeal during the Revolution for the loyal Anthony Wayne, Washington now characterized him as nearly unfit, as too injudicious and "open to flattery; vain, easily imposed upon; and liable to be drawn into scrapes." The cabinet and Thomas Jefferson concurred in Washington's assessments. Among the other candidates, some were inexperienced or unknown quantities, others were heavy drinkers or political appointees, some were judged to be imprudent, illiterate, in ill health, or wanting in spirit. There were some good brigadier generals, especially Charles Cotesworth Pinckney; Washington, however, not only harbored doubts about Pinckney, he thought it unwise to elevate the South Carolinian above several superior officers, a step certain to unleash much anger and a bevy of resignations. The president thought "Light-Horse Harry" Lee was the best candidate of all, but because Lee never had risen above the rank of colonel during the War of Independence, his appointment also was certain to bring on a firestorm of protest. In the end, early in 1792, Washington selected Anthony Wayne, not because he was particularly sanguine about his chances for success, but because he was deemed to be the lesser of the available evils.[45]

The southern frontier was no less combustible than its counterpart to the north, but here Washington chose to pursue a more pacific policy. The immediate results were more beneficial. Four years before his inauguration the backcountry in Tennessee and Georgia ignited, an explosion wrought by the settlers' rapacious quest for land and by the speculators' unquenchable avarice. In 1785 the government under the Articles thought it had settled matters in Tennessee. The Treaty of Hopewell defined the Indian country and United States territory; the United States, moreover, pledged not to protect those of its citizens who resided on the lands of the Cherokees. The United States adhered to the treaty. Its citizens did not, however, and Tennessee Territory alternately simmered and boiled with clashes between the squatters and the tribesmen. The Georgia frontier also burst into flames at about the same moment that the war in Tennessee commenced, friction there arising in part from the desire of southern sodbusters to gain Indian lands that today lie within the south-central part of that state. In its inimitable way the Georgia assembly also stirred the pot by laying claim to the Yazoo Strip.

The Yazoo Strip was a wide belt of no man's land that stretched across the lower portion of present-day Alabama and Mississippi. It was a region claimed both by the United States and Spain, the confusion arising because the two former co-belligerents had signed separate peace treaties with Britain in 1783, neither of which categorically specified the southern boundary of the one's territory nor the northern border of the other's domain. To further complicate matters, at the end of the War for Independence, Georgia also still claimed that zone, and in 1787 its legislators sold 15 million acres within the Strip to three Yazoo land companies. The entrepreneurs began to organize colonists, families that would descend on lands occupied by Cherokees, Choctaws, and Chickasaws, all of whom soon threatened to unsheathe their tomahawks.

As if it was not bad enough to find the frontiers in turmoil upon taking office, President Washington faced an additional quandary in the Southwest: the specter of Spain. Spanish North America included the colonies of Louisiana, West Florida, and East Florida, a continuous region that extended from west of the Mississippi to the Atlantic, and north—according to Madrid—to above the 32nd parallel. Nearly twenty-five thousand whites lived in these dominions, mostly folk of French ancestry. They discovered a natural ally in their Indian neighbors, an affiliation born of trade and a shared desire to stop the advance of the United States frontier. To forestall this human tidal wave Spain fashioned a three-pronged policy: by closing the Mississippi River to American navigation it sought to render the Southwest unattractive for settlement; by enticements of reopening the river, it sought to lure the farmers already in that region away from the United States and into the Spanish Empire; and as frontier wars always had proved a hindrance to migration, it armed the Indians. To one degree or another Spain by 1789 was pursuing each of these policies.[46]

Washington's antidote for the impasse in the Northwest had been to use force. But conditions in the South, especially in Georgia, compelled him to seek a solution through different means. In such a thinly populated area, a large militia force was out of the question. Moreover, if—as he was contemplating—he treated Georgia's Yazoo land deal as an illegal infringement upon United States sovereignty, he could hardly expect to get many trainbandsmen from that state. In addition, having already opted to use the army in the Ohio Country, he did not have enough regulars left over to send to the South. Besides, Washington knew that the northern states abhorred the thought of financing a war for the sole benefit of a southern state. Perhaps for all these reasons Washington and Knox made a genuine effort to secure peace on the southern frontier. From the beginning they viewed war in this region as likely to produce "complicated evils," and they insisted that "no degree of success could render a war [in the South] honorable or profitable." There was no talk of a "just war," only a realization that the trouble in those parts arose from the "corrosave [*sic*] conduct of the whites." Thus Washington sought to accommodate the Native Americans. Such a course might lure the tribesmen from the Spanish. It surely would buy time. At some point the United States would have a stronger hand from which to deal, and at some point, too, one of Europe's interminable wars would embroil and distract Spain, giving the new nation the wedge it needed to resolve its southwest dilemma once and for all.[47]

One of Washington's first acts as president, therefore, had been to dispatch General Lincoln as head of a diplomatic commission to discuss peace terms with the Creeks. Those talks sputtered on through the last days of 1789 with no success. But the next year an occurrence as remote to the Georgia frontier as a July snowfall in Savannah helped transform matters. Spain, already isolated by its Bourbon ally's preoccupation with the revolution sweeping across the French countryside, found itself on the verge of war with Great Britain over rival claims in the Pacific. Suddenly, the Creek leader, Alexander McGillivray, son of a Creek half-breed and a Scottish trader, grew ready to parley. Responding to an invitation from Secretary Knox, McGillivray, accompanied by twenty-nine additional sachems and braves, rode to New York to confer in person with the president.[48] Their transit northward was a spectacle not to be missed, and silent crowds lined the streets in the villages and cities through which they passed, witnesses to a little caravan of chiefs on horseback, warriors in wagons, and a United States envoy ensconced in a sulky and tagging along in their dust.

The entourage reached New York in July 1790, where its leader immediately was welcomed as a head of state. When those festivities were out of the way, McGillivray was escorted to the Macomb House, there to be greeted by a wan, still weak president, only slowly mending from his spring bout with pneumonia. Their discussions were cordial, but brief, for the busy chief executive left most of the negotiating to Secretary Knox. During the next two weeks the obese former general and the thin, almost emaciated chieftian talked, their sessions interrupted frequently by tours of the city, parades, a military review, worship in an Episcopalian church, and one good roaring drunk by the Creek sovereign. Finally the Treaty of New York was completed: boundaries were set, with Georgia getting just about everything in dispute, almost all the land between the Oconee and Ogeechee rivers; compensation was to be paid the Native Americans for the territory they ceded; all United States captives were to be returned; the United States pledged to prevent its citizens from straying beyond its boundaries; trade was to be opened between the Creek nation and the United States; and bribes and payoffs went to the leading Creek officials, including McGillivray, who was made both a brigadier general in the United States Army and an Indian agent, for which he was to be paid twelve hundred dollars annually. On August 7 the sachem and his headmen returned to the President's House for the signing, after which Washington gave each guest a string of beads and a pouch of tobacco, and the Native Americans performed their "song of peace." Talk had bloodlessly secured for the South what force had failed to attain in the North.[49]

The Creek issue resolved, Washington moved immediately to pacify the other major southwestern tribes. McGillivray hardly had departed New York before the president issued a proclamation through which he endeavored to suffocate the Yazoo land bonanza. Barely two years beyond the ratification battle, he did not wish to provoke a fight over the jurisdiction of the new Constitution. Therefore, instead of proclaiming the act of the Georgia legislature to be an unconstitutional usurpation of the federal government's sovereign powers, he maintained that the state's sale of Yazoo lands violated federal treaties with the Choctaw and Chickasaw tribes. The United States, he added, would not aid any of its citizens who moved into that area. Almost simultaneously the administration moved into negotiations with the Cherokees over long-disputed regions in Tennessee, and news of the Treaty of Holston greeted him upon his return to Philadelphia from the southern tour in 1791. Signed early in the summer in Knoxville, it opened to white settlement new areas further down the Tennessee River. At the end of that year, in his third State of the Union Address, Washington was remarkably candid. The wilderness war in the South, he said, had arisen from the frontiers settlers' unrestrained encroachment on Indian lands. His administration, he went on, had sought the "preservation of Peace," hoping to "accomplish it on the most humane principles." With regard to the southwestern frontier, his was an accurate statement.[50]

Nearly four months elapsed between Washington's return to Philadelphia in midsummer 1791 and the commencement of the Second Congress that autumn. Indian affairs kept the president busy during this period, but physical ills occupied almost as much of his attention. Late in July another tumor appeared in Washington's leg, incapacitating him for a week and leaving him debilitated and easily fatigued for an even longer period. He barely was beginning to feel better when ominous news arrived about his nephew and estate manager, George Augustine Washington. Early in the fall Washington's old friend Dr. Craik wrote that the young man was coughing and spitting blood; his cough was not new, but the suddenly progressive severity of the illness was quite alarming. On his doctor's orders the young man had taken leave of his duties and set out on the melancholy ride to Berkeley Springs, bouncing and jostling across the same dreary route that Lawrence Washington had taken four decades before. The president, by now nearly fully recovered from his own ills, hurried home, both to see George Augustine and to oversee the autumn harvest.[51]

A month later Washington was back in the capital, hastening to Philadelphia for the scheduled congressional session. This time he anticipated fewer headaches from the lawmakers than he had experienced in the past. He soon was disappointed. He discovered that the policies of his administration had caused greater polarization than he had realized. Earlier rifts had eddied men toward the formation of rival political parties, and in this session, as well, the legislators hardly had been gaveled to order before the wedge that separated the emerging factions was driven deeper. Once again it was a report by Secretary Hamilton that stirred the fury.[52]

Hamilton had just this one paper left to present, a Report on Manufactures. It was an exposition over which he had labored for two years, and as with his earlier reports this, too, was in response to Congress's direction that he draft a plan "for the . . . promotion of such manufactories as will . . . render the United States independent of other nations for essential, particularly military supplies." The secretary went beyond those bounds to insist that the augmentation of manufacturing not only was necessary for national security but for the nation's economic vitality as well. Remain an agrarian society, he warned, and you will remain an economic colony of industrial Europe. On the other hand, manufacturing would secure the true independence that the late war had failed to gain. Moreover, manufacturing would bind the sections together, linking by economic interest the producers of raw materials to those who purchased their commodities.

But how was it to be accomplished? The government itself would manufacture arms and munitions, he answered, and it would assist in the construction of the roads and canals over which these commodities would flow. In addition, under the "general welfare" clause of the Constitution the government would offer bounties and subsidies and tariffs, the very stuff of British mercantilism.[53]

Hamilton got some of what he wanted. During the next several weeks Congress enacted a new tariff that included eighteen of the twenty-one increased rates that he had recommended, affording some protection for American hemp cotton, steel and iron. But that was about all that he got, and, even so, the Tariff of 1792 in reality was more a revenue-raising measure than a truly protectionist instrument. Hamilton's achievements in 1790 and 1791 had been significant, yet his thoughts on transforming the United States into a manufacturing empire were far too utopian to generate much support. The country was rural and agrarian, and most people wanted to keep it that way. Besides, many harbored a virulent distrust of the bankers and financiers who were synonymous with Hamilton's scheme of things. And there were constitutional questions about the role of the government envisioned by Hamilton, not to mention concern over the new taxes that the subsidies and bounties would occasion. Finally, the South was hardly enthusiastic about a program that offered it virtually nothing. During that winter, engendered by the visionary schemes of the secretary, the embryo of a new and formal opposition to the thrust of the Federalist revolution began to emerge.[54]

Factionalism was inevitable. And, with 1792 an election year, it was to be expected that more clearly defined coalitions would begin to take shape. Already the piquant clashes over the debt question and the constitutionality of the Bank Bill had been polarizing Americans. Hard on the heels of the Bank fight Jefferson and Madison had traveled to New York on a "botanizing excursion," a junket that Hamilton suspected had more to do with rounding up political allies than with searching out flora and fauna. Hamilton undoubtedly read more into the Virginians' excursion than the truth would bear, yet his realization that the resistance to the Federalist program was crystallizing was quite true, and he was shaken by the likelihood that the opposition might be led by Jefferson and Madison.

The "tumults of conflicting parties," as Jefferson referred to the situation early in 1792, took many forms, some, as always is the case in America's party wars, intensely and indecorously personal. Hamilton and Jefferson were ambitious men. For reasons of state each wished to be Washington's principal advisor. Each also wished to be Washington's heir. In part, therefore, this was a struggle for the mind of President Washington. Additionally, each man needed Washington. The president's support for Hamilton not only was an essential "aegis" to the young man's continued political ascent, but the fatherly esteem that Washington showered on him fell like balm on the fatherless, illegitimate secretary. Jefferson's relationship with Washington had an equally emotional and psychic dimension. Despite his extraordinary accomplishments Jefferson was dogged by a sense of inadequacy, by a fear that he was a failure as a man. Indeed, in the one great test of courage to which he had been subjected—Great Britain's invasion of Virginia while he still was that state's governor—many believed his response had been that of a panicky and inept ruler, if not of a coward. Jefferson concurred in that harsh judgment. For a man of such temperament, the respect of General Washington was crucial. During these years Jefferson never seems to have questioned Washington's greatness. He saw his fellow Virginian as strong and fearless (a "Samson in the field"), as America's greatest warrior, as a man of wisdom and common sense. Above all, he saw Washington as the very embodiment of every masculine virtue that he longed to exhibit. The respect of such a commanding figure allayed Jefferson's insecurities just as it met the emotional needs of his cabinet rival.[55]

Of course, the deepening rift in American politics transcended personalities. The debate soon took on strident, ideological air, and each side came to believe that nothing less than the nation's survival was at stake. The Federalist revolution sparked the strife, but the factional battle involved not just conflict over funding and the Bank, over a tariff and, later, over taxation. By endeavoring to erect an American economy built upon an English model and directed through the central government's fiscal creations, and by seeking to preserve a hierarchical society dominated by an elite bent on imitating the privileged class of England, the Federalists resurrected long-moribund issues and images. Indeed, historian John Murrin even has suggested that the decade can best be understood as a time when an attempt was made to deal with the unresolved problems of the Revolutionary era, with the result that the party battles in the "1790s . . . mark[ed] something of a reversion to [the familiar] patterns of provincial politics." But if battles between court and country parties in the pre-Revolutionary period had centered about questions of American autonomy versus English sovereignty, the emerging parties during Washington's presidency clashed over which Americans would exercise authority. Convinced that ordinary men were debased and vicious, the Federalists believed that an elite—the merchant-financiers and their planter allies, of course—must predominate, and that the broad electorate must defer to the governance of its social betters. The antifederals, as the Federalists sought to label their foes, saw such a construct as synonymous with the aristocratic values that had characterized the outlook of the ruling classes in the former parent state. Instead, they argued, human beings possessed the capacity for self-government and were not lacking in the rationality that would enable them to govern in a restrained manner for the good of the community. To those opposed to the Federalists, therefore, the issue had become one of egalitarianism versus privilege, of an elite-managed economic development versus the opportunity for independent individuals to exert themselves.

Hamiltonianism, said Jefferson and his followers, had placed America on the same road that had led not only to the eradication of the English yeoman but to the alleged corruption and degradation of all facets of life in that blighted nation. Sometimes, they even referred to Hamilton's followers as the "British party." Madison, once so close to the administration, asserted that Hamilton and his ilk (he called them "the satellites & sycophants which surround" Washington) had "wound up the ceremonials of government to [such] a pitch of stateliness" that the Washington government had taken on the air of a royal court. If not all Hamilton's foes went that far, they certainly believed that his policies sought to help a special class, the wealthy merchants and financiers of the urban Northeast, and especially the speculators, the bank directors, the holders of public credit, that is, those men of paper wealth who thrived because of government favors. From the South and the rural sections of the middle states came the greatest protest. Republicanism, the disaffected said, could best survive in a nation in which most men were property-owning yeomen possessed of equal rights and equal opportunities, a people who exuded the unsullied virtues of commoners. To such folk Hamiltonianism offered nothing, save the almost certain demise of the great gains of the Revolution.[56]

To Jefferson, Hamilton seemed to be winning the war. In fact, Hamilton even seemed to be on the verge of wresting control of American foreign policy from the secretary of state. There could be no question that Britain was the apotheosis of all that Hamilton admired; an imperial and commercial giant, an industrializing entity, it was, to boot, socially stable and, in Hamilton's eyes, run by the right class of people. It was an order that Hamilton hoped to replicate in America, and one of the best ways to achieve his goal, he thought, was by fostering commercial relations with London, for the revenue that would be generated by Anglo-American trade would fuel America's economic transformation. American foreign policy, therefore, was a key ingredient of Hamiltonianism.

Indeed, the very first clash between Hamilton and his opponents had been stirred by questions of trade with Britain. During 1789 and 1790 Madison had sought to induce Congress to close American ports to Britain. His idea was simple. Not only did Britain still occupy its old fortresses on America's wilderness frontier, but it refused to buy many American goods, it had paid no compensation for the slaves it had seized during the Revolution, and it shunned diplomatic relations with the United States. A retaliatory measure toward Britain, Madison reasoned, might serve as the lever to pry concessions from London. Hamilton, however, used chicanery as well as his clout with Washington to forestall any curtailment of Anglo-American trade.

Unbeknownst to Washington, Hamilton had been meeting secretly since 1789 with a British contact. George Beckwith, formerly a major in the British army, had surfaced in the American capital shortly after Washington's inauguration. Although Beckwith clearly was a foreign agent, Hamilton saw him frequently, even divulging information concerning the president's keen desire for a rapprochement with Britain. In 1790, at the height of Madison's campaign to secure retaliatory measures against British commerce, the treasury secretary at last chose to reveal his clandestine activities to the president, telling him that Beckwith recently had shown him secret documents that demonstrated London's enthusiasm for an alliance with the United States. Do not permit better relations with Britain to be destroyed by Madison's proposed navigation acts, Hamilton advised. In fact, however, Hamilton's allegation concerning Whitehall's intentions was not quite true. Beckwith's documents merely stated that the agent should continue to seek to induce the United States to form an alliance with Great Britain. Nevertheless, whatever Washington's reaction to his cabinet officer's improper behavior, the president swallowed the bait and threw his prestige behind the effort to thwart Madison's initiative. Soon Congress rejected the notion of retaliation, whereupon Washington, again at Hamilton's behest, agreed to dispatch Gouverneur Morris to London in quest of that chimerical alliance.[57]

Britain, of course, was not ready to deal, and the Morris mission was a spectacular failure. But a year later a war scare between Spain and Britain transformed the situation. The contretemps between those old European rivals sprang from a clash over their competing Pacific Ocean designs, a quarrel that began when London sought to move in on Spanish bases on Nootka Sound on Vancouver Island. As these two foes prepared for hostilities, President Washington had to take notice. He summoned his cabinet late in the summer of 1790 and posed a thorny question: if Britain sought to attack Spanish possessions on the American border (Florida, perhaps, or Louisiana or New Orleans), should the United States permit the redcoats to reach their destination by crossing American territory?[58]

Jefferson and Hamilton took opposite sides. If Britain seized that portion of Spain's North American domain, Jefferson warned, the United States would be encircled by its former parent state. This must be prevented, even if war with London was the result. Hamilton on the other hand counseled accommodation. In the end a clash between Britain and Spain was averted, but the Nootka Sound Crisis had troubled Whitehall as much as it had worried President Washington, and in the autumn of 1791 London dispatched its first minister to the United States. Jefferson interpreted these events as evidence that Hamilton had succeeded in moving America closer to the orbit of Great Britain, a step, he feared, that would pose a dire threat to the commercial relations the new nation so painstakingly had constructed with its old ally, France.[59]

Coinciding with the arrival of the British minister, recriminations between Washington's two secretaries and their friends moved from the drawing room to the printed page. Since the beginning of the Washington administration John Fenno's *Gazette of the United States* had served as a virtual house organ for the treasury department, trumpeting Hamilton's policies, pillorying his foes. In the fall of 1791, however, Jefferson and Madison bankrolled a newspaper of their own. They lured Philip Freneau from the editor's desk at a slumbering little journal in Monmouth, New Jersey, and put him in charge of the *National Gazette*. By mid-year Hamilton, writing under various pseudonyms, had begun to stuff Fenno's paper with essays in defense of his economic policies, as well as with pieces that portrayed Jefferson as a disunionist and as empathetic toward the worst excesses of the French Revolution. An answer was not long in coming.[60]

Hamilton's newspaper, according to accusing doggerel in Jefferson's and Madison's new journal, was inclined

> To flatter and lie, to pallaver and puff;
> To preach up in favour of monarchs and titles,
> And garters and ribbons, to prey on our vitals. . . .

By implication, President Washington stood accused of complicity in furthering Hamilton's allegedly nefarious schemes. Washington offered no public defense. In fact, he sought to convey the impression that the rising opposition had not given him "a moments painful sensation," but that surely was not true. He complained to Jefferson that the burgeoning factionalism might divide the populace until governance was impossible. Moreover, Jefferson later recalled that Washington was "extremely affected" by the calumny directed at him. He was "sore and warm" at the attacks, Jefferson remembered, and he added that Washington "feels these things more than any person I ever met with." [61]

One result of the newspaper campaign was to foster the impression that the president was little more than Hamilton's dupe, an apolitical rustic who unwittingly had been led astray by the evil genius at the treasury. Some historians continue to find it difficult not to give credence to such a view, suggesting, as one scholar recently did, that Hamilton's program was "so audacious that almost no one, not even his staunchest supporters, understood it until it had been executed, and few understood it even then." [62] Washington hardly sought to foster the notion that he blindly followed Hamilton, but he postured as a benign administrator who merely carried out the dictates of Congress or the policies collectively agreed upon by his principal counselors. Indeed, as soon as the party battles heated up he instituted formal cabinet meetings, abandoning his earlier practice of simply conferring in private with each department chief. While such a step amounted to a legitimate endeavor to minimize discord within his administration by means of reaching decisions through consensus, the practice, as with his councils of war, also was a stratagem that he adopted to mask disharmony, to reinforce the notion that he listened to and acted on the advice of the majority of his advisors. While collective discussion created the impression of collective responsibility, it always was Washington's style to have someone walk the point for him, to be in front in the line of fire. From his point of view the tactic had one pronounced virtue. If matters went well, he got most of the credit; if things went awry, someone else bore the opprobrium for having failed. Thus, during the war Sullivan or Greene or Lee had taken Washington's army into battle. As for his economic program, it was Hamilton's turn to be the point man.

But if Washington was not Hamilton's credulous booby, what was the president's relationship to the policies of his administration? Some have suggested that circumstances led him to embrace the program of his treasury secretary. Hamilton, according to this logic, was with Washington in the capital from the beginning, whereas Jefferson did not arrive until the new government had been in place for a full year. Hamilton, thus, filled the void. But such a notion trivializes the ideological differences of the era, making them appear to be little more than disputes between rival personalities. Nor does such a view concede much acumen to the president.

Perhaps Washington backed Hamilton for less than noble reasons. Consciously or not, Washington may have seen Hamilton and the faction that he represented as the gravest threat to the ability of the Union to survive. The New-burgh Conspiracy must have alerted him to how far such men were willing to go. Three years after that incident Washington heard voices from the same quar-ter, now murmuring about secession from the Union if the government under the Articles was not strengthened. Surely he realized the dangers that might fol-low if this potent faction was obstructed under the new government. Indeed, the more success that element enjoyed under his presidency, the more he relaxed. Thus, whereas in 1786 he had thought the greatest danger to the Union was the threat of a monarchical counterrevolution by these very people, in 1792 he told Jefferson—who still harbored that fear—that there no longer were ten royalists in all of America. Certainly Washington now denied that Hamilton posed a danger to republicanism. "By some he is considered as an ambitious man, and therefore a dangerous one. That he is ambitious I shall readily grant," said the president. But that was as far as he was willing to go. His secretary was not a menace.[63]

Washington also may have been lured to the side of this powerful inter-est because it normally got what it set out to attain. The earliest opposition to Great Britain had surfaced within the northern maritime colonies; thereafter, its provincial leaders had maintained a steady drumbeat for boycotts and congresses, military resistance and eventually independence. In the 1780s this faction first had attained much of what it had sought when it conspired with the officers at Newburgh, then it had succeeded in overthrowing the Articles of Confederation government. Despite his knowledge of their machinations in the Newburgh Con-spiracy, Washington remained their friend. He became their ally in the campaign against the Articles. Together they enacted the Federalist program. He preferred to bet on a winner.

But the best explanation for Washington's continued support of the Federal-ist program is the simplest. He shared the outlook of the principal Federalists. He was a partisan. Behind the mask he was himself a Federalist. Scholars have been loath to accept such a view. The historian who most recently studied the early presidents and party warfare concluded that Washington was "a patriot leader," not a partisan leader.[64] By Washington's definition of partisanship he was correct. Washington's view had remained consistent with the utopian ideology of repub-licanism that had accompanied the onset of the Revolution. Since, in his view, the sole end of government was to attain the public good, he sought, as a public official, to subordinate his private interests to the greater good of the whole. And to a degree that is remarkable in American history he succeeded. But in a plu-ralistic society there inevitably was more than one definition of the public good, and when President Washington threw his support to one faction that enunciated one definition of what was best for the nation he had become a partisan.

Washington's choice should not have come as a surprise. Nothing could have been more logical, or more consistent with his lifelong quest for cohesion than was his support for the programs offered by his treasury secretary. Hamil-ton's schemes served as the last act in the movement initiated by the Federalists in

1786 to save the Revolution from what they believed imperiled it. His economic nostrums were to be the last remedy for the fragmenting taking place among the states, and as such Hamiltonianism appealed as much to Washington's unconscious side as to his rational self. All his life Washington had displayed a need for something or someone to identify with, for a substitute personna to allay his fears about his own insubstantiality. Identification with the interests of his colony, or with those of Britain in the war with France in the 1750s offered such objects; to secure the recognition and blessing of older, powerful men, figures such as the Fairfaxes and Dinwiddie, Braddock and Shirley, was a second path to enhanced self-esteem. But as he grew older the maintenance and perfection of the new nation that he had helped to create—the "offspring of our choice," as he put it—grew in importance. The Union had become an extension of his person. Its survival was equated with his survival. For it to be weak and dependent symbolized his weakness. For it to remain cohesive and to grow was tantamount to self-fulfillment. From the time Washington had sought to escape Ferry Farm by linking his fortune to the British barons on the Northern Neck in Virginia, his drive for omnipotence had been characterized by his perception of the most powerful figures as his ideal objects. Now he merely repeated what long since had become commonplace behavior. For Washington the Union was the "main Pillar in the Edifice of . . . real independence"; it was a "fortress against . . . internal and external enemies" and the "Palladium of your political safety and prosperity." Strengthen that Union by implementing Hamiltonianism, he in effect said, and America not only would be independent but with independence "the period is not far off when we may defy" all foes, when no nation could afford to "lightly hazard" provocations to the United States. The opposite course promised only "dependence" and a "precarious" state. To him the choice was clear, for the independence he sought, that he always had sought, brought with it "tranquility . . . safety . . . prosperity . . . Liberty." [65]

Nor is there any reason to believe that Washington misunderstood what Hamilton was about. The president supported his secretary's program because it was compatible with his own viewpoint. Hamilton neither led Washington nor misled him. The two shared a common outlook, the frame of reference of the dominant class in the urban North.

Even as a young adult, planting had taken a backseat to other pursuits in Washington's mind, and if in the beginning that was due to his modest prospects for success as a farmer, such a factor can not explain his willingness to abandon his plow in 1775 or in 1789. By the end of the War of Independence Washington not only had discovered satisfactions in the world apart from isolated Mount Vernon but had found readjustment to the quiet pace of a planter to be difficult. To be sure, Washington often expressed his love for the agrarian way of life. It was part of his culture, and there can be little doubt that he uttered the truth when he spoke of the joys of farming. But it would be a mistake to think of Washington merely as a farmer. He had run a large operation at Mount Vernon, a venture that included manufacturing, a fishing industry, and a far-flung trading network. In addition, his interests veered off both into the world of investment securities and into the board rooms of two large business firms. Moreover, it often is forgotten that Washington spent much of his life in urban centers well removed from the bucolic fields of Mount Vernon. He grew to find these entrepots exciting, so much so, in fact, that in many respects the Washington of the 1780s–90s was far more likely to evince the tastes of the sophisticated urban dweller than of the rural farmer. His manner had become more the disposition of modernism, of the emerging bourgeois magnate who would dominate the next century, than of the landed patriarch who had prevailed in his eighteenth-century colonial world. Like the mercantile lords of the urban milieu, he too was oriented toward the goods of this world, and in the city he discovered the place where he could best indulge his acquisitive inclinations. He emulated the gracious style of living enjoyed by the commercial elite. Their pursuits became his pursuits. He was drawn to the theater and to museums; he became an art collector of considerable magnitude; he enjoyed his carriage rides about the city; he even abandoned hunting, the grand pastime, the very badge, of the Virginia landed aristocracy. A man rich in experience and travel, Washington unconsciously had so come to identify with his urban friends and their environment that his rural predispositions had receded. Where Jefferson, another son of the countryside, found cities to be "great sores" of humanity inhabited by "panders of vice," Washington, notably, left behind no such vitriolic appraisal of America's centers of commerce. Indeed, first through his intensive efforts to make his Potomac canal dream a reality, then through his endless endeavor to establish the new federal capital near Alexandria, Washington worked tirelessly to erect a burgeoning urban center on the very doorstep of Mount Vernon.

The diary entries that Washington made on his 1789 trip to New England and his 1791 journey through the South implicitly reveal his partiality for the more commercial societies of the northern states. He seemed to find the South backward and underdeveloped, its farmers generally comfortable but not so prosperous as their counterparts to the north. The people in the North, he found, were more enterprising, and he even commented on their physical attractiveness. His enthusiasm for things scientific and mechanical led him to be absolutely engrossed by what he discovered in the North. Even the "great equality" in the distribution of wealth that he found in the North seemed to him a virtue related to their commercial and manufacturing society. Of everything that he observed on his southern tour, the city of Charleston most impressed him, and it, of course, was a bustling urban trading center whose people seemed to be "wealthy—Gay—& hospitable; appear happy & satisfied. . . ." Of everything that he observed on his trek through New England, nothing elicited a more negative comment than the supposed ignorance of that region's farmers, folk that he portrayed as so stupid as to be incapable of providing accurate directions to a weary traveler.[66]

It was from these predispositions as well that Washington conceived Hamiltonianism to be the best course for the new nation to pursue. He equated the "abundant fruits of . . . plenty" with "a flourishing commerce." Debt retirement fostered "the increasing reputation and credit of the Nation," and it helped to augment "the progressive state of Agriculture, Manufactures, Commerce and Navigation." The Bank restored "confidence in the Government." Taken together these measures held the promise of strengthening the United States militarily, so that it might "convince the refractory" citizenry of the prowess of the new government while at the same time it could deal with the Native Americans and the European powers. No less important, the growing abundance that was to be ushered in by these fiscal measures would elevate the "social happiness" of the American people.[67]

Both Jefferson and Hamilton envisioned the aggrandizement of the West, but Washington believed that Hamiltonianism offered the best hope for realizing that end. Only a strong, armed Union could open the West, Washington thought, and the treasury secretary's program, he concluded, offered the means of most rapidly building the nation's muscle. That alone, the president believed, could dash British and Spanish influence in the West, could induce the Native Americans to part with their lands, could open new frontiers. For Jefferson, moreover, the West was the key to forestalling America's rapid industrialization and urbanization; an agrarian America, he thought, would preserve the uniqueness of the young nation, safeguarding it from a steadily encroaching Europeanization. Washington had a very different vision. For him the West loomed as a quasi-colony of the East, the means by which a province such as Virginia could diversify its economy and enjoy those fruits of civilization that Washington had witnessed in the North. Virginia would be a winner through the transformation, but the nation would win as well, for the deadly divisions that had rent the provinces since the initial anti-British boycott in 1774 soon would be submerged beneath the interests of an integrated, single-minded people.[68]

How the factions would act in 1792 depended on what George Washington did. In some states the two groups were coalescing into political parties, Federalists who supported the administration and an opposition faction that called itself "republican." The appelation was deliberate. Reacting to the fears of monarchy aroused by Washington's formal, aristocratic manner, use of the term "republican," as historian Norman Risjord observed, amounted to "a choice of names that was a standing rebuke to the president."[69] The Republicans planned to contend for some state offices, and at the national level some in the opposition had begun a quiet, concerted campaign to dump Vice President Adams, seeking to replace him with Hamilton's old rival, George Clinton of New York. But whether there would be a contested presidential election was up to Washington. The president remained tight-lipped about his intentions through the interminable first session of the Second Congress, a conclave that dragged from October 1791 into the next spring. As that session was winding down, however, he told each department head that he did not plan to serve a second term, and on May 5 he asked Madison's counsel on the best means of making public his intention to retire. The two men talked at some length that afternoon, and again four days later.

Compelling reasons lay behind Washington's talk of retirement. Two serious illnesses, as well as the recent reappearance of the tumor in his thigh, left him more concerned than ever about the time that he had left. He would be sixty-one at the end of his first term. He had lived longer than had most males in his family, and he knew that precious few years remained, a fact that may have made the tranquility of Mount Vernon more attractive than usual. Besides, he told Madison, what with the bitter division between Hamilton and Jefferson and the upsurge in journalistic vitriol toward his administration, he was anxious to lay aside his burdens before his reputation was sullied permanently. Yet, while Washington's inclination was unmistakable, he was pursuing a familiar pattern, one of hesitating to continue in office until men begged and pleaded for his service. It was a ritual, possibly a virtual exorcising of the guilt that he bore for daring to seek power, a way of convincing himself that he acted not because he loved power but because public weal demanded it.

Madison sought to dissuade him from retirement. The divisions would only grow in his absence, the younger man argued. Moreover, there was no heir apparent. Jefferson had little following in the North. Adams and Jay were too widely suspected of pro-monarchical inclinations to have broad support. Hamilton was out of the question. The new nation needed Washington's service for four more years, or it might not survive. If Washington was moved, he did not change his mind. He asked the young Virginian to prepare a draft of a formal farewell address.[70]

The day after their second conference Washington commenced a whirlwind trip to Mount Vernon (he was back in Philadelphia eighteen days after his departure), and six weeks later he journeyed home again. It was as though he already had begun to disassociate himself emotionally from the presidency, although problems at Mount Vernon also were responsible for both treks. In the spring, word arrived in Philadelphia that George Augustine Washington's health had further deteriorated. The sojourn at Berkeley Springs had done little for the young man, and the doctors in Virginia now prescribed a total abstention from work. The president had witnessed all this once before, watching helplessly as Lawrence fought his forlorn battle with the same disease, occasionally seeming to rally or to hold his own before sinking ever more deeply into the deadly grasp of his adversary. Washington knew he had no choice but to replace his incapacitated nephew, and during his brief spring holiday at home he named Anthony Whiting as his plantation's new manager. It was a logical selection. Whiting had come to work for Washington two years before as the overseer at one of Mount Vernon's five farms, eventually moving up to take charge of all the agricultural operations at this vast Potomac estate. For at least nine months, moreover, he already had run the place, for George Augustine had been absent at the Springs, or resting with Fanny at Eltham, or just too ill to tend to his duties. Still, President Washington wanted to be there to talk to Whiting in person and to scrutinize his work.[71]

Washington departed on his second trip to Virginia in July, knowing that the journey afforded an opportunity to transact one item of public business as well. While on vacation he rode over to the new federal district to meet with the three commissioners and to select a design for the presidential residence. Much had changed in the year since he had ridden with L'Enfant through these thick woods along the Potomac. For one thing, L'Enfant was gone, the victim of his own obstinancy. Trouble first had arisen late in the previous year when the hot-tempered planner clashed with a local landowner who had endeavored to build a house too near one of the projected streets. Without a court order or other such amenities, the Frenchman simply had his workmen tear down the house. Jefferson was appalled. So was Washington, but so loath was he to lose the "en grande" visions of L'Enfant that he only gingerly rebuked him. Within a few weeks another problem, one even more troubling, had cropped up. L'Enfant refused to cooperate with the district commissioners, clashing with his superiors over financial considerations and the work schedule, clawing to secure control of every last detail involving the construction of the city. An exasperated Jefferson spoke bluntly to the voluble architect, in no uncertain terms making it clear that he would be dismissed if he could not work under the commission. Washington then sent out Tobias Lear to reason with his bullheaded engineer. L'Enfant refused to listen to reason or even to speak about the matter with Washington's emissary. Insulted, the president fired L'Enfant in February 1792.[72]

Thus when Washington and the commissioners met that summer to look through the stack of designs that had been submitted for the president's house, L'Enfant's projected palace-country house was not considered. Jefferson anonymously entered two designs, one modeled on a Parisian style that he had admired while serving as a diplomat in France and one bearing a close resemblance to Andrea Palladio's Villa Rotunda. However, Washington's eye fastened on a plan offered by James Hoban, an Irish native who had been trained in Dublin and whose drawings were recommended by an influential Charleston, South Carolina, acquaintance of the president. Washington, leaning toward "the established rules which are laid down" by architects, particularly liked the fact that Hoban's plan was patterned after plates published in English architectural manuals. The commission acquiesced in Washington's recommendation, and orders to commence work on the White House soon were issued.[73]

If Washington made his trip to Mount Vernon hoping to escape public affairs, he failed. While Washington was in Virginia tending to the spring planting, Jefferson dispatched an extraordinary letter to his president, one that combined a brutal philippic against Hamilton with an eloquent appeal for Washington to stay on in power. All his pent-up hatred and jealousy toward the treasury secretary poured out, and when he was finished he had accused his rival of nothing less than plotting to overthrow the government, supplanting it with an American monarchy. This would mean disunion, Jefferson wrote, and only Washington could prevent such a train of events. "North and South will hang together if they have you to hang on," he contended, and he pleaded with Washington to serve at least a portion of another term. The secretary of state even dropped by Mount Vernon to reinforce his appeal, telling Washington that "there was no other person who would be thought anything more than the head of a party." By 1794 or 1795, he went on, his followers would have built a majority in Congress. Then both republicanism and the Union could be safeguarded.[74]

The president waited nearly three months before replying, weighing the counsel of those who urged him to stay on, watching as the rival party newspapers bubbled and boiled throughout the summer, grieving at the "internal dissensions . . . tearing our vitals!" Late in August he composed nearly identical letters to Jefferson and Hamilton, ingenuous missives in which he never mentioned his intention of retiring, although both were heavy with the implication that he would refuse a second term if the bitter carping between the two men did not cease. Fight in private, he told them both, but once a decision was made abide by it, for if "one pulls this way and another that" the policy and ultimately the Union "must, inevitably, be torn asunder." "And," he went on, if the Union disintegrated "the fairest prospect of happiness and prosperity that ever was presented to man, will be lost, perhaps for ever!" [75]

By then he was telling others that whatever he decided, he simply hoped for the best. At one level the president must have genuinely wished to relinquish power. That autumn word came of the death of his neighbor George Mason, and sad tidings persisted of George Augustine's decline; by October, moreover, he knew that Whiting, his new estate manager, also had contracted tuberculosis. He may well have felt that life was too short to squander four more years away from home. But his inner needs seemed also to keep him in the limelight. As early as the beginning of July Hamilton discerned that Washington had softened his threat to resign, although by late autumn the president still had not cleared the personal obstacles that inhibited him from making a forthright announcement that he would accept a second term. In fact, he never made such a declaration. Yet privately he knew he would remain in power. Hamilton and Jefferson had continued to beseech him to stay on, and both promised to curtail their public feud; the treasury secretary, moreover, had reemployed the same argument that he had used successfully when encouraging Washington to accept the office in 1789, once again telling him that his retirement would result in the "greatest evil" to the nation, a circumstance that would be "critically hazardous to your own reputation." In addition, in public rallies and speeches and newspaper essays the great and the small pleaded for his continued service. Finally, as in 1789, his failure to issue a firm disavowal was construed to mean that he was committed to a second term.[76]

Early in 1793 the Electoral College unanimously reelected Washington.

By a margin of one and one-half to one Adams also was reelected. With that Washington at last agreed to remain in office, but only because he was "again called upon by the voice of my Country to execute the functions of its Chief Magistrate." [77] It was a statement of fact.

Two years earlier, when Washington received from Lafayette the key to the Bastille and the etching of its seizure, he had reacted to the events in France in a positive manner. Like most Americans—including even Hamilton, who confessed that he had not felt such a fire in his breast since the days of Lexington and Concord—Washington viewed the prospects of a republican revolution in France with optimism, seeing the movement there to adopt a constitution and to restrain the power of the monarchy as coinciding with his and his fellow Americans' most cherished views. Of course, he had lamented the mob violence that occurred episodically in the streets of Paris, and he had warned Lafayette not to expect tranquility until "your Constitution is fixed, your government organized, and your representative Body renovated." Nevertheless, until 1792 he had remained cheery about the French Revolution, a stance made all the more easy because his beloved Lafayette had played a crucial role in the early reform movement. [78]

While Washington was busy disclaiming any intention of accepting a second term, France, in April 1792, went to war with Austria and Prussia. The most radical Frenchmen favored war as the best means of exporting their revolution. The king also was happy, thinking France surely would be defeated, bringing an immediate end to the domestic upheaval. Lafayette and the moderates hoped it would unite the nation in a blaze of patriotism, simultaneously consuming the most radical zealots. Washington's friend and the monarch guessed incorrectly. The war only further radicalized French politics. In the aftermath of what has been called the "Second French Revolution" in August 1792, Lafayette fell from power; subsequently he was imprisoned in Austria. Early in 1793 Louis XVI was guillotined, and France declared war on Great Britain.

From the moment he learned that France was at war, the president's tone toward the revolution changed. He grew "gloomy," and he found the path taken by the French to be "disagreeable." News of the First Terror, the execution of nearly one thousand Parisians during the initial days of the "Second Revolution," filled him with foreboding. As he turned his eyes toward his second term George Washington understood all that was at stake in the terrible struggle half a world away. Those who value the "happiness of mankind," he wrote, are "watching the progress of things with the greatest solicitude, and consider the . . . [French Revolution] as fixing the fate of man." [79]

17

The Second Term Begins

"Thrown . . . into the flame"

While Washington waited in dreary, wintry-wet Philadelphia for his second inaugural ceremony, dark clouds seemed to be gathering all about him. Some were personal. In mid-February a packet from the South brought the word that he had dreaded. Major George Augustine Washington was dead, a victim of tuberculosis. He had perished at Eltham on February 5. The news was not unexpected, but that made it no easier to abide. Only days before the president had written a long, last missive to his young nephew, an uncustomary letter for Washington in that he sought to be consoling. His feelings were uttered in a rather stilted manner, for with all that he had mastered in his sixty-one years, Washington had not learned to feel comfortable with expressions of tenderness. He reiterated his "sincere regard and friendship," and he told his ailing friend that the ways of God could not be understood, should not be questioned. When the terrible final word came Washington received it stoically. It was God's will.[1]

Washington's formula for coping with such melancholy events was a good one, although it was of less service to him in dealing with the mountainous public woes he was about to confront. What the president had feared was about to occur. Once again stable Europe was spiraling out of control. Miraculously, Washington had gotten through an entire term without having had to pay more than passing heed to the affairs of that continent. To be sure, he had explored solutions to America's long-standing differences with Britain and France. But the events in Europe, cataclysmic as they had been, had had but slight impact on the New World. There was little prospect that his second term could enjoy such a luxury.

With the arrival fifteen months earlier of Great Britain's first minister to the United States, hope had grown for the imminent resolution of some of the divisive issues that separated Britain and America. Washington had been especially anxious to resolve the commercial problems between the two nations. Since 1783 Britain had permitted only America's naval stores and its nonmanufactured goods to be sold in its ports; it also allowed American tobacco, naval stores, and certain comestibles and provisions to be sold in the British West Indies, but it stipulated that these goods must be carried only in British vessels. The administration wished to broaden the trade and to attain shipping rights for United States merchants, and it sought to codify these agreements in a formal treaty. After all,

George Washington at age fifty-eight, by Edward Savage (1790). Courtesy of the U.S. Department of the Interior, National Park Service, Adams National Historic Site, Quincy, Massachusetts, U.S.A. Washington sat for Savage early in his presidency. The work might be compared with that by Joseph Wright, which was completed in the same year.

Martha Washington at age fifty-nine, by Edward Savage (1790). Courtesy of the U.S. Department of the Interior, National Park Service, Adams National Historic Site, Quincy, Massachusetts, U.S.A.

even with the restrictions the commerce was too important to be left to transitory British legislation or whim. Almost one-half of all American exports went to Great Britain, and nearly 90 percent of its taxable imports arrived from the former parent state.[2] But if Washington saw the long-awaited arrival of an envoy from London as a harbinger of hope, he was doomed to disappointment.

George Hammond, at twenty-seven a very junior British diplomat, had arrived in October 1791. He immediately engaged in talks with the secretary of state and even sojourned with the president at Mount Vernon for a spell, mingling tours of the estate with social festivities and official discourse. All the talking bore no fruit. In reality, the negotiations were hopeless from the outset, for Hammond had been directed merely to play for time until the turbid affairs of Europe were more discernible.

Whitehall was only serious about bargaining on one matter. Britain, too, wanted peace on America's frontiers, for with Europe ablaze it was not in a position to offer the Native Americans much help. Hammond, thus, was to seek a new boundary between Canada and the United States so that an Indian buffer state could be erected in the zone between the new and the original border. The Washington administration was not disposed to surrender even an inch of soil, however, and, since Hammond was powerless to talk seriously about anything else, the talks dragged on in session after wearying, meaningless session.[3]

Had Hammond been given any flexibility the result in all likelihood would have been no different. He barely had begun to talk with Jefferson before Alexander Hamilton sabotaged the secretary of state. Jefferson planned to take a tough stance, making it clear that if London did not relax its commercial restraints the United States not only would seek closer ties with France, it would reciprocate with embargoes against British commodities. The man charged with formulating American foreign policy never had a chance to test the power of his threat. Hamilton counseled the envoy to ignore Jefferson. The president, he said in effect, would never countenance such steps. Hammond promptly relayed the felicitous news across the Atlantic, and if Whitehall ever contemplated concessions in 1792 the envoy's dispatches persuaded the Pitt ministry to sit tight.[4]

The treasury secretary's meddling nearly backfired. As the year dragged on with no hope of a breakthrough in the talks with Hammond, Washington instructed Jefferson to seek closer relations with France. What might have resulted can only be guessed at, for France desired even closer ties, and in February 1793 it established a virtual free-trade policy with the United States. But that same month Revolutionary France declared war on Great Britain, Holland, and Spain. Now everything had changed.[5]

When Washington rode to the Senate chamber to once again take the oath of office, he was unaware of the thirty-day-old Anglo-French war. During the two or three weeks preceding the ceremony, disquieting communiqués had arrived from Gouverneur Morris, for the past twelve months the United States minister to

France. Washington's old friend had chronicled the growing mayhem in troubled France, and he had discussed the likelihood of a wider war. But definitive word was lacking. Thus, in his Second Inaugural Address (the briefest such speech ever delivered, a two-paragraph oration) the president ignored foreign policy concerns altogether. That is not to say that those concerns were not on his mind.[6]

Two things about the changing situation in Europe struck the president. Should Spain be caught up in the maelstrom, the United States might face both opportunities and dangers. A beleaguered Madrid might be more willing to concede America's navigation rights on the Mississippi, and it also might surrender its claims to the disputed territory it occupied in the Southwest. On the other hand, Spain might tie these concessions to an agreement by the United States to help defend its New World colonies against French attack. The latter option was something Washington would not countenance, and he directed Jefferson to instruct the two United States commissioners in Madrid—a team appointed late in 1791 to open discussions with the Spanish government—not to consent to any such bargain.[7]

The other thing that Washington had thought through was the question of American involvement in the European war. He was convinced that "sense of our own interest" should be sufficient to keep the United States neutral in the event of a general European war. America's participation could, at most, only minutely affect the course of such a war, whereas the risk of loss to the new nation was considerable. Contrarily, isolation from Europe's woes would permit the United States to develop internally; not many years of peace would pass, he thought, before "we may be ranked not only among the most respectable, but among the happiest people on this Globe."[8]

For the time being the government could only await official word of Europe's true situation. That left Washington with little to do in Philadelphia. Congress had adjourned on March 2 and was not due back until December. Besides, George Augustine's death had left him more eager than ever to return to Mount Vernon, for he feared that the loss of his trusted estate manager would "cause my private concerns to suffer very much." Anthony Whiting, the major's successor, was new and unproven, prompting Washington to average more than one letter each week to him over the past five months, each communiqué a long compendium of explicit directions. Make the "lazy" miller work at night as well as during the day, Washington ordered in a typical missive, while in another letter he instructed Whiting to hire a "White-man" for certain carpentry jobs, as "none of my Negro Carpenters are adequate to the framing" of buildings. Anxious to be with his new man and to personally direct the spring planting, Washington at last was free to travel shortly after the inaugural ceremony had been completed.[9]

Late in March he began the ride south. He did not get out of Philadelphia quite fast enough to escape troubling news. Just an hour or two before he departed a ship arrived bearing fresh rumors that France was at war with Britain and Spain. As he passed through Baltimore three days later he was handed a dispatch from the state department that contained still more reports to that effect. But they were only rumors, and he enjoyed nearly two weeks at home before the long-awaited tidings arrived. Typically, it was Hamilton, not the secretary of state, who first conveyed definitive word that the European conflagration had spread, that war had been declared after both Louis XVI and Marie Antoinette had been guillotined by the government of the French Republic. The following morning, just as dawn slanted over his green fields, the president set out for Philadelphia. Preceding him was a letter he had dispatched the previous day, a note directing Jefferson to devise a plan that would enable the United States to "maintain a strict neutrality." [10]

To Washington's way of thinking strict neutrality meant being truly impartial toward all belligerents. That was not what the concept meant in Europe, however, where "neutral" nations frequently did everything but declare war in order to help themselves or to assist their traditional friends. Moreover, when the president arrived in the capital he discovered that his version of neutrality was not what Hamilton and Jefferson had in mind either. The treasury secretary was the first to see Washington, visiting with him only an hour or so after he had alighted from his mud-spattered carriage. Neutrality was essential to America's interests, he told Washington. It was so important, he went on, that the Franco-American Treaty of Alliance of 1778 should not be permitted to stand in its way. Hamilton's advice was for the United States to refuse to recognize the new republican government in Paris, a ploy by which the treaty could be discontinued. In fact, he added, the alliance should not be applicable because France was responsible for launching an offensive war, and the United States was required to provide succor only if its ally was confronted by a defensive war.

Beneath Hamilton's advice lay his unbridled desire to witness the consummation of an Anglo-American alliance. A commercial treaty was as close as he likely would come to the realization of his goal, yet a trade agreement was serviceable. It not only would augment American power but would secure peace with a great power possessed of the strength to do serious harm to the United States. Economically stronger, and on friendly terms with Britain, the United States then could initiate a diplomatic and, if necessary, even a military offensive against Spain's southern and southwestern possessions. In Hamilton's view this was the first step toward the new United States' government's appropriation of the North American continent. But all was jeopardized by the European war, for he feared that even the suspicion of American favoritism toward France would set Whitehall against the United States.

The following morning at a formal cabinet meeting Jefferson finally saw Washington and expressed his views on the matter. The outlook of the secretary of state was more in keeping with European notions of neutrality. Thinking of the accords with France, Jefferson proposed that the United States should seek the "broadest privileges of neutral nations." Treaties, he said, were made between nations, not governments. Therefore, the French treaty could not be disposed of so simply as Hamilton had suggested. Besides, he went on, the pact's very existence might be used as a lever to pry concessions from London. But Jefferson, too, thought neutrality was in the best interests of his nation, though he counseled that a formal proclamation of neutrality might diminish the chances of wringing an accommodation from Britain. In any event, the secretary of state added, neutrality was for Congress to decide, for it fell within the scope of its war-making powers. When Jefferson concluded his remarks, Henry Knox, a "fool" in the eyes of the secretary of state, immediately sided with Hamilton; Randolph, however, seemed to vacillate indecisively.[11]

Three long, acrid meetings were required to iron out a policy, sessions in which the extent of the raw-edged differences that separated Hamilton and Jefferson became clear to Washington. At the final meeting, conducted early the following week, something that resembled a compromise was reached. Washington agreed to a Proclamation of Neutrality, a document couched in carefully contrived language so as to suggest that its purpose merely was to warn the American citizenry against acting in a partisan manner toward any belligerent nation. In fact, Hamilton pretty much got what he wished, for it now was clear that the administration would not honor its alliance with France, and that issue had been the real key to the quarrel.[12]

Washington harbored no illusions that the Proclamation of Neutrality could both preserve domestic tranquility and secure peace for the new nation. To his chagrin, he soon learned that he was correct. Not only did the statement unleash a firestorm of internal discord, within a few months the United States, neutral or not, seemed on the verge of blows with Great Britain.

A domestic battle flared first, drawing on and further exacerbating the party splits that had begun to show two years earlier. The rival party organs blared apologies for and excoriations of the administration's policy, and by late summer Hamilton and Madison, writing under pseudonyms, were gouging at one another in public. At its most elevated level the issue was constitutional: did the president have the power to promulgate such a foreign policy statement? But beneath the legalisms lay the basic conflict that tore at the nation and the administration. What shape would the new nation take? Foreign policy would have more than a little to do with the answer that finally unfolded. One thing seemed certain. The sentiments of the president and his cabinet did not coincide with popular opinion.[13]

Given the violent anti-British and pro-republican feelings that had taken firm root in the course of the long War of Independence, the great majority in the country prayed for the success of French arms. French victories were hailed and celebrated, and many American nationals took to calling one another "citizen" and "citess." Some even wore the tricolored cockade made popular in revolutionary France. But it was the arrival that spring of the new French minister, Citizen Edmond Genêt, that crystallized the expansive pro-French sentiment within the nation. Dashing, flamboyant, and brillant (he could speak six languages before his tenth birthday), Genêt seemed a good salesman to vend an already fashionable cause. In fact, he was not.[14]

Although the vessel that brought him across the Atlantic continued on to Philadelphia, Citizen Genêt jumped ship in Charleston. He lingered there for eleven days, his time taken up largely in overseeing the outfitting of privateers to hunt down British vessels. That completed, he slowly ascended to the capital, along the way peddling the virtues of republican France and reminding everyone he met of the noble assistance his country so recently had provided revolutionary America. By the time he reached Philadelphia, three weeks after landing in the United States, the enterprising young envoy had received the sort of ecstatic welcome that probably no American—save for Washington—ever had received. Indeed, the crowd that ushered him into the capital on May 16 was greater than the city had witnessed since Washington passed through en route to his inauguration four years before. In some circles, however, the arrival of the ebullient minister produced less ecstasy. Intelligence from South Carolina indicated that Genêt had used a satchel filled with French francs to recruit American citizens to serve on his newly rigged privateers.[15]

The public knew nothing of this though, and Genêt's first two days in the capital were more than rewarding. Each night he was fêted at a banquet, evenings that commenced with stirring renditions of the "Marseillaise" and bombastic toasts offered to republican France. Then he met Washington. Jefferson escorted the minister into the president's company on May 18. The secretary of state knew what was coming, for earlier he had spoken of Washington's "cold caution" toward the French. But Genêt was unprepared, and he must have been startled at the contrast between the public's warm reception and Washington's greeting. Anxious to make it plain that his government planned to be truly neutral, the president was at his chilliest and most formal, even greeting Genêt pointedly beneath paintings of the late French monarch and his queen. Washington must have hoped to communicate to Genêt by the gravity of his manner what he had told others: "I believe it is the sincere wish of United America to have nothing to do with the political intrigues, or the squabbles of European Nations; but [only] to exchange commodities and live in peace and amity. . . ."[16]

The cunning antics of Genêt became Washington's immediate problem, although in the long run America's ability to "exchange commodities" provoked a far more serious crisis. But Genêt was there first, and through that hot, sticky Philadelphia summer Washington was unable to escape entirely the guile of the French envoy. With public opinion so enthusiastically on his side, a more savvy diplomat than Genêt might have successfully exploited it and managed to paint the president into a corner. Instead, France's minister self-destructed.

Much of what France desired was not unreasonable. It could live with American neutrality, but it did insist that the Treaty of Commerce of 1778 be honored, a pact that would admit not only French warships but also the prizes they captured to American ports. In addition, while France did not ask for direct

American involvement in the war in the West Indies, it did urge the United States to provide money, provisions, and military stores for the French armed forces, the very sort of assistance called for by the Treaty of Alliance. Finally, France desired a new commercial treaty, a step which the Washington administration had agreed to consider more than a year before Genêt's arrival.[17]

Genêt wasted no time in informing Washington of Paris's desires. He proposed that the United States pay for the supplies it rendered to the French army and navy through an advance on the debt it owed France. The funds, he suggested, could be laundered so as to make it appear that they came only from private citizens. It was an ancient ruse, one, in fact, that France had utilized during the initial years of the War of Independence when it had funneled aid to Washington's armies through the guise of the Rodrique Hortalez Company. But Washington would have none of it. Although the United States had advanced a considerable sum to France since 1792, the president now refused Genêt's appeal, scuttling the envoy's hope for military succor.[18]

Genêt's entreaties had been anticipated. Other of his actions had not been foreseen, however, and these more dubious ventures led the diplomat into dangerous waters. Before leaving Charleston, Citizen Genêt not only recruited Americans to serve on French privateers, he equipped several marauding vessels and even authorized French consuls in the United States to serve as judges of prize courts. Clearly such actions transgressed the bounds of legality, but it was not until his privateers began to seize British ships that more serious matters arose. Things came to a head in June when the *Little Sarah,* a merchant vessel sailing under the Union Jack, fell to the frigate *L'Embuscade.* The Washington administration discovered that the prize had been brought into the port of Philadelphia where, under the very nose of the United States government, it was being outfitted as a French privateer, a craft that Genêt himself rechristened the *Petite Démocrate.* The neutrality of the United States was compromised. But what could be done? If the vessel sailed, Britain had grounds for war. But to restrain the ship was to risk antagonizing France, and to use force to detain the *Petite Démocrate* was to risk spilling French blood. In the end Washington ordered Genêt not to permit the renovated ship to sail. Genêt's response was intemperate and arrogant, and amounted to a threat to appeal over the president's head to the American public. What is more, the *Petite Démocrate* sailed. In private, the envoy wrote a friend in Paris expressing his exasperation with "Old Washington" who "impedes my course in a thousand ways. . . ."[19]

Genêt's foolish intransigence was the last straw, though Washington had other grounds sufficient for moving against the diplomat. While the full details of Genêt's machinations were not clear, the administration discovered that the busy Frenchman was piecing together armed forces comprised of American frontiersmen to assail Spanish Florida and Louisiana as well as British Canada. He never got very far with his Canadian venture, but the attack on Spain's colonies verged on implementation, for Western yeomen, aggrieved by Spain's aid to

Native Americans and its recalcitrant stand on permitting American shipping on the Mississippi, did not require much browbeating to volunteer as soldiers. Genêt concocted a plan for a three-pronged attack, one through Georgia into East Florida, one into West Florida, and one against New Orleans; George Rogers Clark, the Virginian who had won a reputation in the Revolution as a frontier fighter, was set to lead one of the attacks. Ultimately the projected campaign fizzled before a shot was fired, largely for lack of funds. Nor did the administration's actions help, for Washington moved to forestall conduct that surely would have plunged the United States into the wide net of the European war. He and Jefferson publicly spoke of prosecuting all American participants, and he induced Congress to enact legislation making it illegal for United States citizens to enlist "under the color of a foreign authority" for the purpose of "invading and plundering the territories of a nation at peace with the said United States." [20]

Genêt also was blamed for something for which he was not entirely responsible. During 1793 democratic-republican societies sprang up throughout America, organizations given life as a result of the euphoria that accompanied the republicanization of revolutionary France. The societies openly were pro-French and anti-British, prorepublican and antimonarchial, and they encouraged the United States' adherence to the French alliance. By the end of the year eleven such societies existed; twenty-four others were created in 1794. Philadelphia was home to the first club, and there can be little doubt that Genêt played a key role in its founding. But he did not, as if by magic, launch the movement. The societies drew on the reservoir of revolutionary idealism left over from 1776, modeling themselves not only on the Jacobin clubs of France but on the Sons of Liberty who had flourished in an earlier day in America. Societies of artisans and mechanics also served as a wellspring for the movement, and so too did the simmering partisan newspaper war that had raged for eighteen months before Genêt's arrival. His presence perhaps was catalytic, yet the ground that he trod was fertile for such an occurrence. Indeed, given the magnitude of the French Revolution, democratic societies probably were inevitable. that was not how President Washington saw things, however. He laid what he called "Mob and Club Govt" at the feet of the "diabolical leader G[enê]t." [21]

Into 1794 the societies gave focus to the general unrest and dissatisfaction with the Washington administration. Not only did they scorn the neutrality proclamation and urge assistance for beleaguered France but they villified the domestic policies of Hamiltonian Federalism. Nor was Washington spared. Innuendo and thinly veiled criticism of the president crept into the resolutions of the societies. More alarming were the street demonstrations organized by the Philadelphia "mother society." Generally peaceful affairs patterned after the example of the Sons of Liberty gatherings, chanting crowds nevertheless had a way of unnerving folk. John Adams later recalled the "terrorism excited by Genêt," a campaign that he believed desired nothing less than "a revolution in government." When an octogenarian, Adams recollected scenes in 1793 in which "day after day" mobs led by "old revolutionary Americans" and totaling up to ten thousand fanatics gathered to curse the president; at times, he remembered, they "threatened to drag Washington out of his house." [22]

Adams's memory surely played tricks on him, causing him to exaggerate the street protests. But he was correct in remembering that Washington had been criticized, hardly a turn of events likely to endear Genêt to Washington. Ultimately, the president came to believe that the public demonstrations were "embarrassing" to the government, and like Adams he thought the societies, as a prelude to revolution, hoped to "discredit" his administration. By midsummer 1793, Washington was ready to move against the troublesome envoy whom he held responsible for the rising clamor.[23]

By then Genêt had few defenders left in high places. Even Jefferson, initially friendly toward the diplomat, had lost patience when Genêt acted with disrespect toward the office of the president, threatening to appeal over Washington's head to the American people. No one else in Washington's cabinet had ever exhibited any affection for the man. Certainly not Hamilton, who back in March during a secret tête-á-tête with the British minister, had pledged to work unflaggingly not to let France break America's neutrality. What influence he had with Washington during the initial two months of Genêt's presence cannot be known, but with the cabinet meeting of July 13 he took the lead in the campaign to remove the envoy. Genêt's fate hardly was in doubt. Three meetings in the space of three weeks were required to resolve matters, but the discussions revolved less around saving Genêt than how best to get rid of him without unduly upsetting Paris. Ultimately it was decided to send to his bosses in France copies both of his intemperate correspondence and a covering letter requesting his recall. Because of the communication lag caused by the wide Atlantic, months dragged by while the administration anxiously awaited France's response. At last the answer came, a birthday present for the president: on the day before Washington turned sixty-two in 1794 a new French minister disembarked in Philadelphia. Among his papers were documents prepared by still another revolutionary regime in turbulent France; they called for the arrest and return of Genêt. Graciously Washington spared his life by granting him political asylum, and Genêt lived on quietly near Albany for the next four decades, dying on the forty-fifth anniversary of the fall of the Bastille.[24]

While Washington's attention was absorbed by the Genêt "crisis," Whitehall was instituting a policy that soon plunged the administration into a far more grave situation. In June 1793, Great Britain announced a blockade of the French coast. In the autumn Pitt the Younger's government unveiled an order-in-council that authorized the capture of all neutral vessels carrying goods to or from the French West Indies. It was the same policy the prime minister's father had promulgated during the Seven Years' War, a defense of obstructing trade based on a dictum called the "Rule of 1756." Trade that was illegal in peacetime remained illegal in wartime, trumpeted London. In the time between its proclamation of the two blockades, Britain sent a small force to the Netherlands to fight the French; it dispatched a much larger force to the Caribbean to wrest control of its adversary's priceless sugar islands. Before spring of 1794 some of the smaller French islands were in British hands. So were approximately 250 American vessels, seized by the British navy on the translucent blue-green waters of the Caribbean.[25]

The "vexations and spoilations" of American commerce that resulted from British policy has "thrown them into a flame," Washington soon remarked of his countrymen. It did that and more. American newspapers were crammed with calls for war, a pugnacity soon matched by the similar importunings of the democratic societies. The hysteria reached such a fever pitch that when tattle spread through London that Congress had declared war, knowledgeable officials in Whitehall momentarily believed the rumor. The Republican leadership also chose to use this crisis as a means of luring New England Federalists into their party. Jefferson and Madison introduced resolutions in the House of Representatives that urged discriminatory duties against British imports. It seemed the mildest of the steps that could be taken. In fact, war seemed inevitable. Two years of negotiation with Hammond had proved fruitless. In addition, not only was General Wayne gathering his frontier army for a strike at Britain's Native American allies, but in March word leaked out of a secret speech made to American tribesmen by the governor of Canada, superheated remarks in which that official seemed to concede that Britain planned a war with the United States. Now Britain was violating America's neutral rights, and soon came word that British sailors had begun to board United States' merchant vessels and seize suspected deserters from among the crewman, impressing them into the royal fleet.[26]

But not only were hostilities forestalled, even Jefferson's rigorous retalia-tory measures failed to pass Congress. Adroit rearguard maneuvers by Federalist congressmen stopped those who yearned for drastic action. Pressed by the public clamor for revenge, Federalist leaders in Congress urged defensive preparations, calling for an army of fifteen thousand and the augmentation of what passed for a navy; in addition, they countenanced mild, temporary retributive policies against both British and French shipping. It was a shrewd strategy. Covering their flanks so as not to appear pusillanimous, they nevertheless bought time that ultimately permitted them to adopt a more moderate course. Congress huffed and puffed with invective from the time it assembled early in December until late the following March, then it agreed only to a one-month embargo on all shipping already in American ports. Within a few days of that small gesture, word reached the capital that Whitehall had relaxed its orders-in-council, permitting a resumption of United States trade with the French West Indies. It was a step that "allayed the violence of the heat," as President Washington put it. Moreover, as word trickled in that the French were also committing depredations against American ships, the "heat" that lingered was somewhat deflected. But the death blow to those who hoped to immediately retaliate against Britain came from the president's office.[27]

Since early spring the Federalist leadership in Congress quietly had mulled over the notion of urging Washington to dispatch a special envoy to London to seek to hammer out a treaty that might resolve all differences between the two nations. It was not an entirely new idea. Ironically, the first to propose a mission to London may have been Jefferson. About to retire as secretary of state, Jefferson, early in March, seems to have privately suggested such a step to the president, although he linked it to congressional passage of an American Navigation Act. Jefferson got nowhere. Not only did Washington oppose commercial retaliation, he apparently believed that Britain was bent on war. A few days later Senator Oliver Ellsworth of Connecticut was deputed by some of his Federalist colleagues to visit Washington and to propose that Hamilton be sent to London as a minister plenipotentiary. The president listened, but he was unconvinced. He especially balked at the notion of using Hamilton. Either he feared he would give away the store, or he felt—as he said—that the treasury secretary was too unpopular in his own country to be entrusted with such an assignment.[28]

Three weeks later Washington changed his mind. On March 27 word arrived that Britain had modified its November orders-in-council. The very next day the president summoned both Robert Morris and the new secretary of state, Edmund Randolph, for consultation. Both urged him to send a special envoy to London, one armed with extraordinary powers. But whom should he send? Washington preferred either the vice president, or Chief Justice Jay, or Jefferson. It was logical list. The very act of replacing the regular minister with a special emissary implied that only someone of great stature could be considered. No one—save for Hamilton or Madison—was more eminent than these three men. The president had ruled out his treasury secretary, and Madison was eliminated, if not because of his pro-French leanings, then probably because earlier that same month he had turned down Washington's offer of the post of minister to Paris. That left Jefferson and Jay. Washington wrestled with the matter for nearly three weeks before deciding, and, as with so many other matters, his final decision was influenced by Hamilton.[29]

On April 14 the treasury secretary wrote Washington a long, unsolicited letter on the subject. He began by telling the president that groups with three distinct views toward foreign policy existed in the country: one faction desired war with Britain; to further its political ends, another group sought to "keep alive irritation" with Britain, although it hoped to avoid hostilities; a third element favored peace "if it can be [attained] without absolute dishonor or the ultimate sacrifice of essential rights and interests." Public opinion, Hamilton went on, supported the third position, for the people understood the dangers and uncertainties of war. Since he was certain that Britain also hoped to avoid conflict, the secretary added, every step should be taken to maintain the peace. "[O]ne more experiment of negotiation" was warranted, and "Mr. Jay is the only man in whose qualifications for success there would be thorough confidence." Send him, Hamilton concluded, and send him unaccompanied by retaliatory trade embargoes, for measures of "menace and coertion" only would doom the talks and "precipitate a great conflict." The secretary might have added, said his most recent biographer, that "Jay was among the few men who could be confidently counted on to carry out Hamilton's own ideas." [30]

The following day Washington met with Jay, and the next afternoon he formally nominated him as "Envoy Extraordinary . . . to his britannic majesty." The appointment, said the president, "will announce to the world a solicitude for a friendly adjustment of our complaints, and a reluctance to hostility." The Senate required only a few hours to approve the nomination, although the prospect of Jay's mission inspired the Republicans to redouble their efforts to pass a retributive commercial measure. The House did just that, but a bill to sever trade with Britain failed by one vote—Vice President Adams's tie-breaking ballot—in the Senate. Within the month Jay had embarked, off to seek "justice" by "fair, firm negotiation," as Washington put it. [31]

In his pocket Jay carried instructions signed by the secretary of state. In fact, they were the offspring of Alexander Hamilton's quill. The emissary was told to obtain compensation for the ships and cargoes seized under the secret orders-in-council. In addition, he was to strive to draft a commercial treaty, a pact granting the United States access to the ports of the British West Indies, as well as the right to ship its cereals and manufactured goods to Great Britain and Ireland. Next Jay was to seek Britain's immediate evacuation of the northwestern posts. In return for these British concessions, Jay was to offer to agree to the payment of America's prewar debts to the former parent state. However, in only the most general way—virtually as a matter that "would be interesting to comprehend"— was the envoy to push for indemnification for the slaves liberated by Britain during the War of Independence. First and foremost John Jay had been dispatched on a mission to win favors for the interests of the northern Federalists. Had they been privy to the diplomat's instructions, southern Republicans would have expected even less from this enterprise than they did. As it was many Republicans viewed the mission as tantamount to national humiliation and, as Jefferson wrote the president from Monticello, as unlikely to "force [Britain] to do justice." But time would tell. Meanwhile, Washington said, "what may be the final result . . . no mortal, I believe can tell." [32]

Whatever Jay ultimately brought home, Washington was proud of his own action in sending him. He had preserved the peace, and, at least for the moment, he had avoided a war that he feared might well be disastrous for the fragile, strife-torn political union. "If we are permitted to improve without interruption, the great advantages which nature and circumstances have placed within our reach," he said, then within only a few years "we may be ranked not only among the most respectable, but among the happiest people on this Globe." Besides, he continued, the warfare that plagued Europe was Europe's quarrel. Washington's outlook reflected a cardinal belief of his generation, one best articulated by Benjamin Franklin and Thomas Paine. When Franklin opted for separation from the parent state he spoke of the need to escape a people that ever "will drag us after them in all [their] plundering wars. . . ." Paine testified that the monarchs of the Old World "hath little more to do than to make war." Repeatedly Europe has been reduced to "blood and ashes," compelling many of its inhabitants to flee "the cruelty of the monster" for the sanctuary offered by America. In the crisis of the 1790s Washington reiterated the sentiment, albeit in his customary terse, prosaic manner: it would be "unwise . . . to involve ourselves in the contest of European Nations, where our weight could be but small; tho' the loss to ourselves would be certain." [33]

The president had acted as an American nationalist, unmoved by his feelings toward the European rivals. While he may have longed to win the respect of a powerful England that had so often rejected him, he did not—as did Hamilton— exalt the former parent state. Moreover, although he had been sympathetic to France's early republican reforms, he did not share Jefferson's bubbling zeal for the French Revolution. His break with England had been complete, and he was too little the idealist and ideologue to be swayed philosophically by the events in France. Nor did Washington have an emotional need for war. His actions on the battlefields of two earlier wars had been sufficient to demonstrate whatever he had felt needed to be shown about himself. Never for a moment did he exhibit signs of inner turmoil over his pacific behavior.[34]

Washington's outlook was pragmatic and realistic. With a rich broad continent awaiting its attention, the United States had no need for the spoils of Europe. Nor did it labor under the "mistaken policy" of seeking the "destruction of any nation, under an idea that our importance will be increased in proportion as that of others is lessened." For the United States Washington wished only that it be permitted to reap "all the advantages that nature and it's [sic] circumstances would admit," including the expansion of the "*useful* arts and manufactures," so that their products might be "exchang[ed] on liberal terms" with the nations and colonies of Europe. His goals were shared by most of his countrymen, but to choose the path of peace in order to realize these ends was the most arduous—and the most statesmanlike—route he could have taken.[35]

"I have no relish for formal and ceremonious engagements and only give into them when they cannot be avoided," a weary Washington sighed half way through his presidency. It showed. Senator Maclay twice dined at the President's House, and each time he was struck by Washington's bored, and boorish, behavior. On each occasion the chief executive sat mute and listless at the head of the company, abstractedly drumming his fork against the table. People who rarely attended his levees found them dull affairs, so formal that they smacked more of a royal court than of a republican entertainment. On such occasions Washington dressed somberly in a black velvet suit, strapping to his side a dress sword encased in a white leather scabbard; usually he donned yellow gloves and black stockings, and he always wore his best highly polished buckle shoes. His hair was heavily powdered and drawn back severely, and he carried a cocked hat. As the guests filed past, Washington bowed gravely and solemnly, seldom speaking, never engaging in small talk. The secretary at the British legation felt right at home in such an environment. "I cannot call it republicanism, for . . . it is [a] very *kingly* style," he thought.[36]

If his levees and dinners were business engagements, Washington found other means of entertaining himself. The president hastened to see the circus when it came to Philadelphia, but even then he discovered that it was difficult to escape politics; on one occasion the proprietor of the circus halted the performance to toast the arrival of the First Family, a gesture that so displeased some patrons that "many put on their hats and went out." He also continued to attend the theater, sometimes taking in two plays a week. On occasion he visited Peale's museum and the Philadelphia waxworks, from time to time he enjoyed a concert, and once he paid to see an elephant that some entrepreneur had brought to town. Like the modern executive jogger, Washington enjoyed the opportunity to exercise, continuing both his long-standing practice of riding horseback each morning and his habit of periodically taking a long stroll.[37]

His activity kept him fit for the arduous treks to Mount Vernon, four-to-five-day journeys that he ordinarily undertook partly by horseback, partly by carriage. During his second term he returned home nine times, his visits ranging from only a few days to two eight-week stays. Customarily he lingered at home for about three weeks, and almost always one or two of those days were spent in meetings at Georgetown with the commissioners of the federal district. Although all pursuits took a backseat to business while he was at home, the president usually squeezed in some moments of recreation. He fished, visited with relatives and acquaintances, and dropped in on doings in Alexandria. He continued to disdain hunting, and he refused access to others who wished to hunt on his thousands of acres. In particular Washington zealously safeguarded his growing herd of English deer, and when he learned that someone had killed one of the bucks his fury knew no bounds, even though the animal had broken from his paddock and, when struck down, may not have been on the lands of Mount Vernon.[38]

But these trips home were undertaken more for reasons of business than pleasure. The untimely death of George Augustine, his nephew and estate manager, left Washington anxious for the welfare of his Mount Vernon enterprises, and while isolated in the capital he dispatched about one letter per week to Anthony Whiting, his new manager. These usually were long missives packed with the most detailed instructions (what size gravel to use in his walkways, the requisite distance between newly planted trees, symptoms of dangerous illnesses among his slaves, what sort of fertilizer to use on his lawn). Nothing seemed to concern him more than his various overseers, for these men, in his estimation, were unreliable idlers given to "frolicking." When a rash of robberies occurred at Mount Vernon, Washington directed Whiting to see that the overseers visit "the Negro quarters at unexpected hours." He even ordered his overseers to hide in the thickets alongside the roads leading from the estate so that "the receivers of Stolen goods might be entrapped." Whiting also was to watch after the gardner, another employee whom Washington thought required a constant prod. Strangely, Whiting himself seems to have pulled the wool over his boss's eyes. Washington regarded him as honest, sober, and industrious, but after Whiting's death in the fall of 1793 the president discovered that his manager "had drank freely, kept bad company . . . and was a very debauched person." [39]

With almost his entire second term still facing him, the revelation of Whiting's misdeeds left Washington even more concerned about the subsequent management of his affairs. He immediately wrote to acquaintances seeking their aid in finding a man of experience, discretion, honesty, and talent for managing "the labor . . . done by negroes." Only a few weeks passed before he hired William Pearce, a manager recommended by a planter on Maryland's eastern shore. The two men met in Philadelphia, then at Mount Vernon so Pearce could judge whether "the part of the Country, the accommodations, the water, &ct were to his liking." Pearce required only a day or two of ambling over Washington's green rolling domain to consent to take the post, and after a bit of haggling over wages—the president ultimately agreeing to the prospective employee's demands—a contract was signed. The retention of Pearce was a wise move by Washington. The new manager remained until the very end of Washington's second term, performing his duties so well that his meticulous boss eventually expressed his "perfect confidence . . . in your care, judgment and integrity." [40]

Washington's ceaseless financial worries of the 1780s largely seem to have vanished until near the end of his presidency. He continued to plead economic difficulties to those who approached him for loans, but he assured his young confidant Tobias Lear that his affairs were in good condition. When he decided to dispose of much of his property during the second term, he solemnly told some that he was forced to take that step because of financial straits. Once again, however, he told Lear that he had other motives. Selling now would make his retirement years "more tranquil and freer from cares," he said, and, besides, he added in a section of his letter marked "Private," he planned to free the slaves who lived on the grounds he sold. [41]

Not long after he hired Pearce, Washington announced his intention of leasing three of the farms at Mount Vernon. However, he did not wish to rent the lands to just anyone. As American farmers seemed capable only of destroying the land, he thought, he intended to secure English husbandrymen, yeomen who were "peaceable, industrious and skilled." At the end of his term, more than three years after hatching the idea, his Mount Vernon properties remained unrented. Washington likewise noised about his hope of selling his interest in the James River Canal Company, one hundred shares that had been given to him by Virginia. When Jefferson learned of Washington's plans he urged the president to donate the proceeds from the sale to help defray the cost of transporting the faculty of the University of Geneva scholars, who sought refuge from the war that raged in Europe, to the United States; the Virginia assembly, meanwhile, asked Washington not to sell the stock but to donate it to an educational enterprise in

Virginia. The president did neither. Unable to sell his holdings and unwilling to give them away, they still were in his possession at the time of his death. Washington did find a buyer for his interest in the Dismal Swamp Company. Henry Lee agreed to trade several shares in a newly chartered bank in the Federal City for Washington's swamp lands. The president made no attempt to sell his interest in the Potomac Company.[42]

While Washington frequently returned to Mount Vernon to superintend his business affairs, these treks—including the time spent on the road—amounted to less than 15 percent of the nearly fifteen hundred days of the second term. By contrast, his successor John Adams, spent as much as six months a year at his home in Massachusetts during his term. Washington however, preferred to remain in the capital. Annoyed as he may have been by the ceremonial obligations of his office, he enjoyed the assemblage of glittering personalities that surrounded him. Unlike Jefferson, who felt an "excessive repugnance" to the company of "wealthy aristocrats, the merchants connected closely with England, the new created paper fortunes" with which he was compelled to keep, Washington seemed comfortable in the presence of such people. Not surprisingly, given his facility for a chameleonlike metamorphosis from gravity to ease and mellowness in the presence of women, the president seemed to particularly enjoy the opportunity to mingle with a number of notable ladies. Both he and Martha remained close to Mrs. Robert Morris, and he developed a remarkably close relationship with Henrietta Liston, the Scottish-born wife of Robert Liston, George Hammond's replacement as the British minister to the United States.[43]

Considerably younger than either Washington or her husband, Mrs. Liston had been married but two months when she disembarked in Philadelphia in the spring of 1796. A handsome rather than a beautiful woman, she exuded an arresting mix of urbanity and motherliness, part sophistication, part simple amiability. Washington immediately got on well with her, well enough to talk freely. Strangely, however, while he evidently felt relaxed in her presence, even opening up to her as he did with few others, she thought him quite reserved and guarded in his comments and felt that he selected his every phrase carefully and enunciated his thoughts hesitantly. Still, she thought him polite and "friendly"—again not the word his male acquaintances chose when describing him. For the private man she felt affection. The public Washington awed her with his noble demeanor and his "unaffected dignity"; she felt he comported himself more as a monarch than as an elected official.[44]

But, of the women around Washington, none was closer to him than Elizabeth Willing Powel. A native Philadelphian, she was the daughter of a wealthy merchant, the sister of Thomas Willing, Robert Morris's long-time partner, a man said to bear such an uncanny resemblance to Washington that he often was mistaken for the president. Five years before the war she married Samuel Powel, probably the wealthiest bachelor in town and soon to be the last pre-Revolutionary mayor of the city. He was a merchant, but, like Washington, he was intensely interested in farming, and he even belonged to the Society for Promoting Agriculture. Washington probably first met the Powels in 1774 when he attended the First Continental Congress. At that time Mrs. Powel was thirty-two years old, and had been married for four years. He next must have seen her in the course of his three visits to the city between 1775–77 (his first known letter to her was sent from the Morristown cantonment in 1777), and he certainly saw the couple often during his lengthy sojourn in the city following the victory at Yorktown, for he was their next door neighbor for five months. That Eliza and her husband had been only lukewarm patriots—many believed that the reception they had accorded the redcoats in occupied Philadelphia had gone beyond mere civility—apparently did not concern Washington. After the war he corresponded with Samuel, and while he was in Philadelphia for the Constitutional Convention he frequently visited the Powel's home; later in 1787 he reciprocated their many kindnesses by entertaining them at Mount Vernon.

When the two first met Eliza was a striking brunette, buxom and attractive. By the time Washington moved to Philadelphia as president she was nearly forty-eight, and her greying hair and ever so slightly puffy features lent her a matronly look. Of Eliza's appearance in 1790, Abigail Adams, for instance, merely said that she looked her age. In two surviving paintings, Eliza Powel radiates confidence and strength. However, despite her air of composure and equanimity, she, like Washington, was dogged by a lack of self-esteem, which was reinforced, in her case, by a confessed inability to maintain friendships for long. On her first visit to Mount Vernon she excused herself from the dinner table in the midst of the meal, acting under the mistaken notion that her social ineptitude was spoiling the fun for all the others. Thinking herself dull, she hated social functions, and when thrust into illustrious company she sought to compensate for her presumed shortcomings by talking too much. But Washington, with his talent for getting along with women, put her at ease. Always a good listener, he must have enjoyed her steady prattle. When relaxed, she turned coquettish, exhibiting the sort of playfulness that Washington always enjoyed in women. Yet she was anything but shallow. Cultured and articulate, resolute and dogmatic, she was like many of the young men he had selected to surround him. And like young Hamilton and Reed and Lafayette, she understood this complex man, only she was even more candid with him than they were. When Washington thought of leaving the presidency after one term, she wrote to dissuade him. Because a towering ambition had been the "moving spring of all your acts," she advised, the isolation and insignificance of Mount Vernon only would promote "the keenest sufferings" in his breast. She knew that he could be happy only when he was at the center of power. So did he.[45] The president and Eliza Powel seemed to fill each other's needs. To be admired by such an attractive and urbane woman clearly would have gratified Washington's compulsive desire for approval, whereas she must have found it exhilarating to win the attention and friendship of the nation's most esteemed man. Whether their friendship ever was transformed into intimacy cannot be determined, although it is highly unlikely. For one thing their mates always were nearby, an inhibiting presence even had the two been so inclined. Also, there is no hint that such a connection existed in the records left by contemporaries, a generation that hardly shrank from tittle-tattle. And, in all likelihood, a close friendship was sufficient to fill the emotional needs of these two somewhat shy, insecure people.[46]

The Marquis de Lafayette's son, born in 1780 and named for George Washington, also served a function in the president's emotional life. In 1795, with Lafayette still in an Austrian prison, Washington offered asylum in the United States to his friend's family. Mme. Lafayette promptly dispatched her fifteen-year-old son across the Atlantic, the tab for the voyage largely paid for by Washington. But when George Washington Motier Lafayette arrived, a French exile disembarking in a country in the midst of severely strained Franco-American relations, Washington thought it impolitic to have the youngster live with his family in Philadelphia. Instead, he secured the lad's admission to Harvard College, where he remained for a year while the president paid for his schooling. Near the end of the Washington presidency, however, the boy and his elderly French tutor moved into Mount Vernon, remaining there as Washington's guest for eighteen months. In many ways the young man was unlike his famous father. Henrietta Liston found him to be sad and gentle, others thought him awkward. But a loving father-son relationship grew up between the boy and Washington. Indeed, the president must have been pervaded with a melancholy sense of *déjà vu* when he witnessed the departure of the quiet, polite youngster late in 1797, for he could not but have recalled that snowy day thirteen years before when the boy's father had set out for France. In one final gracious act toward young Lafayette, Washington bore the cost of his return passage.[47]

The president also was close to another namesake, George Washington Craik, the son of his old army doctor, James Craik. Raised in Alexandria, where the Scottish physician had set up his practice following the French and Indian War, young Craik was introduced at any early age to his famous neighbor. Beginning in 1788 the master of Mount Vernon had helped underwrite the boy's formal education, and in the final year of his presidency Washington briefly took young Craik on as one of his secretaries. There young Craik joined another aide to whom Washington was especially close. In 1790 Washington had brought Bartholomew Dandridge to Philadelphia to serve as an aide to Lear. Bat, the son of Martha's brother, had performed well enough. Naturally bright, though with little formal education, Bat could handle those duties, but when Lear resigned in 1793 and Dandridge was elevated to the post of the president's personal secretary, it soon was apparent that he had overstepped his limits. In the summer of 1796 Bat simply deserted his post for more than two months, fleeing perhaps because of the pressures of the job. When he resurfaced begging forgiveness, Washington reinstated him, but he made young Craik his assistant.[48]

After seven years of loyal service, Washington had grown much closer to Lear than to any other aide, but during the second term this talented attendant resigned. Following the death of his wife Polly during an epidemic of yellow fever in 1793, Lear, overcome with grief, opted to leave the First Family and enter business in the new Federal City. Washington lent his assistance by recommending the fledgling enterprise to the commissioners of the Federal District, and later he secured the presidency of the Potomac Canal Company for his onetime amanuensis. But Lear continued to be plagued by ill fortune. His business collapsed, largely because of the ineptitude of his partner. Even worse, in 1795 he married Fanny Washington, George Augustine's widow, a marriage that lasted barely six months before she died at age twenty-nine. Moved by his plight—among other things Lear was left with four small children under the age of ten—Washington gave him generous amounts of cash and land.[49]

The public was unaware of the kindness and the warm benevolence with which Washington treated those close to him. Certainly strangers who encountered Washington only briefly would have been surprised by his compassionate qualities, for almost without exception he struck these people as terribly cold and implacable. His most conspicuous trait was his solemn, formal demeanor. When the young architect Benjamin Latrobe first visited Washington he found a man of "reserve, but no hauteur." He also discovered that the president was difficult to speak with, that he "was frequently silent for many minutes, during which time an awkward silence seemed to prevail." So stilted and quiet was the host at mealtime, in fact, that Labrobe soon "felt a little embarrassed at the quiet reserved air." He quickly added, however, that there was "something uncommonly majestic and commanding" in the way that Washington walked and comported himself." A young relative saw the same characteristic in Washington. The president's "dignity awed all who approached him," he later recollected. Curiously, a craftsman, an English stonemason who encountered Washington in the course of his work on the new federal city, saw another side to the president. Without the need to be on guard around such a man, Washington evidently relaxed, leading the artisan to see him as a down-to-earth man who exhibited "none of the disgusting *hauteur* of a superior." Whatever that worker perceived, there was one thing that almost every witness agreed on who saw Washington during the last two years of his presidency: he looked old and worn and tired.[50]

The many portraits made of Washington during these years confirmed the toll that age and service had begun to exact. Charles Willson Peale's last painting of Washington, the one undertaken during the Constitutional Convention in 1787, depicted a robust subject, a man of fifty-five who could have passed for forty-five, who seemed to brim with energy and, for once, with secure self-confidence. Washington was six months beyond the second major illness of his presidency when he sat for Edward Savage late in 1790. He appeared gaunt and slack-jawed, his eyes staring ahead dully, his once ruddy complexion vitiated, an ineffable fatigue etched into his features. Five years later Washington posed for the most famous American painter of the era. Trained in London, Gilbert Stuart returned to the States during the Washington presidency and first induced the great man to sit for him in 1795; two additional sittings followed the next year. The president now was recovered and healthy. His features had filled out, and, indeed, in the initial of the three Stuart works, the so-called Vaughn portrait, Washington appeared to be more overweight than at any time since he had camped with his army before Boston twenty years earlier. In each painting Washington possesses that air of gravity and taciturnity that most contemporaries witnessed. According to all eyewitnesses, he appeared tight-lipped, assertive, humorless, and majestical. Stuart seemed to have captured the essence of the man as described by so many who met him, except that he depicted him as more robust than he was. To most observers Washington seemed never to have recaptured the vitality stolen from him by his illnesses in 1789 and 1790. Those who knew him thought him slower, weaker, more tired—in essence, older—in the wake of those grave afflictions. But, aside from depicting a receding hairline and a full mane of grey hair, Stuart's brush did not dwell on the ravages of time.

Actually, Washington had been in generally good health since those two serious ailments early in his presidency, although he continued to be nagged by a series of relatively minor discomforts not uncommon to a man of his age. A recurrence of the tumor in his thigh resulted in a temporary illness, and an unhappy but inconsequential bout with a virus—probably the ubiquitous flu bug—also briefly felled him. In addition, in June 1794, while inspecting the progress of the Potomac Canal Company workmen, he injured his back in a fall. For a while the injury made it too painful to mount a horse or even to ride in a jostling carriage, yet after a few days of distress he again was in good fettle. About that same time a prickly, tender spot appeared on his right cheek, a splotch diagnosed as skin cancer. However, after two months of treatment at the hands of a physician "possessed of the valuable secret of curing Cancerous complaints," the disorder disappeared.[51]

Of course, Washington's chronic dental afflictions also continued to distract him, a woe his wife now shared. By the middle of his presidential years Washington had only one natural tooth left in his head; he made do with the dentures fashioned from hippopotamus ivory that he had purchased in 1789, an ill-fitting set that caused his lips to protrude in a bucktoothed manner, and which led him to compensate for that look by severely pursing his mouth. If that was not bad enough, the artificial teeth had begun to turn black, the legacy of drinking port wine, a substance that eroded the color and polish from ivory. Aside from periodic colds and a brief bout with colic, Martha also was in good health during these years, but she too had been driven to wear false teeth. Evidently, although she resorted to a different dentist, she had no better luck. Soon after acquiring her artificial dentures she ordered a new pair, instructing her dentist to make the set "something bigger and thicker in the front and a small matter longer." [52]

The greatest health scare of these years did not harm Washington or his family. Late in the summer of 1793 one of the worst epidemics ever to strike

America laid siege to Philadelphia. Yellow fever had invaded the capital. A score or more died each day, and 325 perished during the last twelve days of August. Hamilton was one of the stricken, for days lingering at death's door, although, unlike so many, he ultimately survived. When the death toll climbed to forty per day early in September, President Washington fled the city for Mount Vernon.

Washington had contemplated leaving thirty days earlier, and he even had asked Eliza Powel and her husband to accompany his family to Virginia. She declined the offer, explaining that her husband "saw no Propriety in . . . flying from the only spot where Physicians conversant in the Disorder . . . could be consulted." She would remain with her husband, she added; the "line of Duty" required that she do so. Curiously, Washington then abandoned his plan to flee, and he did not finally depart until the infestation's net had spread from the city's working-class neighborhoods into the more fashionable districts. To no avail he once again urged the Powels to come with him. Samuel Powel's refusal to leave Philadelphia was a fatal error, for he, too, soon contracted the disease and perished.

President Washington spent several weeks at Mount Vernon, and when he returned north he lived for six weeks in Germantown, a safe haven a few miles outside Philadelphia. There he remained until late in November when the "malignant fever," as he called the malady, at last had spent itself. By then one in every twenty Philadelphians had succumbed to the grim visitor.[53]

A year later, in the summer of 1794, news of another malady reached the capital—a disorder within the body politic. From western Pennsylvania, a region in which Washington had spent some of his most trying days, came word that defiant backwoodsmen had organized a campaign of armed resistance against the federal excise tax on distilled whiskey. The duty had been established in 1791— and modified the next year—at the behest of Hamilton. There is no reason to believe that the secretary of the treasury should have been surprised by the protest movement aroused by the tax. Western farmers had a history of violent dissent, a record that included both the Shaysite episode in the 1780s as well as random resistance to various state excises during that decade. In this instance, too, there was good reason to scorn the law. The tax was considerable (one quarter of the cost of a gallon of whiskey); moreover, the revenue generated by the excise was to be used to rescind the states' debts, in itself never a popular policy out on the frontier. Some scholars even have surmised that Hamilton may have hoped the outlanders would challenge the law, thus presenting the administration with an excuse for demonstrating the power of the new national government.[54]

If he did harbor such wishes, the opportunity to make an example of the defiant westerners arose in mid-1794. For two years the area about Pittsburgh had bubbled and simmered with the rhetoric of discontent, and even with sporadic violence. As early as 1792, when word of the initial disorders reached Philadelphia, Hamilton had urged the use of force to suppress the dissidents. His strident counsel was premature. Washington was unmoved. Fearing that force would be counterproductive—if the endeavor to subdue the yeomenry did not destroy the fledgling central government, he seemed to warn, it would render it impossible in moments of greater crisis ever again to raise an army—the president agreed only to issue a proclamation defending the duties.[55]

By mid-1794 nothing had been resolved. With monotonous regularity couriers arrived in the capital bearing word of increasingly recalcitrant behavior in the West. June brought tidings from Kentucky of remonstrances against the Jay mission, and that in turn was followed in July by lurid accounts of angry protests and inflammatory statements against the excise. Popular evasion was endemic on the frontier, from Pennsylvania to Kentucky, from backcountry Virginia to South Carolina.

Washington also learned that the excise inspector in western Pennsylvania had been assaulted by an anti-tax mob. Other reports indicated that insurgent leaders were seeking to neutralize local militia units in order to prevent the enforcement of the law. Washington's reaction was swift, and in this instance, unlike two summers before, he and his treasury secretary thought along similar lines. From the outset of the crisis both sought a resolution of the frontier commotions through the use of force. Both Washington and Hamilton were anxious to display the power of the new national government. Still, the president and Secretary Hamilton were troubled. Their problem was not over the wisdom of using force, but, as historian Richard Kohn has written, "whether it was possible to use force."[56]

One quandary that faced Washington was simple. Western resistance was widespread, but it took its most overt form in Pennsylvania and Kentucky, and the latter was precisely the region from which the president hoped to find militia assistance for Anthony Wayne's army. Washington's dilemma, therefore, was to find a means by which force might be used against the refractory frontiersmen without at the same time alienating those from the backcountry who were expected to soldier in the war for the Northwest.[57]

Another problem also vexed Washington. He soon discovered that unleashing a federal force was easier said than done. Article IV of the Constitution stipulated that federal troops could be dispatched to a state only upon the petition of the state legislature, or, if the assembly was not in session, as was the case in Pennsylvania in the summer of 1794, on the request of the governor. Washington learned quickly that Thomas Mifflin, Pennsylvania's governor, did not wish to ask for federal troops.

On August 2 Washington summoned his cabinet to consider the unrest on the frontier, and he invited Mifflin and three additional Pennsylvania officials to sit in on the deliberations. While a hot sun blazed away at steamy, stifling Germantown, to which Washington had transferred his residence three days earlier, the cabinet and its guests met for several hours. In that session, as well as in written reports subsequently submitted to the president, Washington discovered that his council was divided. He opened the meeting with the declaration that he was determined to "go every length that the Constitution and Laws would permit, but no further." The remark shed no light on his thinking. But the length to which Hamilton, Knox, and the new attorney general, William Bradford, would go soon was apparent. Each man urged the president to use force to suppress the uprising. Hamilton's view typified the outlook of these three advisors. The anti-tax movement, he said, was the result of an organized conspiracy, and he urged an "immediate resort to Military force." The president, he added, should simultaneously call up the militia and issue another proclamation, a statement demanding compliance with the law; when it became evident that the law would not be obeyed, he went on, Washington should unleash the army.

Among the cabinet members only Secretary of State Randolph eschewed the use of force. In a long, perhaps emotional, statement he appeared to argue that an army was not the proper instrument through which to compel tax evaders to comply with the law. He probably took issue with the notion of an organized conspiracy among the discontented frontiersmen, and, without question, he warned that if Hamilton's end was merely to display the efficacy of federal power under the new Constitution, such a heavy-handed tactic was likely to be counterproductive, for the government ultimately could succeed only if it possessed the affection of the people.

The state authorities concurred with Randolph. Mifflin, joined by Pennsylvania's attorney general and the chief justice of the state, expressed doubts about the conspiracy hypothesis, and they sought to convince Washington that the dissidents still could be dealt with through the courts.[58]

The judiciary it would be, but not as Mifflin had envisioned. Inspired by the memory of Shays's Rebellion, Congress had passed the Militia Act of 1792, a statute that gave the president authority to summon a state militia for the purpose of repelling a foreign invader, enforcing federal law, or suppressing insurrections. All that was needed was a judicial writ certifying that all other avenues toward a peaceful resolution of the crisis had been exhausted. A friendly associate justice of the Supreme Court—one of Washington's appointees, of course—happily signed the paperwork, though, despite the widespread opposition in the backcountry, the administration-prepared document merely declared that Washington and Allegheny counties in western Pennsylvania were in a state of rebellion. With that act Washington had removed his two obstacles to the use of force. He not only had legal sanction to act, he had ingeniously discovered a means by which he could avoid alienating the Kentuckians whom Anthony Wayne might wish to recruit for soldiering. Washington simply had closed his eyes and pretended that the rebellion was confined to western Pennsylvania.[59]

Only one dissenting voice continued to be heard. Secretary Randolph persisted in his objection to the use of force. He urged the president to issue a proclamation and to appoint emissaries to treat with the frontiersmen. At first, it seemed that Washington was listening. On August 7 he published a statement. Whereas "combinations too powerful to be suppressed" by judicial means had acted in a "dangerous and criminal" manner, it was his intention, his Delphic utterance warned, to use force if the insurgents had not dispersed by September 1. He added, however, that he was sending three commissioners to treat with the protestors, agents empowered to offer amnesty in return for compliance with the whiskey tax.[60]

His accommodating public remarks notwithstanding, Washington must already have decided that the use of force would be unavoidable. He could hardly have expected his emissaries to meet with success, inasmuch as he believed—as he now said privately—that the democratic societies were behind the protest, and that their "diabolical leader," Edmund Genêt, had "poison[ed] the minds" of the westerners. In addition, whereas he earlier had believed that the use of force might prove destructive to the new central government, he seemed now to have come to think that to fail to use force might be fatal. Hamilton, moreover, was convinced that his arguments at the August 2 cabinet meeting had proved decisive in winning Washington's commitment to use force; privately, in fact, he even carped that since Washington planned to use force when the commissioners failed in their undertaking, it was both tawdry and unenterprising of the president not to have called up the militia when he issued his proclamation.[61]

The commissioners, therefore, must have been dispatched only for show, as a means of whipping up public support for the pending campaign of armed suppression. There can be little doubt that Washington feared that he might be unable to raise an adequate military force. As what amounted to the United States army still was on an even more remote frontier with Anthony Wayne, the force that would invade western Pennsylvania would have to be composed of volunteers and militiamen, men lured—or dragged—away from America's farms and back-country settlements. It was entirely possible that America's yeomen might have little stomach for killing their counterparts in the Pennsylvania outlands. Thus, the commissioners. And to supplement their endeavors Hamilton was turned loose to conduct a propaganda blitz in the press. He penned a series of essays under the sobriquet "Tully," pieces in which he depicted the insurrection as a "dark conspiracy" hatched by the democratic societies, a plot whose aims included bringing the United States into the European war on the side of France.[62]

When the first pessimistic reports arrived from his emissaries in Pittsburgh, Washington acted quickly to use force. Before the commissioners even opened talks with the insurgent leaders, they reported that there seemed to be no prospect of enforcing the whiskey excise save by resorting to "the Physical strength of the Nation." Within twenty-four hours of reading this gloomy assessment Washington invoked the Militia Act, and he turned to his old friend Henry Lee, now governor of Virginia, and asked him to mobilize his state's trainband units. In the next few days Washington requested assistance from other states. The response was gratifying. The media campaign and the well-publicized reports of the commissioners did the job, as, undoubtedly, did the public's carnival thirst for participating in a martial crusade. In fact, so many volunteers came forward that the government had to close its recruiting offices lest the army become bloated and unwieldy. Even so, Washington soon had more than twelve thousand men under arms, poised to suppress an insurrection of tax evaders presumably confined to just two frontier counties.[63]

Washington did not immediately order the army forward, however. He waited two additional weeks, until early September. On the 8th still more pessimistic reports arrived from the commissioners, and, once again, within twenty-four hours Washington acted. He ordered the army to proceed against the "refractory counties." [64]

On September 30 Washington left the capital to assume command of the invasion army. He intended to ride at least as far as Carlisle, about half way to the war zone. Events thereafter would determine his conduct. On the first night of his journey a messenger bearing important news about the frontier caught up with the president at his resting stop in a German settlement called the Trappe, a few miles beyond Norristown. The tidings, however, were not about the Pennsylvania frontier. Anthony Wayne, the president learned, at last had encountered the Indians in the Northwest. At a battle in Ohio he had accomplished what Harmar and St. Clair had been unable to achieve: the Indians had been dealt a staggering defeat.[65]

Thirty months had elapsed since Wayne had been commissioned to resume the United States offensive in the Northwest Territory. Setting up headquarters at Pittsburgh he had recruited his Legion of the United States, as his force pompously was called, then with pitiless fervor he had sought to whip an army into shape, ordering three malefactors shot and others branded and flogged. Late in the spring of 1793 he finally marched into the Ohio Country, but he remained near present-day Cincinnati for nearly a year. Not until mid-year, 1794, about the time that Washington had begun to consider action against the foes of the whiskey excise, and roughly two months after John Jay had sailed for England, did General Wayne march down the Maumee into disputed territory. Six weeks later, just below the western tip of Lake Erie, his army of thirty-five hundred men clashed with an Indian force only one-seventh its size. The fight took place in what once had been a lush primeval forest, since reduced to a tangle of rubble and refuse by a tornado. The Battle of Fallen Timbers was over in less than an hour. Only fifty tribesmen perished, but Wayne was right to call his victory a "brilliant success," for it had broken the will of these Indians to continue a long war of resistance. Less than a year later the survivors signed the Treaty of Greenville, which formally surrendered much of Ohio and Indiana to the United States. Thereafter, the number of Miami tribesmen shrank steadily, until within twenty years William Henry Harrison, the Northwest Territory's first delegate to Congress, characterized this once grand people as "merely a poor drunken set." A century later fewer than five hundred of the Miamis even existed.[66]

Buoyed by the "pleasing" (the term used in his diary entry by this undemonstrative president) tidings of Fallen Timbers, Washington set off the next morning for the Pennsylvania frontier. He paused at Carlisle, where the Pennsylvania troops were assembling. There he heard a Presbyterian minister "Preach a political Sermon, recommendatory of order & good government," and for the first time in nearly a dozen years he helped organize an army. He also met with two emissaries from frontier settlements, men who had been deputed to tell him that the back of the dissident force already had been broken. Washington was not swayed, and soon he again was on his way. At Cumberland, Maryland, he paused for three days, greeting General Henry Lee, who had arrived with the troops from Virginia, and sitting through an endless succession of dreary staff meetings. When the army broke camp and entered Pennsylvania, Washington rode at its head, but at Bedford he decided to go no further. With Congress about to assemble in Philadelphia, he concluded suddenly, he must return to the capital "to attend the Civil duties of my office." With rather more dramatic effect than the situation merited, he left a "farewell address to the army" to be read to the soldiery, put General Lee in charge, and, on October 21, turned for the six-day ride back to the Delaware.[67]

Washington did not miss much in his absence from the army. Indeed, as Randolph had predicted, no army of "Whiskey Men" awaited the United States force, a realization that must have dawned on Washington as the army pushed further west. The greatest danger to the troops came from within the ranks of the army itself. For instance, while Governor Mifflin, the commander of the Pennsylvania forces, was reeling in an alcoholic stupor, the trainbandsmen of his state shot up the New Jersey militia; as usual, however, the most serious threat came from severe camp diseases, ailments that cropped up randomly to carry many men to a less-than-heroic grave. After Washington's departure the army drove on to the Monongahela, stumbling through incessant autumn rains. In the end it rounded up several hundred farmers for interrogation, actually jailing about 160 luckless sodbusters. Of these, most ultimately were acquitted. Only twenty alleged insurgents were brought back to Philadelphia in shackles, there to be paraded for the curious citizenry to behold. And after all the hysteria just two of these unfortunates were convicted of high treason and sentenced to death. Washington pardoned both. It was well that he did. One of the convicts was thought to be an imbecile, the other to be mad.[68]

By then Washington knew that Randolph had been correct, that Hamilton had erred, regarding the existence of an organized western conspiracy "to sow the seeds of . . . revolution." But to acknowledge his error was not the president's way. Publicly, he never wavered from the line that the democratic societies had fomented rebellion, although he now claimed that they had "precipitated a crisis for which they were not prepared." Nor did he waver from the notion that the army's majestic incursion into the West was warranted, for its end had been to display the supremacy of the new national government.[69]

As the autumn splendor turned quickly to winter's bleakness, the seasonal changes must have reminded Washington that his second term was hastening to its end. The years 1793 and 1794 had been difficult, filled with party strife, domestic turmoil, and international tension. Whatever the future brought, the president knew by Christmas that he would have to face it without Hamilton and Knox. Though these men had exhorted Washington to sacrifice in order to serve the public, each now had announced his own intention to resign early in 1795.

Nevertheless, as he entered these final years of his presidency Washington seemed more confident than ever. Save for the continued warfare in Europe, he reflected, conditions were good. Even the congressional session of 1794–95 was remarkably tranquil compared to some of its predecessors. Only if John Jay's negotiations in London were unsuccessful was real trouble likely, he thought. On that subject, the president was holding his breath.[70]

18

Last Years in Office

"Trouble and perplexities"

President Washington remained in the capital throughout the winter of 1794–95. He would not leave while Congress was in session, and, in fact, he did not seem to mind spending these cold, wet months in Philadelphia. Not only was this the slow season at Mount Vernon, but William Pearce, his estate manager, had established firm control of operations back home.

This was the slow season in the capital as well. The Federalist program was in place, and with their comfortable majority in the Senate they easily could keep their foes under control. The Democratic-Republicans controlled the House, yet while the effects of the Whiskey Rebellion still resonated they seemed inclined to remain mute. From his vantage point as presiding officer of the Senate, Vice President Adams marveled at the serenity within the halls of Congress. Senators "have no feelings this session; no passions; no animation in debate." Was it the calm before the storm, he wondered?[1]

Whatever it was, after the tumult of the preceding twelve months, the president must have welcomed the lull. During these weeks Washington's concern turned principally toward Spain. Hoping to reopen talks that might unsnarl the Mississippi River question, he appointed an "envoy extraordinary" to Madrid. Washington had decided on such a mission months before, though he had delayed filling the post until the time was right. During the summer of 1794 evidence mounted that Madrid was edging toward terminating its alliance with Great Britain and improving its relationship with the United States. More optimistic now, the president offered the post to Jefferson, then to Patrick Henry, and finally, after each had declined the offer, he named Thomas Pinckney the American minister to Britain.[2]

Filling the vacancies left by Hamilton and Knox was more difficult. Timothy Pickering, just back from a diplomatic assignment that had sent him into western New York to parley with the Six Nations, became the new secretary of war. A dozen years younger than the president, the son of a prosperous farmer-businessman in Salem, Massachusetts, Pickering's name first had become familiar at the outbreak of war in 1775 when he published an *Easy Plan of Discipline for a Militia*, a manual of arms that immediately was widely read by drillmasters throughout America. Soon Pickering was bearing arms himself. He saw combat on the Brandywine in 1777, and subsequently he went on to sit on the Board of War and to serve as quartermaster general. Without a fortune or an alternate income, the federal bureaucracy became his livelihood. His administrative experience led to his appointment as postmaster general of the United States in 1791, then to his selection as perhaps the administration's principal diplomat in talks with the Native Americans. His success in keeping the Six Nations neutral in 1794 earned him the secretary of war post. Tall, slender, shy and reserved, severe in appearance, and, in fact, appropriately dour, he was at least his own man and not a tool of Hamilton as his political foes later charged.[3]

That could not be said for the new treasury secretary, Oliver Wolcott, Jr. Also a New Englander, the Connecticut-born Wolcott had considerable experience in dealing with fiscal concerns. After serving briefly as the controller of his state, he had joined the new national government in 1789 as the auditor of the treasury. Two years later, at Hamilton's suggestion, he became the United States controller, a post he still held when Washington named him—once again at the behest of Hamilton—to fill the vacant treasury post. Affable and gentle in appearance, cultivated and courteous in manner, Wolcott's darker side included a penchant for scheming, a compelling urge to do whatever had to be done to get ahead—and to see that in the course of things the Federalists' and Hamilton's interests were served.[4]

Word from John Jay was the most important matter on Washington's mind, however. Early in March 1795, a month after the appointment of Wolcott, the long-awaited packets from the faraway envoy finally arrived. Jay had negotiated a treaty of twenty-eight articles. He believed he had pried as many concessions from the British as could be extracted, he told Washington and Secretary of State Randolph in attached cover letters. "To do more was not possible," was how he put it, adding that much was left unresolved but that, at least, "the door of conciliation is fairly and widely opened." Jay, in fact, had probably obtained the best treaty that he was capable of getting. But that is not to say that another diplomat might not have done better. And Jay might have been capable of more had his feet not been cut from beneath him by American officials in Philadelphia.[5]

Jay had arrived in London in mid-1794, and he had initialed the pact in November, a relatively short space of time for two unfriendly nations to resolve their many crucial differences. Before Jay landed, it now is known, Whitehall already had decided to make major concessions on the issue of the western posts. What else the British were ready to concede cannot now be known. But it is clear that when the talks commenced Britain was chagrined at the course its war with France was taking. Spain seemed on the verge of breaking its ties with Great Britain and concluding peace with France. Reports indicated that the temporary United States embargo had caused real problems in Britain's Caribbean holdings. French armies had scored amazing victories in several theaters. Economic woes had descended on the British isles, and food shortages were being reported. And on the eve of Jay's arrival came word that Sweden and Denmark were busy constructing a coalition for the protection of neutral countries. If a league of armed neutralists was instituted, trade between the French empire and the outside was certain to be augmented; if the United States participated in such an association, the clout of the neutral nations would only be enhanced.[6]

Faced with this increasingly gloomy situation the British set about aggressively courting the American envoy. British agents in New York and Philadelphia had notified Whitehall that Jay would purr like a kitten if his vanity were stroked, prompting the diplomat's counterpart in the pending talks, William Wyndham Grenville, to wheedle and flatter the American. But other information in the hands of the ministry probably resulted in more damage to America's aspirations. Back in the 1780s, while he was secretary of foreign affairs, Jay injudiciously had taken it upon himself to apprise the British consul in New York of his sympathies for Great Britain in its lingering disputes with the United States. Moreover, if Britain did not know how loath Jay had been to break with the parent state in 1776, its officials had not done their homework; indeed, as early as 1776 some contemporaries even suspected that Jay had passed along to London information on the secret undertakings of the Continental Congress.[7]

The evidence suggests that Whitehall, knowing full well how badly Jay wanted to preserve the peace with Great Britain, adopted an unpliable stance. The evidence also suggests that Jay collapsed in the face of British intransigence. What cannot be known, however, is how inflexible Britain all along had intended to be. But armed with a thorough understanding of Jay's wishes, and over the years advised by Hamilton of Washington's similar yearning for peace, Grenville was dealt the sort of powerhouse hand of which every diplomat dreams.[8]

When Washington first read the terms of Jay's Treaty that cold Philadelphia afternoon, he was concerned at the meagerness of his envoy's achievement. He did not find the accord filled with "mischiefs," as he put it, but he found it disconcertingly free of concessions to the United States. Whitehall, in fact, had made just one important concession. It had agreed to withdraw from the United States's western posts by June 1796. A second concession was virtually meaningless. In Article XII Britain agreed to a slight accommodation concerning United States trade in the British West Indies, pledging to admit American ships of seventy tons or less into these ports. This allowance was so modest that there could be no doubt that Britain's carriers clearly would remain predominant in this commerce. For these presentments Jay conceded the right of Britain and its Native American allies to trap and trade on the rivers of the Northwest Territory, including the Mississippi, and he pledged that the United States would not impose discriminatory duties on Great Britain. The treaty said nothing about the impressment of American seamen, and it was silent concerning compensation for the slaves liberated by Britain during the War of Independence, but it did contain a provision for settling the prewar claims of British creditors in America. Moreover, the treaty seemed to give legal sanction to two British policies that were decidedly unpopular in most American circles: American ships were to be prohibited from transporting goods from British ports to France or to other non-aligned nations, and naval stores and virtually all foodstuffs were placed on the contraband list. Finally, the pact made provisions for the eventual solution of two troubling matters. The United States–Canadian border was to be determined by an Anglo-American commission, and it was agreed that binding arbitration should set compensation for American shippers who had lost property in the Caribbean as a result of the orders-in-council.[9]

If Washington's reaction to the Jay Treaty was mixed, he apparently never considered not submitting it to the Senate. For three months, while he carefully kept secret the terms of the pact, the only person to whom the president spoke about the treaty was the secretary of state. Secretary Randolph signaled his lukewarm endorsement of Jay's handiwork, although he did propose that Washington scuttle the article that limited the size of American vessels trading in the British Caribbean; he also favored tying the implementation of the treaty to Britain's repeal of its orders-in-council. When the Senate reassembled for a special session in June, Washington submitted the treaty, accompanied by a statement that revealed a unique interpretation of the constitutional process of treaty ratification. He truly wished to have the Senate's advice. If it failed to consent, the matter was done; only if it consented would Washington agonize over whether to sign the treaty.[10]

The Senate required only two weeks of deliberation before ratifying the Jay Treaty. Still, to secure approval the Federalists had to agree to delete Article

XII, and even then they pushed the accord through with the minimum number of votes necessary. The vote was along the now-familiar partisan lines, and it was accompanied by a strident indignation that had not been present even in the disputes over Hamiltonian economics. Fairly accurate rumors about the contents of the treaty had begun to spread as early as January, talk that elicited the earliest attacks on the document. By the time the Senate at last began its deliberations, the country seemed to be rocking with outrage, and that was just the beginning. Five days after the Senate voted for ratification, a Philadelphia newspaper published the treaty. The public finally glimpsed what it had been howling about. The bellowing increased. It was, said Washington, a cry "like that against a mad-dog." [11]

The protest reflected the deep anti-British mood that persisted in America, and the administration came in for a pounding for allegedly being little better than Whitehall's puppets and lackeys. There also was an economic motive for the opposition. The South, in particular, seemed about to explode with wrath when it learned that the pact was silent on the matter of compensation for the slaves carried away by the British army during the War of Independence. The region had not expected much from Jay. A past president of the New York Society for the Abolition of Slavery, he long had been suspect in the southern states. Now, said Madison, his "extraordinary abandonment" of the South left no room for doubt about whom he represented. But the slavery portion of the pact was not the only reason for southern outrage. The wide-ranging contraband list evoked howls both from the region's yeomenry and from those who eked out a living from the forest industries. The residents of Charleston, it was said, reacted to the pact as they had to the Stamp Act thirty years before.

Although almost every northern senator had voted for the treaty, that region also reverberated with denunciations of an accord that failed to outlaw impressment and that had secured negligible gains for the nation's shippers. A Boston town meeting at Faneuil Hall unanimously disapproved of Jay's handiwork, and to the four corners of the northern states newspapers overflowed with invective. Some rioting occurred, including an ugly scene in Boston when a mob torched a British ship anchored in that city's famous harbor. John Jay was hanged in effigy by more than one throng—and *he* got off lightly. Hamilton was struck by a stone while addressing a forum in New York. So visceral was the public outcry that Federalists were compelled to assume a defensive posture. The treaty, they said, was the best that a small, weak nation could expect. Besides, it was a better bargain than the alternative—another war with Britain. [12]

Still, the Senate had acted positively, leaving the matter for the president to resolve. Washington had watched the Senate debate closely, but he had not intruded. Nor did he make any public comment immediately after its vote. For two weeks he wrestled with the matter, closely following the public debate and almost daily consulting with his secretary of state, Edmund Randolph. On July 7 matters took a bizarre turn. That day news arrived that Britain once again had begun to plunder American ships bound for France. The Pitt ministry apparently had reinstituted its orders-in-council. The president was outraged. On the verge of signing the treaty, he abruptly reversed himself. After conferring with Randolph, he directed the secretary of state to inform the British minister that he never would consent to the treaty while these depradations persisted.[13]

A week later Washington departed for Virginia to begin a long-planned vacation. He had not seen Mount Vernon in three months, and then he had sojourned at his estate for less than a week. The president was not about to permit the treaty crisis to rob him of this excursion. He bumped out of the capital on July 15, commencing the long trek home. Predictably, it was a "disagreeable ride," he told a correspondent upon his arrival, one made all the more unpleasant by his receipt of the news of the action of Boston's town meeting just as his carriage was being readied for the journey. His plan was to remain at home for the next ten weeks, not returning to the capital until early fall. By then Philadelphia's oppressive and unhealthy summer weather should have ended, and, with luck, whatever he chose to do about the Jay Treaty should have become of as ancient history.[14]

The president had been home only a few days before he evinced signs that he missed the excitement that swirled in the capital. Even though his leading cabinet officials assured him that his presence was not required, Washington announced that he might have to return to Philadelphia sooner than planned, and on his fourteenth day at home he decided that he must scrap his vacation. Nevertheless, business and the weather confined him to Mount Vernon for a few additional days. First he wished to attend a board meeting of the Potomac Company, then a spate of torrential rains compelled his continued presence, for he wished to direct the repairs to his fields made necessary by the downpours. But on August 5 he received a mysterious note from the secretary of war. Could he not return to Philadelphia quickly, Pickering asked. A *"special reason"* required the president's presence. He could not divulge that reason in a letter.[15]

Early the next morning Washington's carriage rolled out of Mount Vernon. On August 11 he was back in the sweltering oven of Philadelphia, and that very evening he summoned Pickering to his residence. The secretary arrived to find Washington dining with Secretary of State Randolph. Leaving Randolph alone for the moment, the president and Pickering adjourned to another chamber. While Washington sipped a glass of wine, Pickering unveiled an incredible tale.

Pickering launched into a story about how George Hammond, the British minister, had set in motion a train of events by inviting Secretary Wolcott to his office. There on July 26, Pickering said, Hammond had divulged an intercepted letter written to the French foreign minister by Citizen Genêt's successor, Joseph Fauchet. In the document Fauchet alleged in veiled and indistinct language that Edmund Randolph had sought to play a game of extortion, requesting money from Paris in return for a promise that the United States would pursue a pro-French policy. In addition, the letter could be interpreted to suggest that the secretary of state had passed along state secrets to Fauchet; the French minister's terminology once again was imprecise, however, for he alluded only to "Precious confessions" that Randolph allegedly had made. Fauchet's only categorical charge was that Randolph had helped foment the Whiskey Rebellion as a means of reducing Washington's popularity and influence. Wolcott had secured the original letter, Pickering added, and he had showed it to his two Federalist colleagues in the cabinet. The three agreed upon the necessity for Pickering's urgent letter to Mount Vernon.[16]

The president was shocked. What is most shocking today, however, is that Washington immediately embraced the charge that Randolph had acted as a traitor. He had known and trusted the secretary of state for more than twenty years. Randolph, moreover, had served in his cabinet for six years without the slightest hint of impropriety. Washington had known in 1789 that Randolph was in financial straits, nearly ruined, in fact, by his public service and his wife's protracted and expensive illness. Still, he had selected him to head the justice department, then, contrary to Jefferson's counsel, he had named his fellow Virginian to head the state department. Until his conversation with Pickering, Washington had never expressed the slightest misgiving about Randolph's performance. Now, when presented with no more evidence than an epistle composed in vague and uncertain terms, a letter translated by Pickering (a translation which the president evidently made no attempt to authenticate), which had surfaced from the depths of the British embassy in the midst of a British campaign to see the Jay Treaty finally approved, and which was championed by three Federalist comrades at the expense of the lone non-Federalist in the cabinet—on such slight evidence Washington instantly judged the secretary of state to be guilty as charged.[17]

With that as his starting point, Washington also concluded that Randolph must have deliberately misled him about the Jay Treaty. By urging him not to sign the treaty until Britain rescinded its orders-in-council, the president now surmised, Randolph discreetly had manipulated him into not approving the accord.

Without a word of any of this to Randolph, Washinton mustered his cabinet the following morning. He commenced the meeting by calling for recommendations concerning the Jay Treaty. As he must have anticipated, the three Federalists counseled ratification, while Randolph once again advised against the president's acquiescence until Britain discontinued its policy of seizing American cargoes. To the secretary of state's considerable surprise, Washington soon cut off the discussion and announced his plan to sign the accord. Without a word to the man responsible for American foreign affairs, the president had made an about-face on an issue of paramount importance.[18]

Washington's decision has been attributed to a "fit of rage, or outrage" at Randolph, an act "against his own best judgment and against the advice of his most trusted intimates." Such a conclusion is unwarranted. There can be no doubt that Washington believed that he had been misused by Randolph, yet factors other than personal pique weighed more heavily on his final decision. The Senate had advised ratification. In addition, the strong, even violent, public outcry that had characterized the initial response to the treaty had given way by mid-August to a debate in the press, an emotionally charged battle to be sure, but one that now was peaceful and confined to the printed page. Furthermore, not only had the cabinet recommended that he sign the treaty, it also was clear that the northern merchant community, toward many of whose leading lights he felt a deep kindredship, endorsed the treaty. Finally, Hamilton, as usual, played a crucial role in the evolution of Washington's thinking.[19]

Shortly after the Senate's vote Washington wrote Hamilton to request two favors. On the one hand he virtually urged his young friend to publicly defend the treaty. Hamilton soon complied by publishing thirty-nine open letters under the signature of "Camillus," essays that many scholars regard as equal in quality to his Federalist treatises of 1787–88. The president also requested the private views of Hamilton, credulously suggesting that he wished "to learn from dispassionate men" the pros and cons of the Jay Treaty. Three days later Hamilton drafted the first of seven letters that he would write to Washington in the next two weeks; in addition, he sent along a typically lengthy essay—it spans fifty pages in the modern edition of Hamilton's papers—which enjoined Washington to sign the treaty. The former secretary told Washington that the pact had resolved most Anglo-American differences about "as reasonably as could have been expected." At the same time, he added, it gave the United States the means of "escaping finally from being implicated in the dreadful war which is ruining Europe—and of preserving ourselves in a state of peace for a considerable time to come."

The last of Hamilton's letters arrived at Mount Vernon on July 29. The president's actions on that day indicate that he at last had made up his mind to sign the treaty. He decided to return to the capital where he could meet with his cabinet and divulge his decision. That same day he drafted a missive to Hamilton which all but stated that he was prepared to sign Jay's treaty. Most of the arguments against the accord were erroneous and founded on "misrepresentations," he began, and he went on to suggest that the great virtue of the pact was that it afforded a chance for peace with London. Though his would be an unpopular act, he added, he believed that once "the paroxysm of the fever is a little abated" the "real temper of the people" would change, endorsing his decision. Thus, by the time he departed Virginia, five days before he learned of the allegations against Randolph, Washington appears to have decided to exchange ratifications with Whitehall. The machinations of the Pickering-Wolcott-Hammond cabal, at best, only hastened and colored the inevitable.[20]

On August 18 President Washington signed the Jay Treaty. Only then did he confront Randolph with the evidence of his alleged treason. The cabinet again was assembled at Washington's residence, and following some perfunctory pleasantries the president asked Randolph to read Fauchet's dispatch. By prearrangement Washington and the three Federalists carefully studied Randolph's features as he perused the letter. Whatever they expected, they observed no evidence of discomposure. And Randolph confessed to no crimes. He had neither requested nor received money from France. He denied having ever passed secrets to any foreign government. The charge that he had fomented the unrest in western Pennsylvania was preposterous, he said. Defiantly Randolph pledged to defend himself in writing. The following day he resigned his place in the Washington administration making it quite clear that he believed his old friend, the president, had subjected him to the most base and cruel treatment. Timothy Pickering, who had carried Fauchet's dispatch to Washington, agreed to serve as the acting secretary of state, and in the ensuing personnel shuffle the Washington administration grew unmistakably Federalist.[21]

The president named his wartime aide James McHenry to succeed Pickering at the war department. Steadfastly loyal to Washington, McHenry had served as a Maryland delegate to the Constitutional Convention and he had worked diligently for the document's ratification; since 1791 he had been among the Senate's strongest supporters of the Washington-Hamilton program. Samuel Chase, also of Maryland, was at the same time named to one of two vacancies that materialized suddenly on the Supreme Court. The son of an immigrant preacher from England, Chase had launched his national career as one of the First Continental Congress's most conservative members, supporting Joseph Galloway's Anglo-American reconciliation scheme. Ultimately he swung behind the notion of separation, signed the Declaration of Independence, and won a reputation as one of Washington's staunchest supporters in Congress during the "Conway Cabal" frenzy. Thereafter, however, his political ascent was stymied by his implication in a scandal to use inside government information for personal profit. Washington overlooked that blot on Chase's record to name him to the nation's highest court. Oliver Ellsworth got Washington's nod for the other opening, the post of chief justice of the United States. Ellsworth had the reputation, according to John Adams, of being Washington's "firmest pillar" in the Senate. A graduate of Princeton College, a wealthy Hartford, Connecticut, lawyer, he had been elected to Congress as early as 1778, and he too had sat as a delegate to the Constitutional Convention.[22]

Although each member of the cabinet now was a Federalist, Washington continued to deny the obviously partisan leanings of his administration. A "hundred and an hundred times you have heard me lament" factionalism, he exclaimed. Few were convinced by his disavowal. The Republican press, in fact, turned its guns on Washington and directed a campaign of open invective against him, subjecting him to a litany of vitriolic comments such as he never had previously encountered. Not only was his talent for statesmanship called into question, his style of leadership was mocked, especially his august and stately bearing, a manner best suited, it was said, for monarchy. Strangely, however, Washington's most esteemed critic, and the foe with perhaps the strongest case to make against him, aroused little support, failing even to induce the Republicans to take up his case against the embroiled chief executive. That was Edmund Randolph, who just before Christmas 1795 launched an open assault on his former friend.[23]

Before going public Randolph had communicated his bitterness to the president in several private missives. He was aggrieved that Washington had not consulted him privately before confronting him in the presence of the cabinet; and, he went on, for Washington to have permitted his colleagues on the cabinet to cross-examine him was unconscionable. The case against him, he added, was the outcropping of partisan politics, and Washington should have seen what the Federalist conspirators were about. As Randolph stewed and simmered throughout the autumn, his tone grew more strident, more sarcastic. Late in October his letters—in Washington's estimation—had grown so "full of innuendoes" that the president refused any longer to respond. But that hardly ended matters. During the holiday season the public was let in on what had been occurring in private. Randolph published his version of the affair for all the world to see. He accused Washington of having prejudiced his case, and, more damning, he maintained that beneath Washington's "exterior of cool and slow deliberation" lurked a narrow mind, one that "rapidly catches a prejudice and with difficulty abandons it. . . ." [24]

Randolph's case was strong. The original evidence against his alleged misconduct was worse than feeble. It was based on Pickering's amateurish and error-strewn translation of Fauchet's letters. In addition, Randolph not only had secured from Fauchet a certificate in which the French envoy declared that the former secretary of state had never sought or received bribes from the government of France, but the minister also denied that Randolph ever had communicated state secrets to the French legation. Furthermore, Randolph had secured from Citizen Pierre Adet, Fauchet's successor in Philadelphia, the release of hitherto secret French documents, state papers that revealed a few indiscreet statements by the secretary, yet which seemed to confirm his innocence. Washington might have obtained these same documents before moving against Randolph. Unfortunately, he never made the attempt. [25]

The Randolph episode once again unmasked an unattractive side of Washington's personality, one glimpsed earlier in his fevered behavior toward Generals Lee and Gates. Randolph was the latest to discover the ease with which Washington could be swayed by his "patrons," as he put it. Moreover, it now was his turn to learn that rather than acknowledge an error Washington would "shut [his] mind" and steel himself with an "invincible repugnance to retract" any misjudgment. [26]

In addition, Randolph learned something else. Washington was invulnerable. "I wish he were dead," said former Pennsylvania senator Maclay that fall, an old foe who long before had learned of the president's invincibility. Washington, he believed, could succeed with anything he touched. Now Randolph concurred. The president's touch was magical. Even his most "unpalatable" acts were sanctioned, the former secretary moaned. [27]

On the day that Washington named Oliver Ellsworth to be chief justice, he received welcome news. From Spain came word of the Treaty of San Lorenzo, the fruits of the Pinckney mission to Madrid. The pact secured far more than anyone in Philadelphia had dared to expect.

Pinckney had been fortunate. Fearing that the secret Jay Treaty was but a prelude to a joint Anglo-American assault on Spain's North American empire, Madrid quickly came to terms. The treaty granted the United States the privilege—not the right—to navigation of the Mississippi River and to deposit at New Orleans, and in the accord Spain recognized the thirty-first parallel as the southern boundary of the United States.[28]

For a president troubled lately by little but bad news, the treaty of San Lorenzo had to provide exhilarating reading. The long anxious years of perturbation over the Mississippi, a nagging issue that had helped to pry apart the sections and to weaken support for the Articles of Confederation, seemed at last to have been resolved. Indeed, the only major difference with Spain not addressed in the treaty concerned American commerce with the Spanish West Indies, an omission that led Jefferson to denounce the accord. No one listened. Washington submitted the pact to the Senate on February 26, 1796. Five days later Pinckney's Treaty was unanimously approved.[29] Washington's diplomacy had achieved a coup. Through the treaties negotiated by Jay and Pinckney, each of the three sections—North, South, and West—attained something that it long had sought. Better yet, the life-and-death interests of no section had been compromised in the process.

Nevertheless, while the Senate bubbled with exuberance over Pinckney's handiwork, the House of Representatives was in a less amicable mood. The day before the upper house voted on the Treaty of San Lorenzo influential Republicans in the lower chamber launched a campaign to compel the president to deliver copies of the instructions that John Jay had carried to London. Their motives were numerous, but for many this clearly amounted to an attempt to prevent the funding required by the pact. For others this was a ploy to energize the Jay Treaty question for the elections of 1796.

Not surprisingly Washington turned first to Hamilton for counsel. In a typically long-winded reply the former secretary advised against compliance with the wishes of the Republican majority in the House. That chamber had no constitutional right to play a role in the treaty-making process, he said, and for Washington to comply with its request would set a dangerous precedent. Besides, he added, Washington was dealing from strength, for "the house of representatives have no moral power to refuse the execution of a treaty." Three of the four members of the cabinet proffered similar advice. Only Charles Lee, the new attorney general, advised Washington to heed the call of the House, but he, too, acknowledged that the legislators had no authority to make such a demand. The president followed the recommendation of his principal Federalist friends and aides. It proved to be a safe course. At the end of April the House voted by a margin of three votes to fund the Jay Treaty, a reversal occasioned by the turnabout of several Republican representatives from the middle states. Washington did nothing to induce the about-face. In fact, he believed that public pressure from the urban Northeast—the result of a propaganda blitz by Federalist moguls, including Hamilton—accounted for the apostasy within the opposition's ranks. More likely, greater pressure came from the West, from Republican-leaning frontiersmen who feared that if the House refused to fund the Jay Treaty the British army never would leave American soil. Scotch the treaty, it was rumored in Republican circles, and disunion might result. No one wished to countenance that possibility.[30]

That bitter fight barely was resolved before partisanship helped devour still another Republican. James Monroe was the latest victim. A month after Washington announced Jay's mission to London, he named Monroe, a United States senator from Virginia, as Gouverneur Morris's replacement in Paris. The reason for the appointment was unmistakable. Word of Jay's negotiation with Britain was certain to arouse suspicions in France; while the Federalists did not expect a crisis with republican France, Monroe, a high-ranking Republican who never had sought to hide his Francophile leanings, was to be a placatory instrument, smoothing all ruffled feathers in Paris. He was to "keep the French Republic in good humor with us," as Secretary Randolph instructed him in the autumn of 1794, making it clear that the United States wished to be really neutral toward the European powers; he also was to seek to convince them that Jay was authorized only to procure the removal of British troops from the western posts and to urge compensation for the depradations committed against American shipping.

Monroe had crossed on the *Cincinnatus*, ecstatic at his appointment, confident of success. It was not a very realistic appraisal. Arriving in the aftermath of the contretemps surrounding the improvident Genêt mission, stepping ashore at a time when French suspicion of the United States had been aroused to a white-hot pitch by the Jay-Grenville negotiations, Monroe found relations between the two allies at their lowest ebb in fifteen years. Still he remained confident. To reestablish amity he believed he must openly display his admiration for France; France also would be impressed, he additionally seemed to think, if he openly divulged his partisan loyalties in America's party warfare. In public and in private he reiterated his government's friendship for France, underscoring the fraternal bond between Frenchmen and Americans by openly embracing the president of the National Convention, the French congress, and by presenting the flag of the United States to that body. Soon, too, he helped spring Thomas Paine, now a French citizen who had backed the wrong revolutionary government, from a Gallic cell. Indeed, whereas Morris, his Federalist predecessor, had seen fit to permit Paine to languish for months in prison, Monroe vouchsafed the writer, a symbol of the two great revolutions of the eighteenth century, an invitation to lodge with his family. The doors to his residence also were thrown open to a legion of Jefferson's old friends, all staunch revolutionaries. If nothing that he did was wrong, much of it was indiscreet. And when he aired his views in American newspapers, especially his hostile judgment of the Jay mission, he was downright foolish. The administration tolerated his conduct until the Jay Treaty was safely approved and funded, and until the Directory, the new French government, began to seize American shipping in retaliation for Jay's accord with Great Britain. Then it moved to recall him.[31]

The arch-Federalists in Washington's cabinet long had hoped to be done with such an avowedly Republican envoy. Initially, however, they sought to discredit him in Washington's eyes. Tattle about Monroe's supposed misconduct, including accusations of financial peculation, were leaked to the press. Washington must have believed some of the accusations. He came to think that Monroe was responsible for releasing to the French government private administrative documents, materials that caused the president to appear in a bad light. Incredibly, he also blamed Monroe for France's negative reaction to the Jay Treaty, an unfounded suspicion making the rounds in Federalist circles and predicated on the idea that French hostility could be translated into Republican victories at the polls that autumn. The notion that Monroe was to blame was silly, but it was easier to believe that than to acknowledge that one's own policies had angered America's oldest ally.[32]

Still Washington did not move until it was apparent that Monroe no longer was effective, and, then, in a last-ditch effort to refurbish ties with Paris, the president considered the same remedy he earlier had utilized to normalize relations with Britain and Spain. He prepared to send a special envoy to France, a gesture that in one fell swoop might convince Paris of America's friendship while, at the same moment, removing Monroe. In the end Washington simply recalled Monroe, replacing him with Charles Cotesworth Pinckney, a South Carolina Federalist and the brother of the diplomat who had negotiated the Treaty of San Lorenzo. The president's action was a mixture of statesmanship and partisanship. The minister's indiscreet behavior and his managerial shortcomings (he could not even compose a letter properly, Washington complained) partly accounted for Monroe's fall, but the president also wished to have a "faithful organ" in the French capital, someone who could "explain [the administration's] real views." By implication, the recall of Monroe was an attempt to impose upon the Republicans the blame for the sudden worsening in Franco-American relations.[33]

Sometime in the spring of 1796 Washington decided to resign at the conclusion of his second term. This time he was intransigent. The last four years had been a difficult period, especially those months after he signed the Jay Treaty. Week after week he had watched as his name was villified in the Republican press, causing him to remark that he was pilloried in a manner that would not have been "applied to a Nero; a notorious defaulter; or even to a common pick-pocket." He was depicted as the dupe of Hamilton and his other Federalist "satellites." The president and his "British faction" in the cabinet had thrust the nation into a "gulph of despair," it was said. Even his generalship in the late war was questioned. Some organs depicted Washington as senile. The Old Fellow "must seasonably, and occasionally be rouzed" to an awareness of reality, reported one journal. That was far from the truth, but Washington indeed was getting on in years. Even Jefferson had noticed as early as four years before that Washington's "memory was . . . sensibly impaired by age"; the secretary had added that

Washington occasionally displayed such "listlessness of labor" that he was willing "to let others act and even think for him." Washington might have disputed Jefferson's observations, but he knew full well that he would be nearly seventy before a third term concluded—if he lived to see the end of still another four years in the President's House. In fact, to continue to live, he now thought, it was "indispensably necessary" that he escape the "serious anxiety . . . trouble and perplexities" of office. He must retire.[34]

When Hamilton appeared in Philadelphia in February to argue a case before the Supreme Court, Washington told him of his decision, and a bit later he asked him to scrutinize a draft of a valedictory address that he had prepared. Actually, what Washington sent to Hamilton essentially was the address that Madison had prepared for him in 1792; the president merely had deleted a couple paragraphs and appended a few brief remarks, alterations designed to bring the document up to date. However, Washington's accompanying letter made it clear that he wished to give Hamilton a free hand to alter the document as he saw fit. His only stipulation was that the document was to take the high road, addressing ideas, avoiding personalities; he also stressed that he wished it to be brief and in such a "plain state . . . and . . . simple garb" that the public easily could comprehend it.[35]

Working in his spare moments during the next ten weeks, Hamilton produced two documents. First, he sent to the president a draft of his own handiwork, a paper that incorporated some of the Madison-Washington version, but which also contained a long middle section that he had composed. Ten days later he forwarded an edited copy of the Madison-Washington draft. Not surprisingly, the president preferred Hamilton's original version to the Madison document. It was "more dignified . . . and [contained] less egotism," said Washington, and he added that he thought it would read better in Europe. The president made only a few stylistic modifications, then he returned the document to New York with just two further requests of Hamilton. He desired the addition of a section dealing with the importance of education, and he wished Hamilton to reread and polish the address, inasmuch as it had been "out of sight for sometime." Within three weeks the New Yorker's final revision had been returned to the president. Once again Washington made a few stylistic changes, and he deleted a self-vindicatory passage lest it strike some as a case of "affected modesty." At the end of the summer he submitted the document to his cabinet, where the Federalist membership quickly rubber-stamped Hamilton's and Washington's production. On September 19, 1796, Washington's Farewell Address was published in both *Claypoole's American Daily Advertiser* and in Fenno's *Gazette*.[36]

The address began with the sort of lengthy passage that characterized many of Washington's public pronouncements. He had not sought office, he had been called to the presidency, he reminded his readers, and he hoped that his resignation would not be viewed as a dereliction of duty. Then he turned to more cogent matters. Only the continuance of the Union could insure your "real independence," he argued. The broad national government is the "main Pillar . . . of

George Washington, *The Landsdowne Portrait*, by Gilbert Stuart (1797). Courtesy of the National Portrait Gallery, Smithsonian Institution, Washington, D.C. On indefinite loan to the National Portrait Gallery, Smithsonian Institution, from the Earl of Rosebery.

The Washington Family, by Edward Savage (c. 1796). Courtesy of the National Gallery of Art, Washington, Andrew W. Mellon Collection. George Washington Parke Custis ("Wash") is standing next to the president, Eleanor Parke Custis ("Nellie") is next to Mrs. Washington. A slave stands in the background.

your tranquility at home; your peace abroad; of your safety; of your prosperity; of that very Liberty which you so highly prize." He appealed to his fellow citizens to forego sectionalism, to think in more national terms. While regional differences existed, he went on, presaging remarks that Abraham Lincoln would offer in his First Inaugural Address, he reminded his audience of the citizenry's homogeneity in religious, cultural, and ideological matters. If there were economic differences, he went on, each section offered something to the others, ultimately pulling all together into "an indissoluble community of Interest as *one Nation*."

Aside from the dangers posed by sectionalism, Washington looked upon political parties as the greatest threat to the Union. With a daring seldom equaled in American political history, Washington, in a passage written by the leader of the Federalist party, denounced party leaders as "designing men" who sought to create differences where none existed, and he portrayed parties as the tools of "cunning, ambitious and unprincipled" persons who had succeeded in mobilizing an "artful and enterprizing minority of the Community." In a monarchical society, the president continued, parties were useful weapons for restraining government's impetus toward tyranny, but in a republic parties themselves become despotic, inasmuch as factional rivalry "sharpened . . . the spirit of revenge," provoking retribution and misery until the populace cried out for the strong ruler who could restore order.

Washington offered sparse counsel as to how best to avoid factionalism. He seemed to suggest that rulers emulate his sacrificial example. Govern in a selfless manner, he said. Otherwise, he spoke of religion and morality as the great contributors to human happiness, and he recommended a national commitment to education, for "as the structure of a government gives forces to public opinion, it is essential that public opinion should be enlightened."

Another danger to which Washington alluded was the presence of standing armies. He counseled that a strong Union meant a strong people, a fact that would deter foreign rivals and render it unnecessary to institute "those overgrown military establishments, which under any form of Government are inauspicious to liberty. . . ." Thus, a nation's relationship with other nations was crucial for the maintenance of liberty. "The Nation, which indulges towards another an habitual hatred, or an habitual fondness, is in some degree a slave." Where there exists inveterate ill will toward another, he went on, an atmosphere of passion blinds reason, causing "collisions . . . and bloody contests" where peace might have prevailed. Yet to hang to the coattails of another country is to encourage the hostility of its adversaries, leading perhaps to war and certainly to domestic factionalism. Moreover, a nation could not expect "disinterested favors" from another. To be too close to another state was to ask to be harmed. In the best-remembered section of the address, he advocated commerce with Europe, but he counseled against political and military ties. Sounding like Thomas Paine in *Common Sense*, he reminded his readers that Europe "must be engaged in frequent controversies, the causes of which are essentially foreign to our concerns. . . .'Tis our true policy to steer clear of permanent Alliances, with any part of the foreign world." At certain times—as during the War of Independence—a temporary alliance might be justified, he went on. But now the policy of neutrality laid down by his administration was best, for such a course would "gain time to our country to settle and mature its yet recent institutions, and to progress . . . to that degree of strength . . . which is necessary to give it . . . the command of its fortunes." [37]

Although authored by Hamilton, the ideas broadcast in the address clearly were those of Washington. Some threads in the speech ran as far back as his farewell remarks to the army in 1783, an utterance that similarly resounded with an appeal to the nationalism of his countrymen. Indeed, the principal difference in the two valedictories was that his presidential remarks addressed the rise of political parties and the problems of foreign policy which had occurred only during his two terms in office.[38]

As Washington must have expected, his Farewell Address elicited a partisan response. Acclaim blared forth from the Federalist press, faultfinding held sway in Republican organs. What would have surprised him in all likelihood was the transformation that occurred in the nineteenth century, for within a very few years of his death the valedictory almost universally was revered, and that at a time when the Federalist party had collapsed, leaving the Republicans in command of the nation's cultural and ideological lockbox. Whatever Washington's hopes about the timelessness of the document, contemporaries not unrealistically saw it for what it was—a defense of Federalist philosophy and Federalist governance comingled with an implicit plea that the policies of that faction be permitted to continue. Propounding a dim view of humanity—as greedy, grasping creatures actuated by a "love of power, and [a] proneness to abuse it"—the address was still another statement in the litany of Federalist pronouncements that sought to defend the Federalist counterrevolution. It represented a renewed repudiation of the localist faith of 1776, one that equated dissent and decentralization with chaos and tyranny, which depicted a symbiosis between centralized governance and true independence. In the new creed the government emerged as the great protector of humanity, while the people themselves were the great enemy of the people. That Washington's Farewell Address came to be so universally accepted by subsequent generations was further proof that the real American Revolution of the late eighteenth century was the one that commenced in the constitution-making at the State House in Philadelphia during that hot, dusty summer of 1787.[39]

Although Washington had said good-bye, six months of his term remained. A month of that time was spent amidst the luxurious autumn foliage at Mount Vernon, but from early November onward he remained at the presidential mansion in the capital, enjoying a comfortable, seasonal fall, and then, like the other denizens of the city, suffering though an exceptionally cold, wet winter. At least that winter's miseries did not include extraordinary public woes.[40]

The deterioration in relations with France continued to nag at Washington, and yet only one brief, troubling incident occurred in these months. In November Citizen Pierre Auguste Adet, Fauchet's successor as minister to the United States, vented his displeasure with American foreign policy. That was not unusual, but when he chose to air his views in the press that was an entirely different matter.

Adet's action caught the Federalists by surprise, not least because they liked the envoy, regarding him as educated (he was a chemist by training), cosmopolitan, moderate, and, like themselves, a thoroughly bourgeois urbanite. But Adet found much in Washington's policy toward Britain and France about which to complain. For instance, while the Washington government eagerly had negotiated the Jay Treaty, Adet had experienced no success in moving the administration into talks on a new commercial treaty with France. In truth, however, the French were deeply aggrieved by two more substantive matters. On the one hand, Paris alleged that the administration repeatedly had refused to execute the 1778 treaties of alliance and commerce. Under this heading France lodged two accusations. First, whereas the United States government had denied French cruisers and privateers access to American ports, it not only had admitted British vessels of war into its harbors but had permitted those ships to vend their catches. Second, Paris contended that the Jay Treaty was inimical to its interests, particularly in that the accord increased the items listed as contraband, thus reducing the number of commodities that the United States legally could sell to France. On that matter the French imputation was solidly grounded. As to the first charge, however, the Washington administration claimed correctly that its policy had been to seal its ports to French ships only when those vessels had taken prizes in America's territorial waters, or when the French privateers had been outfitted in an American port; the latter conduct, the administration contended, had not been sanctioned by the 1778 accords with Paris.[41]

By 1796 the French had come to view the Washington administration not merely as unneutral but as a puppet whose strings were pulled in London and in America's pro-British mercantile centers. For more than a year before his last autumn in office, Washington had been fully aware of the displeasure emanating from Paris. Still, that fall he was rocked by two more Gallic announcements. First came news of a decree promulgated by the Directory, a step taken coincidentally on the twentieth anniversary of the day Congress had voted the United States independent of Britain. The French government, Washington learned in October, had announced its intention of dealing with neutral vessels in the same manner as London treated such vessels, meaning that the Directory henceforth would regard as contraband precisely what Great Britain treated as contraband. Thus, American goods that London sought to deny entry to France now would be denied entry to Britain as well. French logic was as impeccable as its action was drastic, for the move, as diplomatic historian Alexander De Conde has pointed out, amounted to a repudiation of the Franco-American commercial and military alliance.[42]

The American people learned of the Directory's action through Citizen Adet, who took the unconventional step of publishing a long note in defense of his government's position, a statement that went on to openly—and undiplomatically—criticize the allegedly nonneutral conduct of the Washington administration. Washington, the envoy maintained, had from the beginning sought to sever the Franco-American alliance. Long ago, he added, Washington had "ceased to be neutral." Turn this government of Federalists out of office, Adet seemed to say on the very eve of the election of 1796, and "you will still find in Frenchmen faithful friends and generous allies." Maintain the Federalist administration, he implied, and France will be your enemy. Adet's intemperate remarks laid clear cold reality. To foil America's rapprochement with Britain, Paris had begun to seize United States vessels, and it had intruded into the murky domestic politics of its once close friend.[43]

President Washington huffed and puffed at these actions, and he solicited Hamilton's advice as to how he should greet Adet upon their next meeting. (Receive the envoy with "a *dignified reserve*" somewhere between "offensive coldness and cordiality," Hamilton rejoined. "[N]o one will know better how to do it," he added with authority, often having seen Washington utilize that very approach.) The president also authorized Pickering to answer the French diplomat in the American press. But when Hamilton proved to be one of the sharpest critics of the administration's reaction, Washington immediately restrained Pickering. The former secretary gently chided the president for stooping to engage in a newspaper war with Citizen Adet. It would have been more sound for Washington to have communicated his displeasure to Congress, he advised. Hamilton also counseled against the indignant tone of the government's official response to Adet's public letter, warning against the danger of provoking "further insult or injury." Henceforth, he added, use the language of moderation, for the United States must seek to avoid a total rupture with France. When Adet published a second essay on November 21, the president did as Hamilton had advised: he turned the matter over to Congress. There, void of harm, things could spin themselves out until Charles Cotesworth Pinckney had an opportunity to assess the mood in France. By then, too, there would be a new president.[44]

That fall Washington watched with interest as the first contested presidential election unfolded. The Federalists put up Vice President Adams, the Republicans supported Thomas Jefferson. If Adet sought to intrude in the election, the president endeavored to remain aloof, making no public announcements on behalf of either candidate. In the end, Adet had less impact on the race than did Alexander Hamilton, who, behind the scenes, plotted the undoing of Adams. Hamilton's scheme was to induce just enough Federalist electors to withhold their votes from the vice president to permit the party's choice for the second slot—Thomas Pinckney—to receive a majority of the electoral votes. His machination almost backfired, enabling Jefferson to win the contest. But Adams squeaked past his foe with just three votes to spare. In the eyes of the Directory the result was as if "old man Washington," as some domestic foes had taken to calling him, was about to serve for four more years.[45]

By 1797 Washington at last was truly thankful that his stay in office was about at an end. He looked forward to the "shades of retirement." He knew that his allotted time was running short. So many old acquaintances and comrades now were gone. Only the previous year the president had learned that Lund Washington, his estate manager during his long wartime absence, had died at Hayfield at the age of fifty-nine. It was another reminder that the sixty-five-year-old president's days were numbered. Back at Mount Vernon, Washington dreamed, he would study many of the tracts on scientific agriculture published in Britain in recent years. Mostly, though, he would be happy to escape the misrepresentation and reprobation of his conduct that had filled the Republican press. Nevertheless, he felt he would depart Philadelphia with the conviction that Adams's election amounted to a popular vindication of his administration. His only regret upon leaving, he said, was that he likely would never again see those men who had served him so faithfully, those "few intimates whom I love." [46]

As he entered the final weeks of his presidency, it was clear that Washington had no doubts about the wisdom of his policies. He had agreed to serve, then to accept a second term, he said in announcing his intention of retiring, because of the "perplexed and critical posture of our Affairs." But the great crisis now was over, he suggested. He believed he had helped solidify the Union, for the notion that it was wise to secure a bonding of "one people is also now dear to you." In external affairs relations with France were strained, but in December 1796 he told Congress that his policies had overcome the "inconveniences and embarrassments" of 1789, an oblique reference to the gains procured by the Jay and Pinckney treaties. Still, he added, "nothing short of a general Peace in Europe" would calm the new nation's beleaguered relations with the great powers.[47]

Washington expressed disappointment on only two matters. Congress had failed to create a military academy for the preparation of the nation's officers, and its earlier reform of the militia system, he believed had been ineffectual. While still commander of the Continental army he first had broached the idea of a military college, and on occasion during his presidency he reiterated his zest for such an institution. In his final message to Congress he returned to that idea. The "Art of War, is at once comprehensive and complicated," he said, and to have an officer corps well-grounded in martial knowledge "is always of great moment to the security of a Nation." While the nation hoped to avoid war, he went on, it never was wise to be without "an adequate stock of Military knowledge."

He also had urged reform of the nation's trainband system since 1783, and he must have been pleased when the Constitution that he helped draft granted

Congress power over the militia. He declared militia reform to be a priority item when he took office in 1789, and three years later, stung by the defeats inflicted on Harmar and St. Clair, Congress acted. But Washington did not get what he wanted. Instead of a nationalized system, Congress responded with the Uniform Militia Act of 1792, legislation that resulted in few changes, and which left the militia thoroughly in state hands. With two months remaining in his presidency, Washington issued a final plea for reform.[48]

Curiously, Washington also waited until the eve of his retirement to recommend that Congress take several other important steps. He urged higher pay for the army's officers, lest all be drawn from the most privileged class, an end that would "proportionally diminish the probability of a choice of Men, able, as well as upright." He proposed that Congress study America's coastal defenses. A United States navy must also be created, he advised, both for the ongoing protection of the nation's commerce and so that "the requisite supply of Seamen" always would be on hand. In his initial State of the Union message Washington had hinted that Congress would be wise to create a national university, but he did not raise the subject of education again until his Farewell Address, then he merely exhorted his countrymen to make "the general diffusion of knowledge" a priority consideration. In 1790 he had spoken of the correlation between sound republican government and enlightened public opinion. In his final address to Congress, Washington once again took up the matter of a national university. It was a subject to which he had given much thought recently. Sometime before 1795 he had prepared a will which bequeathed his fifty shares in the Potomac Canal Company and his one hundred shares in the James River Canal Company toward the establishment of a national university within the new Federal District. But his gift was to be conditional. First a "well digested plan" would have to be approved by Congress before 1800. His remarks now to Congress must have been an attempt to kindle lagging interest. In fact, the legislators had remained so indifferent that he already had altered his will, stipulating that his James River Company shares go instead to the Liberty Hall Academy in Virginia, the precursor of today's Washington and Lee College.[49]

For some time before taking office Washington had spoken privately about the evils of slavery, yet he made no such public statements during his early presidential years, and he remained silent on the matter both in his valedictory and his final address to Congress. Political realities must have been partially responsible for his discretion. To raise the subject was to risk certain discredit in the South, while to let the abolitionist geni out of the bottle was to court the eradication of the Union. In 1790, in fact, when Quaker activists, as well as the Pennsylvania Society for Promoting the Abolition of Slavery, had petitioned for an immediate end to the foreign slave trade, some southern states had raised the threat of secession if their northern brethren dared vote to ban that ugly commerce. Washington had been put off by the Quaker campaign, calling it "an ill-judged piece of business" and expressing his pleasure at the ultimate defeat of their endeavor. Indeed, President Washington's principal activity with regard to slavery was to sign into law the Fugitive Slave Act of 1793, legislation that permitted slaveowners to cross state lines in order "to seize or arrest" runaway slaves.[50]

If President Washington dared not touch slavery, citizen Washington seemed equally reluctant to tamper with the institution. During the war, as we have seen, Washington deplored his status as a slaveowner, although his lamentations stemmed less from moral reservations than from an awareness that his capital could be put to better use. Upon his retirement in 1783 he took no steps to manumit his bondsmen. The reason for his inaction is clear: "imperious necessity," he acknowledged, compelled him to retain ownership of slave laborers. That is, manumission would not permit him to live in the manner to which he was accustomed.[51]

His attitude seems to have undergone no change for ten years or more following the war. Twice in the 1780s Lafayette pleaded unsuccessfully with his famous friend to join with him in emancipation schemes. First, the young Frenchman urged Washington to liberate some of his slaves and post them as tenants on a western estate, where by their example of resourceful farming they might inspire other slaveowners to follow suit. Later, Lafayette proposed that the two celebrated warriors purchase slaves and manumit them to a French Guiana farm that might serve as a model for what a free black population could accomplish. Washington was cool to both suggestions, and nothing came of either plan. While still a Mount Vernon farmer in 1785, he displayed a similar disinclination to aid Methodist clergymen who wished the Maryland legislature to gradually abolish slavery. Washington would act only if the legislature formally considered such a move, he said, knowing full well that such an eventuality was unlikely. In private he equated manumission with the exercise of "humanity," yet he denigrated immediate emancipation as certain to produce "much inconvenience and mischief," and he refused to lend his magical name to the cause of gradual emancipation.[52]

Still, both before and during his presidency Washington clearly was troubled by the institution and by his station as a slaveowner. In 1786 he spoke of his "regret" that the institution existed, and he claimed that "no man living wishes more sincerely than I do to see the abolition of it." His quandary was similar to that faced by many other enlightened contemporaries on plantations throughout Virginia. Men like Jefferson and Madison, for instance, were no less distressed by their role as slaveowners, yet neither was willing to manumit his slaves or to publicly attack the institution. Both, in fact, continued to sell their chattel, occasionally sundering families, a practice that Washington had abandoned years before. The dilemma that faced these men was made no easier by their realization that slavery was not on the brink of extinction, for race fears and secure prices for bondsmen combined to thwart whatever abolitionist tendencies may have existed. Indeed, the 1790s inaugurated an epoch that was to witness slavery's greatest expansion, until half a century later the descendants of the chattel owned by the Revolutionary generation likewise toiled as slave laborers, even into the trans-Mississippi Southwest.[53]

Yet while Washington exhibited distress at his continued involvement with the practice, his slave population continued to grow. He sold nine slaves in the 1780s, and he attempted to sell at least two others in the following decade. Meanwhile, he acquired at least three slaves, one as part payment of a debt, one from his mother's estate upon her death, and a third when he purchased a bricklayer. In 1786 he endeavored to procure six slaves as compensation from another debtor, and later he sought to purchase a slave with a special skill. While these two efforts failed, he frequently rented slaves to labor on his properties. By 1799 Washington owned 317 slaves, nearly a 50 percent increase in this property since the end of the war. His careful inventory showed 11 house servants, 38 skilled artisans, 18 who were too old to work, and 143 children. The remainder, presumably, were field hands.[54]

Troubled by his continued complicity with the institution, Washington sought to convince himself that he left no stone unturned when it came to caring for his chattel. His slaves, he said, lived and worked in means "as easy and comfortable" as their "ignorance . . . would admit." In fact, the evidence pertaining to the condition of his bondsmen is mixed at best. Most of the scores of guests who visited and looked about Mount Vernon left no accounts that might either verify or discredit his claim. An English traveler who paused at the estate late in 1798 concluded that Washington was not "of a humane disposition," adding that he treated his chattel "with more severity" than did any other Virginia planter with whom he lodged. On the other hand, a Polish visitor who dropped in on Mount Vernon six months earlier found that "Gl. Washington treats his slaves far more humanely than do his fellow citizens of Virginia. Most of these gentlemen give to their Blacks only bread, water and blows." By that meager standard Washington must have been an enlightened slaveowner. There can be little doubt that Washington was a more caring master after the war, although the record he left behind in his letters and diary cast doubt on his claim of exceptional altruism.[55]

During his presidential years Washington's racial views were in no way extraordinary for a southern planter—or, for that matter, for any white American of the time. He believed that blacks were ignorant and shiftless, careless, deceitful, and liable to act without "any qualms of conscience." Various individuals that he owned were characterized as "very sly, cunning and roguish," as a "bungler," a "lazy scoundrel," as "never celebrated for her honesty." Of his domestic chattel he wrote, "I know of no black person about the house that is to be trusted." His views were reinforced by Martha's similar outlook. Of a slave that she lent to a niece, she wrote: "I hope you will not find in him much sass. [T]he Blacks are so bad in their nature that they have not the least gratitude for the kindness that may be showed to them."[56]

Washington complained that new, complicated machinery would be "entirely useless" at Mount Vernon because his dim-witted chattel lacked the intelligence to utilize such tools. It would be difficult to find "so idle a set of rascals" as his slave carpenters, he went on, adding that "it would be [best] for me to set them free" and hire free laborers. He did not liberate his slave craftsmen, however. Asserting that any relaxation of discipline inevitably results in habitual malingering, he simply urged his manager to keep these and, indeed, all his slaves, "in their places, and to their duty." In a not uncharacteristic remark he alleged of one of his slaves that "a more lazy, deceitful and imputent huzzy is not to be found." Discovering one of his chattel to be a "misbehaving fellow," Washington sold the man to the West Indies, obtaining in return "one pipe and a quarter cask of wine." Notified of the demise of two of his slaves, he cracked that the "death of Paris is a loss, that of Jupiter the reverse." Upon learning of another slave's death two months later, he hardly was bereaved; the deceased had been "troublesome to all those around her," he merely observed.[57]

Washington would not tolerate idleness among his slaves. "I expect my people will work from daybreaking until it is dusk," he said. He ordered his manager to see that the chattel be at "work as soon as it is light, work till it is dark, and be diligent while they are at it." Do not let anyone be "ruined by idleness," he directed; "let them be employed in any manner . . . that will keep them out of idleness and mischief." When the cook was not cooking, put her to knitting, he commanded. When the spinners and knitters completed their tasks, send them to the fields. He advised that a domestic slave with a light load be made to assist the milkmaid, and he decreed that a habitually malingering outdoor slave be placed behind a spinning wheel. Each bondsman "must be . . . *made* to do a sufficient day's work."[58]

The first trick toward making the chattel work, he observed, was to get them out of their cabins and to their assigned work stations. But not infrequently the slaves complained of illness and begged to be excused from their labor. "I never wish my people to work when they are really sick, or unfit for it," Washington said, and he advised his manager to give them the benefit of the doubt the first time they pleaded illness. The next episode of alleged sickness was to be viewed with skepticism, however. Washington boasted that he could distinguish between real illness and malingering, and he left the clear impression that he thought most slave maladies were contrived disorders. One slave claimed to be lame, but Washington thought he only "pretds to be so." Another pleaded an "Asthmatical complaint," yet Washington was convinced that "Laziness Is . . . his principal ailment." Most other ills, said Washington, arose from the chattels' proclivity for "night walking," that is, for carousing in the slave quarters, activity "which unfit them for the duties of the day." When a slave said he was ill, Washington advised, check first for signs of a fever. "Nobody can be very sick without having a fever," he thought. He also cautioned his managers to be particularly vigilant for signs of "Pleurisies and inflammatory fevers," disorders that should be treated immediately by bleeding and by a diet of sweetened tea, broth, and wine, as well as by patient and kindly nurturing. And, of course, a physician should be called in to examine a truly ill slave.[59]

Considering the size of Washington's holdings, as well as his protracted absences, ultimate responsibility for making the slaves work fell to his overseers. Washington utilized white superintendents until after the war, experimented with black overseers for a time thereafter, then returned to white overlords in his last years. Few of those whom he hired were satisfactory, he concluded. He demanded much. An overseer, he said, must be "sober, attentive to his duty, honest, obliging, and cleanly." He also must be "accustomed to Negros," and he must additionally take safeguards so as not to sink to the same "level with the Negroes." Indeed, the slaves had an adverse effect on their bosses, for the overseers tended to "fall into the slovenly mode" of the chattel they were hired to work. The job required men of "activity and Spirit," but most of his hirelings either were too lenient or too harsh. Usually they erred on the side of cruelty, he discovered, treating the bondsmen "as they do the brute beasts, on the farms." His overseers were not to be merciless, he asserted, but they were to threaten and intimidate the slaves. The chattel with the more desirable duties were to be cajoled with threats of being made into "a common hoe negro." Or, they might be coerced by pledges that they would be sold to the West Indies. If the desired results still were not achieved, the overseers were to transfer the slave to another task, even if in some instances it meant exchanging a hard job for an easier one. And, if necessary, Washington authorized his overseers to resort to the lash. No one was immune. Washington sanctioned the scourging of female slaves, and when confronted by a particularly recalcitrant bondsman he simply directed his manager to "give him a good whipping." The best tactic for obtaining work, however, was constant supervision. Most slaves would work if they were watched, he said, recommending that overseers not assign the slaves to tasks where they could not be observed, that they vigilantly stand over them, and that they check the quality of their labor. But, whatever they did, the overseers were warned not to use the chattel for their own ends. "I expect to reap the benefit of the labour myself," Washington emphasized.[60]

Unremitting labor and coercion were the chattel's fate at Mount Vernon, and their lot does not seem to have been ameliorated in the least by the environment in which they lived. The same Polish visitor who believed that Washington was more beneficent than the ordinary Virginia planter described Mount Vernon's slave quarters as "habitations [that] cannot be called houses," and he hinted at a scene of abysmally squalid destitution, suggesting even that the residences were "far more miserable than the cottages of our peasants" in Eastern Europe. Washington referred to these lodgings as "Negro cabins," or simply as "coverings," whereas his livestock were sheltered in a "shed" and his overseers in a "house." Washington also acknowledged that the slave quarters at Mount Vernon "might not be thought good enough for the workmen or day laborers" of England.[61]

The allocation of victuals at Mount Vernon must also have been meager, for Washington's slaves took the extraordinary step of petitioning their master, claiming they received an inadequate supply of food. Frequently, they maintained, they were made to go as long as forty-eight hours without an allotment of cornmeal. Meat was provided even less regularly. While Washington sought to deny these charges, his remarks lent credence to his chattels' allegation. "It is not my wish . . . that my Negros should have one oz of meal more, nor less, than is sufficient to feed them plentifully," but he defined a "plentiful" diet as a fare that consisted of cornbread, buttermilk, "fish (pickled herring) frequently, and meat now and then." Nor do his chattel seem to have been deluged with other provisions. While he annually spent about five dollars to clothe each bondsman who was on public display at the President's House in Philadelphia, clothing, shoes, stockings, and blankets for each adult slave at remote Mount Vernon cost him less than a dollar per year. As late as Christmas one year he acknowledged that some of his slaves lacked winter garments, and in October of another year, a season when evening temperatures at Mount Vernon averaged only about 50°, he expressed annoyance that the "Negroes are all teazing me" for blankets. The next spring he acknowledged that he had "lost more Negroes [from illness] last winter, than I had done in 12 or 15 years." [62]

Historians have made much of Washington's yearning in the 1790s to free his slaves. There can be little doubt that he had grown uneasy about the institution and his involvement with it. A slaveowner living in a northern city, his discomfort grew to such proportions that he eventually sought to use only white attendants at all public functions, though, out of sight, his black chattel continued to toil for the First Family. Yet he not only took no legal steps to liberate any slaves during his presidential years, he shuffled bondsmen between Mount Vernon and Philadelphia lest any live in a free state long enough to qualify as residents. Moreover, his response to the loss of two slave runaways during these years was revealing. When Hercules, his cook, escaped, Washington sought to purchase another slave with similar talents. Earlier, when a female slave fled from the President's House, he had her hunted down and eventually captured in Portsmouth, New Hampshire. Washington characterized her act as one of "ingratitude" and wished to have her returned to Philadelphia, but when informed that a riot would result if the captive runaway was shipped back to her master, he demured and set her free. [63]

For all of Washington's agonizing over slavery, he took but two steps during his presidential years to emancipate his chattel. Early in the 1790s he concocted a plan to divide and rent his Mount Vernon properties. His hope was to lease the farms to suitable English farmers, while, simultaneously, he manumitted his chattel and made them available for hire as free laborers. Under such a plan Washington would have escaped heavy overhead expenses while he received a steady income in rent money, a combination that would have offset the losses incurred by surrendering his investment in slave property. But no renters surfaced and his plan never was put into operation. When he departed Philadelphia for home in 1797 he took a second step. He left behind some of his house slaves, in effect granting them *de facto* emancipation. It was done so quietly that no one was aware of his act.[64]

As Washington oversaw the packing of his family's possessions in preparation for the final long ride to Mount Vernon, he seemed pleased with his performance as chief executive, and he could not have been more delighted by what he interpreted to be the "approving voice of my Country." Of course, not all his countrymen approved of his policies. Some Republican organs did not attempt to hide their glee at his imminent retirement, and one editor even asserted that if "ever a Nation was debauched by a man, the American Nation has been debauched by Washington."[65]

George Washington had faced a difficult presidency. To the hard economic decisions that he knew he would have to make had been added the warfare that arose from the French Revolution, a contagion unforeseen at the moment of his inauguration in 1789. Every move that he made, moreover, was a step into uncharted territory; each decision was likely to set a precedent for his successors. But what made his two terms especially arduous was that he chose to pursue the goals of a minority faction, policies that often were unpopular with the largest part of the population and which could be implemented at all only because of the unsurpassed esteem in which the president was held. Only Washington's myopia can explain his surprise at the inevitably deep fragmentation brought about by his course.

Washington had approached the presidency with one overriding aim: the establishment of a powerful new national government and the preservation of American unity. Too often before 1789 he had witnessed the iniquities of an enervated government. As deeply as he believed anything, Washington was certain that national impotence must cease. He came to the presidency speaking of fashioning "our National character." Later, as president, he urged the creation of an *"American* character." By the first expression he meant that it was his objective to so augment the strength of America as to render the nation "respectable" to the powers of Europe. By *"American* character" he meant to persuade both his countrymen and European statesmen that "we act for *ourselves* and not for *others.*" His first objective could be realized only by drastic change, and during its two terms the Washington administration, generally thought to be a conservative government, undertook not only a startling and radical economic transformation, but an equally fundamental reorientation of United States foreign policy. Building an *"American* character" was a more protracted undertaking, and at the end of his presidency, in his Farewell Address, he still preached the need for Americans to put America's interest above those of every other nation.[66]

Washington's first term was absorbed with the implementation of Hamiltonianism. There can be little doubt that the system worked as the treasury secretary and Washington hoped it would, for Hamiltonian economics solidified the Union

by eliminating what had been the greatest threat to unity in the Articles of Confederation era—the danger that the forces of entrenched wealth and greed in one
or more sections would scuttle the existing national union rather than submit to
a government too weak to satisfy its acquisitive lust. Hamiltonianism, thus, was
the logical culmination of the movement that had secured the Constitution of
1787, for the secretary's economic program utilized the enhanced powers of the
new national government to safeguard the economic interests of a portion of the
nation's most wealthy citizenry. In so doing the moneyed interests were bound
to the government, fulfilling the nationalistic yearnings of men like Washington.
From the outset of his administration, from even before he departed Mount Vernon to assume the presidency, Washington understood those facts, even though
he probably never fathomed the intricacies of Hamiltonian economics.

Diplomatic perplexities had dominated Washington's second term, but by
1797 he could point to three successes in this area. His government had kept the
United States out of the European war, it had secured the removal of the British
from the Northwest Territory, and it had attained a satisfactory resolution of the
principal differences between the United States and Spain. The gains, however,
had been realized not only at the expense of the termination of the Franco-
American alliance but with the result that relations between the two former allies
had deteriorated to a cold-war status. Yet the loss of the French alliance hardly
caused irreparable harm to the United States. Indeed, it was Washington's genius
to see what his adversaries were unable to fathom: with the end of the war in 1783
the alliance was of little benefit to America. But to squander French friendship was
another matter. With Europe's great powers enveloped in a life-and-death struggle
the administration concluded that little middle ground existed between friendship
and hostility. It was as though Washington surmised that, while he might proclaim
America's neutrality, he was, in fact, compelled to choose between France and
Britain. He opted for Britain.

Washington's choice was not a surprise. Although he sincerely believed
that his actions were in the best interests of the new nation, he was led by deep
emotional impulses to adulate Britain. That far-away country had denied him at
every step, rejecting his youthful entreaties to soldier in its uniform, jeopardizing
his speculative ventures, treating him as a humble provincial, fighting him in a
bitter struggle after 1775, even robbing him of the very people with whom he had
the closest of ties, George William and Sally Fairfax. Yet Britain had remained a
powerful figure for Washington. To win the affirmation of those who would have
been his "lordly masters" remained a driving goal in his quest for self-esteem.
Historians often err in treating the George Washington of the pre-1775 period and
the older Washington, the man of the warrior-statesman persona, as two distinct
characters. The Washington who began his amazing ascent by carefully identifying with the habits and styles of elite—and generally British—role models
never abandoned the practice. After the war he carried on a regular correspondence with several eminent Englishmen, eliciting their advice, basking in their

approbatory remarks about his "patriotic and heroic virtue," and regaling them with predictions of America's impending emergence as a power with which the European capitals would have to reckon. Even while he was chief executive, his letters to the Earl of Buchan, an English philanthropist, rang out with solicitations to "your Lordship" and "my Lord," a form of address that was standard and proper, although one can hardly imagine a republican revolutionary such as Samuel Adams or Thomas Paine persisting in such a habit. In the years after the Revolution he remained drawn to the British example. He made Mount Vernon into a grand English country manor house, carefully fashioned and furnished after its counterparts across the ocean, and had he had his way it would have been worked by English farmers, not by American yeomen. Nor was that all. When choosing a plan for the presidential house in the new federal city, he selected a model from a book of architectural drawings prepared by an Englishman to cater to the tastes of the English gentry. He would have been pleased had he known of the high marks his presidency earned in the eyes of English officials. For instance, Robert Liston, the English minister, lauded Washington's "marked aversion to the extravagences of democratick principles." Others felt at home in the Philadelphia of Washington's administration, finding his style delightfully similar to that of the courts of the Old World's crowned heads of state. An English visitor thought his temper and manner akin to that of "a great European monarch," and British diplomats in the American capital sometimes seemed to forget that they were not serving in a British colony, or at the royal court.[67]

The affirmation of the merchant-financier elite of the urban Northeast was no less important to him. Those to whom he was closest after he departed Virginia in 1775—the Morrises, Samuel and Eliza Powel, Jay, Hamilton—came from that milieu. He tolerated their plotting at Newburgh, joined with them to write and ratify the Constitution of 1787, and surrounded himself with them during his presidency. On his travels he extolled the virtues of their society. As he prepared to leave the presidency he shipped home a household of elegant new furnishings acquired in the merchant coves of New York and Philadelphia, as if to remodel his country estate in the image of a town mansion. He even seemed to grow to prefer living in an urban environment to dwelling in the remote Northern Neck of Virginia, although he could anticipate that his area of the Potomac soon might become a burgeoning mercantile center in its own right, thanks to the new capital which he had helped secure for his neighborhood. Indeed, a year later when he wrote to Sally Fairfax for the first time in twenty-five years, his letter was full of the important changes that had occurred in his region of the Potomac since her departure in 1773, each change seeming to point toward the northernization of that southern entrepot.[68]

Not surprisingly, Washington and the Federalist party, the backbone of whose strength stemmed from the northeastern mercantile classes, saw much to admire in Great Britain. When Washington thought of Great Britain he envisioned a unified, mercantile and manufacturing country, "a mighty Nation" with "inexhaustible" resources, an empire whose "fleets covered the Ocean," whose "troops harvested laurels in every quarter of the globe." The "energetic government" that he sought to establish would result in nothing less for America, he hoped, save that its empire would consist of hegemony over the North American continent coupled with a bountiful free commerce with the great trade centers of Europe. Unity, he knew, would permit expansion, expansion would safeguard against "luxury, dissipation, and corruption," and that would procure "tranquility . . . safety . . . prosperity . . . Liberty." The America he envisioned would become a "fortress," a "Palladium of your political safety and prosperity."

Great Britain, however, held the key to the rapid fulfillment of Washington's dreams. It was as though he could never escape the tentacles of that empire. Frustrated in his youthful ambitions by imperial officials, he had watched in continued frustration after 1783 as America was powerless to compel Britain to adhere to the Treaty of Paris. Ultimately he and Hamilton concluded that ties with Britain were crucial to the realization of their plans for the new American nation. British trade offered the fuel that could drive the American economy, solidify the Union, and bond the mercantile class to the new government. President Washington might have chosen a different route toward the same end. He might have sought leverage against Great Britain through the maintenance of close ties with France, as the Republicans urged, or he might have implemented an American navigation system, also a course advocated by Jefferson and Madison. But each alternative not only presented the risk of extirpating all chance for a rapprochement with Great Britain, but also without question, each promised to earn him the hostility of those whose plaudits he valued above all others. Thus, he permitted Hamilton to make clear to London his desire to normalize relations between the two nations, and with the Jay Treaty he swallowed a bitterly unpopular pact to further that end.

Judged by the standards of peace and prosperity, Washington's foreign policies were a success. They were no less successful for the fulfillment of Washington's inner needs. In one way or another he often had warned, as he did again in his Farewell Address: "Against the insidious wiles of foreign influence (I conjure you to believe me, fellow citizens), the jealousy of a free people ought to be *constantly* awake." At last, in his final great messages as president he could boast that the new nation had moved closer to his goal of true independence. The day was at hand, he said, when "we may defy" all who would seek to exert dominion over the United States. And, as in his own youthful struggle for independence, Washington could with satisfaction now see that his actions would permit his nation to "command its own fortunes."[69]

Washington's last days in office were busy ones, though most of the frantic activity arose from the mad social whirl occasioned by his imminent departure and John Adams's impending inauguration. Many old acquaintances wanted to say good-bye, and Washington, about to return to the isolation of his farm, seemed no less eager to partake of the festive mood that hovered about the capital. The grandest celebration had occurred on Washington's birthday—his sixty-fifth. The day was made an official holiday in Philadelphia, and the citizenry lined the streets beneath flag-draped buildings for a parade and a round of speeches. That evening the president attended a ball in his honor, a great affair at which more than twelve hundred persons jammed Ricketts's Amphitheater to mix exultation at having had Washington for so long with melancholy and foreboding at the thought that he soon would be gone.

Not everyone joined in these celebrations, however. Some Republican legislators, including young Andrew Jackson, refused to consent to a congressional resolution of appreciation for his lengthy service. Presently many Republicans would toast him: "George Washington—down to the year 1787, and no farther." [70]

Soon all that remained was John Adams's inauguration, and it was a brief and, for Washington, a thoroughly pleasant affair. Garbed in his customary, stately black suit, President Washington arrived at Congress Hall a few minutes before the president-elect. Washington was greeted by clamorous cheering as he entered the chamber and took his seat before the congressmen and magistrates, the diplomatic corps and the guests. Jefferson, soon to be vice president, came in moments later and took a seat next to the president. At noon Adams was ushered in, accompanied by a short burst of polite applause. In his usual low, clipped tone, the anxious new president read a succinct address, then he took the oath. The Washington presidency was at an end. Save for Washington, Adams said later, there was not a dry eye in the legislative hall. In fact, Adams added, the general could not have seemed more pleased by these events. His "countenance was . . . serene and unclouded," Adams wrote home the next day. "Methought I heard him say, 'Ay! I am fairly out and you fairly in! See which of us will be happiest!' " [71]

PART FIVE

19

The Last Years

"The shades of retirement"

On the afternoon that he again became a private citizen, Washington walked the short distance from the President's House to the Francis Hotel to call on his successor. A large crowd of Philadelphians walked along with him, silently, respectfully tagging behind to get one last glimpse of America's most renowned son. The ex-president paid no heed until after he had entered the hostelry, then, before climbing the stairs to John Adams's suite, he impulsively stepped back outdoors and waved to the throng. Those who were near the hotel entrance said that tears were streaming down George Washington's cheeks.[1]

The Washingtons lingered in the capital for five days following the inauguration of the new president, packing their belongings and saying their goodbyes, sharing mingled feelings at the impending change in their life, and, at the same time, moving others to a profound sense of loss. Eliza Powel was among those deeply affected by her friend's imminent parting. During Washington's final days in Philadelphia she sent him several missives. The initial notes were addressed to "My dear Sir," the latter to "my very dear Sir." Her earliest letter closed with the salutation, "Your unalterable Friend"; he wrote next, closing with, "Your sincere Affectionate Friend," then "Your affectionate Afflicted Friend," and, finally, "Truly & affectionately . . . your most Obed. & Obliged."[2]

On one of the Washingtons' last nights in town the former First Family was honored at Rickett's Circus, and on another evening he and Martha hosted Adams and Vice President Jefferson. On the 8th Washington called for the last time on the president. It was a social call, yet Washington had personal business on his mind too. Some of the furniture in the President's House had been provided by the taxpayers, but to those items Washington had added curtains, chairs, carpets, even a chandelier, all purchased out of his own pocket. As Mount Vernon already groaned with furnishings, the ex-president had no desire to pay shipping costs to have these superfluous goods conveyed to Virginia. Thus, amidst their goodbyes, the first two presidents of the United States spent some time that afternoon discussing the price of the wares that Washington wished to vend. In the end Adams purchased only a few household articles, and he declined to buy the two horses that Washington also hoped to sell. In fact, Adams intimated to his wife that his predecessor had tried to gouge him on the equine deal, hoping to get a thousand dollars for two nearly middle-aged horses. He may have been correct, for when Washington eventually sold the mares to his friend Eliza Powel, he confided that the horses were older than he had represented them as being to Adams.[3]

During their final days in the city the Washingtons did what country folk have done since time immemorial. They called on several urban merchants, busily shopping for items that were certain to be inaccessible in rural Virginia. When at last they were ready to depart the couple took along two newly acquired side-boards (evidently deciding that Mount Vernon's great room and dining room could accommodate still more furniture), a new set of china, two pipes of Madeira, and several gallons of porter. In addition, Washington purchased a smoking jacket and a pair of new spectacles (for eighty cents apiece), while Martha bought new shoes and a jewelry box. They also paid for shoe repairs and had an artisan mend some broken china, and the two laid in a large supply of nuts, molasses, raisins, lime juice, candles, and assorted medicines. Washington even purchased new farm implements in Philadelphia, as he discovered that they were cheaper in the city than in Alexandria.[4]

Finally, on March 9 everything was packed, all the personal business had been tended, and the Washingtons at last were ready to start home, heading for what Martha hoped would be "a more tranquil theater." They slipped out of town in the morning. This time little ceremony attended the departure, an unusual circumstance for this city that enjoyed festivities, and which so often had fêted Washington with grandiose or solemn ceremonies to mark his comings and goings. By 7:00 A.M. the Washingtons' carriage, buffeted by a strong, cold wind, had rattled over the last of Philadelphia's empty cobblestone streets, swiftly conveying the family from the busy urban neighborhoods into the more serene environs of rustic southeastern Pennsylvania—a transition that could have been taken as a symbol of the transformation that was about to descend over Washington's life. For the third time he was leaving public life and, like the mythic Cincinnatus he so admired, he was bent on withdrawal to Mount Vernon, there, he told himself, "to seek, in the shades of retirement, the repose I had always contemplated." As in earlier times, however, he eventually discovered that he could not remain completely aloof from the vibrant public life he so enjoyed.[5]

Graced by peace, and basking in the guidance of a series of generally competent estate managers, the Mount Vernon to which Washington returned in

1797 was in far better condition than he had found it to be both at the conclusion of his service in the French and Indian War and following the War of Independence. In particular, William Pearce, George Augustine's successor, had done a good job before the gradual worsening of a painful, debilitating rheumatic disorder forced him into retirement. Just before the end of 1796 Washington replaced him with James Anderson, an experienced hand who been recommended by a trusted acquaintance. A Scotsman who had come to America only five years before, Anderson assumed his duties at a difficult time, taking up the reins just after a summer-long drought that had parched the estate's already attenuated soil, then watching helplessly as one of the worst winters in memory afflicted the region from the Chesapeake to New England. Nevertheless, in the first days that followed Washington's return, the owner discovered that the fields were in about as good shape as they ever were likely to be. The mansion, however, had suffered considerably during his long absence.[6]

When Washington had come home the previous fall he had begun to suspect his troublesome cupola once again might need repairs, and it was obvious that rooms that had not been painted for a decade or more begged to be looked after. On this occasion, he had been home less than ten days before, to his surprise, he uncovered several structural matters that required work, and once the repairmen got to work they, in their timeless manner, located still more serious problems that demanded attention. Chimney repairs were in order. A mantel literally was pulling away from the wall. The stairway required attention. Windows had to be replaced. So long as he could not escape "the Music of hammers, or the odoriferous smell of Paint," he arranged to transfer the dining room mantel to another chamber, and he set out to hire a craftsman to install handsome paneling and wainscotting in some rooms. In the midst of all the disorder Washington must have wondered whether there would be room for his possessions. En route from Philadelphia was a sloop bearing ninety-seven boxes, fourteen trunks, forty-three casks, thirteen packages, three hampers, and numerous "other things" that he and Martha had shipped home. Among the "other things" was an extensive collection of art that he had accumulated while president. His presidential papers were coming too. So voluminous were the writings from his long career, in fact, that he had begun to contemplate building an entire house—a presidential library, perhaps—on the grounds at Mount Vernon, a building that would serve as a repository for "my Military, Civil and private Papers which . . . may be interesting."[7]

Outside the mansion only the gardens required work, the legacy, said Washington, of the incompetent artisan who recently had overseen this domain. Otherwise, the proprietor came home confident that his new manager had everything well in hand. Indeed, during his final weeks in Philadelphia Washington cheerfully welcomed several changes recommended by Anderson. The Scotsman wanted to put in a peach orchard and had suggested that the estate would profit from the construction of a threshing machine and the planting of corn at Dogue Run. He had also convinced his employer to permit him to build a still. Washington agreed to everything, although he demanded that the distillery be erected nearer the mansion than Anderson had proposed, "for I fear *at the Mill*, idlers (of which, and bad people there are many around it) . . . could not be restrained from visiting the Distillery, nor probably from . . . robbing the Still." The still, an innovation that Washington had not previously considered, quickly turned into a money maker. Actually, Anderson constructed five stills, putting them in the care of his son. In short order they produced a thousand gallons a month, liquid gold that Washington turned into useful revenue.[8]

Despite that successful venture, Washington's ardor for Anderson began to cool after he had been at home for about a year. By then it was apparent that Mount Vernon's fields had yielded no greater produce than before, a failing that the owner laid at Anderson's doorstep. It was an unfair charge. Not only was the Scotsman about as successful as his predecessors, but Richard Parkinson, the eminent English agriculturalist, visited Mount Vernon and privately advised Washington that indifferent soil was the source of the estate's poor showing. The owner would have none of that, however. While he conceded that Anderson was "a very industrious man; a very honest, zealous, and well intentioned man; and . . . a very sober man" who was not without skills as a farm manager, he felt his manager was doomed to be an underachiever because of his "Want of System," his "Want of foresight" in planning. His great failing, Washington went on, was that he constantly was "shifting from thing to thing, without finishing any thing. . . ."[9]

There was another source of friction. Anderson did not appreciate criticism, and he had the misfortune to work for a man who displayed little restraint in meting out disapproving judgments. Early in 1798, for instance, when Washington questioned matters in Anderson's account books, the irascible manager thought he was being accused of embezzlement and threatened to quit. Washington hurriedly assured him that he was "perfectly well suited with your conduct," and while he acknowledged that he sometimes had questioned Anderson's decisions, he protested that it always had been in "a friendly manner." One reason that Washington was so loath to lose his manager was that he had no earthly idea how to operate the distillery, an expensive and profitable contraption that would be useless if Anderson departed. Thus, while their relationship often was troubled, Washington did what he had to do to keep Anderson aboard through 1798 and 1799. Near the end of the latter year Anderson once again announced his intention of quitting. This time he seemed intransigent, but the two men worked out a deal. The Andersons, father and son, agreed to remain, although only as managers of the distillery and the mill. The elder Anderson must have seen this as a good bargain, a way to remain in familiar surroundings while getting Washington off his back. But there was no immediate deliverance, and, indeed, on the day before he died, Washington wrote Anderson to complain about his allegedly careless maintenance of the cattle pens.[10]

Washington's frequently strained relationship with Anderson did nothing to diminish his zeal for disposing of portions of Mount Vernon. However, in the five years that remained to him after he first advertised his intention of renting the estate, no takers stepped forth. Richard Parkinson was sufficiently interested to drop by for a look, but after a close inspection he told the owner with acerbity that he would not take twelve hundred acres of the place if it was offered free of charge. Just seventy-two hours before he was struck down by his final illness, Washington drafted a three-year plan for agricultural operations at Mount Vernon, suggesting he had abandoned hope of disposing of these mediocre fields. Indeed, his only success in his quest had come in the autumn of 1799 when he rented the mill and distillery to Lawrence Lewis, his nephew.[11]

Washington enjoyed better luck in disposing of his vast western land holdings, tracts in present-day West Virginia, Pennsylvania, Ohio, and Kentucky that totaled approximately 45,000 acres. Most of this realty had been on the market since well before his presidency, but it was not until 1795 that he found a buyer for a small portion of the domain. As usual, Washington proved to be a tough, intractable businessman, one who served notice that he would neither "dispose of the land for a song, nor . . . higgle" over the price. For years he settled for renting a part of his lands, generally receiving wheat in lieu of cash from his tenants. As that grain sold for record prices in the early 1790s, it should have been a good deal for the owner. It was not, however. Little wheat was forthcoming, the fault, Washington charged, as he had a decade before, of a negligent manager. He got a new agent in 1794, while, back in the capital, he worked to swap some of his western lands for a cleared homestead near Philadelphia, a working farm to which he could retreat periodically.[12]

Nothing turned up on his end, but the next year he sold most of his Pennsylvania dominion to two buyers, his Fayette County lands near the remains of Fort Necessity fetching $7.20 per acre, considerably above what he had dreamed of attaining. Nevertheless, as often was the case with Washington's business transactions, the bonanza proved to be less bountiful than it had seemed at first glance. Although the purchaser of the Miller's Run lands made a $3000 down payment and was generally trustworthy about meeting his subsequent obligations, he died in 1798, and his heirs were considerably less faithful. The new owner of the Fayette County tract was a headache from the outset. He made a down payment of $2693, then proceded to drag his feet. Washington directed his agent to tell the vendees "in *decisive terms*" to pay up, threatened legal action, and at the time of his death was planning still another trip to the West, a journey inspired in part by his wish for a face-to-face meeting with the new owners. Washington had expected to receive about $22,000 from these two tracts. At the time of his death he had received only slightly more than half that amount.[13]

In the years following his presidency Washington concluded transactions on much that remained of his other western holdings. In 1798 he swapped his Round Bottom tract on the Ohio—near present-day Moundsville, West Virginia—for cash and property in Alexandria. A bit later he concluded a complicated bargain for his additional Ohio lands between modern Marietta, Ohio, and Point Pleasant, West Virginia, and his Kanawha tracts. According to this deal the purchaser signed a thirty-year lease, paid $5000 down, and pledged to pay off the balance in three annual payments of $50,000 each, beginning in 1806. Shortly before his death Washington acknowledged that through the sale of his frontier lands, as well as with the jobbing of some of his Virginia investments, he had realized approximately $50,000 between 1795 and 1799.[14]

On the other hand his continued interest in the Potomac River Canal Company amounted to a far less profitable business endeavor. After his return to Mount Vernon in 1797 he continued to beat the drums for the venture, and he persisted in his dream that the Potomac one day would serve as the link between the Atlantic and the trans-Appalachian West. In fact, he seemed a victim of his own boosterism and wishful thinking. By the end of his presidency the company had overcome only one major obstacle. In 1794, acting largely at the behest of Washington, the board of directors had hired a new engineer, and after several months of labor under his guidance work was completed on the Little Falls. Yet the optimism which that generated proved to be misplaced, for the company was unable to surmount the more formidable Great Falls. By 1797 about thirty boats a day made the run between Cumberland and Williamsport, a one-and-a-half-day journey down river, a five-day trip upriver. At the Great Falls, however, each craft had to be unloaded, its cargo transferred to wagons and conveyed by land around the impediment, whereupon the freight was returned to another bottom for the final leg of the voyage. During the next three years not only was no progress made in overcoming the engineering obstructions that frustrated the enterprise, but the company's financial plight grew more precarious.[15]

A year into his retirement Washington sought to sell $3494 in government securities in order to make a loan to the beleaguered firm. In addition, he bought additional stock in the ailing company and he served as something of a lobbyist to pry assistance from Virginia and Maryland. His argument was simple. The two states ultimately would derive enormous economic benefits from the endeavor, he counseled, but if they dragged their feet New York or Pennsylvania would be the winner, for one or the other would engineer the "great *high way*" into the interior.

Of course, Washington's efforts were not born of altruism. He envisioned an annual return of 50 percent on his investments in this company. Moreover, he knew that if the undertaking succeeded the Shenandoah Valley, a region where he owned considerable acreage, could be expected to experience an economic boom. The ex-president lived to see Maryland purchase an additional 130 shares, each priced at nearly $600, but he witnessed no further accomplishments in the company's epic battle to subdue nature. As was his custom, he attributed the Potomac Company's failures to human shortcomings, ranting at the "sloth" and the mismanagement that had characterized the conduct of the firm's directors.

Such a view of things kept him naively optimistic to the very end. One or two personnel changes, coupled with Maryland's handsome grant, buoyed his zeal, and in the last week of his life he "rejoice[d], sincerely, that the means are likely to be obtained, to effect so desirable an objective." [16]

After General Washington had been back in Virginia for almost a year, his friend Eliza Powel inquired about the health of "the withered Proprietor" of Mount Vernon, as she jokingly referred to him. He was in good health, much as in the previous year when his spirits "never [had been] in better flow." Washington and Robert Morris had made a compact a few years earlier, each man pledging to live into the next century. If appearances counted for anything, Washington seemed intent on keeping up his end of the bargain. A European traveler who met the general in 1798 thought him "a majestic figure," a "square set, and very strongly built" man. He looked elderly, the visitor related, but he described Washington by quoting Virgil: "Now aged, but a god's old age is hardy and green." Washington, in fact, had maintained a good trim, still weighing 210 pounds, as he had fifteen years before. And he remained active. He rode and walked about his fields daily, moving about so jauntily that one young visitor, twenty-five years his junior, found the older man difficult to keep up with.[17]

Other than the chronic discomfort he experienced from ill-fitting dentures, Washington suffered no complaints until August 1798, when suddenly he was attacked by a fever. For two days he felt poorly, yet he paid little heed; the next day, however, nausea and other baleful symptoms of the ailment descended on him. A physician was fetched, and Washington, who steadfastly refused to take medicine, consented to swallow what was prescribed. For three days he was bedfast and quite ill, then the fever broke and he slowly began to recover. He lost twenty pounds during the ordeal, and for three weeks thereafter he complained of a lingering weakness. In the aftermath of his major illness in 1790 Washington had speculated that he never would survive another ailment. He was wrong. This was his second serious and debilitating bout of sickness since then. Clearly, however, he was all too aware that his time was running out. The best that could be hoped for, a mending Washington told Landon Carter that autumn, was "a gradual decline." [18]

He suspected, though, that his life was "hastening to an end." Yet whether he was tormented by premonitions of imminent death, as historian James Thomas Flexner surmised, is doubtful. While the subject certainly crossed his mind, there is no evidence that he was obsessed with the prospect of his demise. Earlier he had spoken frequently of hailing from a family cursed by a short life expectancy, but that no longer seemed accurate. His mother had lived past her eightieth birthday. He had been sixty-five when he retired, and he had barely arrived back at Mount Vernon when he learned that his sister Betty had died, at age sixty-five. Curiously, the news did not seem to weigh on him. He immediately wrote to George Lewis, Betty's son, but it was a strange letter, one that mixed (in the same paragraph) the obligatory expressions of sorrow with news about his renovation of Mount Vernon; he even queried as to whether the bereaved knew of a joiner that he might hire. Nor did his sister's death cause him to reflect on his own mortality in any of the scores of letters or diary entries that he wrote over the next several months. Indeed, the work on Mount Vernon which he carefully supervised in this period suggests just the opposite tendency: Washington planned to be around for awhile.[19]

Most recent biographers have suggested that Martha was in poor health, even that she had "gone downhill rapidly" by the time the family returned to Virginia. However, there is no evidence to sustain such a belief. She was troubled by occasional lingering colds, and once Washington noted that she was "indisposed by swelling on one side of her face." But during all of 1798 Washington mentioned only one cold that afflicted her, apparently only a brief bout of the wintertime sniffles. A foreign traveler who spent nearly two weeks with the Washingtons that year apparently found her quite healthy, and he went on to characterize her as "extremely agreeable and attractive," a woman "with lively eyes, a gay air," "one of the most estimable persons that one could know, good, sweet, and extremely polite."[20]

When Washington returned to Mount Vernon he took a step that he thought might prolong the good health that he and Martha enjoyed. He asked Lawrence Lewis, one of Betty's five sons, to move to Mount Vernon and "ease me of the trouble of entertaining company" in the evenings. He could not pay him for the work, Washington wrote, but he would cover the expense of housing and feeding his body slave and his horse. "Besides," he went on, "your time, or attention . . . if you have an inclination for it, might be devoted to Reading, as I have a great many instructive Books, on many subjects, as well as amusing ones." Lewis quickly accepted the offer and assumed his duties as surrogate host, but his time and attention soon were devoted less to study than to Nellie Custis. It is not difficult to see why.[21]

Now eighteen, Nelly was a beautiful young woman. Three years earlier an English visitor at the President's House had discovered her to be "a very pleasing young lady." A guest at Mount Vernon in 1798 thought her "a young woman of the greatest beauty," a "celestial" figure, while Benjamin Latrobe, who also met her in Virginia, found her the embodiment of "perfection." Fair-skinned, with raven hair and large, dark, lustrous eyes, she mingled an air of gentle sweetness and resolute confidence. Raised by the Washingtons, she had enjoyed a life of cosmopolitanism unavailable to most other children; tutored, indulged, fêted, she had seen much, met many people, and experienced the best of both the urban and rural worlds. But for all that, John Adams found her to be limited, the product of an environment in which her step-grandparents had been forced to shelter her unduly. Perhaps he was correct, although given the dearth of evidence it is as likely that what he deemed to be over-protection was, in fact, the conscious grooming of a young lady for the position she would, in all likelihood, hold someday as mistress of an isolated southern plantation.[22]

If there can be little doubt that Washington never tired of the company of Nelly, the same cannot be said of his relationship with her brother, Wash. Sixteen years old when Washington entered retirement, George Washington Parke Custis either was a late bloomer or he was acting out an adolescent rebellion against his step-grandfather. In any case his behavior was decidedly similar to that of his father, Jackie Custis, whose blasé indifference to work had caused the general and Martha so much vexation. Washington found this young man to be lazy and rebellious and utterly without ambition. The fact that he had done poorly at the College of Philadelphia—later the University of Pennsylvania—and at Princeton added weight to Washington's judgment. But if the boy easily conceded defeat in these undertakings, his guardian did not. Washington contemplated sending him to William and Mary College, decided instead on Harvard (from which he had an honorary degree, but which he persisted in calling the "University in Massachusetts" or "the University at Cambridge"), and ultimately consented to Martha's wish that he be enrolled closer to home. Thus St. John's College at Annapolis got Wash next. No college-bound student ever left home with better advice ringing in his ears. Study with "zeal and alacrity," Washington counseled the lad, and "your respectability in maturer age, you usefulness to your country, and, indeed, your own private gratification" will be ensured. After only two months, however, the young man was writing home for money, and a month later the Washingtons discovered that he was in love and hoped to marry, though that desire was thwarted by the young lady's parents. Before two more months elapsed Wash was back at Mount Vernon, his college days a thing of the past. Yet, the general refused to surrender, and that autumn he placed the boy under the tutelege of Tobias Lear, the loyal secretary who had returned to Washington's employ earlier in 1798.[23]

Lear did not live at Mount Vernon, as he had during his first stint with Washington. He and his four children resided at nearby Walnut Tree Farm on Clifton Neck, the homestead that Washington had given him for a modest rent as a wedding present in 1795. No doubt the size of his family dictated such a course, but the ceaseless flow of overnight visitors and the abundance of live-ins at Mount Vernon might have contributed to his decision. Lafayette's son had accompanied the Washingtons to Virginia in 1797, and he and his tutor dwelled at Mount Vernon for six months, departing the moment they learned that the senior Lafayette had been liberated from his Austrian confinement. Lawrence Lewis arrived about the same time the sober young Frenchman departed, and so did Eleanor Forbes, a fifty-year-old English widow whom the general hired as a housekeeper. Her function, of course, was to help with Martha's work load, made the more onerous by the sudden flight of Hercules, the Washington's enslaved cook. About the same time that Mrs. Forbes came, Washington hired Albin Rawlins as a clerk, a move he apparently thought necessary inasmuch as Lear was not a resident. The general offered him $100 a year, or $150 if the applicant could "bring sufficient testimony . . . of [his] Sobriety, integrity and good dispositions"; at either price, Washington got him cheap, for he was ready to pay an in-law 30 percent more to accept the same post.[24]

To this house which groaned with inhabitants came a steady stream of visitors. Curiosity brought numerous foreign travelers, including at least two diplomats, the Spanish and British ministers to the United States. Endless numbers of relatives also called on Washington, especially the ubiquitous clan of Dandridge and Washington nephews and nieces from all about Virginia. Planters from throughout the Chesapeake states likewise dropped in, and, seemingly, every son of every aristocrat in the region visited the estate, as if meeting the proprietor of Mount Vernon was a requisite to the completion of one's education. Washington's vanity led him to appreciate the attention, but what especially delighted him was the opportunity to spend an evening with an old acquaintance such as Dr. Craik or Dr. Stuart, the husband of Nelly and Wash's mother. And he welcomed visits from old comrades in arms, such as Henry Lee and General Alexander Spotswood, as well as social calls by former political allies, men like Attorney General Lee and the Pinckney brothers from South Carolina. So rarely was Mount Vernon without a guest that on one such occasion a somewhat startled Washington wrote to Lear: "I am alone at *present*. . . . Unless someone pops in, unexpectedly—Mrs. Washington and myself will do what I believe has not been done within the last twenty years by us—that is to set down to dinner by ourselves." He then asked Lear to come over that evening.[25]

Necessity, said Washington a few months after his return to Virginia, had compelled him to work "from the 'rising of the sun to the setting of the same.' " As was his custom Washington exaggerated his plight, but the reference to a long workday did not stretch the truth. His business interests and his superintendency of Mount Vernon, as well as his commitment of providing hospitality to the neverending line of guests, demanded his time. So did his correspondence, both his current and his past communications. Upon leaving the presidency Washington dug out his letter books from thirty years or more before and proceeded to correct those missives he had written as a young man. He did not seek to alter the meaning of this correspondence, but concerned with history's judgment and, as always, plagued by self-doubt, he sought to replace his earlier plain and occasionally ungrammatical letters with more elegant and proper epistles.[26]

Washington also complained of the time required to "discharge all my [current] epistolary obligations," as if his days were squandered by the task of responding to numerous unsolicited letters. He did write a great deal. During his first year at home he wrote nearly 175 letters, missives that from habit he carefully, painstakingly drafted, going over each word and every clause meticulously to assure that his style was in no way flawed. But he initiated much of the correspondence, especially the exchanges concerned with current political matters. Upon retiring he had proclaimed his intention of leaving politics to others. "To make, and sell a little flour . . . and to amuse myself in Agricultural and rural pursuits," he had said, were his only aspirations. But Eliza Powel had predicted that a man of his temperament would find it difficult to adjust to private life, and she was correct. The general had hardly alighted from his carriage in Virginia before he implored Secretary McHenry to communicate to him "such matters as are interesting." Soon he waxed eloquent about foreign policy concerns in letter after letter, and on more than one occasion he confessed that he waited for news with "no small degree of solicitude." [27]

During his first year at home only one episode verged on luring Washington back into the public arena. When James Monroe, whom Washington had recalled from Paris, arrived in Philadelphia in the summer of 1797, he wasted no time in launching a campaign to vindicate himself of the suspicion that he had betrayed his country's interests through his diplomacy. He authored several spirited newspaper essays, and soon he published *A View of the Conduct of the Executive of the United States*, a very long pamphlet in which he blasted Washington's policy as anti-French. The legacy of Washington's bankrupt policy, he charged, was the Jay Treaty, a humiliating pact made necessary because the administration's open anglophilia gradually had dissipated Paris's friendship.[28]

By early in the new year Washington had obtained a copy of the pamphlet. He read it closely, but he confined his comments to several notations in the margin of his copy. With his unerring feel for such things Washington realized that he had little to gain by engaging in an undignified public war with an insignificant little fellow like Monroe. Besides, he saw Monroe's attack as just another skirmish in the raging party warfare, a fray from which he intended to remain aloof. His interests would be better served, he remarked, by remaining silent and watching as the former minister's "Artillery . . . recoil[ed] upon himself." [29]

Soon the Monroe episode faded away, overshadowed by what seemed a national emergency. Early in Adams's administration relations with France broke down completely. The crisis, it will be recalled, had really begun late in Washington's presidency, and it was to arrest the deteriorating relationship that Hamilton had urged his chief to send a special envoy to Paris. Washington had refused, simply nominating Charles Cotesworth Pinckney to replace Monroe. The former treasury secretary did not surrender easily, however. On the eve of Adams's inauguration he set to work on the incoming president, proposing that it would be wise to dispatch a special diplomatic commission to the French capital. Ostensibly, Hamilton wished to settle the differences between the two nations. Higher on his agenda, however, was his hope that the commission could negotiate the termination of the twenty-year-old Franco-American treaty of alliance. When the Republican leadership also took up the cry for a special mission, Adams was moved to seriously consider the notion. Before Washington left Philadelphia the two men conferred about the matter, and even discussed the names of a few likely candidates for such a mission.

Before he could act, however, Adams learned that the French government not only had refused to receive Minister Pinckney, it had abrogated the Franco-American commercial accord of 1778. A bellicose spirit swept America, yet Adams sought a peaceful resolution of the differences that separated the one-time allies. He announced that he was dispatching a three-member commission to Paris, a trio that would include Pinckney, John Marshall of Virginia, and Elbridge Gerry. Washington watched these events closely, all along believing that conflict would be avoided. Events soon suggested that Washington's optimism surely was misplaced.[30]

On the first anniversary of his inauguration, Adams received dire tidings. France had refused to receive the three American envoys. In addition, it had announced a harsh stance concerning the right of neutral trade. Henceforth, it would seize all ships whose cargo included English goods.[31]

Adams spoke of military action, and the Federalist Congress quickly passed nearly twenty laws designed to ready the country for war. One of those laws empowered Adams to appoint the general officers in a new American army.[32]

When the news of the treatment of the American envoys made its way down to Mount Vernon, Washington's outrage matched that of other Federalists. As his administration had sought "to Treat [France] upon fair, just and honorable ground," he expressed shock at the behavior of Paris. For the first time he conceded that war with France was possible. Until now he had maintained that Paris was sufficiently pragmatic to realize that it could gain nothing from a conflict with the United States. The recent events, however, caused him to reconsider. French dupes in America, he now argued, had encouraged Paris to believe that the United States never would defend itself, and he now feared that French miscalculation could result in war. America must speak with one voice, he urged. For that reason, he added, he supported the Federalist campaign of readiness, including the Alien and Sedition laws limiting free speech.[33] But Washington uttered these thoughts in private, and he played no role in the Federalist preparedness campaign. In fact, when Hamilton, who feared that southern Democratic-Republicans would never support a war with France, urged him to make a tour of the region to rally the populace for hostilities, the ex-president rejected the suggestion. He feared the "malicious insinuations" that such activity would elicit, he said. He added, too, that he doubted that a land war with France would occur. A naval war, perhaps, but he could not believe that France would invade America, though their government, he conceded, was "capable of *any thing bad*."[34]

The thinking in Philadelphia was quite different, and by the 4th of July Washington not only knew of Congress's decision to augment the army, he was aware of talk that he would be summoned from retirement to lead that force. He expressed his customary distaste toward such a notion, although his protests of disinclination were familiar and not terribly credible. Indeed, so that his alleged misgivings would not be misunderstood, Washington told the secretary of war that "principle . . . would not suffer me, in any great emergency, to withhold any services I could render, required by my country." Later that day, garbed in his old buff and blue uniform, he reviewed a military parade in Alexandria. At that very moment one hundred miles to the north, Secretary McHenry was signing the form that made Washington the commander of the newly enlarged army.[35]

The secretary personally brought the commission to Virginia. McHenry also brought along a letter from his real boss, Alexander Hamilton, a missive that urged Washington to accept the appointment as the nation's first lieutenant general. This time Hamilton did not resort to the convoluted arguments he had used in 1788 when he had appealed to Washington to accept the presidency. Now he knew Washington better, and he seems not to have doubted that Washington would come out of retirement. Hamilton seldom misjudged Washington, and once again he correctly understood the master of Mount Vernon.[36]

Washington greeted McHenry at his doorstep on July 11. The two men had much to talk about, and presumably the secretary paid close heed to what Washington said, for Adams had advised him that the general's "opinion on all subjects must have great weight." By the time McHenry set forth on the hot, dusty return trip to the capital, he had secured the general's consent to serve, although Washington made it clear that he wished to remain at home until the "urgency of circumstances" made his presence in the field absolutely necessary. McHenry's satchel also contained a list of the names of the general officers that Washington wished to have serve under him, an enumeration that he had prepared at Adams's behest. The list contained only the names of Federalists. Hamilton headed the tally, followed by Charles C. Pinckney, Hamilton's superior in the last war; Knox, who had outranked both Pinckney and Hamilton, was next. Henry Lee was to be added should any of those on the list decline to accept. All were to hold the rank of major general.[37]

Many reasons could be advanced for placing Pinckney's name, not Hamilton's, at the top of the list. Washington even candidly told Hamilton as much. Pinckney was a more experienced officer and he had outranked Hamilton. Moreover, any French attack must occur in the South, said Washington, and as a southerner Pinckney would be better able than Hamilton to rally men to the colors. Why, then, did Washington name Hamilton? Hamilton had requested the position, and Pickering and McHenry had lobbied Washington on his behalf, even telling the general that the New Yorker would not serve if he was not elevated above everyone save Washington. For reasons that he did not chronicle, Washington believed that Hamilton's participation was essential. His "Services ought to be secured at *almost* any price," he said, adding only that the nation's "entire confidence might be reposed" in the former secretary, and that Hamilton possessed the youth and stamina necessary for another grueling partisan war in the South. If Washington gave any thought to the relationship between the war and Hamilton's or Federalism's political future, he did not divulge it. But, then, why would he have aired such views?[38]

Others, however, had given much thought to such matters. Some Federalists were desperate to get Hamilton back into the government, and to see him made second in command to an old, stay-at-home general was to see him made the real commander. Others may have seen a correlation between an army run by Hamilton and the fortunes of the party. Not only would the army be a rich resource for patronage, but, in the right hands it could, in the words of historian Richard Kohn, become the means for the establishment of "a subterranean Federalist military network to intimidate" domestic foes.[39] One who had mulled over these possibilities was President Adams, and he did not enjoy such thoughts. He was aware of Hamilton's almost unfettered ambition. To his way of thinking there was something unsettling about the former secretary, some dark, menacing side to his character that made him untrustworthy. He was a "Hypocrite," the president charged, an intriguer—power-hungry, duplicitous, and even lascivious, "with as debauched Morals as old Franklin." As it was Adams's plan to "maintain the same conduct towards him I always did, that is to keep him at a distance," the president nearly choked when he learned that General Washington had headed his list of officers with Hamilton's name.[40]

Not only could Adams not abide the thought of Hamilton as second in command, he was perturbed that Knox, a fellow Bay stater and an old friend, had been shoved into third place. Therefore, Adams chose to accept only half of Washington's recommendation. He agreed to the three men that Washington had named, but he decreed that their ranking must be determined by the date of their original commissions. Thus, Knox topped his list, followed by Pinckney, then Hamilton.[41]

If Washington blundered in the first instance by listing the three major generals, his subsequent actions not only compounded his error but stained the virtuous reputation he had labored so long and so hard to establish. Unwittingly, yet inescapably, Washington found himself at the head of a faction that sought to force the hand of the commander in chief. It was an intrigue that was far more real than the "Conway Cabal" which had caused him such anguish twenty years before.

Washington barely had offered his list of officers before a despairing letter from Knox arrived at Mount Vernon, a communiqué in which his faithful old comrade expressed his sense of betrayal at learning that junior men had been recommended over him. The old artillery officer would not accept command under such circumstances. Shaken, Washington's answer was filled with fine-sounding evasion and barely credible logic. Public opinion, as reflected by the sentiments of a majority in Congress, wished to see Hamilton at the top of the list, he replied lamely. He also denied that Hamilton or his friends had worked on him to secure the former secretary's appointment. Sycophantic to the end, Knox accepted Washington's inadequate explanation, even offering to serve as the general's aide de camp should an invasion occur. However, he persisted in his refusal to take a general officer's post.[42]

Washington next turned to Adams. The general proceeded to lecture his commander. "I *accepted* and *retained*" command, he said, on the condition that "the three Major Generals stood, Hamilton, Pinckney, Knox; and in this order I expected their Commissions would have been dated." He had wished no affront to the presidency, he went on; his object only had been to secure the most able lieutenants. He went on to contradict himself, however. He had selected Hamilton because public opinion supported his appointment, he said later in the letter. Appearing to read Adams's mind, Washington hurriedly stated that he had ranked the three men without regard to their political fortunes, and in a passage that must have seemed equally preposterous to the president Washington denied that Hamilton's ambition constituted any danger to the nation. Washington closed by alluding to the problems faced by the army's commander, "be him whom he may," a chilling reminder that he would not serve if Adams refused to consent to his wishes concerning Hamilton's ranking. Adams conceded. He had little choice.[43]

For four months following his appointment Washington remained at Mount Vernon, hardly distracted by his new post. He put Lear on the federal payroll by naming him to be his aide, although while he awaited taking the field the general seems to have used him principally to "overhaul, arrange, and separate" his huge collection of private papers. Meanwhile, there was little else to do. A month after taking command Washington complained to Secretary McHenry that he was being kept in the dark, that he was "ignorant of every step" that had been taken by the war department. Thirty days later, as he was recovering from the serious ailment that struck him toward the end of that summer, Washington again carped at McHenry's failure to keep him abreast of the military's preparations, this time even hinting that he suspected that "important and interesting" matters were being concealed from him. Three weeks later he demanded to "know *at once* and *precisely*" what was going on. By late October about all that Washington had learned was that Pinckney had accepted rank beneath Hamilton, and that McHenry had summoned him and the major generals to the capital for a planning session.[44]

In the eighteen months since he had returned to Virginia, Washington had not strayed more than a few miles from Mount Vernon, only visiting Alexandria and once looking into business matters in the new Federal City. But on November 5 he and Lear, the latter garbed in his new uniform adorned with a colonel's insignia, set off for Philadelphia. Washington must never have expected to make this journey again, much less to be hailed and honored in every little hamlet, much as he had been almost a decade before when en route to assume the presidency. Philadelphia arranged the greatest celebration, and as the general's carriage rumbled into town early on the 10th he was greeted by pealing bells and gaily attired military units.[45]

Washington was in the capital for about a month. Curiously, on his first three nights in town the general was left to dine alone at his lodgings, the Widow White's boardinghouse on 8th Street. Thereafter, however, he had a busy schedule. He dined out seventeen of the other twenty nights that he made diary entries, including one evening at the President's House and another at the British embassy. Surely his most extraordinary meal was the one he took with his old friend Robert Morris, now serving time in the Prune Street Prison, a debtor's jail. Morris was in the early stages of what eventually would be more than a three-year incarceration, the result of a staggering indebtedness that had occurred when the European war provoked the collapse of his financial empire. Eliza Powel did not entertain her friend on any of these evenings, although Washington must have seen her on the night that he dined at her brother's residence. He did visit her home on two or three afternoons, and he breakfasted with her one morning. One of her letters, moreover, hints that she and the general may have taken long walks together, including a lengthy stroll one chilly, rainy Sunday.[46]

If Washington relaxed in the evenings, his days largely were consumed by work. He met frequently with McHenry and Generals Hamilton and Pinckney, and on occasion one or another of Adams's other cabinet ministers requested a meeting. Mostly it was tedious, often mundane work, tending to procuring supplies, organizing the support services, designing uniforms and insignia, selecting sites for magazines. By December 14, the day Washington set out for home, some action at last had been taken "for the proper and successful direction of our military affairs."[47]

Although General Washington could not have known it as his carriage left Philadelphia late that December afternoon, he was departing this city for the final time. Nor could he have realized that his last stint of military service—all thirty-four days of it—was at an end. Of course, for several more months he concerned himself with the cantonment of this or that unit and with various appointments. But there was little glory in what he did, and surely there was less glamour to his role than he must have anticipated when he had "consented to Gird on the Sword." For a time it must have seemed to him that the design of his uniform was his most pressing concern.[48] In fact, his letters soon betrayed his realization that he was little but a figurehead general; "my opinions and inclinations are not consulted," he complained, adding that important matters were decided "not only without my recommendation, but even without my knowledge."[49] Hamilton, for so long a power behind Washington's throne, at last had supplanted even Washington.

While Washington sat grumbling above the chilly banks of the Potomac, the most important decision in the Quasi-War crisis with France was being made elsewhere. A few weeks after the general's return to Mount Vernon—with the air thick with Federalist demands for war—President Adams privately decided to walk one more mile for peace. Early in the year he had received information from the United States minister to the Hague that led him to believe that France sincerely wished to avoid war. Unwittingly, too, Washington influenced the president. In February the general passed along similar advice that he recently had received from one of his former diplomats. Adams seemed profoundly moved. All along he desperately had hoped to avoid conflict, though, at times, his compulsion to ask Congress for a declaration of war must have seemed irrestible, both because of the pressures from his cabinet and his party, and because of his realization that his self-interest might be advanced by a popular war. Such feelings only tormented Adams, however, besetting him with anxiety for harboring wishes that he believed he should not have entertained. Washington's letter, thus, was crucial for Adams. The general, whose courage was beyond doubt, seemed now to counsel the commencement of "Negociation upon open, fair and honorable ground"; such a step, he added, might result in peace "upon just, honorable and dignified terms." [50] Washington's carefully chosen words were identical to those he had used in defending the Jay Treaty, and, in fact, he was suggesting no less than that Adams seek out his own such accord, one that was certain to be unpopular but no less essential to the nation's welfare.

Buoyed by Washington's stand, Adams acted quickly, nominating William Vans Murray as Minister Plenipotentiary to the French Republic. The crisis was not over, but its turning point had been reached, and a year later France and the United States signed a convention that restored—if only briefly—amicable relations. But George Washington did not live to witness his successor's diplomatic triumph.[51]

General Washington had one year and five days of life remaining to him when he alighted at the door of Mount Vernon upon his return from duty in Philadelphia. It was bitterly cold, with snow atop the estate's dormant brown grass, when he returned. The weather provided a good excuse for relaxing indoors, and it was not long before he had an abundance of company with which to relax. Old acquaintances dropped in, often staying for a night or two, as did a plethora of federal officials, ranging in importance from magistrates to generals to Indian agents. Letters from Lafayette that had arrived during his absence probably cheered him more than any visitor, however. The Frenchman now was free and in good health, Washington was delighted to learn, and on Christmas Day the general adjourned to his study to write his cherished friend. Although this was his first letter in a year to Lafayette, Washington wrote of little but diplomacy and Franco-American tensions, a sign once again of how difficult retirement was for this robust public man.[52]

Some of Washington's time during his first days back home were spent in arranging a military commission for Wash, a step that the general must have believed would improve the youngster's character. As soon as Martha and his mother consented, Washington completed the paperwork that made Wash a coronet in a troop of Light Dragoons. He would hold the post for eighteen months, joining several friends and relatives in the service, including Dr. Craik's son, George Washington, and Lawrence Lewis, the stand-in host whom Washington had lured to Mount Vernon in 1797.[53]

Before the army got his services, however, young Lewis had another duty to attend. While Washington was in Philadelphia, Lewis and Nelly Custis had announced their plans to marry, selecting the general's birthday as the date for the wedding. The announcement took everyone by surprise, and Washington the more so, for in his preoccupation with public matters he had remained oblivious even to the tell-tale signs of love that the young couple must have shown.[54] The appointed day was typical of February. A mantle of snow lay over the estate, and a biting wind huffed across the rolling slopes above the Potomac. Toward evening the ceremony was held in the mansion's ballroom, a large chamber illuminated on this night by only a few candles. Washington, who attended the ceremony attired in his military regalia, simply noted in his diary:

> The Revd. Mr. Davis & Mr. Geo. Calvert came to dinner & Miss Custis was married abt. Candle light to Mr. Lawe Lewis.[55]

Soon the beehive that was Mount Vernon was restored to its customary pace. In no time Washington was at work mixing his sputtering public duties with his private business endeavors. He kept a close eye on the construction of his houses in the Federal City, and in the spring he rode to the growing village. He also was concerned about his compensation for his recent active duty. As in the Revolution he had agreed to serve for expenses only, and as he departed Philadelphia he had been given $1039.50. By his calculation he had been shortchanged at least $75.00 and perhaps as much as $400.00 if he was entitled to compensation for the new horse he had purchased for the trip north. Secretary McHenry was more than generous. He appears to have forwarded $520.00 to the general, the equivalent of a month's salary.[56]

Sometime late that spring or early in the summer Washington prepared a new will. This was at least his third will, for he had prepared such a document on the eve of his departure for the military front in 1775 and had drafted a second bequest during his presidential years. As the earlier wills were destroyed, no one can be certain what changes he now made. Certainly, however, he would have deleted passages that referred to the western lands that he recently had sold, and he must have incorporated sections to deal with the property in Alexandria and elsewhere that he had acquired in the past few months. In addition, the provision awarding fifty shares of his Potomac Company stock to a national university in the Federal District probably was new, as in all likelihood was the incorporation of a lengthy paragraph concerning his slaves.

Washington now decreed that Billy Lee, his body slave, was to be freed immediately upon his master's death. In addition, he was to receive an annual annuity of thirty dollars for the rest of his life. Most of the remainder of his 316 slaves were to be liberated upon his death, or at Martha's demise, should she survive him. The exception to this rule pertained to infants without living parents. These slaves were to be assigned to new masters until they reached age twenty-five, whereupon they were to be manumitted; in the meantime, they were to be taught a craft, and they were to learn how to read and write. There was one further stipulation concerning the freedmen. Those who, from old age or illness, could not fend for themselves were to be comfortably clothed, sheltered, and fed by his heirs.[57]

Martha, of course, was to inherit everything. Moreover, all profits from the sale of his lands or businesses were to be invested in bank stock, the dividends belonging to his wife. Following her demise, some of his furniture and mementos would pass to his friends, to Dr. Craik and Dr. Stuart, to Bryan Fairfax and to Lafayette, among others. Tobias Lear immediately was to be given free and clear title to the Walnut Hill farm he now rented. Washington's papers and the contents of his library, as well as the crowning jewel, Mount Vernon itself, would become the property of his nephew Bushrod Washington, the son of his brother John Augustine, and now, as a result of an appointment by President Adams, a justice on the United States Supreme Court. Lawrence and Nelly were to inherit what remained of his spacious Mount Vernon properties, including the mill and the distillery. A lot in the Federal City and 1200 acres near Alexandria were earmarked for Wash. In all he specified 9200 acres that were to pass to close relatives. Everything else was to be sold, with the resulting profits itemized for equal division among twenty-three near and distant relatives.[58]

Aside from a thirty-six-hour absence in August when he attended a Potomac Company Board meeting in Georgetown, Washington spent the long, warm summer at Mount Vernon. On average he still drafted a letter each day, his correspondence divided between his business pursuits and the responsibilities entailed by his military post. And, as had been his habit for years, he was off each morning about 7:30 to inspect conditions about his sprawling estate. That he gave no thought to further public pursuits is clear. Disgruntled by Adams's peace mission and by his frequent and protracted absences from the capital, some Federalists had begun to yearn for still another return of the Cincinnatus from Virginia. This time, however, Washington would have none of it, and in an emphatic manner that was missing from his disclaimers of previous years he quickly brought such thinking to a halt.[59]

Late that summer the uneventful humdrum of daily life at Mount Vernon was shattered suddenly when Martha fell seriously ill. Toward the end of August she had begun to feel poorly, but she had persisted with her daily regimen. Eight days later her stubborn resistance collapsed, and on September 6 she was too ill to rise. Through the day she sank, and an anguished Washington sent for Dr. Craik. It was an "Ague & fever," according to the physician. He prescribed bark. Within twenty-four hours she was better, though still weak and drained of every ounce of energy. That night she suffered a relapse. Couriers were dispatched to alert her grandchildren of the gravity of the situation. But, once again, she soon was better. When her fever broke she steadily improved, although two weeks after the crisis she remained "much indisposed." Six weeks of rest were required before she at last was pronounced "tolerably well again." [60]

Washington, meanwhile, remained in good health. Late in July he felt "unwell," as he tersely noted in his diary, and Dr. Craik was called in. Evidently, the physician did not find anything alarming, for he soon departed. Washington wrote no letters that day or the next, probably because of his minor affliction, but within forty-eight hours he seems to have again felt well and to have resumed his normal activities.[61]

Once Martha was out of danger, Washington must have relaxed and enjoyed himself, undoubtedly reflecting on his good fortune still to have her at his side. He might have been happy too that Mount Vernon was quieter than normal, for the steady onslaught of visitors slowed that autumn, probably in deference to Mrs. Washington's long period of recuperation. Yet, as the fiery red and yellow splendor of a Potomac fall enveloped Mount Vernon, all was not well. Upper Virginia remained in the grip of a drought that had decimated that year's oat and corn crops and which now jeopardized the autumn produce as well. To make matters worse, Washington learned that fall that the Hessian Fly, the great plunderer of late eighteenth-century wheat fields, had invaded his estate, augering, he knew, "great ravages thereon next spring." Ill tidings of a political nature also descended on Mount Vernon that autumn. October brought word of Federalist setbacks in the off-year elections, defeats that seemed to inspire in Washington renewed misgivings about President Adams's decision to send a new envoy to Paris. The most disturbing news, however, reached the Potomac late in September. Charles Washington, save for George the last surviving child of the seven sired by Augustine Washington, was dead, the victim of a lingering, painful illness. Word of his death, said the general in complete candor, produced "awful and affecting emotions." [62]

November was a busy month, and a happier one too, for Washington. Early in the month he was away from Mount Vernon for five days, personally surveying land at Difficult Run, a 275-acre tract west of Alexandria in Loudoun County, land that he had purchased years before from Bryan Fairfax. From there he visited the Federal City. Back home on the 10th he enjoyed a spell of mild weather and even a bit of much-needed rainfall. It was a good month for farmers, a month fittingly capped for Washington when Nelly gave birth at Mount Vernon to a baby girl. Nelly's mother, Eleanor Calvert Stuart, had come to be with her, and at about the same time a midwife was hired and took up quarters at the estate. On November 27, a clear, mild day for so late in the season, her services at last were called for. During the afternoon Frances Parke Lewis was brought into the world.[63]

The birth of this first child of a new generation, arriving, as did Frances, on the cusp of the new century, seemed to turn Washington's thoughts to the future. During the next few days he ordered trees for his new houses in the Federal City, wrote for several bushels of seed for Mount Vernon's tired soil, and drafted a four-year "fixed plan" for "Cropping the Farms" of his estate that rolled back from the green Potomac. In addition, he announced his intention for a spring journey far into the West, there, by his own reckoning, to obtain "a just, and faithful acct. respecting" his Ohio and Kentucky lands. After dinner on December 12, as was his habit, he retreated to his study to deal with his correspondence. Only one missive was penned that night, still another letter that looked toward the future. He wrote to Hamilton, hinting that he should throw his limitless energies into a campaign to erect a national military academy.[64]

His letter to Hamilton sealed and ready to be posted, Washington had completed an unpleasant day. Upon awakening that morning, he had discovered that the generally balmy autumn weather had been banished abruptly. The temperature had plummeted eleven degrees during the night and hovered just above freezing. During the day the thermometer hardly moved, and slate gray clouds enveloped the brown, barren hillsides. From habit, though, Washington rode his rounds throughout that morning. He still was out shortly after noon when it began to snow. A clean white blanket was just beginning to lap over his idle fields when the temperature suddenly climbed a few degrees, turning the snow to sleet, then to "a settled cold Rain." Washington turned back to the warmth of his mansion, but he was an hour reaching his hearth. By then he had spent nearly five hours in the elements, and he was cold and wet.[65]

Washington awakened on the 13th plagued by a sore throat. Cause for concern, not alarm, he thought. During the night the temperature had fallen again. Three inches of snow already lay on Mount Vernon, and it still was snowing. The general decided against his customary daily ride about his farms, though he did slosh outside briefly to mark some nearby trees that he wished to have felled. As night came on he still felt reasonably good, despite the sore throat and a dogged hoarseness that had emerged in the course of the day. He appeared to be in good spirits. That night he read newspaper items to Lear and Martha, then he listened as his aide read to him the transcript of recent debates in the Virginia assembly. Sometime before nine o'clock he recorded his daily diary entry. Then he retired.[66]

Between 2:00 and 3:00 A.M. Washington awakened. He was desperately ill, so much so that he barely could speak and his breathing had grown labored. But he did not send for Dr. Craik. Nor did Martha, whom he awakened and who must have realized that his conditioned had worsened markedly in just a few hours. Not until seven o'clock was Lear aroused and informed of the general's deteriorating state. Rushing to the general's bedchamber he found a gravely ill man. Washington now was unable to swallow, barely able to breathe, seemingly almost suffocating from the edema that rapidly had gripped his lungs and from the distension in his throat. Lear took charge. He dispatched a servant to bring Craik. And at Washington's behest an overseer skilled in the art of bleeding was fetched to the general's bedside.

Despite his ceaseless pain, Washington was lucid. He directed the operation that followed. Between 7:30 and 8:00 he was bled for several minutes, for a longer time than Martha or Lear wished, in fact, but the general silenced their protests and directed the overseer to continue. When the procedure was completed he arose and, with assistance, dressed. For two hours he sat in a chair before a warm fire. During that period, at about 9:00, Martha remembered that Dr. Craik once had counseled that in the event of an emergency she should summon Dr. Gustavus Brown of nearby Port Tobacco. Now, seven hours after the crisis began, a servant was sent to invoke his assistance.

About the same time that the servant was setting out on his cold journey, Dr. Craik reached Mount Vernon. He applied a blister—made of cantharides, Spanish fly—to Washington's throat, erected a vaporizer of vinegar and water, and administered a gargle. Washington failed to respond. Indeed, he almost choked to death on the gargle. Craik then ordered a second bleeding, and at 11:00 he sent for a physician who practiced in Alexandria. In early afternoon Dr. Craik administered a third bleeding, then a fourth. A bit later he gave the general a purgative, and still later he ordered another laxative, one that resulted in "a copious discharge from the bowels."

At 3:30 the physician that Martha had sent for arrived, and thirty minutes later the doctor whose presence Craik had requested reached Mount Vernon. They consulted and continued to work on the patient, but there was little left to be done. They agreed that Washington was afflicted with "inflammatory quinsy," a severe inflammation of the tonsils. Today it is presumed that he suffered from a streptococcus infection, an ailment that resulted in asphyxia as the swelling about the glottis diminished his capacity to draw in air. Such an affliction now can be successfully treated with antibiotic drugs. Without those modern medicines, however, Washington's doctors tried other remedies. Their methods did not help the patient, yet, in all likelihood, their prescriptions did not result in his death.

By late afternoon Washington was too weak to turn himself. Lear lay beside him and, when prompted, wrestled to turn the large man to a more comfortable position. Sometime before 5:00 Washington painfully told Lear that he knew he was dying, that he had known as much since he first had awakened in the dark of that long night. A bit later he told Craik and his colleagues: "I feel myself going. . . . I cannot last long."

About 8:00 fresh blisters were applied to Washington's legs and feet. But all knew it was hopeless. No one understood this better than Washington. "I die hard, but I am not afraid to go," he whispered to Craik. Lear, Martha, and Craik remained in the bedroom, overcome with grief, worn by what must have seemed an endless day of endless anxiety. Outside the cold, black night had descended. Inside the three, together with the general's body slave, sat in the barely lighted, overly warm bedchamber filled with the pungent aroma of medicines, and waited, listening to the labored breathing, straining to detect any sign of change.

Near 10:00 Washington stirred. In almost inaudible tones he told Lear, who was closest to his side, "I am just going." Laboring for each word he issued his final command. "Have me decently buried, and do not let my body be put into the vault in less than two days after I am dead." He knew that death was at hand. " 'Tis well," he said. They were his last words.

A few minutes later Washington took his own pulse. Then he seemed to relax, and his breathing grew more shallow. Quietly, at about 10:30 P.M., December 14, 1799, George Washington, aged sixty-seven, died.[67]

Afterword

Hundreds, perhaps thousands, of eulogies to George Washington reverberated about the nation in the ensuing days, but, for majestic simplicity, none exceeded the sentiments that Eliza Powel conveyed to the general's widow. His, she said, had been a "glorious well spent Life." [1]

For others, life went on. Early on the morning after his death Martha asked Lear to see that a coffin was made in Alexandria, and the following day the brick and mortar that long had sealed the family vault at Mount Vernon was chipped away, opening the crypt so that it could be cleaned, then used once again. The tragic events of December 14 meant a heavier work load than usual for Martha's female slaves, as mourning clothes had to be hurriedly made and food prepared for those who would attend the funeral. Finally, on the clear, cold afternoon of December 18 Washington's body was laid to rest. Just before the coffin was sealed Lear cut a lock of the general's hair, a last remembrance which he carefully entrusted to the widow. [2]

On that still, dark night four evenings before, Martha's first words upon realizing that her husband was gone had been, " 'Tis well. All is now over. I have no more trials to pass through. I shall soon follow him." But she lived longer than she must have thought likely, longer, perhaps, than she wished. "May you long very long enjoy the happiness you now possess and never know affliction like mine," she wrote Abigail Adams a few days after the general's funeral. [3] With Washington's death, Martha's reason for living seemed to have vanished, and her last years were ones of melancholy loneliness.

Martha Washington outlived her husband by two and a half years. Although Nelly and Lawrence, as well as Wash and Lear and Albin Rawlins, the clerk, continued on with her at Mount Vernon, it was not a pleasant time. Recurrent illnesses nagged at her, and her awful sense of loss never abated. Atop these woes were pressing financial concerns. While Washington's estate was estimated to be worth approximately $530,000, little of that amount was in liquid assets. Moreover, without him there to manage affairs, little money came in. The estate's exhausted soil continued to vex its proprietor, and to that problem was added a decline in the supply of labor, for many slaves, perhaps learning that their emancipation was imminent, simply drifted away. Sightseers and the curious troubled the widow too. They continued to flock to the estate, and, as when Washington had been alive, many were fed and lodged. The tax collector made his regular calls as well, taking a sizable bite of Martha's resources, eating up funds earmarked for repairs. Abigain Adams visited Martha just before Christmas 1800, one year after the general's death, and she discovered an estate already wearing a down-at-the-heels air. The once magnificent mansion, she thought, paled even by comparison to her modest little farm in Braintree, Massachusetts. Indeed, in the two years following her husband's demise, Martha was compelled to sell considerable numbers of the farm's livestock, including several of Washington's jackasses and jennys, in order to raise money to maintain the residence. She realized over $3500 by this means, yet that amount hardly arrested the deterioration that had set in.[4]

In the end Martha went as had her husband, struck down suddenly by some violent fever. From the moment of the malady's attack, said her grandson-in-law, she knew she was desperately ill and probably dying. She "prepared for death," he added, even welcoming it, he thought, as a "relief from the infirmities & melancholy of old age." Death came quickly, taking Martha Washington on May 22, 1802.[5]

Following her simple funeral at Mount Vernon, change came over the estate even more rapidly. The vast number of slaves still remaining on these grounds were liberated immediately, though some freedmen elected to continue on at Mount Vernon, the only home they had ever known. Of those who remained, the last died in the autumn of 1828. Soon the mansion's interior reflected the change too, as its contents also were dispersed to the four winds. Some items, like the 561 books and pamphlets in the general's library which went to Bushrod Washington, passed into the hands of heirs as designated in Washington's will. Other pieces, also in accord with the will, were sold at an auction conducted by the estate's executors forty-five days after Martha's death. There was much to be sold. The Washingtons had owned 131 chairs, 142 paintings and 3 pieces of sculpture, 16 assorted tables, 25 trunks, 7 carpets, a settee and a sofa, 12 mirrors, 3 sideboards, 13 beds, and 5 chests. The general had accumulated 7 guns and 7 swords, 11 spyglasses, and a telescope. And that was but a fraction of the inventory of Mount Vernon. Family members outbid rivals for some pieces. Wash purchased his grandparents' carriage, some of the general's jennys and livestock, and a few pieces of farm equipment. Bushrod Washington secured some sheep and cattle. Surprisingly, however, Washington's riding horse was sold outside the family, as were most of the goods. The sale raised $124,928, which under the will was to be divided among certain stipulated heirs.[6]

With Martha's death the other residents of the mansion soon moved on. Nelly and Lawrence, with little Frances, now nearly three years old, moved to Woodlawn, an estate they built on the Dogue Run tract left to them by the general. There Lawrence settled into a life of planting, living on until 1839. Nelly, or Eleanor Parke Lewis as she called herself following her marriage, bore seven additional children, four of whom died before their second birthday. Following

Lawrence's death she moved in with one of her sons at Audley in Clarke County, where she remained for thirteen years, until her death at the age of seventy-three in 1852. She was buried at Mount Vernon.

George Parke Custis—"Wash"—stayed on at Mount Vernon for a time after his grandmother's death, but in 1805, at the age of twenty-five, he married and set out on his own. He wed sixteen-year-old Mary Lee Fitzhugh and moved into a residence that had been under construction since shortly after Martha's demise. Ultimately it grew into a huge Greek Revival mansion set on the twelve-hundred acres in Alexandria which Washington had bequeathed to him, a tract overlooking the Potomac and the emerging Federal City, or Washington, as everyone now called the new national capital. Wash and his wife had four children, but only one survived infancy. Like her great-grandmother, that child, Mary Anne Randolph Custis, eventually married a soldier, in 1831 uniting with young Lt. Robert E. Lee. For all the Washingtons' frenetic hand-wringing over Wash, he turned out to be a sober and successful citizen. An eloquent speaker, he was in demand as a lecturer, and he wrote plays and sold paintings of Revolutionary battles. The crisis year of 1860 witnessed the publication of *Recollection and Private Memoirs of Washington*, his invaluable remembrance of his famous step-grandfather. Wash did not live to see his reminiscences in print, however. He had died three years earlier, in 1857.

By then most of those who had been close to Washington already had passed on. Nelly and Wash's mother, Eleanor Stuart, died in 1811, and their stepfather, David Stuart, passed away three years later. Their last years were spent at Ossian Park, a plantation in Fairfax County. Dr. Craik, though a year older than the general, lived on until 1814. Sally Fairfax, two years older than Washington, died in England in 1811; she was eighty-one at her death. Eliza Powel lived through the semicentennial of the Declaration of Independence. She died in Philadelphia at the age of eighty-seven in 1830. Tobias Lear moved from Walnut Tree Farm to Washington soon after Martha's death, and within a few weeks he was aboard a brig bound for Santo Domingo and an assignment as the United States consul general on that island. A similar position in Algiers followed, and in 1805 he played a key role in negotiating a peace treaty between his country and Tripoli. His treaty stirred a furor, however, and he abandoned the diplomatic service, returning to the capital where he took employment as an accountant for the war department. Lear died in October 1816. Blessed and cursed by a life that had mingled glitter with extraordinary disappointment and sorrow, Lear's days ended in tragic misfortune. He died by his own hand.

Justice Bushrod Washington inherited Mount Vernon upon Martha's death, but he, too, found the property next to useless as a working farm. Unable to live off the estate, he continued in his judicial post, living in Philadelphia and Washington most of the year and residing at Mount Vernon only in the summer months. During the twenty-seven years that he owned the property, he made only one substantive alteration, adding a small porch on the southwest end of the mansion. In 1829 he died suddenly while conducting circuit court proceedings in Philadelphia.[7]

Having no children, Bushrod divided his thirty-six hundred acres at Mount Vernon among three nephews, one niece, and the heirs of still another nephew. John Augustine Washington received the mansion, and he soon moved in. But his was a brief stay. He died less than three years after taking occupancy. His widow, Jane Washington, and her four children remained at the mansion, however, and in 1843 her eldest son, also John Augustine Washington, inherited the property.

By this time Mount Vernon had further deteriorated, falling, in fact, into a dilapidated state. For five years the owner struggled in vain to redeem the lands and the dwelling, only to awaken to the reality that renovating the estate would steal his every cent. In 1848, therefore, he put the place up for sale. Eleven years later the Mount Vernon Ladies Association purchased the mansion and 202 acres surrounding it for $200,000. On February 22, 1860, the 128th anniversary of George Washington's birth, that organization, dedicated to the preservation and restoration of the residence where so much history had occurred, took over Mount Vernon.[8] By then every person, save one, who had resided in that mansion with Washington had followed him to the grave.

Only Frances Parke Lewis, the little girl born to Nelly less than three weeks before Washington's death, still was alive. Raised at Woodlawn, she had married Edward George Washington Butler in 1826. An officer in the United States army, Butler was transferred from base to base, until the family settled at Dunboyne Plantation in Louisiana.[9] There in 1875, almost one hundred years to the day after her famous step-great-grandfather had arrived in Cambridge to take command of the Continental army, the last of Washington's immediate family died.

Within a few months of the death of Frances Butler a great exposition opened its doors in Fairmount Park in Philadelphia. The purpose of the spectacle was to celebrate the one hundredth anniversary of the American Revolution. There was irony in the selection of Fairmount Park as the site for the celebration, for this lush woodland included the gentle, rolling green estate of Mount Pleasant, the house looking upon the Schuylkill that Benedict Arnold had presented to his war bride, Peggy Shippen. But Philadelphia was the logical choice for a celebration of the Revolution. Not only had so many of the great events after 1774 occurred there, but the city epitomized the ultimate triumph of Federalism. Philadelphia had become a hub of manufacturing. Its industries annually spewed out products worth $335 million. The city contained 125,000 buildings, 300 miles of paved streets, 86,000 gas lights, and 8339 businesses, Railroad lines crisscrossed the sprawling metropolis, and 750,000 people were jammed into its distended neighborhoods.[10] Visitors from the prairies and farms and small hamlets of the transmontane region could see in Philadelphia not only the legacy of the Federalist Revolution, they could see what was in store for them once the influence of the mercantile and commercial centers spread like a dark stain over their empire to the west.

George Washington would have taken pride in this city and in the ebullience and the raw dynamism that seemed to pulsate from the iron stalls and the show-cases that made up this Centennial exposition. This was the America of which he had dreamt.

But Washington had always enjoyed success as a dreamer. Seldom do people dream on the grandiose scale that typified his vision. Even more rarely do such dreamers have the opportunity to realize even the least of their longings. In fact, almost never in history has a major leader been able to look back at the end of his life and acknowledge that virtually every grand design he had ever conceived had been realized.

But George Washington could have done just that.

Notes

The following abbreviations are used throughout in each citation of the publications, libraries, and individuals listed below.

AHR / *American Historical Review*.

DGW / Donald Jackson et al., eds. *The Diaries of George Washington*. 6 vols. Charlottesville, Va., 1976–79.

Flexner, *GW*, 1 / James T. Flexner. *George Washington: The Forge of Experience*. Boston, 1965.

Flexner, *GW*, 2 / James T. Flexner. *George Washington in the American Revolution*. Boston, 1968.

Flexner, *GW*, 3 / James T. Flexner. *George Washington and the New Nation*. Boston, 1970.

Flexner, *GW*, 4 / James T. Flexner. *George Washington: Anguish and Farewell*. Boston, 1972.

Freeman, *GW* / Douglas Southall Freeman. *George Washington: A Biography*, completed by J.A. Carroll and Mary W. Ashworth. 7 vols. New York, 1948–57.

GW / George Washington.

GWP / *George Washington Papers: Presidential Papers on Microfilm*. 124 reels. Washington, 1961.

HLQ / *Huntington Library Quarterly*.

Hamilton, *LGW* / Stanislaw Hamilton, ed. *Letters to George Washington and Accompanying Papers*. 5 vols. Boston, 1898–1902.

JCC / Worthington C. Ford et al., eds. *The Journals of the Continental Congress, 1774–1789*. 34 vols. Washington, 1904–37.

MHS / Massachusetts Historical Society.

MVL / Mount Vernon Library.

MW / Martha Washington.

NYHS / New-York Historical Society.

PC / President of Congress.

PCC-NA / Papers of the Continental Congress, National Archives.

PGW / W.W. Abbot et al., eds. *The Papers of George Washington: Colonial Series*. Charlottesville, Va., 1983–.

PMHB / *Pennsylvania Magazine of History & Biography*.

Reed LBK / Joseph Reed Letterbook, New-York Historical Society.

Reed MSS / Joseph Reed Papers, New-York Historical Society.

Reed NYPL / Joseph Reed Papers, New York Public Library.

Sparks, *WGW* / Jared Sparks, ed. *The Writings of George Washington*. 12 vols. Boston, 1834–37.

VMHB / *Virginia Magazine of History and Biography*.

WMQ / *William and Mary Quarterly*.

WW / John C. Fitzpatrick, ed. *The Writings of Washington*. 39 vols. Washington, D.C. 1931–44.

WPPV / Washington Papers Project, Alderman Library, University of Virginia.

Preface

1. Adams to Thomas Jefferson and Thomas McKean, July 30, 1815, in Lester J. Cappon, ed., *The Adams-Jefferson Letters: The Complete Correspondence Between Thomas Jefferson and Abigail and John Adams*, 2 vols. (Chapel Hill, N.C., 1959), 2:451; Adams to Benjamin Rush, Apr. 4, 1790, Benjamin Rush, *Old Family Letters* (Philadelphia, 1892), 55.

2. GW to Dr. James Craik, March 25, 1784, *WW*, 27: 371–72; GW to David Humphreys, July 25, 1785, ibid., 28:203.

3. For the complete citations of these works, as well as for an explanation of the evolving literature on Washington, see the bibliographical essay at the conclusion of this study.

I

Young George Washington

1. Freeman, *GW*, 1:15–47; John C. Fitzpatrick, *George Washington Himself: A Common Sense Biography Written from His Manuscripts* (Indianapolis, 1933), 3–18; Bernhard Knollenberg, *George Washington: The Virginia Period, 1732–1775* (Durham, N. C., 1964), 3–4.

2. Richard L. Morton, *Colonial Virginia*, 2 vols. (Chapel Hill, N.C., 1960), 2:525–26.

3. Thomas J. Wertenbaker, *Patrician and Plebian in Virginia, or the Origin and Development of the Social Classes of the Old Dominion* (New York, 1910), 111–13; Freeman, *GW*, 1:73.

4. Morton, *Colonial Virginia*, 1:207–10, 298; 2:539–42.

5. Flexner, *GW*, 1:14–15.

6. *PGW*, 1:1–4n; Jonathan Boucher, *Reminiscences of an American Loyalist, 1737–1789: Being the Autobiography of the Revd. Jonathan Boucher* (Boston, 1925), 49; Flexner, *GW*, 1:23–24; Freeman, *GW*, 1:64n.

7. Charles Moore, ed., *George Washington's Rules of Civility and Decent Behaviour in Contemporary Conversation* (Boston, 1926), 3–21. Washington was so influenced by Addison's *Cato*, that at Valley Forge he even had the play performed in order to rally the morale of his men. See: Trevor Colbourn, ed., *Fame and the Founding Fathers: Essays by Douglass Adair* (New York, 1974), 284–85n.

8. Elkanah Watson, *Men and Times of the Revolution* (New York, 1857), 43; George Washington Parke Custis, *Recollections of Washington* (New York, 1860), 131.

9. Freeman, *GW*, 1:76.

10. Ibid., 1:64–70; Douglas Edward Leach, *Arms for Empire: A Military History of the British Colonies in North America, 1607–1763* (New York, 1973), 217–19.

11. Freeman, *GW*, 1:70.

12. GW, "Biographical Memoranda" [Oct. 1783], *WW*, 29:37; Freeman, *GW*, 1:39.

13. Flexner, *GW*, 1:30; Charles C. Wall, "Notes on the Early History of Mount Vernon," *WMQ*, 3d ser., 2 (1945), 173–90.

14. Paul L. Ford, *The True George Washington* (Philadelphia, 1898), 60–75; Fitzpatrick, *GW Himself*, 40.

15. Flexner, *GW*, 1:28; Rupert Hughes, *George Washington: The Human Being and the Hero, 1732–1762*, 3 vols. (New York, 1926), 1:37–38.

16. GW, "Biog. Memo.," *WW*, 29:36; Flexner, *GW*, 1:30; Knollenberg, *GW*, 5.

17. Joseph Ball to Mary Washington, May 19, 1747, Freeman, *GW*, 1:198–99.

18. Ibid., 1:200–18.

19. *DGW*, 1:6–23.

20. Wilson M. Cary, *Sally Cary: A Long Hidden Romance of Washington's Life* (New York, 1916), 15–26.

21. Samuel E. Morison, "The Young Man Washington," in Samuel E. Morison, *By Land and By Sea: Essays and Addresses by Samuel Eliot Morison* (New York, 1953), 169; Fitzpatrick, *GW Himself*, 34; Thomas P. Abernathy, *Western Lands and the American Revolution* (New York, 1937), 25; Freeman, *GW*, 1:224, 228, 234.

22. *PGW*, 1:8–37n; GW to Richard [1749–50], ibid., 1:43–44; Abernathy, *Western Lands*, 25; *DGW*, 1:15, 19.

23. Freeman, *GW*, 1:243–44.

24. Ibid., 1:230–33, 241–42, 244, 247.

25. *DGW*, 1:43–72.

26. Ibid., 1:74–83.

27. Ibid., 1:26–29; Lawrence Washington to Col. Fairfax, n.d., in Jared Sparks, ed., *The Writings of George Washington* 12 vols. (Boston, 1834–37), 1:422; Lawrence Washington to a Friend, Apr. 6, 1752, ibid., 2:423.

28. *DGW*, 1:93–116; Freeman, *GW*, 1:256–57.

29. Freeman, *GW*, 1:260.

30. GW to Wm Fauntleroy, May 20, 1752, *WW*, 1:22; Lawrence Washington to a Friend, Apr. 6, 1752, and ND, Sparks, *Writings of GW*, 2:423.

31. Freeman, *GW*, 1:264–66.

32. Ibid., 266–70; Flexner, *GW*, 1:53.

33. *PGW*, 1:57n; Abernathy, *Western Lands*, 8; Charles Ambler, *George Washington and the West* (New York, 1936), 32–36.

34. John Alden, *Robert Dinwiddie: Servant of the Crown* (Charlottesville, Va., 1973), 1–15.

35. Hughes, *GW*, 1:37–38; Fitzpatrick, *GW Himself*, 147; Knollenberg, *GW*, 87; William S. Baker, *Early Sketches of George Washington* (Philadelphia, 1893), 13–14; Tobias Lear, *Letters and Recollections of Washington . . . With a Diary of Washington's Last Days, Kept by Mr. Lear* (New York, 1906), 137.

36. "Commission from Robert Dinwiddie" and "Instructions from Robert Dinwiddie," Oct. 30, 1753, *PGW*, 1:56–61.

37. Ibid., 1:151–54; William M. Darlington, ed., *Christopher Gist's Journal, with historical, geographical and ethnological notes* (Pittsburgh, 1893), 83; Hughes, *GW*, 1:113.

38. *DGW*, 1:154–56; Darlington, *Gist's Journal*, 84–87.

39. *DGW*, 1:161n.

40. On the early days of the Virginia Regiment, and for GW's views on Colonel Fry, see: Dinwiddie to James Patton, Jan. 1754, in Robert A. Brock, *The Official Records of Robert Dinwiddie, Lieutenant Governor of Virginia, 1751–1758*, 2 vols. (Richmond, 1883–84), 1:50–51; Dinwiddie to Lord Holdernesse, Mar. 12, 1754, ibid., 1:93–94; James R. W. Titus, "Soldiers When They Chose to Be So: Virginians at War, 1754–1763" (Ph.D. diss., Rutgers Univ., 1983), 151–85; GW to Loudoun, Jan. 10, 1757, *PGW*, 4:81–87; GW to Dinwiddie, March, 20, 1754, ibid., 1:35–36; Freeman, *GW*, 1:328–29, 337; Flexner, *GW*, 1:81.

41. Dinwiddie to GW, March 15, 1754, *PGW*, 1:75–76. On Fry's inactivity, see: ibid., 1:93n.

42. *DGW*, 1:174–83, 187–88; GW to Dinwiddie, March 9, May 18, and 29, 1754, *PGW*, 1:73–74, 99–100, 116–17; Dinwiddie to GW, March 15, and May 4, 1754, ibid., 1:75–76, 91–92.

43. GW to Fry, May 23, 1754, ibid., 1:100–101; GW to Dinwiddie, May 27, 1754, ibid., 1:104–106; Dinwiddie to GW, March 15, 1754, ibid., 1:75–76; *DGW*, 1:191–94; Freeman, *GW*, 1:366, 375.

44. GW to Dinwiddie, May 29 and June 3, 1754, *PGW*, 1:73–74, 122–25; *DGW*, 1:194–96; Gilbert Leduc, *Washington and "The Murder of Jumonville"* (Boston, 1943), 94–101; Ambler, *Washington and the West*, 64, 67; Freeman, *GW*, 1:331–33. Contemporary accounts of this clash vary. The memoir of an Indian translator who was present, as well as the account by Dinwiddie, who of course was not an eyewitness, maintained that all the French casualties occurred at the hands of the Indians; Washington and the French, however, agreed that the Virginians were primarily responsible for the French casualties. See: Worthington C. Ford, ed., *The Writings of George Washington*, 14 vols. (New York, 1889–93), 1:124n; *PGW*, 1:114–15n.

45. Dinwiddie to GW, May 25 and June 4, 1754, *PGW*, 1:102–104, 126–27; GW to Dinwiddie, May 29, 1754, ibid., 1:116–17.

46. *DGW*, 1:187n; Dinwiddie to GW, May 4, 1754, *PGW*, 1:91–92; GW to Dinwiddie, June 10 and 12, 1754, ibid., 1:129–38; GW, "Biog. Memo.," *WW*, 29:40.

47. *DGW*, 1:203–207.

48. Freeman, *GW*, 1:399–400; Ambler, *Washington and the West*, 214; "Minutes of a Council of War," June 28, 1754, *PGW*, 1:155–56, 125–26n; J. C. Harrington, "The Metamorphosis of Fort Necessity," *Western Pennsylvania Historical Magazine*, 37 (1954–55), 181–88.

49. Dinwiddie to the Lords of Trade, July 24, 1754, Dinwiddie, *Official Records*, 1:239–40; GW, "Biog. Memo.," *WW*, 29:40.

50. Dinwiddie to Lords of Trade, July 24, 1754, Dinwiddie, *Official Records*, 1:240–42; Freeman, *GW*, 1:404–409; *PGW*, 1:163, 165–68.

51. GW to Dinwiddie, June 3, 1754, *PGW*, 1:123–24; Ford, *Writings of Washington*, 1:124n.

52. *PGW*, 1:161–62n.

53. Ibid., 1:162–64n; GW, "Account. . . ." [1786], ibid., 1:172–73.

54. Dinwiddie to GW, Aug. 1 and Sept. 11, 1754, ibid., 1:180–81, 206–207; GW to Wm. Fairfax, Aug. 11, 1754, ibid., 1:183–87; Dinwiddie to Earl of Halifax, Oct. 25, 1754, *WW*, 1:160n.

55. GW to Wm. Fitzhugh, Nov. 15, 1754, *PGW*, 1:226.

56. Ibid., 1:227–35; Charles Cecil Wall, *George Washington: Citizen-Soldier* (Charlottesville, Va., 1980), 17.

2

The Frontier Warrior

1. GW to John Robinson, Oct. 23, 1754, *PGW*, 1:219; GW to Fitzhugh, Nov. 15, 1754, ibid., 1:225–26.

2. GW to Fitzhugh, Nov. 15, 1754, ibid., 1:225–26.

3. Freeman, *GW*, 2:1–7.

4. GW to Wm. Byrd, Apr. 20, 1755, *PGW*, 1:250–51; GW to Carter Burwell, Apr. 20, 1755, ibid., 1:252–53; GW to John Augustine Washington, May 14 and June 28, 1755, ibid., 1:271–72, 319–24.

5. GW to Robert Orme, Mar. 15, 1755, ibid., 1:243–45; GW to Byrd, Apr. 20, 1755, ibid., 1:250–51; GW to Burwell, Apr. 20, 1755, ibid., 1:252–53; GW to Maj. John Carlyle, May 14, 1755, ibid., 1:274; GW to J.A. Washington, May 14 and June 28, 1755, ibid., 1:277–78, 319–24; Orme to GW, Mar. 2 and Apr. 3, 1755, ibid., 1:241, 249; GW to Loudoun, Jan. 10, 1757, *WW*, 1:18. GW's letter to Carlyle, as well as his May 14 letter to his brother, were never sent.

6. Paul E. Kopperman, *Braddock at the Monongahela* (Pittsburgh, 1977), 7–8; GW to J.A. Washington, May 6, 1755, *PGW*, 1:266–67; GW to Wm. Fairfax, June 7, 1755, ibid., 1:298–300; GW, "Biog. Memo.," *WW*, 29:41–42.

7. Orme to Lt. Gov. Robt. Morris, July 18, 1755, Hamilton, *LGW*, 1:71; Oliver L. Spaulding, "The Military Studies of George Washington," *AHR*, 29 (1924), 677.

8. GW, "Poetry," 1749–50, *PGW*, 1:46–47.

9. GW to Wm. Fauntleroy, May 20, 1752, ibid., 1:49; Freeman, *GW*, 1:261–62.

10. GW to Sally Fairfax, Apr. 30, May 14, and June 7, 1755, *PGW*, 1:261, 276–77, 308; GW to Sarah Fairfax, May 14, 1755, ibid., 1:279–80; GW to J.A. Washington, June 28, 1755, ibid., 1:319–24; Fitzpatrick, *GW Himself*, 75.

11. For a more extensive analysis of Washington's attitude and behavior toward Sally Fairfax, see ch. 10.

12. GW to J.A. Washington, June 28, 1755, *PGW*, 1:321, 326n; GW, "Biog. Memo.," *WW*, 29:42; Lawrence Henry Gipson, *The British Empire Before the American Revolution*, 14 vols. (New York, 1958–68), 6:82.

13. Freeman, *GW*, 2:55, 57, 60–61, 64; GW, Memorandum [July 8–9, 1755], *PGW*, 1:331; Kopperman, *Braddock*, 13–14.

14. GW, "Biog. Memo.," *WW*, 29:42; Kopperman, *Braddock*, 18, 31.

15.   Kopperman, *Braddock*, 32–45.

16.   Ibid., 50–76, 164, 176; Stanley Pargellis, "Braddock's Defeat," *AHR*, 40 (1936), 259–62; GW to Dinwiddie, July 18, 1755, *PGW*, 1:339–40; Leach, *Arms for Empire*, 365–66.

17.   Kopperman, *Braddock*, 76–77; GW to Dinwiddie, July 18, 1755, *PGW*, 1:339–40; GW to Mary Ball Washington, July 18, 1755, ibid., 1:336. For the casualty figures, see: *PGW*, 1:337n, 342n.

18.   David Humphreys, manuscript biography of GW [1788], The Rosenbach Museum & Library, Philadelphia; Kopperman, *Braddock*, 84–92; GW, "Biog. Memo., *WW*, 29:43.

19.   GW to Dinwiddie, July 18, 1755, *PGW*, 1:339–40; GW to Mary Ball Washington, July 18, 1755, ibid., 1:336–37; GW to J.A. Washington, July 18, 1755, ibid., 1:343; GW, "Biog. Memo.," *WW*, 29:44–45; Freeman, *GW*, 2:78–81.

20.   GW to Dinwiddie, July 18, 1755, *PGW*, 1:339–40; GW, "Biog. Memo.," *WW*, 29:45. The final toll for Braddock's Anglo-American force was 976 casualties (456 killed and 520 wounded) out of a total army of 1,469. See, *PGW*, 1:338n.

21.   Wm Fairfax to GW, July 26, 1755, *PGW*, 1:345–46; Sally Fairfax, Ann Spearing, and Eliz. Dent to GW, July 26, 1755, ibid., 1:346; Flexner, *GW*, 1:133.

22.   Freeman, *GW*, 2:104–14; Dinwiddie to Col. Th. Dunbar, July 26, 1755, Dinwiddie, *Official Records*, 2:118–20; Ch. Lewis to GW, Aug. 9, 1755, *PGW*, 1:357–58; Warner Lewis to GW, Aug. 9, 1755, ibid., 1:358; GW to Warner Lewis, Aug. 14, 1755, ibid., 1:360–63.

23.   GW to J.A. Washington, Aug. 2, 1755, *PGW*, 1:351–53; GW to Mary Washington, Aug. 14, 1755, ibid., 1:359.

24.   GW, Memorandum, Oct. 8, 1755, ibid., 2:82–83; Orders, Sept. 17 and Oct. 6, 1755, ibid., 2:40, 75–76; GW to Dinwiddie, Oct. 8, 1755, ibid., 2:83–84; Stephen to GW, Oct. 4, 1755, Hamilton, *LGW*, 1:103; Norton, *Colonial Virginia*, 1:710.

25.   GW to Dinwiddie, Sept. 11, Oct. 8 and 11, 1755, *PGW*, 2:29–30, 83–84, 101–106; Orders, Sept. 19, Oct. 5, 10, and 23, 1755, ibid., 2:51–52, 75, 94, 134; Stephen to GW, Oct. 4, 1755, Hamilton, *LGW*, 1:103; Norton, *Colonial Virginia*, 2:710; Flexner, *GW*, 1:140–41.

26.   GW to Dinwiddie, Oct. 11, Dec. 5, 1755, and Jan. 14, 1756, *PGW*, 2:101–106, 200–202, 283–84; GW to Stephen, Dec. 28, 1755, ibid., 2:238–39; Robinson to GW, Dec. 16, 1755, Hamilton, *LGW*, 1:151; Dinwiddie to Shirley, Nov. 4, 1755, and Jan. 24, 1756, Dinwiddie, *Official Records*, 2:261, 330; Freeman, *GW*, 2:154.

27.   Knollenberg, *GW*, 47.

28.   Freeman, *GW*, 2:151–64; Flexner, *GW*, 1:145–47.

29.   GW to Th. Walker, Feb. 1, 1756, *PGW*, 2:312; GW to Wm. Fairfax, Apr. 23, 1755, ibid., 1:257–58; Freeman, *GW*, 2:156.

30.   Shirley to GW, Mar. 5, 1756, Hamilton, *LGW*, 1:201; Freeman, *GW*, 2:164–69; Orders, Sept. 17, 1755, *PGW*, 2:40–41.

31.   GW, "Notes of Journey to Boston," *WW*, 1:298–99; Freeman, *GW*, 2:167.

32.   GW to Dinwiddie, Apr. 16, 18, 19, 24, May 3, 23, June, 25, Aug. 4, Sept. 8, Oct. 10, and Nov. 9, 1756, *PGW*, 3:1–3, 13–15, 20, 44–46, 81–84, 171–73, 222–25, 312–18, 396–400, 430–34, 4:1–6; GW to J. Robinson, Apr. 24, Aug. 5, Nov. 9, 1756, ibid., 3:48–51, 323–31; 4:11–18; GW to Loudoun, Jan. 10, 1757, ibid.,

4:81–84, 86–87; GW to Henry Woodward, May 5, 1756, ibid., 3:96; Orders, May 1, July 6–8, Aug. 30–31, Sept. 1, 1756, ibid., 3:70, 238–39, 382–83; GW to Robt. Morris, Apr. 9, 1756, ibid., 2:345–46. On the composition of Washington's armies, see: John Ferling, "Soldiers for Virginia: Who Served in the French and Indian War?," *VMHB*, 94 (1986), 307–28.

33. GW to Dinwiddie, Apr. 7, 24, Sept. 23 and 28, 1756, ibid., 2:332–35; 3:44–46, 414–18, 420–21; Freeman, *GW*, 2:193–94, 199; Esmond Wright, *Washington and the American Revolution* (New York, 1962), 36–37.

34. GW to Dinwiddie, Feb. 2, Apr. 7, May 3, and Aug. 4, 1756, *PGW*, 2:314–15, 332–35; 3:85–86, 312–18; GW to Robinson, Apr. 16, 1756, ibid., 3:6–8; Wall, *GW*, 20–21.

35. "The Centinel No. X," *Virginia Gazette*, Sept. 3, 1756; Knollenberg, *GW*, 44–45.

36. Fairfax to GW, Apr. 26, May 20, 1756, Hamilton, *LGW*, 1:231–32, 256, 264; A. Washington to GW, Oct. 16, 1756, ibid., 1:375–77; Officers to Col. Stephen, Oct. 4, 1756, *GWP*, ser. 4, reel 30, item 546; Knollenberg, *GW*, 45–46.

37. GW to Sally Fairfax, Sept. 23, 1756, *PGW*, 3:418; GW to Dinwiddie, Nov. 24, Dec. 19, 1756, ibid., 4:29–32, 62–66; Dinwiddie to GW, Nov. 16, 24, Dec. 10 and 19, 1756, Dinwiddie, *Official Records*, 2:507, 523–24, 553, 559–60.

38. GW to Loudoun, Jan. 10, 1757, *PGW*, 4:79–90. A slightly different version of this letter can be found under the date of Jan. 28, 1757, in *WW*, 2:6–19.

39. Edward P. Hamilton, *The French and Indian Wars: The Story of Battles and Forts in the Wilderness* (New York, 1962), 185; Freeman, *GW*, 2:234; Flexner, *GW*, 1:174–75.

40. GW to Stanwix, July 15, 1757, *PGW*, 4:306–307; GW to Robinson, May 30 and July 10, 1757, ibid., 4:174–75, 287–89; GW to Dinwiddie, Sept. 17, 24, and Oct. 5, 1757, *WW*, 2:140; GW, "Remonstrances to Officers," Apr. 16[?], 1757, ibid., 2:25–27.

41. GW to Dinwiddie, Apr. 29, May 30, June 12, 27, July 12, Aug. 27, 1757, *PGW*, 4:149–50, 171–72, 203–204, 267–68, 299–300, 384–87; GW to Dinwiddie, Sept. 27 and Oct. 5, 1757, *WW*, 2:133, 141–43; Alden, *Dinwiddie*, 67–68; John Alden, *George Washington: A Biography* (Baton Rouge, La., 1984), 58. Historian Marcus Cunliffe suggested that Washington, about whom he found "something unlikeable" in these years, manifested a virtual "persecution complex." See his *George Washington: Man and Monument* (New York, 1958), 55.

42. Dinwiddie to GW, Sept. 24, 1757, Dinwiddie, *Official Records*, 2:703; GW to Dinwiddie, Aug. 27, 1757, *PGW*, 4:386–87; GW to Dinwiddie, Sept. 17, Oct. 5, 1757, *WW*, 2:133, 141–42; Knollenberg, *GW*, 53–54; Alden, *Dinwiddie*, 102–109.

43. Dinwiddie to GW, Oct. 19, 1757, Dinwiddie, *Official Records*, 2:707–708.

44. GW to Mary Washington, Sept. 30, 1757, *PGW*, 4:430; Craik to GW, Nov. 25, 1757, Hamilton, *LGW*, 2:246–47; Robt. Stewart to Dinwiddie, Nov. 9, 1757, ibid., 2:231; Freeman, *GW* 2:264, 274–75.

45. "Invoices . . . ," *WW*, 2:23; GW to Th. Knox, Jan. 1758, ibid., 2:162; Worthington C. Ford, *Washington as an Employer and Importer of Labor* (Brooklyn, 1889), 8–9; Flexner, *GW*, 1:181.

46. GW to Sally Fairfax, Nov. 15, 1757, and Feb. 13, 1758, *WW*, 37:479–80; Bernard Fay, *George Washington: Republican Aristocrat* (Boston, 1931), 131.

47. GW to John Blair, Feb. 20, 1758, *WW*, 2:164–65; GW to Richard Washington, Mar. 18, 1758, ibid., 2:168; Freeman, *GW*, 2:277–78.
48. Anne Wharton, *Martha Washington* (New York, 1897), 3–24; Eugene E. Prussing, *The Estate of George Washington, Deceased* (Boston, 1927), 96; Freeman, *GW*, 2:278–301; Knollenberg, *GW*, 26–28.
49. Freeman, *GW*, 2:301.
50. Elswyth Thane, *Potomac Squire* (New York, 1963), 37.
51. GW to Th. Gage, Apr. 12, 1758, *WW*, 2:177.
52. GW to Stanwix, Apr. 10, 1758, ibid., 2:173; GW to Sir John St. Clair, Apr. 12 and 18, 1758, ibid., 2:175, 179; GW to Gen. Forbes, June 19, 1758, ibid., 2:216.
53. Freeman, *GW*, 2:241–42, 242n.
54. GW to Gabriel Jones, July 29, 1758, *WW*, 2:249; GW to Bouquet, July 16, 1758, ibid., 2:238; Knollenberg, *GW*, 54.
55. GW to Bouquet, Apr. 2, July 25, and Aug. 2, 1758, *WW*, 2:246, 252–58; GW to Gov. Fauquier, Aug. 5, 1758, ibid., 2:261–62; GW to Mjr. Halkett, Aug. 2, 1758, ibid., 2:260; GW to Robinson, Sept. 1, 1758, ibid., 2:278; Freeman, *GW*, 2:327–29, 332, 335; Knollenberg, *GW*, 64.
56. If Washington corresponded with Martha Custis during these months, no letters have survived. Following Washington's death, Martha attempted to destroy all remnants of her correspondence with her husband; only two or three letters escaped destruction. See Freeman, *GW*, 2:405–406.
57. GW to Sally Fairfax, Sept. 12, 1758, *WW*, 2:287–89.
58. GW to Sally Fairfax, Sept. 25, 1758, ibid., 2:292–94; Wharton, *Martha Washington*, 40.
59. GW to Fauquier, Sept. 28, Oct. 30, and Nov. 5, 1758, *WW*, 2:295, 300–301; Freeman, *GW*, 2:357–59.
60. Freeman, *GW*, 2:358–59.
61. GW to Forbes, Nov. 16 and 17, 1758, *WW*, 2:302–303, 305; GW to Fauquier, Nov. 28, 1758, ibid., 2:308; Freeman, *GW*, 2:360–66.
62. GW to Fauquier, Dec. 2 and 9, 1758, *WW*, 2:312, 316; Freeman, *GW*, 2:367.
63. GW to Fauquier, Dec. 2, 1758, *WW*, 2:312–14.
64. GW to David Humphreys, July 25, 1785, ibid., 28:203.
65. Freeman, *GW*, 2:317, 383.
66. GW to J.A. Washington, May 28, 1755, *PGW*, 1:289–92.
67. Mercer to GW, Aug. 17, 1757, Hamilton, *LGW*, 2:175.
68. GW to Henry Knox, Apr. 27, 1787, *WW*, 29:209.
69. GW to Richard Washington, Aug. 10, 1760, ibid., 2:345.

3

The Acquisitive Planter

1. Daniel Blake Smith, *Inside the Great House: Planter Life in Eighteenth Century Chesepeake Society* (Ithaca, N. Y., 1980), 151–53; Charles M. Andrews, *Colonial Folkways: A Chronicle of American Life in the Reign of the Georges* (New Haven, Conn., 1919), 86–89; Julia C. Spruil, *Women's Life and Work in the Southern*

Colonies (Chapel Hill, N.C., 1938), 86–87, 94–95; Freeman, *GW*, 2:302, 3:11; George W. Nordham, *George Washington: Vignettes and Memorabilia* (Philadelphia, 1977), 31–32; George W. Nordham, *George Washington's Women: Mary, Martha, Sally, and 146 Others* (Philadelphia, 1977), 29–31.

2. GW to John Alton, Apr. 1, 1759, *WW*, 2:318–19.

3. Paul Wilstach, *Mount Vernon: Washington's Home and the Nation's Shrine* (New York, 1916), 23–24, 55–56; Flexner, *GW*, 1:195–96, 245–46; Wall, *GW*, 63–66.

4. Wilstach, *Mount Vernon*, 68–73, 125–26; Flexner, *GW*, 1:235–36; Wall, *GW*, 90–101.

5. GW to Richard Washington, Aug. 10, 1760, *WW*, 2:344; GW to Robert Cary & Co., Oct. 24, 1760, Apr. 3, 1761, Aug. 1, 1761, and Sept. 18, 1762, ibid., 2:353, 357, 363, 380; Freeman, *GW*, 2:45–46; Flexner, *GW*, 1:237. On tobacco farming in colonial Virginia, see: Melvin Herndon, *Tobacco in Colonial Virginia: "The Sovereign Remedy"* (Williamsburg, Va., 1957), 11–41; T.H. Breen, "The Culture of Agriculture: The Symbolic World of the Tidewater Planter, 1760–1790," in David D. Hall, John M. Murrin, and Thad W. Tate, eds., *Saint and Revolutionaries: Essays on Early American History* (New York, 1984), 255–61.

6. GW to Anthony Bacon & Co., Sept. 10, 1757, *WW*, 2:125; GW to R. Washington, May 7, 1759, and Aug. 10, 1760, ibid., 2:321–22, 344; GW to James Gildart, June 12, 1759, and Apr. 3, 1761, ibid., 2:326, 358; GW to Cary, Apr. 26, 1763, ibid., 2:394; Breen, "Culture of Agriculture," in *Saints and Revolutionaries*, 264–66.

7. GW to Cary, May 28, 1762, Aug., 10, 1764, and Sept. 20, 1765, *WW*, 2:378, 416, 430; Freeman, *GW*, 3:117, 152; Paul L. Haworth, *George Washington, Country Gentleman* (Indianapolis, 1925), 96–97. On the earnings of Virginia planters, and for figures on Washington's production, see: Freeman, *GW*, 3:42–44, 43n, and Thane, *Potomac Squire*, 76.

8. Freeman, *GW*, 3:116, 141, 242–43, 153, 179; Haworth, *GW*, 65, 135, 149–50; Hughes, *GW*, 2:91, 116–17; Ford, *True GW*, 112–37; Marc Egnal and Joseph A. Ernst, "An Economic Interpretation of the American Revolution," *WMQ*, 3d. ser., 29, 1972, 24–28.

9. Flexner, *GW*, 1:284; *DGW*, 1:256–58, 263, 266, 283; Hughes, *GW*, 2:91; Francis R. Bellamy, *The Private Life of George Washington* (New York, 1951), 140–43.

10. Ford, *Washington as an Employer*, 8–10; Ford, *True GW*, 138–45; Wall, *GW*, 56; Donald M. Sweig, "The Importation of African Slaves to the Potomac River, 1732–1772," *WMQ*, 3d ser., 42 (1985), 507–24.

11. GW to Daniel J. Adams, July 20, 1772, *WW*, 3:98–99; GW to Capt. Josiah Thompson, July 2, 1766, ibid., 2:437; *DGW*, 1:215, 230, 236, 266, 276, 309.

12. Wall, GW, 59–60; Charles C. Wall, "Housing and Family Life of the Mount Vernon Negro" [Oct. 1954], 7–8, ms., MVL. For later conditions at Mount Vernon, see ch. 18.

13. James Hill to GW, July 24, Aug. 30, and Dec. 13, 1772, Feb. 5, May 11, July 2 and 23, 1773, Hamilton, *LGW*, 4:136, 147, 168, 182, 200, 223, 241; Joseph Valentine to GW, Aug. 24, 1771, ibid., 4:12.

14. Ford, *Washington as an Employer*, 10, 25; *DGW*, 1:252, 276, 296; 2:37, 77, 164–65; Freeman, *GW*, 3:88, 179, 186, 243.

15. Hughes, *GW*, 2:116–17; Freeman, *GW*, 3:345, 348.

16. For lengthy treatments of Britain's muddled western policy, see: Francis S. Philbrick, *The Rise of the West, 1754–1830* (New York, 1965), 1–52; Jack M. Sosin, *The Revolutionary Frontier, 1763–1783* (Albuquerque, N.M., 1967), 20–38; Ambler, *GW and the West*, 132–51; Abernathy, *Western Lands*, 14–97. For the statements by GW quoted in this section, see: GW to John Posey, June 24, 1767, *WW*, 2:458–59; GW to Crawford, Sept. 21, 1767, ibid., 2:468–70; GW to Gov. Botetourt, Apr. 15, 1770, ibid., 3:9–12; GW to James Wood, Mar. 13 and 30, 1773, ibid., 3:125, 127–29; *DGW*, 2:133, 3:37.

17. *DGW*, 1:319–26; 2:102n; Freeman, *GW*, 3:94, 101–103, 162–63, 175, 208.

18. Ambler, *GW and the West*, 137–40; GW to Botetourt, Dec. 8, 1769, *WW*, 2:528–32; Freeman, *GW*, 3:238–40.

19. *DGW*, 2:289–90, 292–324, 328.

20. GW to Robt. Stobo, Nov. 22, 1771, *WW*, 3:73–74; GW to Robt. Adam, Nov. 22, 1771, ibid., 3:75–77; GW to Ch. Washington, Jan. 31, 1770, ibid., 3:2; GW to Ch. Thruston, Mar. 12, 1773, ibid., 3:124; *DGW*, 3:12, 138, 144; Crawford to GW, Nov. 12, 1773, Hamilton, *LGW*, 4:275; Knollenberg, *GW*, 91–93.

21. GW to George Muse, Jan. 29, 1774, *WW*, 3:179–80.

22. Knollenberg, *GW*, 96–100. Washington had purchased about one-half of his property. The remainder he acquired through inheritance, marriage, or grant; the grant in this case was a 5000-acre tract he received under the Proclamation of 1763 as a former officer.

23. For a sampling of his orders to just one company, see: GW to Cary & Co., June 12 and Sept. 20, 1759, Oct. 12, 1761, Feb. 13, 1764, July 20, 1767, June 6, 1768, July 25, 1769, July 15 and Aug. 12, 1771, July 10, Oct. 6, and Nov. 10, 1773, *WW*, 2:323, 330–36, 369–70, 413–14, 462–64, 488–89, 514; 3:62–63, 94, 141, 155, 165.

24. Thane, *Potomac Squire*, 47; GW to Cary & Co., Aug. 10, 1760, Aug. 1, 1761, Sept. 18, 1762, July 20, 1771, *WW*, 2:333–34, 348–49, 363, 382; 3:56; GW to Maudit & Co., July 20, 1771, ibid., 3:55.

25. For the above three paragraphs see: *DGW*, 1:238; 2:32, 38–39, 67, 73, 91, 120, 139, 148, 154, 157, 203, 209, 219; Paul L. Ford, *Washington and the Theater* (New York, 1899), 20–21; Fitzpatrick, *GW Himself*, 459; GW to Ch. Green, Aug. 26, 1761, *WW*, 2:365; Flexner, *GW*, 1:239.

26. Flexner, *GW*, 1:240.

27. On Washington's religious views and practices, see: Paul F. Boller, *George Washington and Religion* (Dallas, 1963), 26–30, 75–76, 90–112; GW to Bassett, Aug. 28, 1762, in Flexner, *GW*, 1:237.

28. Freeman, *GW*, 3:280–81, 297, 336, 346n, 407n, 595–98; GW to Hugh Mercer, Mar. 28, 1774, *WW*, 3:198–99; GW to Benj. Harrison, Mar. 21, 1781, ibid., 21:341; *DGW*, 3:52–53.

29. *DGW*, 1:256.

30. GW to Bassett, Feb. 15, 1773, *WW*, 3:115; *DGW*, 1:245–46n.

31. *DGW*, 1:245.

32. Ibid., 3:192–93; Freeman, *GW*, 3:306; GW to Fairfax, Feb. 27, 1785, *WW*, 28:83; GW to Sally Fairfax, May 16, 1798, ibid., 36:262–64.

33. GW to Rich. Washington, Sept. 20, 1759, *WW*, 2:357; GW to Elizabeth Parke Custis, Sept. 14, 1794, ibid., 33:501.

34. GW to Cary, Oct. 12, 1761, *WW*, 2:368; GW to C. and O. Hanbury, July 25, 1769, ibid., 2:515–17; GW to Boucher, May 30, 1768, May 13 and Dec. 16, 1770, June 5 and July 9, 1771, ibid., 2:487; 3:14, 35, 45, 51; Boucher to GW, May 9 and 21, and Dec. 18, 1770, May 9 and July 4, 1771, Hamilton, *LGW*, 4:18, 24, 42, 62, 69, 84.

35. Boucher to GW, Jan. 19, 1773, Hamilton, *LGW*, 4:175–76; GW to Boucher, Jan. 7, 1773, *WW*, 37:497; GW to Bassett, Apr. 25, 1773, ibid., 3:134; GW to Benedict Calvert, Apr. 3, 1773, ibid., 3:129–31; GW to Myles Cooper, Dec. 15, 1773, ibid., 3:167–68; *DGW*, 3:181–82.

36. *DGW*, 2:31, 45, 47, 54, 68, 76, 108, 120, 122–23, 128, 141, 168, 177, 195, 197, 201, 209, 257, 272; 3:1, 2, 7, 9, 71, 114.

37. Ibid., 3:188.

38. GW to Bassett, June 20, 1773, *WW*, 3:138; *DGW*, 3:188–205.

39. *DGW*, 3:205; GW to Cary, Nov. 10, 1773, *WW*, 3:164–65.

40. *DGW*, 1:211; 3:62; GW to R. Washington, Oct. 20, 1761, *WW*, 2:371.

41. Tobias Lear, *Letters and Recollections of George Washington, Being Letters to Tobias Lear . . . With a diary of Washington's last days kept by Mr. Lear* (New York, 1906), 136–37; Flexner, *GW*, 1:80n; Alden, *GW*, 11n. On the height of the Virginia soldiers, see: *PGW*, ser. 4, reels 29–30, or Ferling, "Soldiers for Virginia," *VMHB*, 94:312–13.

42. Ford, *True GW*, 45, 57; Fitzpatrick, *GW Himself*, 73; Baker, *Early Sketches*, 77; Custis, *Recollections*, 171, 480–85; Garry Wills, *Cincinnatus: George Washington and the Enlightenment* (New York, 1984), 235.

43. Ford, *True GW*, 45; Baker, *Early Sketches*, 25–27; Bellamy, *Private Life of GW*, 53.

44. DGW, 3:205; *Pennsylvania Journal*, Sept. 27, 1773.

45. *DGW*, 3:208–20.

4

Patrician Revolutionary

1. Benjamin W. Labaree, *The Boston Tea Party* (New York, 1964), 170–93; William Cobbett, ed., *The Parliamentary History of England, From the Norman Conquest, in 1066, to the Year, 1803 . . .* , 39 vols. (London, 1806–20), 17:1167–70, 1184–85, 1195–1340; Jack M. Sosin, "The Massachusetts Acts of 1774: Coercive or Preventive," *Huntington Library Quarterly*, 26 (1963), 235–52.

2. *DGW*, 3:250, 253.

3. Knollenberg, *GW*, 100–06.

4. Carl Van Doren, *Benjamin Franklin* (New York, 1938), 529.

5. Knollenberg, *GW*, 103–106. The flavor of a normal session of the House of Burgesses can be gathered by perusing the body's official journals. See, H. R. McIlwaine and John Pendleton, eds., *Journals of the House of Burgesses of Virginia*, 13 vols. (Richmond, 1905–15); volumes 9–13 span GW's service.

6. Knollenberg, *GW*, 101–102.

7. Jack P. Greene, "An Uneasy Connection: An Analysis of the Preconditions of the American Revolution," in Stephen G. Kurtz and James H. Hutson, eds., *Essays on*

the American Revolution (Chapel Hill, N.C., 1973), 32–80; Jack P. Greene, " 'A Posture of Hostility': A Reconsideration of Some Aspects of the Origins of the American Revolution," American Antiquarian Society *Proceedings*, 87 (1977), 27–68; Merrill Jensen, *The Founding of a Nation: A History of the American Revolution, 1763–1776* (New York, 1968), 36–69.

8. Edmund S. and Helen M. Morgan, *The Stamp Act Crisis: Prologue to Revolution* (Chapel Hill, N.C., 1953), 53–70.

9. *DGW*, 1:388; Morgan and Morgan, *Stamp Act Crisis*, 36–39, 88–98.

10. GW to Francis Dandridge, Sept. 20, 1765, *WW*, 2:425–26; GW to Cary, Sept. 20, 1765, ibid., 2:431.

11. GW to Dandridge, Sept. 20, 1765, ibid., 2:425–26; *DGW*, 1:338–40; Morgan and Morgan, *Stamp Act Crisis*, 261–81.

12. Jensen, *Founding of a Nation*, 239–52; McIlwaine and Pendleton, *Jrnls., Burgesses of Va., 1766–1769*, 170–71; *DGW*, 2:46–47, 51–53.

13. *DGW*, 2:58–59, 70, 100–103, 133.

14. GW to Mason, Apr. 5, 1769, *WW*, 2:500–504.

15. *DGW*, 2:153n; Helen Hill Miller, *George Mason: Gentleman Revolutionary* (Chapel Hill, N.C., 1973), 25–43, 94; Kate Mason Rowland, *The Life of George Mason, 1725–1792*, 2 vols. (New York, 1964), 1:123–38.

16. Baker, *Early Sketches*, 32. A very different perception of Washington's position may be found in Rhys Isaac, *The Transformation of Virginia* (Chapel Hill, N.C., 1982), 251. Isaac sees GW's call for a boycott as ritualistic, a move to "affirm the 'virtue' " of Virginia, a palliative "to nagging doubts about the moral soundness of Virginia society."

17. Works that touch on the economic motives of the planters include: Marc Egnal and Joseph Ernst, "An Economic Interpretation of the American Revolution," *WMQ*, 3d. ser., 21 (1972), 3–23; Joseph Ernst, *Money and Politics in America, 1755–1775* (Chapel Hill, N.C., 1973), 174–96; Merrill Jensen, *The American Revolution Within America* (New York, 1974), 24–38; Emory Evans, "Planter Indebtedness and the Coming of the Revolution in Virginia," *WMQ*, 3d ser., 19 (1962), 511–33; Isaac S. Harrell, *Loyalism in Virginia: Chapters in the Economic History of the Revolution* (Durham, N.C., 1926), 5–35; Louis M. Hacker, "The American Revolution: Economic Aspects," *Marxist Quarterly*, 1 (1937), 46–67. See also n. 24 below.

18. McIlwaine and Pendleton, *Jrnls., Burgesses of Va., 1766–1769*, 216–18; *DGW*, 2:143, 146–53; Jensen, *Founding of a Nation*, 301–305.

19. Jensen, *Founding of a Nation*, 314–33; Pauline Maier, *From Resistance to Revolution: Radicals and the Development of Opposition to Britain, 1765–1776* (New York, 1972), 161–91; Ian Christie and Benjamin W. Labaree, *Empire or Independence, 1760–1776; A British-American Dialogue on the Coming of the American Revolution* (New York, 1976), 119–30, 144–50.

20. Jensen, *Founding of a Nation*, 354–72; GW to Cary, July 25, 1769, *WW*, 2:512–14; GW to Hanbury, July 25, 1769, ibid., 2:515–17.

21. GW to Th. Johnson, July 20, 1770, *WW*, 3:19; GW to Cary, Aug. 20, 1770, and July 20, 1771, ibid., 3:22–23, 56; GW to Crawford, Nov. 24, 1770[?] and Sept. 25, 1773, ibid., 3: 31, 149; GW to Craven Peyton, Feb. 23, 1773, ibid., 3:116, 116n; GW to Earl Duncan, Apr. 13, 1773, ibid., 3:132; Grace L. Nute, "Washington and

the Potomac," *AHR*, 28 (1923), 497–519, 705–22; Ambler, *GW and the West*, 154, 147.

22. Labaree, *Boston Tea Party*, 3–57; Arthur M. Schlesinger, *The Colonial Merchants and the American Revolution, 1763–1776* (New York, 1918), 240–98.

23. Freeman, *GW*, 3:345; GW to Henry Riddell, March 1 and 5, 1774, *WW*, 3:193–96; *DGW*, 3:220–46, 248–49.

24. On the complexities of Revolutionary Virginia, see: Jack P. Greene, "Society, Ideology and Politics: An Analysis of the Political Culture of Mid-Eighteenth-Century Virginia," in Richard M. Jellison, ed., *Society, Freedom, and Conscience: The American Revolution in Virginia, Massachusetts, and New York* (New York, 1976), 65–68; Isaac, *Transformation of Virginia*, 39, 131–38; Thad W. Tate, "The Coming of the Revolution in Virginia: Britain's Challenge to Virginia's Ruling Class, 1763–1776," *WMQ*, 3d. ser., 19 (1962), 324–43; Joseph Albert Ernst, "Genesis of the Currency Act of 1764: Virginia Paper Money and the Partition of British Investments," *WMQ*, 3d. ser., 22 (1965), 33–74; Marc Egnal, "The Origins of the Revolution in Virginia: A Reinterpretation," *WMQ*, 3d. ser., 37 (1980), 401–28; Evans, "Planter Indebtedness," *WMQ*, 19:511–33.

25. McIlwaine and Pendleton, *Jrnls., Burgesses of Va., 1773–1776*, 124; Freeman, *GW*, 3:350–53; *DGW*, 3:153, 250–51.

26. *DGW*, 2:252; McIlwaine and Pendleton, *Jrnls., Burgesses of Va., 1773–1776*, 139–40.

27. GW to Geo. Wm. Fairfax, June 10, 1774, *WW*, 2:224; GW to Bryan Fairfax, July 4 and 20, 1774, ibid., 2:228, 232–34.

28. *DGW*, 3:255–66; Freeman, *GW*, 3:360–66. For a discussion of the authorship of the Fairfax Resolves, see: Donald M. Sweig, "A New-Found Washington Letter of 1774 and the Fairfax Resolves," *WMQ*, 3d. ser., 40 (1983), 283–91.

29. *DGW*, 3:266–69; Freeman, *GW*, 3:367–72.

30. GW to Geo. Wm. Fairfax, June 10, 1774, *WW*, 3:221; *DGW*, 3:269–70; Freeman, *GW*, 3:370–71.

31. GW to Th. Johnson, Aug. 5, 1774, *WW*, 3:235.

32. Quoted in James T. Flexner, *Washington: The Indispensable Man* (Boston, 1969), 47.

33. GW to Bushrod Washington, Jan. 15, 1783, *WW*, 26:39.

34. GW to Mason, Apr. 5, 1769, ibid., 2:500–501; GW to Reed, Jan. 31, 1776, ibid., 4:297; GW to John Augustine Washington, May 31, 1776, ibid., 5:92.

35. *DGW*, 3:271–72; William Wirt Henry, *Patrick Henry: Life, Correspondence and Speeches*, 3 vols. (New York, 1891), 1:213; Garry Wills, *Inventing America: Jefferson's Declaration of Independence* (New York, 1978), 3, 6.

36. *DGW*, 3:272–74.

37. Silas Deane to Eliz. Deane, Sept. 10–11, 1774, in Paul H. Smith, ed., *Letters of Delegates to Congress, 1774–1785* (Washington, 1976–), 1:61–62; L. H. Butterfield, ed., *The Diary and Autobiography of John Adams*, 4 vols. (Cambridge, 1961), 2:117.

38. Carl and Jessica Bridenbaugh, *Rebels and Gentlemen: Philadelphia in the Age of Franklin* (New York, 1942), 1–28, 179–224.

39. Ibid., 1–28; Charles Oltan, *Artisans for Independence: Philadelphia Mechanics and the American Revolution* (Syracuse, N.Y., 1971), 1–32; Gary B. Nash, *The Urban*

Crucible: Social Change, Political Consciousness, and the Origins of the American Revolution (Cambridge, Mass., 1979), 319–25.

40.   Sam Bass Warner, *The Private City: Philadelphia in the Three Periods of Its Growth* (Philadelphia, 1968), 3–21; Billy Smith, "The Material Lives of Laboring Philadelphians, 1750–1800," *WMQ*, 3d. ser., 38 (1981), 163–202.

41.   *DGW.* 3:280; Butterfield, *Adams Diary and Autobiog.*, 2:115–17; William H. Williams, "The 'Industrious Poor' and the Founding of the Pennsylvania Hospital," *PMHB*, 97 (1973), 431–43; Gary B. Nash, "Poverty and Poor Relief in Pre-Revolutionary Philadelphia," *WMQ*, 3d. ser., 33 (1976), 3–30.

42.   *DGW*, 3:276–80.

43.   Ibid., 3:284; John P. Roche, *Joseph Reed: A Moderate in the American Revolution* (New York, 1957), 3–48; Richard A. Ryerson, *The Revolution is Now Begun: The Radical Committees of Philadelphia, 1765–1775* (Philadelphia, 1978), 83–84; Reed to Earl of Dartmouth, Sept. 25 and Nov. 6, 1774, in William B. Reed, *The Life and Correspondence of Joseph Reed*, 2 vols. (Philadelphia, 1847), 1:76–80, 82–83.

44.   For a good summary and analysis of the First Continental Congress, see: David Ammerman, *In the Common Cause: American Response to the Coercive Acts of 1774* (New York, 1974), 35–87.

45.   *DGW*, 3:288–302.

46.   Ibid., 3:290.

47.   Ibid., 3:298, 302; John Alden, *General Charles Lee: Traitor or Patriot?* (Baton Rouge, La., 1951), 1–65.

48.   *DGW*, 3:303–21; Freeman, *GW*, 3:403–406.

49.   GW to John Connally, Feb. 25, 1775, *WW*, 3:268; *DGW*, 3:304.

50.   Ambler, *GW and the West*, 152–58.

51.   GW to Dunmore, Apr. 3, 1775, *WW*, 3:280–83; Dunmore to GW, Apr. 18, 1775, Hamilton, *LGW*, 5:158.

52.   GW to Mercer, Apr. 5, 1775, *WW*, 3:288; *DGW*, 3:321–25.

53.   Mercer to GW, Apr. 26, 1775, Hamilton, *LGW*, 5:162–63; Freeman, *GW*, 3:410–15.

54.   *DGW*, 3:319–23, 325–27; Wall, *GW*, 49–53.

55.   *DGW*, 3:325, 332.

56.   Curtis P. Nettles, *George Washington and American Independence* (Boston, 1951), 158–59.

5

Commander of America's Army

1.   Adams to Wm. Tudor, Sept. 29, 1774, Smith, *Letters of Delegates*, 1:130; Adams to Abigail Adams, Apr. 30 and May 1, 1775, L.H. Butterfield et al., ed., *Adams Family Correspondence*, 4 vols. (Cambridge, Mass., 1963–73), 1:189, 191–92.

2.   Butterfield, *Adams Diary and Autobiog.*, 3:315–16; Jensen, *Founding of a Nation*, 602–13, 616–20.

3.   *JCC*, 2:53, 67.

4.   Ibid., 2:59–60, 86–86.

5.   Adams to Abigail Adams, May 29, 1775, Butterfield, *Adams Fam. Corres.*, 1:207;

Deane to Eliz. Deane, May 12, 1775, Smith, *Letters of Delegates*, 1:347; Butterfield, *Adams Diary and Autobiog.*, 3:322.

6. Diary of Silas Deane, Smith, *Letters of Delegates*, 1:482; Butterfield, *Adams Diary and Autobiog.*, 3:322–23.

7. Butterfield, *Adams Diary and Autobiog.*, 3:323; *Jrnls. Cont. Cong.*, 2:89–90.

8. Deane to Eliz. Deane, June 16, 1775, Smith, *Letters of Delegates*, 1:494; Deane to Jos. Trumbull, June 18, 1775, ibid., 1:506–503; Dyer to Jon. Trumbull, Sr., June 16 and 17, 1775, ibid., 1:496, 499; Adams to Elbridge Gerry, June 18, 1775, ibid., 1:503; John Hancock to Gerry, June 18, 1775, ibid., 1:506–507; Adams to Abigail Adams, June 17, 1775, Butterfield, *Adams Fam. Corres.*, 1:215.

9. *DGW*, 3:336, 339; George W. Corner, ed., *The Autobiography of Benjamin Rush. His "Travels Through Life" together with his Commonplace Book for 1789–1813* (Princeton, N.J., 1948), 113.

10. *DGW*, 3:336, 339; Freeman, *GW*, 3:437–45.

11. *Jrnls. Cont. Cong.*, 2:92, 96.

12. Ibid., 2:93–94.

13. Adams to Elbridge Gerry, June 18, 1775, Smith, *Letters of Delegates*, 1:503; Adams to Josiah Quincy, July 29, 1775, ibid., 1:667.

14. *Jrnls. Cont. Cong.*, 2:94–103. For sketches of many of the general officers, see: George A. Billias, ed., *George Washington's Generals* (New York, 1964).

15. GW to MW, June 18, 1775, *WW*, 3:293–95; Deane to Eliz. Deane, June 16, 1775, Smith, *Letters of Delegates*, 1:494.

16. GW to Jack P. Custis, June 19, 1775, *WW*, 3:299–300; GW to John A. Washington, June 20, 1775, ibid., 3:299; GW to MW, June 23, 1775, ibid., 3:301.

17. GW to Burwell, June 19, 1775, ibid., 3:297.

18. *Jrnls. Cont. Cong.*, 2:100–03.

19. Kenneth R. Rossman, *Thomas Mifflin and the Politics of the American Revolution* (Chapel Hill, N.C., 1952), 40, 43–44; Ch. Pettit to Reed, June 22, 1775, Reed Mss., 2:16; Daniel Cox to Reed, ibid., 2:21.

20. On Howes see: Ira Gruber, *The Howe Brothers and the American Revolution* (New York, 1972); Maldwyn A. Jones, "Sir William Howe: Conventional Strategist," George A. Billias, ed., *George Washington's Opponents: British Generals and Admirals in the American Revolution* (New York, 1969), 37–72; Troyer Steele Anderson, *The Command of the Howe-Brothers During the American Revolution* (New York, 1936). On Bunker Hill, see: John Alden, *General Gage in America* (Baton Rouge, La., 1948), 251–71; Don Higginbotham, *The War of American Independence: Military Attitudes, Policies and Practices* (New York, 1971), 68–77.

21. Adams to Abigail Adams, June 23, 1775, Butterfield, *Adams Family Corres.*, 1:226; Freeman, *GW*, 3:458–59; Flexner, *GW*, 2:23.

22. Freeman, *GW*, 3:460–76; William S. Baker, *Itinerary of General Washington, from June 15, 1775, to December 23, 1783* (Lambertsville, N.J., 1892), 1–9; *Jrnls. Cont. Cong.*, 2:109–10; GW to PC, June 25, 1775, *WW*, 3:301–02; GW to Schuyler, June 25, 1775, ibid., 3:302–04; GW to N. Y. Legislature, June 26, 1775, ibid., 3:305; Bush, *Revolutionary Enigma*, 24–27.

23. Mabel Ives, *Washington's Headquarters* (Upper Montclair, N.J., 1932), 13–40; Flexner, *GW*, 2:60–62.

24. Gen. Orders, July 3, 4, and 5, 1775, *WW*, 3:305–06, 308–12; GW to Mass. Leg.,

July 10, 1775, ibid., 3:319; GW to PC, July 10, 1775, ibid., 3:320–29; Abigail Adams to John Adams, July 16, 1775, Butterfield, *Adams Fam. Corres.*, 1:246–47; Peter Force, comp., *American Archives . . .* , 4th Ser., 2:1630; Freeman, *GW*, 3:493; "The Journal of Dr. Belknap," MHS, *Colls.*, 4 (1858), 83.

25. GW to PC, July 10, 1775, *WW*, 3:322–26; Freeman, *GW*, 3:509.

26. GW to R.H. Lee, July 10, 1775, *WW*, 3:330; GW to PC, July 10, 1775, ibid., 3:326–27; Philip S. Foner, *Blacks in the American Revolution* (Westport, Conn., 1975), 42–44; Benjamin Quarles, *The Negro in the American Revolution* (Chapel Hill, N.C., 1961), 15–17; Walter H. Mazyck, *George Washington and the Negro* (Washington, D.C., 1932), 37–43.

27. Gen. Orders, July 4, 5, 6, 7, 10, 11, 14, 16, 18, Aug. 11 and 18, 1775, *WW*, 3:309, 312–17, 333–34, 338, 341, 346, 414, 429; GW to R.H. Lee, July 10 and Aug. 29, 1775, ibid., 3:331, 450; GW to Lund Washington, Aug. 20, 1775, ibid., 3:432; GW to Mass. Leg., Aug. 7, 1775, ibid., 3:408; Joseph Reed to Esther Reed, Oct. 11, 1776, in William B. Reed, *The Life and Correspondence of Joseph Reed*, 2 vols. (Philadelphia, 1847), 1:243.

28. Gen. Orders July 7, 14, 15, 23, Sept. 6, 1775, *WW*, 3:314, 338, 340, 357, 475; GW to Col. Wm. Woodford, Nov. 10, 1775, ibid., 4:80.

29. GW to PC, July 10 and 20, 1775, ibid., 3:324, 349, 351; GW to Lewis Morris, Aug. 4, 1775, ibid., 3:400; GW to Jos. Palmer, Aug. 7, 1775, ibid., 3:405; GW to R.H. Lee, Aug. 29, 1775, ibid., 3:451; Gen. Orders, Aug. 15, 1775, ibid., 3:425; Jonathan Rossie, *The Politics of Command in the American Revolution* (Syracuse, N.Y., 1975), 27–30, 61–62, 64.

30. GW to PC, July 20, 27, and Aug. 4, 1775, *WW*, 3:347, 369, 393; GW to John A. Washington, July 27, 1775, ibid., 3:372; GW to R.H. Lee, Aug. 29, 1775, ibid., 3:450; Freeman, *GW*, 3:505–507, 516–18.

31. GW to PC, Aug. 4, 1775, *WW*, 3:393; Gen. Orders, July 26, Aug. 9 and 15, 1775, ibid., 3:366, 410, 425; Freeman, *GW*, 3:529.

32. GW to Lund Washington, Aug. 20, 1775, *WW*, 3:435.

33. GW to Schuyler, July 28 and Aug. 20, 1775, *WW*, 3:373–74, 424; Rossie, *Politics of Command*, 33–44; Bush, *Revolutionary Enigma*, 24–40; Benson Lossing, *The Life and Times of Philip Schuyler*, 2 vols. (New York, 1860–73), 1:330–66.

34. GW to Schuyler, Aug. 20, 1775, *WW*, 3:436–37; Freeman, *GW*, 3:532–37.

35. Rossie, *Politics of Command*, 42–43.

36. Freeman, *GW*, 3:535–36.

37. Willard M. Wallace, *Traitorous Hero: The Life and Fortunes of Benedict Arnold* (Freeport, N.Y., 1954), 5–54.

38. GW to Schuyler, Sept. 8, 1775, *WW*, 3:485–86; GW to Arnold, Sept. 14, 1775, and GW's Instructions to Arnold, ibid., 3:491–96; Gen. Orders, Sept. 5, 1775, ibid., 3:473; Wallace, *Treacherous Hero*, 55–61; Rossie, *Politics of Command*, 38–39.

39. Gen. Orders, Aug. 4, 1775, *WW*, 3:384–85; Freeman, *GW*, 3:523–25; Higginbotham, *War of American Independence*, 102–103; Smith, *A New Age*, 1:573; John Sellers, "The Virginia Continental Line, 1775–1780," (-Ph.d. diss. Tulane Univ., 1968), 13; "The Revolutionary War Journal of Aaron Wright, 1775," *Historical Magazine*, 6 (1862), 209–210.

40. GW to General Officers, Sept. 8, 1775, *WW*, 3:483–85; GW to PC, Sept. 21, 1775, ibid., 3:511; Freeman, *GW*, 3:539–41; Reed to Th. Bradford, Sept. 14, 1775, Reed

Mss., 2:126; Reed to [?], Sept. 29, 1775, Reed Lbk; Dave Richard Palmer, *The Way of the Fox: American Strategy in the War for Independence* (Westport, Conn., 1975), 101.

41. Lee to Benj. Rush, Sept. 19, 1775, *The Lee Papers* [1754–1811], NYHS, *Collections*, 4 vols. (New York, 1872–75), 1:206; Eric Robson, *The American Revolution: In Its Political and Military Aspects, 1763–1783* (New York, 1966), 161.
42. Reed to Esther Reed, July 26, 1775, Reed Mss., 2:20.
43. Diary of Samuel Ward, Sept. 13, 1775, Smith, *Letters of Delegates*, 2:10; GW to PC, Sept. 21, 1775, *WW*, 3:505–13.
44. R.H. Lee to GW, Aug. 1, 1775, Smith, *Letters of Delegates*, 1:692; Report of Committee on Powder, ibid., 2:181; Freeman, *GW*, 3:515; GW to Jos. Palmer, Aug. 22, 1775, *WW*, 3:442; GW to Gov. Nicholas Cooke, Aug. 9, 1775, ibid., 3:386–87.
45. PC to GW, Sept. 19, 30, and Oct. 3, 1775, Smith, *Letters of Delegates*, 2:31, 82, 105; Eliphalet Dyer to Jos. Trumbull, Sept. 15, 1775, ibid., 2:14; Diary of Samuel Ward, Oct. 3, 1775, ibid., 2:106; Diary of Richard Smith, Sept. 13, 1775, ibid., 2:8; Ward to GW, Sept. 17, 1775, ibid., 2:27; Butterfield, *Adams Diary and Autobiog.*, 2:181.
46. Adams to Warren, Oct. 13, 1775, Smith, *Letters of Delegates*, 2:178; *Jrnls. Cont. Cong.*, 3:270–71; Freeman, *GW*, 3:555–56.
47. Conf. Minutes, Oct. 23–24, 1775, Smith, *Letters of Delegates*, 2:233–38.
48. *Jrnls. Cont. Cong.*, 3:320–27.
49. Franklin to David Hartley [?], Oct. 3, 1775, Smith, *Letters of Delegates*, 2:103; Butterfield, *Adams Diary and Autobiog.*, 3:354–56, 2:186–217; Jensen, *Founding of Nation*, 617–18, 632–45.
50. *Jrnls. Cont. Cong.* 3:314–15; Nathan Miller, *Sea of Glory: The Continental Navy Fights for Independence, 1775–1783* (New York, 1974), 39–69; Gardner W. Allen, *A Naval History of the American Revolution*, 2 vols. (New York, 1913), 1:58–89; Christopher Ward, *The War of the Revolution*, 2 vols. (New York, 1952), 1:114.
51. GW to Shuyler, Oct. 4, 1775, *WW*, 4:405; Adams to Warren, June 10, 1775, Robert Taylor et al., eds., *Papers of John Adams* (Cambridge, Mass., 1977–), 3:22.
52. Reed to Pettit, Aug. 7, 1775, Reed Mss., 1:116; GW to Schuyler, Oct. 4, 1775, *WW*, 4:405; Nettles, *GW and Independence*, 151–91.
53. GW to PC, Nov. 8 and 11, 1775, *WW*, 4:73–74, 82–83; Nettles, *GW and Independence*, 142–43.
54. Charles Royster, *A Revolutionary People at War: The Continental Army and the American Character, 1775–1783* (Chapel Hill, N.C., 1979), 25–53, 61–69.
55. Gruber, *Howe Brothers*, 41–43, 62–63, 82–83; Anderson, *Command of the Howe Brothers*, 82, 85–104.
56. GW to Ward, Nov. 17, 1775, *WW*, 4:96; GW to John A. Washington, Oct. 13, 1775, ibid., 4:26; GW to PC, Dec. 14, 1775, ibid., 4:162.
57. GW to Gov. Cooke, Dec. 5, 1775, ibid., 4:146; GW to PC, Dec. 4 and 11, 1775, ibid., 4:142, 156; Freeman, *GW*, 3:569–80; Gen. Lee to Rush, Dec. 12, 1775, *Lee Papers*, 1:226.
58. GW to PC, Dec. 4, 11, 18, and 25, 1775, *WW*, 4:143, 156, 173, 183; GW to Reed, Dec. 5, 1775, and Jan. 4, 1776, ibid., 4:166, 211; Higginbotham, *War of American Independence*, 390.

59.   GW to Gov. Trumbull, Dec. 2, 1775, *WW*, 4:137; GW to PC, Dec. 4, 1775, ibid., 4:142; GW to Reed, Nov. 28, 1775, ibid., 4:124; Higginbotham, *War of American Independence*, 104; Thayer, *Greene*, 75–77; Rossie, *Politics of Command*, 65–66.

60.   GW to Reed, Nov. 28, 1775, *WW*, 4:125; GW to Schuyler, Dec. 5, 1775, ibid., 4:148.

61.   Thayer, *Greene*, 73; MW to Betty Ramsey, Dec. 30, 1775, MVL; Nordham, *GW's Women*, 35.

62.   GW to Mass. Leg., Nov. 2, 1775, *WW*, 4:60; GW to PC, Nov. 19, 1775, ibid., 4:101; Gen. Orders, Nov. 19 and 22, 1775, ibid., 4:102, 109; Freeman, *GW*, 3:582–83.

63.   Philip Cash, *Medical Men in the Siege of Boston, April 1775 to April 1776* (Philadelphia, 1973), 68–81, 91–92, 105–112; "Diary of Ezekial Price, 1775–1776," MHS, *Colls.*, 6 (1863), 209–26; "The Journal of James Stevens of Andover, Massachusetts," *Historical Collections of the Essex Institute*, 48 (1912), 58, 62.

64.   GW to Reed, Nov. 27 and Dec. 15, 1775, *WW*, 4:118, 168; GW to PC, Dec. 14, 1775, ibid., 4:162.

65.   William F. Norwood, "Medicine in the Era of the American Revolution," *International Record of Medicine* (1958), 391–407; Whitfield Bell, "Medical Practice in Colonial America," *Bulletin of the History of Medicine*, 31 (1957), 442–53.

66.   GW to PC, Dec. 31, 1775, *WW*, 4:196.

67.   Rossie, *Politics of Command*, 43–44, 50–56; Wallace, *Treacherous Hero*, 60–86; Kenneth Roberts, *March to Quebec* (New York, 1940), 201–206.

68.   GW to Reed, Jan. 4, 1776, *WW*, 4:211–12.

6

At the Brink

1.   Lee to Langdon Cater, Jan. 22, 1776, Smith, *Letters of Delegates*, 3:130.

2.   Ward, *War of the Revolution*, 1:134; Robert L. Scribner and Brent Tarter, eds., *Revolutionary Virginia: The Road to Independence* (Charlottesville, Va., 1979–), 5:14–18; GW to PC, Jan. 4, 1776, *WW*, 4:209–10; GW to Reed, Jan. 4, 1776, ibid., 4:210.

3.   GW to Reed, Jan. 31, 1776, *WW*, 4:297; GW to PC, Jan. 4 and 14, 1776, ibid., 4:208–209, 238; GW to Gov. Trumbull, Jan. 7, 1776, ibid., 4:218; GW to Gen. Sullivan, Jan. 10, 1776, ibid., 4:225; GW to Gen. Montgomery, Jan. 12, 1776, ibid., 4:231; GW to Col. Arnold, Jan. 12, 1776, ibid., 4:232; GW to Mass. Leg., Jan. 13, 1776, ibid., 4:235–36.

4.   GW to Schuyler, Jan. 18, 1776, ibid., 4:255–56; GW to PC, Jan. 19, 1776, ibid., 4:258.

5.   GW to Reed, Jan. 4 and 14, 1776, ibid., 4:210–12, 240–45.

6.   On Washington's character see: Robert Calhoon, " 'Inescapable Circularity': History and the Human Condition in Revolutionary Virginia," *Reviews in American History*, 11 (1983), 41; Smith, *A New Age*, 1:548–53; Edmund S. Morgan, *The Meaning of Independence: John Adams, George Washington, and Thomas Jefferson* (Charlottesville, Va., 1975), 29–41; Edmund S. Morgan, *The Genius of George*

Washington (New York, 1980). For the "to run all Risques" statement, see: GW to Cooke, Aug. 4, 1775, *WW*, 3:386–87.

7. Peter Force, *American Archives* . . . , 4th ser., 6 vols. (Washington, D.C., 1837–46), 4:774–75; GW to Col. McDougall, Jan. 13, 1776, *WW*, 4:234; GW to Lee, Jan. 23, 1776, ibid., 4:267.

8. Gen. Orders, Jan. 21, 22, and 24, 1776, *WW*, 4:264, 266, 275; GW to PC, Jan. 30, 1776, ibid., 4:288; GW to Reed, Jan. 23 and 31, 1776, ibid., 4:268–69, 296–97.

9. Force, *Am. Arch.*, 4th ser., 4:534–35; Freeman, *GW*, 4:17; North Callahan, *Henry Knox: George Washington's General* (New York, 1958), 32–56.

10. GW to Reed, Feb. 1 and 10, 1776, *WW*, 4:299–300, 322; GW to PC, Feb. 18, 1776, ibid., 4:335–36; Bellamy, *Private Life*, 53.

11. Force, *Am. Arch.*, 4th ser., 4:1193; GW to Reed, Feb. 26, 1776, *WW*, 4:348; GW to PC, Feb. 18, 1776, ibid., 4:335–36; Reed to GW, Mar. 15, 1776, Reed, *Reed*, 1:171; Nelson, *Gates*, 45.

12. GW to Lee, Feb. 26, 1776, *WW*, 4:352; GW to Bassett, Feb. 28, 1776, ibid., 4:359; Gen. Orders, Feb. 27, 1776, ibid., 4:355.

13. GW to PC, Mar. 7, 1776, ibid., 4:370–74.

14. Gen. Orders, Mar. 3 and 4, 1776, ibid., 4:363–64, 368–69; GW to PC, Mar. 7, 1776, ibid., 4:370–79; GW to Reed, Mar. 7, 1776, ibid., 4:379–81; Freeman, *GW*, 3:28–35.

15. GW to Reed, Mar. 7, 1776, *WW*, 4:379.

16. Anderson, *Command of the Howe Brothers*, 99–100; Force, *Am. Arch.*, 4th ser., 4:458–59.

17. Boston Selectmen to GW, Mar. 8, 1776, *WW*, 4:377n.

18. GW to PC, Mar. 13, 1776, ibid., 4:390; GW to Cooke, Mar. 17, 1776, ibid., 4:401.

19. GW to PC, Mar. 19, 1776, ibid., 4:403; Freeman, *GW*, 3:50–51.

20. GW to PC, Mar. 19, 1776, *WW*, 4:403–404; GW to Reed, Mar. 19, 1776, ibid., 4:405–406; GW to Schuyler, Mar. 19, 1776, ibid., 4:407; John C. Dann, ed., *The Revolution Remembered: Eyewitness Accounts of the War for Independence* (Chicago, 1977), 10.

21. GW to Reed, Mar. 25, 1776, *WW*, 4:430–31; Freeman, *GW*, 3:56–57.

22. GW to PC, Mar. 27, 1776, *WW*, 4:436–37; GW to Reed, Mar. 28, 1776, ibid., 4:439; GW to Putnam, Mar. 29, 1776, ibid., 4:442–43; Gen. Orders, Mar. 30 and 31, 1776, ibid., 4:444–45.

23. GW to John A. Washington, Mar. 31, 1776, ibid., 4:446, 450; GW to Reed, Apr. 1, 1776, ibid., 4:453.

24. Lee to GW, Jan. 5, 1776, *Lee Papers*, 1:234; GW to PC, Jan. 4, 1776, *WW*, 4:208–209; GW, "Instructions to Major General Charles Lee," Jan. 8, 1776, ibid., 4:221–23; Adams to GW, Jan. 6, 1776, Taylor, *Papers of Adams*, 3:395–96; GW to Adams, Jan. 7, 1776, ibid., 3:397.

25. Alden, *Lee*, 95–103; Lee to Prov. Cong. of New York, Mar. 6, 1776, *Lee Papers*, 1:350–51, 360; Lee, "Report on the Defense of New York," ibid., 1:354–57.

26. GW to PC, May 5 and July 4, 1776, *WW*, 4:20, 219.

27. GW to Knox, Apr. 3, 1776, ibid., 4:462; GW to Morgan, Apr. 3, 1776, ibid., 4:465; GW to Reed, Apr. 15, 1776, ibid., 4:483; Freeman, *GW*, 4:77.

28. Ferling, *A Wilderness of Miseries*, 97, 101; Smith, *A New Age*, 1:711–12.

29. GW to PC, Apr. 15, 1776, *WW*, 4:479–80; Ives, *GW's Headquarters*, 46–65; Royster, *A Revolutionary People at War*, 60–61; Baker, *Itinerary of GW*, 37.

30. Butterfield, *Adams Diary and Autobiog.*, 2:119; GW to PC, Apr. 15 and 27, 1776, *WW*, 4:480, 501–502; GW to NY Comm. of Public Safety, Apr. 17, 1776, ibid., 4:487; Gen. Orders, Apr. 19 and 27, 1776, ibid., 4:491, 526.

31. GW to Lee, May 1, 1776, *WW*, 5:2; GW to NY Leg., May 19, 1776, ibid., 5:59; GW to Gen. Putnam, May 21, 1776, ibid., 5:68; GW to PC, June 20 and July 3, 1776, ibid., 5:161, 215.

32. Lee, "Report," *Lee Papers*, 1:354–57; GW to PC, June 13 and Aug. 5, 1776, *WW*, 5:129, 370–71; GW to NY Leg., May 19, 1776, ibid., 5:59; GW to Putnam, May 21, 1776, ibid., 5:69.

33. Reed to Esther Reed, July 26, 1775, Reed Mss., 2:20; GW to Reed, Jan. 14, 1776, *WW*, 4:240; Roche, *Reed*, 67–70; Freeman, *GW*, 4:72; Lee to GW, Nov. 12, 1775, *Lee Papers*, 1:273.

34. GW to Reed, Nov. 20, 28, 1775, Mar. 7 and Apr. 15, 1776, *WW*, 4:104, 123, 381, 483; Adams to Tudor, June 24, 1776, Taylor, *Papers of Adams*, 4:336.

35. Reed to Esther Reed, June 4, 1776, Reed Mss., 4:14.

36. *WW*, 5:87n; GW to Jesse Root, Aug. 7, 1776, ibid., 5:391; *Jrnl. Cont. Cong.*, 4:399–401; Josiah Bartlett to John Langdon, June 3, 1776, Smith, *Letters of Delegates*, 4:125; Joseph Hewes to Samuel Johnston, May 26, 1776, ibid., 4:78.

37. *Jrnl. Cont. Cong.*, 4:376–78, 388, 394–96, 399–401, 412; Whipple to Joshua Brackett, June 2, 1776, Smith, *Letters of Delegates*, 4:119.

38. Reed to GW, Mar. 3, 1776, Reed Mss., 4:12; Adams to Abigail Adams, Feb. 13 and 18, Apr. 12, 14, and 15, 1776, Butterfield, *Adams Fam. Corres.*, 1:346, 348–49, 377, 382–83; Jensen, *Founding of a Nation*, 632–66.

39. GW to John A. Washington, May 31, 1776, *WW*, 5:91; Freeman, *GW*, 5:101n; Smith, *Letters of Delegates*, 4:9–10n. Cultural historian Kenneth A. Silverman discerns an "embarrassed" look on Washington's face. See: Silverman, *A Cultural History of the American Revolution. Painting, Music, Literature and the Theater in the Colonies and the United States . . .* (New York, 1976), 317.

40. GW to John A. Washington, July 22, 1776, *WW*, 5:327; Flexner, *GW*, 2:95.

41. Gen. Orders, July 2, 1776, *WW*, 5:211; GW to Trumbull, July 9, 1776, ibid., 5:241.

42. GW to Ward, July 11, 1776, ibid., 5:256; Gen. Orders, July 11, 1776, ibid., 5:263; GW to PC, Aug. 2, 1776, ibid., 5:364.

43. Gen. Orders, July 7, 9, 10, 12, 18, 19, 20, 25, Aug. 2, 4, 6, 13, 15, 17, and 20, 1776, ibid., 5:230, 244, 246, 264, 299, 301, 313, 336, 366, 368, 376, 426, 427, 443, 468.

44. Gen. Orders, Aug. 1, 1776, ibid., 5:361; GW to Putnam, Aug. 25, 1776, ibid., 5:488.

45. John Bakeless, *Turncoats, Traitors and Heroes* (New York, 1959), 94–109; Freeman, GW, 4:115–20; Carlos E. Godrey, *The Commander-in-Chief's Guard* (Washington, 1904), 21–35; Gen. Orders, June 28, 1776, *WW*, 5:194–95. After the war a certain "credibility" was given to the action against Hickey when certain of his alleged co-conspirators once again publicly admitted their complicity in the plot;

however, in some cases these were men in quest of a Loyalist pension, a lure that might have colored their testimony.

46. GW to PC, July 12, 14, Aug. 7, 1776, *WW*, 5:264, 275, 382; GW to Trumbull, Aug. 7, 1776, ibid., 390; Freeman, *GW*, 4:135–36, 145–46.

47. Lee to GW, Feb. 14, 1776, *Lee Papers*, 1:295.

48. Ward, *War of the Revolution*, 1:195–201; Whittemore, *Sullivan*, 26–31.

49. GW to PC, June 17 and July 17, 1776, *WW*, 5:152–53, 296; Nelson, *Gates*, 55–57; Whittemore, *Sullivan*, 29–31.

50. GW to Schuyler, May 17, June 7, 13, and 24, 1776, *WW*, 5:52, 102, 130, 171; GW to PC, June 9, 27, and 29, 1776, ibid., 5:112, 183, 199; GW to Sullivan, June 16, 1776, ibid., 5:148; GW to Mass Leg., June 28, 1776, ibid., 5:187–88.

51. GW to Ward, July 29, 1776, ibid., 5:352; GW to Trumbull, Aug. 1, 1776, ibid., 5:363; GW to Col. Samuel Miles, Aug. 8, 1776, ibid., 5:393; GW to Gen. Hugh Mercer, Aug. 8, 1776, ibid., 5:395; GW to NY Leg., Aug. 8, 1776, ibid., 5:401; Charles K. Bolton, *The Private Soldier Under Washington* (New York, 1902), 38–39; Samuel Richards, *Diary of Samuel Richards* (Philadelphia, 1909), 9, 46; R.G. Albion and L. Dodson, eds., *The Journal of Philip Vickers Fithian, 1775–1776*, 2 vols. (Princeton, N.J., 1924), 1:131; 2:20; James Thacher, *A Military Journal of the American Revolution . . . to the Disbanding of the American Army* (Hartford, Conn., 1862), 20, 28, 303; Ferling, *A Wilderness of Miseries*, 121–26.

7

Washington's War Begins

1. GW to PC, Aug. 12, 1776, *WW*, 5:416.

2. Gruber, *Howe Brothers*, 73–76; Rodney Atwood, *The Hessians: Mercenaries from Hessen-Kassel in the American Revolution* (Cambridge, Eng., 1980), 13–14, 22–32.

3. GW to PC, July 14, 1776, *WW*, 5:273–74; Reed to Pettit, July 15, 1776, Reed, *Reed*, 1:204.

4. GW to PC, July 22, 1776, *WW*, 5:321, 321–23n; Reed to Esther Reed, July 20 and 26, 1776, Reed Mss., 4:37, 40.

5. GW, "Address . . . ," *WW*, 4:245.

6. *WW*, 5:57n; Reed to Pettit, Aug. 4, 1776, Reed, *Reed*, 1:212–13; Reed to Esther Reed, July 20, 1776, ibid., 1:208.

7. Atwood, *Hessians*, 53–57, 61.

8. GW to PC, Aug. 16, 1776, *WW*, 5:439–40; Gen. Orders, Aug. 20, 1776, ibid., 5:469.

9. Gen. Orders, Aug. 20, 1776, ibid., 5:469; GW to PC, Aug. 22, 1776, ibid., 5:475.

10. Henry Johnston, *The Campaign of 1776 Around New York and Brooklyn* (Brooklyn, 1878), 49–73, 143; Thomas W. Field, *The Battle of Long Island, with Connected Preceding Events, and the Subsequent American Retreat* (Brooklyn, 1869), 153.

11. GW to Gen. William Heath, Aug. 23, 1776, *WW*, 5:475; GW to PC, Aug. 23 and 26, 1776, ibid., 5:476, 491; GW to Putnam, Aug. 24, 1776, ibid., 5:486–87; Robert Harrison to PC, Aug. 27, 1776, ibid., 5:494; Reed to Livingston, Aug. 30,

1776, Field, *Battle of Long Island*, 397; Alan Valentine, *Lord Stirling* (New York, 1969), 43–49, 55, 153–75.

12. Johnston, *Campaign of 1776*, 148–73; Reed to Livingston, Aug. 30, 1776, Field, *Battle of Long Island*, 397; Freeman, *GW*, 4:159–68.

13. Anderson, *Command of the Howe Brothers*, 134.

14. GW to NY Leg., Aug. 30, 1776, *WW*, 5:498–99.

15. GW to PC, Aug. 31, 1776, ibid., 5:508; Gen. Orders, Aug. 31, 1776, ibid., 5:502; Force, *Am. Arch.*, 5th Ser., 1:1246.

16. George E. Scheer, ed., *Private Yankee Doodle* (Boston, 1962), 27–29.

17. Dann, *Revolution Remembered*, 44.

18. GW to PC, Sept. 2 and 8, 1776, *WW*, 6:5–6, 28; Gen. Orders, Sept. 4, 1776, ibid., 6:16; "Jedidiah Swan's Orderly Book," New Jersey Historical Society *Proceedings*, 2 (1917), 27–28; Freeman, *GW*, 4:180–81.

19. GW to Mass. Leg., Sept. 19, 1776, *WW*, 6:75–76.

20. Reed to Esther Reed, Sept. 2 and 6, 1776, Reed Mss., 4:56, 57.

21. GW to PC, Sept. 2 and 8, 1776, *WW*, 6:6–7, 28–29, 7n.

22. GW to PC, Sept. 8, 14, 16, and 19, 1776, ibid., 6:45, 53–54, 59, 73, and 54n; GW to Gov. Cooke, Sept. 17, 1776, ibid., 6:63; *JCC*, 5:733, 749; Freeman, *GW*, 4:184–90.

23. GW to PC, Sept. 14 and 16, 1776, *WW*, 6:53, 58; Benjamin Trumbull, "Journal of the Campaign at New York, 1776–1777," Connecticut Historical Society, *Collections*, 7 (1899), 195; Atwood, *Hessians*, 70–71. On the peace talks initiated by Howe that September, see: Butterfield, *Adams Diary and Autobiog.*, 3:415–24.

24. GW to PC, Sept. 16, 1776, *WW*, 6:57–58; Victor Paltsits, "The Jeopardy of Washington," *New York Historical Society Quarterly*, 32 (1948), 267–68.

25. Anderson, *Command of the Howe Brothers*, 173–79; Johnston, *Campaign of 1776*, 231–39.

26. GW to PC, Sept. 16 and 18, 1776, *WW*, 6:59, 68–69; GW to Mass. Leg., Sept. 19, 1776, ibid., 6:77; Reed to Esther Reed, Sept. 17, 1776, Reed Mss., 4:59; Scheer, *Private Yankee Doodle*, 41–43.

27. Reed to Esther Reed, Sept. 17, 1776, Reed Mss., 4:59; Freeman, *GW*, 4:204; Scheer, *Private Yankee Doodle*, 46.

28. Anderson, *Command of the Howe Brothers*, 181–82; Gruber, *Howe Brothers*, 127–28; GW to Mass. Leg., Sept. 19, 1776, *WW*, 6:76–77; GW to John A. Washington, Sept. 22, 1776, ibid., 6:95.

29. GW to Gov. Trumbull, Oct. 9, 1776, *WW*, 6:190; GW to PC, Oct. 13, 1776, ibid., 6:197.

30. Force, *Am. Arch.*, 5th ser., 2:1118; Freeman, *GW*, 4:222.

31. George A. Billias, *General John Glover and His Marblehead Mariners* (New York, 1960), 114–23; Ward, *War of the Revolution*, 1:261.

32. GW to PC, Nov. 6, 1776, *WW*, 6:248–50; Reed to Esther Reed, Nov. 6, 1776, Reed, *Reed*, 1:248; Scheer, *Private Yankee Doodle*, 55; Force, *Am. Arch.*, 5th ser., 3:543–44; Freeman, *GW*, 4:374.

33. Force, *Am. Arch.*, 5th ser., 3:618–19; GW to PC, Nov. 16, 1776, *WW*, 6:285–86; GW to Reed, Aug. 22, 1779, ibid., 16:151–52; Freeman, *GW*, 4:242–51.

34. Freeman, *GW*, 4:252.

35. GW to PC, Nov. 16, 1776, *WW*, 6:285–86.

36. GW to PC, Nov. 23, 1776, ibid., 6:303.

37. Adams to Gen. Samuel Parsons, Oct. 2, 1776, Smith, *Letters of Delegates*, 5:286; Adams to Wm. Tudor, Sept. 26, 1776, ibid., 5:240; Adams to Knox, Sept. 29, 1776, ibid., 5:260; Adams to Abigail Adams, Oct. 7, 1776, Butterfield, *Adams Fam. Corres.*, 2:139; Adams to Knox, Sept. 30[?], 1776, Edmund C. Burnett, ed., *Letters of Members of the Continental Congress*, 8 vols. (Washington, D.C., 1921–36), 2:108.

38. Alden, *Lee*, 136–45.

39. Lee to Reed, Nov. 16, 1776, *Lee Papers*, 2:283; Reed to Lee, Nov. 21, 1776, ibid., 2:293–94.

40. Lee to Reed, Nov. 24, 1776, ibid., 2:305–306.

41. On GW's reaction, see his later letter of June 14, 1777, to Reed, in *WW*, 7:247.

42. GW to Reed, Nov. 30, 1776, ibid., 6:313.

43. Reed to Esther Reed, Oct. 11, 1776, Reed Mss., 4:61; Reed to PC, Nov. 28 and Dec. 2, 1776, Reed NYPL.

44. Roche, *Reed*, 100–101.

45. GW to PC, Nov. 14, 27, and 30, 1776, *WW*, 6:279, 310, 314; GW to Lee, Nov. 21, 1776, ibid., 6:298.

46. GW to PC, Nov. 19, 1776, ibid., 6:293, 295.

47. GW to Livingston, Nov. 21, 1776, ibid., 6:302; GW to Lee, Nov. 21 and 27, Dec. 1, 3, 10, 11, and 14, 1776, ibid., 6:299, 309, 318, 326, 341, 348, 370.

48. GW to PC, Dec. 20, 1776, ibid., 6:407; Alden, *Lee*, 151–57.

49. GW to PC, Dec. 1, 2, 8, and 9, 1776, *WW*, 6:321–23, 335–37, 339; Freeman, *GW*, 4:268; Franklin and Mary Wickwire, *Cornwallis and the War of Independence* (London, 1971), 7–46, 90–94; Hugh Rankin, "Charles Lord Cornwallis: A Study in Frustration," Billias, *GW's Opponents*, 193–232.

50. William S. Stryker, *The Battles of Trenton and Princeton* (Boston, 1898), 37; GW to Stirling, Dec. 14, 1776, *WW*, 6:367.

51. GW to PC, Dec. 3, 6, 8, and 20, 1776, *WW*, 6:325, 331, 335, 402, 411; Freeman, *GW*, 4:273, 278–81; Nelson, *Gates*, 72–73; Stryker, *Trenton and Princeton*, 18–19, 34–35.

52. Anderson, *Command of the Howe Brothers*, 204–12; Atwood, *Hessians*, 84–87; Gruber, *Howe Brothers*, 148.

53. GW to Trumbull, Dec. 14, 1776, *WW*, 6:366; Palmer, *Way of the Fox*, 133.

54. GW to Lund Washington, Dec. 17, 1776, *WW*, 6:347; GW to John A. Washington, Dec. 18, 1776, ibid., 6:398; GW to PC, Dec. 5 and 11, 1776, ibid., 6:330–31, 351.

55. GW to PC, Dec. 27, 1776, ibid., 6:441–43.

56. Stryker, *Trenton and Princeton*, 64–65, 86–88, 112–13; GW to PC, Dec. 15, 1776, *WW*, 6:378; GW to Gates, Dec. 14, 1776, ibid., 6:372; GW to Trumbull, Dec. 14, 1776, ibid., 6:366; Conner, *Autobiography of Rush*, 124; Reed to GW, Dec. 22, 1776, Reed, *Reed*, 1:271–73.

57. George F. Scheer and Hugh F. Rankin, eds., *Rebels and Redcoats* (New York, 1957), 212.

58. GW to PC, Dec. 27, 1776, *WW*, 1:441–44; Stryker, *Trenton and Princeton*, 70–192; Scheer and Rankin, *Rebels and Redcoats*, 212; Atwood, *Hessians*, 43, 64, 84–95; Ward, *War of the Revolution*, 1:291–303; Freeman, *GW*, 4:303–24.

59. GW to Cadwalader, Dec. 27, 1776, *WW*, 6:446–47; Freeman, *GW*, 6:327–29.
60. GW to Cadwalader, Dec. 27, 1776, *WW*, 6:447; GW to Heath, Dec. 28, 1776, ibid., 6:447; GW to PC, Dec. 29, 1776, ibid., 6:451.
61. GW to PC, Jan. 1, 1777, ibid., 6:462.
62. Ibid., 6:461–62; *JCC*, 6:1045.
63. Reed, *Reed*, 1:282–83.
64. Scheer and Rankin, *Rebels and Redcoats*, 217; Freeman, *GW*, 4:373–74.
65. Reed, "Narrative," Reed, *Reed*, 1:282–83.
66. Joseph M. Waterman, *With Sword and Lancet: The Life of General Hugh Mercer* (Richmond, Va., 1941), 45–86.
67. Stryker, *Trenton and Princeton*, 255–98; Scheer and Rankin, *Rebels and Redcoats*, 219.
68. GW to PC, Jan. 5 and 7, 1777, *WW*, 6:467–71, 477–78; Freeman, *GW*, 4:343–57; Alfred Hoyt Bill, *The Campaign of Princeton, 1776–1777* (Princeton, N.J., 1948), 95–123; Waterman, *With Sword and Lancet*, 278–98.
69. *The Journal of Nicholas Cresswell, 1774–1777* (Port Washington, N.Y., 1968), 179–81.
70. Piers Mackesy, *The War for America, 1775–1783* (Cambridge, Mass., 1965), 98–102; Gruber, *Howe Brothers*, 191–92, 227; Atwood, *Hessians*, 97–98; Solomon Lutnick, *The American Revolution and the British Press, 1775–1783* (Columbia, Mo., 1967), 77, 79, 95; Royster, *A Revolutionary People at War*, 119.
71. GW to PC, Jan. 5, 1777, *WW*, 6:470.

8

The Campaign of 1777

1. Leonard Lundin, *Cockpit of the American Revolution: The War for Independence in New Jersey* (Princeton, N.J., 1940), 231–33.
2. GW to Heath, Jan. 7, 9, 12, 17, and 19, 1777, *WW*, 6:475, 482–83, 497–98; 7:24, 31; GW to PC, Jan. 7, 9, and Feb. 5, 1777, ibid., 6:477, 487; 7:103; GW to Shippen, Jan. 6, 1777, ibid., 6:473–74.
3. GW to Heath, Feb. 3, 1777, ibid., 7:94–95. Also see, ibid., 7:31n and 96n.
4. GW to PC, Jan. 12, 14, 22, and Feb. 5, 14, 28, 1777, ibid., 6:502; 7:9, 48–49, 105, 146, 205; GW to Reed, Jan. 14, 1777, ibid., 7:15; GW to Schuyler, Jan. 18, 1777, ibid., 7:27; Freeman, *GW*, 4:383n; R. Arthur Bowler, *Logistics and the Failure of the British Army in America, 1775–1783* (Princeton, N.J., 1975), 67–69.
5. Bowler, *Logistics*, 8–11, 92–145; Edward E. Curtis, *The Organization of the British Army in the American Revolution* (New Haven, Conn., 1926), 81–147.
6. GW to Morris, Jan. 19, 1777, *WW*, 7:32; GW to Pa. Council of Safety, Jan. 19, 1777, ibid. 7:35; GW to Gates, Feb. 20, 1777, ibid., 7:176; GW to John Augustine Washington, Feb. 24, 1777, ibid., 7:198.
7. Gruber, *Howe Brothers*, 156–57, 179–80, 188–89; Anderson, *Command of the Howe Brothers*, 214–222; Palmer, *Way of the Fox*, 139; John Adams to Abigail Adams, Sept. 1, 1777, Butterfield, *Adams Fam. Corres.*, 2:335.
8. GW to PC, Jan. 22, Feb. 20, 1777, *WW*, 7:48, 168; Robert K. Wright, Jr., *The Continental Army* (Washington, D.C., 1983), 91–119; James Kirby Martin and

Mark E. Lender, *A Respectable Army: The Military Origins of the Republic, 1763–1789* (Arlington Heights, Ill., 1982), 30–34, 69–78, 87–97; Edward C. Papenfuse and Gregory A. Stiverson, "General Smallwood's Recruits: The Peacetime Career of the Revolutionary War Private," *William and Mary Quarterly*, 3d ser., 30 (1973), 117–32; *JCC*, 6:944–45. The emergence of the new army also has been explained as arising from the economic realities of the war. If the army was composed principally of landowning farmers not enough food would be available for both soldiers and civilians; hence, after 1777 farmers remained at home, while the least productive elements in society soldiered. See: Richard Buel, Jr., "Samson Shorn: The Impact of the Revolutionary War on Estimates of the Republic's Strength," in Ronald Hoffman and Peter J. Albert, eds., *Arms and Independence: The Military Character of the American Revolution* (Charlottesville, Va., 1984), 141–65.

9. Freeman, *GW*, 4:397; GW to Gov. Cooke, Apr. 3, 1777, *WW*, 7:350; GW to Patrick Henry, May 31, 1777, ibid., 8:148; GW to Gen. Parsons, May 25, 1777, ibid., 8:124; GW to Richard Henry Lee, June 1, 1777, ibid., 8:161; GW to PC, Mar. 14, 1777, ibid., 7:285; Buel, *Dear Liberty*, 105, 110–11; Wright, *Continental Army*, 111; Ward, *War of the Revolution*, 1:320–21.

10. Royster, *A Revolutionary People*, 87, 147–51; John Adams to Abigail Adams, Feb. 21, 1777, Butterfield, *Adams Fam. Corres.*, 2:165; GW to PC, Oct. 4, 1776, *WW*, 6:153; GW to Gov. Livingston, Feb. 11, 1777, ibid., 7:134; GW to Col. Livingston, Feb. 20, 1777, ibid., 7:182; GW to Gov. Woodward, Mar. 3, 1777, ibid., 7:140; GW to John Parke Custis, Jan. 23, 1777, ibid., 7:54; GW to Heath, Apr. 10, 1777, ibid., 7:384; Gen. Orders, Feb. 9, Apr. 17 and 23, 1777, ibid., 7:122, 215, 422, 423; 8:23; GW to Gen. Smallwood, May 3, 1777, ibid., 7:13.

11. GW to Arnold, Apr. 3, 1777, ibid., 7:352 and 234n; John Adams to Abigail Adams, May 22, 1777, Butterfield, *Adams Fam. Corres.*, 2:245.

12. Ward, *War of the Revolution*, 1:321; GW to Heath, May 2, 1777, *WW*, 8:2–3; Gw to Bd. of War, June 30, 1777, ibid., 8:318–19; GW to Knox, Jan. 16, 1777, ibid., 7:18–19; GW to Col. Benj. Flower, Jan. 16, 1777, ibid., 7:20–22; Wright, *Continental Army*, 104.

13. GW to PC, Mar. 26 and Apr. 28, 1777, *WW*, 7:319, 490; GW to Heath, Mar. 29, 1777, ibid., 7:332; GW to McDougall, Apr. 28, 1777, ibid., 7:487; Freeman, *GW*, 4:409–411.

14. Gruber, *Howe Brothers*, 199–215.

15. Edward Tatum, ed., *The American Journal of Ambrose Serle* (Los Angeles, 1940), 226; Gruber, *Howe Brothers*, 228.

16. GW to McDougall, May 1, 1777, *WW*, 8:2; GW to Bd. of War, May 10, 1777, ibid., 8:36; GW to Putnam, May 12 and 26, 1777, ibid., 8:74; GW to John Augustine Washington, June 1, 1777, ibid., 8:157.

17. GW to Sullivan, June 14, 15 and 17, 1777, ibid., 8:248, 251–52, 262–63; GW to Schuyler, June 16 and 20, 1777, ibid., 8:253, 275.

18. GW to PC, June 22, 1777, ibid., 8:281–82; GW to Reed, June 23, 1777, ibid., 8:295.

19. GW to PC, June 25, 1777, ibid., 8:298; GW to Putnam, June 22, 1777, ibid., 8:284; GW to Wm. Gordon, June 29, 1777, ibid., 8:316; Tatum, *Journal of Serle*, 234.

20. GW to PC, June 28 and 29, 1777, *WW*, 8:307, 308–309; GW to John Augustine

Washington, June 29, 1777, ibid., 8:314; Tatum, *Journal of Serle*, 235–36; Gruber, *Howe Brothers*, 229; Ward, *War of the Revolution*, 1:326–28; Alan Valantine, *Lord Stirling* (New York, 1969), 202–205.

21.   GW to PC, July 10, 1777, *WW*, 8:376–77.

22.   Ward, *War of the Revolution*, 1:384–411; Rossie, *Politics of Command*, 107–17; Nelson, *Gates*, 58–92; Richard J. Hargrove, *General John Burgoyne* (Newark, Del., 1983), 141.

23.   Hargrove, *Burgoyne*, 117–29, 147–48, 178, 192, 269; Gruber, *Howe Brothers*, 208, 212, 232–33.

24.   GW to PC, July 10, 1777, *WW*, 8:376–77.

25.   GW to PC, July 12, 14, 16, and 22, 1777, ibid., 8:384, 407, 414–15, 453–54, 471–72; GW to Schuyler, July 18, 1777, ibid., 8:427; GW to Heath, July 19, 1777, ibid., 8:439; GW to Gates, July 30, 1777, ibid., 8:499; Freeman, *GW*, 4:446–47.

26.   GW to PC, July 30, 1777, *WW*, 8:502; GW to John Augustine Washington, Aug. 5, 1777, ibid., 9:21; Anderson, *Command of the Howe Brothers*, 279–82.

27.   GW to Samuel Washington, Aug. 10, 1777, *WW*, 9:40; GW to Heath, Aug. 10, 1777, ibid., 9:42; GW to PC, Aug. 10 and 21, 1777, ibid., 9:46–52, 107–109; GW to Gates, Aug. 20, 1777, ibid., 9:102; "Council of War," Aug. 21, 1777, ibid., 9:109–110, 110n.

28.   GW to PC, Aug. 21, 1777, ibid., 9:111.

29.   Gen. Orders, Aug. 23–24, 1777, ibid., 9:125–27, 129; Freeman, *GW*, 4:462; Henry Marchant to Nicholas Cooke, Aug. 24, 1777, Smith, *Letters*, 7:541; John Adams to Abigail Adams, Aug. 24, 1777, Butterfield, *Adams Fam. Corres.*, 2:327–28.

30.   Gruber, *Howe Brothers*, 233–38.

31.   GW to Sullivan, Mar. 15, Aug. 3, 10, and 27, 1777, *WW*, 7:290; 8:6, 44, 135; Whittemore, *Sullivan*, 51–52, 55.

32.   Gen. Orders, Aug. 22, 1777, *WW*, 9:122; GW to Gates, Sept. 1, 1777, ibid., 9:154; Nelson, *Gates*, 89–113; Hargrove, *Burgoyne*, 147–59; Higginbotham, *War for American Independence*, 191.

33.   Atwood, *Hessians*, 117; Gen. Orders, Sept. 5 and 7, 1777, *WW*, 9:181–82, 192; GW to PC, Sept. 9, 1777, ibid., 9:197–98.

34.   Ward, *War of the Revolution*, 1:344–53; Freeman, *GW*, 4:471–84; Thayer, *Greene*, 198–96; Whittemore, *Sullivan*, 56–64; Valentine, *Stirling*, 207–210; GW to PC, Sept. 11, 1777, *WW*, 9:206–207; Mark E. Lender and James Kirby Martin, eds., *Citizen Soldier: The Revolutionary War Journal of Joseph Bloomfield* (Newark, N.J., 1982), 127.

35.   Freeman, *GW*, 4:484–89; Ward, *War of the Revolution*, 1:351, 353–54; Whittemore, *Sullivan*, 56–57; GW to PC, Sept. 11, 1777, *WW*, 9:207–208; GW to Heath, Sept. 30, 1777, ibid., 9:287.

36.   GW to PC, Sept. 16, 17, 19, and 23, 1777, *WW*, 9:230, 231, 238, 258–59; GW to Anthony Wayne, Sept. 18, 1777, ibid., 9:235; GW to Bd. of War, Nov. 3, 1777, ibid., 9:497; GW to Gov. Clinton, Sept. 19[?], ibid., 9:241.

37.   GW to Sullivan, Sept. 21, 1777, ibid., 9:245; GW to PC, Sept. 23, 1777, ibid., 9:257–60; "Council of War," Sept. 23, 1777, ibid., 9:261; Freeman, *GW*, 4:490–98; Ward, *War of the Revolution*, 1:355–61. On the Paoli affair, see: Paul David

Nelson, *Anthony Wayne: Soldier of the Early Republic* (Bloomington, Ind., 1985), 55–57.

38. GW to Heath, Sept. 30, 1777, *WW*, 9:287; Nelson, *Gates*, 103–21.

39. GW to Gates, Sept. 24, 1777, WW, 9:264; GW to Putnam, Sept. 23 and Oct. 1, ibid., 9:253, 290; GW to Thomas Nelson, Sept. 27, 1777, ibid., 9:271.

40. "Councils of War," Sept. 27 and 28, 1777, ibid., 9:259–61, 277–79; Bernard Knollenberg, *George Washington and the American Revolution, A Reappraisal: Gates, Conway and the Continental Congress* (New York, 1941), 24–29.

41. GW to PC, Oct. 5, 1777, *WW*, 9:308–309; Freeman, *GW*, 4:501n.

42. Gen. Orders, Oct. 3, 1777, *WW*, 9:305–306.

43. Ward, *War of the Revolution*, 1:362–71; Freeman, *GW*, 4:502–19; Thayer, *Greene*, 201–202; Whittemore, *Sullivan*, 69–75.

44. GW to PC, Sept. 23, 1777, *WW*, 9:259.

45. "Reports on Fortifying the Delaware," Aug. 6–9, 1777, in Worthington C. Ford, ed., *Defences of Philadelphia in 1777* (Brooklyn, 1897), 5–30; GW to PC, Aug. 10, 1777, *WW*, 9:46–53; W. H. Moomaw, "The Denouement of General Howe's Campaign of 1777," *English Historical Review*, 79 (1964), 500–501.

46. Ford, *Defenses*, 5–45; Freeman, *GW*, 4:527–29.

47. GW to Gen. Newcomb, Oct. 22, 1777, *WW*, 9:418; GW to PC, Nov. 23, 1777, ibid., 10:100; Ward, *War of the Revolution*, 1:372–77; Thayer, *Greene*, 207; Atwood, *Hessians*, 118–29; Gruber, *Howe Brothers*, 246–52, 558–60.

48. GW to Samuel Washington, Oct. 27, 1777, *WW*, 9:451.

49. GW to Gates, Oct. 30, 1777, ibid., 9:465.

50. "Council of War," Oct. 26 [29], 1777, ibid., 9:441–42, 442n, 461–64; GW to PC, Nov. 1 and 17, 1777, ibid., 9:478; 10:73–74; GW to Greene, Nov. 22, 1777, ibid., 10:96, 104–105; Greene to Gw, Nov. 24, 1777, Richard K. Showman et al., eds., *The Papers of Nathanael Greene* (Chapel Hill, N.C., 1976–), 2:208–209, 212.

51. GW to Greene, Nov. 25, 1777, Showman, *Papers of Greene*, 10:104–105; GW to Greene or Varnum or Huntington, Nov. 28, 1777, ibid., 10:120–21.

52. Scheer, *Private Yankee Doodle*, 101; Smith, *Letters*, 8:381n; Freeman, *GW*, 4:561–63.

53. GW to Gates, Dec. 2, 1777, *WW*, 10:133; GW to Reed, Dec. 2, 1777, ibid., 10:133; GW to PC, Dec. 22 and 23, 1777, ibid., 10:186–88, 196; Gen. Orders, Dec. 17, 1777, ibid., 10:167–68; Congress to GW, Dec. 15[?], 1777, ibid., 10:162–63; John F. Reed, *Campaign to Valley Forge, July 1, 1777–December 19, 1777* (Philadelphia, 1965), 381–96; Smith, *Letters*, 8:442n.

9

The New Continental Army

1. GW to John Augustine Washington, Nov. 26, 1777, *WW*, 10:113–14; GW to Henry, Nov. 13, 1777, ibid., 10:53; GW to PC, Nov. 26–27, 1777, ibid., 10:109; Ward, *War of the Revolution*, 2:543.

2. Gen. Orders, Dec. 18, 29, 1777, and Jan. 4, 1778, *WW*, 10:170–71, 235, 262; GW to Gen. Robt. Howe, Jan. 13, 1778, ibid., 10:301; GW to Morris, Feb. 10,

1778, ibid., 10:447; Martha Washington to Mercy Otis Warren, Mar. 7, 1778, ibid., 10:414n; Scheer, *Private Yankee Doodle*, 102; John B.B. Trussell, Jr., *Birthplace of an Army: A Study of the Valley Forge Encampment* (Harrisburg, Pa., 1976), 21.

3. GW, "Circular to the States," Dec. 29, 1777, *WW*, 10:224; GW to Bd. of War, Jan. 2–3, 1778, ibid., 10:251; GW to Putnam, Jan. 22, 1778, ibid., 10:334; GW to Gen. James Potter, Dec. 21, 1777, ibid., 10:182; GW to PC, Dec. 23, 1777, ibid., 10:193; Gen. Orders, Jan. 1, 1778, ibid., 10:243 and 243n; Greene to GW, Jan. 1, 1777, Showman, *Papers of Greene*, 2:241; Ward, *War of the Revolution*, 2:545; Royster, *A Revolutionary People*, 190–94.

4. Gen. Orders, Jan. 13 and 15, 1778, *WW*, 10:300, 306; Ward, *War of the Revolution*, 2:546; Charles H. Lesser, ed., *The Sinews of Independence: Monthly Strength Reports of the Continental Army* (Chicago, 1976), 54–61.

5. GW to John Parke Custis, Feb. 1, 1778, *WW*, 10:414; GW to Capt. Geo. Lewis, Jan. 11, 1778, ibid., 10:290; GW, "General Instructions for the Colonels . . . ," ibid., 10:242; Gen. Orders, Feb. 4, 1778, ibid., 10:421; Flexner, *GW*, 2:282–83; Walter H. Blumenthal, *Women Camp Followers of the American Revolution* (Philadelphia, 1952), 57–90.

6. GW to PC, Mar. 24, 1778, *WW*, 9:139; Greene to GW, Jan. 1, 1778, Showman, *Papers of Greene*, 2:241; Royster, *A Revolutionary People*, 195; Trussel, *Birthplace of an Army*, 90.

7. GW to "Committee of Congress with the Army," Jan. 29, 1778, *WW*, 10:362–65.

8. *JCC*, 11:502–503; Wright, *Continental Army*, 124–25; Royster, *A Revolutionary People*, has the most complete treatment on the officer caste and its drive for professional status; see 190–254.

9. GW to PC, Dec. 22 and 23, 1777, *WW*, 10:183, 192–98; GW to Henry, Dec. 27, 1777, ibid., 10:209; GW, "Circular to the States," Dec. 29, 1777, ibid., 10:224.

10. GW to Gov. Johnson, Nov. 6, 1777, ibid., 10:15; GW to PC, Nov. 11, Dec. 22, 1777, and Jan. 5, 1778, ibid., 10:37, 183, 267; GW to Col. Lutterloch, Dec. 20, 1777, ibid., 10:179; GW to Col. Adams, Nov. 7, 1777, ibid., 10:18; GW to Henry, Dec. 27, 1777, ibid., 10:209; Gen. Orders, Nov. 15, Dec. 15[?], 1777, Jan. 6, 23, and 26, 1778, ibid., 10:70–71, 162–63, 271, 342, 350.

11. *JCC*, 9:1013–15; GW to PC, Jan. 5, 1778, *WW*, 10:267.

12. On Washington's view of the problems at Valley Forge, see: GW to Comm. of Cong., Jan. 29, 1778, ibid., 10:392; GW to Sullivan, Feb. 14, 1778, ibid., 10:460; GW to Trumbull, May 28, 1777, ibid., 7:326; GW to Gerry, Livingston, and Clymer, July 19, 1777, ibid., 7:441.

13. Erna Risch, *Supplying Washington's Army* (Washington, D.C., 1981), 17–18, 80–84, 188–219; Louis C. Hatch, *The Administration of the Revolutionary Army* (New York, 1904), 92–97; James A. Huston, *The Sinews of War: Army Logistics, 1775–1953* (Washington, D.C., 1966), 6–12, 27–36; Victor Johnson, *The Administration of the American Commissariat During the Revolutionary War* (Philadelphia, 1941), 82–102; E. Wayne Carp, *To Starve the Army at Pleasure: Continental Army Administration and American Political Culture, 1775–1783* (Chapel Hill, N.C., 1984), 20, 43–45; 56–72, 89, 92, 116–24; Rossman, *Mifflin*, 75–92; Trussel, *Birthplace of an Army*, 37–38; Wayne K. Bodle and Jacqueline Thibaut, *Valley Forge Historical Research Report*, 3 vols. (Valley Forge, Pa., 1980), 2:112, 155.

14. GW to Henry, Nov. 13, 1777, *WW*, 10:51–53; GW to PC, Nov. 17, 1777, ibid.,

10:76; GW to John A. Washington, Nov. 26, 1777, ibid., 10:114; GW to Conway, Nov. 9, 1777, ibid., 10:30.

15. GW to Conway, Nov. 9, 1777, ibid., 10:30.

16. Craik to GW, Jan. 6, 1778, WPPV. Also see: Nelson, *Gates*, 48, 55, 73–77, 102–103, 163–64; Rossie, *Politics of Command*, 188–202; Higginbotham, *War of American Independence*, 216–22; Bernhard, Knollenberg, *Washington and the American Revolution: A Reappraisal* (New York, 1941), 65–77; Royster, *A Revolutionary People*, 179–89; Rossman, *Mifflin*, 91–139.

17. James Lovell to Robt. Treat Paine, Sept. 24, 1777, Smith, *Letters*, 8:15; Lovell to Samuel Adams, Jan. 20, 1778, ibid., 8:618; Henry Laurens to John Laurens, Oct. 16, and Nov. 15, 1777, ibid., 8:125, 270; Sergeant to Lovell, Nov. 20, 1777, ibid., 8:296; [Anon.], "The Thoughts of a Freeman," Sparks, *WGW*, 5:497–99; Rossie, *Politics of Command*, 191; Knollenberg, *Washington and the Revolution*, 190–98.

18. Rush to Henry, Jan. 12, 1778, Sparks, *WGW*, 5:495–96; Gouverneur Morris to Robt. Livingston, March 10, 1778, Smith, *Letters*, 9:264; Richard Peters to Robt. Morris, Jan. 21, 1778, ibid., 8:651n. On the notion that Washington must be maintained in power, see: Abraham Clark to Wm. Alexander, Jan. 15, 1778, Smith, *Letters*, 8:597; Robt. Morris to Richard Peters, Jan. 21, 1778, ibid., 8:649.

19. Henry Laurens to John Laurens, Oct. 16, 1777, Smith, *Letters*, 8:125–26; Morris to Peters, Jan. 21, 1778, ibid., 8:650; Peters to Morris, Jan. 21, 1778, ibid., 8:651n; John Adams to Abigail Adams, Oct. 28 and 26, 1777, Butterfield, *Adams Fam. Corres.*, 2:361–62, 360–61; Adams to Rush, Feb. 8, 1778, *Microfilm Edition of the Adams Papers* (Boston, 1954–59), Reel 89.

20. Gates to GW, Dec. 8, 1777, *Horatio Gates Papers, 1726–1828* [Microfilm] (Sanford, N.C., 1979), reel 6, no. 111; GW to Gates, Jan. 4, 1778, *WW*, 10:263–65.

21. Gates to GW, Jan. 23, 1778, *Gates Papers*, reel 6, no. 811; GW to Gates, Feb. 9, 1778, *WW*, 10:437–41.

22. Gates to GW, Feb. 19, 1778, *Gates Papers*, reel 6, no. 1026; GW to Gates, Feb. 24, 1778, *WW*, 10:508–509.

23. Conway to GW, Dec. 31, 1777, *WW*, 10:228n.

24. Knollenberg, *Washington and the Revolution*, 43–59; GW to Gates, Jan. 4, 1778, *WW*, 10:265; Conway to Gw, July 23, 1778, WPPV.

25. Butterfield, *Adams Diary and Autiobiog.*, 2:263.

26. On Lafayette see: Howard H. Peckham, "Marquis de Lafayette: Eager Warrior," Billias, *GW's Generals*, 212–38; Louis R. Gottschalk, *Lafayette Comes to America*, (Chicago, 1935); Louis R. Gottschalk, *Lafayette Joins the American Army* (Chicago, 1937); Louis R. Gottschalk, *Lafayette and the Close of the American Revolution* (Chicago, 1942).

27. Rudolph Cronau, *The Army of the American Revolution and its Organizer* (New York, 1923), 13–30; John M. Palmer, *General Von Steuben* (New Haven, Conn., 1937), 3–22, 137–72; Royster, *A Revolutionary People*, 213–54.

28. GW to PC, Dec. 23, 1777, *WW*, 10:197.

29. Wright, *Continental Army*, 121–52; Hatch, *Administration of the Revolutionary Army*, 66; Reed, *Valley Forge*, 49–50.

30. Thayer, *Greene*, 224; GW to the Comm. of Cong., Jan. 29, 1778, *WW*, 10:387–88; Risch, *Supplying Washington's Army*, 40–44.

31. GW to Sullivan, Mar. 10, 1778, *WW*, 11:57–58.

32.   Freeman, *GW*, 2:257; 3:55–56, 61–62, 98; 4:417–18, 535–36; Gen. Orders, Nov. 20, 1777, *WW*, 10:89.

33.   Lee to Laurens, Apr. 17, 1778, *Lee Papers*, 2:389–90; Alden, *Lee*, 164–93.

34.   GW to Comm. of Cong., Jan. 29, 1778, *WW*, 10:389; Gen. Orders, Jan. 20, 1778, ibid., 10:321; GW to PC, Feb. 3, 1778, ibid., 10:418; GW to Col. Geo. Gibson, Feb. 21, 1778, ibid., 10:495; GW to Putnam, Jan. 22, 1778, ibid., 10:334; GW to Smallwood, Jan. 13 and Feb. 25, 1778, ibid., 10:302, 512; Reed, *Valley Forge*, 19.

35.   GW to John Parke Custis, Feb. 1, 1778, *WW*, 10:414; GW to Henry Champion, Feb. 7 and 17, 1778, ibid., 10:425, 474; GW to Wm. Buchanan, Feb. 7, 1778, ibid., 10:427; GW to Henry, Feb. 19, 1778, ibid., 10:483.

36.   Reed, *Valley Forge*, 35–36, 41; Nelson, *Wayne*, 73–75.

37.   Gruber, *Howe Brothers*, 261–91.

38.   John E. Ferling, *The Loyalist Mind: Joseph Galloway and the American Revolution* (University Park, Pa., 1977), 55; John E. Ferling, "Joseph Galloway's Military Advice: A Loyalist's View of the Revolution," *PMHB*, 98 (1974), 171–88.

39.   Quoted in William H. Nelson, *The American Tory* (Oxford, Eng., 1961), 141.

40.   GW to Nelson, Feb. 8, 1778, *WW*, 10:433; GW to Lt. Col. John F. Fitzgerald, Feb. 28, 1778, ibid., 10:529.

41.   Nelson, *Gates*, 170–71.

42.   Ibid., 174–75. A contrary view of the wisdom of the planned invasion is in Ward, *War of the Revolution*, 2:559–62. On the notion that the "cabal" had a hand in this scheme, see: Charlemagne Tower, *The Marquis de La Fayette in the American Revolution*, 2 vols. (Philadelphia, 1895), 1:268–87.

43.   Knollenberg, *Washington and the Revolution*, 78–92; Lafayette to Gates, Mar. 12, 1778, Stanley J. Idzerda et al., eds., *Lafayette in the Age of the American Revolution: Selected Letters and Papers, 1776–1790* (Ithaca, N.Y., 1977–), 1:347; Lafayette to Laurens, Feb. 19, 1778, ibid., 1:295.

44.   Wall, *GW*, 52–55; GW to Lund Washington, Nov. 26, 1775, *WW*, 4:114–15.

45.   GW to Lund Washington, Aug. 19 and Sept. 30, 1776, Aug. 15 and Dec. 18, 1778, Feb. 24 [26], 1779, *WW*, 5:460–62; 6:139; 7:326–28; 8:423–29; 9:147–48; GW to John A. Washington, June 1, 1777, ibid., 8:157–58.

46.   GW to Lund Washington, Feb. 28 and Dec. 18, 1778, ibid., 10:530–31; 13:423–29; Lund Washington to GW, Mar. 18, 1778, ibid., 10:531n.

47.   Wall, *GW*, 56–79.

48.   GW to Lund Washington, Dec. 18, 1778, Aug. 17, 1779, and Feb. 12, 1783, *WW*, 13:424–28; 16:124; 26:126–27.

49.   GW to Jackie Custis, Nov. 14, 1777, ibid., 10:61.

50.   GW to Lund Washington, Feb. 24 [26], 1779, ibid., 14:147–49.

51.   GW to PC, Apr. 18 and Mar. 24, 1778, ibid., 11:276, 138; GW to Cadwalader, Mar. 20, 1778, ibid., 11:117; GW to John Banister, Apr. 21, 1778, ibid., 11:288–90.

52.   GW to PC, May 1 and 4, 1778, ibid., 11:330, 348; After Orders, May 5, 1778, ibid., 11:354–56.

53.   Gen. Orders, May 5 and 7, 1778, ibid., 11:354–56, 362–63; Royster, *A Revolutionary People*, 250–54; John Laurens to Henry Laurens, May 7, 1778, in *The*

Army Correspondence of Colonel John Laurens in the Years 1777–1778 (New York, 1969), 169–70.

54. Gen. Orders, May 7, 1778, *WW*, 11:362; GW to Richard H. Lee, May 25, 1778, ibid., 11:450; J. Laurens to H. Laurens, May 7, 1778, *Army Correspondence of Laurens*, 169.

55. GW to General Officers, Apr. 20, 1778, *WW*, 11:282–83; Council of War, May 8, 1778, ibid., 11:363–66, 366n.

56. GW to PC, May 18, 1778, ibid., 11:415; GW to Pres. Jeremiah Powell, May 19, 1778, ibid., 11:424–25; William B. Willcox, *Portrait of a General: Sir Henry Clinton in the War of Independence* (New York, 1962), 211–25; Robson, *American Revolution*, 192–95; Mackesy, *War for America*, 230.

57. Willcox, *Portrait of a General*, 3–93; Willcox, "Clinton," Billias, *GW's Opponents*, 73–83.

58. GW to R. H. Lee, May 25, 1778, *WW*, 11:451; GW to Gen. Philemon Dickinson, June 5, 1778, ibid., 12:19; GW to PC, June 18, 1778, ibid., 12:84; Tatum, *Journal of Serle*, 300, 309, 311.

59. Council of War, June 24, 1778, *WW*, 12:116.

60. GW to PC, June 28, 1778, ibid., 12:128.

61. Councils of War, June 17 and 24, 1778, ibid., 12:75–78, 115–17.

62. John Shy, "Charles Lee: The Soldier as Radical," in Billias, *GW's Generals*, 41; GW to Lafayette, June 25, 1778, *WW*, 12:117; Lee to GW, June 25, 1778, ibid., 12:119n.

63. On the curious episode of Barren Hill, see Ward, *War of the Revolution*, 2:562–67.

64. Theodore Thayer, *The Making of a Scapegoat: Washington and Lee at Monmouth* (Pt. Washington, N.Y., 1976), 31–33; GW to Lafayette, June 26, 1778, *WW*, 12:119, 121–23.

65. Thayer, *Making of a Scapegoat*, 33.

66. GW to Lafayette, June 25, 1778, *WW*, 12:117; GW to Gates, June 28, 1778, ibid., 12:127; GW to Lee, June 30, 1778, ibid., 12:133; Alden, *Lee*, 213–14.

67. Lee to R. Morris, July 3, 1778, *Lee Papers*, 2:458.

68. Scheer, *Private Yankee Doodle*, 127.

69. Alden, *Lee*, 222; Thayer, *Making of a Scapegoat*, 52.

70. Thayer, *Making of a Scapegoat*, 36–67; Alden, *Lee*, 212–27; Freeman, *GW*, 5:24–37; GW to PC, July 1, 1778, *WW*, 12:139–46; GW to John Augustine Washington, July 4, 1778, ibid., 12:156–57.

IO

The Character of General Washington

1. Lee to GW, June 30, 1778, *Lee Papers*, 2:435–38; GW to Lee, June 30, 1778, *WW*, 12:132–33.

2. Flexner, *GW*, 2:30; Hughes, *GW*, 2:365–66.

3. Higginbotham, *War of American Independence*, 90; Smith, *A New Age*, 2:1134.

4. Thayer, *Greene*, 20–51, 56, 91.

5. GW to Jay, Apr. 14, 1779, *WW*, 14:383–86; Hamilton to Elias Boudinot, July

5, 1778, Harold C. Syrett and Jacob E. Cooke, eds., *The Papers of Alexander Hamilton*, 26 vols. (New York, 1961–1979), 1:512.

6. Alden, *Lee*, 164–65; Greene to Griffin Greene, May 25, 1778, Showman, *Papers of Greene*, 2:406; Greene to Gov. Wm. Greene, May 25, 1778, ibid., 2:408.

7. Thayer, *Making of a Scapegoat*, 73; Hamilton to Boudinot, July 5, 1778, Syrett and Cooke, *Papers of Hamilton*, 1:512.

8. Thayer, *Making of a Scapegoat*, 75.

9. Robert A. Hendrickson, *The Rise and Fall of Alexander Hamilton* (New York, 1981), 93; Thayer, *Making of a Scapegoat*, 76–83.

10. See North Callahan, "Henry Knox: American Artillerist," in Billias, *GW's Generals*, 239–59; Willard M. Wallace, "Benedict Arnold: Traitorous Patriot," ibid., 163–92; Hugh F. Rankin, "Anthony Wayne: Military Romanticist," ibid., 260–90.

11. GW to Reed, Jan. 23, 1776, *WW*, 4:269; W. Jackson Steager, "Tench Tilghman, George Washington's Aide," *Maryland History Magazine*, 77 (1982), 136–53; Jacob E. Cooke, *Alexander Hamilton* (New York, 1982), 13–15.

12. *DGW*, 2:181.

13. Cooke, *Hamilton*, 1–13.

14. Hamilton to Schuyler, Feb. 18, 1781, Syrett and Cooke, *Papers of Hamilton*, 2:564, 566, and 566n; John C. Miller, *Alexander Hamilton: Portrait in Paradox* (New York, 1959), 246.

15. Hamilton to Schuyler, Feb. 18, 1781, Syrett and Cooke, *Papers of Hamilton*, 2:567; Silas Deane to Eliz. Deane, Smith, *Letters of Delegates*, 1:61; Marquis de Chastellux, *Travels in North-America, in the Years 1780, 1781, and 1782*, 2 vols. (New York, 1968), 1:113, 129; Alden, *Lee*, 236, 297.

16. Cunliffe, *GW*, 153, 160, 162–63; Flexner, *GW*, 2:372.

17. Charles Royster, *Light-Horse Harry Lee and the Legacy of the American Revolution* (New York, 1981), 199–204; Freeman, *GW*, 4:411, 411n; 5:158, 192; Chastellux, *Travels*, 1:137–38; Mathieu Dumas, *Memoirs of His Own Time; Including the Revolution, the Empire, and the Restoration*, 2 vols. (Philadelphia, 1839), 1:29; John Adams to Abigail Adams, June 18 and Sept. 1, 1777, Butterfield, *Adams Fam. Corres.*, 2:268, 335; Page Smith, *John Adams*, 2 vols. (New York, 1962), 2:1084; Adams to Jefferson, May 1, 1812, Cappon, *Adams-Jefferson Letters*, 2:301; Jefferson to Wm. Jones, Jan. 2, 1814, Andrew Lipscomb and Albert E. Bergh, eds., *The Writings of Thomas Jefferson*, 20 vols. (Washington, D.C., 1903), 14:48; Evelyn M. Acomb, ed., *The Revolutionary Journal of Baron Ludwig von Closen, 1780–1783* (Chapel Hill, N.C., 1958), 64, 241.

18. Thacher, *Military Journal*, 30; Callahan, *Knox*, 32; Claude Blanchard, *Journal* (Albany, N.Y., 1876), 67, 89, 117–19; Chastellux, *Travels*, 1:119–26, 137; von Closen, *Journal*, 241; James Warren to Adams, Nov. 14, 1775, Taylor, *Papers of Adams*, 3:306; Mercy Warren to Adams, Oct. 25, 1775, ibid., 3:269; Abigail Adams to Adams, July 16, 1775, Butterfield, *Adams Fam. Corres.*, 1:246; Freeman, *GW*, 3:370n; 4:70, 343n, 413, 496, 519n, 581n; "Mrs. Theodorick Bland's Reminiscences on George Washington's HQ at Morristown," New Jersey Historical Society *Proceedings*, 51 (1933), 250–53.

19. GW to Livingston, Gerry, and Geo. Clymer, July 19, 1777, *WW*, 8:439–40; Freeman, *GW*, 5:483; Flexner, *GW*, 2:283; Chastellux, *Travels*, 1:117–28.

20. Freeman, *GW*, 3:290; 4:413; 5:44, 408, 443.

21. *WW*, 6:106n; 7:268n; 11:342n; GW to Lund Washington, Dec. 25, 1782, ibid., 25:472; Freeman, *GW*, 4:453; Chastellux, *Travels*, 1:119.

22. Alden, *Lee*, 297; Freeman, *GW*, 5:436. On the evolution of Washington's "character" in American art, literature, and historiography, see: Bernard Mayo, *Myths and Men: Patrick Henry, George Washington, Thomas Jefferson* (Athens, Georgia, 1959), 25–48.

23. GW to Reed, Feb. 10 and 26, 1776, *WW*, 4:319, 321, 348; GW to PC, Sept. 8, 1776, ibid., 6:28–29, 32; GW to Lund Washington, Sept. 30, 1776, ibid., 6:138; GW to John Augustine Washington, Mar. 31 and Nov. 19, 1776, ibid., 4:450; 6:246.

24. Lee to Gates, Dec. 19, 1779, *Lee Papers*, 3:401; Lee to Sidney Lee, June 22, 1782, ibid., 4:9–11; GW to Lafayette, Dec. 31, 1777, *WW*, 10:236; GW to Landon Carter, May 30, 1778, ibid., 11:493; GW to G. Morris, July 24, 1778, ibid., 11:228; GW to John Augustine Washington, Mar. 31, 1776, ibid., 4:457; GW to PC, May 16, 1776, ibid., 5:62.

25. Henry Laurens to John Laurens, Jan. 8, 1778, Smith, *Letters of Delegates*, 8:546; Lafayette to GW, Dec. 30, 1777, Idzarda, *Lafayette*, 1:204.

26. Mayo, *Myths and Men*, 45.

27. Blanchard, *Journal*, 67; John Adams, *Thoughts on Government*, in Taylor, *Papers of Adams*, 4:91.

28. GW to Lund Washington, May 19, 1780, *WW*, 18:392; GW to Bannister, Apr. 21, 1778, ibid., 11:286–90; Morgan, *Genius of George Washington*, 3–25.

II

The Forgotten Years, 1778–1780

1. GW to Benjamin Harrison, Dec. 18 [–30], 1778, *WW*, 13:462–68.

2. H. Laurens to GW, July 11, 1778, ibid., 12:174n; GW to Sullivan, July 17, 22, and 27, 1778, ibid., 12:184, 201, 237; GW to Lafayette, July 22, 1778, ibid., 12:203; Paul F. Dearden, *The Rhode Island Campaign of 1778: Inauspicious Dawn of Alliance* (Providence, R.I. 1980), 38–39.

3. GW to Heath, Aug. 28, 1778, *WW*, 12:364–65; Ward, *War of the Revolution*, 2:587–93; Dearden, *Rhode Island Campaign*, 105, 107–108.

4. Willcox, *Clinton*, 249–54; GW to d'Estaing, Sept. 11, 1778, *WW*, 12:425–28; GW to John Augustine Washington, Oct. 26, 1778, ibid., 13:156.

5. Henry Lumpkin, *From Savannah to Yorktown: The American Revolution in the South* (Columbia, S.C., 1981), 27–29; Ward, *War of the Revolution*, 2:679–84.

6. Lumpkin, *From Savannah to Yorktown*, 29–40; Ward, *War of the Revolution*, 2:688–94.

7. GW to Lafayette, Oct. 20, 1779, *WW*, 16:492; GW to Gov. Clinton, Oct. 1, 1779, ibid., 16:377.

8. Nelson, *Gates*, 189, 197–205; *JCC*, 12:1042–48.

9. GW to PC, Nov. 11, 1778, *WW*, 13:223–44; GW to H. Laurens, Nov. 14, 1778, ibid., 13:254–57; *JCC*, 13:11–13.

10. Gustave Lanctot, *Canada and the American Revolution* (Cambridge, Mass., 1967), 176, 184–85; Nathaniel Peabody to Nathaniel Folsom, June 14, 1780, Burnett, *Letters of Members*, 5:216; Richard Howley to Gates, June 13, 1781, ibid., 6:119; Lovell to Gates, Apr. 5, 1779, ibid., 4:142. Also see GW to Jay, Apr. 14, 1779, *WW*, 14:378–88.

11. GW to Comm. of Conf., Jan. 8 and 13, 1779, *WW*, 13:485–91; 14:3–12; GW to Stirling, Jan. 1, 1779, ibid., 13:474.

12. GW to Comm. of Conf., Jan. 13, 1779, ibid., 14:4–12; GW to Jay, Aug. 16 and Sept. 7, 1779, ibid., 16:115, 247.

13. GW to Minister Gerard, May 1, 1779, ibid., 14:470–73; GW to G. Morris, May 8, 1779, ibid., 15:24–25.

14. Ward, *War of the Revolution*, 2:638; GW to Bd. of War, Aug. 3, 1778, *WW*, 12:261–66; GW, Remarks to the Comm. of Conference, Jan. [?], 1779, WPPV.

15. Gates to GW, Mar. 16, 1779, *Gates Papers*, reel 9, no. 63; GW to Armstrong, May 18, 1779, *WW*, 15:47; GW to Jay, Apr. 14, 1779, ibid., 14:384; GW to Sullivan, Mar. 6, 1779, ibid., 14:201; GW to Comm. of Cong., Jan. 13, 1779, ibid., 14:9; GW to PC, Aug. 13, 1779, ibid., 15:107.

16. GW to Sullivan, May 4 and 31, 1779, *WW*, 14:492–93; 15:189–93; GW to Schuyler, Dec. 18, 1778, ibid., 13:430.

17. Smith, *A New Age*, 2:1172.

18. R.W.G. Vail, *The Revolutionary Diary of Lieut. Obadiah Gore, Jr.* (New York, 1929), 29, 31; Alfred Hazen Wright, comp., *The Sullivan Expedition of 1779; Contemporary Newspaper Comment and Letters*, Studies in *History*, nos. 5–8 (Ithaca, N.Y., 1943), 6:11, 15; 7:28; Howard Peckham and Lloyd A. Brown, eds., *Revolutionary War Journals of Henry Dearborn, 1775–1783* (Chicago, 1939), 172–90; Barbara Graymont, *The Iroquois in the American Revolution* (Syracuse, N.Y., 1972), 123, 196, 231–32; Whittemore, *Sullivan*, 132–52; Smith, *A New Age*, 2:1173–77.

19. GW to Schuyler, June 9, 1779, *WW*, 15:243; GW to PC, June 11, 1779, ibid., 15:261–62; Willcox, *Clinton*, 275–76.

20. GW to Gates, June 11, 1779, *WW*, 15:260; GW to Wayne, July 10, 1779, ibid., 15:396–99.

21. Wayne to GW, July 16, 1779, ibid., 15:427n; Nelson, *Wayne*, 97–100.

22. Ward, *War of the Revolution*, 2:596–603; GW to PC, July 21, 1779, *WW*, 15:449; GW to Gates, July 25, 1779, ibid., 15:477–78; GW to Lund Washington, May 29, 1779, ibid., 15:180.

23. Royster, *Light-Horse Harry, Lee* 20–21, 25; GW to Stirling, Aug. 28, 1779, *WW*, 16:190–91.

24. GW to Lee, Sept. 10, 1779, *WW*, 16:73; GW to PC, Aug. 23, 1779, ibid., 16:155.

25. GW to Reed, Aug. 22, 1779, ibid., 16:150–52; GW to Heath, Aug. 21, 1779, ibid., 16:144; Gen. Orders, Sept. 11 and Oct. 8, 1779, ibid., 16:265, 433; GW to Gordon, Aug. 2, 1779, ibid., 16:38.

26. GW to Heath, Aug. 21, 1779, ibid., 16:144; Willcox, *Clinton*, 279; Freeman, *GW*, 5:137.

27. Freeman, *GW*, 5:88–89, 95; Risch, *Supplying Washington's Army*, 293–303.

28. GW to Harrison, Oct. 25, 1779, *WW*, 17:20–21; GW to Pendleton, Nov. 1, 1779, ibid., 17:52.

29. GW to Harrison, Oct. 25, 1779, ibid., 17:20–21; GW to Bd. of War, Oct. 2, 1779, ibid., 17:389; GW to Magistrates of New Jersey, Jan. 8, 1780, ibid., 17:362–63; Scheer, *Private Yankee Doodle*, 166, 172; Thayer, *Greene*, 268, 270; Risch, *Supplying GW's Army*, 228, 305; Ives, *GW's HQs*, 204–08; Acct. Bk., *GWP* ser. 5, reel 117.

30. Greene to Reed, May 10, 1780, Reed, *Reed*, 2:191; GW to PC, Oct. 4, 1779, and Mar. 26, 1780, *WW*, 16:406; 17:152n; GW to Pres. Jeremiah Powell, ND [Nov. 22, 1779?], ibid., 17:161n; GW to Bd. of War, Oct. 2, 1779, ibid., 16:389–90; GW to Sullivan, Nov. 20, 1780, ibid., 20:371–72; GW to Lafayette, Mar. 18, 1780, ibid., 28:125; GW to R. Morris, Mar. 2, 1777, ibid., 7:225; Carp, *To Starve an Army*, 171–72; Risch, *Supplying Washington's Army*, 228, 306–307; Thayer, *Greene*, 268, 273.

31. GW to Govs. Trumbull, Clinton, and Livingston, Sept. 27, 1779, *WW*, 16:344–45; GW to Govs. Trumbull and Clinton, Nov. 16, 1779, ibid., 16:107–10.

32. GW to Joseph Jones, May 31, 1780, ibid., 18:453; Richard H. Kohn, "American Generals of the Revolution: Subordination and Restraint," in Don Higginbotham, ed., *Reconsiderations of the Revolutionary War: Selected Essays* (Westport, Conn., 1978), 110, 116.

33. Risch, *Supplying Washington's Army*, 229–32; GW to PC, May 27, 1780, *WW*, 18:428–29; GW to Reed, May 28, 1780, ibid., 18:434–35.

34. Freeman, *GW*, 5:167.

35. Willcox, *Clinton*, 295–99.

36. Ward, *War of the Revolution*, 2:695–703; Lumpkin, *Savannah to Yorktown*, 41–50; Clifford K. Shipton, "Benjamin Lincoln: Old Reliable," in Billias, *GW's Generals*.

37. Higginbotham, *War of American Independence*, 357.

38. Nelson, *Gates*, 216–18, 224–36; Higginbotham, *War of American Independence*, 359–60; Ward, *War of the Revolution*, 2:723–30.

39. Nelson, *Gates*, 239, 242; GW to Greene, Oct. 22, 1780, *WW*, 20:238–40.

40. GW to Reed, June 19 and 25, 1780, *WW*, 19:32, 70-71; GW to PC, July 10 and 15, 1780, ibid., 19:150, 181; GW to Fielding Lewis, May 5 [–July 6], 1780, ibid., 19:129–34; GW to John Augustine Washington, June 6 [–July 6], 1780, ibid., 19:135–37; GW to Col. Brodhead, July 4, 1780, ibid., 19:120.

41. GW to Bd. of War, July 18, 1780, ibid., 19:206–207; GW to Pres. Weare, June 30, 1780, ibid., 19:106.

42. Lee Kennett, *The French Forces in America, 1780–1783* (Westport, Conn., 1977), 36–37, 13; GW to Heath, May 15, 1780, *WW*, 19:361; GW to Gov. Rutledge, May 16, 1780, ibid., 19:375–76; GW to Lafayette, May 16, 1780, ibid., 19:370.

43. Kennett, *French Forces*, 12–14, 29–31; Freeman, *GW*, 5:n.p. (between pp. 275–76).

44. Kennett, *French Forces*, 48–49; GW to Howe, July 27, 1780, *WW*, 19:271; Howard C. Rice, Jr., and Anne S.K. Brown, eds., *The American Campaigns of Rochambeau's Army, 1780, 1781, 1782, 1783*, 2 vols. (Princeton, N.J., 1972), 1:18, 120.

45. GW, "Memorandum," July 15, 1780, *WW*, 19:174–76; Kennett, *French Forces*, 48–56; Mackesy, *War for America*, 350.

46. Kennett, *French Forces*, 51–52.

47. GW to Samuel Washington, Aug. 31, 1780, *WW*, 19:481–82; GW to Reed, July 27, Aug. 20, and 26, 1780, ibid., 19:263, 399, 442; GW to Lafayette, Aug. 3, 1780, ibid., 19:314; GW to Comm. of Cooperation, Aug. 17, 1780, ibid., 19:391; GW to PC, Aug. 20 and 28, 1780, ibid., 19: 405, 462.

48. GW to Chevalier de Bouchet, Oct. 1780, ibid., 20:275; Gen. Orders, June 18, 1780, ibid., 19:21–22.

49. "Conf. at Hartford," Sept. 22, 1780, ibid., 20:76–81; GW to Duane, Oct. 4, 1780, ibid., 20:118; GW to Cadwalader, Oct. 5, 1780, ibid., 20:122.

50. GW to Reed, Oct. 18, 1780, ibid., 20:213–15.

51. Gen. Orders, Aug. 1 and 3, 1780, ibid., 19:302, 313; GW to Arnold, Aug. 3, 1780, ibid., 19:309–310.

52. Wallace, *Traitorous Hero*, 160–259.

53. Smith, *A New Age*, 2:1584; Freeman, *GW*, 5:202–203; GW to Bd. of War, Oct. 25, 1780, *WW*, 20:170–71; GW to PC, Sept. 26, 1780, ibid., 20:91–93.

54. GW to Greene, Sept. 25, 1780, *WW*, 20:84.

55. GW to Gen. Clinton, Sept. 30, 1780, ibid., 20:103–104.

56. Gen. Orders, Sept. 26, 1780, ibid., 20:95; GW to H. Laurens, Oct. 13, 1780, ibid., 20:173; GW to Rochambeau, Sept. 27, 1780, ibid., 20:97; GW to Cadwalader, Oct. 5, 1780, ibid., 20:123; GW to J. Laurens, Apr. 9, 1781, ibid., 21:438; Royster, *Light Horse Harry Lee*, 20; Charles Royster, " 'The Nature of Treason': Revolutionary Virtue and American Reactions to Benedict Arnold," *WMQ*, 3d. Ser., 36, (1979), 163–93.

57. Martin and Lender, *A Respectable Army*, 150–52; Royster, *A Revolutionary People*, 333.

58. GW to Duane, Oct. 4, 1780, *WW*, 20:117–18; GW to PC, Aug. 20 and Oct. 11, 1780, ibid., 19:408; 20:157–67; GW, "Circular to the States," Oct. 18, 1780, ibid., 20:204–12; *JCC*, 18:839, 844.

59. GW to Duane, Oct. 4 and Dec. 26, 1780, *WW*, 20:118; 21:14–15; GW to Trumbull, Dec. 19, 1780, ibid., 20:495; GW to Capt. Buchanan, Dec. 19, 1780, ibid., 20:498.

60. GW to PC, Dec. 22, 1780, ibid., 21:1; GW to Col. Shreve, Dec. 29, 1780, ibid., 21:35; GW to Pickering, Dec. 29, 1780, and Jan. 25, 1781, ibid., 21:36, 141; "Circular to the N. Eng. States," Jan. 5, 1781, ibid., 21:62; Kennett, *French Army*, 80.

61. GW to Wayne, Jan. 3–9, 1781, *WW*, 21:55–58; "Circular to the N. Eng. States," Jan. 5, 1781, ibid., 21:61; GW to PC, Jan. 6, 1781, ibid., 21:65.

62. On the mutiny, see: Carl Van Doren, *Mutiny in January* (New York, 1943); Hugh F. Rankin, "Anthony Wayne: Military Romanticist," Billias, *GW's Generals*, 277–80; Smith, *A New Age*, 2:1600–23; James Kirby Martin, "A 'Most Undisciplined, Profligate Crew': Protest and Defiance in the Continental Ranks, 1776–1783," in Hoffman and Albert, *Arms and Independence*, 119–40; Nelson, *Wayne*, 115–31.

63. GW to Howe, Jan. 22, 1781, *WW*, 21:128–29.

64. GW to Greene, Feb. 2, 1781, ibid., 21:172.

65. Gen. Orders, Jan. 30, 1781, ibid., 21:159; GW to PC, Aug. 20, 1780, ibid., 19:406–407; GW to Jackie Custis, Feb. 28, 1781, ibid., 21:319–20; Mackesy, *War for America*, 385.

I2

Victory and Retirement

1. GW to J. Laurens, Jan. 15, 1781, *WW*, 21:105–10.

2. Ibid., 21:108–109.

3. Ward, *War of the Revolution*, 2:867–69.

4. GW to Rochambeau, Jan. 29 and Feb. 7, 1781, *WW*, 21:152, 197–98; GW to Jefferson, Feb. 6, 1781, ibid., 21:191–92. See Ira D. Gruber, "British Strategy: The Theory and Practice of Eighteenth-Century Warfare," in Higginbotham, *Reconsiderations*, 28–30.

5. Ward, *War of the Revolution*, 2:751–62; Don Higginbotham, "Daniel Morgan: Guerrilla Fighter," in Billias, *GW's Generals*, 304–10.

6. GW to Rochambeau, Feb. 14, 15, and 19, 1781, *WW*, 21:225, 229–32, 247; GW to Destouches, Feb. 22, 1781, ibid., 21:278.

7. GW to Lafayette, Feb. 20 and Mar. 1, 1781, ibid., 21:253–56, 322–23; Freeman, *GW*, 5:262–63.

8. GW to Armstrong, Mar. 26, 1781, *WW*, 21:378.

9. GW to Greene, Mar. 21, 1781, ibid., 21:346; GW to Schuyler, Mar. 23, 1781, ibid., 21:361; GW to Jones, Mar. 24, 1781, ibid., 21:378; GW to Lafayette, Apr. 5, 1781, ibid., 21:419.

10. Kennett, *French Forces*, 98–101; GW to Lafayette, Apr. 5, 1781, *WW*, 21:419; Freeman, *GW*, 5:279.

11. Don Higginbotham, "Reflections on the War of Independence, Modern Guerrilla Warfare, and the War in Vietnam," in Hoffman and Albert, *Arms and Independence*, 21–24.

12. Wickwire, *Cornwallis*, 274–311; Thayer, *Greene*, 307–31.

13. GW to Rochambeau, Apr. 3 and June 7, 1781, *WW*, 21:403; 22:171. On the dearth of provisions in the Carolinas, see: Intelligence Report to GW, Sept. [?], 1780, WPPV.

14. "Conference . . . ," May 23, 1781, *WW*, 22:105–107; Jonathan R. Dull, *The French Navy and American Independence: A Study of Arms and Diplomacy, 1774–1787* (Princeton, N.J., 1975), 239. On Washington's postwar statements, see: GW to Noah Webster, July 31, 1788, *WW*, 30:26–27.

15. GW to Laurens, Jan. 15, 1781, *WW*, 21:105–10; GW to Jones, June 7, 1781, ibid., 22:179; GW to Luzerne, May 23, 1781, ibid., 22:103–104; "Conf.," May 23, 1781, ibid., 22:107; GW to Reed, May 27, 1781, ibid., 22:117–18; GW to Lafayette, May 31, 1781, ibid., 22:143.

16. GW to PC, May 27, 1781, ibid., 22:119.

17. GW to Rochambeau, June 4, 19, and 30, 1781, ibid., 22:157, 234, 293.

18. GW to PC, June 6 and July 6, 1781, ibid., 22:168, 329–31; Freeman, *GW*, 5:297–99; Kennett, *French Forces*, 107, 115–17.

19. GW to Rochambeau, June 13, 1781, *WW*, 22:208; GW to de Grasse, July 21, 1781, ibid., 22:400–402.

20. Samuel Flagg Bemis, *The Diplomacy of the American Revolution* (New York, 1935), 172–88; William C. Stinchcombe, *The American Revolution and the French Alliance* (Syracuse, N.Y., 1969), 153–69.

21. GW to Lund Washington, Apr. 30, 1781, *WW*, 22:14–15; GW to Lafayette, May 4, 1781, ibid., 22:31–32; Wall, *GW*, 163.
22. Wickwire, *Cornwallis*, 325–33; GW to Greene, July 30, 1781, *WW*, 22:430; GW to R.H. Lee, July 15, 1781, ibid., 22:384.
23. Wickwire, *Cornwallis*, 336–53; Willcox, *Clinton*, 401–18.
24. Kennett, *French Army*, 129.
25. *DGW*, 3:397, 405; GW to Lafayette, July 30 and Aug. 15, 1781, *WW*, 22:432–33, 501; Freeman, *GW*, 5:309, 311.
26. Dull, *French Navy*, 243.
27. Gen. Orders, Aug. 22, 1781, *WW*, 23:38; Kennett, *French Army*, 131–34.
28. Willcox, *Clinton*, 418–23; *DGW*, 3:416n.
29. Kennett, *French Army*, 137.
30. GW to Lafayette, Sept. 10, 1781, *WW*, 23:110; Wickwire, *Cornwallis*, 358–64.
31. GW to de Grasse, Sept. 15, 1781, *WW*, 23:116; "Questions . . . ," Sept. 17, 1781, ibid., 23:122–25, 122n; GW to Heath, Sept. 23, 1781, ibid., 23:132; *DGW*, 3:420–21; Dull, *French Navy*, 242–26.
32. *DGW*, 3:422; Scheer and Rankin, *Rebels and Redcoats*, 484.
33. Scheer, *Private Yankee Doodle*, 230–32.
34. Scheer and Rankin, *Rebels and Redcoats*, 484; Thacher, *Journal*, 283.
35. Ward, *War of the Revolution*, 2:886–95; Scheer and Rankin, *Rebels and Redcoats*, 484, 488; Wickwire, *Cornwallis*, 374–84; Kennett, *French Army*, 149.
36. GW to Scammell, Sept. 26, 1781, *WW*, 23:142; GW to Weedon, Sept. 20, 1781, ibid., 23:126; Gen. Orders, Oct. 6 and 10, 1781, ibid., 23:182–83, 205; GW to PC, Oct. 12, 1781, ibid., 23:213; "Questions . . . ," Sept. 25, 1781, ibid., 23:136–37.
37. Gen. Orders, Oct. 6, 1781, ibid., 23:182–83.
38. GW, "Military Expenses," ser. 5, reel 17, 281–82.
39. GW to de Grasse, Sept. 29, 1781, *WW*, 23:13.
40. GW to Rutledge, Oct. 6, 1781, ibid., 23:186; GW, "Questions . . . ," Oct. 17, 1781, ibid., 23:125; GW to Lt. Col. Anthony White, Oct. 8, 1781, ibid., 23:138; Ward, *War of the Revolution*, 2:798–99, 810, 825, 834.
41. GW to Th. McKean, Oct. 6, 1781, *WW*, 23:189; GW to de Grasse, Oct. 1, 11, and 16, 1781, ibid., 23:161, 208, 225; GW to Weedon, Oct. 12, 1781, ibid., 23:215.
42. Wickwire, *Cornwallis*, 385.
43. Flexner, *GW*, 2:460.
44. Freeman, *GW*, 5:378–93; Scheer and Rankin, *Rebels and Redcoats*, 494; Scheer, *Private Yankee Doodle*, 240–41; Thacher, *Journal*, 288–90.
45. Gen. Orders, Oct. 20, 1781, *WW*, 23:245; GW to Gov. Nelson, Oct. 27, 1781, ibid., 23:271–72; GW to PC, Oct. 27 [–29], 1781, ibid., 23:295–97; *DGW*, 3:433–35.
46. John P. Custis to MW, Oct. 12, 1781, MVL; GW to Nelson, Oct. 27, 1781, *WW*, 23:271; GW to Lafayette, Nov. 15, 1781, ibid., 23:340; *DGW*, 3:437–38n.
47. Wall, *GW*, 170.
48. GW to Lafayette, Nov. 15, 1781, *WW*, 23:341–42; GW to Gen. Parsons, Jan. 8, 1782, ibid., 23:433; GW to Sec. of War, Jan. 20, 1782, ibid., 23:454–55; *JCC*, 21:1179–80; Freeman, *GW*, 5:405.
49. GW to Greene, Mar. 18, 1782, *WW*, 24:73; GW to PC, June 24, 1782, ibid., 24:384; Thayer, *Greene*, 395; Mackesy, *War for America*, 494.

50. GW to Greene, Mar. 18, 1782, *WW*, 24:73; Mackesy, *War for America*, 434.

51. GW to Greene, July 9, 1782, *WW*, 24:409; GW to James McHenry, July 18, 1782, ibid., 24:432; GW to Franklin, Oct. 18, 1782, ibid., 25:273.

52. GW to Sec. for For. Aff., May 22, 1782, ibid., 24:271; GW to Rochambeau, June 27, 1782, ibid., 24:382.

53. "Conf.," July 19, 1782, ibid., 24:433–35; Freeman, *GW*, 5:418. On his Canadian plan, see: GW to Hazen, Apr. 10, 1782, *WW*, 24:107–10; "Memorandum," May 1, 1782, ibid., 24:197–99.

54. Kennett, *French Army*, 161–62.

55. GW to Greene, Oct. 17 and Dec. 18, 1782, *WW*, 25:255–56, 448–49; GW to Lafayette, Dec. 15, 1782, ibid., 25:434.

56. GW to Sec. of War, Oct. 2, 1782, ibid., 25:226–29.

57. Hamilton to GW, Feb. 13, 1783, Syrett and Cooke, *Papers of Hamilton*, 3:253–55.

58. *JCC*, 24:295–97. On Gates's role in these machinations, see: Nelson, *Gates*, 270–76.

59. GW to Jones, Mar. 12, 1783, *WW*, 26:213–16; GW to PC, Mar. 12, 1783, ibid., 26:211–12; Gen. Orders, Mar. 11, 1783, ibid., 26:208.

60. *JCC*, 24:298–99.

61. GW, "To the Officers of the Army," Mar. 15, 1783, *WW*, 26:222–27; Josiah Quincy, ed., *The Journal of Major Samuel Shaw* (Boston, 1843), 101–105.

62. Quincy, *Journal of Shaw*, 105; Freeman, *GW*, 5:435–36. On the Newburgh Conspiracy, see: Richard H. Kohn, *Eagle and Sword: The Federalists and the Creation of the Military Establishment in America, 1783–1802* (New York, 1975), 17–39; Royster, *Revolutionary People at War*, 333–41; Nelson, *Gates*, 269–77; C. Edward Skeen, "The Newburgh Conspiracy Reconsidered," *WMQ*, 3d ser., 31 (1974), 273–90; Richard H. Kohn, "Rebuttal," ibid., 31:290–98.

63. GW to Hamilton, Mar. 31, Apr. 4 and 16, 1783, *WW*, 26:276–77, 291–93, 323–26; Wills, *Cincinnatus*, 104.

64. GW to Theodorick Bland, Apr. 4, 1783, ibid., 26:285–91, 293–96; GW to PC, Mar. 18, 1783, ibid., 26:230–32; GW to Lund Washington, Mar. 19, 1783, ibid., 26:246.

65. GW to Jefferson, Feb. 10, 1783, ibid., 26:118; GW to Luzerne, Mar. 19, 1783, ibid., 26:236.

66. GW to Carleton, Apr. 9, 1783, ibid., 26:307.

67. David Howell to Gov. Greene, Sept. 9[?], 1783. Burnett, *Letters of Delegates*, 7:292.

68. Ives, *GW's Headquarters*, 292–300; Charles H. Metzger, *The Prisoner in the American Revolution* (Chicago, 1971), 203–20; Larry Bowman, *Captive Americans: Prisoners During the American Revolution* (Athens, Oh., 1976), 69, 72–74, 100–15.

69. On the end of one soldier's service, see: Scheer, *Private Yankee Doodle*, 273–83.

70. GW to Boudinot, May 10, 1783, *WW*, 26:422–23; Gen. Orders, June 2, 1783, ibid., 26:464; GW to Putnam, June 2, 1783, ibid., 26:462; GW to Supt. of Finance, June 3, 1783, ibid., 26:467; Freeman, *GW*, 5:441–43.

71. GW to Chastellux, Oct. 12, 1783, *WW*, 27:189–90; GW to Clinton, Aug. 12, 1783, ibid., 27:99; "Military Expences," *GWP*, ser. 5, reel 117, no. 435; Freeman, *GW*, 5:450.

72. GW, "Circular to the States," June 8, 1783, *WW*, 26:483–96.

73. GW to Clinton, Aug. 12, 1783, ibid., 27:97; GW to Knox, Aug. 17 and Sept. 23, 1783, ibid., 27:106, 163; Freeman, *GW*, 5:456, 451–52.

74. Freeman, *GW*, 5:446–47.

75. GW, "Address to the Faculty . . . ," Aug. 25, 1783, *WW*, 27:115–16; GW, "Address to Congress," Aug. 26, 1783, ibid., 27:116–17; GW to Duane, Sept. 7, 1783, ibid., 27:133–34; Ives, *GW's HQs*, 304.

76. GW, "Observations on an Intended Report . . . ," Sept. 8, 1783, *WW*, 27:140–44; GW, "Sentiments on a Peace Establishment," [May, 1783], ibid., 26:374–98.

77. GW to Tilghman, Oct. 2, 1783, ibid., 27:177; GW to Lafayette, Oct. 12, 1783, ibid., 27:187.

78. GW to Citizens of New Brunswick, N.J., Dec. 6, 1783, ibid., 27:260; GW to Rochambeau, Nov. 1, 1783, ibid., 27:219; "Farewell Orders," Nov. 2, 1783, ibid., 27:224; Royster, *Revolutionary People at War*, 257.

79. GW, "Address to Congress," Dec. 23, 1783, *WW*, 27:284; GW, "Address to Faculty," Aug. 25, 1783, ibid., 27:115; GW to d'Estaing, May 15, 1784, ibid., 27:402; GW, "Farewell Orders," Nov. 2, 1783, ibid., 27:227.

80. GW to Mason, Mar. 27, 1779, ibid., 14:299; GW to James Warren, Mar. 31, 1779, ibid., 14:313; GW to Harrison, May 5–7, 1779, ibid., 15:6; GW to Gates, June 11, 1779, ibid., 15:259–60; GW to PC, Mar. 15 and July 22, 1780, ibid., 14:243; 19:235; GW to John Augustine Washington, Nov. 26, 1778 and May 12, 1779, ibid., 13:335; 15:59; GW to G. Morris, Oct. 4, 1778, ibid., 13:21–23; GW to Fitzhugh, June 25, 1779, ibid., 15:313; GW to A. Lewis, Oct. 15, 1778, ibid., 13:79; GW to Hazen, Jan. 21, 1780, ibid., 17:418–21; GW to Comm. of Cooperation, May 25, 1780, ibid., 28:416–17.

81. Stinchcombe, *French Alliance*, 142.

82. Royster, *Revolutionary People at War*, 160, 256, 264.

83. GW to Luzerne, Nov. 17, 1783, *WW*, 27:243; GW, "Farewell," Nov. 2, 1783, ibid., 27:222–27.

84. Freeman, *GW*, 5:465–68.

85. "Pocket Day Book," *GWP*, ser. 5, reel 116, no. 549; "Military Expences," ibid., no. 475.

86. Wall, *GW*, 188; Charles Beard, *An Economic Interpretation of the Constitution* (New York, 1913), 145; GW, "Address to Congress . . . ," Dec. 23, 1783, *WW*, 27:284–85; Freeman, *GW*, 5:469–78. On Washington's expense account, see: George Washington, *Account of Expences while Commander in Chief*, with annotations by John C. Fitzpatrick (Boston and New York, 1917).

13

A Brief Retirement

1. GW to Lafayette, Feb. 1, 1784, *WW*, 27:317.

2. Thomas Tilston Waterman, *The Mansions of Virginia* (New York, 1965), 268–307.

3. GW to Bryan Fairfax, July 4, 1774, *WW*, 3:227.

4. Wall, *GW*, 85–101.

5. GW to Samuel Vaughn, Jan. 14, 1784, *WW*, 27:298; GW to Wm. Hamilton, Jan.

15 and Apr. 6, 1784, ibid., 27:303, 388; GW to John Rumney, July 3, 1784 and June 22, 1785, ibid., 27:433; 28:171; GW to Clement Biddle, Jan. 17, 1784, ibid., 27:305; Thayer, *Potomac Squire*, 205.

6.　GW to R. Morris, June 2, 1784, *WW*, 27:413; GW to Wm. Hamilton, Jan. 15, 1784, ibid., 27:303; GW to Tilghman, Aug. 11, 1784, ibid., 27:454–55; GW to Richard Boulton, June 24, 1785, ibid., 28:175; GW to Knox, Feb. 28, 1785, ibid., 28:94.

7.　GW to Biddle, Nov. 3, 1784, ibid., 27:493; GW to Gov. Clinton, Nov. 25 and Dec. 8, 1784, ibid., 27:502; 28:6; GW to George A. Washington, Jan. 6, 1785, ibid., 28:28; GW to Wm. Grayson, Jan. 22, 1785, ibid., 28:38; GW to John A. Washington, Mar. 27, 1786, ibid., 28:396; GW to Wm. Washington, Apr. 10, 1786, ibid., 28:406; GW to Wm. Gordon, Dec. 5, 1785, ibid., 28:346.

8.　GW to Peale, Mar. 13, 1787, ibid., 29:178 and 178n; GW to Benj. Ogle, Aug. 17, 1785, ibid., 28:228; GW to Geo. Wm. Fairfax, June 26, 1786, ibid., 28:468; GW to Rich. Sprigg, Sept. 28, 1787, ibid., 29:281; GW to Andrew Lewis, Feb. 1, 1787, ibid., 29:397; Howarth, *GW*, 152–59.

9.　GW to Tilghman, Mar. 24, 1784, *WW*, 27:367; GW to Rumney, June 22 and Nov. 18, 1785, ibid., 28:171, 317; GW to John Mercer, Nov. 6 and Dec. 19, 1786, ibid., 28:56, 116–18; GW to H. Lee, Feb. 4, 1787, ibid., 28:154; GW to John Lawson, Apr. 10, 1787, ibid., 28:199 and 369n.

10.　"A View of the Work . . . ," [1789], ibid., 30:175–76n GW to Th. Green, Mar. 31, 1789, ibid., 30:262–64; "Agreement with Philip Bater, Apr. 23, 1787, ibid., 29:206–207.

11.　GW to Lund Washington, Dec. 20, 1785, and May 7, 1787, ibid., 28:363–64; 29:212; *DGW*, 4:80–81n, 322; 5:87; Freeman, *GW*, 6:50 and 50n, 53, 160, 392; *DGW*, 4:80–81n.

12.　GW to Geo. Wm. Fairfax, June 30 and Nov. 10, 1785, and June 21, 1786, *WW*, 28:185, 313, 469; "Agreement with James Bloxham," May 31, 1786, ibid., 28:444–46; GW to Wm. Peacey, Aug. 5, 1786, and Jan. 7, 1787, ibid., 28:509, 29:356; GW to Arthur Young, Aug. 6, 1786, ibid., 28:513; *DGW*, 4:315.

13.　Freeman, *GW*, 6:33, 53.

14.　*DGW*, 4:116, 123, 127, 217; GW to Young, Nov. 1, 1787, and Dec. 4, 1788, *WW*, 29:297–98; 30:152–53; GW to Geo. A. Washington, May 27, 1787, and March 31, 1789, ibid., 29:217; 30:251; GW to David Stuart, Dec. 2, 1788, ibid., 30:148; GW to John Bordley, Aug. 17, 1788, ibid., 30:47–52; GW to Levi Hollingsworth, Sept. 20, 1785, ibid., 28:271; GW to Barbe Marbois, July 9, 1783, ibid., 27:55; GW to Gov. Clinton, Nov. 25, 1784, ibid., 27:502. Washington's library was filled with agricultural tracts. For a list of his holdings, see: Alan Fusonie and Donna Jean Fusonie, eds., *A Selected Bibliography of George Washington's Interest in Agriculture* (Davis, Calif. 1976).

15.　GW to Young, Dec. 4, 1788, *WW*, 30:151–52; GW to Lafayette, Sept. 1, 1785, and May 10, 1786, ibid., 28:244, 423; GW to Bushrod Washington, Apr. 13, 1786, ibid., 28:409; GW to Fitzhugh, June 5, 1786, ibid., 28:454; GW to Sprigg, June 28, 1786, ibid., 28:471; Howarth, *GW*, 132.

16.　GW to R. Morris, Apr. 12, 1786, *WW*, 28:408; GW to Lafayette, May 10, 1786, ibid., 28:424; GW to Harrison, May 6, 1783, ibid., 26:401.

17.　Washington's conduct as a slaveowner is analyzed further in ch. 18.

18. GW to Lewis, Feb. 27, 1784, *WW*, 27:345; GW to Mercer, Dec. 20, 1785, and Aug. 12 and Sept. 9, 1786, ibid., 28: 363, 515; 29:6; GW to Lund Washington, May 7, 1787, ibid., 29:212; GW to Mary Ball Washington, Feb. 15, 1787, ibid., 29:158; "Advertisement," Mar. 20, 1784, ibid., 27:253; Robert F. Jones, *George Washington* (Boston, 1979), 77; Freeman, *GW*, 3:62, and 6:113n; Ernst W. Spaulding, *His Excellency George Clinton* (New York, 1938), 231–33; Forrest M. McDonald, *We the People: The Economic Origins of the Constitution* (Chicago, 1958), 72n.

19. GW to Clinton, Nov. 5, 1786, *WW*, 29:52–53; GW to Jefferson, Mar. 29, 1784, ibid., 27:375; GW to Rufus Putnam, June 2, 1784, ibid., 27:411. Some of Washington's woes arose because he did not know the exact nature of his finances, thanks in large measure to Lund's shoddy bookkeeping practices. See: GW to John Harvie, Feb. 10, 1784, ibid., 27:326; GW to Th. Newton, Sept. 3, 1785, ibid., 28:248–49.

20. Jones, *GW*, 78.

21. GW to Hugh Williamson, Mar. 31, 1784, *WW*, 27:378, 380; GW to Jefferson, Feb. 25 and Sept. 26, 1785, ibid., 28:78, 279; GW to John de Neufville, Sept. 8, 1785, ibid., 28:259; GW to John Page, Oct. 3, 1785, ibid., 28:286; GW to Geo. Wm. Fairfax, Nov. 10, 1785, ibid., 28:312; GW to James Madison, Nov. 30, 1785, ibid., 28:377; GW to Robt. Hooe, Feb. 21, 1786, ibid., 28:386; *DGW*, 4:131–32. Pleading a shortage of funds, GW declined Patrick Henry's invitation to participate in a venture to drain and develop the southern portion of the Dismal Swamp. See: GW to Henry, June 24 and Nov. 30, 1785, *WW*, 28:176, 333.

22. Douglas R. Littlefield, "Eighteenth Century Plans to Clear the Potomac River: Technology, Expertise, and Labor in a Developing Nation," *VMHB*, 93 (1985), 293, 296–97; GW to Carter, Aug. 1754, *GWP*, 1:196–97; GW, "Notes on the Navigation of the Potomac River above the Great Falls," July–Aug., 1754, ibid., 1:179; Rick W. Studevant, "Quest for Eden: George Washington's Frontier Land Interests" (Ph.D. diss., Univ. of California, Santa Barbara, 1982), 99–135.

23. GW to Jefferson, Mar. 29, 1784, *WW*, 27:373–75; GW to Harrison, Oct. 10, 1784, ibid., 27:471–80; GW to Jacob Read, Nov. 3, 1784, ibid., 27:488–90; Flexner, *GW*, 3:73–82.

24. *DGW*, 4:140n; GW to Lafayette, July 25, 1785, *WW*, 28:207, 245; GW to R. Morris, Feb. 1, 1785, ibid., 28:49; GW to Jefferson, Aug. 31, 1788, ibid., 30:80; GW to Fairfax, Nov. 10, 1785, ibid., 28:312; Potomac Company Report, 1783, WPPV; Norman K. Risjord, *Chesapeake Politics, 1781–1800* (New York, 1978), 240–44.

25. Littlefield, "Eighteenth Century Plans," *VMHB*, 93:310, 314–16; Sturdevant, "Quest for Eden," 215–38; Cora Bacon-Foster, *Early Chapters in the Development of the Potomac Route to the West* (Washington, D.C., 1912), 33–84.

26. *DGW*, 4:84–85n; 5:37, 40, 52, 54n, 102; 1:241n.

27. GW to Lafayette, Oct. 12, 1783, *WW*, 27:187; GW to Craik, July 10, 1784, ibid., 27:437; GW to Simpson, Feb. 13, 1784, ibid., 27:329–30; Freeman, *GW*, 4:21n.

28. *DGW*, 4:4–6, 32, 34n; GW to Ch. Simms, Sept. 22, 1786, *WW*, 29:11; J. Lawrence Smith, "The 'Lost Washingtons,'" *Wonderful West Virginia*, 40 (Feb. 1985), 26–28.

29. *DGW*, 4:25–34; GW to Th. Smith, July 28, 1786, *WW*, 28:490.

30. *DGW*, 4:38–53.

31. Humphreys, Ms. Biog. of GW, Rosenbach Museum & Library; Custis, *Recollections*, 163–74; Wright and Tinling, *Quebec to Carolina*, 52, 191–95; Fitzpatrick, *GW Himself*, 147; Freeman, *GW*, 6:54; Thayer, *Potomac Squire*, 243.

32. Thayer, *Potomac Squire*, 227; *DGW*, 4:115, 137, 142, 147, 201.

33. *DGW*, 4:139, 160, 241, 275–76, 276n; 5:56.

34. GW to Madison, Nov. 28, 1784, *WW*, 27:504–505; GW to Lafayette, Dec. 8, 1785, ibid., 28:6–7.

35. GW to Knox, June 18, 1785, ibid., 28:169; GW to Stuart, June 5, 1785, ibid., 28:159; GW to PC, June 22, 1785, ibid., 28:174.

36. *DGW*, 4:129–30, 200, 209; GW to Jefferson, Sept. 26, 1785, *WW*, 28:278, 504.

37. GW to Geo. Wm. Fairfax, July 10, 1783, and June 26 and 30, 1786, *WW*, 27:57–60; 28:83, 468, 472–76.

38. GW to Warner Washington, Nov. 9, 1787, ibid., 29:306; GW to Sally Fairfax, May 16, 1798, ibid., 28:262–65.

39. GW to Mary Ball Washington, Feb. 15, 1787, ibid., 29:306; 159; Flexner, *GW*, 3:124; *DGW*, 5:163n, 169n; Custis, *Recollections*, 385–92.

40. GW to State Soc. of the Cincinnati, Oct. 31, 1786, *WW*, 29:32; GW to Gov. Randolph, Mar. 28, 1787, ibid., 29:187; GW to Lafayette, Dec. 8, 1784, ibid., 28:7; Nordham, *GW: Vignettes*, 7.

41. Smith, " 'Lost Washingtons,' " *Wonderful W.Va.*, 40:26–28.

42. GW to Thomson, Jan. 22, 1784, *WW*, 27:312; GW to Benj. Harrison, Mar. 21, 1781, ibid., 21:341–42; GW to John A. Washington, Jan. 16, 1783, ibid., 26:42–44; GW to Mary Ball Washington, Feb. 15, 1787, ibid., 29:159; Wall, *GW*, 171; Miriam Anne Bourne, *First Family: George Washington and his Intimate Relations* (New York, 1982), 120.

43. GW to Mary Ball Washington, Feb. 15, 1787, *WW*, 29:158–62; GW to Knox, Apr. 27, 1787, and June 17, 1788, ibid., 29:209, 517; GW to Rich. Conway, Mar. 6, 1789, ibid., 30:222; GW to Betty Lewis, Sept. 13 and Oct. 12, 1789, ibid., 30:399, 435.

44. GW to Geo. Wm. Fairfax, July 10, 1783, ibid., 27:59–60; GW to Lund Washington, Sept. 20, 1783, ibid., 27:157, 157n; *DGW*, 4:72, 206; Bourne, *First Family*, 100–102.

45. GW to Knox, Jan. 5, 1785, *WW*, 28:23; GW to Humphreys, Feb. 7, 1785, ibid., 28:65; GW to Th. Montgomerie, June 25, 1785, ibid., 28:177.

46. *DGW*, 4:158–59n, 231, 250, 257, 259, 263, 267, 285, 340; 5:26, 30; Haworth, *GW*, 175.

47. *DGW*, 4:337 and 338n.

48. GW to Armand-Tuffin, Oct. 7, 1785, *WW*, 28:289.

49. GW to Lafayette, Dec. 8, 1784, ibid., 27:7; GW to Geo. Wm. Fairfax, June 26, 1786, ibid., 28:468; GW to Alex. Spotswood, Feb. 13, 1788, ibid., 29:414; GW to Marchioness de Lafayette, Apr. 4, 1784, ibid., 27:385; GW to Knox, Feb. 20, 1784, ibid., 27:340; GW to Armand-Tuffin, Oct. 7, 1785, ibid., 28:289; GW to Gov. Clinton, Dec. 28, 1783, ibid., 27:288.

50. Isaac Weld, *Travels Through the States of North America, and the Provinces of Upper and Lower Canada, 1795, 1796, 1797*, 2 vols. (London, 1799), 1:94; GW to Gov. Clinton, Dec. 28, 1783, *WW*, 27:288; Wills, *Cincinnatus*, 18.

14

An End to Retirement

1. GW to Jay, Aug. 1, 1786, *WW*, 28:503.
2. GW to Gov. Harrison, Jan. 18 and Oct. 10, 1784, ibid., 27:305, 474–76; GW to Jefferson, Mar. 29, 1784, ibid., 27:373–74; GW to Jacob Read, Nov. 3, 1784, ibid., 27:487–88; GW to Lafayette, July 25, 1785, 1786, ibid., 28:208.
3. Jefferson to GW, Nov. 14, 1786, Julian P. Boyd et al., eds., *The Papers of Thomas Jefferson* (Princeton, N.J., 1950–), 10:532; Van Doren, *Franklin*, 707–708; Page Smith, *John Adams*, 2 vols. (New York, 1962), 1:570.
4. GW to Hamilton, Dec. 11, 1785, *WW*, 28:352; GW to Trumbull, Apr. 4, 1784, ibid., 27:386; GW to Soc. of Cincinnati, May 4, 1784, ibid., 27:393–98; GW to Madison, Dec. 16, 1786, ibid., 29:113–15; GW to Knox, Apr. 2, 1787, ibid., 29:194–95; GW to Jefferson, May 30, 1787, ibid., 29:222–24; Wills, *Cincinnatus*, 142.
5. GW to Jay, Aug. 1, 1786, *WW*, 28:503; GW to H. Lee, Oct. 31, 1786, ibid., 29:33–34; GW to Madison, Nov. 5, 1786, ibid., 29:52. On the proposal that Washington become America's monarch, an idea that gave him "painful sensations," see: GW to Col. Nicola, May 22, 1782, ibid., 24:272–73.
6. GW to Jay, Aug. 1, 1786, ibid., 28:503. Emphasis added.
7. GW to Harrison, Oct. 10, 1784, ibid., 27:475.
8. Merrill Jensen, *The New Nation: A History of the United States During the Confederation, 1781–1789* (New York, 1965), 154–63, 201–17.
9. Ibid., 403–406; Jensen, *American Revolution within America*, 149–50; Joseph L. Davis, *Sectionalism in American Politics, 1774–1787* (Madison, Wisc. 1977), 84–93.
10. Davis, *Sectionalism*, 93, 106–07, 127, 139–40; Jensen, *New Nation*, 418–20; Richard B. Morris, *The American Revolution Reconsidered* (New York, 1967), 152.
11. Davis, *Sectionalism*, 109–26; Jensen, *New Nation*, 170–73.
12. See Marion L. Starkey, *A Little Rebellion* (New York, 1955).
13. Andrew C. McLaughlin, *The Confederation and the Constitution, 1783–1789* (New York, 1962), 126–28.
14. GW to James Madison, Nov. 18, 1786, *WW*, 29:70–71.
15. GW to Luzerne, Aug. 1, 1786, ibid., 28:500; GW to Jefferson, Aug. 1, 1786, ibid., 28:505; GW to Chastellux, Aug. 18, 1786, ibid., 28:523; GW to Lafayette, July 25, 1785, ibid., 28:208.
16. Knox to GW, Oct. 23, Dec. 17, 1786, Jan. 14, 1787, WPPV; Humphreys to GW, Nov. 9, 1786, and Jan. 20, 1787, WPPV; Noah Brooks, *Henry Knox: A Soldier of the Revolution* (New York, 1980), 191–99; Callahan, *Knox*, 255.
17. GW to Jay, Aug. 1, 1786, *WW*, 28:502; GW to Humphreys, Oct. 22, 1786, ibid., 29:27; GW to H. Lee, Oct. 31, 1786, ibid., 29:34; GW to Madison, Nov. 5, 1786, ibid., 29:51–52; GW to Knox, Dec. 26, 1786, ibid., 29:122.
18. GW to Madison, Nov. 18, 1786, ibid., 29:71; GW to H. Lee, Oct. 31, 1786, ibid., 29:34; GW to Stuart, Nov. 19, 1786, ibid., 29:76; GW to Knox, Dec. 26, 1786, ibid., 29:124; GW to Humphreys, Dec. 26, 1786, ibid., 29:128; GW to Jay, May 18, 1786, ibid., 28:431.

19. GW to Lafayette, Aug. 15, 1786, ibid., 28:521; GW to Rochambeau, July 31, 1786, ibid., 28:493; GW to Samuel Purviance, Mr. 10, 1786, ibid., 28:393; Davis, *Sectionalism*, 13–14, 117–20.

20. Knox to GW, Dec. 17, 1786, Jan. 14 and Apr. 9, 1787, WPPV; GW to Madison, Mar. 31, 1787, *WW*, 29:192; GW to Knox, Feb. 3, 1787, ibid., 29:153; GW to Jay, Aug. 1, 1786, ibid., 28:502. On the Federalist critique of the Articles, as well as the remedies they proposed, see: Gordon S. Wood, *The Creation of the American Republic, 1776–1787* (Chapel Hill, N.C., 1969), 402–405, 410, 416–17, 432, 437, 440–55, 466, 475.

21. Wright and Tinkling, *Carolina to Quebec*, 50; Knox to GW, Jan. 14, 1787, WPPV; GW to Madison, Nov. 5, 1786, *WW*, 29:51.

22. GW to Knox, Apr. 2 and 27, 1787, *WW*, 29:194, 209; GW to State Soc. of Cincinnati, Oct. 31, 1786, ibid., 29: 31; GW to Jay, Mar. 10, 1787, ibid., 29:177; GW to Lafayette, Mar. 25, 1787, ibid., 29:184; GW to Randolph, Mar. 28, 1787, ibid., 29:186–88; Miller, *Mason*, 233; Jensen, *American Revolution within America*, 169; Wills, *Cincinnatus*, 154–57.

23. GW to Randolph, Mar. 28, 1787, *WW*, 29:187; GW to R. Morris, May 5, 1787, ibid., 29:210–11.

24. GW to Knox, Apr. 27, 1787, ibid., 29:209; GW to R. Morris, May 5, 1787, ibid., 29:211; *DGW*, 5:152–56.

25. *DGW*, 5:156–63; Clinton Rossiter, *1787: The Grand Convention* (New York, 1966), 161; Carl Van Doren, *The Great Rehearsal: The Story of the Making and Ratifying of the Constitution of the United States* (New York, 1948), 31.

26. Rossiter, *1787*, 164–66.

27. McDonald, *We the People*, 38–92; Rossiter, *1787*, 142–43.

28. Stanley M. Elkins and Eric McKitrick, "The Founding Fathers: Young Men of the Revolution," *Political Science Quarterly*, 76 (1961), 181–216; Rossiter, *1787*, 139–51.

29. Forrest McDonald, *The Formation of the American Republic, 1776–1790* (Baltimore, 1967), 154.

30. GW to Humphreys, Dec. 26, 1786, and Oct. 10, 1787, *WW*, 29:126, 287; GW to Madison, Nov. 5, 1786, and Mar. 31, 1787, ibid., 29:51–52, 190; GW to H. Lee, Oct. 31, 1786, ibid., 29:34; GW to Jay, Aug. 1, 1786, ibid., 28:503; McDonald, *We the People*, 93–110; McDonald, *Formation of the American Republic*, 174–84.

31. Max Farrand, ed., *The Records of the Federal Convention of 1787*, 4 vols., (New Haven, Conn., 1911), 1:18–19; Jensen, *American Revolution within America*, 167–69; GW to Jay, Aug. 1, 1786, *WW*, 28:502.

32. Wood, *Creation of the American Republic*, 525.

33. Ibid., 471, 475, 476, 477–82; Jackson T. Main, "Government by the People: The American Revolution and the Democratization of the Legislatures," *WMQ*, 3d ser., 23 (1966), 391–407.

34. Farrand, *Records*, 2:644.

35. Edmund S. Morgan, *The Birth of the Republic, 1763–1789* (Chicago, 1956), 139.

36. *DGW*, 5:155–85.

37. Ibid., 5:163, 171; "Accts. & Vouchers," *GWP.*, ser. 5, reel 117.

38. *DGW*, 5:173–75; Silverman, *Cultural History*, 429, 571–73.

39. GW to Humphreys, Oct. 10, 1787, *WW*, 29:287; GW to Knox, Aug. 19, 1787, ibid., 29:261.
40. Jensen, *American Revolution within America*, 206–12.
41. *DGW*, 5:164; Cooke, *Hamilton*, 51; GW to Hamilton, July 10, 1787, *WW*, 29:245–46; GW to Randolph, Jan. 8, 1788, ibid., 29:358.
42. Rossiter, *1787*, 222.
43. Ibid., 170, 174–75, 221–24, 230.
44. GW to Col. John Cannon, Sept. 16, 1787, quoted in Risjord, *Chesapeake Politics*, 632n; *DGW*, 5:185; Rossiter, *1787*, 237.
45. *DGW*, 5:185–87.
46. Ibid., 5:193, 204.
47. McDonald, *Formation of the American Republic*, 209–10; GW to Humphreys, Oct. 10, 1787, *WW*, 29:287.
48. GW to Henry, Sept. 24, 1787, *WW*, 29:278; GW to Madison, Jan. 10, 1788, ibid., 29:373; *DGW*, 5:205, 339; Freeman, *GW*, 6:134–35.
49. GW to Ch. Carter, Dec. 14, 1787, *WW*, 29:339; GW to Lafayette, Apr. 28, 1788, ibid., 29:479–80; Freeman, *GW*, 6:125–30.
50. GW to Lafayette, May 28, 1788, *WW*, 29:507–508; Freeman, *GW*, 6:135–36.
51. Jonathan Elliot, ed., *The Debates in the several State Conventions on the Adoption of the Federal Constitution . . .* , 5 vols. (New York, 1888), 3:44, 151, 278–90, 365–71, 403, 493, 505, 653–55; Wood, *Creation of the American Republic*, 519–24, 527–28, 536–43.
52. *DGW*, 5:349, 351–52, 352n; Freeman, *GW*, 6:139; GW to Ch. C. Pinckney, June 28, 1788, *WW*, 30:9.
53. GW to Pettit, Aug. 16, 1788, *WW*, 30:42; GW to Hamilton, Aug. 28, 1788, ibid., 30:66–67; GW to C. Lee, Sept. 22, 1788, ibid., 30:97–98; GW to Lincoln, Oct. 26, 1788, ibid., 30:118–20; Freeman, *GW*, 6:145–47.
54. Hamilton to GW, Sept.[?], 1788, Syrett and Cooke, *Papers of Hamilton*, 5:220–22; GW to Lincoln, Oct. 26, 1788, *WW*, 30:119, 121.
55. GW to Gordon, Dec. 23, 1788, *WW*, 30:169; GW to Lafayette, Jan. 29, 1789, ibid., 30:185–86.
56. GW to Samuel Vaughn, Mar. 21, 1789, ibid., 30:237; GW to Harrison, Mar. 9, 1789, ibid., 30:224; GW to Conway, Mar. 6, 1789, ibid., 30:222; GW to Madison, Mar. 30, 1789, ibid., 30:255; GW to G.A. Washington, Mar. 31, 1789, ibid., 30:256–60; GW to Knox, Apr. 1, 1789, ibid., 30:268.
57. GW to Thomson, Apr. 14, 1789, ibid., 30:285–86; *DGW*, 5:447n; Freeman, *GW*, 6:165.
58. *DGW*, 5:447–48; Freeman, *GW*, 4:167–84; Stephen Decatur, *Private Affairs of George Washington: From the Records and Accounts of Tobias Lear, Esquire, his Secretary* (Boston, 1933), 5.
59. GW, Inaugural Address, Apr. 30, 1789, *WW*, 30:291–96; Edgar S. Maclay, ed., *Journal of William Maclay, United States Senator from Pennsylvania, 1789–1791* (New York, 1890), 9, 14. On the Inaugural, see: Thomas E.V. Smith, *The City of New York in the Year of Washington's Inaugural* (New York, 1889), 228–35, and Decatur, *Private Affairs of GW*, 7–11.

15

The Early Presidency

1. David Hackett Fischer, *Growing Old in America* (Oxford, Eng., 1978), 99–112; Richard D. Brown, *Modernization in the Transformation of American Life, 1600–1865* (New York, 1976), 74–121.

2. Smith, *City of New York*, 24–25, 91–125, 175–83, 195–208; GW to Capt. Randall, Aug. 30, 1790, *WW*, 31:108.

3. GW to Lincoln, Oct. 26, 1788, *WW*, 30:121.

4. Wills, *Cincinnatus*, 23.

5. GW to Rutledge, May 5, 1789, *WW*, 30:309.

6. GW to Bowdoin, May 9, 1789, ibid., 30:313; GW to Heath, May 9, 1789, ibid., 30:316.

7. GW, "Queries . . . ," May 10, 1789, ibid., 30:319–20.

8. Hamilton to GW, May 5, 1789, Syrett and Cooke, *Papers of Hamilton*, 5:335–37. On his views at the Constitutional Convention, see: ibid., 4:178–207.

9. Smith, *Adams*, 2:752–54.

10. Maclay, *Journal of Maclay*, 351; Flexner, *GW*, 3:196. Forrest McDonald, *The Presidency of George Washington* (Lawrence, Kans., 1974), 28–30; John C. Miller, *The Federalist Era, 1789–1801* (New York, 1960), 5–10.

11. Freeman, *GW*, 6:203–204; GW to Gabriel Van Horne, May 31, 1789, *WW*, 30:341; Decatur, *Private Affairs*, 19.

12. GW to Biddle, June 22, 1789, *WW*, 30:348; GW to de Neufville, June 29, 1789, ibid., 30:350; GW to McHenry, July 3, 1789, ibid., 30:351; GW to R.H. Lee, Aug. 2, 1789, ibid., 30:369; GW to Craik, Aug. 8, 1789, ibid., 30:396; Freeman, *GW*, 6:214–15; Maclay, *Journal of Maclay*, 341.

13. McDonald, *Presidency of GW*, 37–38.

14. GW to Lincoln, Aug. 11, 1789, *WW*, 30:379–80; GW to Bushrod Washington, July 27, 1789, ibid., 30:366.

15. Hamilton to GW, Mar. 10 and Nov. 25, 1785, Oct. 11–15, 1787, Syrett and Cooke, *Papers of Hamilton*, 3:598, 635–36; 4:280–81; GW to Hamilton, Oct. 18, 1787, *WW*, 29:290–91.

16. GW to G. Morris, Oct. 13, 1789, *WW*, 30:443; Dumas Malone, *Thomas Jefferson and his Time*, 6 vols., (Boston, 1948–1981), 2:245.

17. McDonald, *Presidency of GW*, 38; GW to the Assoc. Justices, Sept. 30, 1789, *WW*, 30:424–25, 425n; GW to Hamilton, Sept. 25, 1789, ibid., 30:413; Freeman, *GW*, 6:253n.

18. Miller, *Federalist Era*, 20–21; GW to McHenry, July 31, 1788, *WW*, 30:28–30; GW to Lincoln, Aug. 28, 1788, ibid., 30:63.

19. GW, "Proposed Address . . . ," *WW*, 30:304.

20. GW to Betty Lewis, Oct. 12, 1789, ibid., 30:436; *DGW*, 5:451, 454, 457, 458, 459n.

21. *DGW*, 5:460–73.

22. Ibid., 5:474–75, 475n.

23. Ibid., 5:476; GW to Hancock, Oct. 26, 1789, *WW*, 30:453.

24. *DGW*, 5:477–92.

25. Ibid., 5:493–97.
26. Ibid., 5:498, 504, 508–509; GW to McHenry, Nov. 30, 1789, *WW*, 30:470–72; GW to the Emperor of Morocco, Dec. 1, 1789, ibid., 30:474–76.
27. MW to Frances Washington, June 8 and Oct. 22, 1789, MVL; MW to Mercy Warren, June 12, 1790, ibid.,; MW to Sally Fairfax, Nov. 26, 1798, ibid; Decatur, *Private Affairs*, 21; Custis, *Recollections*, 372.
28. *DGW*, 5:497–512; GW, "Thanksgiving Proc.," *WW*, 30:427–28.
29. GW, Address, Jan. 8, 1790, *WW*, 30:491–94; *DGW*, 6:4–5.
30. Cooke, *Hamilton*, 75.
31. Ibid., 73–84; McDonald, *Presidency of GW*, 47–65; Miller, *Hamilton*, 155, 160, 163–68, 219–37; Gerald Stourzh, *Alexander Hamilton and the Idea of Republican Government* (Stanford, Calif., 1970), 38–75. The Report is printed in Syrett and Cooke, *Papers of Hamilton*, 6:51–168.
32. Miller, *Hamilton*, 122, 311–12; Cooke, *Hamilton*, 78–79; Miller, *Federalist Era*, 41–42.
33. Irving Brant, *James Madison*, 5 vols., (Indianapolis, 1941–61), 3:306–309.
34. *DGW*, 6:26n, 37; Decatur, *Private Affairs*, 118, 121–23.
35. *DGW*, 6:26–37; Freeman, *GW*, 6:225, 251–53; Decatur, *Private Affairs*, 3.
36. Decatur, *Private Affairs*, 35, 39, 40, 42, 48, 101–103, 114, 122–24, 133–34, 152, 164, 190, 328–32; Flexner, *GW*, 3:199n, 202.
37. GW to Stuart, June 15, 1790, *WW*, 31:55; *DGW*, 6:9, 77; Freeman, *GW*, 6:259–61; Decatur, *Private Affairs*, 28; Maclay, *Journal of Maclay*, 265.
38. David L. Lewis, *District of Columbia: A Bicentennial History* (New York, 1976), 4–5; William N. Chambers, *Political Parties in a New Nation: The American Experience, 1776–1809* (New York, 1963), 38; "Editorial Note," Boyd, *Papers of Jefferson*, 19:6–7.
39. On the Compromise of 1790, see: Jacob E. Cooke, "The Compromise of 1790," *WMQ*, 3d ser., 27 (1970), 523–45; Kenneth R. Bowling, "Dinner at Jefferson's: A Note on Jacob E. Cooke's 'The Compromise of 1790,' [With a Rebuttal by Jacob E. Cooke]", ibid., 28 (1971), 629–48; Norman K. Risjord, "The Compromise of 1790: New Evidence on the Dinner Table Bargain," ibid., 28 (1976), 309–14; "Editorial Notes," Boyd, *Papers of Jefferson*, 17:452; 19:6–7; Maclay, *Journal of Maclay*, 312, 328.
40. GW to Rochambeau, Aug. 10, 1790, *WW*, 31:84.
41. GW to Lafayette, Aug. 11, 1790, ibid., 31:85, 85n.
42. GW to Luzerne, Apr. 29, 1790, ibid., 31:40.

16

The End of the First Term

1. Lear to Biddle, Aug. 26, 1790, *WW*, 31:101; Freeman, *GW*, 6:278.
2. GW to Lear, Sept. 5 and 20, 1790, *WW*, 31:110–11, 120.
3. Jefferson to GW, Sept. 14, 1790, Boyd, *Papers of Jefferson*, 19:463; "Editorial Note," ibid., 19:3–5, 21–22.
4. GW to Lear, Sept. 17, 20, 27, Oct. 3, 10, 27, 31, Nov. 7, 14, and 23, 1790, *WW*,

31:116–18, 120–24, 125–27, 128–30, 132–34, 135–37, 139–41, 146–49, 152–54, 159–60.

5. GW, Second Annual Address, Dec. 8, 1790, ibid., 31:164–69.

6. Hamilton, "First Report on . . . Public Credit," Feb. 13, 1791, and "Second Report . . . ," Feb. 13, 1792, Syrett and Cooke, *Papers of Hamilton*, 7:210–342; McDonald, *Presidency of GW*, 61–62; Miller, *Hamilton*, 255–77, 396; Cooke, *Hamilton*, 85–89.

7. Ralph Ketchum, *James Madison: A Biography* (New York, 1971), 319; Merrill D. Peterson, *Thomas Jefferson and the New Nation: A Biography* (New York, 1970), 433–35.

8. GW to Hamilton, Feb. 16, 1791, *WW*, 31:215–16; Hamilton, "Opinion . . . ," Feb. 23, 1791, Syrett and Cooke, *Papers of Hamilton*, 7:63–134; Jefferson, "Opinion . . . ," Feb. 15, 1791, Boyd, *Papers of Jefferson*, 19:275–80; Miller, *Hamilton*, 264.

9. Maclay, *Journal of Maclay*, 378, 401; GW, Proclamation, Jan. 24, 1791, *WW*, 31:202–204; "Editorial Note," Boyd, *Papers of Jefferson*, 19:26–29, 34–40.

10. "Editorial Note," Boyd, *Papers of Jefferson*, 19:47–58.

11. Sturdevant, "Quest for Eden," 256–62.

12. GW to Stuart, Apr. 8, 1792, *WW*, 32:19.

13. *DGW*, 6:102–105; GW, Proclamation, Mar. 30, 1791, *WW*, 31:254–55; Freeman, *GW*, 6:300–301.

14. GW to Wm. Washington, Jan. 8, 1791, *WW*, 31:Archibald Henderson, *Washington's Southern Tour*, 1791 (Boston, 1923), 1.

15. *DGW*, 6:107–12.

16. Ibid., 6:113–22, 157

17. Ibid., 6:123–32, 140n.

18. Ibid., 6:124–40, 158.

19. Ibid., 6:140–63; Henderson, *GW's Southern Tour*, 269; GW to Humphreys, July 20, 1791, *WW*, 31:318.

20. GW to Lear, June 12, 1791, *WW*, 31:291–92; GW to Stuart, Nov. 20, 1791, ibid., 31:420; David L. Lewis, *District of Columbia: A Bicentennial History* (New York, 1976), 7; H. Paul Caemmerer, *Life of Pierre Charles L'Enfant* (Washington, D.C., 1950), 27–28; Elizabeth S. Kite, ed., *L'Enfant and Washington, 1791–1792* (Baltimore, 1929), 1–13.

21. Malone, *Jefferson*, 2:374–75; L'Enfant to Jefferson, n.d., Kite, *L'Enfant*, 47–48; GW to L'Enfant, Apr. 4, 1791, *WW*, 31:270–71; "Editorial Note," Boyd, *Papers of Jefferson*, 20:7–9.

22. Jefferson to L'Enfant, Apr. 10, 1791, Boyd, *Papers of Jefferson*, 20:86; Jefferson to GW, Apr. 10, 1791, ibid., 20:87–88; "Editorial Note," ibid., 20:15–16, 18–19, 23–29; L'Enfant to Hamilton, Apr. 8, 1791, Syrett and Cooke, *Papers of Hamilton*, 8:253; GW to Jefferson, Mar. 31, 1791, *WW*, 31:257.

23. *DGW*, 6:164–65; "Editorial Note," Boyd, *Papers of Jefferson*, 20:29–32; "Report of L'Enfant," June 22, 1791, Kite, *L'Enfant*, 52–58, and see 16, 18–19.

24. *DGW*, 6:167–69.

25. On GW's testimony, see ch. 13 and *WW*, 26:374–98.

26. Francis Paul Prucha, *The Sword of the Republic: The United States Army on the*

Frontier, 1783–1846 (Bloomington: Ind., 1977), 3–18; Knox to GW, May 5, 1789, WPPV

27.   GW to Clinton, Sept. 14, 1791, *WW*, 31:369.

28.   GW to G. Morris, Dec. 17, 1790, ibid., 31: 174; GW to Humphreys, July 20, 1791, ibid., 31:320; GW to Jefferson, Mar. 6, 1792, ibid., 31:501; GW to Pierce Butler, Aug. 10, 1789, ibid., 30:379; GW, "Proposed Address," Apr. [?], 1789, ibid., 30:303.

29.   GW to R.H. Lee, Dec. 14, 1784, ibid., 28:12.

30.   GW to the Cherokee Nation, Aug. 29, 1796, ibid., 25:193–94. GW to Duane, Sept. 7, 1783, ibid., 27:133–40.

31.   GW, Second Annual Address, Dec. 8, 1790, ibid., 31:166; GW to St. Clair, Oct. 6, 1789, ibid., 30:430–31; GW to Lear, Apr. 3, 1791, ibid., 31:267; GW to Jefferson, Mar. 6, 1792, ibid., 31:501.

32.   GW to St. Clair, Oct. 6, 1789, ibid., 30:429.

33.   Ibid., 30:430–31.

34.   Kohn, *Eagle and Sword*, 127, 99–100; Maclay, *Journal of Maclay*, 227, 239–40.

35.   Kohn, *Eagle and Sword*, 100, 102; GW to Lear, Apr. 3, 1790, *WW*, 31:267; GW to G. Morris, Dec. 17, 1790, ibid., 31:174.

36.   Kohn, *Eagle and Sword*, 102–103.

37.   Randolph G. Adams, "The Harmar Expedition of 1790," *Ohio State Archives and History Quarterly*, 50 (1941), 60–62; Howard Peckham, "Josiah Harmar and his Indian Expedition," ibid., 55 (1946), 227–41; Prucha, *Sword of the Republic*, 21.

38.   GW to Knox, Nov. 19, 1790, *WW*, 31:156.

39.   GW, Second Annual Address, Dec. 8, 1790, WW, 31:166–73; GW to Jefferson, Apr. 1, 1791, ibid., 31–260; GW to Clinton, Sept. 14, 1791, ibid., 31:370; Knox to GW, June 4 and Dec. 10, 1790, and Jan. 22, 1791, WPPV; Kohn, *Eagle and Sword*, 108–10; Wiley Sword, *President Washington's Indian War: The Struggle for the Old Northwest, 1790–1795* (Norman, Okla., 1985), 131.

40.   GW to Col. Wm. Dark, Apr. 4, 1791, *WW*, 31:268–69; Custis, *Recollections*, 282–83; Freeman, *GW*, 6:329; Kohn, *Eagle and Sword*, 110.

41.   Frazer E. Wilson, "St. Clair's Defeat," *Ohio Archives and History Quarterly*, 11 (1902), 30–43; Sword, *GW's Indian War*, 195.

42.   Prucha, *Sword of the Republic*, 21–22, 26–27.

43.   GW, "Errors of Government Toward the Indians, [Feb. 1792], *WW*, 31:491; GW to Knox, Aug. 1, 1792, ibid., 32:104; Wilcombe E. Washurn, *The Indian in America* (New York, 1975), 162.

44.   Kohn, *Eagle and Sword*, 122–24.

45.   GW, "Opinion of the General Officers," Mar. 9, 1792, *WW*, 31:509; GW to H. Lee, June 30, 1792, ibid., 32:32; Nelson, *Wayne*, 222–26.

46.   On the turbulent southwestern frontier, see: Arthur P. Whitaker, *The Spanish-American Frontier: 1783–1795. The Westward Movement and the Spanish Retreat in the Mississippi Valley* (Boston, 1927), 78–139; Thomas P. Abernethy, *The South in the New Nation, 1789–1819* (Baton Rouge, La., 1961), 43–101.

47.   Knox to GW, Feb. 15, 1790, *GWP*, ser. 4, reel 99; John W. Caughey, *McGillivray of the Creeks* (Norman, Okla., 1938), 42, 261.

48.   *DGW*, 6:42, 82–83.

49.   Callahan, *Knox*, 330–35; Arthur P. Whitaker, "Alexander McGillivray, 1783–

1789," *North Carolina Historical Review*, 5 (1928), 181–203, 289–300; Caughey, *McGillivray*, 42–45.

50. GW, Proc., Aug. 26, 1790, *WW*, 31:99; GW, Annual Address, Oct. 25, 1791, ibid., 31:397–98.

51. GW to Moultrie, Aug. 9, 1791, ibid., 31:334; GW to Lafayette, Sept. 10, 1791, ibid., 31:363; GW to Lear, Sept. 26 and Oct. 2, 1791, ibid., 31:377–78, 392; Decatur, *Private Affairs*, 245; Freeman, *GW*, 6:323–24n, 330.

52. GW to Vaughn, Aug. 25, 1791, *WW*, 30:346.

53. Hamilton, "Report on Manufactures," Syrett and Cooke, *Papers of Hamilton*, 10:230–340; Miller, *Hamilton*, 278–95; Cooke, *Hamilton*, 97–102. For a different view, see: John R. Nelson, Jr., "Alexander Hamilton and American Manufacturing: A Reexamination," *Jrnl. Am. Hist.*, 65 (1979), 971–95.

54. Miller, *Federalist Era*, 68–69; Miller, *Hamilton*, 299, 311.

55. Fawn M. Brodie, *Thomas Jefferson: An Intimate History* (New York, 1974), 135, 143, 155, 267, 285; McDonald, *Presidency of GW*, 79–80; Malone, *Jefferson*, 2:421.

56. John M. Murrin, "The Great Inversion, or Court versus Country: A Comparison of the Revolutionary Settlements in England (1688–1721) and America (1776–1816)," in J.G.A. Pocock, ed., *Three British Revolutions: 1641, 1688, 1776* (Princeton, 1980), 368–430; Joyce Appleby, *Capitalism and a New Social Order: The Republican Vision of the 1790s* (New York, 1984), 70–83, 93–97; Lance Banning, *The Jeffersonian Persuasion: Evolution of a Party Ideology* (Ithaca, N.Y., 1978), 78–83, 128, 171–89, 199; Noble E. Cunningham, *The Jeffersonian Republicans: The Foundation of Party Organization, 1789–1801* (Chapel Hill, N.C., 1957), 21–41, 89; Joseph Charles, *The Origins of the American Party System* (New York, 1961), 39; Robert Kelley, *The Cultural Pattern in American Politics: The First Century* (New York, 1979), 88, 109–115; Miller, *Hamilton*, 311–42; Cooke, *Hamilton*, 109–20; Miller, *Federalist Era*, 70-98; Ketcham, *Madison*, 310–17. That the Republicans soon included more than just American yeomen, see: Roland M. Baumann, "Philadelphia's Manufactures and the Excise Taxes of 1794: The Forging of the Jeffersonian Coalition," *PMHB*, 106 (1982), 3–40.

57. See Julian P. Boyd, *Number 7: Alexander Hamilton's Secret Attempts to Control American Foreign Policy* (Princeton, N.J., 1964).

58. GW, Queries . . . ," Aug. 27, 1790, *WW*, 31:102–103.

59. Alexander De Conde, *Entangling Alliance: Politics and Diplomacy Under George Washington* (Durham, N.C., 1958), 66–77; Peterson, *Jefferson*, 387–89, 416–67; Gilbert L. Lycam, *Alexander Hamilton and American Foreign Policy* (Norman, Okla., 1970), 121–31.

60. Malone, *Jefferson*, 2:420, 426–27, 457–77; Miller, *Hamilton*, 343–52; Ketchum, *Madison*, 326–34.

61. Malone, *Jefferson*, 2:461; GW to Eliz. Powel, Apr. 23, 1792, *WW*, 32:22; GW to Jefferson, Aug. 23, 1792, ibid., 32:130; Ford, *True GW*, 206.

62. McDonald, *Presidency of GW*, 47.

63. Jefferson, "Anas," in Paul L. Ford, ed., *The Writings of Thomas Jefferson*, 10 vols., (New York, 1892–99), 1:199; GW to J. Adams, Sept. 25, 1798, *WW*, 26:460–61.

64. Ralph Ketcham, *Presidents Above Party: The First American Presidency, 1789–1829* (Chapel Hill, N.C., 1984), 89–93, 193–203. See also, Richard Buel, Jr.,

Securing the Revolution: Ideology in American Politics, 1789–1815 (Ithaca, N.Y., 1972), 1–27.

65.   GW, Farewell Address, Sept. 15, 1796, *WW*, 35:219, 224, 227, 234; GW, Annual Address, Dec. 7, 1796, ibid., 35:315; GW, Proposed Inaugural, 1789, ibid., 30:297, 303, 305, 307.

66.   *DGW*, 6:132, 141, 156, 464, 468, 470, 483.

67.   GW, Annual Addresses, 1790–1791, *WW*, 31:164–65, 396–97; GW to Lafayette, March 19, 1791, ibid., 31:248.

68.   Robert Kelley, "Ideology and Political Culture from Jefferson to Nixon," *AHR*, 82 (1977), 538; Gerald Stourz, *Alexander Hamilton and the Idea of Republican Government* (Stanford, Calif., 1970), 191–92.

69.   Risjord, *Chesapeake Politics*, 343.

70.   GW to Madison, May 20, 1792, *WW*, 32:45–49; Brant, *Madison*, 3:355–56.

71.   GW to Whiting, Apr. 14, 1790, and July 1, 1792, *WW*, 31:36; 32:80–82; Thane, *Potomac Squire*, 300–302, 306, 311–14.

72.   GW to Jefferson, Nov. 30, 1791, Jan. 15, 18, Feb. 22, 26, and Mr. 14, 1792, *WW*, 31:432, 459, 462–63, 482–83, 486–87; 32:3–4; GW to L'Enfant, Dec. 13, 1791, and Feb. 28, 1792, ibid., 31:442–44, 488–89; GW to Fed. Dist. Comm., Dec. 18, 1791, ibid., 31:445–48; L'Enfant to GW, Dec. 7, 1791, Kite, *L'Enfant*, 89–91, 133–34, 152–53; Malone, *Jefferson*, 2:379–84; "Editorial Note," Boyd, *Papers of Jefferson*, 20:57–72.

73.   GW to Fed. Dist. Comm., July 23, 1792, *WW*, 32:94; Flexner, *GW*, 3:343.

74.   Jefferson to GW, May 23, 1792, Ford, *Writings of Jefferson*, 6:1–6; Jefferson, "Anas," ibid., 1:27.

75.   GW to Jefferson, Aug. 23, 1792, *WW*, 32:130–32; GW to Hamilton, Aug. 26, 1792, ibid., 32:132–34.

76.   GW to Randolph, Aug. 26, 1792, ibid., 32:136. Jefferson to GW, Sept. 9, 1792, Ford, *Writings of Jefferson*, 6:101–109; Hamilton to GW, July 30 [–Aug. 3], and Sept. 9, 1792, Syrett and Cooke, *Papers of Hamilton*, 7:177, 344–46; Freeman, *GW*, 6:371.

77.   GW Second Inaugural Address, *WW*, 32:374. Also see, GW to H. Lee, Jan. 20, 1793, ibid., 32:309–10.

78.   GW to Lafayette, July 28, 1791, ibid., 31:324–25; GW to Comte de Moustier, Sept. 5, 1791, ibid., 31:357; GW to Luzerne, Sept. 10, 1791, ibid., 31:361.

79.   GW to Louis Sigeur, May 4, 1792, ibid., 32:33; GW to Jefferson, July 17, 1792, ibid. 32:87; GW to Lafayette, June 10, 1792, ibid., 32:53. On the reports that Washington received on the progress of the French Revolution, see: Louis M. Sears, *George Washington and the French Revolution* (Detroit, 1960), 47–173.

17

The Second Term Begins

1.   GW to George Augustine Washington, Jan. 27, 1793, *WW*, 32:315–16; GW to Frances Washington, Feb. 24, 1793, ibid., 32:354–55; GW to Bryan Fairfax, Mar. 6, 1793, ibid., 32:376.

2. Samuel Flagg Bemis, *The Jay Treaty: A Study in Commerce and Diplomacy* (New Haven, Conn., 1926), 28–50.

3. A.L. Burt, *The United States, Great Britain and British North America: From the Revolution to the Establishment of Peace after the War of 1812* (New York, 1940), 118–23; Peterson, *Jefferson*, 451–55; Malone, *Jefferson*, 2:412–19; Bemis, *Jay Treaty*, 147–82.

4. De Conde, *Entangling Alliance*, 81–82.

5. Ibid., 82; McDonald, *Presidency of GW*, 119.

6. GW, Second Inaugural Address, Mar. 4, 1793, WW, 32:374–75; Freeman, *GW*, 7:9, 26–27.

7. Malone, *Jefferson*, 406–407; Whitaker, *Spanish-American Frontier*, 71–80; Freeman, *GW*, 7:33.

8. GW to Humphreys, Mar. 23, 1793, WW, 32:399; GW to G. Morris, Mar. 25, 1793, ibid., 32:402–403.

9. GW to Humphreys, Mar. 23, 1793, ibid., 32:400; GW to Whiting, Feb. 24 and Jan. 6, 1793, ibid., 32:357–58, 293.

10. GW to Hamilton, Apr. 12, 1793, ibid., 32:416; GW to Jefferson, Apr. 12, 1793, ibid., 32:415; Hamilton to GW, Apr. 5 and 8, 1793, Syrett and Cooke, *Papers of Hamilton*, 14:291, 295–96.

11. Jerald A. Combs, *The Jay Treaty, Political Battlefield of the Founding Fathers* (Berkeley, Calif., 1970), 31–46, 107–108; Jefferson, "Anas," Ford, *Writings of Jefferson*, 1:226–27; Syrett and Cooke, *Papers of Hamilton*, 14:328–29n; Charles M. Thomas, *American Neutrality in 1793: A Study in Cabinet Government* (New York, 1931), 15–39.

12. GW, "Questions . . . ," Apr. 18, 1793, WW, 32:419–20; GW, Proclamation of Neutrality, Apr. 23, 1793, ibid., 32:430–31; De Conde, *Entangling Alliance*, 88; Thomas, *American Neutrality*, 41–49.

13. For Hamilton's series of essays entitled "No Jacobin," see: Syrett and Cooke, *Papers of Hamilton*, 15:145–51, 184–91, 203–207, 224–28, 243–46, 249–50, 268–70, 281–84, 304–306. Madison's rejoinders are in Gaillard Hunt, ed., *The Writings of James Madison*, 9 vols., (New York, 1900–10), 7:133–88.

14. Charles D. Hazen, *Contemporary Opinion of the French Revolution* (Baltimore, 1897), 164–73; Greville Bathe, *Citizen Genět, Diplomat and Inventor* (Philadelphia, 1946), 3–22, 106–18; De Conde, *Entangling Alliance*, 179.

15. Harry Ammon, *The Genět Mission* (New York, 1973), 44–53.

16. Malone, *Jefferson*, 2:93–94; Freeman, *GW*, 7:70–75; Jefferson to Madison, Apr. 28, 1793, Ford, *Writings of Jefferson*, 6:232; WW, 32:468n; GW to Earl of Buchan, Apr. 22, 1793, ibid., 32:428; Ammon, *Genět Mission*, 54–59.

17. De Conde, *Entangling Alliance*, 157–61.

18. Ibid., 197–99; Freeman, *GW*, 7:80–81; Malone, *Jefferson*, 3:90–113.

19. De Conde, *Entangling Alliance*, 200–201, 208–11, 217–26; Malone, *Jefferson*, 3:103; Ammon, *Genět Mission*, 67, 80–93.

20. De Conde, *Entangling Alliance*, 235; GW, Proc., Mar. 24, 1795, WW, 33:304–305.

21. McDonald, *Presidency of GW*, 129–32; GW to Morgan, Oct. 8, 1794, WW, 33:523–24. On the Democratic societies, see: Eugene P. Link, *Democratic-Republican Societies, 1790–1800* (New York, 1942).

22. Adams to Jefferson, June 30, 1813, Adams, *Works*, 10:47; Adams to William Cunningham, Oct. 15, 1813, Timothy Pickering, ed., *A Review of the Correspondence between John Adams and William C. Cunningham, 1803-1812* (Salem, Mass., 1824), 103.

23. GW to H. Lee, Oct. 16, 1793, *WW*, 33:133; GW to Charles Thurston, Aug. 10, 1794, ibid., 32:465; GW to Stuart, Sept. 21, 1794, ibid., 33:506.

24. Jefferson to Madison, July 7, 1793, Ford, *Writings of Jefferson*, 6:338-39; Jefferson, "Anas," ibid., 1:243, 247, 252; De Conde, *Entangling Alliance*, 283-96; Malone, *Jefferson*, 3:114-29; Bemis, *Jay Treaty*, 201; Freeman, *GW*, 7:140, 154; Ammon, *Genĕt Mission*, 171-79; Gilbert L. Lycom, *Alexander Hamilton and Foreign Policy: A Design for Greatness* (Norman, Okla., 1970), 146-74.

25. Anna C. Clauder, *American Commerce as Affected by the War of the French Revolution and Napoleon, 1793-1812* (Philadelphia, 1932), 27-36; McDonald, *Presidency of GW*, 134.

26. GW to Lear, May 6, 1794, *WW*, 33:355; GW to Clinton, Mar. 31, 1794, ibid., 33:310-11; GW to Knox, Apr. 4, 1794, ibid., 33:313-14; Charles, *Origins of the Party System*, 97, 99; Bemis, *Jay Treaty*, 257-64; De Conde, *Entangling Alliance*, 94.

27. GW to Lear, May 16, 1794, *WW*, 33:355; Bemis, *Jay Treaty*, 254-69.

28. Freeman, *GW*, 7:160; "Introductory Note," Syrett and Cooke, *Papers of Hamilton*, 16:261-65. Subsequently Jefferson called the act of sending an envoy without the backing of retaliatory legislation a "degrading measure." See Syrett and Cooke, *Papers of Hamilton*, 16:264n.

29. Combs, *Jay Treaty*, 125; Brant, *Madison*, 3:400; Freeman, *GW*, 7:166.

30. Hamilton to GW, Apr. 14, 1794, Syrett and Cooke, *Papers of Hamilton*, 16:266-79; Cooke, *Hamilton*, 140.

31. GW to Jay, Apr. 15, 1794, *WW*, 33:329; GW to the Senate, Apr. 16, 1794, ibid., 33:332; GW to Randolph, Apr. 15, 1794, ibid., 33:329; GW to Lear, May 6, 1794, ibid., 33:355.

32. Hamilton to GW, Apr. 23, 1794, Syrett and Cooke, *Papers of Hamilton*, 16:319-23, 323-28n; Hamilton to Jay, May 6, 1794, ibid., 16:381-85; McDonald, *Presidency of GW*, 142-43; Jefferson to GW, May 14, 1794, Ford, *Writings of Jefferson*, 6:510; GW to R.H. Lee, Apr. 15, 1794, *WW*, 33:332.

33. GW to Humphreys, Mar. 23, 1793, *WW*, 32:399; GW to G. Morris, Mar. 25, 1793, ibid., 32:402; Franklin to Galloway, Feb. 25, 1775, Labaree, *Papers of Franklin*, 21:509; Paine, *Common Sense*, in Foner, *Writings of Paine*, 1:81-82; John Ferling, "The American Revolution and American Security: Whig and Loyalist Views," *The Historian*, 60 (1978), 492-507.

34. Washington's successor, John Adams, who had never soldiered, offers a revealing contrast. See: John Ferling, " 'Oh that I was a Soldier': John Adams and the Anguish of War," *American Quarterly*, 36 (1984), 258-75.

35. GW to G. Morris, Mar. 25, 1793, *WW*, 32:403; GW to Buchan, May 26, 1794, ibid., 33:383.

36. GW to McHenry, Aug. 12, 1792, ibid., 32:110; Maclay, *Journal of Maclay*, 137, 206; Decatur, *Private Affairs*, 43, 72-73, 267; Custis, *Recollections*, 395-96, 406-407; Ford, *True GW*, 174.

37. Jefferson, "Anas," Ford, *Letters of Jefferson*, 1:245; Freeman, *GW*, 7:58–59, 106, 227, 437; "Washington's Household Account Book, 1793–1797," *PMHB*, 30 (1906), 161, 183–84, 327; 31 (1907), 70, 326.

38. GW to Richard Chichester, Aug. 8, 1792, and Nov. 23, 1793, *WW*, 32:109–10; 33:155.

39. GW to Whiting, Oct. 14 and Dec. 2, 1792, ibid., 32:177, 246; GW to Wm. Tilghman, July 21, 1793, ibid., 33:26; GW to Pearce, Dec. 18, 1793, ibid., 33:192.

40. GW to Tilghman, July 21, 1793, ibid., 33:25–26; GW to Pearce, Aug. 26, 1793, and Nov. 2, 1794, ibid., 33:68–70; 34:11; "Agreement with Wm. Pearce," Sept. 23, 1793, ibid., 33:97–101.

41. GW to Th. Peter, Aug. 31, 1794, ibid., 33:487; GW to Ch. Carter, Mar. 10, 1795, ibid., 34:139–40; GW to Lear, May 6, 1794, ibid., 33:358.

42. GW to Stuart, Feb. 7, 1796, ibid., 34:453; GW to James Anderson, Feb. 15, 1796, ibid., 34:464; GW to Young, Dec. 12, 1793, ibid., 33:174–83; Freeman, *GW*, 7:231–32n, 307–308, 586.

43. Withey, *Dearest Friend*, 217; Jefferson, "Anas," Ford, *Writings of Jefferson*, 1:73.

44. Bradford Perkins, ed., "A Diplomat's Wife in Philadelphia: Letters of Henrietta Liston, 1796–1800," *WMQ*, 3d ser., 11 (1954), 592, 606, 609, 613, 614, 628; Flexner, *GW*, 4:283.

45. Nathaniel Burt, *The Perennial Philadelphians: The Anatomy of an American Aristocracy* (Boston, 1963), 153; Eliza Powel to MW, Nov. 30, 1787, and Aug. 9, 1793, MVL; Eliza Powel to GW, Nov. 17, 1792, MVL; GW to Eliza Powel, Feb. 2, 1777, WPPV; Samuel Powel to GW, Jan. 16, 1786, May 10 and June 30, 1787, WPPV.

46. For a different view, see: Flexner, *GW*, 3:314–22.

47. GW to G.W.M. Lafayette, Nov. 22, 1795, and Feb. 28, 1796, *WW*, 34:367–68, 478; GW to Geo. Cabot, Sept. 7, 1795, ibid., 34:299–301; Thane, *Potomac Squire*, 341, 356, 373; Perkins, "Diplomat's Wife," *WMQ*, 11:603; Flexner, *GW*, 4:350.

48. GW to John Dandridge, July 11, 1796, *WW*, 35:135–36; GW to Wolcott, Aug. 1, 1796, ibid. 35:162; Thane, *Potomac Squire*, 235, 239, 285, 299, 321, 352.

49. Flexner, *GW*, 4:91, 404n; Thane, *Potomac Squire*, 340, 352.

50. William S. Baker, *Washington after the Revolution, 1784–1799* (Philadelphia, 1898), 349–50; Weld, *Travels*, 60n; Freeman, *GW*, 7:267n 383–84.

51. *WW*, 32:478n; GW to Knox, June 25, 1794, ibid., 33:411; GW to Th. Pinckney, Feb. 25, 1795, ibid., 34:125.

52. GW to John Greenwood, Jan. 20 and 25, 1797, *WW*, 35:370–71, 374–75; Flexner, *GW*, 4:308–309; MW to Eliza Powel, Apr. 24, 1793, MVL; MW to Fanny Bassett, Feb. 10, 1794, ibid., MW to Whitlock, Apr. 17, 1794, ibid.

53. GW to John Howard, Aug. 25, 1793, *WW*, 33:66; GW to Buchan, May 26, 1794, ibid., 34:382; GW to Knox, Sept. 9, 1793, ibid., 33:86; GW to Lear, Sept. 25 and Nov. 8, 1798, ibid., 33:104, 150; Eliza Powel to MW, Aug. 9, 1793, MVL. The paragraph on the epidemic is based on J.H. Powell, *Bring Out Your Dead: The Great Plague of Yellow Fever in Philadelphia in 1793* (Philadelphia, 1949).

54. Miller, *Federalist Era*, 155–56; McDonald, *Presidency of GW*, 145–46.

55. Hamilton to GW, Sept. 1, 1792, Syrett and Cooke, *Papers of Hamilton*, 12:312; GW to Hamilton, Sept. 17, 1792, *WW*, 32:153–54. On the historiography of

the Whiskey Rebellion, see: Jacob E. Cooke, "The Whiskey Insurrection: A Re-Evaluation," *Pennsylvania History* 30 (1963), 316–46.

56. Richard H. Kohn, "The Washington Administration's Decision to Crush the Whiskey Rebellion," *Journal of American History* 59 (1972), 567–84. The quotation is on p. 568.

57. Mary K. Bonsteel Tachau, "George Washington and the Reputation of Edmund Randolph," *Jrnl. Am. Hist.*, 73 (1986), 21.

58. "Conference Concerning the Insurrection in Western Pennsylvania," Aug. 2, 1794, Syrett and Cooke, *Papers of Hamilton*, 17:9–13; Hamilton to GW, Aug. 2 and 5, 1794, ibid., 17:15–19, 24–58; Hamilton and Knox to GW, Aug. 5, 1794, ibid., 17:21; Freeman, *GW*, 7:188–90; Kohn, "Decision to Crush the Whiskey Rebellion," *Jrnl. Am. Hist.*, 59:572.

59. Tachau, "GW and Randolph," *Jrnl. Am. Hist.*, 73:22.

60. GW, Proclamation, Aug. 7, 1794, *WW*, 33:457–61.

61. GW to H. Lee, Aug. 26, 1794, ibid., 33:476. Syrett and Cooke, *Papers of Hamilton*, 17:23n.

62. The "Tully" essays are in Syrett and Cooke, *Papers of Hamilton*, 17:132–35, 148–50, 159–61, 175–80.

63. GW to H. Lee, Aug. 26, 1794, *WW*, 33:476; Hamilton, "Minutes . . . ," Aug. 24, 1794, Syrett and Cooke, *Papers of Hamilton*, 17:135–38. On Washington's thinking, see: GW to Hamilton, Aug. 21, 1794, *WW*, 33:472; GW to Morgan, Oct. 8, 1794, ibid., 33:523–24; GW, State of Union Message, Nov. 19, 1794, ibid., 33:34; GW to Burgess Ball, Sept. 25, 1794, ibid., 33:506; Miller, *Hamilton*, 407; McDonald, *Presidency of GW*, 145–46; Charles, *Origins of the Party System*, 84; Leland D. Baldwin, *The Whiskey Rebels* (Pittsburgh, 1939), 215.

64. GW, Proclamation, Sept. 25, 1794, *WW*, 33:507–509; Hamilton to Mifflin, Sept. 9, 1794, Syrett and Cooke, *Papers of Hamilton*, 17:210–11.

65. *DGW*, 6:178–79, 179n.

66. Prucha, *Sword of the Republic*, 29–38; Nelson, *Wayne*, 228–68; Sword, *GW's Indian War*, 299–311, 335.

67. *DGW*, 6:178–98.

68. Miller, *Hamilton*, 408–13; Miller, *Federalist Era*, 159.

69. GW to Randolph, Oct. 16, 1794, *WW*, 34:3–4; GW, Sixth Annual Message, Nov. 19, 1794, ibid., 34:34.

70. GW to Jay, Sept. 1[–5], and Dec. 18, 1794, ibid., 34:16, 61.

18

Last Years in Office

1. Quoted in Flexner, *GW*, 4:193.

2. DeConde, *Entangling Alliance*, 251.

3. On Pickering, see Gerald H. Clarfield, *Timothy Pickering and the American Republic* (Pittsburg, 1980).

4. In the absence of a modern biography of Wolcott, see the *Dictionary of American Biography* (New York, 1928–37), 20:443–45.

5. Paul A. Varg, *Foreign Policies of the Founding Fathers* (East Lansing, Mich., 1963), 105–106.

6. Combs, *Jay Treaty*, 145–49.

7. Ibid., 153–58; DeConde, *Entangling Alliance*, 105; Jensen, *Founding of the American Republic*, 571.

8. DeConde, *Entangling Alliance*, 106–109; Bemis, *Jay Treaty*, 279–87, 368–73.

9. GW to R. Livingston, Aug. 20, 1795, *WW*, 34:278; GW to Randolph, July 22, 1795, ibid., 34:244; Bemis, *Jay Treaty*, 252–71; Burt, *Anglo-American Relations*, 145–51.

10. Combs, *Jay Treaty*, 165.

11. GW to Hamilton, July 29, 1795, *WW*, 34:262; Combs, *Jay Treaty*, 159; Charles, *Origins of the Party System*, 104–105; Varg, *Foreign Policies*, 111–13.

12. Donald L. Robinson, *Slavery in the Structure of American Politics* (New York, 1971), 348–52, 358; Lycan, *Hamilton and American Foreign Policy*, 240–46; Combs, *Jay Treaty*, 162–64; Bradford Perkins, *The First Rapprochement: England and the United States, 1795–1805* (Philadelphia, 1955), 34–35.

13. Freeman, *GW*, 7:260–62; W.C. Ford, ed., "Edmund Randolph on the British Treaty, 1795," *AHR*, 12 (1906–1907), 587–99.

14. GW to Hamilton, July 29, 1795, *WW*, 34:262; GW to George Lewis, July 27, 1795, ibid., 34:249.

15. GW to Randolph, July 29, 1795, ibid., 34:258; GW to R. Lewis, July 27, 1795, ibid., 34:252; Freeman, *GW*, 7:277–78.

16. GW to Randolph, Aug. 20 and Sept. 27, 1795, *WW*, 34:276–77, 316; Moncure Conway, ed., *Omitted Chapters of History Disclosed in the Life and Papers of Edmund Randolph* (New York, 1888), 271–81.

17. Irving Brant, "Edmund Randolph, Not Guilty!," *WMQ*, 3d ser., 7 (1950), 180.

18. Peter Daniel, ed., *A Vindication of Edmund Randolph, Written by Himself and Published in 1795* (Richmond, Va., 1855), 1–4.

19. McDonald, *Presidency of GW*, 165.

20. GW to the Boston Selectmen, July 28, 1795, *WW*, 34:253; GW to Hamilton, July 3 and 29, 1795, ibid., 34:227, 262–63; Alexander Hamilton, "Remarks on the Treaty . . . ," Syrett and Cooke, *Papers of Hamilton*, 18:404–54; Cooke, *Hamilton*, 163; De Conde, *Entangling Alliance*, 116; Freeman, *GW*, 7:275. The seven letters that Hamilton wrote to Washington that July have been lost. See Syrett and Cooke, *Papers of Hamilton*, 17:403, 456, 460, 464, 473, and 475.

21. Daniel, *Vindication*, 1–4; Conway, *Omitted Chapters*, 282–89.

22. Miller, *Hamilton*, 44. On the background of the new cabinet officers, see: Bernard C. Steiner, *The Life and Career of James McHenry* (Cleveland, 1907); James Haw et al., *Stormy Patriot: The Life of Samuel Chase* (Baltimore, 1890); William G. Brown, *The Life of Oliver Ellsworth* (New York, 1905).

23. GW to Randolph, Oct. 25, 1795, *WW*, 34:344; Freeman, *GW*, 7:319.

24. Randolph to GW, Aug. 19, Oct. 2, 8, and 24, 1795, Daniel, *Vindication*, 2–4, 13, 15–16, 17–18, 36–45; GW to Randolph, Oct. 25, 1795, *WW*, 34:34.

25. Daniel, *Vindication*, 4–6, 7–10; Brant, "Randolph," *WMQ*, 7:190–98; Tachau, "GW and Randolph," *Jrnl. Am. Hist.*, 73:24–34.

26. Daniel, *Vindication*, 43–44.

27. Harry M. Tinkcom, *The Republicans and Federalists in Pennsylvania, 1790–1801* (Harrisburg, Pa., 1950), 30; Daniel, *Vindication*, 44.

28. Samuel Flagg Bemis, *Pinckney's Treaty: America's Advantage from Europe's Distress, 1783–1800* (New Haven, Conn., 1926), 245–84, 343–62; McDonald, *Presidency of GW*, 166–67. For another explanation of Spain's motivation, see: Arthur P. Whitaker, "Godoy's Knowledge of the Terms of Jay's Treaty," *AHR*, 35 (1930), 804–10, and Whitaker, *Spanish-American Frontier*, 201–202.

29. GW to the Senate, Feb. 26, 1796, *WW*, 34:477–78; GW to Pinckney, Mar. 5, 1795, ibid., 34:485; Malone, *Jefferson*, 3:254.

30. Hamilton to GW, Mar. 29, 1796, Syrett and Cooke, *Papers of Hamilton*, 20:85–103; Charles, *Origins of the Party System*, 109–12; GW to Pinckney, May 22, 1796, *WW*, 35:62; Freeman, *GW*, 7:354, 363.

31. DeConde, *Entangling Alliance*, 342–79; Harry Ammon, *James Monroe: The Quest for National Identity* (New York, 1971), 112–50.

32. GW to Monroe, Aug. 25, 1796, *WW*, 35:182; DeConde, *Entangling Alliance*, 380–86.

33. GW to Hamilton, May 8, 1796, *WW*, 35:41; Pickering, Wolcott, and McHenry to GW, July 2, 1796, Ford, *Writings of GW*, 216n; DeConde, *Entangling Alliance*, 383; Ammon, *Monroe*, 153.

34. [Phil.] *Aurora*, Jan. 12, 19, Mar. 3, Apr. 7, 21, and June 8, 1796; Jefferson, "Anas," in Ford, *Writings of Jefferson*, 1:68; GW to Jefferson, July 6, 1796, *WW*, 35:120; GW to Jay, May 8, 1796, ibid., 35:37.

35. [GW-Madison], Farewell Address [first draft], May 15, 1796, *WW*, 35:51–61; GW to Hamilton, May 15, 1796, ibid., 35:48–51.

36. GW to Hamilton, Aug. 25, Sept. 2 and 6, 1796, ibid., 35:190–92, 199–201, 204–20; Hamilton, "Draft of GW's Farewell Address," Syrett and Cooke, *Papers of Hamilton*, 20:265–88; Hamilton, "Draft on the Plan of Incorporating," ibid., 20:294–303. See also: "Introductory Note," ibid., 20:169–73, and Victor Hugo Palsits, *Washington's Farewell Address* (New York, 1935).

37. GW, Farewell Address, Sept. 19, 1796, *WW*, 35:214–38.

38. GW, Farewell, Nov. 2, 1783, ibid., 27:222–27; Felix Gilbert, *To the Farewell Address: Ideas of Early American Foreign Policy* (Princeton, N.J., 1961), 121–33.

39. Miller, *Federalist Era*, 198; Gilbert, *To the Farewell Address*, 132–33. See also Wood, *Creation of the American Republic*, 519–44.

40. Freeman, *GW*, 7:423.

41. Gardner W. Allen, *Our Naval War with France* (Boston, 1909), 1–23; De Conde, *Entangling Alliance*, 424–46.

42. De Conde, *Entangling Alliance*, 438.

43. Ibid., 439–40.

44. GW to Hamilton, Nov. 2, 3, and 21, 1796, *WW*, 35:251–55, 255–56, 287–89; GW to Congress, Jan. 19, 1797, ibid., 35:369–70; Hamilton to GW, Nov. 4 and 5, 1796, Syrett and Cooke, *Papers of Hamilton*, 20:372–73, 374–75.

45. Stephen G. Kurtz, *The Presidency of John Adams: The Collapse of Federalism, 1795–1800* (Philadelphia, 1957), 127–32; Miller, *Federalist Era*, 199.

46. GW to Sir John Sinclair, Dec. 10, 1796, *WW*, 35:321–23; GW to Knox, Mar. 2, 1796, ibid., 35:408–10.

47. GW, Farewell Address, Sept. 19, 1796, ibid., 35:215–16, 218; GW, Annual Address, Dec. 7, 1796, ibid., 35:311–18; GW to Humphreys, June 26, 1797, ibid., 35:481.

48. GW, Annual Messages, Dec. 3, 1793, Dec. 7, 1795, and Dec. 7, 1796, ibid., 33:165–66; 34:386–93; 35:317; Kohn, *Eagle and Sword*, 128–38.

49. GW, Annual Address, Dec. 7, 1796, *WW*, 35:313–18; GW, Farewell Address, Sept. 15, 1796, ibid., 35:230; Leonard Helderman, *George Washington: Patron of Learning* (New York, 1932), 28, 36, 38–39, 42–49. On GW's initial will, prepared in the 1790s, see: *WW*, 34:59–60n.

50. GW to Stuart, Mar. 28 and June 15, 1790, *WW*, 31:30, 52; Thomas E. Drake, *Quakers and Slavery in America* (New Haven, Conn., 1950), 100–13; Robinson, *Slavery in the Structure of American Politics*, 285–88, 302–304.

51. GW to Lear, May 6, 1794, *WW*, 33:358.

52. GW to Lafayette, Apr. 5, 1783, and May 10, 1786, ibid., 26:300; 28:424; Flexner, *GW*, 4:112–25; Ford, *True GW*, 153–54.

53. Wall, "Housing and Family Life of the Mount Vernon Negro," 7–8, MVL; Flexner, *GW*, 4:122, 124; GW to Wolcott, Sept. 1, 1796, ibid., 35:201–202; GW to Joseph Whipple, Nov. 28, 1796, ibid., 35:296–98; GW to Lewis, Nov. 13, 1797, ibid., 36:70; William W. Freehling, "The Founding Fathers and Slavery," *AHR*, 77 (1972), 81–91; William Cohen, "Thomas Jefferson and the Problem of Slavery," *JAH*, 56 (1969), 503–26; Ketcham, Madison, 148–49; Robert McColley, *Slavery and Jeffersonian Virginia* (Urbana, Ill., 1973), 114–32, 182–85.

54. GW to David Stuart, Dec. 11, 1787, Jan. 18 and 22, 1788, *WW*, 29:335, 387, 390; GW to Pendleton, Mar. 1, 1788, ibid., 29:429; GW to Ch. Lee, Apr. 4, 1788, ibid. 29:460–61; GW to John Lawson, Apr. 10, 1787, ibid., 29:199; GW to John Fowler, Feb. 2, 1788, ibid., 29:398; GW to Geo. Lewis, Nov. 13, 1797, ibid., 36:70; GW to Eliz. Lewis, Sept. 1, 1789, ibid., 30:400; GW, "Estimate of the Cost of . . . Negroes on Dogue Run . . . ," [1790], ibid., 31:186–89; GW, Inventory, June, 1799, ibid., 37:256–68; *DGW*, 4:277–83; Affadavit, May 28, 1795, WPPV; Ford, *True GW*, 138–39.

55. Flexner, *GW*, 4:121; GW to R. Morris, Apr. 12, 1786, *WW*, 27:408; Richard Parkinson, *George Washington: Statement of George Washington* (Baltimore, 1909), 16; Richard Parkinson, *A Tour of America*, 2 vols., (London, 1805), 2:121–23; Julian Ursyn Niemcewicz, *Under Their Vine and Fig Tree: Travels Through America*, trans. by Metchie J.E. Budka (Elizabeth, N.J., 1965), 100–101.

56. GW to Whiting, Jan. 6 and Feb. 17, 1793, *WW*, 32:293, 348; GW to H. Lewis, Aug. 18, 1793, ibid., 33:53; GW to Anderson, Dec. 21, 1797, ibid., 36:114; GW to Spotswood, Sept. 14, 1798, ibid., 36:445; GW to Ch. Vancouver, Nov. 5, 1791, ibid., 31:410; GW to Pearce, Feb. 9, July 13 and 27, 1794, June 7, July 5, Oct. 25, 1795, and May 1, 1796, ibid., 33:267, 447; 34:212, 231, 343; 35:34; GW to Lear, June 19, 1791, ibid., 31:302; MW to Fanny Washington, May 24, 1795, MVL.

57. GW to Vancouver, Nov. 5, 1791, *WW*, 31:440; GW to Pearce, Feb. 22, Aug. 3, 1794, Feb. 1 and March 8, 1795, ibid., 33:275, 452; 34:12, 135; GW to Whiting, Oct. 14, 1792, ibid., 32:184; Ford, *True GW*, 145.

58. GW to Whiting, Nov. 4, Dec. 9, 1792, and Jan. 6, 1793, *WW*, 32:205, 256–57,

293, 295; GW, Memorandum, Nov. 5, 1796, ibid., 35:265; GW to Bloxham, Jan. 1, 1789, ibid., 30:175n.

59.   GW to Pearce, Jan. 12, May 18, July 20, 1794, and May 22, 1795, ibid., 33:242, 369, 435; 34:153; GW, Inventory, June, 1799, ibid., 37:256; GW to Whiting, Oct. 14 and 28, 1792, ibid., 32:184, 197.

60.   GW to Spotswood, Sept. 14, 1798, ibid., 36:445; GW to Pearce, Oct. 27 and Dec. 18, 1793, Jan. 19, 1794, Jan. 25, Mar. 1, May 10, and Dec. 13, 1795, ibid., 33:33, 142, 191, 243; 34:103, 128, 193, 393; GW to Whiting, Jan. 20, Feb. 23, Mar. 3, and May 19, 1793, ibid., 32:307, 358, 366, 465; GW, "To the Overseers at Mount Vernon," July 14, 1793, ibid., 33:11.

61.   Niemcewicz, *Under Their Vine and Fig Tree*, 100; Wall, "Housing and Family Life of the Mount Vernon Negro," 23–24, MVL: GW to Young, Dec. 12, 1793, *WW*, 33:178.

62.   GW to Whiting, Oct. 14, 1792, May 12 and 26, 1793, *WW*, 32:184, 458, 474–75; GW to Pearce, Dec. 22, 1793, ibid., 33:205; GW, "Estimate of the Cost . . . ," [1790?], ibid., 33:186–87; GW to Lear, Oct. 7, 1791, ibid., 31:385; "Washington's Household Account Book," *PMHB*, 30 (1905), 43, 321; 31 (1906), 67, 73.

63.   Flexner, *GW*, 4:432–34.

64.   GW to Young, Nov. 9, 1794, *WW*, 34:21; Flexner, *GW*, 4:432–34.

65.   GW to Knox, Mar. 2, 1797, *WW*, 35:409; Louis M. Sears, *George Washington* (New York, 1932), 484.

66.   GW to Duane, Apr. 10, 1785, *WW*, 38:124; GW to Henry, Oct. 9, 1795, ibid. 34:335. See also Morgan, *Genius of GW*, 20–25.

67.   GW to Rush, Apr. 28, 1788, *WW*, 29:481; GW to Buchan, June 30, 1790, May 1, 1792, and Apr. 22, 1793, ibid., 31:63; 32:25, 429; Liston to Lord Grenville, Dec. 21, 1799, WPPV; Richard Parkinson, *George Washington: Statement of Richard Parkinson* (Baltimore, 1909), 27.

68.   GW, Farewell Address, Sept. 19, 1796, *WW*, 35:237.

69.   GW, Proposed Inaugural Address, 1789, ibid., 30:297, 299, 303, 305, 307; GW, Farewell Address, Sept. 19, 1796, ibid., 35:219, 224, 227; GW, Annual Address, Dec. 7, 1796, ibid., 35:315.

70.   Baker, *GW after the Revolution*, 340–41, 343; Freeman, *GW*, 7:432–35; Mayo, *Myths and Men*, 35–36.

71.   Freeman, *GW*, 7:436–37; Smith, *Adams*, 2:917–18; Withey, *Dearest Friend*, 247.

19

The Last Years

1.   Bellamy, *Private Life of GW*, 375–76.

2.   Eliza Powel to GW, Feb. 6, 8, Mar. 6 and 11, 1791, MVL.

3.   Eliza Powel to GW, Feb. 6 and 8, 1797, MVL; GW to Dandridge, Apr. 3, 1797, *WW*, 35:428–29; GW to Mary White Morris, May 1, 1797, ibid., 35:441–42; Freeman, *GW*, 7:438–44; GW, "Household Furniture" [Memorandum], Feb.[?], 1797, WPPV.

4.   "GW's Household Account Book," *PMHB*, 31:341–47; GW to Anderson, Feb. 5, 1797, *WW*, 35:385.

5. MW to Catherine Greene, Mar. 3, 1797, MVL; Freeman, *GW*, 7:236; GW to Citizens of Alexandria, Mar. 23, 1797, *WW*, 35:423.

6. GW to Pearce, Dec. 4 and 11, 1796, *WW*, 35:307, 332; GW to Anderson, Aug. 18, 1796, ibid., 35:182; GW to Dr. James Anderson, Apr. 7, 1797, ibid., 35:432; GW, Memorandum, Nov. 5, 1796, ibid., 35:256–58, 266; GW to Sir Edward Newenham, Aug. 6, 1797, ibid., 36:4; Thane, *Potomac Squire*, 359.

7. GW, Memorandum, Nov. 5, 1796, *WW*, 35:266; GW to Pearce, Nov. 20, 1796, ibid., 35:286; GW to Lear, Mar. 25, 1797, ibid., 35:424–25; GW to Lewis, Apr. 9, 1797, ibid., 35:434–35; GW to McHenry, Apr. 3, 1797, ibid., 35:431. On the contents of GW's art collection, see Flexner, *GW*, 4:356–70.

8. GW to Anderson, Jan. 8, 29, Feb. 5, Apr. 7, 1797, and Feb. 6, 1798, *WW*, 35:352–53, 377–78, 384; 36:154; GW to Lewis, Jan. 26, 1798, ibid., 36:141; GW to Wm. Augustine Washington, Feb. 27, 1798, ibid., 36:172–73; Niemcewicz, *Under Their Vine*, 100.

9. GW to Fitzhugh, May 30, 1798, *WW*, 36:278; Parkinson, *GW: Statement of Parkinson*, 16, 18, 24.

10. GW to Anderson, Feb. 6, 1798, Oct. 1 and Dec. 13, 1799, *WW*, 36:153–55; 37:382–85, 473–74; GW to Lawrence Lewis, Sept. 28, 1799, ibid., 37:376–77.

11. Parkinson, *GW*, 18; Flexner, *GW*, 4:451; GW, River Farm [Plans], Dec. 10, 1799, *WW*, 37:463–72; GW to Lewis, Sept. 20, 1799, ibid., 37:369; GW to Wm. A. Washington, Oct. 29, 1799, ibid., 37:415.

12. GW to Ebenezer Tucker, Jan. 24, 1790, *WW*, 31:2; GW, Land Memorandum, May 25, 1794, ibid., 33:376–80.

13. GW to Wolcott, June 7, July 3, 1797, ibid., 35:461, 486; GW to Israel Shreve, Sept. 1, 1797, June 10, 1799, ibid., 36:23–25; 37:85–87; GW to Judge A. Addison, Nov. 24, 1799, ibid., 37:439; Sturdevant, "Quest for Eden," 293–328.

14. GW to Lewis, Aug. 18, 1799, *WW*, 37:339; Sturdevant, "Quest for Eden," 345–60; Roy Bird Cook, *Washington's Western Lands* (Strasburg, Va., 1930), 75, 80, 88.

15. GW to John Mason, Jan. 2, 1798, *WW*, 36:116; Sturdevant, "Quest for Eden," 264–83.

16. GW to Biddle, May 28, 1798, *WW*, 36:276; GW, Last Will and Testament, [1799?], *WW*, 37:301; GW to Wm. Berkeley, Aug. 11, 1799, ibid., 37:330; GW to J. Mason, Dec. 8, 1799, ibid., 37:457; Sturdevant, "Quest for Eden," 372–79.

17. Eliza Powel to MW, Jan. 7, 1798, MVL; MW to Eliza Powel, Dec. 17, MVL; Niemcewicz, *Under Their Vine*, 84, 311, 104.

18. GW to Greenwood, Dec. 7 and 12, 1798, *WW*, 37:27–28; GW to Bushrod Washington, Aug. 27, 1798, ibid., 36:419–20; GW to David Stuart, Sept. 10, 1798, ibid., 31:435; GW to Spotswood, Sept. 14, 1798, ibid., 36:444; GW to Carter, Oct. 5, 1798, ibid., 36:484.

19. GW to Th. Erskine, July 7, 1797, ibid., 36:489–90; GW to Lewis, Apr. 9, 1797, ibid., 35:434–35; Flexner, *GW*, 4:341.

20. Flexner, *GW*, 4:346; Freeman, *GW*, 7:480; GW to McHenry, Apr. 3, 1797, *WW*, 35:430; GW to G.W.P. Custis, Aug. 29, 1797, ibid., 36:22; GW to Stuart, Feb. 26, 1798, ibid., 36:171; Niemcewicz, *Under Their Vine*, 85, 103.

21. GW to Lewis, Aug. 4, 1797, *WW*, 36:2–3.

22. Baker, *GW after the Revolution*, 277, 349–50; Niemcewicz, *Under Their Vine*, 97;

Flexner, *GW*, 4:196; GW to G.W.P. Custis, Apr. 15, 1798, *WW*, 36:246; *DGW*, 6:288n.

23. GW to John McDowell, Sept. 16, 1798, *WW*, 36:449; GW to Stuart, Jan. 22, 1798, ibid., 36:136; GW to G.W.P. Custis, Aug. 29, 1797, Mar. 10, May 10, June 13, and July 24, 1798, ibid., 36:21, 187, 259, 288, 363; *DGW*, 4:284; Bourne, *First Family*, 181–83.

24. *DGW*, 6:261, 271, 287, 252n, 272n, 287n; GW to Rawlins, Jan. 31 and Feb. 12, 1798, *WW*, 36:150–51, 165–66; GW to Wm. A. Washington, Feb. 27, 1798, ibid., 36:171–72.

25. GW to McHenry, May 29, 1797, *WW*, 35:455; *DGW*, 6:258, 264–65, 268, 285, 297–98, 312, 327; Freeman, *GW*, 7:469; Flexner, *GW*, 4:346.

26. GW to William Vans Murray, Dec. 3, 1797, *WW*, 36:88; GW to Strickland, July 15, 1797, ibid., 35:409; GW to Sally Fairfax, May 16, 1798, ibid., 36:262–64; *PGW*, 1:xvii–xviii.

27. GW to McHenry, Apr. 3, 1797, *WW*, 35:430; GW to C.C. Pinckney, June 24, 1797, ibid., 35:471; GW to Wolcott, May 15 and 29, 1797, ibid., 35:447, 457.

28. Ammon, *Monroe*, 165–67.

29. GW, "Remarks on Monroe's View . . . ," [Mar. 1798], *WW*, 36:194–237; GW to McHenry, Aug. 14, 1797, ibid., 36:8.

30. GW to Pickering, Aug. 29, 1797, ibid., 36:18–19; Alexander DeConde, *The Quasi-War: The Politics and Diplomacy of the Undeclared War with France, 1797–1801* (New York, 1966), 3–29; Ferling, " 'Oh that I was a Soldier,' " *American Quarterly*, 36:271–75.

31. DeConde, *Quasi-War*, 36–54.

32. Ferling, " 'Oh that I was a Soldier,' " 272–73; DeConde, *Quasi-War*, 90–92, 96.

33. GW to James Lloyd, Apr. 15, 1798, *WW*, 36:246; GW to Pickering, Aug. 29, 1797, ibid., 36:19; GW to Sally Fairfax, May 16, 1798, ibid., 36:263; GW to Pres. Adams, July 13, 1798, ibid., 36:328; GW to Spotswood, Nov. 22, 1798, ibid., 37:23.

34. Hamilton to GW, May 19, 1798, Syrett and Cooke, *Papers of Hamilton*, 21:467; GW to Hamilton, May 27, 1798, *WW*, 36:271–73.

35. GW to McHenry, July 4, 1798, *WW*, 36:305; Freeman, *GW*, 7:516–17, 519.

36. Hamilton to GW, July 8, 1798, Syrett and Cooke, *Papers of Hamilton*, 21:534–35.

37. *WW*, 36:326n; GW to Pickering, July 11, 1798, ibid., 36:323–27; GW to Pres. Adams, July 13, 1798, ibid., 36:327–29; GW to Hamilton, July 14, 1798, ibid., 36:331; GW to Knox, July 16, 1798, ibid., 36:344; Adams to McHenry, July 6, 1798, Adams, *Works*, 7:574.

38. GW to Hamilton, July 14, 1798, *WW*, 36:332; GW to Pickering, July 11, 1798, ibid., 36:323–24; Pickering to GW, July 2, 1798, ibid., 36:324n; GW to McHenry, July 4, 1798, ibid., 36:304–12; GW to Pres. Adams, July 4, 1798, ibid., 36:312–15; Hamilton to GW, June 2, 1798, Syrett and Cooke, *Papers of Hamilton*, 21:479.

39. Kohn, *Eagle and Sword*, 227.

40. Ferling, " 'Oh that I was a Soldier,' " 273.

41. Smith, *Adams*, 2:972, 974.

42. Knox to GW, July 29, 1798, Sparks, *Writings of GW*, 11:534–37; GW to Knox, Aug. 9, 1798, *WW*, 36:396–401; Freeman, *GW*, 7:531.

43. GW to Pres. Adams, Sept. 25, 1798, *WW*, 36:453–62; Adams to GW, Oct. 9, 1798, Adams, *Works*, 8:600–601.

44. GW to Lear, Aug. 2, 1798, *WW*, 36:381; GW to Pickering, Sept. 9, 1798, ibid., 36:434; GW to McHenry, Aug. 10, Sept. 14, 16, and Oct. 23, 1798, ibid., 36:402, 441–42, 463, 514.

45. *DGW*, 6:322–23; Freeman, *GW*, 7:549–50.

46. *DGW*, 6:323–26; Eliza Powel to GW, Dec. 3, 1798, MVL; Freeman, *GW*, 7:554n; GW to Eliza Powel, Nov. 17, 1798, WPPV.

47. GW to McHenry, Dec. 13 and 16, 1798, *WW*, 37:32–38, 60–62.

48. GW to McHenry, Oct. 27 and Nov. 5, 1799, ibid., 37:413, 419.

49. GW to McHenry, Jan. 27, Feb. 10, Mar. 25, May 13, and July 7, 1799, ibid., 37:110–12, 127–29, 157; 209, 271; GW to James McAlpin, May 12, 1799, ibid., 37:206–207.

50. DeConde, *Quasi-War*, 174; GW to Pres. Adams, Feb. 1, 1799, *WW*, 37:119–20; Ferling, " 'Oh that I was a Soldier,' " 142–43, 418.

51. DeConde, *Quasi-War*, 174–79; GW to Pickering, Mar. 3 and Nov. 3, 1799, *WW*, 37:142–43, 418.

52. *DGW*, 6:327; GW to Lafayette, Dec. 25, 1798, *WW*, 37:64–72.

53. GW to Stuart, Dec. 30, 1798, *WW*, 37:77–78; GW to Lewis, Jan. 23, 1799, ibid., 37:105–106.

54. GW to Dandridge, Jan. 25, 1799, ibid., 37:108.

55. *DGW*, 6:335.

56. Ibid., 6:350; GW to McHenry, Jan. 6, 1799, *WW*, 37:84–85; Freeman, *GW*, 7:561n.

57. GW, Inventory, June, 1799, *WW*, 37:256–68; GW, Last Will and Testament, ibid., 37:276–77.

58. GW, Last Will and Testament, ibid., 37:275, 278–307. See also, John C. Fitzpatrick, ed., *The Last Will and Testament of George Washington and Schedule of his Property* (Mount Vernon, Va., 1939).

59. *DGW*, 6:359; GW to Gov. Trumbull, July 21, 1799, *WW*, 37:314.

60. *DGW*, 6:363, 363–64n; GW to Th. Peter, Sept. 7, 1799, *WW*, 37:353; GW to Samuel Washington, Sept. 22, 1799, ibid., 37:374; GW to Wm. A. Washington, Oct. 29, 1799, ibid., 37:415.

61. *DGW*, 6:358.

62. Freeman, *GW*, 7:606; GW to Lewis, Aug. 18 and 23, 1799, *WW*, 37:339, 341; GW to Peter, Dec. 3, 1799, ibid., 37:452; GW to Murray, Oct. 26, 1799, ibid., 37:400; GW to Hamilton, Oct. 27, 1799, ibid., 37:409–10; GW to Ball, Sept. 22, 1799, ibid., 37:372.

63. GW to Fairfax, Nov. 30, 1799, *WW*, 37:447; 447; Freeman, *GW*, 7:608; *DGW*, 6:374, 377; ibid., 4:250n.

64. GW to Wm. Thornton, Dec. 1, 1799, *WW*, 37:448; GW to Biddle, Dec. 8, 1799, ibid., 37:458; GW to Anderson, Dec. 10, 1799, ibid., 37:459, 462; GW [Plans, 1799], ibid., 37:463–72; GW to Hamilton, Dec. 12, 1799, ibid., 37:473.

65. DGW, VI, 378–79; Lear, *Letters and Recollections*, 129.

66. *DGW*, 6:379n; Freeman, *GW*, 7:619.

67. Lear, *Letters*, 130–36; "Statement of Attending Physicians," *Alexandria Times*,

Dec. 19, 1799, reprinted in Freeman, *GW*, 7:640–41. On Washington's death, see also, "A Comparative Critique of Washington's Last Illness," Freeman, *GW*, 7:637–47; Creighton Barker, "A Case Report," *Yale Journal of Biology and Medicine*, 9 (1936–37), 185–87; Wyndham Bolling Blanton, *Medicine in Virginia in the Eighteenth Century* (Richmond, Va., 1931), 305–12; Fielding O. Lewis, "Washington's Last Illness," *Annals of Medical History*, 4 (1932), 245–48; Rudolph Marx, "A Medical Profile of George Washington," *American Heritage*, 6 (1955), 43–47, 106–107; Walter A. Wells, "The Last Illness and Death of George Washington," *Virginia Medical Monthly*, 53 (1926–27), 629–42.

Afterword

1.   Eliza Powel to MW, Dec. 24, 1799, MVL.
2.   Lear, *Letters*, 139; Freeman, *GW*, 7:626–29.
3.   Lear, *Letters*, 135; MW to Abigail Adams, Jan. 5, 1800, MVL.
4.   Prussing, *Estate of GW*, 98; Charles W. Akers, *Abigail Adams: An American Woman* (Boston, 1980), 173–74.
5.   Th. Law to John Law, May 23, 1802, Mount Vernon Ladies Association *Annual Report, 1981* (Mount Vernon, Va., 1981), 15.
6.   Prussing, *Estate of GW*, 159, 137, 410–47, 204; Public Sales [Ledger] . . . , Mar. 5, 1800–June 5, 1803, WPPV.
7.   Prussing, *Estate of GW*, 204.
8.   Ibid., 205–206.
9.   Billy J. Harbin, "Letters from John Parke Custis to George and Martha Washington, 1778–1781," *WMQ*, 3d ser., 43 (1986), 267.
10.   Dennis Clark, "Philadelphia 1876: Celebration and Illusion," in Dennis Clark, ed., *Philadelphia 1776–2076: A Three Hundred Year View* (Port Washington, N.Y., 1975), 41–63.

Select Bibliography

From the moment George Washington became an officer in the Virginia Regiment he understood that he was a public figure, and that historians and concerned citizens who were his contemporaries, as well as those from generations yet unborn, would scrutinize his activities. In 1754 he not only began to make copies of his letters but apparently commenced the practice of preserving the correspondence that he received. By the time of his death forty-five years later, his accumulated papers were massive, testing even spacious Mount Vernon's capacity for housing the materials.

The work of sorting and classifying Washington's papers began in 1781. Even before the Battle of Yorktown, Congress appointed Lt. Col. Richard Varick to superintend the arrangement of the commander's papers and, in addition, to make copies of this vast array of documents (GW to PC, Apr. 4, 1781, *WW*, 21:411–12. See also *GWP*, ser. 1, 1:xiii–xix; ser. 2, 1:xvii–xxi). Although Washington looked upon these materials as public property, he brought them with him to Mount Vernon in 1783.

During the next five years Washington sought to "overhaul and ajust" those of his papers that antedated the war years, documents that were left in disarray when they were hastily removed from an imperiled Mount Vernon in 1781 (GW to Geo. Wm. Fairfax, Feb. 27, 1785, *WW*, 28:84). He returned to that task following his presidency, devoting many "leisure hours . . . to the arrangement and overhaul of my voluminous . . . papers." (GW to McHenry, July 29, 1798, *WW*, 36:373–74). The "overhaul" to which Washington alluded was just that, for during his last years, and probably in the 1780s as well, he set out to repair his earlier missives, seeking to refine his youthful style so that posterity would see a more correct and elegant version of his correspondence.

Washington's work was in progress when he was stricken by his final illness. Following his death, his papers, a vast collection that included his correspondence, diaries, exercise books, surveys, financial records, ledger books, and military records, passed to Bushrod Washington, and subsequently to his heir, George Corbin Washington. Before the Civil War, what survived of the collection— Bushrod Washington had permitted at least three early biographers and compilers to remove some of the documents from Mount Vernon—was sold to the federal government. Today it is housed in the Library of Congress, and it is available both in the Manuscript Division of that facility and on 124 reels of microfilm, published as the *George Washington Papers: Presidential Papers on Microfilm* (Washington, D.C., 1961).

This collection has been the source for several published editions of Washington materials. In the nineteenth century two editions of Washington's letters were issued: Jared Sparks, ed., *The Writings of George Washington: Being His Correspondence, Addresses, Messages, and Other Papers, Official and Private, Selected and Published from the Original*, 12 vols. (Boston, 1833–37), and Worthington Chauncey Ford, ed., *The Writings of George Washington*, 14 vols. (New York, 1889–93). In addition, two editions of letters written to Washington were produced from that collection: Jared Sparks, ed., *Correspondence of the American Revolution: Being Letters of Eminent Men to George Washington*, 4 vols. (Washington, D.C., 1853), and Stanislaus M. Hamilton, ed., *Letters to Washington and Accompanying Papers*, 5 vols. (Boston and New York, 1898–1902).

Until recently the most complete edition of Washington's correspondence was that of John C. Fitzpatrick, ed., *The Writings of Washington from the Original Manuscript Sources, 1745–1799*, 39 vols. (Washington, D.C., 1931–44). These volumes, however, consisted almost solely of the Washington correspondence housed in the Library of Congress, and virtually no letters written to Washington were included.

Publication of a modern, comprehensive edition of Washington's papers was long overdue, and scholars rejoiced in the 1970s at the news that the University of Virginia had begun such a project. The endeavor discovered Washington items in over four hundred libraries and in the hands of hundreds of private owners. To date the venture has issued complete editions of the following: Donald Jackson and Dorothy Twohig, eds., *The Diaries of George Washington*, 6 vols. (Charlottesville, Va., 1976–79), and Dorothy Twohig, ed., *The Papers of George Washington: The Journal of the Proceedings of the President, 1793–1797* (Charlottesville, Va., 1981). Under the direction of W.W. Abbot, Dorothy Twohig, Beverly H. Runge, Frederick Hall Schmidt, and Philander D. Chase, eds., *The Papers of George Washington* (Charlottesville, Va., 1983–), the definitive edition of Washington's correspondence and other materials has begun to appear. These items are being published simultaneously in three series, one spanning the years to 1775, a second covering the War of Independence era, and the last comprising the post-Revolutionary period. Lamentably, only four volumes were available before the completion of this study of Washington.

Numerous biographies of Washington have been published. The best to appear in the nineteenth century was Paul Leicester Ford's *The True George Washington* (Philadelphia, 1896), although it focused heavily on Washington's early years. Otherwise, Washington Irving's *The Life of George Washington*, 5 vols. (New York, 1856–59) was the most readable effort, while the works of John Marshall, *The Life of George Washington*, 5 vols. (London, 1804–7), Henry

Cabot Lodge, *George Washington*, 2 vols. (Boston, 1889), and Woodrow Wilson, *George Washington* (New York, 1897), added little to contemporary knowledge or understanding of the man. It was unfortunate that Washington's first biographer, Mason Locke Weems played the largest part in forming the public's notion of the subject, for his was a distorted portrayal. His *The Life of George Washington: With Curious Anecdotes Equally Honorable to Himself and Exemplary to His Young Countrymen* passed through several editions. The ninth edition, published originally in 1809, is available in a modern reprint and is accompanied by a useful introductory essay by the editor. See: Marcus Cunliffe, ed., *The Life of Washington by Mason L. Weems* (Cambridge, Mass., 1962).

This century has witnessed several exceptional biographies of Washington. The encyclopedic work of Douglas Southall Freeman, J.A. Carroll, and M.W. Ashworth, *George Washington: A Biography*, 7 vols. (New York, 1948–57), is the most complete. More readable and, happily, quite reliable, is James Thomas Flexner's *George Washington*, 4 vols. (Boston, 1965–72). A single-volume condensation of Flexner's study is available as *Washington: The Indispensable Man* (Boston, 1969), but it omits rather too much.

The Freeman and Flexner studies overwhelmed some earlier works of value. Rupert Hughes's *George Washington*, 3 vols. (New York, 1926–30), a study that carried the subject only to 1781, was the best of these works. Other fine biographies published early in this century included: William Roscoe Thayer, *George Washington* (Boston, 1931); Louis Martin Sears, *George Washington* (New York, 1932); John C. Fitzpatrick, *George Washington: A Common Sense Biography Written from His Manuscripts* (Indianapolis, 1933); and Nathaniel W. Stephenson and Waldo H. Dunn, *George Washington*, 2 vols. (New York, 1940). The Freeman and Flexner works also crowded out William E. Woodward's *George Washington: The Image and the Man* (New York, 1926), a distorted attempt at debunking the Washington legend, but probably the most widely read of the Washington biographies published in the initial decades of this century. That period also saw the publication of Bernard Fay's *George Washington: Republican Aristocrat* (Boston, 1931) and Shelby Little's *George Washington* (New York, 1929), neither of which contributed significantly to an understanding of the man.

Several brief biographies of Washington have appeared since mid-century. The most analytical and provocative is that of Marcus Cunliffe, *George Washington: Man and Monument* (London, 1959). The works by John Alden, *George Washington: A Biography* (Baton Rouge, La., 1984) and Esmond Wright, *Washington and the American Revolution* (New York, 1962) are thoughtful and useful. For slender but worthy pieces contemplating Washington, see the essays by Edmund S. Morgan, *The Genius of George Washington* (New York, 1980) and *The Meaning of Independence: John Adams, George Washington, and Thomas Jefferson* (Charlottesville, Va., 1975), and that of Bernard Mayo, *Myths and Men: Patrick Henry, George Washington, and Thomas Jefferson* (Athens, Ga., 1959). Sound and standard biographies were produced by North Callahan, *George Washington: Soldier and Man* (New York, 1972), and Robert F. Jones, *George Washington* (Boston, 1979).

Washington has been the subject of numerous specialized studies. On his early years, Bernhard Knollenberg's *George Washington: The Virginia Period, 1732–1775* (Durham, N.C., 1964) is the best effort. Of value, however, is Charles H. Ambler, *George Washington and the West* (Chapel Hill, N.C., 1936) and Samuel E. Morison, "The Young Man Washington," in his *By Land and By Sea: Essays and Addresses by Samuel Eliot Morison* (New York, 1953). Contemporary evaluations of young Washington can be found in William S. Baker, *Early Sketches of George Washington* (Philadelphia, 1893).

A good introduction to Washington the private citizen and farmer can be found in Charles Cecil Wall's *George Washington: Citizen Soldier* (Charlottesville, Va., 1980) and the popular and quite readable *Potomac Squire* (New York, 1963) by Elswyth Thane. Something of value can be found in Paul L. Haworth, *George Washington, Farmer* (Indianapolis, 1915) and Francis R. Bellamy, *The Private Life of George Washington* (New York, 1951). George W. Nordham's *George Washington: Vignettes and Memorabilia* (Philadelphia and Ardmore, Pa., 1977) is interesting. Of more usefulness, however, are Paul L. Ford, *George Washington, Country Gentleman* (Indianapolis, 1925) and Moncure D. Conway, *George Washington of Mount Vernon* (Brooklyn, 1889). For a fine chronicle of Washington's beloved estate, see Paul Wilstach, *Mount Vernon: Washington's Home and the Nation's Shrine* (New York, 1916). Important, too, is Charles C. Wall's "Notes on the Early History of Mount Vernon," *William and Mary Quarterly*, 3d ser., 2 (1945), 173–90.

Eugene E. Prussing's *The Estate of George Washington, Deceased* (Boston, 1927) focuses on Washington's property, investments, and philanthropic inclinations. The extent of Washington's property holdings at the time of his death can be seen in John C. Fitzpatrick, ed., *The Last Will and Testament of George Washington and Schedule of his Property* (Mount Vernon, Va., 1939). Also reliable in this area is George Washington Nordham, *George Washington and Money* (Washington, D.C., 1982).

Washington the slavemaster is scrutinized in Worthington C. Ford, *Washington as an Employer and Importer of Labor* (Brooklyn, 1889), and in Walter H. Mazyck, *George Washington and the Negro* (Washington, D.C., 1932). The Mount Vernon Library contains two fine, though unfortunately unpublished, typescript essays on this subject. These are by Charles C. Wall, "Housing and Family Life of the Mount Vernon Negro" (1962), and Frank E. Morse, "About General Washington's Freed Negroes" (1968).

Other aspects of Washington's private life are treated in Paul F. Boller, *George Washington and Religion* (Dallas, 1963), Paul L. Ford, *Washington and the Theater* (New York, 1899), and Leonard Helderman, *George Washington: Patron of Learning* (New York, 1932). On Washington's library, see: Alan and Donna

Jean Fusonic, eds., *A Selected Bibliography of George Washington's Interest in Agriculture* (Davis, Calif., 1976).

One can gain an acquaintance with the many members of Washington's family in Miriam Anne Bourne's *First Family: George Washington and his Intimate Relations* (New York, 1982) and in Elswyth Thane, *Mount Vernon Family* (New York, 1968). The *Annual Reports* issued since 1945 by the Mount Vernon Ladies Association of the Union occasionally contain newly discovered letters written by Washington and members of his family, as well as useful articles pertaining to the family and Mount Vernon. The dearth of primary sources has stymied those seeking to write a good biography of Martha Washington, but see Elswyth Thane, *Washington's Lady* (New York, 1954) and Anne Hollingsworth Wharton, *Martha Washington* (New York, 1897).

The literature on Washington's generalship in the War of Independence is almost limitless. It begins with Thomas C. Frothingham's *Washington: Commander in Chief* (New York, 1930). Better and more useful treatments can be found in Bernhard Knollenberg, *Washington and the American Revolution: A Reappraisal* (New York, 1941), and Curtis P. Nettles, *George Washington and American Independence* (Boston, 1951). For two excellent assessments of his leadership, see: Marcus Cunliffe, "George Washington's Generalship," in George Athan Billias, ed., *George Washington's Generals* (New York, 1964), and Don Higginbotham, *George Washington and the American Military Tradition* (Athens, Ga., 1985). Students of Washington additionally should read Dave Richard Palmer's *The Way of the Fox: American Strategy in the War of Independence* (Westport, Conn., 1975). For a brilliant essay on General Washington, though it was published too late for use in this study, readers would be well advised to see John Shy, "George Washington Reconsidered," in Henry S. Bausum, ed., *The John Biggs Cincinnati Lectures in Military Leadership and Command, 1986* (Lexington, Va., 1986). Another aspect of Washington's conduct is investigated in John C. Fitzpatrick, ed., George Washington, *Account of Expences while Commander in Chief* (Boston and New York, 1917); a humorous treatment of the subject is provided by Marvin Kitman, *George Washington's Expense Account* (New York, 1970). Washington's travels and his domiciles in these years can be glimpsed in William S. Spahn's *Itinerary of George Washington from June 15, 1775, to December 23, 1783* (Philadelphia, 1892), and in Mabel L. Ives, *Washington's Headquarters* (Upper Montclair, N.J., 1932). For his relationship with his young aides, see: Emily Stone Whiteley, *Washington and His Aides-de-Camp* (New York, 1936).

Washington's presidential years have received considerably less scrutiny than the period of his military service. The recent slender volume by Forrest McDonald, *The Presidency of George Washington* (Lawrence, Kans., 1974), is the only one-volume assessment of his presidency, although John C. Miller's *The Federalist Era, 1789-1801* (New York, 1960) offers an excellent survey of that turbulent decade. Washington's conception of the office is assayed in Ralph

Ketchum's *President's Above Party: The First American Presidency, 1789–1829* (Chapel Hill, N.C., 1984).

For Washington's private life in this period of public service, see Stephen Decatur, Jr., ed., *Private Affairs of George Washington from the Records and Accounts of Tobias Lear* (Boston, 1933).

On President Washington's frontier policy readers would profit from Wiley Sword's *President Washington's Indian War: The Struggle for the Old Northwest, 1790–1795* (Norman, Okla., 1985). A good treatment of his administration's foreign policy is Louis Martin Sears's *George Washington and the French Revolution* (Detroit, 1960). The best study of Washington's diplomacy is Alexander De Conde, *Entangling Alliance: Politics and Diplomacy under George Washington* (Durham, N.C., 1958).

Two excellent articles should be consulted on Washington and the Whiskey Rebellion. The most provocative in that by Mary K. Bonsteel Tachau, "George Washington and the Reputation of Edmund Randolph," *Journal of American History*, 73 (1986), 15–34. On Washington's decision to raise the army in this instance, see: Richard Kohn, "The Washington Administration's Decision to Crush the Whiskey Rebellion," *Journal of American History*, 59 (1972), 567–84.

Two recent studies have contributed greatly to our understanding of Washington's meaning to contemporaries, as well as to succeeding generations in ante-bellum America. One should see Garry Wills, *Cincinnatus: George Washington and the Enlightenment* (Garden City, N.Y., 1984), and Barry Schwartz, "The Character of Washington: A Study in Republican Culture," *American Quarterly*, 38 (1986), 202–22. On this subject one should also see Barry Schwartz, *George Washington: The Making of an American Symbol* (New York and London, 1987), a study that appeared too late for use in this biography.

The best contemporary account of Washington's death is in Tobias Lear, *Letters and Recollections of Washington . . . With a Diary of Washington's Last Days* (New York, 1906). For other accounts of Washington's final illness, see: Creighton Barker, "A Case Report," *Yale Journal of Biology and Medicine*, 9 (1936–37), 185–87; Fielding O. Lewis, "Washington's Last Illness," *Annals of Medical History*, 4 (1932), 245–48; and Walter A. Wells, "The Last Illness and Death of George Washington," *Virginia Medical Monthly*, 53 (1926–27), 629–42.

For additional secondary and primary works that pertain to the great events of Washington's lifetime, see the notes that accompany this study. Full citation of a particular work may be found in its first appearance in the notes.

Index

The First of Men: A Life of George Washington was designed
by Dariel Mayer, composed by Tseng Information Systems, Inc.,
printed and bound by Arcata Graphics/Kingsport.
The book is set in Times Roman with Galliard display
and printed on 50-lb. Glatfelter B-16 machine finish.